Experiencing Race, Class, and Gender in the United States

SEVENTH EDITION

Roberta Fiske-Rusciano

Rider University

ROWMAN & LITTLEFIELD
Lanham • Boulder • New York • London

Executive Editor: Mark Kerr
Editorial Assistant: Courtney Packard

Credits and acknowledgments for material borrowed from other sources, and reproduced with permission, appear on the appropriate page within the text.

Published by Rowman & Littlefield
An imprint of The Rowman & Littlefield Publishing Group, Inc.
4501 Forbes Boulevard, Suite 200, Lanham, Maryland 20706
www.rowman.com

6 Tinworth Street, London SE11 5AL, United Kingdom

British Library Cataloguing in Publication Information Available

Library of Congress Cataloging-in-Publication Data

Names: Fiske-Rusciano, Roberta, author.
Title: Experiencing race, class, and gender in the United States / Roberta Fiske-Rusciano, Rider University.
Description: Seventh Edition. | Lanham, Md. : Rowman & Littlefield, [2019] | Revised edition of the author's Experiencing race, class, and gender in the United States, c2013.
Identifiers: LCCN 2018059768 | ISBN 9781538114933 (pbk. : alk. paper)
Subjects: LCSH: United States—Social conditions—1980– | United States—Race relations. | United States—Ethnic relations. | Social classes—United States. | Cultural pluralism—United States. | Women—United States—Social conditions. | Gays—United States—Social conditions. | Discrimination—United States.
Classification: LCC HN59.2 .E96 2019 | DDC 305.800973—dc23
LC record available at https://lccn.loc.gov/2018059768

For Becky

Contents

Preface   ix

Identity

Part I   Racial and Ethnic Identity   3

1.   Just 'Cause I'm Mixed *by Afro DZ ak (Peter Shungu)*   6
2.   American Anthropological Association "Statement on Race"   6
3.   Ethnicity in American Life: The Historical Perspective *by John Hope Franklin*   8
4.   Toward a More Perfect Union *by Barack Obama*   14
5.   The Loudest Voice *by Grace Paley*   20
6.   To Be Hopi or American *by Polingaysi Qoyawayma (Elizabeth Q. White)*   23
7.   People of Color Who Never Felt They Were Black *by Darryl Fears*   25
8.   Rosa Wakefield *by John Langston Gwaltney*   27
*9.   I'm Not Your Miss Saigon *by Jillian Montilla*   30
10.   Before the Great Gorge *by Carlos Cumpián*   31
11.   Race in a Genetic World *by Harvard Magazine*   32
*12.   Exploring the Cuban Conundrum: Exiles, Immigrants, Americans, or Illegals? *by Mercedes R. Diaz, PhD*   34

Suggestions for Responding to Part I   48

Part II   Gender and Sexual Identity   49

*13.   Adam Rippon: When I Came Out Is When I Started to Own Who I Am as a Person *by Karen Price*   51
*14.   Why Are White Men Stockpiling Guns? *by Jeremy Adam Smith*   52
15.   The Male Role Stereotype *by Doug Cooper Thompson*   54
16.   Transgender Rights in the United States: A Short History *by Tom Head*   56
17.   A Transsexual's Story *by Jessica R. Stearns*   58

Suggestions for Responding to Part II   71

Part III   Economics and the American Dream   73

18.   Decloaking Class: Why Class Identity and Consciousness Count *by Janet Zandy*   75
19.   The Truth about Growing Up Rich *by Sallie Bingham*   83
20.   Daddy Tucked the Blanket *by Randall Williams*   86
*21.   Homeless in America *by Sabena Siddiqui*   88

Suggestions for Responding to Part III   89

Suggestion for Responding to *Identity*   90

Power

Part IV   Power and Racism   93

*22.   Why *Birth of a Nation* Still Matters in American Politics *by Frank Louis Rusciano*   96

*23.   ICE Spokesman Quits, Bashes Trump Administration on Immigration Raids *by Willa Frej*   103

24.   Historical Discrimination in the Immigration Laws *by U.S. Commission on Civil Rights*   104

25.   Immigration Laws since 1980: The Closing Door *by Barbara Franz*   109

*26.   The Year in Hate: Trump Buoyed White Supremacists in 2017, Sparking Backlash among Black Nationalist Groups *by Southern Poverty Law Center*   117

*27.   What Is White Privilege, Really? *by Cory Collins*   118

28.   Native Americans vs. the U.S. Government *by Michael Dorris*   123

29.   Urban Native Americans *by Roberta Fiske-Rusciano*   125

30.   Sex, Class, and Race Intersections: Visions of Women of Color *by Carol Lee Sanchez*   128

31.   Crimes against Humanity *by Ward Churchill*   131

32.   Anti-Semitism in the United States *by Robert Cherry*   136

33.   Behind Barbed Wire *by John Hersey*   138

34.   Asian Americans Battle "Model Minority" Stereotype *by Robert Daseler*   147

35.   Jim Crow Revived in Cyberspace *by Greg Palast and Martin Luther King III*   150

*36.   It's Not Just Starbucks: White Fear Is an American Problem *by Renée Graham*   151

37.   Emmett Louis Till, 1941–1955 *by Southern Poverty Law Center*   153

38.   Blacks Feel Indignities *by Robert Anthony Watts*   154

Suggestions for Responding to Part IV   156

Part V   Power and Sexism   157

39.   Citizenship and Violence *by The American Prospect*   160

*40.   For Women's History Month, a Look at Gender Gains—and Gender Gaps—in the United States *by Abigail Geiger and Kim Parker*   162

*41.   Sexual Harassment at Work in the Era of #MeToo *by Nikki Graf*   163

*42.   Breaking Down Gender Bias in the Construction Industry *by Kate Stephenson*   164

43.   Why Doesn't She Just Leave? *by Clarethia Ellerbe*   166

44.   Rape and Sexual Assault *by James A. Doyle*   168

45.   "The Rape" of Mr. Smith *by Unknown*   171

*46.   *Roe v. Wade* Turns Forty-Five, but There's No Time to Celebrate *by Ilyse Hogue*   172

*47.   Unions Are Fighting for Families *by Liz Shuler*   174

Suggestions for Responding to Part V   175

Part VI   Power and Classism   177

 48. Warren Buffett Calls for Higher Taxes for U.S. Super-Rich *by Graeme Wearden* 181

 49. Bulging Jails Are Other American Exception *by Albert R. Hunt* 182

 50. Institutionalized Discrimination *by Robert Cherry* 183

 *51. Why People Love "Assistance to the Poor" But Hate "Welfare" *by Ashley Jardina* 189

 *52. The Tainted Water Crisis in Upstate New York That Andrew Cuomo Can't Shake *by Alexander C. Kaufman* 190

Suggestions for Responding to Part VI   195

Part VII   Race, Class, and Gender during the Obama and Trump Administrations: A Comparative Look   197

 *53. How America Changed during Barack Obama's Presidency *by Michael Dimock* 199

 *54. *The Atlantic*'s Adam Serwer: The Politics of Racism in Trump's America *by Nilagia McCoy* 199

 *55. The Trump Administration Isn't Just Curtailing Women's Rights; It's Systematically Eroding Trust in Women *by Annalisa Merelli* 201

 *56. Environmental Justice in the Age of Trump *by Michael J. Brogan* 203

 *57. The Power to Count: Citizenship and the Census *by Victor Thompson* 208

Suggestions for Responding to Part VII   212

Suggestions for Responding to *Power*   213

Change

Part VIII   Taking Action   217

 58. Attorney General Eric Holder Speaks at the Lyndon Baines Johnson Library and Museum *by Eric Holder* 219

 59. Diversity and Its Discontents *by Arturo Madrid* 223

 60. Breakfast at Perkins *by Derek Schork* 228

 *61. Five Ways to Help Prevent Domestic Violence *by Richard Tolman* 229

 62. Going Public with Our Vision *by Charlotte Bunch* 230

 63. A Manifesto for Men *by Andrew Kimbrell* 235

 64. Freedom for the Thought We Hate *by Gerald Gunther* 238

 *65. The Oklahoma Teachers' Strike Is Twenty-Six Years in the Making *by Jon Hazell* 240

Suggestions for Responding to Part VIII   242

Part IX   Change Makers   243

 66. Victory at Arnot *by Mary Harris "Mother" Jones* 245

 67. Free at Last *by Southern Poverty Law Center* 247

 68. The Movement *by Anne Moody* 251

 69. Freedom Is a Constant Struggle *by Muriel Tillinghast* 254

 70. "Don't Tell Us It Can't Be Done" *by Michael Ryan* 258

 71. Cecilia Fire Thunder: She Inspires Her People *by Ann Davis* 260

72.   Claiming Respect for Ancestral Remains: Repatriation and the Caddo Nation of
       Oklahoma *by Robert L. Cast, Bobby Gonzalez, and Timothy K. Perttula*   263

*73.   The Weinstein Effect *by Linda Burstyn*   265

Suggestions for Responding to Part IX   266
Suggestions for Responding to *Change*   266
Credits   269
Index   273

*New to this edition

Preface

THE FIRST TWO DECADES of the new millennium have been saturated with debate concerning fundamental ideals and principles by which people live worldwide. Large migrations of populations, due to shifts in economic opportunities, natural disasters, and especially war, have thrown into sharp relief the need for reassessing who we are and where we are heading as a society. As a nation, are we best able to care for ourselves by following more of an isolationist set of policies, both abroad and domestic? These new positions feature "America First" slogans, followed by conversations and a reversal of laws making decisions regarding who is American, who is not, and who is marginalized. The seventh edition of *Experiencing Race, Class, and Gender in the United States* offers an opportunity to look at many of these issues as experienced by the diverse population of this country and of the world. This is also the best way to learn about ourselves. Collecting details of the "American experience" is an ongoing effort that requires each of us to keep our eye on the shifts and different reflections of this richly varied and complex society. Learning more about the past and present through many voices will help us all problem solve with balance and wisdom as valuable, participating members of this country and of the world.

Experiencing Race, Class, and Gender in the United States, seventh edition, introduces students to basic concepts of multiculturalism and to seminal debates taken up by social scientists, physical scientists, and political commentators. Some points, however, can be made only by the poets and literary writers included herein. This text encourages readers to examine their own lives by challenging notions of hierarchy and stereotypes that often seem natural and largely go unchallenged. Such a journey is transforming and lengthy, and it is part of an ongoing American experience. *Experiencing Race, Class, and Gender* is a guide for students in thoughtful exploration of issues that surround personal and institutionalized bigotry. It encourages informed debate and avoids being doctrinaire, for learning to think through these issues is a far greater commitment than carefully agreeing with the professor.

Organization of the Book

This book is divided into three main divisions: *Identity* (Parts I–III), *Power* (Parts IV–VII), and *Change* (Parts VIII–IX). The first division, *Identity*, guides the reader to examine his or her own life and those of others by exploring the many layers that make up our selves and how those layers are affected by the lived experience of race, ethnicity, religion, gender, sexuality, and socioeconomic class.

The text then shifts its focus to a wider context in the second division, *Power*, in order to examine how our lives are shaped by specific social powers. Understanding one's social skin includes an acknowledgment of how we are all tied to institutions, groups, ongoing conflicts, and supportive networks. Exploring the differing circumstances and seeing patterns that reflect groups' varying experiences within our society gives us a better intellectual grip on inequalities that persist or emerge in the United States, often made clearer after natural and manmade disasters.

As some of us have become used to the idea that only governmental institutions or business conglomerates can change social policies and broad economic circumstances, the acknowledgment of inequities and human rights abuses leaves many feeling powerless, angry, and convinced that "there will always be poverty (or racism, sexism, etc.), so I just have to take care of myself." The third division of this text, *Change*, guides students to the knowledge that they can indeed effect change. Part VIII, *Taking Action*, introduces students to the stages of identifying a problem, visualizing the needed change, and going forward with a collective plan of action while armed with the knowledge of how to handle resistance. Part IX, *Change Makers*, brings the reader into the experiences of ordinary people who have changed many lives by refusing to give up their human rights and those of their community.

The introductions to the text's three main divisions and nine parts are intended to situate the concepts of the readings in a particular context, but students and instructors are encouraged to challenge the editor's and authors' assumptions. Some theoretical terms are highlighted by boldface type, and term definitions follow some of the readings. Each reading is followed by a set of "Understanding the Reading" questions to aid in critical thinking and classroom discussion, as well as "Suggestions for Responding," which encourage further study for those who are interested.

New to the Seventh Edition

The seventh edition has twenty-five new readings. As with the previous edition, the text remains a combination of social science and the humanities, drawing on the strengths of a multidisciplinary approach that ideally will add to the flexibility of the collection's use and provide broader exposure to knowledge as we grapple with these most basic questions in our society. Other new readings focus upon divisions in our understanding of U.S. history and the consequences. In verse, a young Asian American woman rejects the words and behavior of those who feel entitled to assign her to specific sexual stereotypes. The details of the different Cuban American "vintages" give us a more complex palette of "the American experience." In part II, *Gender and Sexual Identity*, an Olympic champion talks about the importance of coming out in his life, and another essay asks "Why Are White Men Stockpiling Guns?" In the *Power and Racism* section, an essay analyzes why the 1915 silent film *Birth of a Nation* still matters in American politics, and another discusses governmental reactions to recent immigration raids. Still another essay examines how the Trump administration encouraged white supremacists, and another article discusses what white privilege actually is. The essay by Renée Graham examines White fear as an American problem. In part III, *Economics and the American Dream*, a new essay on homelessness in America focuses upon California and New York City. In the *Power and Sexism* section, essays on gender gaps and gender gains are examined, as well as sexual harassment at work during the #MeToo era and gender bias in the construction industry, There is also focus on the present-day status of *Roe v. Wade*, now that this landmark decision supporting women's right to choose is forty-five years old.

Part VII, *Race, Class, and Gender during the Obama and Trump Administrations: A Comparative Look*, is new to this edition. These new essays deal with changes in human rights policies, behavior, and laws from 2010 to 2018, which include two terms of the Obama presidency and the first year of Trump's presidency. Some of the themes are racial politics, women's rights, environmental justice, and marginalization. Part VIII, *Taking Action*, highlights specific powerful but peaceful reactions to long-standing societal problems in the United States, including "The Oklahoma Teachers' Strike Is Twenty-Six Years in the Making." Part IX, *Change Makers*, includes an essay on "The Weinstein Effect."

*The preface explaining what has changed in the new edition is not included in this book, but it can be downloaded at https://textbooks.rowman.com/RaceClassGender.

Acknowledgments

I am deeply grateful to colleagues and former students at Rider University who have directly guided me to readings, contributed their own original material, or helped me think through ideas that have found their way into this book: Frank Rusciano, Barbara Franz, Victor Thompson, Mercedes Diaz, Michael Brogan, Jillian Montilla, Kelvin D. Clark, and especially the late Virginia Cyrus, who created the first three editions of this book.

My heartfelt thanks go to everyone at Rowman & Littlefield who helped in innumerable ways and patiently waited as I crafted the book, including Mark Kerr, editor; Courtney Packard, assistant editor; Janice Braunstein, production manager; and Patricia Stevenson, production editor.

Finally, I thank the Norwegian Nobel Institute in Oslo, Norway, especially Asle Toje, the director of research, for making me a fellow of the institute, which gave me time to complete this book, an office with a window, and lively luncheon conversations as we all ate our sandwiches.

Roberta Fiske-Rusciano

Identity

WHO ARE YOU? The way you answer this question depends on many factors, not the least of which is the context in which it is asked. Most frequently—meeting a professor, for instance—you give your full name, but when you arrive at your dorm, you might instead respond that you are the new roommate. At a big family reunion with lots of relatives you have never met, you might identify yourself as Stan and Ruth's daughter. Think about the many other ways you could respond. "I'm a college student." "I'm an economics major." "I'm a big fan of yours." "I'm your new neighbor." "I'm Tony's spouse." "I'm Puerto Rican." "I'm the place kicker." "I'm the babysitter." "I'm a New Yorker." "I'm an American." The list is almost endless.

In fact, you are all these things. Your individual identity is a unique blend of the many aspects of your life. These elements include your gender, your age, your placement in your family, your religion and your devotion to it, your race, your ethnic heritage and how (or even whether) your family has preserved it, your sexual orientation and experience, your education, your employment history, your socioeconomic background. What else would you add?

Identity incorporates both those personal characteristics by which we recognize an individual and those that define one's affiliation with a group. American culture has put considerable emphasis on the former. From Daniel Boone to Rambo, we make heroes of the nonconforming loner who acts independently, often in opposition to or in defiance of society. Advertisers promote their products as having what it takes to set us apart from the crowd and demonstrate our unique individuality. Increasingly now there are superheroes who defy the status quo and work for others while cooperating, such as Diana/Wonder Woman.

This view of identity seems to make some sense, in that some psychologists suggest that a personal sense of identity begins when a child first recognizes his or her mother as a separate being, who in turn recognizes the child as an individual. From there, however, we go through innumerable developmental stages, as we perceive and accept or reject the values and distinctions established by our particular life circumstances.

Despite the myth of American individualism, our **identity**—our self-definition or sense of selfhood—actually is shaped not by separation but by affiliation, by bonding and identifying with others. As children, we observe the people around us and learn the qualities associated with those who seem like us, especially in terms of such characteristics as gender, race, age, and religion. For example, we learn what it means to be female or male by our interactions with the women or men around us. Then we **internalize**, accept as part of our own thinking, the characteristics that we recognize as appropriate to various facets of our identities.

Psychologists have differing theories about how this internalization takes place. Some see it as a cognitive process by which we learn how people are labeled and accept those labels for ourselves. Others think it is behavioral, that we learn how to act in response to rewards and punishments. Still others believe internalization to be the emotional desire to feel connected with others like us.

Whatever the process may be, all agree that what we learn about who we are in childhood is central to how we perceive ourselves and act as adults. Even though most of us continue throughout our lives to develop new and more inclusive identities, the "new me" is most accurately understood as an integration of some new or newly discovered facet of ourselves with our previous identifications and self-images. Our individuality, our identity, is actually a constellation of the various affiliations we accept and that are attributed to us.

In this division, *Identity*, we look at how race and ethnicity, gender, and socioeconomic status influence identity formation in American culture. Part I, *Racial and Ethnic Identity*, explores the nature of race and ethnicity by considering them from both theoretical and personal perspectives and in both historical and contemporary contexts. Part II, *Gender and Sexual Identity*, examines how we learn to be male or female in our society and how gender roles affect the way we relate to and interact with one another. Because of the complexity of this topic, we shall focus on the physicality and the accompanying social forces of sexual experiences, through several case studies. Part III, *Economics and the American Dream*, shows that, despite the belief that America is a classless society or that everyone is middle class, sharp disparities in the distribution of wealth determine individual and group values and access to opportunity.

The purpose of the *Identity* division is to help us consider our own identity in the context of race, ethnicity, class, and gender. Even though any single reading selection may not speak specifically to your personal experience, the themes the readings explore will help you recognize and evaluate your place in the overall mosaic. As we come to realize that we actually have a great deal in common with some people who initially seemed different from us, when we discover that they and their experiences are more like our own than we had thought, we are more capable of understanding and sympathizing with the discrimination to which some people are subjected.

Part I
Racial and Ethnic Identity

YOU MAY BE SURPRISED TO LEARN THAT RACE AND ethnicity are not as easily distinguished from each other as is commonly assumed. Even though we use these terms in everyday conversations, most of us do not have an accurate understanding of what they really mean and how imprecise they actually are.

In the United States, when we identify someone as a member of an **ethnic** group, we mean that he or she belongs to some identifiable group with common ancestral or geographical origin.

Ethnic subgroups are defined by many complex, often variable, traits, such as religion, language, culture, customs, traditions, physical characteristics, and, probably most important in this country, ancestral origin. Ancestral origin is the reason we often label ethnic groups as "compound Americans": African Americans, German Americans, Filipino Americans, Chinese Americans, and so on.

"Wait a minute," you are probably saying. "Some of those groups are racial, not ethnic." Do not be so sure.

One definition of **race** in *The American Heritage Dictionary* is "any group of people united or classified together on the basis of common history, nationality, or geographical distribution." In this sense, race does not differ substantially from ethnicity. Traditionally in the United States, people identify race solely in terms of physical characteristics, such as skin color, texture and color of hair, and other attributes, especially facial features. However, these attributes are not as discrete or self-evident as it might seem at first. From earliest times, human populations have migrated and intermingled, mixing and blending their biological makeup. Precise lines of racial demarcation are blurred, so that, at best, systematic classifi-

cations of race are complex and must be carefully qualified and questioned.

For this reason, scientists and an increasing part of the general public have come to believe that race is less a scientific actuality than it is a **social construct**—a classification based on social values. "Racial" lines are blurry, as shown by genetic analysis, yet remain deep in the psyche of Americans. Originally articulated and ordered as a way to cement a hierarchy on this continent, our history is a record of official policy discrimination against certain groups in the United States. In the twenty-first century we continue to see the results of the inequities originally assigned approximately four hundred years ago. While many laboratories now offer DNA testing kits and analyses, where a simple swab of one's mouth reveals the geography of one's ancestral origins, our cities and their schools reveal the surface color of urban poverty. What effect will genetics testing have on our future understanding of ourselves and others?

Today, many of us tend to think of African Americans, Asian Americans, and Native Americans as racial groups and Jewish Americans, Italian Americans, and Irish Americans as ethnic groups. In the early part of the twentieth century, however, each of the latter three was called a race and was said to have distinctive physical features that marked group identity, a belief that now strikes us as quaintly absurd.

Although we tend to consider both ethnic and racial identity fixed and unalterable, in fact, they are fluid and quite subjective. You may call yourself German American because your forebears came from what is now Germany, but they may have seen themselves instead as Prussian or Bavarian, or members of one of the many other nation-states that only later were united to form the Germany we know today.

3

Our current racial and ethnic groupings reflect another blind spot in social thought: our insensitivity to the realities of cultural heritage. The label *European American*, for example, camouflages the differences between Scandinavians and the French and between those two groups and the Poles, the British, and the many other distinct European cultures, such as the indigenous Sami of Arctic Europe. While the term *Native American* is most often used by non-Indians and academicians, most Indians identify themselves as Sioux, or Lakota Sioux, Arapaho, and so on, or simply Indian.

Similarly, when we classify all African Americans as one homogeneous group, we ignore the extreme divergence of African cultures. The Ethiopian Plains culture differs tremendously from that which developed in Morocco or West Africa; moreover, like Native Americans, Africans are more likely to consider themselves Zulu, Ibo, Hausa, or Yoruba than South African or Nigerian—or even African. Finally, today there are at least nineteen Asian and Pacific Island populations lumped together under the *Asian American* label. These include the Hmong, Cambodians, Laotians, Sikh, and Burmese in addition to the more widely recognized groups representing Japan, China, Korea, India, and the Philippines.

Finally, it is important to note that all these subgroups exist within the American context, and every subgroup has been transformed by the influences of this larger society. Nevertheless, even when many historical features of the subgroup have been lost or altered, members may continue to identify with the re-created group. These are the compound Americans.

The readings in part I present a sampling of the innumerable accounts that are part of this evolutionary process. Some of them and some of the themes they present may reflect your heritage; others may not. However, each of them is part of the American experience, and we need to understand them if we are to understand what it means to be American. This is where we are now: learning about and becoming sensitive to the multiplicity and complexity of the ethnic and racial cultures that have shaped the America we know today and that will mold our nation in the future.

Reading 1 is by Afro DZ ak, the poet/musician and educator presently working and performing in Illinois.

Reading 2, the American Anthropological Association "Statement on Race," introduces some social scientists' recent position on the theoretical and practical questions surrounding our understanding and use of race as a category.

Reading 3 provides a general perspective on ethnic identity and explores several related issues. John Hope Franklin discusses historical changes in Americans' attitudes about and treatment of immigrants and ethnic groups, illuminating the distance between the American ideal that "all men are created equal" and the reality of exclusion. The fourth reading, by then-senator Barack Obama, focuses on our need and ability to form a more perfect union, as we promised in the U.S. Constitution.

Readings 5 and 6 describe the effects of **assimilation**, the process by which minority groups—under overt or subtle pressure from the majority group—abandoned the unique features of their former cultures and adapted to the values and norms of European American culture, which was dominated by the Anglo-Protestant ethic. In Grace Paley's story, Jewish immigrant parents see that their daughter's selection as the narrator of her public school's Christmas play is a difficult but necessary part of assimilation into American society. Polingaysi Qoyawayma, renamed Elizabeth Q. White by white missionaries, tells of a similar conflict when she returns for a visit to her traditional Hopi parents after her conversion at the Christian mission; her rejection of her parents' beliefs about the spiritual power of nature is painful to all three members of her family.

Reading 7, by Darryl Fears, "People of Color Who Never Felt They Were Black," describes the experience of many immigrants from Latin America and Brazil who were never considered black until they entered the United States. Similarly, in her interview with John Langston Gwaltney in reading 8, Rosa Wakefield describes what being black means to her, but her contemplation of the differences between blacks and whites and among blacks exposes how complex and subjective ethnic identification is.

Reading 9, "I'm Not Your Miss Saigon" by Jillian Montilla, is a young Asian American woman's rejection of the hurtful stereotypes made clear by many around her—colleagues and strangers. Many Americans struggle to understand their distinctive identity, achieving self-acceptance in different ways.

Reading 10 directly addresses the complexities of living in our diverse nation, as Chicano poet Carlos Cumpián reflects on Thanksgivings past and present.

Reading 11 ("Race in a Genetic World") explores how recent DNA uses have situated themselves in the debate on the meaning of race, among scientists, politicians, and the public. Finally, in reading 12, Mercedes Diaz analyzes the complex identities of Cuban Americans in "Exploring the Cuban Conundrum."

By the time you have finished the readings in part I, you will have some sense of the elements most central to ethnic identity and may have thought about your family and your life in light of those factors.

1

Just 'Cause I'm Mixed

Afro DZ ak (Peter Shungu)

Just 'Cause I'm Mixed, that don't mean that I'm
    mixed up
Inherently confused or I need to be fixed up
Just 'Cause I'm Mixed, that don't mean I'm a mule
So don't call me "mulatto," thinkin it's cool
Just 'Cause I'm Mixed, that don't mean I'm adopted
Yes, she's white, and yes, she's my biological mama
But whether or not I was adopted, you ain't got the
    right
To stare or make comments 'cause my mother is
    white
Just 'Cause I'm Mixed, that don't mean I'm "not
    black"
Cuz the concept we can have only one identity is
    wack
And I stand proudly with all my people of color
Painting broad concepts of "sister" and "brother"
Just 'Cause I'm Mixed, that don't mean I'm ill-
    conceived
As words like "miscegenation" would have you
    believe
Just 'Cause I'm Mixed, that don't mean I'm ashamed
Cuz the "race" of my mom and my dad ain't the
    same
Just 'Cause I'm Mixed, that don't mean I'm
    predictable
So sayin "mixed people all do this" or "mixed people
    are all like that" is despicable
Just 'Cause I'm Mixed, and I rock a big fro
Don't mean I'm Maxwell, Lenny Kravitz, Bob
    Marley, Jimi Hendrix, or "that guy in that
    commercial for jeans, beer, or cologne"
Just 'Cause I'm Mixed, that don't mean that I'm
    "Other"
Miscellaneous, Oreo, or the "half & half brother"
Just 'Cause I'm Mixed, that don't mean racism has
    ended
As some ignorant conservative politicians have
    pretended
Just 'Cause I'm Mixed, that don't mean that I'm
    perfect
Like some kind of "hybrid vigor" has made my genes
    superior to mere earthlings
Cuz being Multiracial is a blessing and a curse
It's better and it's worse, it's last and it's first

It's nothing and it's everything, it's yin and it's yang
It's the apocalypse, the creation, and the big bang
It's a subject that inspires me to write
It's a commonality which has helped me unite
With other Mixed people who can relate all across
    the earth
But being Mixed does not define my personal worth
                      [2011]

Understanding the Reading

1. Why does the poet defend his being "mixed"?
2. Discuss "Cuz the concept we can have only one
   identity is wack."
3. Do you recognize the stereotypes to which he is
   referring? Give examples.
4. Discuss "Cuz being Multiracial is a blessing and a
   curse."

Suggestions for Responding

1. Speak to friends who are multiracial; bring ideas
   to the class.
2. Research "miscegenation" and its history in the
   United States.

2

American Anthropological Association "Statement on Race"

The following statement was adopted by the Executive Board of the American Anthropological Association, acting on a draft prepared by a committee of representative American anthropologists. It does not reflect a consensus of all members of the AAA, as individuals vary in their approaches to the study of "race." We believe that it represents generally the contemporary thinking and scholarly positions of a majority of anthropologists.

In the United States both scholars and the general public have been conditioned to view human races as natural and separate divisions within the human species based on visible physical differences. With the vast expansion of scientific knowledge in this century, however, it has become clear that human populations are not unambiguous, clearly demarcated, biologically distinct groups. Evidence from the analysis of genetics (e.g., DNA) indicates that most physical variation, about 94 percent, lies *within* so-called racial groups. Conventional geographic "racial" groupings differ from one another only in about 6 percent of their genes. This means that there is greater variation within "racial" groups than between them. In neighboring populations there is much overlapping of genes and their phenotypic (physical) expressions. Throughout history whenever different groups have come into contact, they have interbred. The continued sharing of genetic materials has maintained all of humankind as a single species.

Physical variations in any given trait tend to occur gradually rather than abruptly over geographic areas. And because physical traits are inherited independently of one another, knowing the range of one trait does not predict the presence of others. For example, skin color varies largely from light in the temperate areas in the north to dark in the tropical areas in the south; its intensity is not related to nose shape or hair texture. Dark skin may be associated with frizzy or kinky hair or curly or wavy or straight hair, all of which are found among different indigenous peoples in tropical regions. These facts render any attempt to establish lines of division among biological populations both arbitrary and subjective.

Historical research has shown that the idea of "race" has always carried more meanings than mere physical differences; indeed, physical variations in the human species have no meaning except the social ones that humans put on them. Today scholars in many fields argue that "race" as it is understood in the United States of America was a social mechanism invented during the eighteenth century to refer to those populations brought together in colonial America: the English and other European settlers, the conquered Indian peoples, and those peoples of Africa brought in to provide slave labor.

From its inception, this modern concept of "race" was modeled after an ancient theorem of the Great Chain of Being, which posited natural categories on a hierarchy established by God or nature. Thus "race" was a mode of classification linked specifically to peoples in the colonial situation. It subsumed a growing ideology of inequality devised to rationalize European attitudes and treatment of the conquered and enslaved peoples. Proponents of slavery in particular during the nineteenth century used "race" to justify the retention of slavery. The ideology magnified the differences among Europeans, Africans, and Indians, established a rigid hierarchy of socially exclusive categories, underscored and bolstered unequal rank and status differences, and provided the rationalization that the inequality was natural or God-given. The different physical traits of African Americans and Indians became markers or symbols of their status differences.

As they were constructing U.S. society, leaders among European Americans fabricated the cultural/behavioral characteristics associated with each "race," linking superior traits with Europeans and negative and inferior ones to blacks and Indians. Numerous arbitrary and fictitious beliefs about the different peoples were institutionalized and deeply embedded in American thought.

Early in the nineteenth century the growing fields of science began to reflect the public consciousness about human differences. Differences among the "racial" categories were projected to their greatest extreme when the argument was posed that Africans, Indians, and Europeans were separate species, with Africans the least human and closer taxonomically to apes.

Ultimately "race" as an ideology about human differences was subsequently spread to other areas of the world. It became a strategy for dividing, ranking, and controlling colonized people used by colonial powers everywhere. But it was not limited to the colonial situation. In the latter part of the nineteenth century it was employed by Europeans to rank one another and to justify social, economic, and political inequalities among their peoples. During World War II, the Nazis under Adolf Hitler enjoined the expanded ideology of "race" and "racial" differences and took them to a logical end: the extermination of 11 million people of "inferior races" (e.g., Jews, Gypsies, Africans, homosexuals, and so forth) and other unspeakable brutalities of the Holocaust.

"Race" thus evolved as a worldview, a body of prejudgments that distorts our ideas about human differences and group behavior. Racial beliefs constitute myths about the diversity in the human species and about the abilities and behavior of people homogenized into "racial" categories. The myths fused behavior and physical features together in the public mind, impeding our comprehension of biological variations and cultural behavior, implying that both are genetically determined. Racial myths bear no relationship to the reality of human capabilities or behavior. Scientists today find that reliance on such folk beliefs about human differences in research has led to countless errors.

At the end of the twentieth century, we now

understand that human cultural behavior is learned, conditioned into infants beginning at birth, and always subject to modification. No human is born with a built-in culture or language. Our temperaments, dispositions, and personalities, regardless of genetic propensities, are developed within sets of meanings and values that we call "culture." Studies of infant and early childhood learning and behavior attest to the reality of our cultures in forming who we are.

It is a basic tenet of anthropological knowledge that all normal human beings have the capacity to learn any cultural behavior. The American experience with immigrants from hundreds of different language and cultural backgrounds who have acquired some version of American culture traits and behavior is the clearest evidence of this fact. Moreover, people of all physical variations have learned different cultural behaviors and continue to do so as modern transportation moves millions of immigrants around the world.

How people have been accepted and treated within the context of a given society or culture has a direct impact on how they perform in that society. The "racial" worldview was invented to assign some groups to perpetual low status, while others were permitted access to privilege, power, and wealth. The tragedy in the United States has been that the policies and practices stemming from this worldview succeeded all too well in constructing unequal populations among Europeans, Native Americans, and peoples of African descent. Given what we know about the capacity of normal humans to achieve and function within any culture, we conclude that present-day inequalities between so-called "racial" groups are not consequences of their biological inheritance but products of historical and contemporary social, economic, educational, and political circumstances.

Understanding the Reading

1. How do anthropologists argue that human populations are never biologically distinct groups?
2. What was the Great Chain of Being?
3. How did we ever come to believe in the superiority and inferiority of races?

Suggestion for Responding

1. Have a debate on whether U.S. society should collect data on "racial" and ethnic groups.

3

Ethnicity in American Life: The Historical Perspective

JOHN HOPE FRANKLIN

The United States is unique in the ethnic composition of its population. No other country in the world can point to such a variety of cultural, racial, religious, and national backgrounds in its population. It was one of the salient features in the early history of this country: and it would continue to be so down into the twentieth century. From virtually every corner of the globe they came—some enthusiastically and some quite reluctantly. Britain and every part of the continent of Europe provided prospective Americans by the millions. Africa and Asia gave up great throngs. Other areas of the New World saw inhabitants desert their own lands to seek their fortunes in the colossus to the North. Those who came voluntarily were attracted by the prospect of freedom of religion, freedom from want, and freedom from various forms of oppression. Those who were forced to come were offered the consolation that if they were white, they would someday inherit the earth, and if they were black, they would someday gather their reward in the Christian heaven.

One of the interesting and significant features of this coming together of peoples of many tongues and races and cultures was that the backgrounds out of which they came would soon be minimized and that the process by which they evolved into Americans would be of paramount importance. Hector St. Jean de Crevecoeur sought to describe this process in 1782 when he answered his own question, "What, then, is the American, this new man?" He said, "He is either an European, or the descendant of an European, hence that strange mixture of blood, which you will find in no other country. . . . He is an American, who, leaving behind him all his ancient prejudices and manners, receives new ones from the new mode of the life he has embraced, the new government he obeys, and the new rank he holds. He becomes an American by being received in the broad lap of our great *Alma Mater.* Here individuals of all nations are melted into a new race of men, whose labours and posterity will one day cause great changes in the world."

This was one of the earliest expressions of the

notion that the process of Americanization involved the creation of an entirely new mode of life that would replace the ethnic backgrounds of those who were a part of the process. It contained some imprecisions and inaccuracies that would, in time, become a part of the lore or myth of the vaunted melting pot and would grossly misrepresent the crucial factor of ethnicity in American life. It ignored the tenacity with which the Pennsylvania Dutch held onto their language, religion, and way of life. It overlooked the way in which the Swedes of New Jersey remained Swedes and the manner in which the French Huguenots of New York and Charleston held onto their own past as though it was the source of all light and life. It described a process that in a distant day would gag at the notion that Irish Catholics could be assimilated on the broad lap of Alma Mater or that Asians could be seated on the basis of equality at the table of the Great American Feast.

By suggesting that only Europeans were involved in the process of becoming Americans, Crevecoeur pointedly ruled out three-quarters of a million blacks already in the country who, along with their progeny, would be regarded as ineligible to become Americans for at least another two centuries. To be sure, the number of persons of African descent would increase enormously, but the view of their ineligibility for Americanization would be very slow to change. And when such a change occurred, even if it merely granted freedom from bondage, the change would be made most reluctantly and without any suggestion that freedom qualified one for equality on the broad lap of Alma Mater. It was beyond the conception of Crevecoeur, as it was indeed beyond the conception of the founding fathers, that Negroes, slave or free, could become true Americans, enjoying that fellowship in a common enterprise about which Crevecoeur spoke so warmly. It was as though Crevecoeur was arguing that ethnicity, where persons of African descent were concerned, was either so powerful or so unattractive as to make their assimilation entirely impossible or so insignificant as to make it entirely undesirable. In any case Americanization in the late eighteenth century was a precious commodity to be cherished and enjoyed only by a select group of persons of European descent.

One must admit, therefore, that at the time of the birth of the new nation there was no clear-cut disposition to welcome into the American family persons of any and all ethnic backgrounds. Only Europeans were invited to fight for independence. And when the patriots at long last relented and gave persons of African descent a chance to fight, the concession was made with great reluctance and after much equivocation and soul-searching. Only Europeans were regarded as full citizens in the new states and in the new nation. And when the founding fathers wrote the Constitution of the United States, they did not seem troubled by the distinctions on the basis of ethnic differences that the Constitution implied.

If the principle of ethnic exclusiveness was propounded so early and so successfully in the history of the United States, it is not surprising that it would, in time, become the basis for questioning the ethnic backgrounds of large numbers of prospective Americans, even Europeans. Thus, in 1819, a Jewish immigrant was chilled to hear a bystander refer to him and his companion as "more damned emigrants." A decade later there began a most scathing and multifaceted attack on the Catholic Church. On two counts the church was a bad influence. First, its principal recruits were the Irish, the "very dregs" of the Old World social order; second, its doctrine of papal supremacy ran counter to the idea of the political and religious independence of the United States. Roman Catholics, Protestant Americans warned, were engaged in a widespread conspiracy to subvert American institutions, through parochial schools, the Catholic press, immoral convents, and a sinister design to control the West by flooding it with Catholic settlers. The burning of convents and churches and the killing of Catholics themselves were indications of how deeply many Americans felt about religious and cultural differences for which they had a distaste and suspicion that bordered on paranoia.

Soon the distaste for the foreign-born became almost universal, with Roman Catholics themselves sharing in the hostility to those who followed them to the new Republic. Some expressed fear of the poverty and criminality that accompanied each wave of immigrants. Some felt that those newly arrived from abroad were a threat to republican freedom. Some saw in the ethnic differences of the newcomers an immediate danger to the moral standards of Puritan America. Some feared the competition that newcomers posed in the labor market. Some became convinced that the ideal of a national homogeneity would disappear with the influx of so many unassimilable elements. Soon, nativist societies sprang up all across the land, and they found national expression in 1850 in a new organization called the Order of the Star Spangled Banner. With its slogan, "America for

Americans," the order, which became the organizational basis for the Know-Nothing party, engendered a fear through its preachments that caused many an American to conclude that his country was being hopelessly subverted by the radical un-Americanism of the great variety of ethnic strains that were present in the United States.

If there was some ambivalence regarding the ethnic diversity of white immigrants before the Civil War, it was dispelled by the view that prevailed regarding immigrants in the post–Civil War years. The "old" immigrants, so the argument went, were at least assimilable and had "entered practically every line of activity in nearly every part of the country." Even those who had been non-English speaking had mingled freely with native Americans and had therefore been quickly assimilated. Not so with the "new" immigrants who came after 1880. They "congregated together in sections apart from native Americans and the older immigrants to such an extent that assimilation had been slow." Small wonder that they were different. Small wonder that they were barely assimilable. They came from Austro-Hungary, Italy, Russia, Greece, Rumania, and Turkey. They dressed differently, spoke in unfamiliar tongues, and clung to strange, if not exotic customs. It did not matter that Bohemians, Moravians, and Finns had lower percentages of illiteracy than had the Irish and Germans or that Jews had a higher percentage of skilled laborers than any group except the Scots. Nor did it matter that, in fact, the process of assimilation for the so-called "new" group was about as rapid as that of the so-called "old" group.

What did matter was that the new nativism was stronger and more virulent than any anti-immigration forces or groups of the early nineteenth century and that these groups were determined either to drive from the shores those who were different or to isolate them so that they could not contaminate American society. Old-stock Americans began to organize to preserve American institutions and the American way of life. Those who had been here for five years or a decade designated themselves as old-stock Americans and joined in the attack on those recently arrived. If the cult of Anglo-Saxon superiority was all but pervasive, those who were not born into the cult regarded themselves as honorary members. Thus, they could celebrate with as much feeling as any the virtues of Anglo-Saxon institutions and could condemn as vehemently as any those ideas and practices that were not strictly Anglo-Saxon. Whenever possible they joined

the American Protective Association and the Immigrant Restriction League; and in so doing they sold their own ethnicity for the obscurity that a pseudo-assimilation brought. But in the end, they would be less than successful. The arrogance and presumption of the Anglo-Saxon complex was not broad enough to embrace the Jews of eastern Europe or the Bohemians of central Europe or the Turks of the Middle East. The power and drive of the Anglo-Saxon forces would prevail; and those who did not belong would be compelled to console themselves by extolling the virtues of cultural pluralism.

By that time—near the end of the nineteenth century—the United States had articulated quite clearly its exalted standards of ethnicity. They were standards that accepted Anglo-Saxons as the norm, placed other whites on what may be called "ethnic probation," and excluded from serious consideration the Japanese, Chinese, and Negroes. It was not difficult to deal harshly with the Chinese and Japanese when they began to enter the United States in considerable numbers in the post–Civil War years. They simply did not meet the standards that the arbiters of American ethnicity had promulgated. They were different in race, religion, language, and public and private morality. They had to be excluded; and eventually they were.

The presence of persons of African descent, almost from the beginning, had helped whites to define ethnicity and to establish and maintain the conditions by which it could be controlled. If their color and race, their condition of servitude, and their generally degraded position did not set them apart, the laws and customs surrounding them more than accomplished that feat. Whether in Puritan Massachusetts or cosmopolitan New York or Anglican South Carolina, the colonists declared that Negroes, slave or free, did not and could not belong to the society of equal human beings. Thus, the newly arrived Crevecoeur could be as blind to the essential humanity of Negroes as the patriots who tried to keep them out of the Continental Army. They were not a part of America, these new men. And in succeeding years their presence would do more to define ethnicity than the advent of several scores of millions of Europeans.

It was not enough for Americans, already somewhat guilt-ridden for maintaining slavery in a free society, to exclude blacks from American society on the basis of race and condition of servitude. They proceeded from that point to argue that Negroes were inferior morally, intellectually, and physically. Even as he reviewed the remarkable accomplishments of Benjamin Banneker, surveyor, almanacker, mathematician, and clockmaker, Thomas Jefferson had serious doubts about the mental capabilities of Africans, and he expressed these doubts to his European friends. What Jefferson speculated about at the end of the eighteenth century became indisputable dogma within a decade after his death.

In the South every intellectual, legal, and religious resource was employed in the task of describing the condition of Negroes in such a way as to make them the least attractive human beings on the face of the earth. Slavery was not only the natural lot of blacks, the slaveowners argued, but it was also in accordance with God's will that they should be kept in slavery. As one sanctimonious divine put it, "We feel that the souls of our slaves are a solemn trust and we shall strive to present them faultless and complete before the presence of God. . . . How ever the world may judge us in connection with our institution of slavery, we conscientiously believe it to be a great missionary institution—one arranged by God, as He arranges all moral and religious influences of the world so that the good may be brought out of seeming evil, and a blessing wrung out of every form of the curse." It was a difficult task that the owners of slaves set for themselves. Slaves had brought with them only heathenism, immorality, profligacy, and irresponsibility. They possessed neither the mental capacity nor the moral impulse to improve themselves. Only if their sponsors—those to whom were entrusted not only their souls but also their bodies—were fully committed to their improvement could they take even the slightest, halting steps toward civilization.

What began as a relatively moderate justification for slavery soon became a vigorous, aggressive defense of the institution. Slavery, to the latter-day defenders, was the cornerstone of the republican edifice. To a governor of South Carolina, it was the greatest of all the great blessings which a kind Providence had bestowed upon the glorious region of the South. It was, indeed, one of the remarkable coincidences of history that such a favored institution had found such a favored creature as the African to give slavery the high value that was placed on it. A childlike race, prone to docility and manageable in every respect, the African was the ideal subject for the slave role. Slaveholders had to work hard to be worthy of this great Providential blessing.

Nothing that Negroes could do or say could change or seriously affect this view. They might grad-

uate from college, as John Russwurm did in 1826, or they might write a most scathing attack against slavery, as David Walker did in 1829. It made no difference. They might teach in an all-white college, as Charles B. Reason did in New York in the 1850s, or publish a newspaper, as Frederick Douglass did during that same decade. Their racial and cultural backgrounds disqualified them from becoming American citizens. They could even argue in favor of their capacities and potentialities, as Henry Highland Garnet did, or they might argue their right to fight for union and freedom, as 186,000 did in the Civil War. Still, it made no sense for white Americans to give serious consideration to their arguments and their actions. They were beyond the veil, as the Jews had been beyond the veil in the barbaric and bigoted communities of eastern Europe.

The views regarding Negroes that had been so carefully developed to justify and defend slavery would not disappear with emancipation. To those who had developed such views and to the vast numbers who subscribed to them, they were much too valid to be discarded simply because the institution of slavery had collapsed. In fact, if Negroes were heathens and barbarians and intellectual imbeciles in slavery, they were hardly qualified to function as equals in a free society. And any effort to impose them on a free society should be vigorously and relentlessly resisted, even if it meant that a new and subordinate place for them had to be created.

When Americans set out to create such a place for the four million freedmen after the Civil War, they found that it was convenient to put their formulation in the context of the ethnic factors that militated against complete assimilation. To do it this way seemed more fitting, perhaps even more palatable, for the white members of a so-called free society. And they had some experience on which to rely. In an earlier day it had been the Irish or the Germans or the free Negroes who presented problems of assimilation. They were different in various ways and did not seem to make desirable citizens. In time the Irish, Germans, and other Europeans made it and were accepted on the broad lap of Alma Mater. But not the free Negroes, who continued to suffer disabilities even in the North in the years just before the Civil War. Was this the key to the solution of the postwar problems? Perhaps it was. After all, Negroes had always been a group apart in Boston, New York, Philadelphia, and other northern cities. They all lived together in one part of the city—especially if they could find no other place to live. They had their own churches—after the whites drove them out of theirs. They had their own schools—after they were excluded from the schools attended by whites. They had their own social organizations—after the whites barred them from theirs.

If Negroes possessed so many ethnic characteristics such as living in the same community, having their own churches, schools, and social clubs, and perhaps other agencies of cohesion, that was all very well. They even seemed "happier with their own kind," some patronizing observers remarked. They were like the Germans or the Irish or the Italians or the Jews. They had so much in common and so much to preserve. There was one significant difference, however. For Europeans, the ethnic factors that brought a particular group together actually eased the task of assimilation and, in many ways, facilitated the process of assimilation, particularly as hostile elements sought to disorient them in their drive toward full citizenship. And, in time, they achieved it.

For Negroes, however, such was not the case. They had been huddled together in northern ghettoes since the eighteenth century. They had had their own churches since 1792 and their own schools since 1800. And this separateness, this ostracism, was supported and enforced by the full majesty of the law, state and federal, just to make certain that Negroes did, indeed, preserve their ethnicity! And as they preserved their ethnicity—all too frequently as they looked down the barrel of a policeman's pistol or a militiaman's shotgun—full citizenship seemed many light years away. They saw other ethnic groups pass them by, one by one, and take their places in the sacred Order of the Star Spangled Banner, the American Protective Association, the Knights of the Ku Klux Klan—not always fully assimilated but vehemently opposed to the assimilation of Negroes. The ethnic grouping that was a way station, a temporary resting place for Europeans as they became Americans, proved to be a terminal point for blacks who found it virtually impossible to become Americans in any real sense.

There was an explanation or at least a justification for this. The federal government and the state governments had tried to force Negroes into full citizenship and had tried to legislate them into equality with the whites. This was not natural and could not possibly succeed. Negroes had not made it because they were not fit, the social Darwinists[1] said. Negroes were beasts, Charles Carroll declared somewhat inele-

gantly. "Stateways cannot change folkways," William Graham Sumner, the distinguished scholar, philosophized. The first forty years of Negro freedom had been a failure, said John R. Commons, one of the nation's leading economists. This so-called failure was widely acknowledged in the country as northerners of every rank and description acquiesced, virtually without a murmur of objection, to the southern settlement of the race problem characterized by disfranchisement, segregation, and discrimination.

Here was a new and exotic form of ethnicity. It was to be seen in the badges of inferiority and the symbols of racial degradation that sprang up in every sector of American life—in the exclusion from the polling places with its specious justification that Negroes were unfit to participate in the sacred rite of voting; the back stairway or the freight elevator to public places; the separate, miserable railway car; the separate and hopelessly inferior school; and even the Jim Crow[2] cemetery. Ethnic considerations had never been so important in the shaping of public policy. They had never before been used by the American government to define the role and place of other groups in American society. The United States had labored hard to create order out of its chaotic and diverse ethnic backgrounds. Having begun by meekly suggesting the difficulty in assimilating all groups into one great society, it had acknowledged failure by ruling out one group altogether, quite categorically, and frequently by law, solely on the basis of race.

It could not achieve this without doing irreparable harm to the early notions of the essential unity of America and Americans. The sentiments that promoted the disfranchisement and segregation of Negroes also encouraged the infinite varieties of discrimination against Jews, Armenians, Turks, Japanese, and Chinese. The conscious effort to degrade a particular ethnic group reflects a corrosive quality that dulls the sensitivities of both the perpetrators and the victims. It calls forth venomous hatreds and crude distinctions in high places as well as low places. It can affect the quality of mind of even the most cultivated scholar and place him in a position scarcely distinguishable from the Klansman or worse. It was nothing out of the ordinary, therefore, that at a dinner in honor of the winner of one of Harvard's most coveted prizes, Professor Barrett Wendell warned that if a Negro or a Jew ever won the prize, the dinner would have to be canceled.

By the time that the Statue of Liberty was dedicated in 1886, the words of Emma Lazarus on the base of it had a somewhat hollow ring. Could anyone seriously believe that the poor, tired, huddled masses "yearning to breathe free" were really welcome here? This was a land where millions of black human beings whose ancestors had been here for centuries were consistently treated as pariahs and untouchables! What interpretation could anyone place on the sentiments expressed on the statue except that the country had no real interest in or sympathy for the downtrodden unless they were white and preferably Anglo-Saxon? It was a disillusioning experience for some newcomers to discover that their own ethnic background was a barrier to success in their adopted land. It was a searing and shattering experience for Negroes to discover over and over again that three centuries of toil and loyalty were nullified by the misfortune of their own degraded ethnic background.

In the fullness of time—in the twentieth century—the nation would confront the moment of truth regarding ethnicity as a factor in its own historical development. Crevecoeur's words would have no real significance. The words of the Declaration of Independence would have no real meaning. The words of Emma Lazarus would not ring true. All such sentiments would be put to the severe test of public policy and private deeds and would be found wanting. The Ku Klux Klan would challenge the moral and human dignity of Jews, Catholics, and Negroes. The quotas of the new immigration laws would define ethnic values in terms of race and national origin. The restrictive covenants[3] would arrogate to a select group of bigots the power of determining what races or ethnic groups should live in certain houses or whether, indeed, they should have any houses at all in which to live. If some groups finally made it through the escape hatch and arrived at the point of acceptance, it was on the basis of race, now defined with sufficient breadth to include all or most peoples who were not of African descent.

By that time ethnicity in American life would come to have a special, clearly definable meaning. Its meaning would be descriptive of that group of people vaguely defined in the federal census returns as "others" or "non-whites." It would have something in common with that magnificent term "cultural pluralism," the consolation prize for those who were not and could not be assimilated. It would signify the same groping for respectability that describes that group of people who live in what is euphemistically called "the inner city." It would represent a rather earnest search for a hidden meaning that would make

it seem a bit more palatable and surely more sophisticated than something merely racial. But in 1969 even a little child would know what ethnicity had come to mean.

In its history, ethnicity, in its true sense, has extended and continues to extend beyond race. At times it has meant language, customs, religion, national origin. It has also meant race; and, to some, it has always meant only race. It had already begun to have a racial connotation in the eighteenth century. In the nineteenth century, it had a larger racial component, even as other factors continued to loom large. In the present century, as these other factors have receded in importance, racial considerations have come to have even greater significance. If the history of ethnicity has meant anything at all during the last three centuries, it has meant the gradual but steady retreat from the broad and healthy regard for cultural and racial differences to a narrow, counterproductive concept of differences in terms of whim, intolerance, and racial prejudice. We have come full circle. The really acceptable American is still that person whom Crevecoeur described almost two hundred years ago. But the true American, acceptable or not, is that person who seeks to act out his role in terms of his regard for human qualities irrespective of race. One of the great tragedies of American life at the beginning was that ethnicity was defined too narrowly. One of the great tragedies of today is that this continues to be the case. One can only hope that the nation and its people will all someday soon come to reassess ethnicity in terms of the integrity of the man rather than in terms of the integrity of the race.

[1989]

Terms

1. Social Darwinism: The theory that applied Darwin's theory of evolution, "survival of the fittest," to society; it assumed that upper classes were naturally superior, and the failure of the lower classes was the result of their natural inferiority, not of social policies and practices.
2. Jim Crow: Laws and practices, especially in the South, that separated blacks and whites and enforced the subordination of blacks.
3. Restrictive covenants: Codes prohibiting members of some groups—often blacks, Jews, and Asians—from buying real estate in certain areas.

Understanding the Reading

1. Today, why do we find de Crevecoeur's 1782 definition of "the American, this new man" inadequate or inappropriate?
2. How did the principle of ethnic exclusion that omitted people of African descent affect later immigrant groups in the nineteenth century?
3. What does nativism mean?
4. How was the exclusion of African Americans from American society justified?
5. How was it maintained?
6. How did the treatment of African Americans affect other groups in the twentieth century?

Suggestions for Responding

1. According to Franklin, America has not lived up to its ideals. Do you think his pessimistic views are justified? What arguments would you offer to support or refute his analysis?
2. Is the "really acceptable American" today still that person whom de Crevecoeur described, as Franklin claims? Why or why not?

4

Toward a More Perfect Union

Barack Obama

"We the people, in order to form a more perfect union."

Two hundred and twenty-one years ago, in a hall that still stands across the street, a group of men gathered and, with these simple words, launched America's improbable experiment in democracy. Farmers and scholars; statesmen and patriots who had traveled across an ocean to escape tyranny and persecution finally made real their declaration of independence at a Philadelphia convention that lasted through the spring of 1787.

The document they produced was eventually signed but ultimately unfinished. It was stained by this nation's original sin of slavery, a question that divided the colonies and brought the convention to a stalemate until the founders chose to allow the slave trade to continue for at least twenty more years, and to leave any final resolution to future generations.

Of course, the answer to the slavery question was already embedded within our Constitution—a Constitution that had at its very core the ideal of equal citizenship under the law; a Constitution that promised its people liberty, and justice, and a union that could be and should be perfected over time.

And yet words on a parchment would not be enough to deliver slaves from bondage, or provide men and women of every color and creed their full rights and obligations as citizens of the United States. What would be needed were Americans in successive generations who were willing to do their part—through protests and struggle, on the streets and in the courts, through a civil war and civil disobedience and always at great risk—to narrow that gap between the promise of our ideals and the reality of their time. This was one of the tasks we set forth at the beginning of this campaign—to continue the long march of those who came before us, a march for a more just, more equal, more free, more caring and more prosperous America. I chose to run for the presidency at this moment in history because I believe deeply that we cannot solve the challenges of our time unless we solve them together—unless we perfect our union by understanding that we may have different stories, but we hold common hopes; that we may not look the same and we may not have come from the same place, but we all want to move in the same direction—towards a better future for our children and our grandchildren.

This belief comes from my unyielding faith in the decency and generosity of the American people. But it also comes from my own American story.

I am the son of a black man from Kenya and a white woman from Kansas. I was raised with the help of a white grandfather who survived a Depression to serve in Patton's Army during World War II and a white grandmother who worked on a bomber assembly line at Fort Leavenworth while he was overseas. I've gone to some of the best schools in America and lived in one of the world's poorest nations. I am married to a black American who carries within her the blood of slaves and slaveowners—an inheritance we pass on to our two precious daughters. I have brothers, sisters, nieces, nephews, uncles and cousins, of every race and every hue, scattered across three continents, and for as long as I live, I will never forget that in no other country on Earth is my story even possible.

It's a story that hasn't made me the most conventional candidate. But it is a story that has seared into my genetic makeup the idea that this nation is more than the sum of its parts—that out of many, we are truly one.

Throughout the first year of this campaign, against all predictions to the contrary, we saw how hungry the American people were for this message of unity. Despite the temptation to view my candidacy through a purely racial lens, we won commanding victories in states with some of the whitest populations in the country. In South Carolina, where the Confederate Flag still flies, we built a powerful coalition of African Americans and white Americans.

This is not to say that race has not been an issue in the campaign. At various stages in the campaign, some commentators have deemed me either "too black" or "not black enough." We saw racial tensions bubble to the surface during the week before the South Carolina primary. The press has scoured every exit poll for the latest evidence of racial polarization, not just in terms of white and black, but black and brown as well.

And yet it has only been in the last couple of weeks that the discussion of race in this campaign has taken a particularly divisive turn.

On one end of the spectrum, we've heard the implication that my candidacy is somehow an exercise in affirmative action; that it's based solely on the desire of wide-eyed liberals to purchase racial reconciliation on the cheap. On the other end, we've heard my former pastor, Reverend Jeremiah Wright, use incendiary language to express views that have the potential not only to widen the racial divide but also to denigrate both the greatness and the goodness of our nation—that rightly offend white and black alike.

I have already condemned, in unequivocal terms, the statements of Reverend Wright that have caused such controversy. For some, nagging questions remain. Did I know him to be an occasionally fierce critic of American domestic and foreign policy? Of course. Did I ever hear him make remarks that could be considered controversial while I sat in church? Yes. Did I strongly disagree with many of his political views? Absolutely—just as I'm sure many of you have heard remarks from your pastors, priests, or rabbis with which you strongly disagreed.

But the remarks that have caused this recent firestorm weren't simply controversial. They weren't simply a religious leader's effort to speak out against perceived injustice. Instead, they expressed a profoundly distorted view of this country—a view that sees white racism as endemic, and that elevates what is wrong with America above all that we know is right

with America; a view that sees the conflicts in the Middle East as rooted primarily in the actions of stalwart allies like Israel, instead of emanating from the perverse and hateful ideologies of radical Islam.

As such, Reverend Wright's comments were not only wrong but divisive, divisive at a time when we need unity; racially charged at a time when we need to come together to solve a set of monumental problems—two wars, a terrorist threat, a falling economy, a chronic health care crisis and potentially devastating climate change; problems that are neither black nor white or Latino or Asian, but rather problems that confront us all.

Given my background, my politics, and my professed values and ideals, there will no doubt be those for whom my statements of condemnation are not enough. Why associate myself with Reverend Wright in the first place, they may ask? Why not join another church? And I confess that if all that I knew of Reverend Wright were the snippets of those sermons that have run in an endless loop on the television and YouTube, or if Trinity United Church of Christ conformed to the caricatures being peddled by some commentators, there is no doubt that I would react in much the same way.

But the truth is, that isn't all that I know of the man. The man I met more than twenty years ago is a man who helped introduce me to my Christian faith, a man who spoke to me about our obligations to love one another; to care for the sick and lift up the poor. He is a man who served his country as a U.S. Marine; who has studied and lectured at some of the finest universities and seminaries in the country, and who for over thirty years led a church that serves the community by doing God's work here on Earth—by housing the homeless, ministering to the needy, providing day care services and scholarships and prison ministries, and reaching out to those suffering from HIV/AIDS.

In my first book, *Dreams from My Father*, I described the experience of my first service at Trinity:

"People began to shout, to rise from their seats and clap and cry out, a forceful wind carrying the reverend's voice up into the rafters. . . . And in that single note—hope!—I heard something else; at the foot of that cross, inside the thousands of churches across the city, I imagined the stories of ordinary black people merging with the stories of David and Goliath, Moses and Pharaoh, the Christians in the lion's den, Ezekiel's field of dry bones. Those stories—of survival, and freedom, and hope—became our story, my story; the blood that had spilled was our blood, the tears our tears; until this black church, on this bright day, seemed once more a vessel carrying the story of a people into future generations and into a larger world. Our trials and triumphs became at once unique and universal, black and more than black; in chronicling our journey, the stories and songs gave us a means to reclaim memories that we didn't need to feel shame about . . . memories that all people might study and cherish—and with which we could start to rebuild."

That has been my experience at Trinity. Like other predominantly black churches across the country, Trinity embodies the black community in its entirety—the doctor and the welfare mom, the model student and the former gang-banger. Like other black churches, Trinity's services are full of raucous laughter and sometimes bawdy humor. They are full of dancing, clapping, screaming and shouting that may seem jarring to the untrained ear. The church contains in full the kindness and cruelty, the fierce intelligence and the shocking ignorance, the struggles and successes, the love and yes, the bitterness and bias that make up the black experience in America.

And this helps explain, perhaps, my relationship with Reverend Wright. As imperfect as he may be, he has been like family to me. He strengthened my faith, officiated my wedding, and baptized my children. Not once in my conversations with him have I heard him talk about any ethnic group in derogatory terms, or treat whites with whom he interacted with anything but courtesy and respect. He contains within him the contradictions—the good and the bad—of the community that he has served diligently for so many years.

I can no more disown him than I can disown the black community. I can no more disown him than I can my white grandmother—a woman who helped raise me, a woman who sacrificed again and again for me, a woman who loves me as much as she loves anything in this world, but a woman who once confessed her fear of black men who passed by her on the street, and who on more than one occasion has uttered racial or ethnic stereotypes that made me cringe.

These people are a part of me. And they are a part of America, this country that I love.

Some will see this as an attempt to justify or excuse comments that are simply inexcusable. I can assure you it is not. I suppose the politically safe thing would be to move on from this episode and just hope that it fades into the woodwork. We can dismiss Rev-

erend Wright as a crank or a demagogue, just as some have dismissed Geraldine Ferraro, in the aftermath of her recent statements, as harboring some deep-seated racial bias.

But race is an issue that I believe this nation cannot afford to ignore right now. We would be making the same mistake that Reverend Wright made in his offending sermons about America—to simplify and stereotype and amplify the negative to the point that it distorts reality.

The fact is that the comments that have been made and the issues that have surfaced over the last few weeks reflect the complexities of race in this country that we've never really worked through—a part of our union that we have yet to perfect. And if we walk away now, if we simply retreat into our respective corners, we will never be able to come together and solve challenges like health care, or education, or the need to find good jobs for every American.

Understanding this reality requires a reminder of how we arrived at this point. As William Faulkner once wrote, "The past isn't dead and buried. In fact, it isn't even past." We do not need to recite here the history of racial injustice in this country. But we do need to remind ourselves that so many of the disparities that exist in the African American community today can be directly traced to inequalities passed on from an earlier generation that suffered under the brutal legacy of slavery and Jim Crow.

Segregated schools were, and are, inferior schools; we still haven't fixed them, fifty years after *Brown v. Board of Education*, and the inferior education they provided, then and now, helps explain the pervasive achievement gap between today's black and white students.

Legalized discrimination—where blacks were prevented, often through violence, from owning property, or loans were not granted to African American business owners, or black homeowners could not access FHA mortgages, or blacks were excluded from unions, or the police force, or fire departments—meant that black families could not amass any meaningful wealth to bequeath to future generations. That history helps explain the wealth and income gap between black and white, and the concentrated pockets of poverty that persists in so many of today's urban and rural communities.

A lack of economic opportunity among black men, and the shame and frustration that came from not being able to provide for one's family, contributed to the erosion of black families—a problem that welfare policies for many years may have worsened. And the lack of basic services in so many urban black neighborhoods—parks for kids to play in, police walking the beat, regular garbage pick-up and building code enforcement—all helped create a cycle of violence, blight and neglect that continue to haunt us.

This is the reality in which Reverend Wright and other African Americans of his generation grew up. They came of age in the late fifties and early sixties, a time when segregation was still the law of the land and opportunity was systematically constricted. What's remarkable is not how many failed in the face of discrimination, but rather how many men and women overcame the odds; how many were able to make a way out of no way for those like me who would come after them.

But for all those who scratched and clawed their way to get a piece of the American Dream, there were many who didn't make it—those who were ultimately defeated, in one way or another, by discrimination. That legacy of defeat was passed on to future generations—those young men and increasingly young women who we see standing on street corners or languishing in our prisons, without hope or prospects for the future. Even for those blacks who did make it, questions of race, and racism, continue to define their worldview in fundamental ways. For the men and women of Reverend Wright's generation, the memories of humiliation and doubt and fear have not gone away; nor has the anger and the bitterness of those years. That anger may not get expressed in public, in front of white co-workers or white friends. But it does find voice in the barbershop or around the kitchen table. At times, that anger is exploited by politicians, to gin up votes along racial lines, or to make up for a politician's own failings.

And occasionally it finds voice in the church on Sunday morning, in the pulpit and in the pews. The fact that so many people are surprised to hear that anger in some of Reverend Wright's sermons simply reminds us of the old truism that the most segregated hour in American life occurs on Sunday morning. That anger is not always productive; indeed, all too often it distracts attention from solving real problems; it keeps us from squarely facing our own complicity in our condition, and prevents the African American community from forging the alliances it needs to bring about real change. But the anger is real; it is powerful; and to simply wish it away, to condemn it without understanding its roots, only serves to widen the chasm of misunderstanding that exists between the races.

In fact, a similar anger exists within segments of the white community. Most working- and middle-class white Americans don't feel that they have been particularly privileged by their race. Their experience is the immigrant experience—as far as they're concerned, no one's handed them anything, they've built it from scratch. They've worked hard all their lives, many times only to see their jobs shipped overseas or their pension dumped after a lifetime of labor. They are anxious about their futures, and feel their dreams slipping away; in an era of stagnant wages and global competition, opportunity comes to be seen as a zero sum game, in which your dreams come at my expense. So when they are told to bus their children to a school across town; when they hear that an African American is getting an advantage in landing a good job or a spot in a good college because of an injustice that they themselves never committed; when they're told that their fears about crime in urban neighborhoods are somehow prejudiced, resentment builds over time.

Like the anger within the black community, these resentments aren't always expressed in polite company. But they have helped shape the political landscape for at least a generation. Anger over welfare and affirmative action helped forge the Reagan Coalition. Politicians routinely exploited fears of crime for their own electoral ends. Talk show hosts and conservative commentators built entire careers unmasking bogus claims of racism while dismissing legitimate discussions of racial injustice and inequality as mere political correctness or reverse racism.

Just as black anger often proved counterproductive, so have these white resentments distracted attention from the real culprits of the middle-class squeeze—a corporate culture rife with inside dealing, questionable accounting practices, and short-term greed; a Washington dominated by lobbyists and special interests; economic policies that favor the few over the many. And yet to wish away the resentments of white Americans, to label them as misguided or even racist, without recognizing they are grounded in legitimate concerns—this too widens the racial divide, and blocks the path to understanding.

This is where we are right now. It's a racial stalemate we've been stuck in for years. Contrary to the claims of some of my critics, black and white, I have never been so naïve as to believe that we can get beyond our racial divisions in a single election cycle, or with a single candidacy—particularly a candidacy as imperfect as my own.

But I have asserted a firm conviction—a conviction rooted in my faith in God and my faith in the American people—that working together we can move beyond some of our old racial wounds, and that in fact we have no choice if we are to continue on the path of a more perfect union.

For the African American community, that path means embracing the burdens of our past without becoming victims of our past. It means continuing to insist on a full measure of justice in every aspect of American life. But it also means binding our particular grievances—for better health care, and better schools, and better jobs—to the larger aspirations of all Americans—the white woman struggling to break the glass ceiling, the white man who's been laid off, the immigrant trying to feed his family. And it means taking full responsibility for own lives—by demanding more from our fathers, and spending more time with our children, and reading to them, and teaching them that while they may face challenges and discrimination in their own lives, they must never succumb to despair or cynicism; they must always believe that they can write their own destiny.

Ironically, this quintessentially American—and yes, conservative—notion of self-help found frequent expression in Reverend Wright's sermons. But what my former pastor too often failed to understand is that embarking on a program of self-help also requires a belief that society can change.

The profound mistake of Reverend Wright's sermons is not that he spoke about racism in our society. It's that he spoke as if our society was static, as if no progress has been made, as if this country—a country that has made it possible for one of his own members to run for the highest office in the land and build a coalition of white and black, Latino and Asian, rich and poor, young and old—is still irrevocably bound to a tragic past. But what we know—what we have seen—is that America can change. That is [the] true genius of this nation. What we have already achieved gives us hope—the audacity to hope—for what we can and must achieve tomorrow.

In the white community, the path to a more perfect union means acknowledging that what ails the African American community does not just exist in the minds of black people; that the legacy of discrimination—and current incidents of discrimination, while less overt than in the past—are real and must be addressed. Not just with words, but with deeds—by investing in our schools and our communities; by enforcing our civil rights laws and ensuring fairness in our criminal justice system; by providing this generation with ladders of opportunity that were unavailable for previous generations. It requires all Americans to realize that your dreams do not have to come at the expense of my dreams; that investing in the health, welfare, and education of black and brown and white children will ultimately help all of America prosper.

In the end, then, what is called for is nothing more, and nothing less, than what all the world's great religions demand—that we do unto others as we would have them do unto us. Let us be our brother's keeper, Scripture tells us. Let us be our sister's keeper. Let us find that common stake we all have in one another, and let our politics reflect that spirit as well.

For we have a choice in this country. We can accept a politics that breeds division, and conflict, and cynicism. We can tackle race only as spectacle—as we did in the OJ trial—or in the wake of tragedy, as we did in the aftermath of Katrina—or as fodder for the nightly news. We can play Reverend Wright's sermons on every channel, every day, and talk about them from now until the election, and make the only question in this campaign whether the American people think that I somehow believe or sympathize with his most offensive words. We can pounce on some gaffe by a Hillary supporter as evidence that she's playing the race card, or we can speculate on whether white men will all flock to John McCain in the general election regardless of his policies.

We can do that.

But if we do, I can tell you that in the next election, we'll be talking about some other distraction. And then another one. And then another one. And nothing will change.

That is one option. Or, at this moment, in this election, we come together and say, "Not this time." This time we want to talk about the crumbling schools that are stealing the future of black children and white children and Asian children and Hispanic children and Native American children. This time we want to reject the cynicism that tells us that these kids can't learn; that those kids who don't look like us are somebody else's problem. The children of America are not those kids, they are our kids, and we will not let them fall behind in a twenty-first-century economy. Not this time.

This time we want to talk about how the lines in the Emergency Room are filled with whites and blacks and Hispanics who do not have health care; who don't have the power on their own to overcome the special interests in Washington, but who can take them on if we do it together.

This time we want to talk about the shuttered mills that once provided a decent life for men and women of every race, and the homes for sale that once belonged to Americans from every religion, every region, every walk of life. This time we want to talk about the fact that the real problem is not that someone who doesn't look like you might take your job; it's that the corporation you work for will ship it overseas for nothing more than a profit.

This time we want to talk about the men and women of every color and creed who serve together, and fight together, and bleed together under the same proud flag. We want to talk about how to bring them home from a war that never should've been authorized and never should've been waged, and we want to talk about how we'll show our patriotism by caring for them, and their families, and giving them the benefits they have earned.

I would not be running for president if I didn't believe with all my heart that this is what the vast majority of Americans want for this country. This union may never be perfect, but generation after generation has shown that it can always be perfected. And today, whenever I find myself feeling doubtful or cynical about this possibility, what gives me the most hope is the next generation—the young people whose attitudes and beliefs and openness to change have already made history in this election.

There is one story in particularly that I'd like to leave you with today—a story I told when I had the great honor of speaking on Dr. King's birthday at his home church, Ebenezer Baptist, in Atlanta.

There is a young, twenty-three-year-old white woman named Ashley Baia who organized for our campaign in Florence, South Carolina. She had been working to organize a mostly African American community since the beginning of this campaign, and one day she was at a roundtable discussion where everyone went around telling their story and why they were there.

And Ashley said that when she was nine years old, her mother got cancer. And because she had to miss days of work, she was let go and lost her health care. They had to file for bankruptcy, and that's when Ashley decided that she had to do something to help her

mom. She knew that food was one of their most expensive costs, and so Ashley convinced her mother that what she really liked and really wanted to eat more than anything else was mustard and relish sandwiches. Because that was the cheapest way to eat.

She did this for a year until her mom got better, and she told everyone at the roundtable that the reason she joined our campaign was so that she could help the millions of other children in the country who want and need to help their parents too.

Now Ashley might have made a different choice. Perhaps somebody told her along the way that the source of her mother's problems were blacks who were on welfare and too lazy to work, or Hispanics who were coming into the country illegally. But she didn't. She sought out allies in her fight against injustice.

Anyway, Ashley finishes her story and then goes around the room and asks everyone else why they're supporting the campaign. They all have different stories and reasons. Many bring up a specific issue. And finally they come to this elderly black man who's been sitting there quietly the entire time. And Ashley asks him why he's there. And he does not bring up a specific issue. He does not say health care or the economy. He does not say education or the war. He does not say that he was there because of Barack Obama. He simply says to everyone in the room, "I am here because of Ashley."

"I'm here because of Ashley." By itself, that single moment of recognition between that young white girl and that old black man is not enough. It is not enough to give health care to the sick, or jobs to the jobless, or education to our children.

But it is where we start. It is where our union grows stronger. And as so many generations have come to realize over the course of the two hundred and twenty-one years since a band of patriots signed that document in Philadelphia, that is where the perfection begins.

[2008]

Understanding the Reading

1. Why does Barack Obama state that the Declaration of Independence of 1787 was "ultimately unfinished"?
2. What were the gaps between the ideals of the U.S. Constitution and the reality of living those ideals? (Trace from the eighteenth century to the twenty-first century.)

3. Why was Obama's former pastor so controversial, and why during Obama's first presidential campaign did he not simply disown him?
4. What are some of the legacies of slavery and Jim Crow, according to this article?

Suggestions for Responding

1. Discuss how some politicians and talk show hosts build their careers by exploiting people's fear of crime and unemployment.
2. Have a classroom discussion that responsibly focuses upon racial injustice and the working-class immigrant experience.

5

The Loudest Voice

GRACE PALEY

There is a certain place where dumb-waiters boom, doors slam, dishes crash; every window is a mother's mouth bidding the street shut up, go skate somewhere else, come home. My voice is the loudest.

There, my own mother is still as full of breathing as me and the grocer stands up to speak to her. "Mrs. Abramowitz," he says, "people should not be afraid of their children."

"Ah, Mr. Bialik," my mother replies, "if you say to her or her father 'Ssh,' they say, 'In the grave it will be quiet.'"

"From Coney Island to the cemetery," says my papa. "It's the same subway; it's the same fare."

I am right next to the pickle barrel. My pinky is making tiny whirlpools in the brine. I stop a moment to announce, "Campbell's Tomato Soup. Campbell's Vegetable Beef Soup. Campbell's S-c-otch Broth . . ."

"Be quiet," the grocer says, "the labels are coming off."

"Please, Shirley, be a little quiet," my mother begs me.

In that place the whole street groans: Be quiet! Be quiet! but steals from the happy chorus of my inside self not a tittle or a jot.

There, too, but just around the corner, is a red brick building that has been old for many years. Every morning the children stand before it in double lines which must be straight. They are not insulted. They are waiting anyway.

I am usually among them. I am, in fact, the first, since I begin with "A."

One cold morning the monitor tapped me on the shoulder. "Go to Room 409, Shirley Abramowitz," he said. I did as I was told. I went in a hurry up a down staircase to Room 409, which contained sixth-graders. I had to wait at the desk without wiggling until Mr. Hilton, their teacher, had time to speak.

After five minutes he said, "Shirley?" "What?" I whispered.

He said, "My! My! Shirley Abramowitz! They told me you had a particularly loud, clear voice and read with lots of expression. Could that be true?"

"Oh yes," I whispered.

"In that case, don't be silly; I might very well be your teacher someday. Speak up, speak up."

"Yes," I shouted.

"More like it," he said. "Now, Shirley, can you put a ribbon in your hair or a bobby pin? It's too messy."

"Yes!" I bawled.

"Now, now, calm down." He turned to the class. "Children, not a sound. Open at page 39. Read till 52. When you finish, start again." He looked me over once more. "Now, Shirley, you know, I suppose, that Christmas is coming. We are preparing a beautiful play. Most of the parts have been given out. But I still need a child with a strong voice, lots of stamina. Do you know what stamina is? You do? Smart kid. You know, I heard you read 'The Lord is my shepherd' in Assembly yesterday. I was very impressed. Wonderful delivery. Mrs. Jordan, your teacher, speaks highly of you. Now listen to me, Shirley Abramowitz, if you want to take the part and be in the play, repeat after me, 'I swear to work harder than I ever did before.'"

I looked to heaven and said at once, "Oh, I swear." I kissed my pinky and looked at God.

"That is an actor's life, my dear," he explained. "Like a soldier's, never tardy or disobedient to his general, the director. Everything," he said, "absolutely everything will depend on you."

That afternoon, all over the building, children scraped and scrubbed the turkeys and the sheaves of corn off the schoolroom windows. Goodbye Thanksgiving. The next morning a monitor brought red paper and green paper from the office. We made new shapes and hung them on the walls and glued them to the doors.

The teachers became happier and happier. Their heads were ringing like the bells of childhood. My best friend Evie was prone to evil, but she did not get a single demerit for whispering. We learned "Holy

Night" without an error. "How wonderful!" said Miss Glacé, the student teacher. "To think that some of you don't even speak the language!" We learned "Deck the Halls" and "Hark! The Herald Angels.". . . They weren't ashamed and we weren't embarrassed.

Oh, but when my mother heard about it all, she said to my father, "Misha, you don't know what's going on there. Cramer is the head of the Tickets Committee."

"Who?" asked my father. "Cramer? Oh yes, an active woman."

"Active? Active has to have a reason. Listen," she said sadly, "I'm surprised to see my neighbors making tra-la-la for Christmas."

My father couldn't think of what to say to that. Then he decided, "You're in America! Clara, you wanted to come here. In Palestine the Arabs would be eating you alive. Europe you had pogroms.[1] Argentina is full of Indians. Here you got Christmas. . . . Some joke, ha?"

"Very funny, Misha. What is becoming of you? If we came to a new country a long time ago to run away from tyrants, and instead we fall into a creeping pogrom, that our children learn a lot of lies, so what's the joke? Ach, Misha, your idealism is going away."

"So is your sense of humor."

"That I never had, but idealism you had a lot of."

"I'm the same Misha Abramovitch, I didn't change an iota. Ask anyone."

"Only ask me," says my mama, may she rest in peace. "I got the answer."

Meanwhile, the neighbors had to think of what to say too.

Marty's father said, "You know, he has a very important part, my boy."

"Mine also," said Mr. Sauerfeld.

"Not my boy!" said Mrs. Klieg. "I said to him no. The answer is no. When I say no! I mean no!"

The rabbi's wife said, "It's disgusting!" But no one listened to her. Under the narrow sky of God's great wisdom she wore a strawberry-blond wig.

Every day was noisy and full of experience. I was Right-hand Man. Mr. Hilton said, "How could I get along without you, Shirley?"

He said, "Your mother and father ought to get down on their knees every night and thank God for giving them a child like you."

He also said, "You're absolutely a pleasure to work with, my dear, dear child."

Sometimes he said, "For God's sakes, what did I

do with the script? Shirley! Shirley! Find it." Then I answered quietly, "Here it is, Mr. Hilton."

Once in a while, when he was very tired, he would cry out, "Shirley, I'm just tired of screaming at those kids. Will you tell Ira Pushkov not to come in till Lester points to that star the second time?"

Then I roared, "Ira Pushkov, what's the matter with you? Dope! Mr. Hilton told you five times already, don't come in till Lester points to that star the second time."

"Ach, Clara," my father asked, "what does she do there till six o'clock she can't even put the plates on the table?"

"Christmas," said my mother coldly.

"Ho! Ho!" my father said. "Christmas. What's the harm? After all, history teaches everyone. We learn from reading this is a holiday from pagan times also, candles, lights, even Chanukah. So we learn it's not altogether Christian. So if they think it's a private holiday, they're only ignorant, not patriotic. What belongs to history, belongs to all men. You want to go back to the Middle Ages? Is it better to shave your head with a secondhand razor? Does it hurt Shirley to learn to speak up? It does not. So maybe someday she won't live between the kitchen and the shop. She's not a fool."

I thank you, Papa, for your kindness. It is true about me to this day. I am foolish but I am not a fool.

That night my father kissed me and said with great interest in my career, "Shirley, tomorrow's your big day. Congrats."

"Save it," my mother said. Then she shut all the windows in order to prevent tonsillitis.

In the morning it snowed. On the street corner a tree had been decorated for us by a kind city administration. In order to miss its chilly shadow our neighbors walked three blocks east to buy a loaf of bread. The butcher pulled down black window shades to keep the colored lights from shining on his chickens. Oh, not me. On the way to school, with both my hands I tossed it a kiss of tolerance. Poor thing, it was a stranger in Egypt.

I walked straight into the auditorium past the staring children. "Go ahead, Shirley!" said the monitors. Four boys, big for their age, had already started work as propmen and stagehands.

Mr. Hilton was very nervous. He was not even happy. Whatever he started to say ended in a sideward look of sadness. He sat slumped in the middle of the first row and asked me to help Miss Glacé. I did this, although she thought my voice too resonant and said, "Show-off!"

Parents began to arrive long before we were ready. They wanted to make a good impression. From among the yards of drapes I peeked out at the audience. I saw my embarrassed mother.

Ira, Lester, and Meyer were pasted to their beards by Miss Glacé. She almost forgot to thread the star on its wire, but I reminded her. I coughed a few times to clear my throat. Miss Glacé looked around and saw that everyone was in costume and in line waiting to play his part. She whispered, "All right. . . ." Then:

Jackie Sauerfeld, the prettiest boy in first grade, parted the curtains with his skinny elbow and in a high voice sang out:

Parents dear We are here
To make a Christmas play in time.
It we give
In narrative
And illustrate with pantomime.

He disappeared.

My voice burst immediately from the wings to the great shock of Ira, Lester, and Meyer, who were waiting for it but were surprised all the same.

"I remember, I remember, the house where I was born. . . ."

Miss Glacé yanked the curtain open and there it was, the house—an old hayloft, where Celia Kornbluh lay in the straw with Cindy Lou, her favorite doll. Ira, Lester, and Meyer moved slowly from the wings toward her, sometimes pointing to a moving star and sometimes ahead to Cindy Lou.

It was a long story and it was a sad story. I carefully pronounced all the words about my lonesome childhood, while little Eddie Braunstein wandered upstage and down with his shepherd's stick, looking for sheep. I brought up lonesomeness again, and not being understood at all except by some women everybody hated. Eddie was too small for that and Marty Groff took his place, wearing his father's prayer shawl. I announced twelve friends, and half the boys in the fourth grade gathered round Marty, who stood on an orange crate while my voice harangued. Sorrowful and loud, I declaimed about love and God and Man, but because of the terrible deceit of Abie Stock we came suddenly to a famous moment. Marty, whose remembering tongue I was, waited at the foot of the cross. He stared desperately at the audience. I groaned, "My God, my God, why hast thou forsaken

me?" The soldiers who were sheiks grabbed poor Marty to pin him up to die, but he wrenched free, turned again to the audience, and spread his arms aloft to show despair and the end. I murmured at the top of my voice, "The rest is silence, but as everyone in this room, in this city—in this world—now knows, I shall have life eternal."

That night Mrs. Kornbluh visited our kitchen for a glass of tea.

"How's the virgin?" asked my father with a look of concern.

"For a man with a daughter, you got a fresh mouth, Abramovitch."

"Here," said my father kindly, "have some lemon, it'll sweeten your disposition."

They debated a little in Yiddish, then fell in a puddle of Russian and Polish. What I understood next was my father, who said, "Still and all, it was certainly a beautiful affair, you have to admit, introducing us to the beliefs of a different culture."

"Well, yes," said Mrs. Kornbluh. "The only thing . . . you know, Charlie Turner—that cute boy in Celia's class—a couple others? They got very small parts or no part at all. In very bad taste, it seemed to me. After all, it's their religion."

"Ach," explained my mother, "what could Mr. Hilton do? They got very small voices; after all, why should they holler? The English language they know from the beginning by heart. They're blond like angels. You think it's so important they should get in the play? Christmas . . . the whole piece of goods . . . they own it."

I listened and listened until I couldn't listen any more. Too sleepy, I climbed out of bed and kneeled. I made a little church of my hands and said, "Hear, O Israel . . ." Then I called out in Yiddish, "Please, good night, good night. Ssh." My father said, "Ssh yourself," and slammed the kitchen door.

I was happy. I fell asleep at once. I had prayed for everybody: my talking family, cousins far away, passersby, and all the lonesome Christians. I expected to be heard. My voice was certainly the loudest.

[1956]

Term

1. Pogrom: An organized and often politically encouraged massacre or persecution of a minority group—in particular, one conducted against Jews.

Understanding the Reading

1. Characterize Shirley's family and neighbors.
2. What objections do the adults have to her part in the Christmas play?
3. Why do her parents allow her to participate?
4. What does she learn from this experience, and how does it change her?

Suggestions for Responding

1. Describe a situation in which you had to participate or at least confront a cultural activity that conflicted with or was alien to your own beliefs or values.
2. What does this story reveal about the lives and values of Jewish immigrants?

6

To Be Hopi or American

POLINGAYSI QOYAWAYMA (ELIZABETH Q. WHITE)

Like many converts to a new religion, Polingaysi was overly zealous. She was young, she was courageous, she was brash—brash enough to challenge her Hopi elders and the whole beautifully interwoven cultural pattern of Hopi life. Had she at that time been able to do so, she would have abolished all the age-old rites, the kiva[1] rituals, the sprinkling of sacred cornmeal, and especially the making of *pahos*, or prayer sticks.

At the same time, tempering her radical approach, she had a deep and unsatisfied curiosity concerning the very things that aroused in her the strongest resentment. As she walked across the field one day after visiting her family at New Oraibi, she saw a *paho* thrust into the sand on a little hillock, its single eagle feather fluttering at the end of a short length of white cotton string.

Prayer sticks, either the long, wandlike ones with many feathers tied to them or the short, sharpened sticks called *pahos*, are held in reverence by the Hopi people. For four days after the "planting" of a prayer, these sticks are thought to possess the essence of the offered prayer and to be very powerful and sacred. To disturb one before it has lost its power is to court disaster. Accident, even death, Polingaysi had been taught, might result.

Well known to her was the story of the white woman who took prayer sticks from a shrine, then fell and broke her leg. Behind this accident the Hopi people saw the work of the invisible forces. The spirits had resented her action and had tripped her, they were convinced.

As she bent to pull the *paho* from the sand, Polingaysi felt a wave of superstitious fear sweep over her. But she was a Christian now, she reminded herself, and need not fear the magic in a stick with a feather on it. Defiantly, she carried it home and challenged her father with it.

"What does this stick mean to you and to the Hopi people?" she asked with more arrogance than she realized. "To me, pah! It means nothing. It has no power. It's just a stick with a bit of cornhusk and a feather attached to it. Why do you, in this day and age, when you can have the message of the Bible, still have faith in sticks and feathers?"

Her father, true Hopi that he was, recoiled from the proffered *paho*, refusing to touch it. There was a worried look in his eyes.

"Must you know?" he asked.

"Of course, I must know," Polingaysi declared. "Why shouldn't I know?"

"Lay it on the table," her father said, "and I will tell you."

She placed the stick on the rough board table which she had goaded the little man into making, and the two of them bent over it.

"Do you see that blue-green, chipped-off place here at the top?" her father asked, pointing. "That is the face of the prayer stick. It represents mossy places, moisture. Now this below is the body of the prayer stick. A red color, as you can see, like our colored sand. That represents the earth. Moisture to the earth, then, is what the *paho* is for."

"A prayer for rain?"

"That, yes, and more. The stick carries a bundle on its back."

"The bit of cornhusk, bound with string? What is it for? What does it mean?"

"I don't know what is bound up in the cornhusk," her father said, "and I won't open it to find out. However, I think you might find there some grass seeds, a pinch of cornmeal, a pinch of pollen, and a drop of honey."

"But, why, why?" Polingaysi demanded impatiently. "What good does it do?"

The little Hopi man had been carving a Kachina doll[2] from the dried root of a cottonwood. He turned away and went back to his work, sitting down cross-legged on the floor and picking up his knife and the unfinished doll. Polingaysi stood looking down at him, waiting for his answer. He thought before he began to speak.

"The good it does depends on many things, my daughter. It depends most of all on the faith of the one who made the *paho*. If all those things I mentioned are inside the little bundle that it carries on its back, it would mean that the one making the *paho* planted it in Mother Earth as a prayer for a plentiful harvest, with moisture enough to help Earth produce full ears of corn, plump beans, sweet melons." He looked up at her and his small face was worried. "Surely you have not forgotten the meaning of the feather? Feathers represent the spirits that are in all things. This one represents the spirit that is in the prayer the *paho* offers up."

Polingaysi turned away and took the *paho* in her hands. About to tear open the cornhusk, she looked down to see her father's hands stilled and horror in his expression. Suddenly she could not open the *paho*'s treasure without his permission. She could not fly in the face of tradition to that extent, knowing it would offend his spirit, however silent he remained, however little he reproached her openly.

"May I open it?"

Her father bent his head, possibly questioning the propriety of such an action and fearing the harm it might do him and his daughter. After a moment of hesitation, he sighed, saying, "It seems well weathered. I think it is more than four days old. If so, its purpose has been served and the power has left it. Use your left hand."

Gently, in spite of her pretended scorn, Polingaysi opened the bit of wrapped cornhusk. It had been folded while still green into a tiny triangle. In this little pouch there was a bit of material about the size of a pea. Seeds, cornmeal, pollen, held together with honey, as her father had predicted.

"Can't you see there's nothing of value in here?" Polingaysi cried.

"Not to you," her father agreed. "Not to me. But to the one who made it in prayer."

She would have questioned him further, but he took his work and went outside, his face enigmatic.

"For pity's sake, Mother," Polingaysi burst out, turning to Sevenka, who had been working quietly on a basket during the discussion, "does everything in the life of a Hopi have a hidden meaning? Why, for

instance, should I use my left hand to open that thing?"

"It seems foolish to you because you are young and do not understand everything," her mother said patiently. "Perhaps you are foolish because you do not understand Hopi ways, though you are a Hopi. I will tell you about the left hand.

"The left hand is on the heart side of the body. It is the hand that moves most slowly. It selects, instead of grabbing as the right hand does. It is cleaner. It does not touch the mouth during the eating of food, nor does it clean the body after release of waste materials.

"Do you remember watching our medicine man—the Man With Eyes—at his work? In his healing rites and also in his religious ceremonies he uses the left hand, for those reasons I have just given you. The left hand, then, is the hand that is of the heart and the spirit, not of nature and the earth."

Polingaysi struggled to deny the beauty of the words her mother had spoken. She sought a scoffing answer, but found none. After a moment the older woman continued.

"One more thing I will tell you about the *pahos*. They must be kept free of the white man's ways if they are to have the full power of old times. That is why Hopi people do not sharpen them to a point with white man's steel blades, but grind them to sharpness on sandstone."

At that moment Polingaysi saw one of her mother's brothers passing the window. He knew nothing of the discussion and she had no desire to reopen it. With her left hand she placed the *paho* on the window sill.

"Polingaysi!" the old man cried, his face crinkling into a big smile of welcome. "It is a great treat to my spirit to see you after so long a time. We are always happy to see our child come home, even if she does make us sit at a wooden platform when we eat."

Polingaysi lost some of her contentiousness and laughed. He had always complained about sitting at the table, insisting that he could not keep his feet warm while he was eating unless he sat on them, Hopi-fashion. Her little grandmother had been completely mystified by the table, and though Polingaysi had patiently explained its use, the old lady had laboriously climbed up onto it, instead of seating herself on the wooden bench that served as a chair.

She looked at her uncle and thought of all the new ideas she had gleaned during her life among white people. The old man had no desire to share her knowledge. To him, the old way was best. He asked little of life: enough food to keep the breath in his thin, worn old body, a little heat in the fireplace, a drink of water when he was dry.

It was she who was forever holding out her cup to be filled with knowledge.

[1964]

Terms

1. Kiva: An underground room used by Hopi men for ceremonies or councils.
2. Kachina doll: A doll made of wood and decorated with paint, feathers, and other materials that represents various spirits to Native Americans in the Southwest.

Understanding the Reading

1. Why does Polingaysi respond to the *paho* with both fear and arrogance?
2. Explain what Polingaysi means when she asks, "Does everything in the life of a Hopi have a hidden meaning?"
3. What does this selection tell you about "Hopi ways"?
4. Why would it be important that *pahos* "be kept free from white man's ways"?
5. What does the closing sentence mean?

Suggestions for Responding

1. Describe a generational conflict, especially one based on an ethnic tradition, between you and an older family member. What were the immediate and the long-term outcomes?
2. Both Paley and Qoyawayma describe the experience of assimilation. Some people feel this process was essential to creating a unified American society, whereas others believe that the costs—both the loss of cultural variety and the pain to individuals and families—were too high. Which position do you support? Why?

7

People of Color Who Never Felt They Were Black

DARRYL FEARS

At her small apartment near the National Cathedral in Northwest Washington, Maria Martins quietly watched as an African American friend studied a picture of her mother. "Oh," the friend said, surprise in her voice. "Your mother is white."

She turned to Martins. "But you are black."

That came as news to Martins, a Brazilian who, for 30 years before immigrating to the United States, looked in the mirror and saw a *morena*—a woman with caramel-colored skin that is nearly equated with whiteness in Brazil and some other Latin American countries. "I didn't realize I was black until I came here," she said.

That realization has come to hundreds of thousands of dark-complexioned immigrants to the United States from Brazil, Colombia, Panama and other Latin nations with sizable populations of African descent. Although most do not identify themselves as black, they are seen that way as soon as they set foot in North America.

Their reluctance to embrace this definition has left them feeling particularly isolated—shunned by African Americans who believe they are denying their blackness; by white Americans who profile them in stores or on highways; and by lighter-skinned Latinos whose images dominate Spanish-language television all over the world, even though a majority of Latin people have some African or Indian ancestry.

The pressure to accept not only a new language and culture but also a new racial identity is a burden some darker-skinned Latinos say they face every day.

"It's overwhelming," said Yvette Modestin, a dark-skinned native of Panama who works as an outreach coordinator in Boston. "There's not a day that I don't have to explain myself."

E. Francisco Lopez, a Venezuelan-born attorney in Washington, said he had not heard the term "minority" before coming to America.

"I didn't know what it meant. I didn't accept it because I thought it meant 'less than,'" said Martins, whose father is black. "'Where are you from?' they ask me. I say I'm from Brazil. They say, 'No, you are from Africa.' They make me feel like I am denying who I am."

Exactly who these immigrants are is almost impossible to divine from the 2000 Census. Latinos of African, mestizo and European descent—or any mixture of the three—found it hard to answer the question "What is your racial origin?"

Some of the nation's 35 million Latinos scribbled in the margins that they were Aztec or Mayan. A fraction said they were Indian. Nearly 48 percent described themselves as white, and only 2 percent as black. Fully 42 percent said they were "some other race."

Between Black and White

Race matters in Latin America, but it matters differently.

Most South American nations barely have a black presence. In Argentina, Chile, Peru and Bolivia, there are racial tensions, but mostly between indigenous Indians and white descendants of Europeans.

The black presence is stronger along the coasts of two nations that border the Caribbean Sea, Venezuela and Colombia—which included Panama in the nineteenth century—along with Brazil, which snakes along the Atlantic coast. In many ways, those nations have more in common racially with Puerto Rico, Cuba and the Dominican Republic than they do with the rest of South America.

This black presence is a legacy of slavery, just as it is in the United States. But the experience of race in the United States and in these Latin countries is separated by how slaves and their descendants were treated after slavery was abolished.

In the United States, custom drew a hard line between black and white, and Jim Crow rules kept the races separate. The color line hardened to the point that it was sanctioned in 1896 by the Supreme Court in its decision in *Plessy v. Ferguson*, which held that Homer Plessy, a white-complexioned Louisiana shoemaker, could not ride in the white section of a train because a single ancestor of his was black.

Thus Americans with any discernible African ancestry—whether they identified themselves as black or not—were thrust into one category. One consequence is that dark-complexioned and light-complexioned black people combined to campaign for equal rights, leading to the civil rights movement of the 1960s.

By contrast, the Latin countries with a sizable black presence had more various, and more fluid, experiences of race after slavery.

African slavery is as much a part of Brazil's history as it is of the United States's, said Sheila Walker, a visiting professor of anthropology at Spelman College in Atlanta and editor of the book *African Roots/American Cultures*. Citing the census in Brazil, she said that nation has more people of African descent than any other in the world besides Nigeria, Africa's most populous country.

Brazil stands out in South America for that and other reasons. Unlike most nations there, its people speak Portuguese rather than Spanish, prompting a debate over whether Brazil is part of the Latino diaspora.

Brazilian slavery ended in 1889 by decree, with no civil war and no Jim Crow—and mixing between light- and dark-complexioned Indians, Europeans, Africans and mulattoes was common and, in many areas, encouraged. Although discrimination against dark-complexioned Brazilians was clear, class played almost as important a role as race.

In Colombia, said Luis Murillo, a black politician in exile from that country, light-complexioned descendants of Spanish conquistadors and Indians created the "mestizo" race, an ideology that held that all mixed-race people were the same. But it was an illusion, Murillo said: A pecking order "where white people were considered superior and darker people were considered inferior" pervaded Colombia.

Murillo said the problem exists throughout Latin American and Spanish-speaking Caribbean countries with noticeable black populations. White Latinos control the governments even in nations with dark-complexioned majorities, he said. And in nations ruled by military juntas and dictators, there are few protests, Murillo said.

In Cuba, a protest by Afro-Cubans led to the arming of the island's white citizens and, ultimately, the massacre of 3,000–6,000 black men, women and children in 1912, according to University of Michigan historian Frank Guridy, author of *Race and Politics in Cuba, 1933–34*.

American-influenced Cuba was also home to the Ku Klux Klan Kubano and other anti-black groups before Fidel Castro's revolution. Now, Cuban racism still exists, some say, but black, mulatto and white people mix much more freely. Lopez, the Afro-Venezuelan lawyer, said, "Race doesn't affect us there the way it does here," he said. "It's more of a class thing."

Jose Neinstein, a native white Brazilian and executive director of the Brazilian-American Cultural Institute in Washington, boiled down to the simplest terms how his people are viewed. "In this country," he said, "if you are not quite white, then you are black." But in Brazil, he said, "If you are not quite black, then you are white."

The elite in Brazil, as in most Latin American nations, are educated and white. But many brown and black people also belong in that class. Generally, brown Brazilians, such as Martins, enjoy many privileges of the elite, but are disproportionately represented in Brazilian slums.

Someone with Sidney Poitier's deep chocolate complexion would be considered white if his hair were straight and he made a living in a profession. That might not seem so odd, Brazilians say, when you consider that the fair-complexioned actresses Rashida Jones of the television show *Boston Public* and Lena Horne are identified as black in the United States.

Neinstein remembered talking with a man of Poitier's complexion during a visit to Brazil. "We were discussing ethnicity," Neinstein said, "and I asked him, 'What do you think about this from your perspective as a black man?' He turned his head to me and said, 'I'm not black,'" Neinstein recalled. ". . . It simply paralyzed me. I couldn't ask another question."

By the same token, Neinstein said, he never perceived brown-complexioned people such as Maria Martins, who works at the cultural institute, as black. One day, when an African American custodian in his building referred to one of his brown-skinned secretaries as "the black lady," Neinstein was confused. "I never looked at that woman as black," he said. "It was quite a revelation to me."

Those perceptions come to the United States with the light-and dark-complexioned Latinos who carry them. But here, they collide with two contradictory forces: North American prejudice and African American pride.

[2002]

Understanding the Reading

1. Why are some Latin Americans and Brazilians pressured to accept a different racial identity in the United States?
2. What is the reaction of many African Americans when Latin Americans are reluctant to identify as black?
3. Why is the United States' view on race different from that of Brazil and many other Latin American countries?

Suggestions for Responding

1. Research the history of slavery in Brazil.
2. Research the Ku Klux Klan Kubano.
3. Listen to Brazilian music from Salvador, Bahia.

8

Rosa Wakefield

JOHN LANGSTON GWALTNEY

Florida-born, Miss Rosa Wakefield has known me practically all my life, and I have always thought of her as a worthy senior with so much dignity that the last thing she needs to think about is standing upon it. She is seventy-eight and hale and preeminently sound-minded. Her buttermilk pies and watermelon pork are as fine as they were when I was a fifth-grader puzzling with her over a text which asserted confidently that the Nigerian Hausa[1] were not black. I do not know anyone who has done more people more good with less noise than Miz Wakefield.

You understand that I am not an educated person. I was born with good sense and I read everything I can get to read. At least I know that I don't know very much. Now, if you still think I can help you, I'll be very glad to answer any question I can for you. I can't answer for nobody but myself. I will tell you what I think and why I happen to think that way. I was never the first person you heard when you came to my father's house or a party, but that never meant that I wasn't thinking as fast as some of these loud folks was talking.

Now, this first question is something I have thought about a great deal ever since I was a little girl. I think that I think more about anything I might think about than most people. That's because I was my father's oldest daughter and my mother died early, so I always had to think for more than one person. And that is a responsibility. It's bad enough when you make a mistake for one person, but when you make a mistake for more than one person—you know, when you make a mistake that's going to hurt somebody who can't think for herself or hisself—then you really feel that more than you would if you had just hurt yourself. I always thought about that. My father and

I sort of brought the others up. Now, I don't want to brag on myself, but I guess we didn't do but so bad. Now, the truth is that I think we did a good job.

But now, right there you have one of the big differences between blackfolks, or colored folks, or whatsoever you might call us, and whitefolks. We don't like to spell things out but so much. We know what we mean, like you knew what I meant. You know that I don't really mean that I think we did a pretty good job in raising all those children. You know that I mean that it was very hard to do so and we did it right.

White people are some writing folks! They will write! They write everything. Now, they do that because they don't trust each other. Also, they are the kind of people who think that you can think about everything, about whatever you are going to do, before you do that thing. Now, that's bad for them because you cannot do that without wings. I think that maybe you can't even do that *with* wings. They say that God's brightest angel fell. Now, ask yourself! Do you think God would have made this brightest angel if He knew that this angel was going to turn against Him? Now, it don't make one bit of sense to think that He would have done that. If He knew this brightest angel was going to ape up, what would He want to go and make this angel for? Now, if the Lord can be surprised, who are we to think that we can think about everything before it happens? All you can do is do what you know has got to be done as right as you know how to do that thing. Now, white people don't seem to know that.

I worked hard to put the others through school, and now they help me so the old lady can stir up a little sweet bread and talk to nice people like you. But, you see, there is hard work behind everything we do. You know that this sweet bread didn't make itself. I was telling you about my trips. You know that trip to Africa and that trip to Norway didn't pay for themselves! But, you see, if you eats these dinners and don't cook 'em, if you wears these clothes and don't buy or iron them, then you might start thinking that the good fairy or some spirit did all that. They asked a little white girl in this family I used to work for who made her cake at one of her little tea parties. She said she made it, and then she hid her face and said the good fairies made it. Well, you are looking at that good fairy.

Blackfolks don't have no time to be thinking like that. If I thought like that, I'd burn cakes and scorch skirts. But when you don't have anything else to do, you can think like that. It's bad for your mind,

though. See, if you think about what is really happening, you will know why these things are happening. When I get these cards on my birthday or Easter, I know that's because I sent my younger brother to school as clean as I could send him and made him get some sense into his head by seeing that he did what that teacher told him to do. They all send me a card on Mother's Day because they say that I was a mother to them. Now, they know that I am living all these other days, too, and they see to it that I don't want for anything I really need and a lot of things the old lady might just want. Rosa has washed her dishes and a lot of other folks' dishes for a long time, so she doesn't really need any machine to wash dishes, but she got one sitting right there in that kitchen! Now, Rosa didn't buy it and she didn't tell anybody to buy it, but it was bought. Now, my youngest brother is a professor too, but if he comes in here and sees something that has to be done, from washing dishes to scrubbing that floor, the next thing you know he just goes on and does it like anybody else. I never married, but any niece or nephew I got will come here if they *think* I need something and go wherever I want to send them.

Now, our children are more mannerable, but now so many of our children are trying to act like white children that it's hard to tell the difference just by the way they act these days. Some of these sorry things passing for young men and ladies that you see in the streets these days are enough to make you hang your head in shame! But so far, praise God, all our children have kept level heads and are doing just fine. In the summer we get together more and they tell me some things that are really hard to believe. I tell them to be nice to everybody that is nice to them and not to do every fool thing that they see being done. Little Rosa, my niece, brought a girl from Nigeria and a girl from Sweden. Now, that pleased me because I have read about those places and I have seen those countries and people there were nice to me, so I was glad to be nice to one of their girls.

We are revern' colored folks! We don't all have the same color skin, but we all have a strong family resemblance. My niece's mother is a German woman, and a finer lady you will never meet. But all you have to do is take one look at my niece and you will know that she is my niece. We all have a very strong family resemblance and we are a family that helps each other. If you know one of us, you know us all. We try to look out for each other. I told my brother about you and those mules and he said you looked just like a Wakefield. All you got to do to look just like a Wakefield is be black and do something good. But he's right this time—you do look a lot like us. You're quiet like we are, too. I guess in your work you have to be quiet because once you get us blackfolks talking, you won't get much of a chance to make much noise! But once a lady was out here, and she couldn't pay for her taxi because that driver had charged her way too much. We helped her and she swore that I looked just like her. Now, I'm a brown woman and this lady I'm telling you about looked as white as any white woman you will ever see. People like to claim kin with people they like. White people do that much more than we do, though. They can' stand the idea of anything good being black. If a black person does something good, they say he did that because of the white in him.

My father was sickly, but he worked hard all his life. He taught me and I tried to help teach the others. People have to go to school now, but they wouldn't have to do that if they would take up time with one another. I went to one college course to learn about the Negro. I'm sorry I did that now because all they did was to sit there and tell each other how they felt—I mean, how it felt to be black. Shoot! I have been feeling black all my life because I am not white! Now, what I wanted to know was not how they felt, because I already knew that; I wanted to know something about our great people and where we came from and how we kept on being folks all through slavery time.

My church and my folks got together and sent the old lady to Spain and Morocco. Everywhere I went I saw some of us. There was colored everywhere I set my foot. Now, I couldn't understand them, but I was looking at them, and if I'm black, and we both know I am, there is nothing else in God's world for them to be but black too. There was all kinds of colors! Some of them were white like the people that call themselves white over here. Some of them looked mighty Wakefield. Now, I saw that in Spain and I saw that in Africa. In Morocco some of those people could have been your brother or mine. Some of them had kinky hair and some of them had straight hair and some had wavy hair. Some of them looked like Jews and Italians, but there was all kinds of folks. Most of those people looked like what we used to call munglas. I have read that the Moroccans are white and I know that Americans are supposed to be white, but it looks to me like they are just as mixed up as we are over here. Half of these whitefolks I see out here look like they are passing[2] to me. That's the same way it is

in Cuba and Puerto Rico. I have seen those countries and I know that most of those people are colored, just like most of those people in Morocco. I'm telling you what I saw, not what somebody told me. A lot of these people from those foreign countries may not speak English, but you can look at them and see that they are Aun' Hagi's[3] children. A lot of them don't want to admit their color because they are afraid that these whitefolks over here would give them a hard time. Now, they are right about that.

I have been a cook and a maid and a housekeeper, and I have worked in hospitals. I still do every now and then, but I was in the hospital not long ago and I met this doctor that they said was an Arab. Well, he was darker than many people in my own family. I was proud to see one of the race better hisself. But, you know, that devil didn't want to hear a thing about his color! They had a lot of doctors from India and Jordan working there too. Now, a lot of the colored people didn't want to have anything to do with them because they said if they will pass like that, maybe they are not really doctors, either. I know folks that pass, but these doctors were just plain fools about it! I know people who pass to get a job that they should be able to get anyway, but they don't try to act like them all the time. There was this young Iraqian doctor there and he was darker than me, but he sure did everything he could think of and then some to show how white he was supposed to be. I don't trust anybody who would deny their color like that. And if Rosa Wakefield can't put her trust in you, you will never get your hands on her blood pressure or her diabetes or anything else!

[1980]

Terms

1. Nigerian Hausa: Black people of Niger and northern Nigeria.
2. Passing: A reference to light-skinned blacks trying to "pass" as whites.
3. Aunt Hagi: A reference to the biblical figure Hagar, the servant of Sarah and Abraham and the mother of Abraham's son, Ishmael.

Understanding the Reading

1. What values does Rosa Wakefield hold?
2. What characteristics does she think differentiate "blackfolks" from "whitefolks"?
3. Explain her beliefs about racial identity.

4. What questions do you think Gwaltney posed to elicit Wakefield's responses?

Suggestions for Responding

1. What advice do you think Rosa Wakefield might give to any one of the preceding writers?
2. If you were collecting oral histories from your family or your community, what kinds of information would you want to focus on? In other words, what characteristics and values do you expect to identify? What questions would you ask to obtain that information?

9

I'm Not Your Miss Saigon

JILLIAN MONTILLA

Fifteen-year-old girl
I love how you feast on the world
experiences dripping from your supple lips
your hands eagerly grabbing for
seconds
wait a second—
there are eyes
brown ones and blue ones and green ones
eyes that are nestled in the heads of grown white
*   men*
eyes that feast on your porcelain body
body unfamiliar like immigrants in a new land
body blooming like cherry blossoms on misty
*   mountains*
body that chafes you like whatever oriental imagery
*   you think I'll say next*

Sixteen-year-old girl
I can see something transform in your face
"Like a new-born baby's face, you can often see it
change before your very eyes."
But I am not Taylor Mali
and you are not a baby anymore
and that face of yours is inch thick with too light
*   foundation*
You get hired to waitress at a Thai restaurant
*   because everyone jokes you are*
"ambiguously asian"
Wow, you speak english real good. What's your
    ethnic name "Jill"?
They ask as if dipping your identity in sweet and
*   sour sauce*

savoring the novelty of your paradox
saliva-soaked skepticism as if they were Immigration
*   demanding to see your green card*
when all you asked for were their drink orders
Let your tongue ferment for two more years and you
*   would have burned their egos like fine sake*
"It's Jill and yes, I speak English well.
Do you hate that I speak 'your' language better than
*   you?"*
But you are still only sixteen
you are little Miss Saigon
you are the Madame Butterfly of Acasia
you smile and stick to the script.

Seventeen-year-old girl
I see you
unseen by the boys in your school
by that girl on your lacrosse team
I see as the skirts climb up your thigh like Oxford
*   ivy*
I see as the necklines plunge
down
your
wonderbra chest
I see that the only stares you catch belong to lonely
*   men who saunter into the restaurant*
greasy smiles wrinkling their faces, gold rings
*   choking tight on their left fingers, oily strands of*
*   hair across shiny foreheads to tie the whole*
*   package together*
Say something in your language, baby.
Let me guess—you're Thai. No, wait—Chinese. I
    love me some Chinese girls.
What size shoe do you wear? Gotta be a 5 or a 6.
    Asian chicks always have small feet.
I want my food as hot as you think I am.
You smile and tell yourself that it's "just for the tip"
I know you smile because you are finally "seen"
You are Pburg's very own Lucy Liu

Eighteen-year-old woman
That tongue you used to submit into a floral fan of
*   femininity*
is now as forked as the one's belonging to the
*   dragons badly tattooed on their hairy upper arms*
You don't take their bull
Your words are a bull
charging violently the red-hot waving of their
*   ignorance*
Red hot you burn their magazines of mail order
*   brides*
Red hot you let them burn in their yellow fever

You make mincemeat of the vile corpses of their
    tongues
You butcher their euphemisms
You slaughter their stereotypes
You imprison their egos within internment camps of
    enlightenment

Never again
a vessel
patiently waiting to be filled with
His American Dream

Never again
patiently waiting for
His red, white, and blue to rescue
your yellow

Eighteen-year-old woman
you are creator
not his creation of
subservience
of submission
not Bird of Paradise, not Happy Ending, not
    porcelain doll

Eighteen-year-old woman
you are creator
and you will never be his Miss Saigon again

Understanding the Reading

1. What does the author remember about her teen years?
2. How does her understanding of men's reactions to her change as the poem progresses?
3. In what way does she become "the creator"?

Suggestions for Responding

1. Have a class discussion about how and if you have been stereotyped.
2. Are you aware of your own use of stereotypes?

10

Before the Great Gorge

CARLOS CUMPIÁN

She raised the oven's temperature,
he unpeeled the plump poultry
from its factory plastic wrap,
they chopped onion, garlic, celery,
poured teaspoons of salt and sage,

stirred together ground black pepper
green parsley, a moon of dry bread to expand
beneath steaming giblet broth, as the round
dining table sprouted silver knives, forks and spoons.
Back during Squanto's time, wild bird meat
    simmered with acorn stuffing
and hot honey pumpkin
joined sweet yams in bright buttery optimism,
releasing great appetites among Pilgrims in the new
    Massachusetts' air.
No parade of football mascots' sportsbabble had
    spread like unbelted American waistlines. But
    even then, bald babies and tipsy husbands took
    satisfied afternoon naps,
while tired women did all the work.
Squanto's great, great, great, great grandchildren
    take Thanksgiving in stride, drink cokes, coffee
    or beer after finishing tonight's meal made from
    reservation
deer,
someone offers fat and meat scraps to backyard dogs,
    another clears
the table as three sisters talk about finding work
    before Christmas,
cars fill up to drive mothers, uncles, aunties and
    cousins home,
teenagers smoke cigarettes, their words cloud
    around school,
past due assignments, and basketball, no one speaks
    of the dark Dutch
or English sailing ships that landed
on these shores long ago or pale-eyed captains
    conquering
a "savage-continent" for pagan crown and Christ.
What was Squanto's peoples' reward after more
    sullen travelers survived?
Warrior-proud Wampanogs or Algonquins did not
    serve them like some
brown-skinned waiters and waitresses, happy in
    Pocahontas feathers
with hands eager for jive-glass bead wampum tips,
    or acting Tonto phonies, "You smart, Kemo sabe,"
    after sharing a thousand-year-old tradition, then
    to be told,
"Thanks for the popcorn chief, now head West!"

[1996]

Understanding the Reading

1. Why does the poet describe the food of a modern Thanksgiving, followed by that of the seventeenth century?

2. What is different and what is similar between the celebrations?
3. Do the American Indians of today celebrate Thanksgiving in this poem?
4. What is the poet's view of this day?
5. What does the last paragraph mean?

Suggestions for Responding

1. Read about early colonial history and relationships with northeastern American Indian nations.
2. Research the contemporary legal battle between the Oneida Nation and New York State.
3. Research how much land owned by American Indian nations has been contaminated, used as a toxic waste dump by large commercial concerns.

11

Race in a Genetic World

HARVARD MAGAZINE

"I am an African American," says Duana Fullwiley, "but in parts of Africa, I am white." To do fieldwork as a medical anthropologist in Senegal, she says, "I take a plane to France, a seven-to eight-hour ride. My race changes as I cross the Atlantic. There, I say, '*Je suis noire*,' and they say, 'Oh, okay—*métisse*—you are mixed.' Then I fly another six to seven hours to Senegal, and I am white. In the space of a day, I can change from African American, to *métisse*, to *tubaab* [Wolof for 'white/European']. This is not a joke, or something to laugh at, or to take lightly. It is the kind of social recognition that even two-year-olds who can barely speak understand. '*Tubaab*,' they say when they greet me."

Is race, then, purely a social construct? The fact that racial categories change from one society to another might suggest it is. But now, says Fullwiley, assistant professor of anthropology and of African and African American studies, genetic methods, with their precision and implied accuracy, are being used in the same way that physical appearance has historically been used: "to build—to literally *construct*—certain ideas about why race matters."

Genetic science has revolutionized biology and medicine, and even rewritten our understanding of human history. But the fact that human beings are 99.9 percent identical genetically, as Francis Collins

and Craig Venter jointly announced at the White House on June 26, 2000, when the rough draft of the human genome was released, risks being lost, some scholars fear, in an emphasis on human genetic difference. Both in federally funded scientific research and in increasingly popular practice—such as ancestry testing, which often purports to prove or disprove membership in a particular race, group, or tribe—genetic testing has appeared to lend scientific credence to the idea that there is a biological basis for racial categories.

In fact, "there is no genetic basis for race," says Fullwiley, who has studied the ethical, legal, and social implications of the human genome project with sociologist Troy Duster at UC Berkeley. She sometimes quotes Richard Lewontin, now professor of biology and Agassiz professor of zoology emeritus, who said much the same thing in 1972, when he discovered that of all human genetic variation (which we now know to be just 0.1 percent of all genetic material), 85 percent occurs *within* geographically distinct groups, while 15 percent or less occurs *between* them. The issue today, Fullwiley says, is that many scientists are mining that 15 percent in search of human differences by continent.

Last October, Fullwiley and colleagues from 14 academic institutions around the country articulated some of their concerns about ancestry testing in *Science* magazine. More than half a million people have paid between $100 and $900 for such tests, and for some—those seeking to establish membership in a Native American tribe poised to open a lucrative casino, for example—the stakes can be high. Unfortunately, the *Science* authors noted, the tests have serious limitations.

Most tests focus on just two types of DNA: the paternally inherited Y sex chromosome that only men carry, and mitochondrial DNA, which is passed exclusively from mothers to their children. Scientists favor these markers with good reason: because only one parent can pass them to offspring, they are not subject to recombination, the reshuffling of genetic data that normally occurs in each generation. But they represent less than 1 percent of a subject's DNA, and each tells about only one ancestor per generation. Two generations back, a customer might learn about one of four grandparents; three generations back, about one of eight great-grandparents; and by 10 generations back (roughly 250 years ago), such genetic tests reference just one of the 1,024 ancestors in that generation. It doesn't take long to reach the point when, mathematically, a person's ancestors start to outnumber the sum total of all people who have ever lived.

Nor can genetic tests verify a person's race or ethnicity. Genes that affect skin pigmentation or blood proteins involved in malarial resistance, the authors note, may not measure direct and unique ancestry (for example, a founder effect) but reflect instead an evolutionary response to "shared environmental exposures." Furthermore, the tests are based on comparisons to databases of DNA from living populations, and are therefore vulnerable to "systematic bias" because of "incomplete geographic sampling" or the fact that "present-day patterns of residence are rarely identical to what existed in the past." One testing company even uses an underlying model that "reinforces the archaic racial view that four discrete 'parental' populations (Africans, Europeans, East Asians, and Native Americans) existed in the past" even though "there is little evidence that four biologically discrete groups of humans ever existed."

Recently, Fullwiley's concerns have centered on a new kind of genetic testing. For a substantial fee, companies such as 23 and Me will "tell you what your propensity is for hypertension, schizophrenia, breast cancer, lactose intolerance, and high or low IQ," she says. But the studies that have established links between genes and these outcomes are probabilistic, she says, and convey, like ancestry tests, what might be called a false precision. Except for known Mendelian traits or conditions (such as Huntington's disease) only a fraction of people with a gene variant linked to a disease actually become ill.

Lost in the discussion about genes, she fears, are "epigenetic" influences: factors that affect gene expression but are not part of one's genetic code, such as prenatal nutrition (which may influence rates of heart disease late in life). Such biosocial factors—environmental, cultural, and economic—can sometimes be more influential than genes. Fullwiley questions, for example, whether the prevalence of diabetes among Native Americans on reservations, or of asthma among U.S. Latinos, is only genetic. Her research in Senegal has reinforced that doubt. Scientists have long searched for a genetic difference that would explain why many Senegalese experience a relatively mild form of sickle cell disease. Fullwiley's work suggests that many of them may instead be mitigating their symptoms with a widespread cultural practice: phytotherapy—the ingestion of roots from a plant that, preliminary studies suggest, triggers pro-

duction of fetal hemoglobin, a blood-cell type that doesn't sickle. "When environmental history, or evolutionary history, gets reduced to racial or ethnic difference," she says, "that's a big mistake."

Not all genetics projects are so potentially divisive, however. In February, Spencer Wells, Ph.D. '94, a former Lewontin student, came to Harvard to tell a story of human connectedness. Wells, who heads the joint National Geographic Society–IBM nonprofit Genographic Project, spent an afternoon with student members of the Harvard Foundation, which represents 72 student organizations "from the Albanian Society to the Vietnamese Society," says director S. Allen Counter. Wells had previously invited the students to participate in the Genographic Project by sending in cheek swabs with their DNA for analysis. "The idea," says Counter, "was to show a diverse group of students how they connect to the rest of humanity."

Spencer Wells tells student volunteers of the Harvard Foundation about their deep ancestors' ancient migrations. Wells has created a human family tree that traces "the journey of man" (as he titled his 2002 book) in populating the entire planet from a homeland in Africa. The project has used linguistic and genetic studies to guide its sampling of indigenous populations from around the globe—many of them isolated and remote—and now has the world's largest and most representative anthropological database of human DNA.

At Harvard, a Pakistani American student whose family had always told her they were originally from an area near the Arabian Sea had this confirmed by her DNA result. "Your family was part of the first migration out of Africa," noted Wells. "You share that with the Australian aborigines." An African American student with ancestors from East Africa carried a genetic signature characteristic of that region. But an Asian American student was surprised to find that she carried almost the same genetic markers as a Mexican American student. Wells explained, "There is only one change, but you are fairly different because your lines diverged a long time ago. Still, you are part of the same branch of the tree": the Native Americans who populated the Western Hemisphere originally came from Asia.

The Genographic Project aims to tell people "where their ancestors were living as indigenous people" at different points in time, but can't, for example, tell most African Americans precisely where in Africa they are from because, Wells explains, "the database isn't quite there yet." Echoing Fullwiley's reservations about all such tests, he says he's "a bit concerned about some of the African-American DNA testing companies purporting to trace you back to your ancient tribe." Ancestry is actually *more* complex for the average African American, he says, not only because people in West Africa (where most of the slave trade occurred) have moved around a lot in the last 500 years but also because "group composition within Africa has changed over time." Furthermore, because only a small number of humans survived the journey out of Africa some 50,000 years ago (and the slave trade on that continent was relatively localized), "there is more diversity *in* the average African village," Wells notes, "than there is outside of Africa combined."

When asked about the question of race, Wells's answer was unequivocal. "Racism is not only socially divisive, but also scientifically incorrect. We are all descendants of people who lived in Africa recently," he says. "We are all Africans under the skin." The kinds of differences that people notice, such as skin pigmentation, limb length, or other adaptations are "basically surface features that have been selected for in the environment. When you peer beneath the surface at the underlying level of genetic variation, we are all much more similar than we appear to be. There are no clear, sharp delineations."

The Human Family Tree

The movements of particular genetic markers—those from the male Y chromosome in blue, and those from maternally inherited mitochondrial DNA in orange—have been plotted on a map by the National Geographic Society–IBM Genographic Project to show the routes humans took as they moved out from an ancestral homeland in East Africa to populate the entire planet. For more information, visit www.nationalgeographic.com/genographic.

Fullwiley's own ethnographic research among genetic scientists suggests that much of current medical genetics may reinforce ideas of racial difference. Because certain diseases occur at higher frequencies in some populations (sickle cell anemia in blacks, Tay-Sachs disease in Jews of eastern European ancestry), they have become linked to the idea of race, even when the disease does not result from common ancestry. Sickle cell trait, for example, has arisen independently in several populations as an evolutionary response to malaria. The genetic change appeared first in India and then in Africa; it is also found in Greeks and Italians. But in the United States, Fullwiley says, sickle cell trait is very much linked to African American racial identity through the history of medicine.

She says the potential for racialization of medical genetics has been institutionalized because "you can't get a grant from the NIH unless you recruit in racial groups, label people by census category, and then report back the data in terms of outcomes by racial type." The original intent—to counter the widespread use of the white male body as the working research norm—is "fine and good," she says, but there "ought to be some flexibility to these race categories, and some thinking about what they mean. This new construction of race . . . *is* socially inflected—but it is not *solely* a social construct because biology is front and center."

Understanding the Reading

1. What are the limitations of ancestry testing?
2. What are concerns that scientists have about the popularity of genetic testing?
3. How can genetics projects give us information on "the journey of man"?

Suggestion for Responding

1. Research objections various social groups have to being genetically tested, especially Native Americans.

12

Exploring the Cuban Conundrum: Exiles, Immigrants, Americans, or Illegals?

Mercedes R. Diaz, PhD

When Fidel Castro died on November 25, 2016, at the age of ninety, less than a month after the 2016 presidential election, some funny memes circulated on social media. One showed a fierce-looking Castro railing, "I will not die until America is destroyed!" The second panel on that meme depicted a smiling president-elect Donald Trump; the third showed Castro lying in state. The implication was that Castro could now rest in peace, knowing that Trump would destroy America. Not to be outdone, Trump supporters spread their own meme using similar images, but their text read, "Trump gets elected November 9th. 2 weeks later, Castro dies. Coincidence?"

The memes are jokes, of course; Castro never said that (at least not publicly), and Trump had nothing to do with his death (as far as we know). None of that is real. What is real is that Castro's victory in January 1959 polarized Cuba, dividing communities—and even families—between those who supported "the Revolution" and those who could or would not. Thousands died; millions fled—most to the United States, Cuba's sworn enemy at the time. Many of them eventually settled in Miami, Florida, building an exile community of more than three-quarter million that changed the city forever. Their arrival tossed the formerly sleepy retirement haven into a political tempest that has yet to abate.

Trump's election to the White House has caused similar divisions here in the United States—even among stalwart Cuban exiles in the GOP stronghold of Miami where traditionally Democrats have struggled and Republican candidates of all stripes have coasted into office. Consider the following: In July 2016, when Donald Trump became the official GOP nominee for president, Cuban-born Miami billionaire and long-time major Republican "rainmaker" Miguel "Mike" Fernandez changed his political affiliation from Republican to "nonaffiliated" (an Independent in Florida). A few months later, Fernandez pledged millions of dollars and helped found the Immigration Partnership & Coalition Fund (IMPAC), an organization devoted to "fundraising for the defense of non-felon undocumented residents to protect families" (Pelaez, 2017). IMPAC has an enviable list of supporters that cross party lines, including notable celebrities Alonzo Mourning, David Hernandez, Ana Navarro, Andy Garcia, and Emilio and Gloria Estefan ("Mission," 2017).

Fernandez's founding of IMPAC is unusual. Traditionally, Cuban exiles have sided with the GOP hardliners on illegal immigration, mainly because, by law, it is almost impossible for a Cuban exile to be an illegal alien.[1] Throughout the latter half of the twentieth century, U.S. lawmakers passed numerous edicts—from the Cuban Adjustment Act to Helms-Burton to "Wet-foot/Dry-foot"—designed more to punish Castro as an agent of the Cold War than to

reward the Cuban people. [Editor's note: The Cuban Adjustment Act of 1966 is a policy to adjust one's immigration status for people who were born in Cuba or who have Cuban nationality, who were lawfully admitted or paroled into the United States, and who have lived in the United States for at least one year. The "Wet-foot/Dry-foot" policy (1995) gave Cubans who were able to reach U.S. soil permission to stay and apply for a green card. The Helms-Burton Act, enacted in 1996, is one of the six laws that codify enforcement of the economic embargo against Cuba that was begun by Eisenhower in 1960 and continues today.] They were the pawns—willing pawns in most cases, but pawns nonetheless—in the chess match between Washington, D.C., and Havana (and, by extension, Moscow).

Fernandez's defection from the Republican Party and his rejection of GOP nominee Trump also is curious. Fernandez, a dapper man in his sixties who arrived in the United States as a teenager, has been—like many Cuban exiles—a staunch Republican for most of his life. In 2012, the *Tampa Bay Times* listed Fernandez as a "big time donor to Super PACs" after he gave tens of thousands of dollars to support Mitt Romney against Barack Obama. Like many Cuban exile Republicans, he opposed most of Obama's policies, especially his deportation policy. He broke ranks with his GOP brethren only once during the Obama administration: he was one of the few who approved of Obama's attempts toward rapprochement with Havana. Nevertheless, during the 2016 presidential campaign, he poured millions into the campaign of Republican candidate Jeb Bush.

But when Trump won the GOP nomination, Fernandez reversed course—and spent millions in advertising to keep Trump *out* of the White House, even contributing to and endorsing Hillary Clinton. What happened?

The short answer: Trump happened.

The long answer is much more complicated. In this article, I will discuss how Cubans in Miami's exile community reacted after Trump's election, especially considering Trump's seemingly anti-immigrant agenda. I will explain how U.S. Cold War policies both helped and alienated Cuban exiles, leading to the issues they confront today. Finally, I will discuss why Trump is the mirror that Cuban exiles might

---

1. There are some exceptions: Cubans who have been convicted of felonies and narcotics-related crimes (including multiple misdemeanors) will never be eligible for permanent residency. They are slated for deportation if relations ever normalize between the two countries.

need to help them see themselves the way the rest of American society sees them, thus helping them move forward as a part of U.S. life in the twenty-first century.

A Primer on Population: Cuban "Vintages" in the United States

Before we go further, it might help to describe the characteristics of this group. The 2010 Decennial Census and American Community Survey enumerated 1,873,585 persons living in the United States who identified as being Cuban or Cuban American. Of those, 1,104,679 were Cuban-born émigrés; the balance—768,906—were U.S.-born Cuban Americans. Although the data show that persons of Cuban descent are dispersed among every state (the result of the policies that were instituted after the Cuban Adjustment Act was passed in 1966), the largest communities are in Florida, the New York/New Jersey metro area, California and Texas ("T139. Place of Birth for the Foreign-Born Population . . . Social Explorer," 2018; T15. "Hispanic or Latino by Specific Origin . . . Social Explorer," 2018). Data show that 70 percent of all Cubans or Cuban Americans either live in or have some connection to Florida (Krogstad, 2014).

Data collected by the Census Bureau also show that the Cuban community in the United States is not monolithic. It is the result of several "vintages" of migration, a word that in this context pertains to "waves" of periodic migration by a specific nationality of people. Demographer Eton F. Kunz explained that each vintage is "distinctly different in character, background and avowed political faith" (1973, 137).

Although there is a tendency to use the term *exile* to describe all Cubans, that is technically incorrect. *Exile* is the socio-political (not legal) term that is used to label those Cubans who immigrated to the United States *after* 1959.[2] Those who immigrated before 1959 are simply "immigrants," regardless of why they immigrated to the United States. By now, most of

that population would be over sixty and are (or would have been) naturalized citizens.

The present-day Cuban exile community in Miami is not unique; it is just the latest vintage in a history stemming from as far back as the 1860s, rivaling that of European immigration to the United States. In fact, the word *vintage* for this group might not be entirely accurate. Perhaps a better term to describe the exiles might be *macro-vintage* since the current exile community comprises several *micro-vintages*, each differing in average age, education, racial composition, and political leanings (Pedraza, 1998).[3] Furthermore, even though "exile" is what we call those who arrived post-1959, not all of them are true exiles; many of the newer arrivals can and have retained contact with Cuba and can travel relatively freely to the island to visit relatives. A recent development is that some have been able to retain their Cuban residency even while still living abroad (even in the United States), the result of reforms in Cuban emigration policies, which has caused some conflict among U.S. legislators (Moreno, 2018).

Research shows that the Cuban population in the United States is, generally, older and more conservative than other Hispanics/Latinos. They have higher educational attainment and income when compared to other Hispanic groups, but their numbers are lower than non-Hispanic whites. Cubans in general—but the exile cohort in particular—are more likely to identify their racial classification as "white," even though there are many Cubans who are of mixed or Afro-Cuban heritage. While most Cubans profess to be Catholics, they are more secular compared to other Latin Americans and have been that way since before the Revolution, even though the church played a role in evacuating refugees after the Revolution. Many also adhere to some form of syncretic religion, as evidenced by the celebrations that take place each December in both Miami and Havana to celebrate the feast day of St. Lazarus/Babalu Aye.

Cubans also tend to seek naturalization at higher rates (60 percent) than all other foreign born (53 per-

2. The exiles were first described as *refugees,* the legal UN term for a nationally displaced person. After the Bay of Pigs invasion failed, the refugees started to be called *exiles* by the CIA and the Kennedy and Johnson administrations; the name stuck.

3. The oldest vintage who arrived between 1959 and 1975 were older, whiter, more educated, wealthier, and more conservative. The "Mariel Boatlift" vintage (1980s) was more racially and sexually diverse, less educated, and poorer. The latest vintages (mid-1990s to present) comprise people born after the Revolution. They tend to be well educated, entrepreneurial, and more liberal leaning than their counterparts; they, unlike the others, are more likely to vote Democrat and advocate normalizing relations with Havana.

cent) (Flores, López, and Radford, 2017). Unlike other Hispanic groups, Cubans also appear to be conflicted about their identities as minorities in the United States; as Alvarez (2016) highlights in his article, Cubans more inclined toward the ideals of pan-Americanism are more comfortable identifying as "Hispanic," but many others are not, preferring to identify as either "Cubans" or "Americans."

In addition, while it is true that Cubans and Cuban Americans are more inclined to support the Republican Party than other Hispanic/Latino groups, not all Cubans vote Republican. In Miami, Cubans are known for voting Republican (83 percent) more often than Democrat (17 percent) on the national level, but their voting patterns on the local level are more mixed. Cubans living outside of Miami (especially those in the New York Metro area) are a swing vote more likely to vote Democrat, their voting patterns more in line with the rest of the Hispanic population in the country. Preference of one party over another differs by vintage: "vintages" that arrived prior to 1959 (or their descendants) and those who arrived during the Mariel Boatlift of 1980 and after the 1990s are more likely to be more receptive to Democratic Party candidates than those who arrived in the years immediately following the Cuban Revolution (López, 2015; "Cubans in the US: A Profile," 2006; Latino Decisions, 2016).

The Cuban tendency to support Republican candidates is longstanding. It predates the exile cohort, extending back to the late 1860s, when Cubans began to migrate to the United States. Writer and intellectual Jose Martí, who was part of one of the first vintages to settle in the United States in the 1880s, and who became the first "president" of Cuba,[4] admired Abraham Lincoln and the Republican Party. Among those first immigrants who advocated Cuban independence, many also were abolitionists and supporters of Lincoln. When Lincoln was assassinated, they mourned his death as deeply as many U.S. citizens. Additionally, at the turn of the twentieth century, Tampa, Florida, was the hub of the thriving Cuban community of *tabaqueros* ("tobacco makers") who came to be known as *Tampeños*. Their integrated factories and relatively liberal mutual aid societies became targets of segregationists, mostly Democrats and members of the now-defunct American Party (also known as the Know-Nothing Party), who pressured immigrant leaders to comply with Jim Crow laws.[5] It is understandable that Cubans would feel some measure of hostility and distrust toward the party. It was not until many *Tampeños* migrated north to New York during the Depression that they became acquainted with New Deal Democrats.

A 2014 report published by the Pew Hispanic Center shows that between 2002 and 2013, the number of Cubans who said they supported the Republican Party dropped from a high of 64 percent to less than half (47 percent). Further dissection of the data reveals that the division is generational: Cubans between the ages of eighteen and forty-nine are more inclined to vote for the Democratic candidate (56 percent), while those older than fifty remain staunchly Republican (44 percent). While the differences might not appear like much, the split was enough to grant Barack Obama slim victories in Florida over his Republican opponents in both 2008 and 2012 (Krogstad, 2014).

Despite this shift, the public political "faces" of the Cuban American community in the United States—with some notable exceptions, like New Jersey's senator Bob Menendez (D-NJ)—are almost all Republicans. Almost all—again, except Menendez—are related to the "exile" cohort. Most interesting of all, perhaps, is the fact that with regard to Hispanic/Latino political representation on the national level, Cubans are disproportionately represented. There are thirty-six representatives of Hispanic/Latino descent in the House of Representatives; of those, five are of Cuban descent, and one of those five, Ileana Ros-Lehtinen (R-FL), has held office since 1989. All are either exiles or descendants of exiles. Of the four senators of Hispanic/Latino descent that currently hold

---

4. Martí was "elected" president in 1895, right before the start of the Cuban War for Independence, and before Cuba was an independent country.

5. Originally, the various ethnic clubs and mutual aid societies, while not integrated, were not entirely segregated either. Blanket invitations extended to workers to attend an activity hosted by one of the societies were inclusive for black workers as well. The liberal attitude drew the ire of Florida segregationists who were suspicious of immigrants and, gradually, all the aid societies were brought into compliance. The only integrated/nonsegregated mutual aid society in Tampa was *Sociedad La Union Marti-Maceo*, which was named after the most influential two Cubans of the Independence movement: Jose Martí, who was white, and General Antonio Maceo, who was black ("Sociedad La Union Marti-Maceo," 2017).

office, only Catherine Cortez Masto is of Mexican descent. The other three are of Cuban descent: Marco Rubio (R-FL), Ted Cruz (R-TX), and Menendez. Menendez, one of the few Cuban American Democrats, is the only one whose parents immigrated to the United States before the 1959 vintage.

All of this means little until one considers that in 2015, of the estimated fifty-six million people who identified as Latino or Hispanic in the United States, Cubans made up only 2.115 million—a mere 3.7 percent of the population. They ranked a distant fourth after Mexicans and Mexican Americans (more than 35.7 million and 63 percent of Hispanic/Latinos), Puerto Ricans (5.3 million, 9.5 percent), and El Salvadorans, who inched out Cubans by about fifty thousand people at 2,173 million and 3.8 percent of the population ("T15. Hispanic or Latino by Specific Origin [31]—Social Explorer Tables . . . ," 2018; "T139. Place of Birth for the Foreign-Born Population [123]—Social Explorer Tables . . . ," 2018).

Reacting to the Trump Win

On November 16, 2016—just eight days after Trump won the election, when many Americans were still grappling with the significance of his win—*Univision* commentator Giancarlo Sopo sought to dispel the notion that the Cuban vote had anything to do with it:

> As Cuban-Americans we can take pride in our achievements: we're a hard-working community with good values; we played a vital role in Miami's transformation from a sleepy beach town to a global city; our contributions to the arts, commerce, and civic life of this country are innumerable; and yes, Pitbull is one of our own. Electing Donald Trump as President is not among our achievements. (Sopo, 2016)

But an article written by University of Virginia professor Cristina Lopez-Gottardi and published in *U.S. News and World Report* that same day contradicted him. In it, Lopez-Gottardi asserted that Trump had indeed taken "between 52 and 54 percent of the Cuban American vote in Florida, according to polls conducted by CNN and Latino Decisions" (2016). Later that month, Latino Decisions, a market research and opinion polling firm headed by academics from Stanford and UCLA, released its final exit poll data on the election. Although the aggregate final

tally of all Cubans nationwide shows that they cast more votes for Clinton (50 percent) than Trump (48 percent) (Naren Ranjit, 2016), polls conducted in Miami on or about the date of the election showed that Miami Cuban exiles had cast more votes for Trump (52 percent) than for Clinton (47 percent) (Latino Decisions, 2016). Trump's lead in that community, though slim, was enough of a margin to hand him the state.

Other Latino Decisions regional and national data showed that Trump had garnered only 18 percent of the overall Hispanic/Latino vote nationwide: only 8 percent of Dominicans had voted for him; Puerto Ricans, at 19 percent, registered the highest percentage of support behind the Cubans. These findings were consistent with findings of polls conducted by various organizations including Univision, NBC/Telemundo, and Florida International University, which suggested that Trump's support among Hispanic/Latinos hovered somewhere between 13 and 19 percent. Those findings were not surprising given the strident anti-immigrant—and particularly anti-Mexican—rhetoric that Trump had used during the campaign.

Aside from Sopo and Lopez-Gottardi, there was a smattering of analysis and questions. The most insightful was a November 15 piece in the *New York Times Magazine* by Marcela Valdes (2016) that attempted to find some reason why Cubans, who are considered Hispanic under the definition set forth by the U.S. Census Bureau, would vote in such numbers for a man who seemed so hostile toward Hispanic immigrants. Trump was on the record opposing the Cuban Adjustment Act (CAA) and its special provisions for entry for Cuban nationals. He was supported by the Federation for American Immigration Reform (FAIR), a group that had been critical of the CAA for years and whose methods had earned it the classification of "hate group" by the Southern Poverty Law Center. Throughout the election, Trump had sounded like a demagogue—he was the very type of leader that Cubans had tried to escape when they fled Cuba. What had motivated so many of them to vote for him?

Understanding the Cuban Vote

Sopo's initial belief that Cubans had withheld their wholesale support for Trump is understandable; prior to the 2016 election, researchers had noted that Cubans and Cuban Americans appeared to be shifting left of the political divide, as discussed above. But Cubans can and always have been a swing vote; the

Obama campaigns had proven that although Cubans tended to vote Republican, they could vote for a Democrat just as easily.

In her article, Valdes (2016) quoted *Univision* news anchor Jorge Ramos as saying that there was a "hidden, secret Latino vote," which signaled a "new divide" among Hispanics, and that the "wall that Trump was talking about is clearly apparent now within the Hispanic community."

But anyone following Cuban exile politics knows that Cuban exiles' bias toward Republican candidates—even Trump—is neither hidden nor secret. A Democrat who "sins" against the community is excoriated, while a Republican who does the same might receive the benefit of the doubt. As early as 2014, there were signs that Democrats were "in the doghouse" with the Cubans again, so to speak: Obama drew the ire of the exile community when he signaled that his administration would be open to pursuing rapprochement with the Cuban government.

In "Old Cuban Exiles in the US Are Filled with Rage," Raf Sanchez interviewed exiles and listed their grievances. Their biggest one: that Obama was naïve and easily manipulated into sending back to Havana one of the "Cuban 5," a team of Cuban spies who had infiltrated Miami's anti-Castro groups in the 1990s. The spy Obama released had been sentenced to life in prison for his role in the downing of two planes flying for Brothers to the Rescue, an anti-Castro organization that monitored the waters between Cuba and Florida looking for rafters escaping from Cuba.[6]

Obama's faux pas with the Cubans was the latest in a long list of unforgivable slights from the Democrats. It had started with John F. Kennedy and his refusal to provide Cuban rebels with military support during the Bay of Pigs invasion. It had continued with Jimmy Carter's overtures toward Havana in the 1970s. The Carter administration's diplomatic efforts restored conditional travel between Cuba and the United States, but exiles argue that they also were the impetus for the Mariel Boatlift that occurred a few years later. Cubans still have not forgiven the Clinton administration for the late-night raid in April 2000 that forcibly removed little Elian Gonzalez from the home of his Miami relatives in order to return him to his father, who wanted to take him back to Cuba. If you contrast these contentious relationships with the cozy ones that existed in the 1980s between Reagan and Bush and officials from the Cuban American National Foundation (CANF),[7] what is surprising is that any Cubans voted for Clinton or Obama at all. The fact that they did does not necessarily signal a "wall" in the Hispanic community, but it does point to a growing split in the Cuban exile community.

It was expected that Obama's overtures toward Cuba at the end of his second term in office would prompt differences of opinion between Cubans of different classes, races, generations, and migration "vintages." Specifically, U.S.-born Cubans and those who arrived before 1950 had been urging normalization between the countries since the 1970s. What was surprising was that this possibility also sparked division within the exile community itself because, since their arrival in the 1960s, the exile community (by virtue of the circumstances under which it came to exist) has been collectivistic. Collectivism is defined as the principal or practice of prioritizing the needs of the group, community, or society over individual gain ("Individualism—collectivism," 2006).

The first aspect that bound those first vintages of Cuban exiles together into a collective whole was having experienced the Cuban Revolution. Many of those who arrived in that first decade had fought on both sides of that struggle. The oligarchs, Batista's ministers, corporate managers, and high-level professionals were among the first to flee to Florida; eventually they were followed by a succession of different groups.

Even though Fidel Castro eventually became the "face" of the Revolution, he and his band of fighters started out as relatively marginal players in that

---

6. On February 24, 1996, Cuban fighter jets spotted two Cessna planes looking for Cuban rafters in the Straits of Florida. They left Cuban airspace to shoot them down, killing four pilots.

7. CANF was founded in 1981 at the urging of Ronald Reagan's National Security Adviser Richard Allen as an organization to promote taking a hardline political stance against the Castro regime. It was instrumental in shaping all Cuba-related legislation from the start of the Reagan administration through the end of the first term of the Clinton administration, including the Cuban Democracy Act of 1992and Helms-Burton in 1996, and the establishment of Radio and TV Martí. CANF and its associated PAC were instrumental in getting Ileana Ros-Lehtinen elected, as well as others who are sympathetic to their hardline stance on Cuba. However, the organization faced controversy in 2006 when one of its former board members alleged that the group had plotted a paramilitary raid to invade Cuba and kill Castro in the late 1990s (Cancio Isla, 2006).

drama. The "revolution" had begun—and had been won—by a coalition of more than a dozen disparate groups who had banded together with three goals in mind: to depose Batista, reinstate the Cuban Constitution of 1940 that Batista had suspended, and hold free elections.

It was a populist, nationalist revolution aimed at taking back the country from foreigners.[8] Batista's Cuba had been a "sin mecca." His presidency was tainted by rampant corruption and ties with organized crime boss Meyer Lansky, who was on Batista's payroll as an unofficial, but salaried, minister of gaming. Millions of dollars of domestic capital were poured into attracting foreign investors who opened hotels and businesses to attract gamblers from around the world and sex tourists who wanted to engage in every kind of debauchery imaginable. More than a tenth of all profits were funneled into graft payments for public officials, including the president, but since Batista's incentives included waiving taxes on new investments for ten years, the Cuban people saw little in return (Worrall, 2016). Despite the massive wealth circulating through the economy, Cuba was characterized by chronic unemployment and underemployment, high illiteracy, and endemic racism. Foreigners owned almost everything of value, and Cubans had become serfs in their own country (Reiss, 2001).

Castro was one of the few coalition leaders to survive the fighting. When he was first considered for prime minister, he appeared to want to create a government that was representative of the coalition that had won the day. He had made promises to his coalition partners that all would be heard, but within months of the victory he betrayed them. Eventually, anyone who disagreed with the path that Castro

wanted to take met the same fate: some were executed, some imprisoned, many were exiled.

The use of exile to quell dissent had been used by Cuban governments since colonial times. The Spanish found that exiling troublemakers was more effective than killing them and making them martyrs to a cause. After the Spanish were ousted, the Cuban governments that followed used exile just as effectively; Fidel Castro himself had been exiled from Cuba after his release from prison in 1955. The government that Castro built also used exile to quell dissent, but to prevent others from doing what they themselves had done, the new leaders passed a law dictating that anyone who left would be barred from returning. All the exiles' property would be confiscated, they would relinquish their Cuban citizenship, and they would effectively be "erased." Furthermore, Cubans who communicated with dissident family members living abroad risked losing their livelihood, and their children could be barred from admission to the university (Torres, 2014, 51–52). Given the years of violence and mayhem that followed Castro's accession to power, Cubans who feared for their safety were forced to make an impossible choice: to stay and remain a patriot or express the desire to leave and be branded a traitor. The moment a person requested a visa to leave the country, they lost their livelihood, all their personal property, and their citizenship, and they would be subjected to acts of repudiation[9] by their neighbors.

U.S. immigration policy toward the exiles served to isolate them further. Since U.S. foreign policy toward the Castro government largely consisted of using the outmigration to delegitimize it, the U.S. government did everything it could to entice people to leave. Facilitation off the island began with Operation Peter

---

8. On the eve of the Revolution, foreigners—mostly Americans—owned more than 75 percent of all the best land, sugar plantations and mills, and mines and manufacturing. The mob, headed by Lansky, controlled the casinos and the associated "vice industries" for which Cuba was notorious, using them to launder money that had been made illegally in the United States. President Batista routinely pocketed a tenth of all foreign investment for himself, while offering generous tax cuts and matching funds to entice the new investors. When Conrad Hilton finally assented to building a hotel in Havana, the pension fund from the Cuban restaurant workers' union financed the $23 million project (Reiss, 2001).

9. Members of the Committees for the Revolution did (and still do) organize people who live in a community to harass neighbors considered dissidents. Once a migrant has applied for a travel visa, he or she can be subjected to intense and frequent verbal and physical abuse and intimidation violent enough to warrant the concern of Amnesty International. Inciting civilians to engage in this kind of groupthink behavior cements cohesiveness among those "patriots" who choose to stay in Cuba against the "traitors" who want to leave. This kind of public humiliation severs the victim's ties with the community, fostering contempt in the perpetrators and bitterness in the victims who feel betrayed by their neighbors. The public nature of the humiliation also serves to put any potential dissidents on notice and instill fear in group members who might be thinking in ways considered nonconformist (Amnesty International, 2017).

Pan,[10] followed by a visa waiver program that allowed thousands to migrate to Miami. Twice-weekly "Freedom Flights" off the island were instituted in 1965 and continued through the mid-1970s. Those who made it to the United States were aided with stipends, food, and housing assistance. The Cuban government used this knowledge to paint the exiles as opportunists who had been paid to betray their country, fostering resentment among the Cubans who remained and were struggling to rebuild the island. The aid program also angered U.S. natives—mainly rural whites and poor African Americans—who resented that foreigners were being given assistance that was denied to them.

At first the exiles did not care that they were reviled in both their native and host countries, since they did not expect to stay in the United States very long. They expected that Eisenhower would do what the United States always did in Latin America: send in Marines to make short work of the usurpers and install someone for whom the status quo would be business as usual. But the Eisenhower administration, having exhausted whatever good will it had left in Cuba through defending Batista for so long, was reluctant to engage in direct military confrontation with Castro. Eisenhower's "hands-off, wait-and-see" attitude backfired badly. By the time he approved an armed intervention of the island in early 1960—an act he would have to leave to the incoming Kennedy administration to implement—the revolutionaries had had more than a year to become entrenched, solidify their position, and eliminate any internal dissent. They also had established connections with a new ally—the Soviet Union—who promised them everything unconditionally that Washington had offered with conditions to try to bring Castro's government to heel (Smitha, 1998). By January 1961,

what remained of the relationship between the United States and Cuba was in tatters. The debacle of the Bay of Pigs invasion in April of that year, followed by the Cuban Missile Crisis in 1962, effectively killed whatever hopes the exiles had of a quick return to Cuba.[11]

Another aspect of the foreign policy toward Cuba that made it difficult for exiles to assimilate was the CIA decision to train and use Cuban nationals to invade and destabilize the island. Many members of the invasion army for the Bay of Pigs operation also had been members of the coalitions that had fought *for* the Revolution. Now, ironically, they were being used to promote the foreign policy goals of the United States. The involvement of the CIA in their training for the Bay of Pigs operation, and their continued use by the agency and its Latin American counterparts to carry out the assassinations of leftist politicians in Latin America and the United States,[12] along with "dirty" dealings for Republican administrations in the United States, tainted them among Hispanic immigrants in the States, many of whom had come from countries where the CIA had deposed or destabilized their governments (Landau, 1999; Torres, 2014, 82, 158). Resentment by native-born Americans and distrust from their Latin American immigrant brethren galvanized the collective bond between the exiles. That collectivism helped them to survive and thrive in Miami and the other communities where they were resettled, but it was also a curse. When the coalition gathered by the CIA to liberate Cuba failed to do so, it became restive. Violence ensued, and the late 1960s and the 1970s were marked by the assassinations of Cuban coalition leaders throughout the country. Bombings rocked Miami, the New York Metro area, Los Angeles, Chicago, and Havana, while members of the Cuban exile community who sup-

---

10. The literacy campaigns of the early 1960s frightened many Cuban parents who believed the campaigns were a ploy to take their children away. In response, the Catholic Church initiated Operation Peter Pan, a series of flights that whisked away some fourteen thousand children to live in the United States between 1960 and 1961. About half of the children ended up reunited with their parents, while the rest ended up in foster care, under the supervision of the church.

11. Torres (2014) writes that after Cubans began arriving to Miami en masse and it became clear that they would not be repatriated quickly, local authorities complained that local resources in Miami could not support such a population and that they should be resettled to alleviate overcrowding. Working in concert with the U.S. Catholic Conference, the federal government resettled more than three hundred thousand refugees throughout the country by 1978 (73–74). Eventually, many who were resettled moved back to Miami.

12. Cuban exiles were implicated in 1970s assassinations associated with Operation Condor, during which leftists from Argentina, Chile, Uruguay, Paraguay, and Bolivia who were in exile from their countries were assassinated in their countries of asylum. In the United States, for example, Cuban exiles with ties to the CIA/DINA were convicted for the 1976 murder of former Chilean ambassador Orlando Letelier and his American assistant Ronni Moffitt in Washington, D.C. Cuban exiles were also instrumental in carrying out the Watergate break-in during the Nixon administration.

ported dialogue with Cuba were suppressed, sometimes violently. The exile community appeared to turn a blind eye to the unrest, further damaging their credibility with the rest of the country.[13]

In the 1980s, exile leaders like Jorge Mas Canosa succeeded in gaining political legitimacy by currying favor with the Reagan administration, but the act of aligning themselves with an administration that was openly hostile to minorities only widened the gap between Miami's exile community and the other Hispanic and minority groups in the country. This is one reason why today, even though they have been in the country for almost sixty years, many members of the exile community are still reluctant to identify themselves as Hispanics in the United States.

This disinclination to identify with Hispanic/Latinos and Hispanic/Latino issues surfaced during the Trump campaign and contributed, in part, to his support among those in the exile community. When Latino Decisions polled Latinos in Miami who were registered to vote and asked them whether they agreed with the statement that the rhetoric coming from the Republican Party was "anti-immigrant" or "anti-Latino," 41 percent of Puerto Ricans and 44 percent of other Latinos agreed that it was; only 26 percent of Cuban exiles agreed. When this same group was asked whether they thought the Republican Party was "hostile" to immigrants and Latinos, 31 percent of Puerto Ricans and 26 percent of other Latinos said yes; only 15 percent of Cubans agreed with them. The most marked difference in responses was when they were asked specifically whether they believed Donald Trump cared about Hispanic voters: 37 percent of Cubans said he "truly cared," while only 16 percent of Puerto Ricans and 13 percent of other Latinos agreed with them. Only 31 percent of the Cubans who responded considered Trump hostile toward Latinos, compared to 60 percent of the Puerto Rican respondents and 53 percent of other Latinos. Cubans also scored lower than the other two groups in response to the question of whether the act of voting, to them, is a means to "support and represent the Latino community" in the United States:

while 46 percent of the Puerto Ricans and 35 percent of other Latinos agreed with the statement, only 28 percent of Cubans agreed (Latino Decisions, 2016).

One can argue that Cubans responded the way they did because, since most do not have immigration issues, they are not concerned about anti-immigration rhetoric. However, Puerto Ricans, who are citizens and certainly do not have immigration issues, seemed to be sensitive to the rhetoric and take offense to it, so this explanation does not make sense. What is more likely is that Cuban exiles in Miami either are not aware of or do not care about attacks on groups other than themselves. This response is in line with the fact that even after all this time, there is an element of the Cuban exile community that continues to isolate itself from the concerns of other minority groups.

It also seems to indicate that there is some disconnect between how they and others in the country might perceive themselves as a minority group in the United States. Quite simply, most Cuban exiles in Miami *do not* consider themselves part of a minority group. The fact that there are about one million of them living within a relatively confined geographic area lends credence to this notion—in Miami, Cubans are *not* a minority group because they are a majority. Furthermore, the fact that they form much of the economic and political backbone of the city, that they enjoy a high level of political representation in Washington, D.C., and that so many Cubans and Cuban Americans are affluent compared to other Hispanic groups reinforces this perception. Research findings by the Pew Hispanic Center suggest that "Hispanics see race as a measure of belonging and 'whiteness' as a measure of inclusion, or perceived inclusion"; Cubans seem to bear out this finding. Since many identify as white, they feel that their interests align more with people who are white, and not with those who are minorities since they do not see themselves as such. To many Cubans, being a minority means being poor and disenfranchised; the Cuban community in Miami, with its perceived political influence, sees itself as anything but.

---

13. This period also saw the rise of Cuban exile terror cells like Alpha 66 and Omega 7. In addition to taking responsibility for planting hundreds of bombs and killing dozens of exile "dissidents," these groups plotted to assassinate high-ranking Cuban officials, including the Cuban ambassador to the United Nation in 1968 (Kaplan, 1968). By 1975, the situation had become so critical that the mayor of Miami asked the federal government to help create an anticrime task force to stamp out the terror threat from the exiles (*New York Times*, 1975). The violence continued unabated until the indictment in 1978 of five Cuban exiles connected to the murder of Orlando Letelier exposed the links between the terror cells, militant exile groups, and the U.S. and Latin American intelligence communities (Branch, 1978).

From Exiles to . . . Immigrants . . .
to Americans . . . or Cubans

However, the reality is that some Cubans *are* poor and disenfranchised, whether the community admits it or not. Many are employed or underemployed and struggling to make ends meet; they live in the deep South—one of the regions paying the lowest wages in the country—in a no-state-tax state that does not provide many subsidies for the poorest of its residents. This is a reality that also drew many Cuban exile voters to Trump.

The fact that the Miami Cubans are splintered politically, and that Trump's anti-immigrant stance might alleviate this "dilution" through detentions, deportations, and immigration limits, is attractive to some. Trump's decision not to reinstate the "Wet-foot/Dry-foot" policy that Obama abolished and his allusion that CAA is unfair and might be on the chopping block sit just fine with some of them, since fewer immigrants in general—even fellow exiles—would mean fewer competitors for jobs and resources, and fewer people who disagree about what should be done with Cuba (Lopez-Gottardi, 2016).

Conservatism also is a factor that drove the vote. Florida talk-show host Roberto Rodriguez Tejera told author Marcela Valdes that he expected many Cubans to vote for Trump. Valdes writes, "Rural white voters, he explained, aren't the only ones frightened by the specter of feminism, Muslim immigrants and L.G.B.T. rights. 'For many Hispanic Americans, the cultural changes of the past 15 years have been very hard. Trump, for many, is a return to the mother's womb'" (Valdes, 2016).

Finally, there is the issue of what it means to be a Cuban exile today. Fifty years ago, Cuban exiles were the "soldiers" on the front line of the Cold War. Today, that war is technically over. The Cuban government makes it possible for Cubans to live abroad and still be Cuban. Some Cubans who were once "erased" can now be permitted to return to Cuba to live as part-time or full-time residents, depending on the circumstances of their departure (Moreno, 2018).

Good news? Maybe . . . but it is a double-edged sword. In 2015, the *Sun Sentinel* ran a series titled "Plundering America: The Cuban Criminal Pipeline." The articles detailed how loopholes in the CAA were allowing Cuban exiles to illegally funnel money to the island and live in Cuba on welfare benefits from the United States. Others were engaging in fraud schemes and other crimes, only to flee to Cuba when they were about to be arrested or face trial. U.S. Marshals estimate there may be as many as 130 fugitives living in Cuba; the number may be higher, but there is no way to confirm where they are. What is frustrating is that, currently, there is no recourse available to extradite them; if they are caught and convicted, there is no way to deport them once they complete their sentences (O'Matz, 2018).

The series was an embarrassment to an exile community that still identifies with the name it was given in the early 1960s, at the start of their odyssey: The Golden Exiles. The problem, as they see it, is with the vintages that followed theirs. Alvarez (2016) quotes a Cuban exile from an earlier vintage who is a Trump supporter: "Cubans who arrived here after 1980 came for economic reasons, not because of political repression, so they should be treated the same as any other immigrant. A lot of them come in, collect benefits, and then go right back to Cuba. That's not fair." It is no wonder that Cuban exiles who support Trump would not be averse to repealing or modifying the CAA to prevent these issues, even if it means that, in the future, Cubans who wish to emigrate and settle in the United States end up as illegal aliens.

Then there are Cubans who like Trump for reasons that are hard to quantify. Cuban culture is achievement oriented, with a large dash of machismo thrown in. Some might consider Trump, with his billions and his private plane, many lavish homes, and beautiful younger wife, the epitome of what they hope to achieve. That he is unfiltered and authoritarian adds to the appeal since, to be honest, Cubans seem to be attracted to leaders who have a streak of the "strongman" in them (Fontova, 2017). If not, there is no way that Gerardo Machado, then Fulgencio Batista, and later Castro could have lasted in power for as long as they did. Lest we think it is an island-only phenomenon, we have only to examine the life of Jorge Mas Canosa, who served as the unofficial spokesman and kingmaker for the exile community through the Reagan, Bush, and Clinton administrations. Mas Canosa, who aspired to be president of Cuba once Castro was deposed, was known for intimidating opponents, including the *Miami Herald*, over negative publicity. Saul Landau (1999) writes that during Mas Canosa's feud with the newspaper, "*Herald* executives received death threats. Vandals smeared excrement on its sidewalk vending machines." A few years later, Mas Canosa challenged Miami City Commissioner Joe Carollo to a duel after the official claimed that Mas Canosa had pushed the city into awarding him a contract. Given all this, the community's support of Trump really comes as no surprise.

But not all Cubans are attracted to strongmen. A year after the election, when transcripts were released showing that Trump had told Mexican president Enrique Peña Nieto that he had won the election "with a large percentage of Hispanic voters," and that he had earned "84 percent, with the Cuban-American vote" (Miller, Vitkovskaya, and Fischer-Baum, 2017), an article in the *Miami Herald* quickly rebutted the contention. Nora Gámez Torres (2017) painstakingly examined postelection voter data looking for Trump's evidence; she finally acknowledged that the Cuban vote in Miami had been instrumental in helping Trump win the election, but in no way did it approach "84 percent," as he had alleged.

Cuban lawmakers also are not on board with Trump. Since taking office, he has had a contentious relationship with Ros-Lehtinen, who has publicly opposed him. Rubio also has gone on the record opposing Trump. Still, for all their opposition, they have voted to approve some of his policy initiatives. Ros-Lehtinen is on the record saying that she will resign at the end of 2018 and will not seek reelection. It remains to be seen whether the person who replaces her will represent those who support Trump or those who do not.

This leads us back to Republican-turned-independent Mike Fernandez, who has been far from silent. In an interview with Politico's Matt Dixon (2017), the billionaire called Trump an "abortion of a human being" and called out Republican lawmakers and administration officials who side with the president. He said it is "demoralizing" to "see adults worshipping a false idol" and that he can't "continue to write checks" for politicians who are "egomaniacs."

Fernandez identifies as Hispanic and a pan-Americanist, with close business ties with Latin America. He also identifies with immigrants, having entered the United States from Cuba via Mexico. He says immigrants are the "key to the fiber and economic survival of the country," and they are doing jobs that "nobody would do" (Mazzei, 2017). He is concerned that his fellow exiles "live in a bubble in Miami" and that their support for Trump shows a lack of empathy toward others. He related how he was stopped by a trooper in Utah, where he owns a home; the trooper assumed that he was a parolee. For Fernandez, it was a revelation: "Cubans forget that in the eyes of most we are all the same" (Pelaez, 2017).

How Cubans decide to come to terms with their identity in this country is an open question. Another layer to the conundrum was added on April 18, 2018, when the last Castro relinquished the Cuban presidency to his vice president, a relatively unknown politician by the name of Miguel Díaz-Canel. For the first time in almost sixty years, a Castro will not helm the government in Cuba. For so many Cuban exiles who said they would only return when Castro was dead or gone, this could be the moment of truth.

Or maybe not. Most Cuban exiles are skeptical, believing that this change is simply a shuffling of the board when the game is still rigged. Raul will still be first secretary of the Communist Party under Díaz-Canel, they say, and some younger Cubans, newer arrivals, trust Díaz-Canel even less than they did Raul ("Cuba's Presidential Transition . . . ," 2018).

But for some older exiles, most of whom arrived in the 1990s, living in the United States has been an exercise in adaptation. It had not always been successful. It is expensive here; the politics of cohabitating in this country as an immigrant can be complicated and vexing. Worst of all, there is a loneliness to life in the United States that only an immigrant can recognize, which exacerbates the struggle. My own father, who emigrated from Cuba in the 1950s, used to say, "In Cuba, we worked to live. In the United States, Americans live to work." It is a fundamental difference in worldview that has made some exiles pause and consider an alternative they never thought they would: to return.

Last year, more than eleven thousand Cuban exiles requested repatriation. In 2016, thirteen thousand applied. The Cuban government, finally taking a page from the U.S. playbook, has made it all too easy to return: Cuban citizens can live anyplace in the world for up to two years without losing residency, and they need only periodically return home to the island to "reactivate" it (Moreno, 2018). The idea of repatriation is unpopular in Miami; but some exiles are willing to risk the ire of the community to return. They miss their families and don't want to be barred from their country forever. They want to go home.

Bibliography

Alvarez, J. (2016, March 17). Trump Disrupts Cuban-American Politics. *The Atlantic*. Retrieved April 4, 2018, from https://www.theatlantic.com/politics/

archive/2016/03/trump-disrupts-cuban-american
-politics/474165/.

Amnesty International. (2017). *"Your Mind Is in Prison": Cuba's Web of Control over Free Expression and Its Chilling Effect on Everyday Life*. London: Amnesty International. Retrieved from https://www.amnesty.org/en/documents/amr25/7299/2017/en/.

Barreto, M. (2016). *2016 Latino Election Analysis [PowerPoint slides]*. LatinoDecisions.com. Retrieved April 27, 2018, from http://www.latinodecisions.com/index.php/download_file/view/702/384/.

Branch, T. (1978). The Letelier Investigation. *New York Times*, 7. Retrieved from https://www.nytimes.com/1978/07/16/archives/the-letelier-investigation-the-venezuelan-connection-proppers-first.html.

Bustamante, M. J. (2016, November 10). Is the Cuban Adjustment Act in Trouble? *Cuba Counterpoints*. Retrieved April 4, 2018, from https://cubacounterpoints.com/archives/1069.

Camarioca Crisis in 1965. (2017, November 17). *The Swiss Confederation: Federal Department of Foreign Affairs (FDFA)*. Retrieved April 6, 2018, from https://www.eda.admin.ch/eda/en/home/news/dossiers/alle-dossiers/schweizer-schutzmachtmandate-usa-kuba/camarioca-krise.html.

Cambridge Academic Content Dictionary. (2018). Exile. Retrieved April 26, 2018, from https://dictionary.cambridge.org/us/dictionary/english/exile.

Cancio Isla, W. (2006). Former CANF Board Member Admits to Planning Terrorist Attack against Cuba. *El Nuevo Herald*. Retrieved from http://havanajournal.com/cuban_americans/entry/former-canf-board-member-admits-to-planning-terrorist-attack-against-cuba/.

Cannon, T. (1983). *Revolutionary Cuba*. La Habana: Jose' Marti'.

Cubans in the US: A Profile. (2006, August 25). Retrieved April 6, 2018, from Pew Hispanic Center/Kaiser Family Foundation website: www.pewhispanic.org/files/factsheets/23.pdf.

Cuba's Presidential Transition Bringing No Joy to Its Exiles. (2018). *WTOP*. Retrieved April 30, 2018, from https://wtop.com/national/2018/04/cubas-presidential-transition-bringing-no-joy-to-its-exiles/.

Dixon, M. (2017, July 20). Billionaire Florida Donor Rails against Trump. Politico. Retrieved April 4, 2018, from https://www.politico.com/states/florida/story/2017/07/20/billionaire-gop-donor-out-of-politics-calls-trump-abortion-of-a-human-113528.

Fields, S. (2018). Ybor City: Cigar Capital of the World. NPS.gov. Retrieved April 16, 2018, from https://www.nps.gov/nr/twhp/wwwlps/lessons/51ybor/51Ybor.htm.

Flores, A., G. López, and J. Radford. (2017). Facts on U.S. Latinos, 2015. Pew Research Center's Hispanic Trends Project. Retrieved April 22, 2018, from http://www.pewhispanic.org/2017/09/18/facts-on-u-s-latinos-current-data/.

Fontova, H. (2017). Cuban-Americans Voted for Trump at Higher Rate Than "White" Americans. *The Daily Caller*. Retrieved April 28, 2018, from http://dailycaller.com/2016/11/21/cuban-americans-voted-for-trump-at-higher-rate-than-white-americans/.

Gallagher, P. L. (1980). *The Cuban Exile*. New York: Arno Press.

Gámez Torres, N. (2017, August 7). Trump Says He Won 84 Percent of the Cuban-American Vote. Fake News? *Miami Herald*. Retrieved April 10, 2018, from http://www.miamiherald.com/news/nation-world/world/americas/cuba/article165450707.html.

Grant, W. (2018). Cuba after the Castros. *BBC News*. Retrieved April 21, 2018, from http://www.bbc.co.uk/news/resources/idt-sh/Cuba_after_the_Castros.

Individualism—collectivism. (2006). In R. H. Schaffer, *Key Concepts in Developmental Psychology*. London: Sage UK. Retrieved from http://bcc.ezproxy.cuny.edu:2048/login?url=https://search.credoreference.com/content/entry/sageukdp/individualism_collectivism/0?institutionId=307.

Kaplan, M. (1968). 9 Cuban Exiles Held in 6 Bombings Here. *New York Times*, 1, 18. Retrieved from https://www.nytimes.com/1968/10/24/archives/9-cuban-exiles-held-in-6-bombings-here-9-cuba-refugees-held-in.html.

Kestin, S., M. O'Matz, and J. Maines. (2015, April 9). Poll: Floridians Question Special Treatment Afforded Cuban Immigrants. *Sun Sentinel* [Palm Beach]. Retrieved from http://www.sun-sentinel.com/news/florida/fl-cuba-poll-20150409-story.html.

Key Migration Terms. (2018). *International Organization for Migration*. Retrieved April 26, 2018, from https://www.iom.int/key-migration-terms#refugee.

Krogstad, J. (2014). After Decades of GOP Support,

Cubans Shifting toward the Democratic Party. *Pew Research Center*. Retrieved April 22, 2018, from http://www.pewresearch.org/fact-tank/2014/06/24/after-decades-of-gop-support-cubans-shifting-toward-the-democratic-party/.

Kunz, E. (1973). The Refugee in Flight: Kinetic Models and Forms of Displacement. *International Migration Review* 7(2), 125–146. doi:10.2307/3002424.

Landau, S. (1999). No Mas Canosa: The Death of Cuban Political Figure Jorge Mas Canosa—Obituary. LatinAmericanStudies.org. Retrieved April 30, 2018, from http://www.latinamericanstudies.org/exile/canosa.htm.

Latino Decisions. (2016). 2016 Florida Election Eve Poll—National and State Crosstabs. Washington, D.C. Retrieved from http://www.latinodecisions.com/index.php/download_file/view/673/384/.

Leary, A. (2012, October 13). Meet Florida's Big-Time Donors to Super PACs. *Tampa Bay Times*. Retrieved April 3, 2018, from http://www.tampabay.com/news/politics/national/meet-floridas-big-time-donors-to-super-pacs/1256128.

López, G. (2015, September 15). Hispanics of Cuban Origin in the United States, 2013. Retrieved April 8, 2018, from http://www.pewhispanic.org/2015/09/15/hispanics-of-cuban-origin-in-the-united-states-2013/.

Lopez-Gottardi, C. (2016, November 16). The Complex Cuban Vote. *U.S. News & World Report*. Retrieved April 10, 2018, from https://www.usnews.com/opinion/op-ed/articles/2016-11-16/2016-highlighted-the-growing-complexity-of-the-cuban-american-vote.

Luscombe, R. (2016, December 3). Florida's Cubans Take Sober Look at Ties with Homeland after Post-Castro Party. *The Guardian* [London]. Retrieved from https://www.theguardian.com/us-news/2016/dec/03/florida-cubans-fidel-castro-trump.

Mabry, D., and W. Wolfe. (2018). Cuba, 1898–1959. *Historical Text Archive: Electronic History Resources, online since 1990*. Retrieved April 26, 2018, from http://www.historicaltextarchive.com/sections.php?action=read&artid=122.

Mazzei, P. (2017, May 10). Miami Billionaire Plans Political Fund to Defend Unauthorized Immigrants. *Miami Herald*. Retrieved April 4, 2018, from http://www.miamiherald.com/news/politics-government/article149797499.html.

Mazzei, P., L. Clark, and N. G. Torres. (2017, January 14). Don't Expect Trump to Reinstate Special Immigration Status for Cubans. *Miami Herald*. Retrieved April 4, 2018, from http://www.miamiherald.com/news/politics-government/election/donald-trump/article126507569.html.

Miller, G., J. Vitkovskaya, and R. Fischer-Baum. (2017, August 3). "This Deal Will Make Me Look Terrible": Full Transcripts of Trump's Calls with Mexico and Australia. [online graphic]. *Washington Post*. Retrieved from https://www.washingtonpost.com/graphics/2017/politics/australia-mexico-transcripts/?utm_term=.42dc2157503f.

Mission. (2017). *The Immigration Partnership & Coalition Fund*. Retrieved April 3, 2018, from https://impacfund.org/mission/.

Moreno, S. (2018). Thousands of Cuban Exiles Are Exploring an Unusual Option: Returning to Cuba to Live. *Miami Herald*. Retrieved from http://www.miamiherald.com/news/local/community/miami-dade/article204732234.html.

Naren Ranjit, L. (2016). *2016 Latino Election Eve Poll*. Latinovote2016.com. Retrieved April 28, 2018, from http://www.latinovote2016.com/app/#cuban-national-all.

New York Times. (1975). Miami Seeks Help to Combat Terror, 43. Retrieved from https://www.nytimes.com/1975/03/02/archives/miami-seeks-help-to-combat-terror-mayor-cites-violence-and-threats.html.

New York Times. (1978). Legacy of Terror, 8. Retrieved from https://www.nytimes.com/1978/07/16/archives/legacy-of-terror.html.

New York Times. (1979). Pro-Castro Cubans in Puerto Rico Are Terrorists' Target, 54. Retrieved from https://www.nytimes.com/1979/10/21/archives/procastro-cubans-in-puerto-rico-are-terrorists-target-exiles-second.html.

O'Matz, M. (2018). In Cuba, Fugitive Declines Invitation to Return to U.S. Sun-Sentinel.com. Retrieved April 29, 2018, from http://www.sun-sentinel.com/news/nationworld/fl-marshals-service-wanted-cuba-20150222-story.html.

Ordoñez, F. (2016). Will Obama's Cuba Opening Cost Clinton a Win in Florida? *Miami Herald*. Retrieved from http://www.miamiherald.com/latest-news/article111043217.html.

Pedraza, S. (1998). Cuba's Revolution and Exodus. *Journal of the International Institute* 5(2). Retrieved from https://quod.lib.umich.edu/j/jii/4750978.0005.204?view=text;rgn=main.

Pelaez, C. (2017, May 31). Why This Cuban American Billionaire Is Raising Millions for Undocumented Immigrants. *NBC News*. Retrieved April 3, 2018, from https://www.nbcnews.com/news/latino/why-cuban-american-billionaire-raising-millions-undocumented-immigrants-n764576.

Perez, L. A. (1995). Cubans in Tampa: From Exiles to Immigrants 1892–1901. In *Essays on Cuban History: Historiography and Research*, 25–35. Miami: University Press of Florida.

Perez, L. A. (1999). *On Becoming Cuban: Identity, Nationality, and Culture*. Chapel Hill: University of North Carolina Press.

Phillips, R. H. (1959, January 2). Batista and Regime Flee Cuba; Castro Moving to Take Power; Mobs Riot and Loot in Havana. *New York Times*. Retrieved April 8, 2018, from https://archive.nytimes.com/www.nytimes.com/learning/general/onthisday/big/0101.html#article.

Portes, A. (1984). The Rise of Ethnicity: Determinants of Ethnic Perceptions among Cuban Exiles in Miami. *American Sociological Review* 49(3), 383–397. Retrieved from http://www.jstor.org/stable/2095282.

Reiss, M. (2001). The Batista-Lansky Alliance. *Cigar Aficionado*. Retrieved April 23, 2018, from https://www.cigaraficionado.com/article/the-batista-lansky-alliance-7197.

Republican Presidential Nomination Process. (2017). *The Green Papers: 2016 Presidential Primaries, Caucuses and Conventions*. Retrieved April 10, 2018, from http://www.thegreenpapers.com/P16/FL-R.

Sanchez, R. (2014). Old Cuban Exiles in the US Are Filled with Rage. *Business Insider*. Retrieved April 28, 2018, from http://www.businessinsider.com/old-cuban-exiles-in-the-us-are-filled-with-rage-2014–12.

Sierra, J. A. (1996). Camilo Cienfuegos. Historyof Cuba.com. Retrieved April 7, 2018, from http://www.historyofcuba.com/history/camilo.htm.

Smitha, F. (1998). Cold War: the Eisenhower Years—Castro and Eisenhower. FSmithA.com. Retrieved April 24, 2018, from http://www.fsmitha.com/h2/ch24t-cuba2.htm.

Sociedad la Union Marti-Maceo. Ybor Chamber of Commerce. (2017). Ybor.org. Retrieved April 16, 2018, from http://ybor.org/sociedad-la-union-marti-maceo/.

Sopo, G. (2016, November 16). Clinton, Trump and the 2016 Cuban Vote in Florida. *Univision*. Retrieved April 10, 2018, from https://www.univision.com/univision-news/opinion/clinton-trump-and-the-2016-cuban-vote-in-florida.

Suarez, C. (2018). Cuban Exiles in Miami's Little Havana View Cuban President as Castro's Puppet [WPLG Local10 news]. Retrieved from https://www.local10.com/news/local/miami/cuban-exiles-in-miamis-little-havana-view-cuban-president-as-castros-puppet.

Torres, M. D. L. A. (2014). *In the Land of Mirrors: Cuban Exile Politics in the United States*. Retrieved from https://ebookcentral.proquest.com.

Valdes, M. (2016, November 15). "We're Looking at a New Divide within the Hispanic Community." Retrieved January 8, 2019, from https://www.nytimes.com/interactive/2016/11/20/magazine/donald-trumps-america-florida-latino-vote.html.

Whitefield, M., and N. Gámez Torres. (2017). Cuban Leader Raúl Castro Will Stay in Power Past February. *Miami Herald*. Retrieved from http://www.miamiherald.com/news/nation-world/world/americas/cuba/article190998519.html.

White House. (1975). Castro (37). Washington D.C. Retrieved from https://www.archives.gov/files/research/jfk/releases/docid-32112987.pdf.

Worrall, S. (2016). When the Mob Owned Cuba. Smithsonian. Retrieved April 22, 2018, from https://www.smithsonianmag.com/travel/mob-havana-cuba-culture-music-book-tj-english-cultural-travel-180960610/.

US Census Bureau Tables

Cuba—T064_032—Foreign Born (White Population)—Social Explorer Tables (SE)—Surveys: Census 1870/1880/1890/1900/1940/1970 Census Tract, County, State and US—Social Explorer. (2018) [online] Available at: https://www.socialexplorer.com/data/C1940CompDS/metadata/?ds=SE&var=T064_032.

Cuba—T139_094—Place of Birth for the Foreign-Born Population—Social Explorer Tables: ACS 2016 (5-Year Estimates) (SE)—Survey ACS 2016 (5-Year Estimates)—Social Explorer. (2018). Socialexplorer.com. Retrieved April 22, 2018, from https://www.socialexplorer.com/data/ACS2016_5yr/metadata/?ds=SE&var=T139_094.

T15. Hispanic or Latino by Specific Origin [31]—Social Explorer Tables: ACS 2010 (1-Year Estimates) (SE)—ACS 2010 (1-Year Estimates)—Social Explorer. (2018). Socialexplorer.com. Retrieved April 22, 2018, from https://www.social

explorer.com/data/ACS2010/metadata/?ds = SE& table = T015.

Understanding the Reading

1. Describe some of the Cuban "vintages."
2. What are some of the splits among Cuban Americans?
3. What was the "Wet-foot/Dry-foot" policy?

Suggestion for Responding

1. Further research the details of the Mariel Boatlift of the 1980s.

Suggestions for Responding to Part I

1. Write a paper analyzing the racial and ethnic features of your identity. Consider your ancestral origins and how your heritage has influenced who you are today. Reflect on such factors as physical characteristics, language, religion, and family customs and traditions. Also, think about such expressive behaviors as dress, music, dance, family stories, holidays, and celebrations. These all may be markers of your ethnic heritage.

   If you think you have nothing to write about, remember that in the United States everyone has a racial and ethnic heritage. Whereas it is central to some people's identity, others may not be conscious of it at all. This is often because they are members of the dominant racial and ethnic culture, which assumes its values and traditions are "universal" or at least most significant or appropriate. If you belong to this group, look at yourself from the outside, from the perspective of another cultural system, several of which have been represented in these readings.

2. In response to the Gwaltney selection (reading 10), you may have written questions you would ask if you were conducting an oral history interview. Singly or as a member of a group, evaluate those questions again. Then use them to interview an older person in your family or community.

   A tape recorder is useful, especially if you plan to prepare a word-for-word transcript, but always ask your informant for permission before you switch it on.

   Your final report could resemble reading 10 (a verbatim transcription of the words of your informant), or it may be more interpretive. In either case, listen to the recording and reread your notes *several* times before you begin to write, and refer to them after you have completed your report to confirm its accuracy.

3. Your instructor may want you to make an oral presentation of your ethnicity analysis or your oral history. In this case, prepare *brief* notes. Try to talk naturally and not read word for word. Rehearse your presentation several times to be sure you stay within the required time limit. You will feel more comfortable in front of your class if you have rehearsed at least once before an audience (a friend or roommate, for example). If this isn't possible, try speaking to a wall mirror. Above all, relax. Try to look at your audience, even if it seems difficult, because their reactions will be encouraging. Remember, you are talking to friends.

4. After completing part I, how would you answer the questions "Who is an American?" and "Is there an American culture?" Support your responses with evidence from the readings.

Part II
Gender and Sexual Identity

"Is it a girl or a boy?" This is inevitably the first question asked about a new baby. As we grow older, many of us identify ourselves and each other as boys or girls, as women or men. In American culture, gender is the most salient feature of one's identity. It shapes our attitudes, our behavior, our experiences, our beliefs about ourselves and about others. Gender is so central to our perception of social reality that we often are not even conscious of how it shapes our behavior and our social interactions.

Consider to what extent our traditional definitions of masculinity and femininity have changed. In the recent past a "real man" should be **masculine**—that is, he should be strong and mechanically oriented, ambitious and assertive, in control of his emotions, knowledgeable about the world, a good provider. A "real woman," in turn, was to be **feminine**—that is, passive and domestic, nurturing and dependent, emotional, preoccupied with her appearance, and maternal. These gender-appropriate characteristics and behaviors affect many areas of our lives: physical and psychological aspects, occupational choices, interpersonal relations, and so on.

The basis for gender distinctions is not wholly clear as of now, and the "nature/nurture" debate—whether or to what degree gendered behavior is controlled by biology or by socialization—continues. Scientists are investigating the roles that hormones, genes, chromosomes, and other physical features play in women's and men's psychological development, but these issues are complex. Central to this discussion must be the understanding that gender identity is a very personal experience and may or may not line up with one's assigned sex at birth.

We will also concentrate on the view of many social scientists who study the diversity of appropriate or "natural" male and female behaviors in different cultures and other times. They see in this diversity strong evidence of the central role that culture plays in creating gender roles. As a result, they distinguish between **sex**, the biological "fact" of one's physiological and hormonal characteristics, and **gender**, the social categories that ascribe roles, behaviors, and personality traits to women and men, yet accepting that there is a wide range of gender experiences and expressions. In this sense, male and female **sex roles** are differences in reproductive traits. The masculine and feminine behaviors are features of **gender roles**.

Social scientists believe that we learn our gender roles by a process called **socialization**. Gender roles are only one kind of role we learn. A **role** is any socially or culturally defined behavioral expectation that is presumed to apply to all individuals in the category. Socialization includes the many pressures, rewards, and punishments that compel us to conform to social expectations. These are deeply embedded in every aspect of our culture. Our treatment of infants and children, language, education, mass media, religion, laws, medical institutions and mental health systems, occupational environments, intimate relationships—all teach and reinforce appropriate gender behaviors. Yet as is discussed in this part, we live in a time where the many expressions of our gender experience are being recognized and increasingly respected and celebrated by our society.

The first article in part II (reading 13) is about an Olympic athlete recounting his story of publicly coming out. Reading 14 looks at the relationship a particular group of American men have to their guns and how that is embedded in their identities. Reading 15 considers male gender roles. Doug Cooper Thompson describes the male stereotype and analyzes what it costs men to conform to those expectations.

This part also sheds light on the distinct areas that affect our sexual orientations. Tom Head gives us a short history of transgender rights in the United States in reading 16. As the author of reading 17, Jessica R. Stearns, writes, "First, there is the anatomical sex of a person (M/F); second, the gender (M/F); then, third, sexual orientation (Hetero/Homosexual)." Although most people have all three segments the same and are heterosexual, there can be any combination. Most of us have been brought up to think only in terms of male and female. Both of these authors help us relearn this important piece of being human. Jessica R. Stearns, in "A Transsexual's Story," writes of her life, which began in 1940 as John Robert Stearns in rural Alabama. From her earliest memories, she remembers having the feeling of being a girl, but in the 1940s and 1950s there was very little known about transgendered people in this country. She joined the air force, became a pilot, and flew missions into Berlin and Vietnam. She eventually had very high security clearance but said, "If they had ever known!" Under great pressure from the military to conform to a particular masculine image, she married, became a father, and eventually flew for Continental Airlines. When she decided to go for the sex reassignment operation (strongly supported by her family and doctors), Continental Airlines fired her. Jessica sued and won. She made national headlines, was featured on the *Sally Jessy Raphael* show, and here writes her story for the first time.

The readings in this part encourage us to assess our own gender identity and give us fuller insight into the experiences of the opposite sex. A clearer sense of some of the consequences of traditional gender roles and gender expectations may encourage us to question just how "natural" traditional gender roles are. It will also help us consider whether we want to see changes in gender roles and sexual relationships and how to act on our decisions. Also, students and professors can discuss, debate, and pursue the implications of all the information within each essay. For example, when is sexual assignment surgery ethical, if ever? Gay marriage is a national right in the United States, but it is constantly being challenged. Does the law reflect your principles? Should gay couples adopt? Why or why not? Would you prefer to know whether your professor is gay or lesbian, or should the professor maintain that distance? Are there differing circumstances? What sorts of public policies would change if we acknowledged the existence of five sexes? Would an intersexed person be allowed to marry, and would it be to a man or to a woman? How would we organize the separation of sexes in prisons? Would they be eligible for a military draft?

Because of the complexity of sexuality, where external organs, internal organs, and our endocrine system all help sort out who we are and what makes us happy, there is a constant tension in our society when the jigsaw pieces do not fit the way we have been told they should. On June 26, 2003, the Supreme Court overruled a Texas sodomy law, legalizing gay sexual conduct. In dissent, Justice Antonin Scalia declared it a cultural war. On August 5, 2003, the Episcopal Church's first openly gay bishop was approved, the Reverend Gene Robinson of New Hampshire, and on November 18, 2003, Massachusetts' highest court ruled that gay couples have the right to marry. In contrast, in May 2007, before the end of the Iraq War, the *International Herald Tribune* reported that the Department of Defense was discharging linguists, including Arabic speakers, because they were gay. (Ten thousand have been discharged in the past decade because of sexual orientation.) In a time when national security was supposed to be top priority, and Arabic linguists were badly needed in Iraq and elsewhere, sexual orientation trumped the war on terrorism. There is a great deal of politics surrounding our sexuality these days, and the geographical fault lines show fairly clearly that the United States is split on subjects dealing with sexual identity. The repeal of the Don't Ask, Don't Tell policy in 2011 ended the mandate requiring military personnel who were not heterosexual to hide their sexual orientation. While this change is a milestone in our country's history, President Trump is attempting to ban all transgendered people from serving in active duty in the U.S. military.

13

Adam Rippon: When I Came Out Is When I Started to Own Who I Am as a Person

Karen Price

Adam Rippon is just twenty-seven, but he speaks with a level of wisdom and insight far beyond his years.

Perhaps it's innate, or perhaps it's the result of denying one's true self only to come out on the other side embracing the person once kept hidden. No matter how or why, Rippon now movingly and enthusiastically shares his journey to becoming an openly gay man and athlete, hoping that his story will help others.

"Being gay isn't what defines me, but it's a big part of who I am and I like to talk about my coming out because that's when I started to own who I was as a person," said Rippon, who spoke to TeamUSA.org on the topic in honor of June's LGBTQ Pride Month. "That's what's important, not the being gay part but at some point—gay or straight—you need to own who you are. You can't be afraid of who you are or else you're afraid of your own potential, and if you don't own who you are then you can't grow.

"When I came out was when I was able to breathe. When everyone knew, I didn't feel like I was hiding anything. I didn't feel like I was putting on a show. I was being me and it was easy. It was a lot easier to be me than to be who I thought I was supposed to be."

For years, Rippon didn't want to believe that he was gay. He was male, and he was a figure skater, so people sometimes assumed he was gay, but the fact that it was assumed made him want to deny it even more.

"A lot of times it's taboo, especially with boys, like, 'You skate, you're gay,'" he said. "That's not always the case, but that being said, you feel a little shame. Being gay and a skater, you don't want it to be true."

The truth was often easy to ignore because of his schedule. For athletes competing at such a high level, there's not much time for a social life. Parties and dating and hanging out take a backseat to training and practice and competition, so Rippon wasn't often forced to confront what he was feeling.

That all changed with one event.

"For as many years as I was like, 'No, I'm not gay,'" he said. "The first time I kissed a boy, I'm like, 'I definitely am gay.'"

Rippon came out to his friends and family in his early twenties and met with so much support that coming out to the world at large in October 2015 felt comfortable. He revealed his sexuality in public for the first time in a story for *SKATING* magazine that featured him and his best friend and training partner Ashley Wagner. The reaction was overwhelmingly positive. The few rude or negative comments, he said, were flushed away by all the people offering encouragement and love.

The fact that so many people still liked him and wanted to be around him after he came out gave him confidence that spilled over into his career as a skater. If people still liked him knowing who he truly was, he reasoned, then they might like his ideas as well. He found the courage to take risks he wouldn't have dreamed of before, and the evidence showed up in everything from his choices of hair color and musical selections to where he wanted to compete.

"I went out and I felt like I was performing as myself and not a character," he said. "That's really what helped push me to win my first national title."

Rippon won the U.S. championships title in 2016, skating to "Who Wants to Live Forever" by Queen for his short program and a Beatles medley for his free skate. He was unable to defend his title this year, however, after breaking his foot during training not long before nationals.

He is now healed enough that he's back to training at nearly 100 percent, though he watches out for repetition of certain elements that might stress his foot too much. Even with that stipulation, he doesn't feel as if he's being held back in his preparation for what will be his most important season yet.

"There's so much to practice all the time that I can always find something to work on and improve," said Rippon, who hopes to make the 2018 Olympic team.

If he does, he will add his name to the list of openly gay Olympic athletes that is steadily growing. *Outsports* magazine estimated that at least forty-seven publicly gay athletes competed in Rio in 2016, the most ever for an Olympic Games. Last summer also saw the first-ever same-sex married couple compete in the Olympics (British field hockey players Helen and Kate Richardson-Walsh) and the first Olympics to accept transgender athletes, although none competed. And after Russia passed antigay legislation prior to hosting the Games in 2014, the International Olympic Committee added language to its host city contracts prohibiting discrimination on the grounds of sexual orientation.

Rippon hopes that one day an athlete coming out won't be a story, but until that happens, he willingly shares his own. Reading about celebrities and athletes coming out helped his own situation feel more normal, he said, and gave him the courage to do the same. Whenever someone tells him that his story was an inspiration, it brings everything full circle and reinforces the responsibility he happily accepts to support and encourage others in their journeys.

"(Pride) is a moment of celebration to see how far we have come, but it's also a reminder that we have so much farther to go," Rippon said. "I think as we get older we owe it to the people who look up to us to stand up for them and say something to make the path easier. We owe it to ourselves and the people around us to continue to pave that road forward."

Understanding the Reading

1. How did Adam's being an athlete both help and challenge his decision to come out?
2. How did coming out change his abilities and his life?

Suggestions for Responding

1. Bring a gay/lesbian/bisexual/transgender group into your classroom to discuss their experiences.
2. Discuss generational, political, and religious divides on the LGBTQ community.

14

Why Are White Men Stockpiling Guns?

JEREMY ADAM SMITH

March 14, 2018

Since the 2008 election of President Obama, the number of firearms manufactured in the United States has tripled, while imports have doubled. This doesn't mean more households have guns than ever before—that percentage has stayed fairly steady for decades. Rather, more guns are being stockpiled by a small number of individuals. Three percent of the population now owns half of the country's firearms, says a recent, definitive study from the Injury Control Research Center at Harvard University.

So, who is buying all these guns—and why?

The short, broad-brush answer to the first part of that question is this: men, who on average possess almost twice the number of guns that female owners do. But not all men. Some groups of men are much more avid gun consumers than others. The American citizen most likely to own a gun is a white male—but not just any white guy. According to a growing number of scientific studies, the kind of man who stockpiles weapons or applies for a concealed-carry license meets a very specific profile.

These are men who are anxious about their ability to protect their families, insecure about their place in the job market, and beset by racial fears. They tend to be less educated. For the most part, they don't appear to be religious—and, one study suggests, faith seems to reduce their attachment to guns. In fact, stockpiling guns seems to be a symptom of a much deeper crisis in meaning and purpose in their lives. Taken together, these studies describe a population that is struggling to find a new story—one in which they are once again the heroes.

Whatever Happened to Hard Work?

When Northland College sociologist Angela Stroud studied applications for licenses to carry concealed firearms in Texas, which exploded after President Obama was elected, she found applicants were overwhelmingly dominated by white men. In interviews, they told her that they wanted to protect themselves and the people they love.

"When men became fathers or got married, they started to feel very vulnerable, like they couldn't protect families," she says. "For them, owning a weapon is part of what it means to be a good husband and a good father." That meaning is "rooted in fear and vulnerability—very motivating emotions."

But Stroud also discovered another motivation: racial anxiety. "A lot of people talked about how important Obama was to get a concealed-carry license: 'He's for free health care, he's for welfare.' They were asking, 'Whatever happened to hard work?'" Obama's presidency, they feared, would empower minorities to threaten their property and families.

The insight Stroud gained from her interviews is backed up by numerous studies. A 2013 paper by a team of United Kingdom researchers found that a one-point jump in the scale they used to measure racism increased the odds of owning a gun by 50 percent. A 2016 study from the University of Illinois at Chicago found that racial resentment among whites fueled opposition to gun control. This perception drives political affiliations: a 2017 study in the *Social Studies Quarterly* found that gun owners had become 50 percent more likely to vote Republican since 1972—and that gun culture had become strongly associated with explicit racism.

For many conservative men, the gun feels like a force for order in a chaotic world, suggests a study published in December of last year. In a series of three experiments, Steven Shepherd and Aaron C. Kay asked hundreds of liberals and conservatives to imagine holding a handgun; they found that conservatives felt less risk and greater personal control than liberal counterparts.

This wasn't about familiarity with real-world guns—gun ownership and experience did not affect results. Instead, conservative attachment to guns was based entirely on ideology and emotions.

Who Wants to Be a Hero?

That's an insight echoed by another study published last year. Baylor University sociologists Paul Froese and F. Carson Mencken created a "gun empowerment scale" designed to measure how a nationally representative sample of almost six hundred gun owners felt about their weapons. Their study found that people at the highest level of their scale—the ones who felt most emotionally and morally attached to their guns—were 78 percent white and 65 percent male.

"We found that white men who have experienced economic setbacks or worry about their economic futures are the group of owners most attached to their guns," says Froese. "Those with high attachment felt that having a gun made them a better and more respected member of their communities."

That wasn't true for women and nonwhites. In other words, they may have suffered setbacks, but women and people of color weren't turning to guns to make themselves feel better. "This suggests that these owners have other sources of meaning and coping when facing hard times," notes Froese—often religion. Indeed, Froese and Mencken found that religious faith seemed to put the brakes on white men's attachment to guns.

For these economically insecure, irreligious white men, "the gun is a ubiquitous symbol of power and independence, two things white males are worried about," says Froese. "Guns, therefore, provide a way to regain their masculinity, which they perceive has been eroded by increasing economic impotency."

Both Froese and Stroud found pervasive antigovernment sentiments among their study participants. "This is interesting because these men tend to see themselves as devoted patriots, but make a distinction between the federal government and the 'nation,'" says Froese. "On that point, I expect that many in this group see the 'nation' as being white."

Investing guns with this kind of moral and emotional meaning has many consequences, the researchers say. "Put simply, owners who are more attached to their guns are most likely to believe that guns are a solution to our social ills," says Froese. "For them, more 'good' people with guns would drastically reduce violence and increase civility. Again, it reflects a hero narrative, which many white men long to feel a part of."

Stroud's work echoes this conclusion. "They tell themselves all kinds of stories about criminals and criminal victimization," she says. "But the story isn't just about criminals. It's about the good guy—and that's how they see themselves: 'I work hard, I take care of my family, and there are people who aren't like that.' When we tell stories about the Other, we're really telling stories about ourselves."

How to Save a White Man's Life

Unfortunately, the people most likely to be killed by the guns of white men aren't the "bad guys," presumably criminals or terrorists. It's themselves—and their families.

White men aren't just the Americans most likely to own guns; according to the Centers for Disease Control and Prevention, they're also the people most likely to put them in their own mouths and pull the trigger, especially when they're in some kind of economic distress. A white man is three times more likely to shoot himself than a black man, while the chances that a white man will be killed by a black man are extremely slight. Most murders and shootouts don't happen between strangers. They unfold within social networks, among people of the same race.

A gun in the home is far more likely to kill or wound the people who live there than a burglar or serial killer. Most of the time, according to every single study that's ever been conducted about interpersonal gun violence, the dead and wounded knew the people who shot them. A gun in the home makes it five times more likely that a woman will be killed by her husband. Every week in America, 136 children and teenagers are shot—and, more often than not, it's a sibling, friend, parent, or relative holding the gun. For every homicide deemed justified by the police, guns are used in seventy-eight suicides. As a new study published this month in *JAMA Internal Medicine* once again shows us that restrictive gun laws don't prevent white men from defending themselves.

What are the solutions? That study and many others suggest that restricting the flow of guns and ammunition would certainly save lives. But no law can address the absence of meaning and purpose that many white men appear to feel, which they might be able to gain through a social connection to people who never expected to have the economic security and social power that white men once enjoyed.

"Ridicule of working-class white people is not helpful," says Angela Stroud. "We need to push the 'good guys' to have a deeper connection to other people. We need to reimagine who we are in relation to each other."

Understanding the Reading

1. According to this article, why are some American men struggling to find a new story? What is the crisis?
2. Why doesn't this seem to apply to women and people of color?
3. Do you agree with this analysis?

Suggestions for Responding

1. Research gun ownership and the social consequences in other countries outside the United States.
2. Do you think there should be stricter controls on guns in the United States? Why or why not?

15

The Male Role Stereotype

Doug Cooper Thompson

When you first consider that many men now feel that they are victims of sex role stereotyping, your natural response might be "Are you kidding? Why should men feel discriminated against? Men have the best jobs; they are the corporation presidents and the political leaders. Everyone says, 'It's a man's world.' What do men have to be concerned about? What are their problems?"

It is obvious that men hold most of the influential and important positions in society, and it does seem that many men "have it made." The problem is that men pay a high cost for the ways they have been stereotyped and for the roles that they play.

To understand why many men and women are concerned, we need to take a look at the male role stereotype. Here is what men who conform to the stereotype must do.

Code of Conduct: The Male Role Stereotype

1. Act "Tough"
   Acting tough is a key element of the male role stereotype. Many boys and men feel that they have to show that they are strong and tough, that they can "take it" and "dish it out" as well. You've probably run into some boys and men who like to push people around, use their strength, and act tough. In a conflict, these males would never consider giving in, even when surrender or compromise would be the smartest or most compassionate course of action.

2. Hide Emotions
   This aspect of the male role stereotype teaches males to suppress their emotions and to hide feelings of fear or sorrow or tenderness. Even as small children, they are warned not to be "crybabies." As grown men they show that they have learned this lesson well, and they become very efficient at holding back tears and keeping a "stiff upper lip."

3. Earn "Big Bucks"
   Men are trained to be the primary source of income for the family. So men try to choose occupations that pay well, and then they stick with those jobs, even when they might prefer to try something else. Boys and men are taught that earning a good living is important. In fact, men are often evaluated not on how kind or compassionate or thoughtful they are, but rather on how much money they make.

4. Get the "Right" Kind of Job
   If a boy decides to become a pilot, he will receive society's stamp of approval, for that is the right kind of a job for a man. But if a boy decides to become an airline steward, many people would think that quite strange. Boys can decide to be doctors, mechanics, or business executives, but if a boy wants to become a nurse, secretary, librarian, ballet dancer, or kindergarten teacher, he will have a tough time. His friends and relatives will

probably try to talk him out of his decision, because it's just not part of the male role stereotype.

5. Compete—Intensely
Another aspect of the male role stereotype is to be super-competitive. This competitive drive is seen not only on athletic fields but also in school and later at work. This commitment to competition leads to still another part of the male stereotype: getting ahead of other people to become a winner.

6. Win—At Almost Any Cost
From the Little League baseball field to getting jobs that pay the most money, boys and men are taught to win at whatever they may try to do. They must work and strive and compete so that they can get ahead of other people, no matter how many personal, and even moral, sacrifices are made along the way to the winner's circle.

Those are some of the major features of the male stereotype. And certainly, some of them may not appear to be harmful. Yet when we look more closely, we find that many males who do "buy" the message of the male role stereotype end up paying a very high price for their conformity.

The Cost of the Code: What Men Give Up

1. Men who become highly involved in competition and winning can lose their perspective and good judgment. Competition by itself is not necessarily bad, and we've all enjoyed some competitive activities. But when a man tries to fulfill the male stereotype, and compete and win at any cost, he runs into problems. You've probably seen sore losers (and even sore winners)—sure signs of overcommitment to competition. Real competitors have trouble making friends because they're always trying to go "one-up" on their friends. And when cooperation is needed, true-blue competitors have a difficult time cooperating.

   The next time you see hockey players hitting each other with their hockey sticks or politicians or businessmen willing to do almost anything for a Senate seat or a big deal, you know that you are seeing some of the problems of the male sex role stereotype: an overcommitment to competition and the need to win at any cost.

2. Hiding emotions can hurt. For one thing, hiding emotions confuses people as to what someone's real feelings are. Men who hide their emotions can be misunderstood by others who might see them as uncaring and insensitive. And men who are always suppressing their feelings may put themselves under heavy psychological stress. This pressure can be physically unhealthy as well.

3. The heavy emphasis that the male stereotype puts on earning big money also creates problems. Some men choose careers they really do not like, just because the job pays well. Others choose a job which at first they like, only later to find out that they would rather do something else. But they stay with their jobs anyway, because they can't afford to earn less money.

   In trying to earn as much as possible, many men work long hours and weekends. Some even take second jobs. When men do this, they begin to lead one-track lives—the track that leads to the office or business door. They drop outside interests and hobbies. They have less and less time to spend with their families. That's one reason why some fathers never really get to know their own children, even though they may love them very much.

4. Many men who are absorbed by competition, winning, and earning big bucks pay a terrible price in terms of their physical health. With the continual pressure to compete, be tough, earn money, with little time left for recreation and other interests, men find themselves much more likely than women to fall victim to serious disease. In fact, on the average, men die 8 years sooner than women. Loss of life is a high cost to pay for following the code of the male role stereotype.

5. Those boys and men who do not follow the male code of conduct may also find their lives more difficult because of this stereotype. For example, some boys choose to become nurses rather than doctors, kindergarten teachers rather than lawyers, artists rather than electricians. Social pressure can make it terribly difficult for males who enter these nonstereotyped careers. Other boys and men feel very uncomfortable with the continual pressure to compete and win.

   And some boys do not want to hide their feelings in order to project an image of being strong and tough. These males may be gentle, compassionate, sensitive human beings who are puzzled with and troubled by the male role stereotype. When society stereotypes any group—by race, religion, or sex—it becomes difficult for individuals to break out of the stereotype and be themselves.

[1985]

Understanding the Reading

1. How are the six characteristics of the male role stereotype connected?
2. What characteristics does Cooper Thompson omit, and how do they relate to his six?
3. Explain the costs to men of conforming to this stereotype.
4. What other costs might the author have included?

Suggestions for Responding

1. Have masculine and/or feminine stereotypes undergone changes in recent years? If you think so, describe those changes and explain what has caused them. If not, explain why you think they have not changed.
2. Using Cooper Thompson's analysis as a model, analyze the "Code of Conduct" and the "Cost of the Code" of the female role stereotype.

16

Transgender Rights in the United States: A Short History

TOM HEAD

There's nothing new about transgender and transsexual individuals—history is replete with examples, from the Indian hijras[1] to the Israeli sarisim (eunuchs) to the Roman emperor Elagabalus[2]—but there is something relatively new about transgender and transsexual rights, as a national movement in the United States.

1868

The Fourteenth Amendment to the U.S. Constitution is ratified. The equal protection and due process clauses in Section 1 would implicitly include transgender and transsexual persons, as well as any other identifiable group:

> No State shall make or enforce any law which shall abridge the privileges or immunities of citizens of the United States; nor shall any State deprive any person of life, liberty, or property, without due process of law; nor deny to any person within its jurisdiction the equal protection of the laws.

While the Supreme Court has not fully embraced the Amendment's implications for transgender rights, these clauses will presumably form the basis of future rulings.

1923

German physician Magnus Hirschfeld[3] coins the term *transsexual* in a published journal article titled "The Intersexual Constitution" ("Die inter-sexuelle Konstitution").

1949

San Francisco physician Harry Benjamin pioneers the use of hormone therapy[4] in the treatment of transsexual patients.

1959

Christine Jorgensen, a transwoman,[5] is denied a marriage license in New York on the basis of her birth gender. Her fiancé, Howard Knox, was fired from his job when rumors of their attempt to marry became public.

1969

The Stonewall riots,[6] which arguably sparked the modern gay rights movement,[7] is led by a group that includes transwoman Sylvia Rivera.

---

1. http://atheism.about.com/b/2006/05/28/gender-and-identity-just-male-and-female-book-notes-with-pleasure.htm
2. http://ancienthistory.about.com/cs/biocategory/a/elagabalus_2.htm
3. http://worldfilm.about.com/library/weekly/aafpr011503.htm
4. http://plasticsurgery.about.com/od/ glossary/g/Hormone-Therapy.htm
5. http://civilliberty.about.com/od/gendersexuality/g/TranswomanTranssexual-Woman.htm
6. http://manhattan.about.com/od/glbtscene/a/stonewallriots.htm
7. http://civilliberty.about.com/od/gendersexuality/tp/History-Gay-Rights-Movement.htm

1976

In *M. T. v. J.T.*, the Superior Court of New Jersey rules that transsexual persons may marry on the basis of their gender identity, regardless of their assigned gender.

1989

Ann Hopkins is denied a promotion on the basis that she is not, in the opinion of management, sufficiently feminine. She sues, and the U.S. Supreme Court rules that gender stereotyping can form the basis of a Title VII[8] sex-discrimination complaint; in the words of Justice Brennan, a plaintiff need only prove that "an employer who has allowed a discriminatory motive to play a part in an employment decision must prove by clear and convincing evidence that it would have made the same decision in the absence of discrimination, and that petitioner had not carried this burden."

1993

Minnesota becomes the first state to ban employment discrimination on the basis of perceived gender identity with the passage of the Minnesota Human Rights Act. In the same year, transman Brandon Teena is raped and murdered—an event that inspires the film *Boys Don't Cry* (1999) and prompts a national movement to incorporate anti-transgender hate crimes into future hate crime legislation.

1999

In *Littleton v. Prange*, the Texas Fourth Court of Appeals rejects the logic of New Jersey's *M.T. v. J.T.* (1976) and refuses to issue marriage licenses to opposite-sex couples in which one partner is transsexual.

2001

The Kansas Supreme Court refuses to allow transwoman J'Noel Gardiner to inherit her husband's property, on the basis that her non-assigned gender identity—and, therefore, her subsequent marriage to a man—was invalid.

2007

Gender identity protections are controversially stripped from the 2007 version of the Employment Non-Discrimination Act,[9] but it fails anyway. Future versions of ENDA, beginning in 2009, include gender identity protections.

2009

The Matthew Shepard and James Byrd, Jr. Hate Crimes Prevention Act,[10] signed by President Barack Obama, allows for federal investigation of bias-motivated crimes based on gender identity in cases where local law enforcement is unwilling to act. Later that same year, Obama issues an executive order banning the executive branch from discriminating on the basis of gender identity in employment decisions.

2010

Proposition 8 is found unconstitutional by a federal judge.

2011

"Don't Ask, Don't Tell" is repealed, ending a ban on gay men and lesbians from serving openly in the military.

2012

The Democratic Party becomes the first major U.S. political party in history to publicly support same-sex marriage on a national platform at the Democratic National Convention.

2015

The U.S. Supreme Court hears oral arguments on the question of the freedom to marry in Kentucky, Tennessee, Ohio, and Michigan. On June 26, the Supreme Court rules that states cannot ban same-sex marriage. The 5–4 ruling has Justice Anthony Kennedy writing for the majority. Each of the four conservative justices writes their own dissent.

8. http://careerplanning.about.com/od/federallawsus/a/civilrightsact.htm
9. http://gaylife.about.com/od/gayatwork/a/enda.htm
10. http://gaylife.about.com/od/hatecrimes/p/Matthewshepardjamesbyrdact.htm

2017

President Donald Trump announces via Twitter, "After consultation with my Generals and military experts, please be advised that the United States Government will not accept or allow Transgender individuals to serve in any capacity in the US Military."

Understanding the Reading

1. Who is Christine Jorgensen?
2. What is the Minnesota Human Rights Act?
3. What was the basis for disallowing J'Noel Gardiner's property inheritance in 2001?

Suggestion for Responding

1. Research transgender rights in other countries.

17

A Transsexual's Story

Jessica R. Stearns

What is a transsexual? For a great part of my life the term was little known. It was not even included in the dictionary. During the 1960s I could find no reference to the term in any dictionary or in any reference book in the public library. It was not until the late 1970s that Webster's included a definition. It was "*Transsexual:* 1. One predisposed to become a member of the opposite sex. 2. One whose sex has been changed externally by surgery and by hormone injections."

By the 1990s the term *transsexual* was becoming replaced by the more inclusive term *Transgendered*. This new term was meant to reduce the harsh narrow term of transsexual and to include a broader group of people who may identify as transsexual but do not have the desire or means to undergo sex reassignment surgery and may include cross dressers, transvestites and others who did not fit more restricted categories. The term continues to change with medical research, legal advances, and societal factors.

Though the term was first used by Dr. Harry Benjamin, author of the book *Transsexual Phenomenon*, and came to public attention by the sex change of Christine Jorgenson in 1952, it seemed that it was such a provocative term that it was talked around, not

used. I was 12 years old at the time of Christine's surgery. The impact on me was very powerful, it scared me. How could I be such a person, what would become of me if I was such a person? I was very troubled by this news. Some 51 years later I can remember the four photos published and most of the text of that *Sunday Parade* magazine article. To even use the "T" word is difficult at best for a true transsexual.

What is a true transsexual? Dr. Benjamin developed a sexual orientation scale, one to six. On a scale of five a person was defined as wanting to be a member of the opposite sex, but not desiring to undergo surgery. A person rated as a six was a true transsexual who had to have surgery in order to have a chance of happiness and even survive. At first it was considered a mental disease thought curable by psychiatric treatment. One of the theories was that as a person got older the urge to change their sex would decrease. Perhaps the rate of suicide for older transsexuals helped discredit this theory.

Only in the past 15 years has the subject of transsexuality/transgender become a topic talked about through TV talk shows, news media, and progress has been made to legally protect the Transgender. Steps to protect the Transgender through the courts have met with great resistance. Only with great persistence, struggle, and dedicated legal help has any progress been made. The Gay/Lesbian community has had more success at getting anti-discrimination laws passed. The average attorney not only lacks training in handling a transgender case but also is unwilling for fear of being adversely labeled.

One more thing about sex/sexual orientation; first, there is the anatomical sex of a person (M/F); second, the gender (M/F); then, third, sexual orientation (Hetero/Homosexual). These are distinct areas of a person's makeup. Of course they can occur in combinations with many variances. For most of the human population these three factors are the same, so that an individual only thinks in terms of male/female with no thoughts given to other factors. At a very early age, most say from their early memories, transsexuals identified with the opposite sex. However, the socialization process governs the process of growing up. A child rapidly learns to adapt to expectations of the sexual role in which they are born. The inner conflict of feeling that they were born in the wrong body is there from the start. It will never go away.

The desire to change sex is a matter of identity. Who am I? What am I? I feel like a girl, but I have a male body. The conflict is intense. This occurs at an age when the child can't understand why those feelings exist. Parents only desire a normal child. Even when they perceive that the behavior patterns are somewhat different, they will strive to reinforce what they perceive as normal behavior. This of course will only lead to greater conflict.

My story began on August 3, 1940. Born as John Robert Stearns in Birmingham, Alabama, I was the first grandchild to a family of farmers in Blount Co. My father, at the time, a traveling salesman from New York City, had been married to my mother only a year. My mother was 16 when married and had never been off the farm. I can't even recall if she finished high school. I know that we moved several times because I have photos of me as an infant in Jacksonville, FL. My sister was born in New Orleans, LA (no photos). My brother was born in Kansas City, MO. I do remember some events from when we lived in Little Rock, Arkansas. I also remember my father's brutality to my mother. I am the only one of the three of us to have any childhood memories of their being together. They were divorced when I was three-and-a-half . My mother moved to Birmingham to find work. Most of the time that was at being a waitress. My grandparents had had six children; the first died in infancy, two had their own families, one was engaged to be married, the youngest was in high school and served as an older sibling, and my mother, who was struggling in Birmingham. Having to raise three more children was now a burden for my grandparents.

In 1946 my mother married a taxi driver who lived in Birmingham. Not only did he refuse to permit us to live with them, but he was also an alcoholic who was verbally and physically abusive to my mother. The task of our rearing fell upon my grandparents. We got to visit with our mother on rare occasions. Our grandparents were to become our sole caregivers for the next few years.

I can remember identifying with the female members of our family before I was four. I wanted to help my grandmother in the kitchen and about the house rather than be with the male members in the barns or fields. Our farm was typical of the time and area. Electricity had not been routed to our farm and the roads were unpaved. Mules were used to work the fields. Grandfather did have a 1935 Chevy truck; I still remember the WWII lend lease symbol on the doors. Everyone was expected to do all sorts of farm work. The day started by 5:00 AM and didn't stop until after dark. Almost every thing we ate was grown on our farm and processed by us. Work was long,

hard and never ending. Still, the lessons I learned have always been of benefit. Just because a task was difficult, it had to be done and there was a certain satisfaction of doing it well. I learned to see a correlation between effort expended and rewards reaped.

Though I preferred helping my grandmother, all of us had assigned chores to accomplish day or night, every day, and without fail. Shirking was not tolerated and failure was severely punished. On the morning of my sixth birthday my grandfather called me into the living room. He told me that since I was getting to be a pretty big boy, he would only tell me to do something once. Then he gave me a small penknife, and wished me a happy birthday. I can still remember the few times he told me twice. Each time I wasn't able to sit for several hours. Grandfather was a stern disciplinarian and did not tolerate noncompliance. Still, I learned a lot from him that would help me cope with future trials.

During the summer my two female first cousins would travel by train to spend the summer with us. My oldest cousin Gail was only three months younger than me and very much a tomboy. We enjoyed playing with each other more than with the others. Many hours were spent exploring the wooded hollows on the farm and playing in the three streams that flowed through the farm. We climbed trees, built hay forts in the barn mow, picked blackberries, ate wild strawberries and persimmons that grew on the farm, and sometimes snitched a watermelon from a neighboring farm, though there were acres of them on our farm. My grandmother had stored boxes of her old clothes in one of the sheds on the farm. One day Kate and I found them, called the other children to join us and spent the afternoon dressing up. I not only found it fun but also suddenly felt that this was the proper clothing for me. When grandmother found out about this, she scolded us and told us not to do it anymore. However, I would play dress up when I could do so without the fear of being caught. When I was seven, my grandmother actually punished me by making me wear one of my sister's dresses. I would hide behind the wood-burning stove in the kitchen, out of sight from prying eyes, and contentedly stay until called out and told to change into my boy clothing. No one knew that my punishment was actually very pleasing. I did not know why, except that somehow I really felt that I wanted to be a girl.

My early years were a mixture of very mixed feelings about myself. As a boy, my grandparents expected me to adhere to the male path. However, from the time that I was five until I was about 14 years old, my health was marginal. I easily caught colds, caught the whooping cough frequently, suffered from bronchitis, and other respiratory-related ailments. My tonsils were removed at age six, but that didn't help much. The doctor at the country clinic told my grandparents that I'd probably not survive my childhood. To assist my health I was often restricted indoors. This I really didn't mind as I liked to help my grandmother and enjoyed being able to read any newspaper, magazine or book that I could get my hands on. Whenever I found an article about aviation I would read it over and over. On my very first day in school, my first grade teacher, Miss Haynes, asked us all to stand in turn and state what we wanted to be when we grew up. I was next to last and announced in a determined voice that I would grow up to be an airplane pilot. The spring before starting school I had seen two yellow Army Air Corps trainers fly low over the field we were working in, and knew at that instant what I wanted to be when I grew up—if I did.

I repeated fourth grade because of being very ill. I think that this prompted my grandparents to insist that my father come for a visit from Brooklyn, NY, to assess my health during the summer of 1950, as well as get to know his three children whom he hadn't seen in over six years. The visit was short but the financial help improved. New store-bought clothes were a treat to wear versus the home-made ones usually made from chicken feed sacks. Though we didn't have much, our status was the same as all the other farm families around us, so we didn't know different and accepted life as we knew it.

A decision was made to send my brother and me to visit my father in Brooklyn, NY during the summer of 1951. Grandmother packed our cardboard suitcases, a box of food to last the 24-hour train trip from Birmingham to NYC. The conductors had been instructed to look after us. Our faces were glued to the windows viewing the changing countryside as the train rolled north. We arrived in NYC's Grand Central Station about 5:00 PM the next day, totally lost and not knowing where to look for our dad. The size of the station and throng of people was overwhelming. It seemed like an eternity before he found us, scared and close to tears. For us it was like arriving in a foreign country. We could hardly understand the language and our senses were on overload from the hustle and bustle of the big city. Occasional trips to Birmingham had not prepared us for this.

Dad worked in a hotel at Gramercy Park. My brother and I were left on our own at the apartment to read, play games and try to amuse ourselves. There was no TV or radio. We were top floor of a fifth-floor walk up. The roof was used to hang laundry and it afforded us a bird's-eye view of Brooklyn Heights. We started exploring the area using some of the high buildings as reference marks, just as I had learned to use tall trees or hills on the farm. Off we went to find and play in small city parks, or wander along the palisade overlooking the East River and docks. Within two weeks we wandered too far and became lost. Since I was the oldest the responsibility was mine, and I knew that if we didn't get home before Dad arrived, I would really be in trouble. At last I spotted a tall building that I recognized. It was a long walk home. Dad had called the police, but he saw us first and had to call the police to say that we'd returned. I didn't sit down for a few hours.

Dad decided to keep us with him in Brooklyn. After finding a suitable apartment, we were enrolled in school. Me in the fifth grade and my brother in the fourth. Because of our very southern accent and lack of city smarts, we were the targets of neighborhood bullies. We learned to take a different route each time we went to school or any other destination. A classmate introduced me to his friends at a local church that had an after-school program. Soon my brother and I were able to play in the gym. I became a member of the boy's choir when I found out that I'd be paid 15 cents for practice and 25 cents for Sunday service. That winter the church put on the play *Show Boat* and each of us had several parts. The cast was short of girls and I was talked into playing two scenes as a girl. I was embarrassed because of the teasing of the boys, but decided that I was brave enough to do it. Strangely, once I was dressed and made up, I secretly enjoyed it. I still have a photo taken of us girls and years later when a flight attendant friend saw it she couldn't pick me out from the other girls.

After a year in Brooklyn, my dad decided that we needed to move from the big city, but where? During the summer of 1952 we visited all the towns and cities between NYC and Boston. He could not find work, so we backtracked and by late August found ourselves in Philadelphia. He was able to find work at a small hotel and a fifth-floor-walkup apartment a few blocks away. This would be our home for the next few years. It was during the fall of 1952 that the newspapers carried the sensational story of Christine Jorgenson. Its impact on me was profound. I felt scared. I didn't want to be like this person, but somehow I knew that I was. I couldn't tell anyone. There was no one to tell. If I told my dad, I was terribly afraid of his reaction. I had to keep my feelings a secret, no matter what. Besides, it would ruin my chances of becoming a pilot. It would ruin my life.

My sister joined us a year later. The apartment was just too small for four of us. Dad refused to get a larger one. During this time my sister and I became quite close, often playing together, or going to pretend shop for clothes, as we did not have money to buy any. I started running errands, bagging groceries, selling flowers for a street vendor, or anything I could do to earn money. I soon found that half of what I earned had to go to the household; then I could buy clothes for the three of us. As the oldest, I had to cook, clean house, shop for food, do laundry, and supervise my brother and sister.

The family situation began to deteriorate. Three of us were too much for my dad. My sister was literally shipped off to my grandparents, who by this time had sold the farm in Alabama and moved to Logansport, IN, to be near their oldest son and his family, plus some cousins. I deeply missed my sister and being able to interact with her on a daily basis. For the rest of my teen years I would only see her for brief visits in Logansport.

It was becoming very clear to me that if I were to escape a life of hardships, then doing my best in school was imperative. I did well in the sixth grade, but upon entry to Jr. HS I still had a very heavy southern accent and was assigned to a remedial grade section. The first report period I received all A's, but I was made to wait to the next semester to be placed in the advanced section. I threw myself into my schoolwork. I avoided the rough and tumble activities of the boys while getting the two really smart girls to help me with English or any other area of study that I was weak in.

In 1953 I joined the Boy Scouts. I enjoyed outdoor activities because I had enjoyed the outdoors of the farm. Most of what was taught I already knew. It was also a way for me to get out of the apartment one or two nights a week. The scoutmaster raised funds by collecting newspapers to sell at two cents per pound. Once a month three of us would make the rounds in his 1930s LaSalle, pack it full of newspapers, deliver them to the scrap dealer, and have enough to pay for a troop outing. He was everything my father wasn't, and I learned a lot from him.

Throughout my teen years I did very well in school but was never comfortable socializing with boys. I did

so at a level that helped me fit in so that I would not be harassed. In Jr. High I felt an attraction to some of the girls in my class but was too shy to get to know them well. Puberty had commenced, and I felt uncomfortable with the male changes taking place. I did not look forward to shaving. It seemed that I wanted to live in a world that I could not enter. On weekends I went to the main library of Philadelphia to get any book that I could find on aviation and space. I also spent hours thumbing through books in the psychology section, but in those days there was nothing to explain what I felt I was going through. I needed knowledge, but it was not there.

One of my disappointments was not getting into Central HS for Boys. I needed to score 110 on the entrance exam. I scored 109.5. The school principal just told me that I didn't measure up. I desperately wanted to get into a four-year high school and going to So. Philly HS where gangs were rampant was not in my plans. Fortunately, a friend told me of a small selective HS in the northwest section of the city that had both academics and agricultural tracks. The schedule called for doing three weeks of academics in two weeks, then spending a week learning agricultural subjects. Although it meant riding the bus for over two hours a day, I talked my father into letting me interview for a slot. The principal asked me to describe milking a cow. Well, I knew, but my graphic description embarrassed his secretary, who was taking notes. I was admitted with no further questions.

The summer of 1955 was spent at the school farm working in the barn, in the fields, and maintaining the school grounds. It was like being on the farm, but in the city at the same time. The school also provided contacts to local residents for students to mow grass and maintain yard work. A nearby family hired me to take care of their place. The dollar an hour would be used (after a 50 percent contribution to the household) to build up my bank account for future flying lessons. At the time I didn't know that this relationship would someday be my salvation. My routine was study, work and more work. Scouting and an occasional movie were my only recreation.

My relationship with my father was on the down slope. He could not be pleased. I determined to do the best that I could, as I now knew that my future depended solely on my efforts. I began to pay my brother to do some of my chores so that I would have more time for work and he would have his own money to spend. Dad was always bringing boxes of used clothing home for me to make repairs on; then he'd resell them. It was in this way that I accumulated a few female articles and wore them in secret. It was my only moments of being in tune with my identity. I was never sure if my brother ever found me out. He never said so.

For a couple of years I had been building model airplanes and rockets. Some flew and some didn't. When Dad would get angry with me, he'd smash some of them. One day after he'd done just that, I told him that I would never build another model and that I would start taking flying lessons in a real airplane. I was almost 16 and had saved about $500 toward that goal. The weekend after my birthday I showed up at a flight school at the Philadelphia International Airport for my first lesson. When asked if my parents approved, I said that they didn't, but I had the money and knew what I wanted. On August 27, I came back and told them that I wasn't leaving until I had received a flight lesson. I'll never forget that 30-minute flight. I was at home in the air and now knew that my future would be in aviation. After each flight lesson, I would go over to the airport weather room, control tower, and radar room. The men took me under their wings and taught me many valuable things about aviation. I became their mascot, and their knowledge filled me as water fills a sponge. On my sister's birthday, October 27, 1957, I passed my private pilot's flight test. However, storm clouds were on the horizon. I had also joined the Civil Air Patrol and loved every aspect of the program. I was the only cadet actually flying.

In the winter of 1957, my father suddenly bought a farm in New Portland, Maine. It was a very small town, isolated, and 20 miles from the nearest high school located in another county. The four-room school that my brother and I were to attend was not even accredited, and Dad wouldn't pay for us to go to the school in Farmington. I could see that this was not going to work. In addition, Dad had become very temperamental and physically abusive to us. He had a Jekyll and Hyde personality that was impossible to live with. One summer day, as I had just finished roofing the house, he started beating my brother. I came down from the roof to stop him. When he raised his fists at me, I blocked the blows and told him that he'd no longer hit us. He blew up, ordering us out of the house. We each packed a suitcase and walked a mile to our only friends' house. The couple agreed to let us stay in one of their three hunter's cabins. For two weeks I tried to find a way for us to get home to our grandparents. Living with Mother

was out of the question. I had fifteen dollars to my name. The local Red Cross refused to help. After two weeks, the couple took us to Portland, Maine. I bought bus tickets to Boston. We arrived there on a Monday evening just before the Traveler's Aid Society office closed. I had 50 cents left in my pocket.

The caseworker was in a state of disbelief after I told him our story. After he called my friends in New Portland, he took us to a rooming house, gave us five dollars, and told us to be at his bus station office at 9:00 AM. We were assigned a new caseworker. For the next week, we lived on five dollars a day while it was determined who would take us and when we would leave. Finally, a week later we were given bus tickets to Birmingham and forty dollars for expenses. I did not really want to return to what I knew would be a life of hardship. We had to change buses in NYC, so when we reached there I put my brother on the bus to Birmingham, gave him twenty dollars, and I took the one to Philadelphia. I had twenty dollars, enough money to last me two or three days. My goal was to find a job, a place to live, and finish my last year of school.

As I spent the day downtown looking for work, not having any luck, I was walking along Broad St. when I heard my name called. It was my old boss who owned a Center City newsstand. After a brief talk, he agreed to sublease his news stand to me. That would provide the money to live on. Next I went to my school to see about enrolling. They were very happy to see me and agreed that if I could find a sponsor, there would be no tuition. As I walked back to the bus stop, I saw the people whose yard I had maintained for three years. After hearing my story, they gave me a room to live in and at the end of the first week invited me to stay with them on a permanent basis. I was to work off my room and board by doing chores and maintaining the yard. They arranged with my mother to have guardianship. Their three children had completed college, moved on, and were raising families of their own. Robert and Anne F . . . were the first people to treat me as a son and take a real interest in my life and goals. I thrived in this atmosphere. For a while I was able to sublimate all feminine desires.

It was during this year that I had to register for the draft. I knew that upon graduation from high school I would be called up unless I was accepted to college or was rated Four F, not fit. My final year of school went very well. Once again, I was flying, earning a good living, and competing for scholarships. In 1959, scholarships were few and no college would let me work part time and go to school part time. I had scored very high on the Air Force Officer Qualifying Tests but was only selected for an alternate slot for the academy. The principal candidate decided to go to the Air Force Academy, so I lost out. Sure enough, I received my draft notice. I went to the AF recruiter and was selected for pilot training as a cadet. While awaiting orders I managed a small farm until my assignment came. That was not to be. The USAF decided that they had too many pilots, so the class was cancelled and the program shut down. I had to get into flying. I went back to the recruiter and was told that the Aviation Cadet Navigator program was still open. I signed up.

On June 20, 1960, I reported to start training; little did I know of the challenges facing me. The month I started training the AF decided that they had too many navigators. The washout rate was about 66 percent for my class. Bust one exam or flight check, and you were done for. I learned to live one half day at a time. Somehow I got through the next ten months, and graduated as a transport navigator and was commissioned a second lieutenant. I was not an AF pilot, but at least I was flying, and becoming a pilot was very much a possibility. My first operational assignment was to Dover AFB, DE. Over the next five years I would see a great deal of the world.

The pay of a second lieutenant was just enough to survive on. Still, I was close enough to drive to Philadelphia and visit with my foster family and friends. I still had my old room. During this period I met a young lady and we began to date. I had dated occasionally but never cemented a relationship. Over the next four years we dated to the point that when I was 24 we actually thought of marriage. During this period, I gave her many gifts that I'd bought around the world, many of them of an intimate nature. I was also in a very confused state of mind about my own sexuality. I knew that I was not homosexual but could not determine the source of my feelings. In private, I had acquired a limited female wardrobe. Dressed in these garments in private, I felt a sense of relief but also felt that I was committing a sin of sorts. I did not like the feeling. I often drove through Wilmington on the way to Philadelphia. I looked up a psychiatrist to try to find out what was going on with me. After three visits, he asked whether I had ever had sex. Finding that I was still a virgin, he told me to go have sex and that after a dozen or so times, I'd give up my foolish notions when I found how good it was. I left there

even more confused. I tried, but it didn't work. My thoughts kept drifting back to the Christine Jorgenson case. I was scared and had no one to turn to.

When a transsexual gets up each morning and looks in the mirror, he/she sees a picture that doesn't match the mental image of who they want to be. As I grew older, the disparity between mirror image and who I felt I was began to diverge. All around me I saw my friends getting married and fitting the societal image that I knew would probably not be mine. The current image of a military officer was a married one. My superiors would ask me about my prospects at least once a month. I had to develop a fantasy life to keep their curiosity at bay. All I wanted to do was fly and be left alone. Besides, if any of them suspected anything, my career would be over in 24 hours. When I was not on a trip, I tried to get away from the base. In those days the world seemed to be in constant conflict and we pulled a lot of alert duty. Being in close contact with five other crewmembers for days at a time could lead to some very prying questions. I became very adept at revealing little and what I did say protected me.

I was in the Philippines when I received my promotion to captain and orders to pilot training. My engagement had ended, and I felt free to concentrate on my dream of becoming a jet pilot. I reported to Graig AFB in Selma, Al. to start class in June 1966. By now, I was a seasoned officer and knew what to concentrate on so that I'd graduate in the top 10 and get a choice assignment. By now I had 3,300 hours of navigator flight time and 300 hours as a civilian pilot. During the first week I took the final exams for most of the academic courses. Since I was a captain, I assisted with the administration of my classmates and did a lot of tutoring. Most of the students were second lieutenants and needed close supervision. Some would not survive the rigors of flight training. For me it was a time to excel, and I did.

As a single officer I was required to live on base, but I found a nice apartment in Selma and gave the phone number to my training officer. It rang at both locations, so most never knew where I really lived. The privacy was essential at this time. I was crossdressing frequently when in my apartment. I felt so relaxed and my concentration for study was much better. On nonflying weekends I would go visit relatives in north Alabama, take in a play in Birmingham, or drive down to the gulf coast for a weekend on the beach. Life was good. By now I had given up the thought of marriage, though the official pressure was still there. About six weeks into training a classmate talked me into going to a mixer dance in Montgomery. He was not familiar with the area and I was.

Little did I know that I would meet my future wife that evening. When we met it was the meeting of two lost souls who had been searching for each other for a long time and had finally arrived at the same time in space. Still, I was uncertain about having a relationship that may lead to places in life I was afraid to go to. I had already faced serious danger in flight, had dealt with it, and survived. It was the emotional part of life that I was ill prepared for. To date, I had found very little information about the subject of transsexuality. I couldn't define it, let alone understand how and if it related to me, or how it would impact marriage.

As our relationship grew more intimate, I really began to feel that marriage was the solution. I purged my closet of all female things and, with her on my arm at base social functions, basked in the warmth of having finally arrived. In five months my life consisted of flying and building a life with Beth. The way my superiors treated me now that I had a beautiful woman in my life gave me confidence that it would work. Little did I realize the deceptions that lay ahead. By January we made the decision to get married before I graduated. We were married at the base chapel with a few family members, friends, and some classmates present. To get a weekend off, I had flown two training flights daily for two weeks. We moved into a duplex near the base and set up housekeeping. While I was flying, she was getting to know the other wives and learn about AF life. We were only married ten days when a mid-air collision with a hawk almost did me in. Upon arriving home I stripped off a rather foul-smelling flight suit, stuffed it into a trash bag, and went inside for a good stiff drink. It was her introduction to flying can be dangerous. There would be many more close calls in the future.

Graduation day finally came. We said our goodbyes and headed off to my first operational assignment as a USAF pilot. I'd got my pick and chose to fly a C-141 Starlifter at Warner Robbins AFB, GA. Flying a heavy jet was a good way to move ahead in my career. We bought a small house in a nice neighborhood and got busy becoming part of the community. In 1967 the war in Vietnam was really heating up. My turn to fly combat came sooner than I expected. Already, most of my flying in the C-141 was to Vietnam, hauling in supplies and often flying the

wounded and bodies out. No one talked on the body bag flights. They still haunt me.

I started my training as a forward air controller in late 1968. FACs flew light unarmed aircraft and controlled the air strikes by directing fighter aircraft to enemy targets. That's a nice way of saying that I killed people by telling the fighters where to drop the bombs. I arrived in Vietnam in April of 1969. What I didn't know was whether I could keep the bomb from going off inside me. I flew up to two times a day; three times when a battle was raging. The disparity of who I was and who I felt I should be was also raging. I even rationalized that it would be better to die a war hero rather than live with the internal conflicts that raged within me. I guess that I did have a desire to live, as I returned to base each day unscathed, though the army ground commanders were sure that my aircraft had taken hits.

At the nine-month point Beth and I met in Hawaii for a five-day R & R. It was tough getting reacquainted, but we did have a good visit. I made sure that she departed on her flight before I left on mine. I shall never forget the look of sorrow on her face at that time. Six weeks later I received a tape telling me that we were now expectant parents. This news encouraged me to be a little more cautious in my flying. After a year in the hell of Vietnam and 381 combat missions, I got on the "Freedom Bird" and 18 hours later found myself in NJ exposed to an ungrateful nation.

For the next six years McGuire AFB would be our home. The flying continued to be a joy, but I knew that it would just be a matter of months before I would be tapped for a staff assignment. Our daughter was born in October, and I was assigned to the training division at the same time. This permitted me to control my schedule to be able to be home most nights to help with the care of our little girl. Life seemed to be on track, except for . . .

The internal pressure continued to grow. Beth had suspected something was wrong after my return from Vietnam. I finally screwed up the courage to tell her about how I felt. We came close to separating, but I promised to seek help so we decided not to do anything until we knew more. Besides, we did have a very good life together and our love was sound. Our daughter was two, and I really loved her. It took months of searching to find a doctor in Philadelphia who was experienced with transsexuals. What a disappointment! On the second visit he gave me an injection of testosterone, saying, "If this doesn't cure you in six months, then we'll reverse the hormones." On the drive home I felt so distraught that he might as well have injected me with arsenic. That night I walked the base golf course crying and screaming, "God—why me?"

I called every hospital and was told that the Pennsylvania Hospital had a doctor with the expertise that I needed. I made an appointment with him immediately. He gave me every test that was known and after six sessions made his pronouncement. He said that I was a true transsexual, but since I had been able to cope with military life for thirteen years, he believed as I got older the urge would decrease and therefore he would not recommend surgery. He referred me to a psychologist for group therapy. At the time this seemed a better course of action to me. Upon examination by the new doctor, group therapy was ruled out. Instead, he put me on a very low dose of hormone treatment to help me cope with the stress and inner conflicts. The new course of treatment enabled me to cope with the stress and help me delay decision time until I had more information. Simply stopping the hormones would reverse the treatment.

My spouse and I talked over the situation. We decided to remain together and live life as normally as possible. I made a promise to complete my AF career so that we would always have a modicum of income. I would also not do anything until our daughter had completed high school. We both began to get counseling so that we could keep open communications and cope with the high level of stress caused by my problem. From all outward appearances, we were the model of a very normal military family.

In the spring of 1976, I obtained my last staff assignment. I was to be a liaison and training officer. My new assignment took us to the Sacramento area of California. Though stationed at Mather AFB, I worked over the six western states of our region. Once again I purged myself of my feminine wardrobe and tried to be a normal straight guy. Within a year I had failed. The hunt for a new doctor began. Finally I found one nearby who was experienced. He felt that he should work with both of us to fully understand how we had coped and stayed together for so long. Once again I was put on a low dose of hormones, but not enough to cause any outward changes. I still had to pass my annual AF flight physicals.

My last four years passed quickly, as I enjoyed my work, the flying, and our life in CA. I was retired from active duty at the end of June 1980. Now I had to find a new career. Flying jobs were scarce. The air-

lines were not hiring and related fields were stagnant. I had taken the management exam for the major Bell Company and was hired to supervise an installation and repair crew of ten technicians. I mastered the technical aspects of the job in short order, but the other managers resented an outsider. It took three months for them to come around. During my three years with the company, I had three management jobs. However, I was hired just as deregulation had been ordained. The company went through several rounds of reorganization and layoffs. Two weeks shy of three years and tenure, my pink slip arrived. I decided that it was time to get back into the flying business.

Though I had flown four engine heavy jets in the Air Force, I did not have the required airline transport pilot rating or flight engineer rating required for an interview. I went back to giving flight instruction and flying charter to hone my skills. One job I had was to deliver bank checks in the wee hours of the morning, bad weather or not. Many a young pilot has bought the farm doing this type of flying. As soon as I had the written exams and ATP flight check passed, my resumes went to all the airlines. In the spring of 1984, I interviewed with People Express Airlines at Newark, NJ. Fortune was with me and I was to start training in August. The move back to NJ was a tough one. We managed to get almost everything into a large rental truck and the overflow into a trailer. We found a rental house near Princeton and settled in for the next phase of our lives.

While making the move, I decided to purge once more. Besides, I had left my doctor in CA and felt that for my and my family's sake I should try once again to be a real man. Getting the household set up, getting settled in the community, and getting checked out as a Boeing 727 flight engineer kept me so busy that I didn't have time to think about gender problems. No matter how I tried to sublimate my feelings, like a cancer, they came back with a vengeance. By the spring of 1985 I knew that I needed help. Again, the lack of information made it extremely difficult to find help. The doctor that I had gone to in Philadelphia had moved on. Through a medical listing I started blanket calling psychiatrists on the list, finally finding one in north NJ. My telephone interview with him was very unsatisfactory. It seemed that he was more interested in the weekly fee, which was very steep, than my well-being. The needle in the haystack search began once more. I went to the NYC Public Library to start the search. There I found an article written by Dr. Leo Wollman, who had been an associate of Dr. Harry Benjamin. A check of the telephone directories was next. No listing under medical, physicians, or doctors could be found. I checked the residential listings next. To my amazement, his name and number was there, more so when I nervously dialed the number and he answered. My heart raced as I told him how I felt. Suddenly, he simply said, "Come to my office on Coney Island next week, we need to talk." Oh, how I looked forward to that.

It was a cold, rainy day as I drove to the office located in a nondescript building on Mermaid Avenue in the Coney Island section of Brooklyn. I had remembered it as a bustling place with a grand boardwalk, the Cyclone and Parachute Jump from 1951. Now it was run down, bleak as the weather that day and I feared for my safety. Arriving at the office, I signed in and took a seat among the very poor of the neighborhood. I really felt out of place, but I was as desperate as those around me. I was scheduled as the last patient, and as Dr. Wollman called me in, he told his nurse that she could go home. Just the two of us to deal with my future. Dr. Wollman pointed to a chair at the side of his desk for me to sit in. He then pulled his chair to a position directly in front of me with little distance between us. I briefly told him of my life and occupation. He cut me off and asked a question: "Tell me, who are you?" I tried to answer in an indirect manner but once again he asked, "Who are you?" He looked me in the eyes. I knew that I had to answer directly. Finally, I stammered, "I am a woman." He leaned back and then said, "And what are you going to do about that?" I stated that I was here to begin the process and needed his help. He said okay, but it's going to be very difficult and that he would make sure that I knew what faced me, and that there would be many tests.

I suddenly felt very much better and asked him what his medical training consisted of. He told me that he'd started as a general practitioner, and then became a gynecologist, then a surgeon, then an endocrinologist, and finally a psychiatrist, and had worked with many transsexual patients before retiring. He explained that he became bored, so he set up a community clinic for the poor, started treating transsexuals, and volunteered at a nearby military hospital. He called a local pharmacy to confirm that they had female hormones, wrote out a prescription, and, since my flying schedule changed each month, told me to call him for an appointment. It was snowing as I left, but to me it seemed like the spring of my life.

Throughout the next four years I would meet once a month on a Saturday at his home with a group of other transgendered people. One was post op, a couple were well along and no longer resembled their former selves, and the few others had been in the program a year or so. They immediately made me feel welcome and comfortable. Still, there was a lot that I didn't understand, but my education had begun.

As I took the hormones, my body slowly began to change. One day I asked Dr. Wollman about it and he asked whether I had experienced a short or long puberty. I said long. He then told me that as I changed, the male hormones would fight back and that I'd experience a long puberty once again. There was a war going on in my body. After an injection I would be nauseous and even have morning sickness for a while. So this is what women go through, I thought. It would take two to three years before my physical changes would become noticeable, and I didn't want to call undue notice to myself. By 1988 my family doctor had picked up on my changed appearance during an annual physical and told me that he was requesting a mammogram. I told him what was going on and he said that that was my business, but it was his business to keep me healthy. The radiologist was taken aback, but I took the position that they only needed to know enough to accomplish what my doctor had ordered. It worked. Each year I also had to get a flight physical from an FAA Aero medical doctor. The medical certificate is necessary to exercise pilot privileges. Again, the doctor was surprised but wished me the best and issued the medical certificate. Both doctors demonstrated a compassion for my well-being that I would find lacking in most of society.

Throughout the period from 1985, when I started taking hormones, to my decision point, the matter of my transsexuality weighed more heavily on the lives of my wife and daughter. Beth and I still enjoyed closeness, were affectionate and intimate, and really tried to effect, at least from outward appearances, a normal relationship. It was difficult for her to see that she was slowly losing her husband. We discussed how it would affect our relationship, the difficulties of my transition, legal and financial matters. It seemed that no matter how logically and methodically I continued, a disaster was in the making. In the AF, I had learned how to write operations plans. I did so now. My plan had sections for medical, legal, financial, logistics, etc. We would go over it from time to time and she asked a lot of "what if" questions. The unknown had to be thought of and dealt with. The plan was revised many times.

One of the most critical aspects facing me was that of money. I had monthly retirement income from the military, Beth worked full time, I made a good salary as an airline pilot, and I would have to—as I had done so far—pay the full expense of the surgery. Transsexual surgery is an elective procedure according to insurance companies. They won't pay for it. They ignore the suicide rate for TS victims. Though the FAA was the agency that finds a pilot fit and capable of flying, I anticipated that my company would probably fire me for some business or medical reason. The future was very uncertain. Flying was the one place I truly felt at home, and I would have to fight to stay there. At the same time I also knew that if I didn't achieve a union of body and psyche, I had no future. I squirreled away money as I could to fund the plan.

We had rented a house since we'd moved to NJ. We had to leave California at a time when the interest rates were 18 percent and we were forced to sell for the amount of the loans. All equity was lost. We started off in NJ at a time of rapidly increasing housing costs. My salary in the first four years was not enough to purchase a home, so we rented. By the spring of 1989, our daughter was working and living with friends so we started house hunting. We found a nice townhouse nearby and bought it using my VA loan entitlement. Now we had the advantages of home ownership at a cost much less than renting. In the event I was fired, the mortgage was affordable.

During my daughter's last three years of high school, she became much more aware of my problem. Though she didn't talk directly to me about it, I knew that she had read my books on the subject that I had placed in the bookcases. She did start to ask her mom what was going on. I was in counseling when my wife sought counseling at our church. One of the priests, a woman, felt that something deeply troubled us. She made herself available and we both went to talk with her, singly and together. She also helped us find a psychologist for our daughter to talk to. At last we were able to express our innermost fears, concerns, and feelings with each other through the priest and doctor, and at times directly. In one session when my daughter was asked how she felt about my impending change, she replied, "I don't want to lose my father figure, but he's not happy and he deserves happiness, so I guess that I'll learn to accept him." Having her say this in front of me in the presence of her mother and the doctor brought tears to my eyes. Much

debate had gone on between Beth and me about my future name. That was solved one day when my daughter arrived home from school. I was "dressed at the time" and didn't expect her home for another hour. She called up to the second floor where I was working on administrative matters in the office and announced that when she finished her snack, she wanted to talk with me. Surprised, I told her to wait until I changed clothes. She said, don't bother—it doesn't matter. A short time later she came into the office and pulled up a chair. I asked what she wanted to talk about but was not prepared for what was to follow.

When she was born, we had a difficult time deciding on her first name. Two names were finalized but we couldn't seem to agree on which one. On the ninth day the head nurse gave us an ultimatum: decide today or it will be "Baby Girl." With that prompt, my choice won out. My daughter knew this, so she said, "Since you got to name me I think it's only right for me to name you." I sat there stunned, then looked at her and said, "OK, what's it going to be?" "Jessica Page," she said. I had not tried Jessica, and suddenly it seemed to fit. I told her that I liked the first name but wanted to keep my initials of JRS. She told me that was okay and that we'd think of something. As she left, she turned and said, "Nice pumps—why don't I have some like that?" I told her to buy some if she wanted. Two weeks later she was wearing her pair. Though I knew that our troubles were far from over, this had given me hope that our relationship would survive. I am proud to have been named by my daughter.

The decision to undergo sex reassignment surgery must never be taken lightly and without thorough preparation. Once done, there is no going back. I did not know when I would arrive at my decision point. It happened the second Sunday of September 1989. As my wife and I knelt in church to recite the Lord's prayer and as I said "thy will be done," I felt seized by only what I can say was the Holy Spirit and instantly knew what had to be done. As we left the church, she suddenly turned to me and spoke, "You've made your decision." It was not a question, but a statement of fact. In reply, I simply said yes to her statement. We then went for brunch and only discussed the subject when we returned home.

The FAA had just completed the evaluations of the many exams required of me, and informed me by letter that I was cleared to proceed. Upon completion of surgery, I was to send the documents needed to obtain new pilot and medical certificates. I knew it would be different with the airline. I wrote a detailed letter explaining my situation, enclosed a copy of the FAA letter, and waited for the fireworks. I went to fly one early morning in November and as I tried to pull up the trip schedule in the computer, could not find it. When my Assistant Chief Pilot showed up two hours later, he told me that I had been administratively grounded and he didn't know why. We stepped into his office, closed the door, and I told him why. We'd known each other in the AF and he told me that he'd always thought the best of my flying and staff work. He promised to do what he could do to help me but thought that the decision made at the highest level, by one of the most despised airline CEOs, would be impossible to overcome. Fortunately, we had a pilots' union and contract, but that would only enable me to go through the prescribed grievance process.

The company said that I was psychologically unsound, not fit to fly, would be a hazard in the cockpit, and passengers would not fly with me. The VP for Flight Operations ordered me to see the company drug abuse specialist and psychologist in LA. In early December my wife and I flew out to see Dr. GB. The company didn't know that he'd already helped several people like me and knew what was going on. He strongly recommended that I be returned to flying and be permitted to fly as a woman. The company rejected that idea, but I was returned to duty for a short time. In February 1990, the second letter came. I was fired. My fight had begun in earnest. Before I went to Vietnam as a forward air controller, I was fighter qualified. When a flight of fighters arrives over the target they set up a wheel formation so that when they roll off their high altitude perch, they can be most effective at striking from any direction. I now put myself in this mental mode of striking back. I needed help, though: a tough, go-for-the-throat attorney who would not be afraid to take on a large corporation, and who would be understanding of my finances. I had read of a local attorney who liked to take on tough, unusual, and challenging cases. He had just beaten a large university in two cases. He sounded like the man for me. When I explained why I needed him, he was in a state of disbelief. He finally said okay, then looked at me and said that I would have to educate him. I paid his retainer and told him that on the next visit he would be seeing Jessica.

I had filed a discrimination complaint with the state and was quickly scheduled for a hearing. At the time my attorney was a little uncomfortable with me as a female, so for the hearing he asked that I appear in men's clothing. Mentally, I had made the switch to female and having to appear dressed as a man was very distressing to me. Of course, the airline attorney and chief pilot jumped on that and tried to discredit me. He realized his mistake and quickly told them in very stern terms that it was he who was uncomfortable and that from then on he would treat me properly, as a woman. He apologized, and the hearing was completed. As we walked from the room, he put his arms around me, apologized again, and told me that the airline was going to be in for one hell of a fight. A couple of months later I was notified that the Division on Civil Rights had found for me, but that didn't mean that I could readily get my job back.

My date for surgery was set for August 28, 1990 in Trinidad, Colorado. My sister, who was still uncertain about my decision, told me that she would be going with me. The hospital stay was scheduled for ten days and travel afterward was going to be difficult and painful. Her car was a Lincoln Town Car. The ride would prove to be very beneficial for me on the journey home. Her daughter lived in Topeka, Kansas, which was about halfway between Indianapolis and Trinidad, so we stopped there both ways. During 1989 I had made the rounds of relatives and close friends to inform them of my plans. This came as a shock to most, but after the news sank in and they began to understand my feelings, most reacted with feelings of love and support. I don't recommend this as a way to find out who your real friends are, or who truly loves you, but you'll soon know. The level of love and support surprised me, and that helped to sustain me during some very dark hours. My sister and I spent a weekend at Colorado Springs. We felt like two sisters on vacation. The weather was perfect as we took the cog rail train to the top of Pikes Peak, walked about the Garden of the Gods, shopped and dined in quaint restaurants.

About an hour from Trinidad my sister told me that it was OK with her if I changed my mind, that she'd love me just as much if I said no. My life was ahead, and as a woman. In my mind, there was no going back. Dr. Biber gave me my final exam on a Monday morning and I was admitted to the hospital that afternoon. Final checks were made, paperwork completed, and fees paid. I met all the staff involved and was given every chance to change my mind. For the first time in my life I felt totally at ease. All that I despised would soon be removed.

I was awakened at 6:30 AM Tuesday morning, rechecked and given a last chance to say no. By 7:00 I was in the operating room. Within seconds of being given a sedative I was asleep. I was told that the surgery took over four hours. When I awoke, numb as a log, the wall clock said 2:10 PM; Dr. Biber and the O.R. nurses were standing at the foot of my bed, with my blood on their scrubs, and smiling. Dr. Biber said to me, "Welcome to the world, Sleeping Beauty." Those words I'll never forget. I was truly born again. It would be a week before I was allowed out of bed. The pain was intense. I endured it, as I knew it would recede as my body healed. My sister came each morning and spent a lot of time with me and the other four new girls in our special section of the ward. Liz, Margaret and I bonded, and to this day we consider ourselves sisters. My strength gradually returned, and on day eleven I was released into the world.

My sister did most of the driving on the return trip. The back seat of the town car was my bed. We spent two nights in Topeka with her daughter, and then drove on to Indianapolis. For two days I rested there before heading back to NJ in my car. I could go about one and a half hours between stops for rest and a change of bandages. When I arrived back in Princeton I truly felt that I had started over. Now I could focus on the legal fight ahead. Though my funds were low, I was getting unemployment, and earning some money from photography. In a short time I would find some part time work to pay for rent and living expenses. For now, I needed to concentrate on learning in months, what the normal female has years to learn. Fortunately, I had a lot of help from friends and family. Never once during my transition had I been challenged about who I was. That had given me a lot of confidence.

As the legal battle began, my airline filed for bankruptcy. Now I had to petition Federal Bankruptcy Court in Delaware in order to sue for reinstatement. More expense but I prevailed. After a lot of legal jousting, my case was taken by the Federal District Court in Trenton, NJ. No argument that the airline presented impressed the court. My case was put on a fast track, and we were kept busy with research, presentations, and legal arguments. At each hearing, the results favored me. Just before a trial was set to start, a summary court hearing was conducted. During the hearing, the judge suddenly ordered the airline attorney and mine to his chambers. He told the company that they would want to settle with me, as they were going to lose. They were given thirty days to come to

terms. I wrote out the terms, and though they tried to weasel, I said to them, "Agree or I'll see you at trial." They gave in.

Almost two and a half years had passed since I'd been fired. I was excited about returning to the profession that I loved. I had made the national news twice and a level of public support had begun which gave me confidence that I could win. I had been on several TV and radio talk shows that helped me deal with public perception and questions about functioning and fitting in with society. Still, I knew that there would be many who didn't want me there, let alone fly with me. During a special interview with the company VP of Flight Operations, I told him that I was back to fly and do my job as a professional, not because they wanted me, but because a federal court had ordered it. If any pilot had a problem with who I was, it was their problem, not mine. Many of the pilots actively supported me; others had a wait-and-see attitude, while some tried to make my life miserable. On July 21, 1992 I reported to training for requalification. It was good to be home.

Because I had beaten the company, stood up for my rights, and went after any pilot that harassed me, the flight attendants and gate agents were open about how they felt. I'd become a folk hero of sorts. They warmly greeted me for each flight, made sure I had a bottle of water, made fresh coffee for me, and saved first-class meals when possible. Many of the employees would let me know about the plots of those who wanted to embarrass or cause me problems. It took a while to get used to being stared at by pilots in the crew room. I knew that it would take some time to be accepted, but I earned it by conducting myself in a professional and friendly manner at all times. Those who crossed me learned that I knew how to use published pilot policies to stop harassment immediately. One of my captain friends told me one day that the word was "Don't mess with Jess."

Of over five thousand pilots, my company only had sixty-three female pilots in 1993. It was rare to fly with another female, but a treat when it happened. I had upgraded to captain before having an entire female crew. We had a lot of fun and it was amusing to see some of the passengers' expressions and hear their comments when they found out that the whole crew was female. When I flew to Mexico or South America airport, employees, mostly male, reacted with surprise and amazement upon seeing a female captain, especially one who wore a skirt instead of slacks. Some even whistled at me.

After I healed from surgery and had resumed as normal a life as I could, I started to become more social. I had to find out how I felt about men in a more intimate way. I was attractive enough that as I went about my daily routine I became aware of how others were looking at me. When I went to a dance, it was as if I could read the minds of the men in the room. I knew exactly what they wanted. The question was, do I or how far do I let them go? I considered myself heterosexual before surgery; now how would I feel in the intimate company of men? I needed to find out. I had met a scientist at a church singles group, and he always arranged to have me in the discussion group that he led and at the monthly dance would dance with me often. One Sunday he told me that he wanted to get to know me better. I invited him to dinner one cold winter evening when I had the house to myself. I discovered after dinner that his interests were more physical than intellectual. Now I'd been there in the past, but was I going to let him do to me what I knew he wanted? It was the situation every female finds herself in and has to decide—do I, or don't I? Well, I did and thus began my journey into the intimacy of being female. In a year I knew that I enjoyed being the object of men's desires.

How do men react when they find out that the woman they are attracted to turns out to have had that very different past? Those who are confident of their own sexuality have told me that since they only knew me as Jessica, it didn't matter. Others run immediately, while others become fearful of what their peers will think. I found that some men are very intimidated by a woman who has advanced education, highly developed technical skills, has coped with extreme danger, and has not had to ask a man to do it for her. My lady friends have done a reasonable job of teaching me, so that I don't scare off the prospective suitor. Of course, I could now write volumes about how women are treated at the local garage, hardware store, car dealership, etc. I won't, but I use that knowledge to my advantage.

In summary, I like to stress that no human chooses to be a transsexual. I feel that half of my life's energy was spent in coping with this. Statistics available in 1990 indicated that the population of transsexual people, both male and female, was about .0004 percent. Of that number only 10 percent will achieve the goal of surgery. In a nation concerned about human health and well-being, we are left to fend for ourselves with little help. The situation has got somewhat better because some of us have been willing to educate, speak out, go to court (I was the first to win in a federal court), and insist that we deserve and have the right to happiness promised to all. Today one needs only to go to the World Wide Web to find support groups and resources for the transgendered. In the past few years, many local and state governments have passed antidiscrimination laws to help protect gays, lesbians, and transgendered people. Many companies have been in the lead as they value the employee and realize that disharmony in the work place affects profits.

When asked if I am happy, I can say without a doubt that I am. I have no regrets about having lived my life as I did. There's no going back, only forward with the total continuity of "freedom of identity."

[2003]

Understanding the Reading

1. What is a transsexual?
2. Do you think Jessica was born this way, or is it because of something in her background?
3. Describe her personality, as you see her.
4. In what different ways did she attempt to deal with her transsexuality throughout her life?
5. After her surgery, how did her employer react?
6. What was the legal outcome?

Suggestions for Responding

1. Research laws concerning transsexuality and report on them.
2. Find out what the U.S. Armed Forces' policy is toward transsexuals. What would have happened to her career had they known about her transsexuality?
3. Have a class discussion on why you think Jessica sought a career in flying, as traditionally it has been a very masculine arena.

Suggestions for Responding to Part II

1. The readings in this part have examined both traditional and changing gender and sexual roles in our society. As the introduction suggested, our socialization into gender-specific behavior is complex and both subtle and overt. Consider how you learned to behave acceptably in terms of your gender. Think back to your earliest memories. When were you first aware of being male or female? How did your placement in your family (first-born, only child, etc.) affect your family's expectations about you as a girl or a boy? If you have siblings of the other sex, were they treated differently than you or held to different standards of behavior? At various points in your life, you were probably quite self-consciously masculine or feminine. Can you explain those moments? Also, your attitudes toward your femininity or masculinity have probably undergone changes; record these changes and try to figure out what triggered them. After you have reflected on these matters, write an autobiography of your gender development. If you do not consider yourself either male or female, write about that.

2. The importance of gender and sexuality in our society can scarcely be overstated. Whether we accept or reject all the social mandates of our assigned gender role, we cannot escape its influence. However, try to imagine that you were born a different sex. How would your life have been different, and what would you be like today? Think about specific moments in your life when the switch would have been especially important—from your earliest childhood through adolescence into adulthood. Consider how it would influence and alter your expectations for your own future. Write an autobiography of this imaginary you.

3. Describe your versions of the female stereotype and of the male stereotype. Then describe your ideal woman and your ideal man. Analyze the differences between the two pairs and explain what this reveals about stereotypes and reality.

4. Many of the selections in part II focus on the difficulties of traditional femininity or masculinity; yet most of us are quite content to be who we are. Write an essay about why you like being the sex you are. You probably want to look at both its advantages and rewards and the disadvantages and difficulties of another sex.

5. The selections in this section can be disturbing and confusing, for some of us have been brought up with the straightforward understanding that there are clear-cut divisions between males and females. To confront the information that sometimes the borders are blurry, and that as members of a society we must acknowledge that fact in personal relations and public policy, can be challenging. For some the knowledge is a great relief. Begin researching on the internet to see what recent information is available about transsexual, transgendered, gay, lesbian, bisexual, and intersexual individuals.

6. Today there are many support groups for members of these communities, as opposed to thirty or forty years ago. Do more internet research and discuss in class or with friends how such organized groups help or hurt our society.

7. Discover the roles or consequences other cultures offer for being a member of the transsexual, transgendered, gay, lesbian, bisexual, or intersexual communities. Several cultures are changing their official stances as a response to world opinion on human rights demands, or as a means of "having it under control." (See Iran's policy of paying for sex change operations.)

Part III
Economics and the American Dream

THE AMERICAN DREAM! WE ALL KNOW WHAT THAT means—a good job with plenty of opportunity for advancement, a good family, a nice house with at least one car (probably two) in the driveway, plenty of good food and frequent dining out with enough money left over for the kids' education at good schools, a few luxuries, and an annual vacation. Each of us can add specific details—appliances, electronic games, and so on—but we would probably agree on the general features of the dream.

This dream arrived on our shores with the early Puritans, who held to the doctrine that God rewarded virtue with earthly wealth; to them, economic success was a way to glorify God. Thus, the **Protestant work ethic** became a core principle of American culture. This ethic is the belief in the importance of hard work and productivity and the corresponding faith that this behavior will be rewarded appropriately. In the eighteenth century, national icon Benjamin Franklin and his "Poor Richard's" maxims advocating frugality, initiative, industry, diligence, honesty, and prudence secularized and popularized the doctrine. Franklin personified the ethic, both for his contemporaries and for succeeding generations, right up to today.

Franklin also represents another facet of the American Dream: the ideal of the self-made man (who, of course, adheres to the Protestant work ethic). The **self-made man** has appeared throughout this country's history. In the nineteenth century, Horatio Alger made a fortune with his popular fictional heroes who rose "from rags to riches" by "luck and pluck and hard work." One of the most admired American presidents is the log-cabin-born, rail-splitting Abraham Lincoln, another self-made man. Recent presidents have also tended to flaunt their humble beginnings, from grocer's son Richard Nixon to peanut farmer Jimmy Carter to alcoholic's son Ronald Reagan. George H. W. Bush preferred to be seen as an oilfield wildcatter rather than as a privileged Yale graduate, and Bill Clinton focuses on the single-parent family of his early childhood. George W. Bush, despite his family wealth, places himself as an antielitist, with a folksy way of speaking, shown frequently on his Texas ranch doing manual labor. Barack Obama, our first African American president, identifies with both his black and his white family members, and, like Clinton, he was raised by his mother. As for Donald Trump's story, few would consider him "self-made" due to his inherited wealth and father's credit worthiness; however, recognizing the power available in this myth, he writes of himself in his 1987 book *The Art of the Deal*, "I play to people's fantasies . . . a very effective form of promotion." One might say that in America if you are self-made, you have "made it," and in the twenty-first century that certainly includes women.

The myth of the American Dream, based as it is on the assumption that opportunities are boundless and that success depends solely on one's character, has a flip side that makes the dream more like a nightmare for many Americans. If individuals are responsible for their own success, they must also be responsible for their own failure and, therefore, deserving of their fate. Even in the twenty-first century, we still hold to these myths, which conceal the realities of class distinctions. We like to think of the United States as a **classless society**; we don't even like to talk about class, except to claim that we all belong to the middle class. This thinking makes it possible for us to ignore the problems created by inequitable economic distribution.

The disparity between the wealthiest and the poorest members of society is, in fact, extensive; while 21 percent of U.S. children lived in poverty in 2015, the richest 1 percent controlled 40 percent of the nation's wealth. In 2015 there were fifteen million children living below the poverty line in the United States, according to the National Center for Children in Poverty. Yet there is resistance to changing the system because we have faith in **upward mobility**, the possibility that we will someday strike it rich ourselves—the good old American Dream.

Janet Zandy's essay (reading 18) is an analysis of what class is—more than the amount of money one has, class is also defined by economic privilege and power and access to resources. Zandy suggests five ways we can use to see and understand class and our own class positions. She also points out how the dominant class controls knowledge, especially historical knowledge, and has distorted our understanding of our national past. She closes with student responses to her argument when she presented it as a lecture. The next selection speaks to the issue of upward mobility. In reading 19, Sallie Bingham describes the disadvantages of being a woman in a very wealthy family. She argues that such women are suppressed and controlled to serve the interests of the family wealth, to which they have only indirect access.

Upward mobility may create its own difficulties. In addition, poverty is accompanied by many stresses unknown to those who have not experienced it. In reading 20, growing up in poverty that he hated, Randall Williams was ashamed to take friends to his house.

In reading 21, we learn that in 2017 25 percent of U.S. homeless were in California, facing epidemics, especially hepatitis A, and consequently oftentimes death. Siddiqui's article raises the question of why the rate has risen for the first time in seven years after the recession.

Although the myth of a classless, middle-class America is an appealing concept, the readings in part III reveal that it is a myth and not an accurate description of our nation. It masks many cruel realities that are embedded in our economic system. In addition, our faith in the American Dream and its underlying principles of hard work and self-reliance allow us to ignore the problems of those who are ill served by the system and even to *blame those victims* for their plight. However, upward mobility, while possible, exacts a considerable toll on those who are forced to choose between the behavior patterns, beliefs, values, and even family and friends of their original world and the chance to "move up," to enter a culture that is both alien and alienating. Thus, in many senses, class in our "classless" society is problematic.

18

Decloaking Class: Why Class Identity and Consciousness Count

JANET ZANDY

To be sure, class is one of those "where do you begin?" subjects. It is a kind of ghost issue, there but not there. Often it is named as part of a cluster of multicultural concerns, but then it seems to disappear, eclipsed by other identities. This is understandable because class is so complex and so mystified, especially in a country as large and diverse as the United States. I use the word "decloaking" in my title not only because I love *Star Trek* but also because the term fits the process of revealing what is clearly there, but cloaked and hidden. To reveal class involves crossing several time zones, of simultaneously having a sense of the past, the present, and the future.

Also, it involves seeing class as both personal and public, a kind of inheritance we carry with us as individuals and as a country. In other words, class is too important to ignore. I wish I could offer you a neat package of class information that would be psychologically comforting and intellectually satisfying. But, frankly, that would be about as real as a hologram on a holodeck. Instead, I want to speak out of my own experience, and to leave you with more questions than answers.

Class Identity

How many of you are first-generation college students or college graduates? How many of you have grandparents who do not have college degrees? How many think that working class and middle class are essentially the same thing? How many of you are uncomfortable with these questions?

Questions about class identity seem to evoke feelings and responses that are different from questions about other identities. If I asked how many of you are from Italian or Irish ancestry, Caribbean, or Asian, there would probably be little hesitation in your response. But class identity is not so evident. Students may be from significantly different economic circumstances—in terms of whether you need to work to stay in school or whether you have significant loans to repay after graduation or whether someone else is paying your tuition—but those differences are not apparent. And except for the styles of dress of different majors, you can't tell class difference by appearance.

Even bringing up the issue of class seems vaguely impolite, even un-American. People respond by saying, "I don't care about class identity; I treat everyone the same. What does it matter what class you come from, we are all equal."

The truth is that class does count. It shapes our lives and intersects with race, ethnicity, gender, and geography in profound ways. What is class? I offer this as a working definition: Class is an experience of shared economic circumstances and shared social and cultural practices in relation to positions of power. Unlike caste (slavery), there is some mobility between classes. That is, it is possible to be born poor and acquire great wealth. (But, not likely.) Conversely, it is possible to keep a sense of one's original class identity as one moves into different economic circumstances. What needs to be understood is that although class identity is shaped by income and wealth, money is only a part of the story. It is what economic privilege can purchase in terms of access and power that really marks class difference.

Each of us is born into a family with a particular class identity and class history—sometimes it is a mixed or hybrid identity—but almost always it is part of a network of other relationships—to other families in a community, to work and jobs, and to institutions. For example, if you are born into a family that owns lands and buildings, a family that has access to the best lawyers and doctors, and has sent generations of sons (and more recently daughters) to boarding schools and then on to Yale or Dartmouth or Harvard, then you have a different class history from someone whose parents may own one small house, whose grandparents had to drop out of school to go to work, who does not have easy access to lawyers and doctors, not to mention judges and lobbyists, and whose parents work long hours at a job site they do not own or control, performing labor that may be physically exhausting and even dangerous. It is conceivable that the sons and daughters from both families might even call themselves "middle class," but in terms of power, autonomy, and opportunity, they clearly are not the same.

How do we measure class? Well, it is the academic way to begin with data, definitions, and statistics. To be sure, we have plenty of statistics—most of which come from government sources. Even a cursory look at wealth distribution reveals the reality of the economic landscape. At the top, is a tiny, tiny percent of people who control and own an enormous amount of wealth. (And that wealth has increased dramatically in the last 15 years.) At the bottom, are the official poor (whose numbers are growing, about 32 million—about 60 percent of those people are working poor—that is, that have jobs but don't make enough to support their families). And between the rich and the growing number of poor are the middle and working classes. This is where the classification gets blurred. Although there are about twice as many working-class people as middle class (about 50 percent to 20 percent), there is a media and political tendency to avoid the term working class and to lump anyone who isn't either very rich or very poor into the amorphous middle (sometimes called "working middle"). I think it is important to unpack the differences between the working class and middle class. To perceive these differences you need to go beyond definitions of a middle salary and look at the nature of work: the degree of autonomy a job has, who is managed, who is the manager; the physicality of work, working-class jobs tend to be harder on the human body, are sometimes even dangerous; the degree of control or ownership one has over one's own labor; and differences of status, options, expectations, language, education, and culture.

Both the middle class and the working class have experienced change: There are fewer well-paying, blue-collar jobs, more low-paying white and pink collar jobs. There are fewer independent middle-class storekeepers and farmers and more professionals and managers. What the middle class and the working class have in common is a downward economic pull. The middle class is losing autonomy and security, and the working class is getting poorer as union jobs decline. Both groups are experiencing the economic frustration of being on a no-fat economic diet of little or no income gain in the last decade. However, the number of people reporting incomes of more than a half million increased in the same decade 985 percent. When class resentments surface, those in positions of power encourage a criticism aimed downward—at the poor—increasingly the scapegoats for people's economic frustrations—and not upward at the rich. This is perhaps a truer reflection of who owns and controls the media than it is of which class is really oppressing another.

But numbers and definitions are not sufficient to decloak class. We need to understand better the everyday class experiences of ordinary people and we need to ask what is missing or distorted in our own notions about class. I'd like to suggest some ways to break down and think about this large concept.

First, think across generations. Consider how class identity changes or stays the same from one generation to the next. For example, your class experience may be different from your parents' and significantly different from your grandparents', but, on the other hand, there may be common values, attitudes, ways of using language that continue from generation to generation. That is the cultural aspect of class. Also, if you look across generations, you can see how tools and technology may have changed—bank clerks use computers instead of adding machines—but the structure of power relationships remains fairly consistent.

Second, consider the concept of relationship as a key to understanding class. That is, class is most visible in juxtaposition or in relationship to something else. You begin to know your class identity when you cross class borders and see your own circumstances through someone else's eyes. For some of you these insights come through community service. For others, class difference was evident when you left home or on your first day in college when you notice what kind of stuff students bring with them. But tangible material differences are only a part of class relationships. There are other relational questions—especially in discerning differences between the middle and working class: For example, in order to advance in the world (and what that means is not always clear), do you need to leave your home and community or can you develop within it? What are the expectations of your family? Are you encouraged to get a secure job with a future and a pension, or are you encouraged to experiment, take a year off, and find yourself? When you went to school as a child, was the language that the school teachers used in first grade familiar to you? Or was it different from the language that you heard at home? And I am referring to the dialects of spoken English, not just other languages. The middle-class child does not have to switch language patterns at home and at school; the working-class child often does. Also, class difference can be seen in the relationship one has to community. Do you feel alone or do you feel that you are part of a network of people and traditions? These are questions that pull us closer to understanding class as a lived experience and not just an academic category.

Third, consider the intersections between class identity and other identities, especially race and ethnicity. I think that the issue of multiculturalism would be complicated in a positive way if class is factored in. That is, it would be a very healthy thing for working-class people of all different backgrounds to know each other's work history. This would mean also that this huge category of whiteness would have to be broken down and understood in relation to issues of power. This does not mean that there is no such thing as white skin privilege; rather, it means that all whites do not have the same degree of privilege. And, of course, in terms of gender issues, all men do not have the same degree of power.

Fourth, if you want to understand class, look at how work is constructed. There are careers, there is work, and there are jobs. Each is nuanced differently. Most of us are so busy either preparing for future work or struggling to sustain what we have that there isn't much time to step back and look at how our work is managed or how it fits into a larger social context. Also, how often do we see the working conditions of other people? How aware are we of the production process behind the goods we consume? It is a fact that most people on this planet do not own or control their own labor, but must sell it in order to survive. And few of them can afford to give their own children the toys and clothes they are assembling for other markets. How work is shaped, who controls and defines it, whether it is scarce or plentiful are all class relational questions.

Fifth, consider the meaning of class consciousness. Consciousness is an awareness, an opening. Class consciousness is an awareness of mutual interests and desires. We are all bombarded with messages coaxing us to identify our interests with those at the economic top. The usual model for this kind of consciousness is the ladder—climbing in an individualistic and competitive way, higher and higher rung by rung. But there are other models. Another is the web—that is, we see ourselves as having a place in a complex network of mutually interrelated positions, and that our individual well being depends on the well being of the group (including the least privileged). This is closer to a model that you find among native peoples and it is closer to the model of a working-class consciousness. It is a sense that survival depends on helping each other out, on a sense of mutuality, not exclusion. Success—if the word is used at all—lies with collective well being, not merely individual achievement—a sense of pushing everything up with us as we rise.

HOW CLASS IS CLOAKED

Let me begin with a small incident that happened several years ago at an academic conference I attended. These conferences are usually in big hotels in big cities. The usual routine is to get up early and begin attending sessions on different topics in hot crowded hotel rooms. On this occasion, I am standing in the hotel lobby and another English professor makes small talk with me. He asks, "What is your field?" I answer, "American working-class literature." After a significant pause, he replies, "Oh, I didn't know there was a working class anymore." I suggest to him that there still is a working class as I glance around the hotel lobby to see people clearing tables, carrying food, cleaning ashtrays, washing windows, setting up chairs, etc. The room hummed with human activity, but it wasn't visible. These individual workers blurred into the deep background of academic humanism.

It seems to me that this small event is telling of a larger pattern in American culture. It is a problem of seeing—an "unequal distribution of visibility." It works on two levels: People are literally invisible to each other, but also their intelligence and experience are devalued. Sometimes the working class—the class that holds everything up—has to literally punch through in order to be seen.

Part of the problem of visibility is a problem of knowledge—how knowledge is constructed, layer after layer, generation after generation. Working-class people have not had much say about how school knowledge is constructed. Textbooks, curricula, course design were developed by other class interests—initially by an elite intelligentsia or more recently driven by business and corporate needs. The formation of knowledge has not included the subjectivities and experiences and histories of working people in any significant way.

Why is this omission important to understand? It means that the point of view of the majority of people—living today and in the history of the country—has not been included in the big history story—the story that gets delivered to school kids at a very young age. Perhaps it has changed since I was a student or since my children were young, but I noticed that what is taught—who won what battle and who was president at the time—doesn't seem to have a lot of connection or relevance to the lives of ordinary people. What seems to be remembered, is not a rich and dense, conflicted and complex U.S.

history, but a kind of Disney-like nostalgic history. Youngsters learn about someone called Betsy Ross sweetly sewing the American flag, but nothing about the noisy, sweaty history of textile work. Or they learn about George Washington chopping down the cherry tree and not telling a lie, but not about the unsafe history of the logging industry or how many lies were told to acquire Indian land. These simplistic little stories have amazing endurance in people's memories and reference points. Indeed, children seem to be protected from serious American history.

And serious American history is violent. It is not safe; it makes people uncomfortable. Class difference and class struggle were—from the very beginning— part of the story. Recent labor and social historians often use words like "hidden," "forgotten," "untold" to tell this other story. Some of this untold story is now part of the history curriculum—but it wasn't when I was a student. I had to learn for myself how to see the point of view in the historical story, how to adjust my angle of vision to look from the bottom up instead of the top down. This adjustment in perspective makes relationships more visible: for instance, in a world of finite resources, if a small group of people own and control vast amounts, it is likely that a large group of people will have very little—no matter how hard they work. And it makes it easier to see how this imbalance is maintained by coaxing people to identify with the very forces that oppress their own kin.

When it comes to the history of class disparity there is a great deal to uncover. At the very beginning of the new nation, Alexander Hamilton advised George Washington to give to the "rich and well born . . . a distinct permanent share in the government." And he did. The very first Congress provided money for bankers to set up a national bank and manufacturers were subsidized in the form of tariffs. In the 1850s state governments gave railroad speculators 25 million acres of public land, free of charge! The first transcontinental railroad was built with government land and money.

When the story is told from the top down, we learn about the feat of building the railroad, how it opened new frontiers and provided jobs. We may not hear that 10,000 Chinese and 3,000 Irish got the opportunity to earn about $1 a day; and die by the hundreds building those *railroads*. And how those very same Chinese workers were hounded and driven out after the job was done. And how none of the workers who built the railroad could claim ownership or even a free ride.

Today, information highways have replaced railroads, but government benefits for businesses and corporations continue. And I am speaking of huge corporate entities, not small businesses or middle-class family-owned companies. One reason the national debt is so enormous is because of the shifting of the tax burden from corporations to individuals. In the 1950s, corporate share of federal income tax collected was 39 percent, in the 1980s it was 17 percent. By 1991 it was down to 9.2 percent, while the corporate share of state and local taxes stayed about what it was in 1965. This is trickle-down economics. But I haven't seen any new cars or fur coats trickle down lately; have you?

But this is only one side of the story. What role did ordinary working people play in shaping their own economic lives? This history, what some historians call "the other civil war," is a record of resistance and endurance in the face of great odds. It seems unfair to the majority of Americans not to know it. To know, for instance, that people fought back. From time to time ordinary citizens—because of unsafe working conditions, long hours, and unlivable wages—would spontaneously refuse to work. The railroad strike of 1877, sometimes called the "great uprising of 1877," was the first national strike in United States history. Within two weeks the strike which began among the railroad workers in Martinsburg, West Virginia (triggered because of five years of wage cuts for workers on the Baltimore & Ohio line) spread through four states—Pennsylvania, Ohio, Indiana and Missouri. It was a general, national strike that included mill workers, miners, laborers, and steel workers; 100,000 workers were on strike at the same time. But they were defeated when federal troops were sent in and, at the end, 100 people were dead. This was neither the first nor the last general strike: between the years 1881 and 1885 there were 500 strikes a year. In 1886 there were 1,400 strikes, involving 500,000 workers. In 1934 there was a general strike in San Francisco and 130,000 workers went out. That same year, 325,000 textile workers in the South struck.

What is troubling to learn is that so many strikes were lost because the National Guard or the army were employed by business and government against working people. Workers were literally outgunned in battles with soldiers who came from the same working-class backgrounds. One brief example: In 1913, in Ludlow, Colorado, miners went on strike because of low wages and dangerous working conditions against the Rockefeller-owned Colorado Fuel &

Iron Corporation. The miners were evicted from their company-owned shacks and set up tents near the coal fields during the cold winter of 1913–1914. The National Guard was called; the miners and their families, waving American flags, thought the soldiers were there to protect them. They didn't know that the Rockefellers were paying the salaries of the soldiers. On April 20, 1914 the National Guard began a machine gun attack on the tents. Women and children dug pits beneath the tents to escape the gunfire. The Guard then set fire to the tents. The next day the charred bodies of eleven children and two women were found. That became known as the Ludlow Massacre. One miner said, "Well, they value their mules more."

Seeing history from the bottom up illuminates other issues in American culture, some surprisingly current. For example, when you look at differences within the working class as a whole, you see a pattern on the part of the owners to pit one ethnic or racial group or gender against another in competition for scarce jobs. It is a strategy of divide and conquer—of terracing skills—so that one race or ethnic group comes to understand that they cannot advance beyond a certain level because they are Hispanic or Hungarian or Italian or women. But even deeper than this, and crucial to our coping with racial tensions today, is how the category of "whiteness" is used to block class awareness. What happens is that the white working class comes to think of its interests in terms of race difference rather than class oppositions. The insecurities that white workers feel about their own status—and the tensions between the ideology of equality and the reality of economic inequality—is displaced by a psychological wage of whiteness, a wage of false superiority because they are white. And so they would compensate for their feelings of class alienation by defining themselves against blackness.

This is just a sliver of American history told from the perspective of working people. It is not history as a sporting event—who won and who lost. I like to imagine what it would mean if this workers' history were embedded in people's consciousness today. What if labor history were half as well known as entertainment trivia? What if the Ludlow massacre were as familiar to school children as sightings of Elvis?

But generally I suspect that most people don't know this history or understand these power relationships. The media does not focus on ordinary people pooling their resources and overcoming differences of language and culture to engage in common struggle. Instead, we have distractions—sports, sensational murder stories (sometimes sports and murder are combined), race and gender antagonisms, and false promises. Instead of examples of how collective effort can change conditions, we have an almost religious reverence for a single leader. Instead of narratives of worker consciousness, we have narratives of minuscule possibility—stories of winning, stardom, and lucky breaks. Practice every day, wear these sneakers, and you will make it to the NBA. Right. Play LOTTO and you'll make it big. Hey, you never know. Indeed, you never know. There's a lot of talk about "empowerment" these days, but it doesn't appear to me that ordinary people feel particularly powerful.

TODAY'S VIRTUAL WORK REALITY

Now why should people who are just beginning their careers pay any attention to this history? What are the connections, if any, between individual achievement and communal well-being? I want to share with you a bit of student writing that caused me to think about these questions. This was something a student of mine wrote in her journal in December 1988. You may remember that this particular December a bomb exploded on Pam Am Flight 103 over Lockerbie, Scotland. Two hundred and seventy people were killed, including a number of upstate New York students who were on the way home for the holidays after a semester abroad. In response to this event, this RIT student wrote, "From 31,000 feet they had no chance to save themselves. Thirty-eight students, thirty-eight fewer people competing for jobs."

I have to ask myself why this student reacted to the explosion of a packed airplane in terms of job competition. I wonder whether she was completely unique in her reaction or she voiced something that others think, but may not write down. I don't know. I wonder, though, if she reflects the experience of growing up with a different set of historical circumstances and more rigid economic opportunities. Has she gotten the message that life is a game based on scarcity, and the rules say that if someone else loses, I may win?

In a number of ways the rules have changed. Middle-class families are getting new and disturbing labels—they are being called the fear of falling class or the anxious class. Part of it is uncertainty about the future. There are no guarantees—no one can say what tomorrow's cutting edge will be or where the jobs will be in ten, even five years from now, or whether there will be any employment continuity in a project-driven work environment. It may be hard to believe that your parents' generation was once on the cutting edge too but now many of them are being downsized (I understand the current term is "right-sized") out. The cutting up of the work force is a class issue. What are the implications for family or community if workers are disposed of like so many Bic razors? This uncertainty is coupled with the reality of enormous college debt faced by graduating college students and their families. My generation—the 1960s generation—was in some ways luckier. We had greater access to grants and scholarships rather than loans and second mortgages. And so there were many working-class kids like myself who had full scholarships to get educations their parents could never afford to give them. Also, twenty years earlier, over two million service men and women of the generation of the 1940s were able to take advantage of Public Law 346, commonly known as the G.I. Bill. Free education and a subsistence allowance to any eligible veteran. It was an enormous leap, a great opportunity to become engineers, educators, judges, lawyers and get degrees from Princeton, Yale, and Stanford via the G.I. Bill.

Today we have what some are calling job virtual reality (now the job exists, now it doesn't). We have a lot of interesting technology. And a great deal of pressure to be technically prepared to face this changing world. But, there doesn't seem to be a lot of time—unless students do it for themselves—to consider how the pleasures of engineering or the writing of an elegant computer program or the crafting of a beautiful table—how the work we enjoy doing—relates to a larger community of people. We don't have time to ask how technology conforms to existing power relationships. The computer scientist Richard Stallman asserts that "the greatest scarcity in the United States is not technical innovation, but rather the willingness to work together for the public good. It makes no sense [he says] to encourage the former at the expense of the latter."

By speaking about history tonight I was reminding myself and others whose shoulders we stand on as we climb. The theologian Dorothee Soelle says we need alternative visions to see what she describes as "work [that] is communal, not only in the space of a given community but also in time, as the shared memory of what we have received from the past that accompanies us into the future."

I realize that we academics in liberal arts tend to frustrate students by delivering a lot of critical information but not offering any solutions. But of course you know that the solutions are not simple because the issues are so complex. Frankly, I would be skeptical of anyone who offers simplistic answers to complex questions. Maybe the better way to go—if we are going to salvage a sense of community—is to figure out the right questions, especially in relation to issues of power and class.

Using Class Difference Personally and Collectively

Since I was the first woman in my family to earn a college degree, I was driven to take in knowledge as hard and fast as I could, but not to think very critically about it. Along the way, I sensed a distance, sometimes even a rupture, between the lived experience of my working-class family and what I learned in school. In myriad subtle and not so subtle ways, I was taught in school not to value nor to see the dignity and worth of my own heritage. The message that I received as a young woman wanting to be an educated person was my working-class identity had to be discarded—like a dark and heavy coat—at the university door. Getting clear about that identity was a long and complicated process. Claiming that identity as crucial to who I am and the work that I want to do in the world was at once liberating and reconciling. My work is sustained because of a sense of kinship and responsibility to my beginnings—not despite them. This is not about survivor's guilt, nor is it about romanticizing economic hardship; there's nothing romantic about not having enough money. Rather, it is trusting what you know even if it is not part of officially sanctioned knowledge. I realized that I could write, research, and act out of my own sense of class difference. And that what I needed to do was to use my resources and privileges to provide a space for some of this history and culture that was so frequently ignored or even despised. And the work had to be collective, not just my own story.

In *Calling Home* I wanted to create a book that would prove that working-class women have created their own written literary culture, that an aesthetic sense is shaped by class but does not belong to one class. I also wanted to show that the experiences of working-class women were not the same as those of working-class men or of middle-class women. Without any lofty expectations of what might happen, I began collecting writing by working-class women and putting it into shoe boxes and then bigger boxes, and finally filling two file drawers. I shaped the material around the interplay of different and linked voices—I, we, and they. And finally—ten years later—I mustered the courage to send it out. No one was more surprised than I was when two prestigious university presses competed for this book. To produce it, I used the tools that I learned in the academy, but the writing itself is grounded outside the academy in the work lives of people like my parents.

In this second book, *Liberating Memory: Our Work and Our Working-Class Consciousness*, I wanted to show how this effort of linking working-class lived experience to cultural work was not unique to me. I wanted to make visible how other working-class people like myself managed to use their class experiences in culturally productive ways. I asked for memory, not nostalgia. That is, not a sugar-coated celebration of the past, a self-congratulating, "look how far I've come," but rather a painful reconstruction of class experiences and loss, a way of using grief to tell a larger story. These essays written by photographers and painters and academics and secretaries and musicians and social activists all begin with a biographical record: I was born at this time and in this place and this is the work that my parents and my grandparents did. All of the writers grew up with the uncertain economic rhythms of working-class life. Their parents' work included: seamstress, short order cook, chemical factory worker, auto line worker, welder, rubber plant worker, bookkeeper, tenant farmer, truck driver, riveter, millwright, domestic, and housewife. All the writers bring the knowledge of physical labor either personally or through the lives of their parents into the current work that they do. This is a knowledge of the body that is not easily articulated and not often part of bourgeois intellectual circles. All of the contributors oppose the dehumanization of workers—of turning human beings who do not own and control their own labor into things. They all see risk taking as necessary for their cultural work—not because they are more heroic than anyone else—but because it is strategically necessary in order to accomplish democratic change. All of the contributors know what it feels like to be cut out of the action, even though they are of the majority class, the working class. And they all love learning and books.

I'll finish with this short excerpt from the introduction to *Liberating Memory* that describes an episode of class consciousness among working people. It takes place on April 28, Workers Memorial Day.

For the last five years, hundreds of communities across the country have held memorial services on this day to remember dead and injured workers. In Rochester we meet late in the afternoon on a windy knoll in Highland Park. The setting is landscaped with junipers and white and yellow daffodils. Nested in the grass is a small memorial plaque inscribed with Mother Jones' feisty injunction to "Pray for the dead, but fight like hell for the living."

The event is organized by the local labor council. Dignitaries, public officials, politicians, and the media often show up—though how many depends on whether it is an election year. The crowd is mostly a mixture of activists, union leaders, and working people. Some are retired; some were able to get off early from work. We do not necessarily know each other, but faces are familiar and recognizable year after year. We hold red carnations and carry names of fallen workers. We are working class people who have come to honor our own.

The ceremony begins. After the speeches, the display of public language, comes the remembrance. One by one we walk to the podium and read the name of a worker who has died or been injured in the Rochester area, and we place a carnation on the memorial. Sometimes people use this moment at the podium to remember special friends, co-workers, heroes of the labor movement. This year Cesar Chavez was remembered along with the three women social service workers who were gunned down in their offices. One by one, the names are read, and the blood-red carnations accumulate on the memorial.

The reading of the names opens us to each other. Not just the names, but the experience of unsafe work behind the names. A shift occurs. We are no longer an assemblage of strangers, but a community who share a special knowledge about work and struggle. Two local men died this year. In accidents that didn't have to happen. One was digging a tunnel, laying the foundation for a new Taco Bell. Perhaps because of the heavy spring rains, or because of inadequate shoring, the earth gave way, and he was buried alive. The other was a young carpenter. He was injured on the job and died within a week. There were many blue carpenter's union caps this year, the man's family was there, his wife and two young sons. The look on the wife's face was familiar—the flat stare of shock. It is the body's way of absorbing the knowledge of loss. Then shock wears off and grief permeates the body.

Grief is physical. On this chilly April afternoon we share communal grief. It is a particular kind of knowledge—of the body at risk because of the conditions of work, of swift and sudden economic uncertainty. How to live with this knowledge is a personal question. How to put this knowledge to good use is a public and cultural question. That is the question I want to leave with you.

William: I actually took the opportunity to watch the video of this lecture twice, taking several days to think about the topic between viewing. I enjoyed the lecture very much. I could quickly identify with the awareness that I do not come from the same class background as many of my friends or even my peers in the workplaces. I come from a working-class family and am experiencing many changes as I prepare to graduate. It's a sobering feeling to realize that in a few weeks I will begin the first job of my career with a starting salary higher than my father ever made in his life, working overtime and supporting a family of four. Class does matter. It affects who I believe I am and what I believe I'm capable of.

While there were many provocative points to the lecture, I really felt strongly about the teachings of other class perspectives in the classroom. As I recall the history lessons I was taught in both elementary and high school, I remember covering essentially the same material year after year: "The Great Roman Empire fell when . . . The Renaissance started in this country . . . The cause of World War was . . ." The stories were lifeless and had nothing to do with me. . . . I liked very much hearing the quote about having a sense of community in time, and I think that's a very important issue that is not being addressed in our educational system.

Gaetana: I understood what you meant by having to work even harder in school because you were the first to attend college . . . with my family it is the same. I was the first to go to school and I had so much pressure on me it seemed all the time to do well and not smear the family name. I wonder how many students could actually relate to that? My parents were not educated. I even was almost held back from first grade because I could not speak English well, just Italian. So I have had to work at everything 100 per-

cent all alone since I could not lean on my parents to help me with my academic career. Even today my dad makes me laugh because he insists on weekends I have to come home since I don't have school . . . he thinks that on weekends, breaks, or even after school you have no homework to do.

Charles: The central theme of Decloaking Class was the problems faced by people in this world against the stigma of class and the struggles to not only recognize it but to see class for what it is. . . . Being a 29-year-old full-time student and worker, class identification is more noticeable to me now than ever before. I see it everywhere I go, in school, at work, and even places I go to eat. . . . The sad fact is that I've experienced it firsthand, I lived in the inner-city growing up and when friends of mine learned that, it was enlightening how their attitudes toward me changed. The one incident that Professor Zandy referenced which was especially poignant to me was the Ludlow incident of April 20, 1914. I have taken many history classes during school and I never recall hearing of this before this lecture. To me this is a perfect example of class invisibility.

Michael: Professor Zandy's examples of the working class being erased, distorted and omitted from history stand out the most to me. For me, and most every one else attending the lecture, it was the first time I had ever heard about the Ludlow Massacre, the National Strikes otherwise known as the Great Uprising of 1877, or the treatment of the Chinese who built the railroad. I think that many of my high school history teachers were good at what they did, but now, when I look back on it, I realize they often spent a lot of time on the important characters in history such as George Washington and Abe Lincoln. They often spent little time, if any, on the working class. I can remember learning all about the wealthy Rockefeller, Morgan, and Carnegie families, but very little about the workers they used to gain their wealth.

Jennifer: Being a college student, you get used to everyone being pretty much like yourself—poor. You usually don't have much spending money to speak of, chances are you live in a hole in the wall, whether it's on or off campus, and it's expected that you'll be especially broke around the first of the month. For us, there is very little class distinction. But growing up, I felt that my family was definitely part of the lower-working class. All you had to do was walk by our house to see that. It never occurred to me that my parents might be ashamed of the way we lived. I just figured, one day I'll get out of this. No big deal. I never thought about my parents never getting out of it, never being able to keep the Joneses in sight, let alone keep up with them. I didn't think about the fact that while I'll probably eventually have a better life than them, they'll die that way. I don't want them to die ashamed. I'm scared that my Dad already has.

Your lecture was the first time I had ever heard of Workers Memorial Day or the Ludlow massacre. It's very frightening to think that huge numbers of Americans will go through life totally ignorant of what goes on in our society, of how small a percentage of people control such enormous amounts of power and wealth. The majority of us fall into the category of working and lower classes. Do the majority of us feel desolate and ashamed? Your point about invisibility is something I see every day here at school. I was so glad to hear it mentioned. Maybe that is the first step. Maybe decloaking class and teaching people that because they are struggling doesn't mean they have to be ashamed is possible. My father said he wanted me to have a better life than he did. I now wish I had told him that I hoped I was half as good a person as he was, instead of telling him that someday I'd buy him the Cadillac he always wanted.

Mike: Professor Zandy, in your lecture "Decloaking Class: Why Class Identity and Consciousness Count," you have raised very important, but not easy to talk about issues. I would like to talk about wealth distribution. In three months I will be graduating from RIT as a Financial Manager and I am worried. My professors gave me knowledge and ability to comprehend complex economic and financial problems. I excelled at it, and I have my grades and letters of recommendation to show my future employers. I, probably, should be happy, go out, get a job, make a pot of money and live happily ever after. However, I am worried. I will always remember what [my professor] said in his Corporate Finance course. He said that our knowledge is a very powerful "sword," and our decisions will affect other people's lives, and that we need to be careful in how we make our decisions. That's why I am worried.

Before coming to the United States, I thought that there are no classes. Six years taught me a lot. In my opinion, people are judged by who they are more often than not. If you are born to a wealthy family, your chances of becoming poor are almost nil, but if you are born in a ghetto, your chances of becoming rich are almost nil. We always hear that if you work hard, you will eventually succeed. I find it difficult to believe.

Distribution of wealth in the society plays an important role in how we live our lives, what values we value, how we communicate with each other. How could the richest country in the world have so many poor and homeless people? Believe me, being born in the former Soviet Union, I am not a socialist. However, I am for social justice.

The United States remains a land of opportunity, although I wish this opportunity was available for everyone.

[1996]

Understanding the Reading

1. What does Zandy mean when she calls class a "ghost issue"?
2. How does Zandy define class?
3. What are the differences between the working class and the middle class?
4. How does power factor into our understanding of class?
5. What impact does class have on the construction of knowledge?
6. Explain the role of government in the strikes of the late nineteenth and early twentieth centuries.
7. In what ways have the rules changed today since earlier generations (the 1960s and the 1940s)?
8. What did Zandy want her books to accomplish?
9. Explain the purpose and impact of the Workers Memorial Day ceremony.

Suggestions for Responding

1. Write a paper responding to Zandy's questions in the first paragraph of the "Class Identity" section.
2. Research and report on one of the labor strikes Zandy mentions.
3. Write your response to the Zandy selection—what you learned and how you now feel about the working class.

19

The Truth about Growing Up Rich

SALLIE BINGHAM

Very few people think of rich women as being "highly vulnerable." We are usually portrayed as grasping and powerful, like Joan Collins's character in the television miniseries *Sins*. Yet in reality, most rich women are invisible; we are the faces that appear behind well-known men, floating up to the surface infrequently, palely; the big contributors, often anonymous, to approved charities, or the organizers of fund-raising events. Rich women have been so well rewarded by an unjust system that we have lost our voices; we are captives, as poor women are captives, of a system that deprives us of our identities.

Growing up a daughter in a very rich family placed me in this special position. It was important to avoid all displays of pride; what made me unusual, after all, was not really my own. I hadn't earned it. It had been given to me, willy-nilly, along with a set of commandments, largely unspoken, that enforced my solitariness:

- Always set a good example.
- Do not condescend to those who have less.
- Never ask the price of anything.
- Avoid being conspicuous in any way.

These commandments were backed by fear. Rich women are always vulnerable to criticism; we do not share the justifications of the men who actually made the money. We neither toil nor spin; yet we have access to a wide range of material comforts. But here there is a delicate line: the jewels must not be too big, nor the furs too obvious.

Often in a rich family the jewels are inherited, obscuring, with their flash and dazzle, the ambivalent feelings of the women who first wore them. In my family, attention was focused on a pair of engagement rings, one made of diamonds, the other of sapphires, which had belonged to our grandmothers. When the time came to divide the rings, my two older brothers, then adolescents, were allowed to choose. Knowing nothing about the value of jewels, but liking the color of the sapphires, the oldest chose it for his eventual bride; the younger brother took possession, by default, of the much more valuable diamonds.

Both those rings were conspicuous, which broke a cardinal tenet of my childhood. It was a rule I had broken before. All bright children are naturally conspicuous; they talk in loud voices and move about in unhampered ways. But when the whole world is watching for a mistake, this natural exuberance must be curbed. And when the child in question is a girl, the curbing is especially intense: As a sexual object, she represents the family's peculiar vulnerability to outsiders, predators—husbands. The little rich girl

must learn to sit with her legs firmly crossed and her skirt prudently down at the same time she is learning to modulate both the tone of her voice and the color of her opinions. The result is paleness.

Her models are pale as well. The hard-driving ancestor who made the fortune is not a good choice for his retiring granddaughter. Yet her female relatives, because of their learned conformity, offer little color or originality to the small girl; their rebellions are invisible, their opinions matched to the opinions of their male counterparts. The most sympathetic woman may be a maid or nurse, but her educational and social limitations restrict her effectiveness as a model. This, in turn, can lead to a split between love and admiration: the cozy, uneducated nurse is loved; the remote, perfect mother is admired. How can one satisfactory role be forged out of two contradictions?

The little rich girl realizes, with a chill, that she must treat the women around her differently. When I was a very small child, I kissed my nurse and the servants when I felt like it; as I grew older, I realized that such displays embarrassed them. As a very small child, I pitied my nurse because she had to work so hard, tending five children; a little later, I realized that such pity was inappropriate. The love doesn't change, but the little girl must look elsewhere for someone to imitate.

Obeying all the rules can never be enough, however. No amount of proper behavior can place a rich woman on comfortable terms with a world where there is so much poverty and suffering. She will always be suspect in a democracy, either as a decoration for a tyrant or as a parasite with little feeling for women struggling to survive.

Another obligation is added to the role of the third- or fourth-generation heiress, whose male relatives have led lives nearly as protected as her own. From private boarding school and Ivy League college, these men return to the family fold and a lifetime career managing assets or running the family business. The harsh bustle and hard knocks of independent life have been avoided, at some cost. Yet, since these sheltered individuals are men, they are expected to play roles of some importance in society, as executives or politicians, donors or secret political kingmakers. Unused to stress and criticism, they must be protected if they are to survive; here, the rich woman's role as peacemaker becomes crucial.

Most women are expected to balance demands for equity with a special sensitivity to human needs. We are asked to value compassion more than fairness, understanding more than critical judgment. Since family fortunes and family businesses usually descend to male heirs, this protective duty becomes essential to the maintenance of the whole structure. If the inheriting males are revealed as vulnerable and uncertain, the whole enterprise is likely to fall. And so the role of rich women becomes, essentially, that of buttressing rich men.

From this buttressing and sheltering springs an intolerance for conflict, for the harsh give-and-take that characterizes most families. A silken silence prevails, a nearly superhuman attempt to agree on every issue. This is the example provided for the children, who are at the same time secretly or openly competing for affection and favor. Emotional inhibition does not really quell raging emotional needs, which are seldom satisfied in families that value appearances highly. And since there can be no open conflict, no channels are carved out for carrying off animosity. Everything must go underground. This is a recipe for an explosion.

Explosions don't wreck most families. At worst, they cause hurt feelings and temporary alienation. But where there are no channels for the resolution of conflict, an explosion leaves nothing but desolation behind it. No one knows how to proceed.

In addition, explosions in rich families may cause a widespread tremor. Employees may be laid off, elaborate households may be dismembered because of a purely personal falling-out. The rich family supports a large number of dependents: domestics, poor relations, down-at-heel friends, the managers of charitable foundations and their grantees, enormous business ventures with their scaled layers of managers and employees, and a huge retinue of legal and financial advisers. All these people tremble when the family that supports them disagrees. This is a strong inducement to contrived peace.

But to preserve a contrived peace, some people will be permanently silenced. And since the point of view of women is generally less acceptable than the point of view of men, it will be women, in rich families, who are silenced for the sake of peace.

This leads to a good deal of distance between the women in such families. Young girls, like young boys, usually express some degree of rebellion. However, there is no way to express such a rebellion inside such a family without causing the tinkling of crystal chandeliers, which sounds too much like tears. And so the rebellious girl will never find an ally to moderate or encourage her in mother, sister, grandmother, or

aunt. They have subscribed to a system that supports them in comfort, and so the system cannot be questioned. The rebel must learn silence or leave.

Rich families shed, in each generation, their most passionate and outspoken members. In the shedding, the family loses the possibility of renewal, of change. Safety is gained, but a safety that is rigid and judgmental. And the price, for the mothers, is terrible: to sacrifice their brightest, most articulate children to the dynasty.

So around the main fire of the wealthy family one usually sees the little winking campfires of the cast-out relatives. Lacking in skills, these relatives may spend their lives on the fringes of poverty, dependent on an occasional check from home. Often they retain emotional ties with the main fire, strengthened by unresolved conflicts, but they will never thrive either within its glow or in outer darkness. Some of these cast-out souls are women.

No matter how well paid we are for our compliance, in the end, we do not inherit equally. Most rich families work on the English system and favor male heirs. There's an assumption that the women will marry well and be taken care of for life; there's an assumption that the men will do the work of the world, or of the family, and should be adequately compensated for it. When the will is read, the women inherit houses, furniture, and jewels; the men inherit cash, stocks, and securities. Yet the same commandments that rule out conspicuous behavior prevent rich women from fighting for their inheritance. Instead, we learn early to accept, to be grateful for what we are given. The slave mentality abounds in the palaces of the rich, even when the slave is decked in precious attire. We are dependent, after all, on the fickle goodwill of those who will never proclaim us their heirs.

What a fruitless arrangement this is for families, as well as for the society as a whole, may be seen in the absence of wealthy women from positions of power and influence. Without strong women models and allies, we sink into silence. Bribed by material comfort, stifled by guilt, we are not strong leaders, strong mothers, or strong friends. We are alone. And, often, we are lost.

For what personal ethic can transcend, or transform, the ethic of the men in our lives? What sense of self-justification can grow out of a sheltered, private, silenced life?

A fine sense of decorum often prevents us from cherishing friendships with women, friendships that are often untidy, provocative, and intimate. The same sense of decorum makes us hesitate to join groups that may also contain unruly elements. Our good looks and fine clothes are separating devices as well; our smooth, sophisticated deportment doesn't encourage intimacies. And so the most envied women in this country today are probably the loneliest, the least effective, the most angry and forlorn. Yet we have everything. How do we dare to complain?

"Everything" is largely material. It's the charge cards, the jewelry, the clothes. We are not taught skills, self-discipline, or self-nurturing; we are left, by and large, to fend for ourselves inside prohibitions that discourage us from experimenting. And if we are unable to persuade or force our daughters to follow our example, we will lose them in the end. And in the end, we may find ourselves totally dependent on our male relatives for friendship, status, affection, a role in life—and financial support. Such total dependence breeds self-distrust, bitterness, and fear.

It doesn't have to be this way. But in order to change, the women in a rich family must realize that its covenants are simply self-perpetuating prejudices: a prejudging of events and individuals so that no untoward thought or action will upset the family's ethic, which is, first and foremost, to preserve the status quo.

Young girls growing up isolated by wealth must find their allies, whether inside or outside the family. They must get themselves educated and prepared for careers, not at the Eastern establishments that are geared toward perpetuating male leadership, but at schools and colleges that are sympathetic to the special fears and vulnerabilities of women. And they must rid themselves of their guilt and their compulsion to smooth the way for the heirs.

This is a large bill. But the releasing of energy and hope, for this small group of wealthy women, would have results, in the country at large, far out of proportion to our numbers. What a difference it would make, for example, if rich women contributed their wealth to the causes that benefit poor women rather than to the sanitized, elitist cultural organizations favored by their fathers, brothers, and financial advisers.

What a difference it would make to women running for political office if they could draw on the massive resources of rich women, as men political candidates have drawn on the rich for generations.

What a difference it would make if wealthy women, who hire so many professionals, made sure

those professionals were women lawyers, doctors, bankers, and advisers.

What a difference it would make to women as a whole if we, who are so misperceived, became visible, actively involved in working out our destiny.

Wealthy men have always influenced the course of this nation's history. Wealthy women have, at best, worked behind the scenes. We share our loneliness, our sense of helplessness, and our alienation from the male establishment with all our sisters. Out of our loneliness and alienation, we can learn to transform the world around us, with a passion for equality that we learned, at close hand, from observing the passionate inequalities practiced by wealthy families.

[1986]

Understanding the Reading

1. What does Bingham mean when she says rich women are captives?
2. What is the responsibility of a rich woman to her family, especially to its males?
3. Why is conflict especially difficult in rich families?
4. Why are rich women "silenced" and lonely?
5. What effects would changing the lives of rich women have on society?

Suggestions for Responding

1. Most of us dream that being rich would make us happy; however, as Bingham points out, wealth has disadvantages. What drawbacks, beyond those she describes, do you think you might face if you were a female or a male member of a very wealthy family?
2. Can you think of any advantages a working-class life would have over a wealthy one?

20

Daddy Tucked the Blanket

RANDALL WILLIAMS

About the time I turned 16, my folks began to wonder why I didn't stay home anymore. I always had an excuse for them, but what I didn't say was that I had found my freedom and I was getting out.

I went through four years of high school in semirural Alabama and became active in clubs and sports; I made a lot of friends and became a regular guy, if you know what I mean. But one thing was irregular about me: I managed those four years without ever having a friend visit at my house.

I was ashamed of where I lived. I had been ashamed for as long as I had been conscious of class.

We had a big family. There were several of us sleeping in one room, but that's not so bad if you get along, and we always did. As you get older, though, it gets worse.

Being poor is a humiliating experience for a young person trying hard to be accepted. Even now—several years removed—it is hard to talk about. And I resent the weakness of these words to make you feel what it was really like.

We lived in a lot of old houses. We moved a lot because we were always looking for something just a little better than what we had. You have to understand that my folks worked harder than most people. My mother was always at home, but for her that was a full-time job—and no fun, either. But my father worked his head off from the time I can remember in construction and shops. It was hard, physical work.

I tell you this to show that we weren't shiftless. No matter how much money Daddy made, we never made much progress up the social ladder. I got out thanks to a college scholarship and because I was a little more articulate than the average.

I have seen my Daddy wrap copper wire through the soles of his boots to keep them together in the wintertime. He couldn't buy new boots because he had used the money for food and shoes for us. We lived like hell, but we went to school well clothed and with a full stomach.

It really is hell to live in a house that was in bad shape 10 years before you moved in. And a big family puts a lot of wear and tear on a new house, too, so you can imagine how one goes downhill if it is teetering when you move in. But we lived in houses that were sweltering in summer and freezing in winter. I woke up every morning for a year and a half with plaster on my face where it had fallen out of the ceiling during the night.

This wasn't during the Depression; this was in the late 1960s and early 1970s.

When we boys got old enough to learn trades in school, we would try to fix up the old houses we lived in. But have you ever tried to paint a wall that crumbled when the roller went across it? And bright paint emphasized the holes in the wall. You end up more frustrated than when you began, especially when you know that at best you might come up with only enough money to improve one of the six rooms in the house. And we might move out soon after anyway.

The same goes for keeping a house like that clean. If you have a house full of kids and the house is deteriorating, you'll never keep it clean. Daddy used to yell at Mama about that, but she couldn't do anything. I think Daddy knew it inside, but he had to have an outlet for his rage somewhere, and at least yelling isn't as bad as hitting, which they never did to each other.

But you have a kitchen which has no counter space and no hot water, and you will have dirty dishes stacked up. That sounds like an excuse, but try it. You'll go mad from the sheer sense of futility. It's the same thing in a house with no closets. You can't keep clothes clean and rooms in order if they have to be stacked up with things.

Living in a bad house is generally worse on girls. For one thing, they traditionally help their mother with the housework. We boys could get outside and work in the field or cut wood or even play ball and forget about living conditions. The sky was still pretty.

But the girls got the pressure, and as they got older, it became worse. Would they accept dates knowing they had to "receive" the young man in a dirty hallway with broken windows, peeling wallpaper and a cracked ceiling? You have to live it to understand it, but it creates a shame which drives the soul of a young person inward.

I'm thankful none of us ever blamed our parents for this, because it would have crippled our relationships. As it worked out, only the relationship between our parents was damaged. And I think the harshness which they expressed to each other was just an outlet to get rid of their anger at the trap their lives were in. It ruined their marriage because they had no one to yell at but each other. I knew other families where the kids got the abuse, but we were too much loved for that.

Once I was about 16 and Mama and Daddy had had a particularly violent argument about the washing machine, which had broken down. Daddy was on the back porch—that's where the only water faucet was—trying to fix it and Mama had a washtub out there washing school clothes for the next day, and they were screaming at each other.

Later that night everyone was in bed and I heard

Daddy get up from the couch where he was reading. I looked out from my bed across the hall into their room. He was standing right over Mama and she was already asleep. He pulled the blanket up and tucked it around her shoulders and just stood there and tears were dropping off his cheeks, and I thought I could faintly hear them splashing against the linoleum rug.

Now they're divorced.

I had courses in college where housing was discussed, but the sociologists never put enough emphasis on the impact living in substandard housing has on a person's psyche. Especially children's.

Small children have a hard time understanding poverty. They want the same things children from more affluent families have. They want the same things they see advertised on television, and they don't understand why they can't have them.

Other children can be incredibly cruel. I was in elementary school in Georgia—and this is interesting because it is the only thing I remember about that particular school—when I was about eight or nine.

After Christmas vacation had ended, my teacher made each student describe all his or her Christmas presents. I became more and more uncomfortable as the privilege passed around the room toward me. Other children were reciting the names of the dolls they had been given, the kinds of bicycles and the grandeur of their games and toys. Some had lists which seemed to go on and on for hours.

It took me only a few seconds to tell the class that I had gotten for Christmas a belt and a pair of gloves. And then I was laughed at—because I cried—by a roomful of children and a teacher. I never forgave them, and that night I made my mother cry when I told her about it. In retrospect, I am grateful for that moment, but I remember wanting to die at the time.

[1975]

Understanding the Reading

1. How did Williams feel about his life as a child? Why?
2. Why did Williams's parents fight?
3. How did Williams's parents really feel about each other?
4. What impact do peers and the media have on impoverished children?

Suggestions for Responding

1. Write a short essay describing why you think Williams's parents finally divorced.

2. Research how problems of poverty and homelessness are solved in other modern industrial nations. How do their rates of poverty compare to ours?

21

Homeless in America

Sabena Siddiqui

Even as California became the sixth-largest economy between the United Kingdom and France, as well as the world's wealthiest subnational entity, it hit the headlines for more dismal reasons, as 25 percent of the people without a roof over their heads in the United States happen to be in sunny California. Around 55,188 people lack shelter in Los Angeles, while 76,501 have been recorded in New York City. Homelessness has spiked for the first time in seven years after the recession, and California is responsible for this surge. In 2017, nearly 554,000 Americans "slept rough," and one out of every five of these were from either New York City or Los Angeles, according to the U.S. Department of Housing and Urban Development report.

Unexpectedly, it is the rich Santa Clara County, home to the famous Silicon Valley, with seventy-six thousand millionaire households, that saw the highest increase in homelessness from 2016 to 2017. Having the largest income gap and facing the highest number of homeless deaths, this rich state now has nearly 134,000 shelterless people. Sleeping in vehicles, living in makeshift tents on Los Angeles thoroughfares, or hiding in uninhabitable places, these Americans have no place to call home.

Usually the headcount is carried out on a specific date in January annually and can vary, but these figures were the highest compiled in seven years. Cities in the coastal states of California, Oregon, and Washington showed spiraling statistics that prompted nearly ten city and county governments to declare a state of emergency since 2015.

Perceiving no end in sight to the crisis, working in Los Angeles since 1984, Bob Erlenbusch complains, "I never in a million years thought that it would drag on for three decades with no end in sight." Around one-third of the homeless are African Americans, mostly living in tents. Furthermore, those who work with these communities often say there is an undercount, as a proper survey cannot be carried out in a single night. The same survey is submitted in front of Congress and government agencies responsible for distributing money for programs to help the homeless. Facing disease outbreaks and hygiene issues, the homeless population in California had a devastating hepatitis A epidemic, and a state of emergency had to be announced in October.

Ostensibly the national poverty rate fell to the same level as before the recession, but economic growth indirectly contributed to homelessness as housing became more expensive and beyond the reach for the average wage earner. Hourly wages grew at a snail's pace over the decades, from $16.74 in 1973 to just $17.86 in 2016, as reported by the Economic Policy Institute.

Consequently, when the suitable hourly wage for renting a one-room apartment becomes $27.29 in New York City and $22.98 in Los Angeles, homelessness is unavoidable. Acknowledging this factor, Housing and Development Secretary Ben Carson observed that rents were rising "much faster" than incomes in cities like Los Angeles and New York.

Despite a vibrant stock market and a growing gross domestic product, poor Americans struggle to make ends meet. The suburbs are getting poorer, and the race for survival is getting tougher, as rents have escalated beyond affordability while wages have not registered the same increase. Thomas Butler Jr., one of the tent dwellers in downtown Los Angeles, says, "A lot of people in America don't realize they might be two checks, three checks, four checks away from being homeless."

Making matters worse, homeless people receive no rental assistance from the government even though it prefers to spend double on giving wealthy Americans a reduction in housing taxes. Government schemes for affordable housing could have solved the problem, but the tax reforms passed by Congress only make funding more difficult.

Trying to find solutions, the people of Los Angeles taxed themselves and raised billions, but California still has the highest poverty rate if housing costs are considered—around 20.4 percent. Commenting on the crisis, Sara Kimberlin from the California Budget and Policy Center was disappointed that the vibrant state economy hadn't "translated into a quality of life improvement for a lot of Californians." Meanwhile, small makeshift housing colonies have come up in Oregon and Washington State, while Hawaii is working on tent encampments on a self-help basis.

Meeting more success in resolving the issue, New York City has come up with a system whereby people can get a cot to sleep; thus, even though it has 76,000 homeless, only 5 percent are considered without shelter. On an urgent footing, the U.S. government needs to work with communities and nonprofit organizations working on the ground to resolve the crisis, as California alone needs an estimated 180,000 new housing units yearly to keep up with its population growth.

Understanding the Reading

1. What has caused this increase in homelessness in California and New York City?
2. Describe the federal government's response to the homeless.
3. Why is this extensive homelessness a problem for all in the United States, both nearby and across the country?

Suggestions for Responding

1. Research the extent of homelessness in your state, and separately in at least two counties.
2. Does the U.S. government have a duty to form and enact housing policy for those in poverty?

Suggestions for Responding to Part III

1. Most of the writers in part III discuss in one way or another how family values and attitudes, language, leisure activities, manners, dress, possessions, and education influence and reflect socioeconomic class. Describe how your socioeconomic class was reflected in such features during your own childhood and youth. Since socioeconomic class is strongly influenced by race and ethnicity, some of your considerations may overlap. Careful thinking should help you sort out the economic factors and come to a fuller understanding of another of the complex factors that shape your identity.

2. If you no longer live in the socioeconomic class into which you were born, consider how and why the change took place. In what ways have you retained the influences of your earlier class experience? What characteristics, behaviors, and values of that class have you rejected, either consciously or unconsciously? Evaluate the strengths of both classes.

3. In recent years, homelessness has become a severe problem throughout the country. Research the manifestations of homelessness in your region. What are the estimated number and proportion of homeless people? What demographic categories—such as gender, age, and racial and ethnic groupings—do they represent? To what causes can your local homelessness problem be attributed? What programs, both governmental and private sector, exist to assist homeless people? What additional services are needed?

Suggestion for Responding to Identity

Apply the concepts you have explored in *Identity* to write an autobiographical report about how your present identity has been shaped by your race and ethnicity, your gender, and your economic class.

Power

POWER IN ITS SIMPLEST SENSE means the ability to do, act, think, and behave as we like, to have control over our own lives. Because we are members of society as well as individuals, however, there are substantial restrictions on our ability to exercise this kind of personal power. Society influences who we are, what we can do, how we act, what we believe or think about, and—central to our purposes here—how we interact with others.

Most interpersonal relationships reflect the relative power of the individuals involved, and the individual with the greater power can exercise greater control. We derive power from our capacity to distribute rewards or punishment, from being liked or admired, or from our position of authority or expertise. If, for example, John is more in love with Shelby than she with him, she can exercise power over him, deciding where they go for dinner or how often they go out. She can reward him with her company or punish him by refusing to see him. Similarly, you may proofread a paper more carefully for a professor you like than for one whose lectures you find boring. Physicians and plumbers have power over their clients who need their expert services. However, not all social power differentials are determined by or are under the control of the individual.

Our society is organized **hierarchically**—that is, it is structured according to rank and authority—and power is distributed unevenly within this hierarchy. Moreover, membership in a particular group, in and of itself, tends either to enhance or to reduce one's power because some groups of people have more power and others have less. Access to power and our place in the social hierarchy both depend on a number of variable factors, including gender, race, sexual orientation, socioeconomic class, age, and religion.

In our society, men often have more power than women, white people more power than people of color, heterosexuals more than homosexuals, wealthy people more than workers, and so on. The intersection of these hierarchies confers the greatest social power on the group at the "top" of each scale: white heterosexual men *as a group*. Their power relative to other groups both rests on and reflects their greater wealth, more prestigious positions, and greater access to information and education. Thus, even though individual men may be relatively powerless (a gardener employed by a wealthy widow, for instance), *as a group* white, heterosexual men are better able to control their own lives, to influence and control others, and to act in their own interests.

People who have established power under any social system find it beneficial to retain that system and maintain the status quo. The interests and needs of members of less powerful social groups are not relevant to their goals. In fact, within any social system, mechanisms operate to **marginalize**, confine to the edges of society, and subordinate its less powerful members. This is often accomplished by projecting stereotypes onto others.

A **stereotype** is a set of assumptions and beliefs about the physical, behavioral, and psychological characteristics assigned to a particular group or class of people. If we know that someone belongs to a given group, we make other suppositions about that person by attributing to him or her those qualities and characteristics we associate with that group. Stereotypes exist for every class of people imaginable; they can be based on such identifiers as age, education, profession, regional origin, economic status, family role, interests, sexual orientation, and disability. Stereotypes assigned by gender, race and ethnicity, and socioeconomic class, however, are the ones most deeply embedded in our culture, and the ones that we examine in the *Power* division.

Even though we may not like to admit that we stereotype people, we all do it. Stereotyping makes it easier to function in a world filled with unknowns. We use the oversimplified and exaggerated generalizations of stereotypes to filter and interpret the complexities of reality. They provide us with an easy way to both respond to and interact with this often confusing world; they also provide a simplified way to structure our social relationships.

The trouble with stereotypes, however, is that the filter also blocks our perceptions. If we see people in terms of the standardized pictures we project onto a group to which they belong, we do not see or interact with them as individuals. Worse still, we usually block and deny any characteristics that do not fit our preconceived ideas. The word *stereotype* originally referred to the solid metal plate of type used in printing. This origin reveals the truth about stereotypes: not only are they rigid and inflexible, but they also perpetuate unchanging images.

Although some stereotypes may seem harmless enough, in general, stereotyping is hardly a benign process. This is made clear by the fact that none of us likes to be pigeonholed. We actively resist seeing ourselves and those with whom we are intimate in stereotypic ways; we insist on our individuality. We apply stereotypes only to others—to those who are unknown to us or who are different from us. And herein lies the rub.

Because difference often makes us uneasy and because we tend to fear the unknown, our collective characterizations of "others" incorporate many undesirable or less valued traits or behaviors. This provides the basis for prejudice against members of those groups. Without knowledge of specific individuals or examination of how they present themselves, we make adverse judgments about them. We come to believe in their inferiority based solely on such traits as race, ethnicity, sex, class, age, disability, or sexual orientation. It is, in fact, a way of denying the inner life of that individual. These images become belief, and we often act on these beliefs.

In *Power*, we look at what happens when these **prejudices**, belief in the inferiority of people because of their membership in a certain group, are acted on. **Discrimination** is behavior that disadvantages one group in relation to another group and maintains and perpetuates conditions of inequality. In our culture, it is practiced most often against women, people of color, lesbians and gay men, and poor people. Both individuals and organizations can discriminate, either consciously or unconsciously, and discrimination can be institutionalized, built into the system. **Institutionalized discrimination** includes those policies, procedures, decisions, habits, and acts that overlook, ignore, or subjugate members of certain groups or that maintain control by one group of people over another group—lighter-skinned people over darker-skinned individuals or groups, men over women, heterosexuals over homosexuals, rich over poor. Such discrimination creates obstacles and barriers for its targets and provides unfair privileges for its beneficiaries.

In part IV, *Power and Racism*, we examine the experience of racism, discrimination against and subordination of a person or group because of color. Part V, *Power and Sexism*, takes a comparable look at discrimination against men and women in our society and the corollary mistreatment of lesbians and gays. We also focus on the power of the federal government, as they argue about women's rights in cases of violence within domestic relations. In part VI, *Power and Classism*, we consider the impact of socioeconomic class in the United States, focusing on the forces that cause economic inequities and poverty. Part VII, *Race, Class, and Gender during the Obama and Trump Administrations: A Comparative Look*, shows a time of rapid changes in the United States that crystallizes many of the ideas that we are exploring in this text.

We like to think of America as a place of liberty, equality, and justice for all, but, as the readings in *Power* document, this ideal has yet to be realized. Racism, sexism, and classism, as we will see, are intertwined and augment and reinforce one another. Moreover, they are not simply problems for minorities, women, and people who are economically disadvantaged; they are also, as a bumper sticker declares, "a social disease." The more fully each of us understands these problems, the closer we all will be to finding, if not a cure, a greatly improved society, where the pursuit of happiness is more possible and the goal is closer at hand.

Part IV
Power and Racism

RACISM IS NOT SIMPLY A BLACK AND WHITE ISSUE; IT IS the subordination of any person or group because of skin color or other distinctive physical characteristics. As discussed in the introduction to part I, racial identity is not as fixed and immutable as we think. It is a social construct—a classification based on social values—that could be said to exist only in the eye of the beholder. At one point or another, many different peoples have been considered to be racial groups—Jews, Muslims, Irish, Italians, Poles, Latinas, Latinos, Native Americans, Asian Americans, and African Americans—and have been subjected to racist treatment.

With few exceptions, Americans agree that racism is a bad thing, but there is less consensus about precisely what racism is or how it actually operates. The U.S. Commission on Civil Rights identifies two levels of racism. The first, **overt racism**, is the use of color and other visible characteristics related to color as subordinating factors. The roots of overt racism lie in our national history: the institution of slavery, the belief in the "manifest destiny" of European Americans to rule the entire North American continent, and the sense of America as a Christian nation, to name just three.

These beliefs provided the basis for and justification of racially discriminatory laws, social institutions, behavior patterns, language norms, cultural viewpoints, and thought patterns. Even after the Civil War and the abolition of slavery, new segregationist laws and practices, known as **Jim Crow**, extended overt racism against African Americans into the middle of the twentieth century. Shifting federal policies—such as removals, termination of tribal status, Indian boarding schools—greatly harmed much of the Native American culture and population. Exclusionary immigration laws and **restrictive covenants**, excluding members of certain groups from living in specified areas, limited the opportunities of Jews and Asian Americans.

The civil rights movement of the 1950s and 1960s awakened most white Americans to the evils of overt racism. However, this change of attitude by itself has been inadequate to address the residual racial inequities that survive in the second level of racism, indirect institutional subordination. More subtle, often invisible, **institutionalized racism** does not explicitly use color as the subordinating mechanism. Instead, decisions are based on such other factors as skill level, residential location, income, and education—factors that appear to be racially neutral and reasonably related to the activities and privileges concerned.

In reality, however, such practices continue to produce racist inequities because they fail to take into account the problems created by a three-hundred-year history of overt racist practices. For example, having a parent with insufficient job training is likely to mean that a child will grow up poor and attend poor schools, without access to sufficient job training, leading to another generation of deprivation and poverty. In this way, no matter how unintentionally, a wide variety of policies, procedures, decisions, habits, attitudes, actions, and institutional structures perpetuate racism—the subordination and subjugation of people of color.

Part IV examines the behavioral extension of racial prejudice: racial discrimination. One can be **prejudiced**, believing in the inferiority of certain kinds of individuals based on their membership in a certain group, but not **discriminate**, not act on those beliefs. As stated earlier, discrimination is individual, organizational, or structural behavior that disadvantages one group in relation to another group and that maintains and perpetuates conditions of inequality for members of the disadvantaged group.

Reading 22, "Why *Birth of a Nation* Still Matters in American Politics" by Frank Louis Rusciano, discusses the 1915 silent film, easily the most racist U.S. film ever made, which tells the story of two fictional families during and after the Civil War. The heroes are the Ku Klux Klan members who form to save the South. Reading 23 is a news article by Willa Frej, reporting on an Immigration and Customs Enforcement official resigning from a job that has become abhorrent to him, under the Trump administration. In reading 24, the U.S. Commission on Civil Rights reports on immigration policies, codified in a series of racial exclusion orders beginning with the 1882 Chinese Exclusion Act, which was extended to 1924 to Japanese, Koreans, Burmese, Malayans, Polynesians, Tahitians, and New Zealanders. Unfortunately, as the report makes clear, these were not the only immigration laws enacted for racist purposes. Reading 25 by Barbara Franz brings us up to date with immigration laws since 1980. Reading 26 is an article by the Southern Poverty Law Center, analyzing the effect President Trump has had on white supremacists, inciting them to active violence. Then Cory Collins (reading 27) highlights the need to understand the concept "white privilege" in its historicity, "where it comes from and why it has staying power."

Readings 28, 29, 30, and 31 consider racist treatment to which Native Americans have been and continue to be subjected. As Michael Dorris reports, the federal government has consistently initiated policies that regulate and restrict Native Americans, despite legal treaties between the Indian nations and the U.S. government. Even today, Native Americans face continued encroachments on their rights. In "Urban Native Americans," by Roberta Fiske-Rusciano, we learn of the history of the U.S. government's attempt to speed up the process of assimilation of American Indians, by enticing them to leave their communities and relocate to large U.S. cities. Although relocation of the 1950s was a failure, Indians from many tribal nations have found a place, permanently or seasonally, in America's largest cities, often forming large communities of kin.

Carol Lee Sanchez (reading 30) shows how, over the past 150 years, novels, movies, and even children's games have negated the humanity of American Indians. She also offers five actions non-Indians can take to counteract the stereotypes—to everyone's benefit. On a subtler level, as Ward Churchill argues in reading 31, the exploitation of Indian names, images, and symbols by mainstream society is racist and degrading and should be eliminated.

In reading 32, Robert Cherry reviews the various theories that historians have offered to explain one manifestation of religion-based racism: the widespread anti-Semitism of the late nineteenth and early twentieth centuries.

Most of us know the shameful episode in our national history when 40,000 Japanese aliens and 70,000 Japanese American citizens were evacuated from the entire West Coast to inland relocation camps during World War II. John Hersey's detailed narrative (reading 33) makes clear the racism implicit in that policy. As Asian Americans understand, even being assigned a positive stereotype is damaging; in reading 34, Robert Daseler demonstrates how the thirty-year-old claim that they are the "model minority" is destructive to Asian Americans, as well as to other minority groups, which are compared with them.

Next, Greg Palast and Martin Luther King III, in "Jim Crow Revived in Cyberspace" (reading 35), discuss the computerized purges of voter rolls as a threat to minority voters. In reading 36, Renée Graham states that white fear in the United States is pervasive and dangerous.

Teenager Emmett Till was one of more than forty people murdered between 1955 and 1968 in Mississippi and Alabama by white terrorists who wanted to "set an example" to blacks and civil rights workers. As the Southern Poverty Law Center reports in reading 37, Till was murdered and mutilated because he "thought he was as good as any white man."

Today, overt racism may be generally unacceptable, but in reading 38, Robert Anthony Watts describes experiences that blacks are perpetually subjected to, regardless of their achievements, that demonstrate the persistence of subtler forms of racism.

Racism continues to exist in our society because the subordination of people of color benefits those who do the subordinating. These psychological, economic, and political benefits will be reduced if racism is eliminated. However, the social costs of excluding a substantial proportion of our population from full participation in society—contributing to as well as benefiting from its bounty—are immense. Hearing the voices of those subjected to racism gives us fuller and more sympathetic insight into the problem. Even those of us who personally reject overt racism still need to take responsibility for its less visible institutionalized tentacles.

22

Why Birth of a Nation *Still Matters in American Politics*

FRANK LOUIS RUSCIANO

The silent film *Birth of a Nation* premiered in the United States more than one hundred years ago. It is noted for its cinematic technique, epic scope, and racist message, which, among other things, portrays the Ku Klux Klan (KKK) as the saviors of the South in the post–Civil War period. It is also perhaps the first political film ever produced, with a view of American history that tragically still resonates a century later.

History and memory have a symbiotic relationship, especially when the memory constructed in a film's narrative manipulates social values to turn historical facts on their head. *Birth of a Nation* presents the perennial theme of racial conflict in American politics in a manner palatable to the dominant group. This article deconstructs the film's step-by-step subversion of U.S. history to describe how its implied values are still salient in American politics.

Too often, the United States treats racial conflicts as discrete events that have little to do with past ideas or conflicts, as if each was a phenomenon peculiar to this point in history, and no other. A film such as *Birth of a Nation* should thereby be an interesting historical piece having little to do with the present racial climate in American society. But film narratives and historical narratives have synergistic relationships. The depictions of the "Wild West" in countless Westerns or the antebellum South in *Gone with the Wind* stand as examples. The former portrays a frontier tamed by gunmen and individual self-reliance when in fact guns were taken away from men entering towns and the federal government provided free land, a canal system, and troops to protect settlers from Indian attacks. The latter portrays a genteel pre–Civil War South, without reference to the horrors of slavery or the vast majority of white southerners who lived in wretched poverty.

Such tropes would just be of cultural interest if American history did not repeat them so often; the "rugged individualism" that supposedly built the West, for example, is generally viewed as an essential part of the American character. Historical and political "realities" are social constructions that reflect a society's values, and those values are, in turn, reflected in the narratives of our movies.

Hence, *Birth of a Nation*'s overall narrative is not easily dismissed; the structural racism embodied in the film's values still pervades American society and politics. The narrative's continued significance is reflected in contemporary news stories, criticisms of former president Barack Obama, political controversies, and public opinion data. Memory and history can be reconstructed when filtered through the medium of film.

"The Bringing of the African to America": "You Knew I Was a Snake . . ."

Birth of a Nation is history disguised as religious metaphor. It shows the "Eden" of a new American nation destroyed by the serpent, a civil war that resulted from the nation's sins, and the dream restored when the Aryan race takes its homeland back. Slavery was the United States' Original Sin, compounded continuously during and after the "peculiar institution's" existence. But the film turns responsibility for this sin upside down. Its first image is an African standing before a white colonist while the story explains, "The bringing of the African to America: the first seeds of disunion are sown." The passive voice in this sentence belies responsibility: traders brought Africans to America to be enslaved. Yet the film never clarifies why "the African" is here in the first place, much less who brought him; indeed, it is curious that in this film about the Civil War and Reconstruction the word *slavery* is never used. Instead of offering any explanation, the film then moves to an abolitionist meeting; the juxtaposition of the two scenes suggests that the abolitionists somehow were responsible for the blacks' presence in America, as if they were conducting what would be considered a bizarre social experiment regarding racial equality. These metaphors define the rest of the film—the serpent (the African) has been released into Eden, and the naïve abolitionists (and other whites with similar opinions) are the Eves seduced by him.

These themes arise in recent efforts to scrub American history books clean of the institution of slavery. Pressure groups wished to denote black slaves as "immigrants" who were "farm workers" in textbooks. Most of these efforts failed, but they represent a lingering notion that slavery is irrelevant to understanding the present state of American politics. Nothing could be further from the truth.

Consider the so-called birther movement that argued Barack Obama was not eligible to be president because he was born in Kenya, and his mother (and other unnamed co-conspirators) somehow forged headlines in Hawaiian newspapers announcing his birth. Even when Obama released his full birth certificate, many argued that it was fraudulent. The false claim, absurd as it was, defined Obama as "the Other," the foreigner who has no birthright in the United States; the catcalls to blacks common in the civil rights movement to "go back where you came from" echoed similar racist tropes. The birther argument is merely another example of the "bringing of the African to America"—in this case, to somehow make him president of the United States. *Birth of a Nation* is a cautionary tale of what would occur if blacks achieved equality and political power in the nation. The birther falsehood echoes the film's narrative, as Obama becomes the "serpent" who seduces the nation with words and causes its fall from grace.

This theme is not limited to blacks, despite their common depiction in American history. In the 2016 presidential election, Donald Trump often read lyrics from the song "The Snake" to characterize the entry of Muslim refugees and undocumented immigrants into the United States. The song describes a "tender-hearted woman" who finds a half-frozen snake, takes him home, and nurtures him with milk and honey by the fire. When she arrives home the next day:

> She clutched him to her bosom, "You're so beautiful," she cried
> "But if I hadn't brought you in by now you might have died"
> She stroked his pretty skin again and kissed and held him tight
> Instead of saying thanks, the snake gave her a vicious bite.

The snake provides the moral of the story: "'Oh shut up, silly woman,' said the reptile with a grin/'You knew damn well I was a snake before you took me in.'"

Once again, the serpent appears and is "brought in" by a naïve woman, seduced by its beauty and its "pretty skin." This Oscar Brown Jr. song was a warning about misplaced trust in a male/female relationship, given its phallic representations. Trump's use of the song on the campaign trail emphasized the "bringing of the snake into Eden" metaphor that *Birth of a Nation* uses so well. The woman in the song is equivalent to the naïve abolitionists who believed racial equality was possible. This symbolism, and the birther movement that Trump promoted, suggest a cycle of naiveté, seduction, and destruction evident in the film.

A key question regarding societies is where they store their concept of evil. The usual place is in its depictions of "the Other" who intrudes upon, disrupts, and corrupts the community. Blacks have traditionally filled this role throughout American history, with other groups (most recently Muslims and undocumented immigrants) also contributing threatening visages. As representations of evil, these particular groups can never be legitimate members of the community. While the blame for this exclusion clearly lies with the society itself, it is blamed upon those who are disenfranchised. *Birth of a Nation* lays the onus of responsibility on the former slaves, justifying the actions of the southerners to repress them.

This blame is similarly meted out in contemporary American politics. Many of Barack Obama's critics stated that racial divisions in the United States worsened while he was president and he is responsible despite his rigorous efforts throughout his career to state that the artificial divisions in American society could be overcome. Past history is irrelevant; he is to blame for racial antagonisms because he is the first black president, rather than those who refuse to accept him.

The Roots of the Civil War: What Are We Fighting For?

Birth of a Nation focuses primarily on two families: the Stonemans of Philadelphia and the Camerons of South Carolina. At the beginning of the film, the Stoneman sons come to visit the Camerons. It is unclear how they formed a relationship, given that one family is led by an avowed abolitionist while the other family keeps slaves. Despite these potential conflicts, the visit is congenial, the brothers bond with one another, and Ben Cameron instantly falls in love with Stoneman's daughter Elsie when he sees her photo, which he keeps. These scenes will underscore the "brother against brother" tragedy of the Civil War; we know the two sets of brothers will end up fighting for opposite sides when hostilities begin. What is left oddly unclear is why they will be fighting.

The Stonemans are shown around the Camerons' plantation and witness slaves picking cotton; despite their father's opposition to slavery, the northern brothers do not seem at all disturbed by the slaves working. Indeed, they barely notice them, except when the slaves entertain them by dancing during their "two-hour dinner break after ten hours of work." The implicit implication is that slavery is a seemingly benevolent system. But if this is so, why was the Civil War fought in the first place?

The Cameron family patriarch answers this question. Clutching a newspaper, he declares, "If the North wins the election, the South will secede!" It is unclear what he means by "the North winning the election." This problem is reified later in the film when Abraham Lincoln appears as a benevolent figure, "the best friend the South had," even though he was the North's antislavery candidate whose election prompted the Civil War.

This contradiction follows from another historical revision that the film perpetrates. The Civil War was not caused by states' rights so much as the rights of the U.S. territories. After the Louisiana Purchase and the Mexican War, the newly acquired land areas were designated territories that could elect to become states once their population reached a certain level. However, the question arose as to whether these new states would enter the Union as free or slave states. The conflict arose because the new states would decide this status for themselves.

The United States struggled with slavery versus antislavery issues in politics for some time before the Constitution was written. Several compromises were designed to allay southern fears that the northern states would ban slavery if they ever gained a majority. Provisions like the Three-Fifths Compromise in the Constitution gave the slave-holding states a political advantage over the nonslave states by providing extra representation based upon partial counting of a slave population that could not vote.

The introduction of new states from the territories threatened to upset the delicate balance between free and slave states. As a result, the territories often became battlegrounds for slavers and abolitionists; for example, the phrase *bleeding Kansas* described the violence there prior to the decision on slavery. Finally, the U.S. Supreme Court's *Dred Scott* decision (1854) decided that slaves, as property, still belonged to their owners, even if they were brought to a free state. This decision, in effect, sanctioned slavery in all states so long as slaves were legally purchased elsewhere.

The film is vague on these causes for two reasons. First, this vagueness allows the director D. W. Grif-

fith to avoid the topic of slavery by never calling it by its name. It also perpetuates the myth that the Civil War was actually a "War between the States," or a matter of "sectionalism" or "states' rights." The conflict's roots actually grew out of states' rights, as the new states had the right to decide whether they would enter the Union as free or slave. Fearing a potential majority of free states politically and geographically, the southern states seceded from the United States.

Compounding the Original Sin: The Strange Case of the "Mulatto"

One of the film's defining characters is the person of mixed white and black race, referred to as the "mulatto." These are the most dangerous characters in *Birth of a Nation*—a combination of white intelligence married to black savagery. The negative stereotypes of other black characters show them as feral beings unrestricted by reason or morality (with the exception of a few former loyal slaves). But mulattos are an unholy combination of man and beast, the Calibans of the Americas. Moreover, the character threatens the very distinction between blacks and whites. As long as the races are kept separate, the issue of identity is supposedly solved; if the races intermix, however, racial identity becomes a question of percentages muddying the distinctions upon which white supremacy rests. Hence, anyone who had "even one drop of black blood in them," as the oft-repeated phrase stated, was black. Put another way, anyone who was not completely white was black. In the United States' contemporary political climate, even the most liberal individuals cite Barack Obama as the first black president, despite the fact that he is mixed race with an African father and a Caucasian mother.

James Baldwin raises the most important issue that *Birth of a Nation* avoids concerning "the mulatto":

> But how did so ungodly a creature as the mulatto enter this Eden, and where did he come from?
>
> The film cannot concern itself with this inconvenient and impertinent question . . . We need not pursue it, except to observe that almost all mulattoes, and especially at that time, were produced by white men, and rarely indeed by an act of love. The mildest possible word is coercion, which is why white men invented the crime of rape.

One might reasonably argue that Baldwin overstates the case when he says white men "invented the crime of rape." Yet "mulattos" were virtually always originated when white slavemasters raped their black female slaves. One of the film's most outrageous misrepresentations is that there were few mulattos in the South; consider that it only includes two mixed-race characters. Modern DNA testing debunks this illusion by exposing how common mixed-race ancestry is in the United States. DNA was not even necessary to refute the film's claim back in 1915; it was an open secret that such rapes and subsequent births occurred. This practice was privately known but never publicly discussed, and *Birth of a Nation* continues that silence.

The mulatto's origins are a particular problem in *Birth of a Nation*. Slavery is the Original Sin of the United States—a sin compounded and amplified by the rape of female slaves. One may more or less elide the discussion of how and why "the bringing of the African" to America occurred, but questions would still linger about mulattos' origins.

D. W. Griffith solves this problem by introducing the second character, the mulatto servant—and apparent mistress—of the abolitionist Senator Stoneman. The film bemoans the relationship between the master and servant, implying that the woman's manipulations compel Stoneman to deceive himself about the possible equality of blacks and whites. In one scene, she is asked to retrieve the hat of a white male visitor. She defiantly drops the hat in front of the man and responds arrogantly when he orders her to pick it up and give it to him. As he leaves, the servant tears her blouse and falls to the floor, feigning an attempted sexual assault. At first, the whole scene appears misplaced—as does the servant, who disappears entirely from the film after the first half. But her behavior suggests how she (and other black women) feigned sexual assault while seducing their white masters. Hence, the white masters, while perhaps not blameless, were caught in a moment of weakness by black seductresses who later claimed they were raped. Once again, the society's evil lies within its victims.

This scene also justifies much of what occurs in the second half, which deals with the Reconstruction Period—black men seek sex with white women, even when the women do not consent (which the film implies they would never do in any case). By planting this idea in the viewers' heads, the real issue becomes not the rape of black women by white masters but the rape of white women by black men.

These tropes are repeated in contemporary American politics and culture. The depiction of the black male as predator has helped fill U.S. prisons with African American men in numbers disproportionate to those in the population. As former speaker of the U.S. House of Representatives Newt Gingrich stated in the late 1980s, "If I am standing next to a black man as opposed to a white man, chances are better that the black man is a criminal," echoing the sentiments displayed in *Birth of a Nation*.

The image of the black woman as a manipulative seductress also prevails to this day. When Barack Obama was first running for president, his wife, Michelle, was accused of being a racist. Once in the White House, she adopted a social cause, as first ladies have done since Jacqueline Kennedy first chose to redecorate the White House. Michelle Obama's program focused on addressing the epidemic of childhood obesity by emphasizing exercise and healthy eating. Critics, most notably Sarah Palin, accused her of trying to dictate to mothers how they should raise their children, as if playing outside and eating fruits and vegetables were part of a conspiracy. The underlying theme was that the black woman was trying to usurp the rights of white women, especially in the sacred position of motherhood. In many ways, mistrust of the black woman mirrors the mistrust of the black man in the film—both are viewed as sexual predators in their different roles as male and female.

The Civil War and Its Aftermath: Reconstructing Reconstruction

Some of Griffith's most masterful scenes depict the Civil War and its costs, although these are mostly felt by the South; the one reference to northern sacrifices is Stoneman's loss of his two sons in the fighting, despite the North's higher death toll on the battlefield. One sees increasing poverty in the South as the war drags on, as well as a brilliant depiction of Sherman's march across Georgia with weeping women on a hillside overlooking the carnage. The last image of the first half of the film shows Union and Confederate soldiers lying dead on the battlefield, after which a signboard describes this as "War's legacy." Even in the midst of the battles, however, the Union and Confederate soldiers show a deep sense of camaraderie. When Stoneman's son is about to bayonet a Confederate soldier and recognizes him as an old friend from the Cameron family, he rejoices, only to be cut down by a bullet and die next to him. When Ben Cameron rushes the Union lines in a final dash forward, he takes time to give water to a fallen Union soldier, drawing cheers from his enemies before he collapses on their front lines. And when a captured Colonel Cameron is recovering in a Union hospital and finds out he will be executed as a spy, his mother and sister successfully petition President Lincoln (described here as "The Great Heart") to pardon him.

The supposed camaraderie between Union and Confederate soldiers foreshadows a later scene in which former Confederates are saved from black troops by two former Union soldiers, in a show of solidarity for their shared "Aryan race." Indeed, the tragedy of the war is depicted in the white soldiers' deaths on both sides, despite the high death toll of black soldiers fighting for the North. More confusing is the portrayal of Abraham Lincoln in the film. He is shown positively, arguing that the South should not be punished but welcomed back into the Union "as if they had never tried to leave." By contrast, Stoneman and others feel the South should be penalized for secession and war. Another incongruity helps to explain this apparent contradiction in Lincoln's depiction. When the film's Lincoln welcomes the South back into the Union, he does not mention the Emancipation Proclamation. That document, issued in 1863, freed all slaves in the "rebellious territories"—that is, the southern states that tried to secede. Even if the southern states were treated as if they had never left, they could no longer keep their slaves. This meant Lincoln was responsible for the black freedmen who presented such a threat to the southerners in the second half of the film. Like all references to slavery, however, this point is ignored in the joyous scene when Cameron and his family set out to "rebuild the South" after the war. After Lincoln is assassinated by a sinister-looking John Wilkes Booth (whom the film neglects to mention was a southerner disgruntled over the outcome of the Civil War), his death allows the more "radical" elements in government to take over policy toward the South, and the northerners' "naïve" beliefs about racial equality precipitate a disaster.

This disaster unfolds as whites from the North "buy" votes from former slaves with promises of "forty acres and a mule." Black voters pack the ballot boxes with extra votes while black soldiers block southern whites from voting. As a consequence, Silas Lynch (a rather unfortunately named mulatto character) is elected lieutenant governor of South Carolina, the state legislature has a black majority, and the courts are filled with black judges and juries. None of this is historically correct. A black majority legislature passes laws that require whites to salute black officers in uniform and allow interracial marriage, while the black courts acquit black defendants as aggrieved white victims watch helplessly.

These circumstances never occurred in history, but their meaning in the film remains significant. The mere election of a mulatto executive and black legislators is sufficient reason for concern, without any discussion of their qualifications. Equal access to public areas is interpreted as an affront to whites. Marriage equality between the races prompts black legislators to leer at white southern women in the gallery, implying that blacks cannot distinguish between marriage and rape. When the black courts acquit a black man, his guilt or innocence is never discussed; the sorrowful faces of the whites in the courtroom are sufficient evidence that an injustice has been done. Two lessons are learned: First, offering equality to blacks necessarily means depriving whites of their rights. A black using the public space implies that whites may not, and blacks marrying whites foreshadows the rape of white women (even though, until very recently, husbands had the right to rape their wives regardless of color). Further, blacks winning in court implies that whites lose, regardless of the case's circumstances. Equality necessarily becomes a zero-sum game between whites and blacks.

However, the dire scenarios depicted in the film are inaccurate. Whites were not prevented from voting, although their states had to declare an end to their rebellion before being readmitted to the Union. The supposed promise of "forty acres and a mule" for black votes was not policy; rather, it referred to an order by General William Tecumseh Sherman during his advance through the South. Former slaves attached themselves to Sherman's advancing army; to avoid a large refugee problem, he ceded to slaves forty acres of abandoned land and some unneeded army mules to encourage them to settle as he advanced. The order existed only for a year, but it became a symbol of supposed black entitlement at the cost of whites' lands. Moreover, although blacks did dominate some state legislatures (notably for a short time in Mississippi), these bodies were neither more nor less corrupt than former ones had been. Some citizens complained of high taxation, but the revenue was needed for improvements in education for newly freed slaves.

Within the movie, the supposed indignities imposed on whites by blacks who gained power justify extending the American Original Sins of slavery and rape into the post-Reconstruction period. In reality, after federal troops were removed from the South, there was mass disenfranchisement, manipulation of the justice system according to race, and racial dominance of elected positions and power. But these were conditions imposed on blacks by whites in the southern states. Sadly, the U.S. federal government did nothing to interfere with southern tactics like literacy tests, poll taxes, intimidation, segregation, and—when all else failed—violence, including the lynching of blacks viewed as a threat.

These actions become justified by inverting the victimhood of rape in the film. A black soldier named Gus sees the youngest Cameron sister getting water from a stream and follows her, causing her to flee in fear. He yells that he wants to "marry her," which, as noted in the film, is a euphemism for rape to black men. The sister climbs a mountain to escape and threatens to jump if he comes closer; when he advances, she jumps to her death and is found and borne off by her brother Ben Cameron. Given the black dominance of the courts, it falls to the Ku Klux Klan to act as vigilante force to bring Gus to justice. They "judge" him guilty, kill him, and dump his body on the Lieutenant Governor Silas Lynch's doorstep. In response, Lynch orders Union soldiers (who for some reason are all black) to arrest or kill any individuals with Klan uniforms. The soldiers find a uniform in the Cameron household, Stoneman's daughter Elsie breaks off her relationship with Ben Cameron as a result, and the old Cameron family patriarch is arrested in chains. He is freed with the help of the "faithful souls" (former household slaves who remain loyal to the family, even though they are never given names or justifications for their "faithfulness"). The rescuers flee and take refuge in the cabin of two former Union soldiers, where their shared "Aryan heritage" is sufficient reason for their former enemies to shelter them from the approaching black troops.

At the same time, Silas Lynch proposes marriage to Elsie; she rudely refuses him, so he states that he will force the nuptials. In a telling scene, Lynch informs Stoneman that he intends to marry a white woman. Stoneman congratulates him profusely—until he learns the woman is his daughter, upon which he protests vehemently. Ignoring these pro-

tests, Lynch moves to force this marriage (read: rape) upon Elsie, using black troops to compel her consent.

These two dramas set up the film's finale, as the Ku Klux Klan rallies its members and rides to the rescue. In scenes that would later be reminiscent of the cavalry arriving just in time, the Klan rescues the Camerons and the Union soldiers, and it prevents Lynch from forcing marriage upon Elsie. The Klan rides triumphantly down their newly conquered streets, and Elsie happily joins an unhooded Ben Cameron in the parade. The KKK subsequently disarms the blacks and prevents them from voting in any further elections.

Historical inversions about black and white actions in these scenes frame the film's emotional narrative. There were few (if any) "renegade" black soldiers in the South, since the Union forces, white and black, were strictly disciplined; moreover, all blacks were mustered out of the armed forces by 1867, long before Reconstruction ended in 1876.

Further, it is never explained why two former Union soldiers settled in the heart of the former Confederacy, or why they turn against the cause for which they fought; we are just supposed to assume they are motivated by their shared "Aryan heritage" with the escapees. The most critical inversion, however, involves the actions of Silas Lynch and Gus. The specter of blacks raping white women is the overriding justification for the Klan's actions; while such incidents could have happened occasionally, it was nowhere near the rate of serial rape of black slave women by white masters. By redefining the renegade black man as the danger, the film denies—and thereby washes away—the Original Sins of slavery and rape, and it provides the ultimate reason why blacks were not to be trusted with power: the life, liberty, happiness, and purity of white women and their race would be stained.

The film concludes with two marriages—Ben Cameron with Elsie and Stoneman's surviving son with Elsie's sister. Against the backdrop of an idyllic seaside honeymoon, the narration celebrates their unions as symbolic of the remaking of the national Union. The audience is treated to a vision of Hell in which the evil are punished and a vision of Heaven with an overlay of Christ's image, in which the good reside peacefully. The religious message is consummated: Eden is restored and the serpent is banished.

Of course, this ending begs the question of what happened to the blacks. The last we see of them in the film, they are being prevented from voting. If the

Union is Paradise regained, and we witness the birth of a true (white) nation, what is to become of the substantial black population?

James Baldwin described *Birth of a Nation* as "really an elaborate justification for mass murder." At first, such a statement seems like hyperbole; after all, nowhere does the film actually advocate the mass extermination of blacks. But even the most hideous of dictators seldom call overtly for mass murder. They signal their desires by analogy, symbolism, or default, usually as a response to an "if/then" statement.

Fritz Hippler, the Nazi propagandist, produced the anti-Semitic hate film *The Eternal Jew*, in which he compared Jews to rats that spread disease. Years afterward, he still claimed that he and his colleagues never thought the Jews would be killed but would instead be sent to an unpleasant area of Eastern Europe. Bill Moyers responded that one purpose of propaganda and political communication was to stimulate people to action—and when you compare people to rats, the action that you wish to stimulate is rather clear.

The same is true of "serpents." Since blacks were responsible for the divided nation, once that division is healed, it is obvious what action should be taken. Nowhere does Griffith state that blacks should be exterminated; he merely notes that the newborn nation has no place for them. The default action implied in *Birth of a Nation* sanctions sufficient violence against blacks to intimidate others into submission. Segregation of housing, education, and public facilities easily follows, as many in the South and beyond struggled to eliminate African Americans' humanness, if not their very presence, in white life.

Segregation and disenfranchisement by law were deemed illegal in the United States by the Civil Rights Act of 1964 and the Voting Rights Act of 1965, respectively. Yet the film's messages still resonate. When Lynch mentions marrying a white woman, Stoneman approves heartily; when Lynch reveals the woman is Stoneman's daughter, the senator responds with outrage and disgust. Those of us who grew up during and after the U.S. civil rights movement in the 1960s have heard this before. Countless times when someone argued for full citizenship for African Americans, the retorts would come: "Oh, really? Well, how would you like it if one of them moved next door to you? How would you like if your daughter brought one of them home?" The dehumanizing phrase *one of them* echoes throughout American history, underscoring the message that

racial equality is acceptable only in theory and from a "safe" distance—with the implicit warning that whites needed to ensure that they were safe.

When all is said and done, segregation—whether de jure (which is now illegal) or de facto (which thrives due to economic inequalities)—is not only about keeping whites safely away from blacks. It was also meant to invalidate the black person's existence. In the classic film *The Long Walk Home* about the Montgomery bus boycott, a white matriarch announces that blacks want everything for nothing and without working; she makes this statement right in front of the black maid who has cooked and is serving her Christmas dinner. The maid ignores the comment and continues serving. The horrors of segregation portrayed in this movie reflect the lessons of *Birth of a Nation*, for there is no reason to make someone disappear if you can render them silent and more or less invisible. Either way, their personhood is erased.

Conclusions: Birth of a Nation *Redux in American Politics Today*

It is comfortable to argue that while some of the film's themes reappear briefly in American politics today, they are mere vestiges of past attitudes, anachronisms in a postmodern society. But then one would need to ignore the contrived controversy over Barack Obama's U.S. citizenship and Donald Trump's equation of Muslim refugees and undocumented immigrants with snakes.

One would also need to ignore the controversy surrounding the Black Lives Matter movement in the United States. This movement's name seems benign and self-evident; after all, who can argue that black lives do not matter? Yet the group has been described as "terrorists" for decrying police violence against blacks and blamed for horrific shootings of police by lone black assassins with no relationship to the movement. The issue, however, is evident in this response to the group's name: "What do you mean, 'black lives matter'? All lives matter!" A similar retort references the police: "Blue lives matter." But simple logic decrees if all lives matter, black lives matter; if it is not true that black lives matter, then it is not true that all lives matter. The two statements are not thesis and antithesis unless one assumes there is an inherent contradiction between them. Regarding the statement "blue lives matter," that phrase is only a retort if one assumes that the lives of police and blacks are antithetical.

This contradiction is perhaps the strongest lesson of *Birth of a Nation*. The implication is that if black lives matter, white lives—and, in particular, white policemen's lives—do not matter. Critics of the movement argue its name claims a special privilege for blacks. Yet the existential value of black lives is only a special privilege if one assumes that it is not extended to everyone. The critics essentially argue that black lives and white lives cannot both be valued, especially if one utters the seemingly magic words that "black lives matter."

Birth of a Nation implies that blacks benefit if whites lose, even if that benefit is the mere security of life. Supposed black entitlement is an issue continuously manipulated to foment white discontent. But where is the entitlement when individuals merely claim the "certain inalienable rights, among them Life, Liberty, and the Pursuit of Happiness," which our founding document claims are granted by the Creator? Of course, this document, like *Birth of a Nation*, never mentions slavery—and the United States has been struggling with that contradiction ever since.

This article begins by noting the often symbiotic relationship between films and our interpretations of history. While few (if any) would accept *Birth of a Nation* as historical fact, it inverts U.S. history and creates a social construction of historical and political reality that resonates to this day. Its narrative is based upon values that persist in American culture and are often invoked for political gain. We also believe that each incident of racial conflict is new in and of itself. *Birth of a Nation* shows the vestiges of narratives that we have not left behind. They exist as vestigial organs that become infected time and time again until—in the words of the black poet Langston Hughes—they "fester like a sore and then run."

Understanding the Reading

1. Describe a few of the ways this 1915 film "inverts" history.
2. Why does the author use biblical references, such as "the Garden of Eden," to analyze the film's storyline?
3. Why does this film still matter today in U.S. politics? What are the similar themes and devices surrounding racial tensions?

Suggestions for Responding

1. Read at least one slave narrative (e.g., *The Classic Slave Narratives*, ed. Henry Louis Gates).
2. See the documentary *Motherland: A Genetic Journey*, in which three British citizens take a genetic test to find precisely where their African Caribbean ancestors originated. They each found that the father line was European and the mother line was African, which was the sexual politics of slavery.

23

ICE Spokesman Quits, Bashes Trump Administration on Immigration Raids

WILLA FREJ

A spokesman for Immigration and Customs Enforcement in San Francisco resigned over the Trump administration's handling of a recent immigrant raid in the Bay Area.

James Schwab told the *San Francisco Chronicle* late Monday that administration officials, including Attorney General Jeff Sessions and President Donald Trump, grossly exaggerated the number of undocumented immigrants who avoided arrest after Oakland mayor Libby Schaaf tipped off the public days before the raid began on February 25.

"I quit because I didn't want to perpetuate misleading facts," Schwab said. "I asked them to change the information. I told them that the information was wrong, they asked me to deflect, and I didn't agree with that. Then I took some time and I quit."

Schwab added that even if there had been no prior warning about the raid, "We were not ever going to be able to capture 100 percent of the target list."

ICE said 232 people were arrested in the sweep but claimed the number could have been higher. "Efforts by local politicians have shielded removable criminal aliens from immigration enforcement and created another magnet for more illegal immigration, all at the expense of the safety and security of the very people it purports to protect," the agency said in a statement.

Acting ICE director Thomas Homan claimed that 864 "criminal aliens" escaped arrest, and Trump railed that close to one thousand people would have been swept up, calling Schaaf's warning "a disgrace." Sessions accused the Oakland mayor of promoting "a radical open-borders agenda."

Schwab disputed the claims and told CNN he could no longer "bear the burden—continuing on as a representative of the agency and charged with upholding integrity, knowing that information was false."

Schaaf applauded Schwab's decision. "Our democracy depends on public servants who act with integrity and hold transparency in the highest regard," the mayor said in a statement.

Sessions escalated the dispute last week by filing a lawsuit against the state of California over its so-called sanctuary cities—areas that limit cooperation with federal immigration authorities. California governor Jerry Brown (D) characterized the move as "basically going to war against the state of California."

The timing is uncanny, as Trump begins his first visit as president to California on Tuesday to check out prototypes for a border wall and attend a Republican fundraiser.

Understanding the Reading

1. Why did the ICE representative quit his job?
2. What is the central tension between the state of California and the federal government?
3. Why is the Trump administration focusing on undocumented immigrants?

Suggestion for Responding

1. Research how much tax money is paid annually by undocumented immigrants in the United States.

24

Historical Discrimination in the Immigration Laws

U.S. COMMISSION ON CIVIL RIGHTS

The Early Years

During the formative years of this country's growth, immigration was encouraged with little restraint. Any restrictions on immigration in the 1700s were the result of selection standards established by each colo-

nial settlement. The only Federal regulation of immigration in this period lasted only two years and came from the Alien Act of 1798, which gave the president the authority to expel aliens who posed a threat to national security.

Immigrants from Northern and Western Europe began to trickle into the country as a result of the faltering economic conditions within their own countries. In Germany, unfavorable economic prospects in industry and trade, combined with political unrest, drove many of its nationals to seek opportunities to ply their trades here. In Ireland, the problems of the economy, compounded by several successive potato crop failures in the 1840s, sent thousands of Irish to seaports where ships bound for the United States were docked. For other European nationals, the emigration from their native countries received impetus not only from adverse economic conditions at home but also from favorable stories of free land and good wages in America.

The Nativist Movements

As a result of the large numbers of Catholics who emigrated from Europe, a nativist movement began in the 1830s. It advocated immigration restriction to prevent further arrivals of Catholics into this country. Anti-Catholicism was a very popular theme, and many Catholics and Catholic institutions suffered violent attacks from nativist sympathizers. The movement, however, did not gain great political strength and its goal of curbing immigration did not materialize.

Immigrants in the mid-nineteenth century did not come only from Northern and Western Europe. In China, political unrest and the decline in agricultural productivity spawned the immigration of Chinese to American shores. The numbers of Chinese immigrants steadily increased after the so-called Opium War, due not only to the Chinese economy but also to the widespread stories of available employment, good wages, and the discovery of gold at Sutter's Mill,[1] which filtered in through arrivals from the Western nations.

The nativist movement of the 1830s resurfaced in the late 1840s and developed into a political party, the Know-Nothing Party.[2] Its western adherents added an anti-Chinese theme to the eastern anti-Catholic sentiment. But once again, the nativist movement, while acquiring local political strength, failed in its attempts to enact legislation curbing immigration. On the local level, however, the cry of "America for Americans" often led to discriminatory state statutes that penalized certain racially identifiable groups. As an example, California adopted licensing statutes for foreign miners and fishermen, which were almost exclusively enforced against Chinese.

In the mid-1850s, the Know-Nothing Party lost steam as a result of a division over the question of slavery, the most important issue of that time. The nativist movement and antiforeign sentiment receded because of the slavery issue and the Civil War. It maintained this secondary role until the Panic of 1873 struck.

Chinese Exclusion

The depression economy of the 1870s was blamed on aliens who were accused of driving wages to a substandard level as well as taking away jobs that "belonged" to white Americans. While the economic charges were not totally without basis, reality shows that most aliens did not compete with white labor for "desirable" white jobs. Instead, aliens usually were relegated to the most menial employment.

The primary target was the Chinese, whose high racial visibility, coupled with cultural dissimilarity and lack of political power, made them more than an adequate scapegoat for the economic problems of the 1870s. Newspapers adopted the exhortations of labor leaders, blaming the Chinese for the economic plight of the working class. Workers released their frustrations and anger on the Chinese, particularly in the West. Finally, politicians succumbed to the growing cry for exclusion of Chinese.

Congress responded by passing the Chinese Exclusion Act of 1882. That act suspended immigration of Chinese laborers for ten years, except for those who were in the country on November 17, 1880. Those who were not lawfully entitled to reside in the United States were subject to deportation. Chinese immigrants were also prohibited from obtaining U.S. citizenship after the effective date of the act.

The 1882 act was amended in 1884 to cover all subjects of China and Chinese who resided in any other foreign country. Then in 1888, another act was enacted that extended the suspension of immigration for all Chinese except Chinese officials, merchants, students, teachers, and travelers for pleasure. Supplemental legislation to that act also prohibited Chinese laborers from reentering the country, as

provided for in the 1882 act, unless they reentered prior to the effective date of the legislation.

Senator Matthew C. Butler of South Carolina summed up the congressional efforts to exclude Chinese by stating:

> [I]t seems to me that this whole Chinese business has been a matter of political advantage, and we have not been governed by that deliberation which it would seem to me the gravity of the question requires. In other words, there is a very important Presidential election pending. One House of Congress passes an act driving these poor devils into the Pacific Ocean, and the other House comes up and says, "Yes, we will drive them further into the Pacific Ocean, notwithstanding the treaties between the two governments."

Nevertheless, the Chinese exclusion law was extended in 1892 and 1902, and in 1904 it was extended indefinitely.

Although challenged by American residents of Chinese ancestry, the provisions of these exclusion acts were usually upheld by judicial decisions. For example, the 1892 act mandated that Chinese laborers obtain certificates of residency within one year after the passage of the act or face deportation. In order to obtain the certificate the testimony of one credible white witness was required to establish that the Chinese laborer was an American resident prior to the passage of the act. That requirement was upheld by the United States Supreme Court in *Fong Yue Ting v. United States*.

Literacy Tests and the Asiatic Barred Zone

The racial nature of immigration laws clearly manifested itself in further restrictions on prospective immigrants who were either from Asian countries or of Asian descent. In addition to extending the statutory life of the Chinese exclusion law, the 1902 act also applied that law to American territorial possessions, thereby prohibiting the immigration of noncitizen Chinese laborers not only from "such island territory to the mainland territory" but also "from one portion of the island territory of the United States to another portion of said island territory." Soon after, Japanese were restricted from free immigration to the United States by the "Gentleman's Agreement"[3] negotiated between the respective governments in 1907. Additional evidence would be provided by the prohibition of immigration from countries in the Asia-Pacific Triangle as established by the Immigration Act of 1917.

During this period, congressional attempts were also made to prevent blacks from immigrating to this country. In 1915 an amendment to exclude "all members of the African or black race" from admission to the United States was introduced in the Senate during its deliberations on a proposed immigration bill. The Senate approved the amendment on a 29 to 25 vote, but it was later defeated in the House by a 253 to 74 vote, after intensive lobbying by the NAACP.[4]

In 1917 Congress codified existing immigration laws in the Immigration Act of that year. That act retained all the prior grounds for inadmissibility and added illiterates to the list of those ineligible to immigrate, as a response to the influx of immigrants from Southern and Eastern Europe. Because of a fear that American standards would be lowered by these new immigrants who were believed to be racially "unassimilable" and illiterate, any alien who was over sixteen and could not read was excluded. The other important feature of this statute was the creation of the Asia-Pacific Triangle, an Asiatic barred zone, designed to exclude Asians completely from immigration to the United States. The only exemptions from the zone were from an area that included Persia and parts of Afghanistan and Russia.

The 1917 immigration law reflected the movement of American immigration policy toward the curbing of free immigration. Free immigration, particularly from nations that were culturally dissimilar to the Northern and Western European background of most Americans, was popularly believed to be the root of both the economic problems and the social problems confronting this country.

The National Origins Quota System

Four years later, Congress created a temporary quota law that limited the number of aliens of any nationality who could immigrate to 3 percent of the United States residents of that nationality living in the country in 1910. The total annual immigration allowable in any one year was set at 350,000. Western Hemisphere aliens were exempt from the quota if their country of origin was an independent nation and the alien had resided there at least one year.

The clear intent of the 1921 quota law was to confine immigration as much as possible to Western and

Northern European stock. As the minority report noted:

The obvious purpose of this discrimination is the adoption of an unfounded anthropological theory that the nations which are favored are the progeny of fictitious and hitherto unsuspected Nordic ancestors, while those discriminated against are not classified as belonging to that mythical ancestral stock. No scientific evidence worthy of consideration was introduced to substantiate this pseudoscientific proposition. It is pure fiction and the creation of a journalistic imagination. . . .

The majority report insinuates that some of those who have come from foreign countries are nonassimilable or slow of assimilation. No facts are offered in support of such a statement. The preponderance of testimony adduced before the committee is to the contrary.

Notwithstanding these objections, Congress made the temporary quota a permanent one with the enactment of the 1924 National Origins Act. A ceiling of 150,000 immigrants per year was imposed. Quotas for each nationality group were 2 percent of the total members of that nationality residing in the United States according to the 1890 census. Again, Western Hemisphere aliens were exempt from the quotas (thus, classified as "nonquota" immigrants). Any prospective immigrant was required to obtain a sponsor in this country and to obtain a visa from an American consulate office abroad. Entering the country without a visa and in violation of the law subjected the entrant to deportation without regard to the time of entry (no statute of limitation). Another provision, prohibiting the immigration of aliens ineligible for citizenship, completely closed the door on Japanese immigration, since the Supreme Court had ruled that Japanese were ineligible to become naturalized citizens. Prior to the 1924 act, Japanese immigration had been subjected to "voluntary" restraint by the Gentleman's Agreement negotiated between the Japanese government and President Theodore Roosevelt.

In addition to its expressed discriminatory provisions, the 1924 law was also criticized as discriminatory against blacks in general and against black West Indians in particular.

The Mexican "Repatriation" Campaign

Although Mexican Americans have a long history of residence within present United States territory,

Mexican immigration to this country is of relatively recent vintage. Mexican citizens began immigrating to this country in significant numbers after 1909 because of economic conditions as well as the violence and political upheaval of the Mexican Revolution. These refugees were welcomed by Americans, for they helped to alleviate the labor shortage caused by the First World War. The spirit of acceptance lasted only a short time, however.

Spurred by the economic distress of the Great Depression, federal immigration officials expelled hundreds of thousands of persons of Mexican descent from this country through increased Border Patrol raids and other immigration law enforcement techniques. To mollify public objection to the mass expulsions, this program was called the "repatriation" campaign. Approximately 500,000 persons were "repatriated" to Mexico, with more than half of them being United States citizens.

Erosion of Certain Discriminatory Barriers

Prior to the next recodification of the immigration laws, there were several congressional enactments that cut away at the discriminatory barriers established by the national origins system. In 1943 the Chinese Exclusion Act was repealed, allowing a quota of 105 Chinese to immigrate annually to this country and declaring Chinese eligible for naturalization. The War Brides Act of 1945 permitted the immigration of 118,000 spouses and children of military servicemen. In 1946 Congress enacted legislation granting eligibility for naturalization to Filipinos and to races indigenous to India. A presidential proclamation in that same year increased the Filipino quota from 50 to 100. In 1948 the Displaced Persons Act provided for the entry of approximately 400,000 refugees from Germany, Italy, and Austria (an additional 214,000 refugees were later admitted to the United States).

The McCarran-Walter Act of 1952

The McCarran-Walter Act of 1952, the basic law in effect today, codified the immigration laws under a single statute. It established three principles for immigration policy:

1. the reunification of families,
2. the protection of the domestic labor force, and
3. the immigration of persons with needed skills.

However, it retained the concept of the national origins system, as well as unrestricted immigration from the Western Hemisphere. An important provision of the statute removed the bar to immigration and citizenship for races that had been denied those privileges prior to that time. Asian countries, nevertheless, were still discriminated against, for prospective immigrants whose ancestry was one-half of any Far Eastern race were chargeable to minimal quotas for that nation, regardless of the birthplace of the immigrant.

"Operation Wetback"

Soon after the repatriation campaign of the 1930s, the United States entered the Second World War. Mobilization for the war effort produced a labor shortage that resulted in a shift in American attitudes toward immigration from Mexico. Once again Mexican nationals were welcomed with open arms. However, this "open arms" policy was just as short lived as before.

In the 1950s many Americans were alarmed by the number of immigrants from Mexico. As a result, then United States Attorney General Herbert Brownell, Jr., launched "Operation Wetback," to expel Mexicans from this country. Among those caught up in the expulsion campaign were American citizens of Mexican descent who were forced to leave the country of their birth. To ensure the effectiveness of the expulsion process, many of those apprehended were denied a hearing to assert their constitutional rights and to present evidence that would have prevented their deportation. More than 1 million persons of Mexican descent were expelled from this country in 1954 at the height of "Operation Wetback."

The 1965 Amendments

The national origins immigration quota system generated opposition from the time of its inception, condemned for its attempts to maintain the existing racial composition of the United States. Finally, in 1965, amendments to the McCarran-Walter Act abolished the national origins system as well as the Asiatic barred zone. Nevertheless, numerical restrictions were still imposed to limit annual immigration. The Eastern Hemisphere was subject to an overall limitation of 170,000 and a limit of 20,000 per country. Further, colonial territories were limited to 1 percent of the total available to the mother country (later raised to 3 percent or 600 immigrants in the 1976 amendments). The Western Hemisphere, for the first time, was subject to an overall limitation of 120,000 annually, although no individual per-country limits were imposed. In place of the national origins system, Congress created a seven category preference system giving immigration priority to relatives of United States residents and immigrants with needed talents or skills. The 20,000 limitation per country and the colonial limitations, as well as the preference for relatives of Americans preferred under the former selections process, have been referred to by critics as "the last vestiges of the national origins system" because they perpetuate the racial discrimination produced by the national origins system.

Restricting Mexican Immigration

After 1965 the economic conditions in the United States changed. With the economic crunch felt by many Americans, the cry for more restrictive immigration laws resurfaced. The difference from the nineteenth-century situation is that the brunt of the attacks is now focused on Mexicans, not Chinese. High "guesstimates" of the number of undocumented Mexican aliens entering the United States, many of which originated from Immigration and Naturalization Service sources, have been the subject of press coverage.

As a partial response to the demand for "stemming the tide" of Mexican immigration, Congress amended the Immigration and Nationality Act in 1976, imposing the seven category preference system and the 20,000 numerical limitation per country on Western Hemisphere nations. Legal immigration from Mexico, which had been more than 40,000 people per year, with a waiting list two years long, was thus cut by over 50 percent.

Recent Revisions of the Immigrant Quota System*

Although the annual per-country limitations have remained intact, Congress did amend the Immigration and Nationality Act in 1978 to eliminate the hemispheric quotas of 170,000 for Eastern Hemisphere countries and 120,000 for Western Hemisphere countries. Those hemispheric ceilings were replaced with an overall annual world-wide ceiling of 290,000.

In 1980 the immigrant quota system was further revised by the enactment of the Refugee Act. In addition to broadening the definition of refugee, that statute eliminated the seventh preference[5] visa category by establishing a separate worldwide ceiling for refugee admissions to this country. It also reduced the annual worldwide ceiling for the remaining six preference categories to 270,000 visas, and it increased the number of visas allocated to the second preference[6] to 26 percent.

[1980]

Terms

1. Sutter's Mill: The site where gold was discovered in 1848, precipitating the California gold rush.
2. Know-Nothing Party: A political movement in the mid-nineteenth century that was antagonistic to Catholics and immigrants.
3. Gentleman's Agreement: The 1908 treaty between Japan and the United States to restrict, but not eliminate altogether, the issuance of passports allowing Japanese immigration to the United States, except that wives could enter, including "picture brides," who were married by proxy.
4. NAACP: National Association for the Advancement of Colored People.
5. Seventh Preference: Refugee status.
6. Second Preference: Spouses and unmarried children of U.S. citizens.

Understanding the Reading

1. What were the nativist movement and the Know-Nothing Party?
2. Explain the Chinese exclusion laws.
3. Explain the national origins quota system.
4. What was Operation Wetback?
5. How do the 1965 amendments perpetuate racial discrimination?

Suggestions for Responding

1. Explain what current immigration policy is and why you think it is good and/or bad.
2. Research and report on one law or policy that was mentioned in the article.

*After the terrorist attacks on 9/11/01, the Immigration and Naturalization Service was folded into the Department of Homeland Security, whose main priority is to protect the country against attacks and to gather intelligence. The broad liberties given to the federal government by the Patriot Act have frightened many immigrants, who are afraid of being targeted, and have slowed down all immigration procedures.

25

Immigration Laws since 1980: The Closing Door

Barbara Franz

Since the 1980s, both refugee and immigration status are becoming harder to attain in the United States. Refugee protection in the United States has changed from a Cold War foreign policy tool to a policy of refugee deterrence and institutionalized exclusion. Increasingly, refugees and displaced people must remain close to or in regions of civil or environmental distress. Often states have chosen to repatriate displaced populations to their areas of origin after the initial civil or environmental misery has receded. These patterns of exclusion are reflected in the 1996 Welfare and Illegal Immigration Reform and Immigration Control Acts.

Undocumented immigration has become a key issue in the U.S. immigration debate. Laws such as the 1986 IRCA (Immigration Reform and Control Act) and the 1990 Immigration Act, state-based referenda such as Proposition 187, the post 9/11 Department of Homeland Security (DHS) and Immigration and Customs Enforcement (ICE) schemes to deport thousands of illegal immigrants.

The Immigration Reform and Control Act of 1986

Legal immigration and refugee admissions remained a minor problem during the 1970s and 1980s. What concerned the U.S. public and government was the great number of undocumented immigrants.

Although employer sanctions were at the heart of the Simpson-Mazzoli bill, it also provided for a new version of the existing H-2 visa program, which allowed for the admittance of aliens for temporary jobs. After ten years, in October 1986, the bill, which then included a compromise that satisfied the growers, won final approval in Congress.[1]

It was in a context of contradictory economic and political pressures that the U.S. Congress enacted this bill named Immigration Reform and Control Act of 1986 (IRCA). The three fundamental components of IRCA: (1) its legalization provision allowed undocumented immigrants who had been in the United States on an illegal basis since before January 1, 1982, to apply for legal residence. (2) Sanctions made it illegal for an employer to knowingly hire undocumented workers. (3) The Special Agricultural Workers provision allowed certain undocumented workers in the agricultural sector to apply for legalization and provided for the admission of additional farm workers in times of farm labor shortages. Overall the IRCA's most significant consequence was the legalization of millions of undocumented farm migrants who for years have survived on the black market. However, employer sanctions—IRCA's political centerpiece—have had little concrete impact. The most comprehensive study of their effect on illegal border crossings concludes that the initial reduction in apprehensions was less a product of employer sanctions than a predictable consequence of the IRCA's legalization provisions (by 1990, the IRCA had legalized close to 3 million immigrants). Observing the political decision-making process of IRCA were watchful voluntary organizations such as the Federation for American Immigration Reform (FAIR), the American Immigration Control Foundation (AICR), and the Center for Immigration Studies, all trying to create a "Nation of Americans." Not only have these voluntary organizations been instrumental in perpetuating the anti-immigrant sentiment that swept the nation through such projects as "Light the Border" or Proposition 187 in 1994, but they also have commissioned studies on the economic impact of immigration and financed opinion polls that reflect a growing public resentment of illegal immigration.[2]

The IRCA remains an outstanding example of U.S.

1. Barbara Franz, "Refugees in Flux: The Resettlement of Bosnian Refugees in Austria and the United States, 1992–2000" (Syracuse University, 2001): 315; David Bennett, *The Party of Fear: From Nativist Movements to the New Right in American History* (Chapel Hill: The University of North Carolina Press, 1988), 371–73.

2. Kitty Calavita, "U.S. Immigration and Policy Responses: The Limits of Legislation." In *Controlling Immigration: A Global Perspective*, edited by Wayne Cornelius, Philip Martin, and James Hollified (Palo Alto, CA: Stanford University Press, 1994), 55–82; Keith Crane, Beth Ash, Joanna Zorn Heilbrunn, and Danielle Cullinane, *Effect of Employer Sanctions*

ambivalent legislation and regulatory practices of immigration. In response to widespread public pressure to curtail the flow of illegal immigration across the U.S.-Mexico border, the act included, for the first time, employer sanctions that made hiring undocumented workers punishable and illegal. However, the employer sanctions were largely symbolic. Not only did the law include provisions like the Special Agricultural Worker and Replenishment Agricultural Worker, which made it possible for farmers and growers to employ temporary Mexican workers, but it also included an "affirmative defense clause that protects employers from prosecution as long as they request documentation from workers, regardless of the validity of the documents presented." IRCA was a response to the general public's demand for restricted movement of illegal immigration across the southern border, thus acting against the interests of agricultural and industrial employers; it also, however, paid attention to the latter's lobbying for light sanctions that would not disrupt their business.[3]

The Immigration Act of 1990

Today four major principles underlie current U.S. policy on permanent immigration: the reunification of families, the admission of immigrants with needed skills, the protection of refugees, and the diversity of admissions by country of origin. These principles are embodied in the Immigration and Nationality Act (INA). The Immigration Act of 1990 constituted a major revision of the 1952 Immigration and Nationality Act. Its primary focus was the numerical limits and the preference system regulating permanent and legal immigration. It provided for an annual worldwide limit of 700,000 permanent immigrants, with certain exceptions for close family members. The legal immigration changes included increases in total immigration under an overall flexible cap and in annual employment-based immigration (from 54,000 to 140,000), as well as a permanent provision for the

admission of "diversity immigrants" from underrepresented countries. Besides legal immigration, the act dealt with many other aspects of immigration law ranging from nonimmigrants to criminal aliens to naturalization. The act established the four-track preference system for family-sponsored, employment-based, refugee, and diversity immigrants. Additionally, the act significantly amended the work-related nonimmigrant categories for temporary admission.[4]

In the Fiscal Year 2014, 225,000 visas were issued for family reunification, 140,000 visas were employment based, 85,000 were issued for refugees and 50,000 were allotted for the diversity lottery.[5]

The 1990s legislation also addressed a series of other issues, a number of which have been overturned by the Trump administration. For example, the 1990 legislation provided undocumented Salvadorans with temporary protected status (TPS). More broadly, it amended the Immigration and Nationality Act to authorize the attorney general to grant temporary protected status to nationals of designated countries subject to armed conflict or natural disasters. Overall, the act significantly revised the political and ideological grounds for exclusion and deportation which had been controversial since their enactment in 1952. After it was signed into law in 1990 by George H. W. Bush, TPS became one of America's most effective humanitarian programs, providing residence for people in need.

Currently, there are still about 320,000 TPS recipients residing in the United States. However, the Trump administration has begun an assault on undocumented immigrants, using (among other tools) the dismantling of TPS as a method to do so. In October 2017, 2,500 Nicaraguans lost temporary protection, followed by 59,000 Haitians in November 2017. In January 2018, the administration ended TPS for 250,000 Salvadorans. A built-in 18-month enforcement delay was designed to provide time for these residents, most of whom have lived in the

on the Flow of Undocumented Immigrants to the United States (Lanham, MD: University Press of America, 1990); Franz (2001): 315–16.

3. Kitty Calavita, *Inside the State: The Bracero Program, Immigration, and the I.N.S.* (New York: Routledge, 1992), pp. 8, 169; Ali Behdad, "Nationalism and Immigration to the United States," *Diaspora* 6, no. 2 (Fall 1997): 155–78; Franz (2001): 317.

4 Calavita, *Inside the State*: 8, 169; Behdad, "Nationalism and Immigration": 155–78; Franz (2001): 317.

5. American Immigration Council, "How the United States Immigration System Works," August 12, 2016, downloaded on March 21, 2018, from https://www.americanimmigrationcouncil.org/research/how-united-st ates-immigrat ion-system-works.

United States since 2001, to find other ways to stay in the country—or to leave. The DHS estimates that, all things being equal, about 200,000 Salvadorans will be without status in September 2019. Along with construction of the proposed border wall, these policies confirm that the Trump administration is willing to trample on due process, human decency, community well-being, and even protections for vulnerable children and people, in pursuit of what Omar Jadwat, the director of the ACLU's Immigrants' Rights Project, calls "a hyper-aggressive mass deportation policy." The current assault on immigrants and other (temporary) protected residents is, of course, not the first of such attacks.[6]

Los Indocumentados *and Proposition 187*

The traditional issue of tension in U.S. immigration politics—undocumented migrants—however, did not go away after the passage of IRCA in 1986. Moreover, with Proposition 187 Californian nativism fueled a backlash against illegal workers which spread over the entire United States. While commentators agreed that many immigrants came to California to find jobs, backers of Proposition 187 felt that free public education, health care, and additional welfare benefits served as magnets for illegal immigrants and drained the state budget (with education costs alone estimated by some at close to $2 billion in the early 1990s, and $7.7 billion in 2006). A series of federal court rulings declared most of the proposition's major sections to be unconstitutional. Underlying most of the rulings was the argument that California was attempting to regulate immigration, a responsibility that solely belonged to the federal government.[7]

The Proposition 187 movement spread to other states, and brought to light deep-seated feelings held by many Americans about immigration and refugee issues which influenced the congressional debate on immigration and welfare legislation.[8]

The Welfare Reform Act of 1996 and the Illegal Immigration Reform and Immigration Responsibility Act

Nativist fears and patriotic subjects also influenced congressional debates over the passage of the U.S. 1996 Illegal Immigration Reform and Immigration Responsibility Act (IIRIRA). IIRIRA derived at least in part from the influx of Haitians into the United States. The so-called Haitian crisis was perhaps the biggest U.S. refugee dilemma in the 1990s. Washington began to forcibly return Haitian refugees without a hearing. This forced return of more than 40,000 Haitian refugees in and after 1991 was soundly criticized for violating national and international prohibitions against *refoulement* (forced return) and selectively discriminating against Haitians. The U.S. government's treatment of Haitians contrasts sharply with that accorded to Cubans, who for years have journeyed to the United States to escape Fidel Castro's communism. While Haitians have been routinely sent back, Cubans have been automatically allowed into the United States.[9]

The 1996 IIRIRA ushered in the era of enforcement-dominated immigration policy. Because the law mandated the detention of certain immigrants and asylum seekers, the INS detained (prior to September 11, 2001) more than 200,000 immigrants and refugees annually at more than 900 sites, the

6. Miriam Jordan, "Trump Administration Says That Nearly 200,000 Salvadorians Must Leave," *New York Times*, January 8, 2018, downloaded on March 21, 2018, from https://www.nytimes.com/2018/01/08/us/salvadorans-tps-end.html; "ACLU Comments on Trump's Mass Deportation Instructions," downloaded on March 21, 2018, from https://www.aclu.org/news/aclu-comment-trumps-mass-deportation-instructions.

7. Patrick McDonnell summarized the claims of Proposition 187 for the *Los Angeles Times*. The proposition called for the following changes regarding illegal immigrants: prohibiting of enrollment in all public schools; requirement of parents or guardians of all school children to show legal residence; obligatory reporting by school administrators of suspected illegal immigrants; denial of nonemergency public health care, including pre-natal and postnatal services, to those who could not prove legal status; cutoff of many state programs dealing with troubled youth, the elderly, the blind and others with special needs; requirement of law enforcement agencies to cooperate fully with INS officials; and increased penalties for the sale and use of fraudulent documents. Patrick McDonnell, "Proposition 187 Turns Up Heat in US Immigration Debate," *Los Angeles Times*, August 10, 1994; Michael McBride, "Migrants and Asylum Seekers: Policy Responses in the United States to Immigrants and Refugees from Central America and the Caribbean," *International Migration* 37, no. 1 (1999): 298.

8. Behdad, "Nationalism and Immigration": 174; Franz (2001): 318–19.

9. Barbara Franz, "Immigration und nationale Sicherheit in der EU und den USA: Die Demontage des *Flüchtlingsrechts*," *AWR Bulletin: Quarterly on Refugee Problems*, Nos. 3–4 (2004): 58–71.

majority of which were county and local jails. The chair of the American Bar Association's Immigration Pro Bono Development and Bar Activation Project, Llewelyn G. Pritchard, argued in February 2001 that "immigration detainees have become the fastest growing segment of the incarcerated population in the United States." Even prior to the terrorist attacks of September 11, 2001, the INS budgeted approximately one billion dollars for refugee and immigration detention and removal.[10]

In addition, the 1996 Welfare Reform Act severely limited welfare aid for legal immigrants and the IIRIRA signaled a more coordinated attempt by the government to stop the flow of illegal immigration. Undocumented migrants became ineligible for most federal or state PA programs, in particular supplemental SSI, AFDC, Medicaid, and food stamps. In addition, the IIRIRA provided for 1,000 new border guards and 300 new INS agents each year through 2002 to strengthen border controls and to investigate unlawful hiring and the smuggling of illegal immigrants. Moreover, a fourteen-mile triple fence was to be constructed along parts of the border near San Diego, California. While the Border Patrol might not have been successful in keeping all the illegal migrants out, it has established a pattern of social control and generalized mode of surveillance in the border regions, if not throughout the country.[11]

The 1996 immigration and welfare reform also included several provisions to limit legal immigration or make it more difficult for potential asylum seekers to enter the country. Those who sponsored legal immigrants needed to earn now more than 125 per-cent of the poverty level to ensure that new arrivals would not need welfare assistance. Asylum seekers have to prove a "credible fear of persecution" at an initial meeting with an INS officer. The final bill provided for a review hearing within seven days before an immigration judge, with no appeals of the judge's decision possible. Moreover, those ordered to leave would be held in mandatory detention until departure, and anyone entering the country without proper documentation would be subject to deportation. Many observers agree that the 1996 expedited removal clause led to arbitrary decisions and possible violations of international guidelines. These policies present special problems for immigrants and refugees from Latin America and the Caribbean.[12]

Then-Republican presidential candidate Patrick Buchanan, cited in the *Los Angeles Times*, tied immigrants to declining living standards, the widening income gap, the evils of free trade, high crime rates, declining property values, and the general sense that communities were veering out of control.[13]

Along the same lines, FAIR, one of the strongest advocates of cuts in legal immigration, stated that

near-record levels of immigration are deforming the nation's character. The inexorable influx . . . could have dire long-term consequences: overpopulation, rampant bilingualism, reduced job opportunities for native-born, and demographic shifts that could result in dangerous ethnic separatism.[14]

As a consequence, the 1996 legislation greatly expanded the grounds on which noncitizens (includ-

---

10. In 1996, Congress passed the Anti-Terrorism and Effective Death Penalty Act (AEDPA). Combined with IIRIRA, this law made it virtually impossible for a lawful permanent resident who had committed a crime to remain in the United States. Under IIRIRA, most immigrants subject to deportation for crimes also became subject to mandatory detention for 90 days following the issuance of a final removal order. IIRIRA permits the INS to detain immigrants for a period beyond 90 days. This gave rise to the population of detainees known as "lifers" because the INS interpreted the law to allow indefinite detention. USCR, "Ashcroft Responds to Supreme Court Ruling Against Indefinite Detention," Worldwide Refugee Information: http://www.refugees.org/world/articles/ashcroft_rr01_7.htm (downloaded on March 7, 2004); Llewelyn G. Pritchard, "The INS Issues Detention Standards Governing the Treatment of Detained Immigrants and Asylum Seekers," USCR: http://www.refugees.org/world/articles/developments_rr01_02.cfm (downloaded on March 4, 2004).

11. Robert Pear, "G.O.P Governors Seek to Restore Immigrant Aid," *The New York Times*, January 25, 1997, 1; Robert Pear, "Panel Urges That Immigration Become Further Americanized," *The New York Times*, October 1, 1997, A20; Mirta Ojito, "Painful Choices for Immigrants in US Illegally," *The New York Times*, September 25, 1997, 1; Behdad, "Nationalism and Immigration": 174.

12. Pear, "Panel Urges": A20; McBride, "Migrants and Asylum Seekers": 299, Franz (2001): 320–21.

13. McBride, "Migrants and Asylum Seekers": 299; Patrick McDonnell, "California: Immigration Hot Button Awaits GOP Candidate," *Los Angeles Times*, March 2, 1996, A10; Franz (2001): 322.

14. FAIR cited in: Patrick McDonnell, "Activists See Dire Immigration Threat," *Los Angeles Times*, August 11, 1996, A3.

ing legal permanent residents) could be deported. The act essentially gives the police a blank check to trigger the deportation of any suspected immigrant.

The Post-9/11 Reaction

The attacks of September 11 provided the political decision makers in the United States with greater justification to increase the securitization of immigration policies. The mainstream public supported and often collaborated with these measures after September 11, 2001, because of the widespread misperception that the terrorists involved in the attacks arrived on immigration visas. Following this logic, immigration policies needed to be restructured to "close the loopholes" through which terrorists entered the United States. In reality, all but one of the terrorists had entered the United States legally on temporary tourist visas with entry permits for six months, and only one held an F-1 student visa. Only one of the hijackers was in the United States prior to July 2001, and not one of the hijackers had immigration status. Nevertheless, the attacks legitimized a number of large-scale immigration searches and expulsions that began late in 2001 and denied the newcomers' constitutional rights, such as due process and fair trial rights.[15]

The U.S. government quickly created a new cabinet-level department and engaged in large administrative restructuring. In January 2003, the Department of Homeland Security (DHS) was established to centralize and coordinate strategic functions within the federal government to "synchronize policy and structure on the U.S. 'war against terrorism.'" The Immigration and Naturalization Service (INS) immigration enforcement and service components have been separated from each other in the DHS. According to the National Network for Immigrant and Refugee Rights (NNIRR), all immigration matters are now "overwhelmingly dominated by so-called 'national security' concerns." Two pieces of legislation, passed shortly after September 11, 2001, the

USA PATRIOT Act (in October 2001) and the Enhanced Border Security and Visa Entry Reform Act (May 2002), amplified the powers of agencies such as the FBI and DHS and authorized significant increases in personnel and technology for border enforcement. The United States, moreover, accelerated its pursuit of bilateral deportation and repatriation agreements with countries that had previously refused to take deportees, such as Cambodia and Nigeria. With Canada the United States signed a safe-third country agreement in 2002.[16]

The consequences of these legislative acts and a number of interagency operations were disastrous for particular immigrant communities in the United States. The crackdown on suspected terrorists within U.S. territory soon degenerated into witch hunts for immigrants accused of criminal offenses or whose records simply indicated processing irregularities. It is well known that thousands of immigrants were detained and deported without access to legal representation in the aftermath of the September 11 attacks. In June 2003, the U.S. Justice Department's Office of the Inspector General (OIG) released a 239-page report outlining the FBI-led terrorism investigations following the attacks. The report criticized the treatment of 762 Arab and Muslim immigrants, documenting how detainees were beaten, kept from contacting lawyers and family members, and jailed for months under an official "no bond policy." The FBI and INS cooperated to detain immigrants by labeling the detainees "of interest" to the terrorism investigations, violating their due process rights, even when there were no grounds for suspicion.[17]

Many people who have been arrested during the investigation of September 11, 2001, attacks were charged with immigration violations, such as visa discrepancies. The detainees were frequently portrayed as possible "sleeper" terrorists by the mainstream media, but little was known initially about their actual treatment and accusations. Some were held for months in solitary confinement. Others suffered

15. Federation for American Immigration Reform (FAIR), "Identity and Immigration Status of 9/11 Terrorists," http://www. fairus.org/ImmigrationIssueCenters/ImmigrationIssueCenters.cfm?ID 51205&c514 (downloaded on March 5, 2004).

16. Heba Nimr, *Human Rights and Human Security at Risk: The Consequences of Placing Immigration Enforcement and Services in the Department of Homeland Security* (National Network for Immigrant and Refugee Rights, September 2003), 1.

17. David Caruso, "FBI Agents Raid Immigrants' Stores," *The Washington Post*, July 9, 2002, http://www.washington post.com/wp-dyn/articles/A42205-2002Jul9.html (downloaded on July 12, 2002).

physical and psychological torture—some were beaten by INS guards, kept in cold cells and refused blankets, and others received no *halal* food (which conforms to specific dietary laws) or toilet paper for weeks. One detainee died of a heart attack while imprisoned. Moreover, as a result of frequent raids of stores, kiosks, and stands in the following year dozens of foreigners, mostly from Pakistan, were detained or questioned and more than 500 detainees were eventually deported, but none of those rounded up has been charged with terrorism.[18]

Soon the investigations' focus shifted entirely from security concerns to immigration-related issues. With the start of the "Absconder Apprehension Initiative," "fugitive apprehension teams" invaded and searched homes throughout the United States for persons with outstanding deportation orders. At this point the officials were no longer engaged in terrorist or national security investigations; instead, the operation shifted to cracking down on immigration violators. Other initiatives emerged to crack down on illegal immigrants.

For example, the Immigration and Customs Enforcement's (ICE) Detention and Removal Operations (DRO) cites as its purpose promoting public safety and national security by deporting all removable aliens through the enforcement of immigration laws.

The new procedures that the INS developed to regulate immigration (Expedited Removal of Aliens, Detention and Removal of Aliens, Conduct of Removal Proceedings), the USA PATRIOT Act, and the ongoing ICE's DRO do not significantly affect the nation's security, but they do add to the insecurity of certain migrant and foreign groups in the country.

The Obama Years—A Mixed Bag

Like most presidents before him, the first African American president, Barack Obama, the son of a Kenyan immigrant, entered the White House promising to reform America's immigration system. Facing a Republican Congress whose members opposed the president on principled and racist grounds, nothing came of this promise. In 2012, Obama signed an executive action providing a legalized status for minors who entered the country clandestinely. The Deferred Action for Childhood Arrivals (DACA) granted those minors renewable two-year periods of deferred action from deportation and eligibility for study and work permits. The executive action only applied to immigrants who entered before their sixteenth birthday and had lived in the country continuously since at least June 15, 2007. By 2017, 800,000 DACA recipients were, in all but one regard, full-fledged members of society—people who had demonstrated their commitment to community and country but were not given a path to citizenship.[19]

Under Obama, ICE's enforcement priorities changed from the large worksite raids, which were frequently used during the Bush administration, to the enforcement of immigration laws in cases of threats and serious criminals. The Obama administration also shifted its focus to apprehending and deporting clandestine entrants from the big factories, agro businesses, hotels, and construction sites in the interior to the borders. In terms of immigration policy, the defining characteristic of Obama's administration was the record high number of deportations. From 2009 to 2016, more than 2.7 million people were deported—more than were expelled under any other president in U.S. history. Many of these deportees were children and unaccompanied refugee minors who had started entering the United States in 2014.[20]

Thousands of such unaccompanied minors from Central American countries (mostly Honduras, El Salvador, and Guatemala) have arrived at the southern U.S. border, fleeing violence in their home countries and seeking asylum in the United States. They turned themselves in to the Border Patrol and asked for protection. However, the large number of them

18. Anne-Marie Cusac, "Ill-Treatment on Our Shores," *The Progressive* (March 2002): 24–28; Barbara Franz, "American Patriotism and Nativist Fears after September 11: A Historical Perspective," *AWR Bulletin: Quarterly on Refugee Problems*, No. 1–2, (2003), also accessible at: http://www.braumueller.at/service/downloads/, pp. 10–11.

19. Katie Heinrich and Daniel Arkin, "What Is DACA?" NBC News, September 5, 2017, downloaded on March 21, 2018, from https://www.nbcnews.com/storyline/immigration-reform/what-daca-here-s-what-you-need-know-about-program-n798761; Barbara Franz, "Call Trump the Dream-Killer-in-Chief," *Morristown Daily Record*, September 14, 2017.

20. Sarah Gonzales, "Nobody Expected Obama Would Deport More People Than Any Other President," *WYNC*, January 19, 2017, downloaded on March 21, 2018, from https://www.wnyc.org/story/no-one-thought-barack-obama-would-deport-more-people-any-other-us-president/.

overwhelmed the Departments of Homeland Security and Health and Human Services, which was required to shelter and care for the minors after they were apprehended. For the most part, the Obama administration did not treat this influx as a humanitarian issue, but rather as an enforcement issue. Instead of ensuring a fair process for refugees to present their claims, many were subjected to a rushed deportation process, often without access to attorneys. As a result, the Obama administration deported, to some of the most unstable and insecure countries in the world, many who should have been protected.[21]

Obama left office with a mixed legacy on immigration. While he received the well-deserved label "Deporter-in-Chief" and failed to get a comprehensive immigration reform law passed, he took important steps toward protecting DACA recipients and focusing enforcement priorities.

The Trump Administration: The End of Humanitarianism and the Rise of White Exclusivism

In one of his first acts as president, Donald Trump signed Executive Order 13767 demanding the "immediate construction of a physical wall" in order to secure the southern border. Currently, fencing already exists along more than 650 miles of the southern border, and the Rio Grande provides a natural border for more than 300 miles. According to a 2017 report by the Government Accountability Office, the U.S. Customs and Border Protection spent about $2.3 billion constructing pedestrian and vehicle fencing along the southern border between the fiscal years 2007 and 2015.

Since Trump took office, the number of minors and parents apprehended at the U.S.-Mexico border has actually decreased. However, the family separation policy exemplifies the federal government's unprecedented escalation of immigration enforcement and control.

Trump issued open-ended travel restrictions to apply to government officials from Venezuela, and both restrict travel and limits admission of refugees from Iran, Libya, Syria, Yemen, Somalia, Chad, and North Korea. The U.S. Supreme Court allowed this travel ban to go into full effect even as legal challenges continue in lower courts.[22]

The GOP administration's new refugee and immigration policy exemplifies the government's new nativist and exclusivist stance. President Trump more than halved the Obama administration's FY 2017 admissions ceiling for refugees from 110,000 to 50,000 and suspended all refugee admissions for 120 days. The administration also set the refugee ceiling at 45,000 for FY 2018, the lowest level since the program began in 1980. For example, in terms of Syrian refugees, there are currently more than 5 million Syrian refugees registered in Turkey, Lebanon, Jordan, Iraq and Egypt. Countries outside of the Middle East, North Africa, and Western Europe received only negligible numbers of Syrian refugees. By the end of 2017, Canada had resettled about 40,000 Syrians and the United States about 20,900.[23] Trump also pulled the plug on DACA and exposed 800,000 young people to potential deportation.

The secret to understanding Trump's immigration policy is that it does not focus on addressing the actual problems that exist within the immigration system; rather, it is an attempt to engineer a less brown demographic future. Unfortunately for Trump and his base, the demographic shifts under way in the country may be slowed but cannot be stopped! According to the Center for American Progress, every month some 66,000 Latinos in the United States turn 18, and Asians are the fastest growing segment of the U.S. population. Thus, these policies (proposed by people whose ancestors were immigrants!) can slow the stream of new immigrants and refugees, but they cannot bring back the United States that was dominated by whites—the "great" America to which Trump and his supporters hope to return.

Conclusion

America's "Golden Door" is slowly closing for refugees and immigrants alike. The 1986 IRCA at-

21. Guillermo Cantor and Tory Johnson, "Detained, Deceived, and Deported: Experiences of Recently Deported Central American Families," American Immigration Council, May 18, 2017, downloaded on March 21, 2018, from https://www.americanimmigrationcouncil.org/special-reports/deported-central-american-families.

22. Reuters, "Enacting a Travel Ban," August 2017, downloaded on March 21, 2018, from http://fingfx.thomsonreuters.com/gfx/rngs/TRUMP-EFFECT-IMMIGRATION/010050ZX28W/index.html.

23. Reuters, "Limiting Refugees," August 2017, downloaded on March 21, 2018, from http://fingfx.thomsonreuters.com/gfx/rngs/TRUMP-EFFECT-IMMIGRATION/010050ZX28W/index.html.

tempted to regulate the country's increasing number of illegal immigrants. While allowing millions of mostly agricultural workers to legalize their status the IRCA's political focus, employer sanctions, had few concrete consequences for the planters and farmers. In part responding to mounting xenophobic pressures, the IRCA remains a noteworthy piece of legislation because of its ambivalent character and its rather successful balancing of farming and industrial interests with the general public's stipulation for restrictions on the movements of undocumented immigration across the southern border. The 1990 Immigration Reform Act changed legal immigration by including an overall cap, an increase in the annual employment-based immigration, and a provision for the admission of immigrants from underrepresented countries.

The 1996 IIRIRA increased the enforcement component of immigration law by mandating the detention of certain immigrants and asylees. It also included an expedited removal clause for asylees whose claims of persecution in their countries of origin were not deemed credible by the INS officer. The act also enlarged the border personnel and initiated the triple fence along the California border. The 1996 Welfare Reform Act strictly reduced public assistance for legal immigrants. By the mid-1990s, not only undocumented immigrants but also more documented immigrants and asylees were forced to live under increased governmental surveillance and scrutiny, often while making ends meet in the lowest economic strata with no or very limited public assistance.

After the September 11, 2001, terrorist attacks, these developments multiplied. The USA PATRIOT Act and the Enhanced Border Security and Visa Entry Reform Act and institutions such as ICE of the newly formed DHS, for all practical purposes did away with due process rights of many Arab-looking immigrants who had the misfortune of being arrested in the aftermath of the September 11 attacks. Many of the operations and procedures that initially were designed to make the United States safe from terrorists soon deteriorated into witch hunts for certain immigrants and contributed less to the security of the country than the insecurity and anxiety of immigrants.

The proposed legislation in 2006 attempts solutions: from turning illegal immigrants into guest workers, to deploying thousands of National Guard troops to the southern border and to building a 10-foot-high steel wall. Almost all of these proposals misunderstand undocumented immigration as a border control and regulation problem, while in reality it is an issue of supply and demand. As long as Mexico and other Latin American countries have a surplus of labor (exacerbated by the North American Free Trade Agreement's (NAFTA) agricultural policies that have plunged hundreds of thousands of Mexican farmers into severe economic hardship), and the United States a surplus of manual seasonal and/or low-wage jobs, immigrants from the global South will find ways to enter the country. The oscillation of American immigration policies, focusing either on regulating immigrants and refugees or on limiting access to the country and/or its services for clandestine immigrants during the past 35 years, has led to at times a severe limiting of civil and human rights of certain newcomer groups. There have been periodic witch hunts among immigrant populations and an understanding of permanent social control in the cities and neighborhoods where immigrants subsist. Immigrants remain the victims of America's ambivalent and inconsistent policies.

[2008]

Terms

1. Refoulement: Forced to return to a country from which one has fled because of fear of bodily harm.
2. Xenophobic: Highly fearful of anyone of foreign origin.

Understanding the Reading

1. Why do U.S. employees continue to hire undocumented immigrants?
2. What are the controversies surrounding the H-2 visa?
3. What is Proposition 187?
4. Describe the different treatment accorded Cuban refugees as opposed to Haitian refugees to the United States.
5. What actions did the U.S. government take that collapsed the categories of "immigrant" and "terrorist"?

Suggestions for Responding

1. Research the "Protocol Relating to the Status of Refugees," which was signed by the United States in 1967. Forced return, or *refoulement*, is in direct

defiance of our signed principles. Discuss this in class.

2. Design your own solution to controversial U.S. immigration policies, or offer a partial solution.

26

The Year in Hate: Trump Buoyed White Supremacists in 2017, Sparking Backlash among Black Nationalist Groups

SOUTHERN POVERTY LAW CENTER

February 21, 2018

"President Trump in 2017 reflected what white supremacist groups want to see: a country where racism is sanctioned by the highest office, immigrants are given the boot and Muslims banned," said Heidi Beirich, director of the SPLC's Intelligence Project. "When you consider that only days into 2018, Trump called African countries 'shitholes,' it's clear he's not changing his tune. And that's music to the ears of white supremacists."

It was a year that saw the "alt-right," the latest incarnation of white supremacy, break through the firewall that for decades kept overt racists largely out of the political and media mainstream.

- Trump appointed key administration advisers with ties to the radical right, including Stephen Bannon, the head of *Breitbart News* who boasted of turning the website into "the platform for the alt-right." The president thrilled white supremacists with his policy initiatives, such as revving up the country's deportation machinery and curtailing civil rights enforcement.
- Reinvigorated white supremacists staged their largest rally in a decade—the demonstration in Charlottesville, Virginia, that left an antiracist counterprotester dead and Trump equivocating over condemning racism. Former Klan boss David Duke called the rally a "turning point" and vowed that white supremacists would "fulfill the promises of Donald Trump" to "take our country back."
- White supremacist groups ramped up their recruiting of college students. White nationalist

leader Richard Spencer—who previously had prompted Nazi salutes from a postelection audience in Washington when he shouted "Hail Trump"—held a rally at the Lincoln Memorial and appeared on college campuses. The SPLC documented some three hundred incidents of racist flyers being distributed on more than two hundred campuses.

The SPLC's Year in Hate and Extremism report identifies 954 hate groups—an increase of 4 percent from 2016. The rise was driven in part by a backlash from the Nation of Islam and other fringe black nationalist groups that see Trump as an avatar of the rising white supremacist movement, a powerful reassertion of the same centuries-old racism that has always fueled their desire to break away from white America.

Typified by their anti-Semitic, anti-LGBT, anti-white rhetoric, and conspiracy theories, these black nationalist groups should not be confused with activist groups such as Black Lives Matter and others that work for civil rights and to eliminate systemic racism.

Nation of Islam leader Louis Farrakhan blamed Trump for encouraging a "growing sentiment" to "put the Black, the Brown, the Red back in a place they have cut out for us." His newspaper, *The Final Call*, wrote that "separation from White America" is the "divine solution" to the rise of white supremacy.

Not surprisingly, the ranks of black nationalist hate groups—groups that have always been a reaction to white racism—expanded to 233 chapters in 2017, from 193 the previous year.

Even with the growth, black nationalist groups lagged far behind the more than six hundred hate groups that adhere to some form of white supremacist ideology—and they have virtually no supporters or influence in mainstream politics, much less in the White House.

Within the white supremacist movement, neo-Nazi groups saw the greatest growth—from 99 groups to 121. Anti-Muslim groups rose for a third straight year. They increased from 101 chapters to 114 in 2017—growth that comes after the groups tripled in number a year earlier.

Ku Klux Klan groups, meanwhile, fell from 130 groups to 72. The decline is a clear indication that the new generation of white supremacists is rejecting the Klan's hoods and robes for the hipper image of the more loosely organized alt-right movement.

The overall number of hate groups likely understates the real level of hate in America, because a growing number of extremists, particularly those who identify with the alt-right, operate mainly online and may not be formally affiliated with a hate group.

The Year in Hate and Extremism report also examines how the tech industry cracked down on hate groups after the Charlottesville rally by banning the social media accounts of prominent white supremacists, removing website domains of hate groups, and canceling services such as PayPal that help hate groups to raise money.

A separate SPLC investigation, released earlier this month, found that forty-three people were killed and sixty-seven wounded by young men associated with the alt-right over the past four years. Seventeen of the deaths came in 2017.

Also, for the first time, the SPLC added two male supremacy groups to the hate group list: A Voice for Men, based in Houston, and Return of Kings, based in Washington, D.C. The vilification of women by these groups makes them no different from other groups that demean entire populations, such as the LGBT community, Muslims, or Jews, based on their inherent characteristics.

Aside from hate groups, the SPLC identified 689 active antigovernment groups that comprised the "Patriot" movement in 2017, up from 623. Of these, 273 were armed militias.

Historically, these groups rise during Democratic presidencies out of fear of gun control measures and federal law enforcement action against them. They typically decline under GOP presidencies. This has not been the case under Trump, whose radical views and bigotry may be energizing them in the same way he has invigorated hate groups.

Understanding the Reading

1. What is the "alt-right," and why do its members see Trump as a leader for their cause?
2. Besides African Americans, what other groups are marginalized by these groups?

Suggestions for Responding

1. Have a class discussion on our right to free speech and free press, balanced with the existence of hate speech that possibly incites some people to violence.
2. Have a class discussion as to whether this is sim-

ply propaganda and politics or an imminent social danger.

27

What Is White Privilege, Really?

Cory Collins

Today, white privilege is often described through the lens of Peggy McIntosh's groundbreaking essay "White Privilege: Unpacking the Invisible Knapsack." Originally published in 1988, this essay helps readers recognize white privilege by making its effects personal and tangible. For many, white privilege was an invisible force that white people needed to recognize. It was being able to walk into a store and find that the main displays of shampoo and pantyhose were catered toward your hair type and skin tone. It was being able to turn on the television and see people of your race widely represented. It was being able to move through life without being racially profiled or unfairly stereotyped. All true.

This idea of white privilege as unseen, unconscious advantages took hold. It became easy for people to interpret McIntosh's version of white privilege—fairly or not—as mostly a matter of cosmetics and inconvenience.

Those interpretations overshadow the origins of white privilege, as well as its present-day ability to influence systemic decisions. They overshadow the fact that white privilege is both a legacy and a cause of racism. And they overshadow the words of many people of color, who for decades recognized white privilege as the result of conscious acts and refused to separate it from historic inequities.

In short, we've forgotten what white privilege really means—which is all of this, all at once. And if we stand behind the belief that recognizing white privilege is integral to the anti-bias work of white educators, we must offer a broader recognition.

A recognition that does not silence the voices of those most affected by white privilege; a recognition that does not ignore where it comes from and why it has staying power.

Racism versus White Privilege

Having white privilege and recognizing it is not racist. But white privilege exists because of historic, enduring racism and biases. Therefore, defining white privilege also requires finding working definitions of racism and bias.

So, what is racism? One helpful definition comes from Matthew Clair and Jeffrey S. Denis's "Sociology on Racism." They define **racism** as "individual- and group-level processes and structures that are implicated in the reproduction of racial inequality." **Systemic racism** happens when these structures or processes are carried out by groups with power, such as governments, businesses, or schools. Racism differs from **bias**, which is a conscious or unconscious prejudice against an individual or group based on their identity.

Basically, racial bias is a belief. Racism is what happens when that belief translates into action. For example, a person might unconsciously or consciously believe that people of color are more likely to commit crime or be dangerous. That's a bias. A person might become anxious if they perceive that a black person is angry. That stems from a bias. These biases can become racism through a number of actions ranging in severity and from individual- to group-level responses:

- A person crosses the street to avoid walking next to a group of young black men.
- A person calls 911 to report the presence of a person of color who is otherwise behaving lawfully.
- A police officer shoots an unarmed person of color because he "feared for his life."
- A jury finds a person of color guilty of a violent crime despite scant evidence.
- A federal intelligence agency prioritizes investigating black and Latino activists rather than investigate white supremacist activity.

Both racism and bias rely on what sociologists call **racialization**. This is the grouping of people based on perceived physical differences, such as skin tone. This arbitrary grouping of people, historically, fueled biases and became a tool for justifying the cruel treatment and discrimination of non-white people. Colonialism, slavery, and Jim Crow laws were all sold with junk science and propaganda that claimed people of a certain "race" were fundamentally different from those of another—and they should be treated accordingly. And while not all white people participated directly in this mistreatment, their learned biases and

their safety from such treatment led many to commit one of the most powerful actions: silence.

And just like that, the trauma, displacement, cruel treatment, and discrimination of people of color, inevitably, gave birth to white privilege.

So, What Is White Privilege?

White privilege is—perhaps most notably in this era of uncivil discourse—a concept that has fallen victim to its own connotations. The two-word term packs a double whammy that inspires pushback. (1) The word *white* creates discomfort among those who are not used to being defined or described by their race. And (2) the word *privilege*, especially for poor and rural white people, sounds like a word that doesn't belong to them—like a word that suggests they have never struggled.

This defensiveness derails the conversation, which means, unfortunately, that defining white privilege must often begin with defining what it's *not*. Otherwise, only the choir listens; the people you actually want to reach check out. White privilege is *not* the suggestion that white people have never struggled. Many white people do not enjoy the privileges that come with relative affluence, such as food security. Many do not experience the privileges that come with access, such as nearby hospitals.

And white privilege is *not* the assumption that everything a white person has accomplished is unearned; most white people who have reached a high level of success worked extremely hard to get there. Instead, white privilege should be viewed as a built-in advantage, separate from one's level of income or effort.

Francis E. Kendall, author of *Diversity in the Classroom and Understanding White Privilege: Creating Pathways to Authentic Relationships across Race*, comes close to giving us an encompassing definition: "having greater access to power and resources than people of color [in the same situation] do." But in order to grasp what this statement means, it's also important to consider how the definition of white privilege has changed over time.

White Privilege through the Years

In a thorough article, education researcher Jacob Bennett tracked the history of the term *white privilege*. Before the Civil Rights Act of 1964, it was less commonly used but generally referred to legal and systemic advantages given to white people by the United States, such as citizenship, the right to vote, or the right to buy a house in the neighborhood of their choice.

It was only after discrimination persisted for years after the Civil Rights Act of 1964 that people like Peggy McIntosh began to view white privilege as being more psychological—a subconscious prejudice perpetuated by white people's lack of awareness that they held this power. White privilege could be found in day-to-day transactions and in white people's ability to move through the professional and personal worlds with relative ease.

But some people of color continued to insist that an element of white privilege included the aftereffects of conscious choices. For example, if white business leaders didn't hire many people of color, white people had more economic opportunities. Having the ability to maintain that power dynamic, in itself, was a white privilege, and it endures. Legislative bodies, corporate leaders, and educators are still disproportionately white and often make conscious choices (laws, hiring practices, discipline procedures) that keep this cycle on repeat.

The more complicated truth: White privilege is both unconsciously enjoyed and consciously perpetuated. It is both on the surface and deeply embedded in American life. It is a weightless knapsack—and a weapon.

It depends on who's carrying it.

White Privilege as the "Power of Normal"

Sometimes the examples used to make white privilege visible to those who have it are also the examples least damaging to people who lack it. But that does not mean these examples do not matter or that they do no damage at all.

These subtle versions of white privilege are often used as a comfortable, easy entry point for people who might push back against the concept. That is why they remain so popular. These are simple, everyday things, conveniences white people aren't forced to think about.

These often-used examples include the following:

- The first-aid kit having "flesh-colored" Band-Aids that only match the skin tone of white people.
- The products white people need for their hair being in the aisle labeled "hair care" rather than

in a smaller, separate section of "ethnic hair products."
- The grocery store stocking a variety of food options that reflect the cultural traditions of most white people.

But the root of these problems is often ignored. These types of examples can be dismissed by white people who might say, "My hair is curly and requires special product," or "My family is from Poland, and it's hard to find traditional Polish food at the grocery store."

This may be true. But the reason even these simple white privileges need to be recognized is that the damage goes beyond the inconvenience of shopping for goods and services. These privileges are symbolic of what we might call "the power of normal." If public spaces and goods seem catered to one race and segregate the needs of people of other races into special sections, that indicates something beneath the surface.

White people become more likely to move through the world with an expectation that their needs be readily met. People of color move through the world knowing their needs are on the margins. Recognizing this means recognizing where gaps exist.

White Privilege as the "Power of the Benefit of the Doubt"

The "power of normal" goes beyond the local CVS. White people are also more likely to see positive portrayals of people who look like them on the news, on TV shows, and in movies. They are more likely to be treated as individuals, rather than as representatives of (or exceptions to) a stereotyped racial identity. In other words, they are more often humanized and granted the benefit of the doubt. They are more likely to receive compassion, to be granted individual potential, to survive mistakes.

This has negative effects for people of color, who, without this privilege, face the consequences of racial profiling, stereotypes, and lack of compassion for their struggles.

In these scenarios, white privilege includes the facts that:

- White people are less likely to be followed, interrogated, or searched by law enforcement because they look "suspicious."
- White people's skin tone will not be a reason

people hesitate to trust their credit or financial responsibility.

- If white people are accused of a crime, they are less likely to be presumed guilty, less likely to be sentenced to death, and more likely to be portrayed in a fair, nuanced manner by media outlets (see the #IfTheyGunnedMeDown campaign).
- The personal faults or missteps of white people will likely not be used to later deny opportunities or compassion to people who share their racial identity.

This privilege is invisible to many white people because it seems reasonable that a person should be extended compassion as they move through the world. It seems logical that a person should have the chance to prove themselves individually before they are judged. It's supposedly an American ideal.

But it's a privilege often not granted to people of color—with dire consequences.

For example, programs like New York City's now-abandoned "Stop and Frisk" policy target a disproportionate number of black and Latinx people. People of color are more likely to be arrested for drug offenses despite using at a similar rate to white people. Some people do not survive these stereotypes. In 2017, people of color who were unarmed and not attacking anyone were more likely to be killed by police.

Those who survive instances of racial profiling—be they subtle or violent—do not escape unaffected. They often suffer from post-traumatic stress disorder, and this trauma in turn affects their friends, families, and immediate communities, who are exposed to their own vulnerability as a result.

A study conducted in Australia (which has its own hard history of subjugating black and Indigenous people) perfectly illustrates how white privilege can manifest in day-to-day interactions—daily reminders that one is not worthy of the same benefit of the doubt given to another. In the experiment, people of different racial and ethnic identities tried to board public buses, telling the driver they didn't have enough money to pay for the ride. Researchers documented more than 1,500 attempts. The results: 72 percent of white people were allowed to stay on the bus. Only 36 percent of black people were extended the same kindness.

Just as people of color did nothing to deserve this unequal treatment, white people did not "earn" disproportionate access to compassion and fairness.

They receive it as the byproduct of systemic racism and bias.

And even if they are not aware of it in their daily lives as they walk along the streets, this privilege is the result of conscious choices made long ago and choices still being made today.

White Privilege as the "Power of Accumulated Power"

Perhaps the most important lesson about white privilege is the one that's taught the least.

The "power of normal" and the "power of the benefit of the doubt" are not just subconscious byproducts of past discrimination. They are the purposeful results of racism—an ouroboros of sorts—that allow for the constant re-creation of inequality.

These powers would not exist if systemic racism hadn't come first. And systemic racism cannot endure unless those powers still hold sway.

You can imagine it as something of a whiteness water cycle, wherein racism is the rain. That rain populates the earth, giving some areas more access to life and resources than others. The evaporation is white privilege—an invisible phenomenon that is both a result of the rain and the reason it keeps going.

McIntosh asked herself an important question that inspired her famous essay on white privilege: "On a daily basis, what do I have that I didn't earn?" Our work should include asking the two looming follow-up questions: *Who built that system? Who keeps it going?*

The answers to those questions could fill several books. But they produce examples of white privilege that you won't find in many broad explainer pieces.

For example, the ability to accumulate wealth has long been a white privilege—a privilege created by overt, systemic racism in both the public and the private sectors. In 2014, the Pew Research Center released a report that revealed the median net worth of a white household was $141,900; for black and Hispanic households, that number dropped to $11,000 and $13,700, respectively. The gap is huge, and the great "equalizers" don't narrow it. Research from Brandeis University and Demos found that the racial wealth gap is not closed when people of color attend college (the median white person who went to college has 7.2 times more wealth than the median black person who went to college, and 3.9 times more than the median Latino person who went to college).

Nor do they close the gap when they work full time, or when they spend less and save more.

The gap, instead, relies largely on inheritance—wealth passed from one generation to the next. And that wealth often comes in the form of inherited homes with value. When white families are able to accumulate wealth because of their earning power or home value, they are more likely to support their children into early adulthood, helping with expenses such as college education, first cars, and first homes. The cycle continues.

This is a privilege denied to many families of color, a denial that started with the work of public leaders and property managers. After World War II, when the G.I. Bill provided white veterans with "a magic carpet to the middle class," racist zoning laws segregated towns and cities with sizeable populations of people of color—from Baltimore to Birmingham, from New York to St. Louis, from Louisville to Oklahoma City, to Chicago, to Austin, and in cities beyond and in between.

These exclusionary zoning practices evolved from city ordinances to redlining by the Federal Housing Administration (which wouldn't back loans to black people or those who lived close to black people), to more insidious techniques written into building codes. The result: people of color weren't allowed to raise their children and invest their money in neighborhoods with "high home values." The cycle continues today. Before the 2008 crash, people of color were disproportionately targeted for subprime mortgages. And neighborhood diversity continues to correlate with low property values across the United States. According to the Century Foundation, one-fourth of black Americans living in poverty live in high-poverty neighborhoods; only one in thirteen impoverished white Americans lives in a high-poverty neighborhood.

The inequities compound. To this day, more than 80 percent of poor black students attend a high-poverty school, where suspension rates are often higher and resources often more limited. Once out of school, obstacles remain. Economic forgiveness and trust still has racial divides. In a University of Wisconsin study, 17 percent of white job applicants with a criminal history got a callback from an employer; only 5 percent of black applicants with a criminal history got callbacks. And according to the National Bureau of Economic Research, black Americans are 105 percent more likely than white people to receive a high-cost mortgage, with Latino Americans 78 per-cent more likely. This is after controlling for variables such as credit score and debt-to-income ratios.

Why mention these issues in an article defining white privilege? Because the past and present context of wealth inequality serves as a perfect example of white privilege.

If privilege, from the Latin roots of the term, refers to laws that have an impact on individuals, then what is more effective than a history of laws that explicitly targeted racial minorities to keep them out of neighborhoods and deny them access to wealth and services?

If white privilege is "having greater access to power and resources than people of color [in the same situation] do," then what is more exemplary than the access to wealth, the access to neighborhoods, and the access to the power to segregate cities, deny loans, and perpetuate these systems?

This example of white privilege also illustrates how systemic inequities trickle down to less harmful versions of white privilege. Wealth inequity contributes to the "power of the benefit of the doubt" every time a white person is given a lower mortgage rate than a person of color with the same credit credentials. Wealth inequity reinforces the "power of normal" every time businesses assume their most profitable consumer base is the white base and adjust their products accordingly.

And this example of white privilege serves an important purpose: It re-centers the power of conscious choices in the conversation about what white privilege is.

People can be ignorant about these inequities, of course. According to the Pew Research Center, only 46 percent of white people say that they benefit "a great deal" or "a fair amount" from advantages that society does not offer to black people. But conscious choices *were* and *are* made to uphold these privileges. And this goes beyond loan officers and lawmakers. Multiple surveys have shown that many white people support the idea of racial equality but are less supportive of policies that could make it more possible, such as reparations, affirmative action, or law enforcement reform.

In that way, white privilege is not just the power to find what you need in a convenience store or to move through the world without your race defining your interactions. It's not just the subconscious comfort of seeing a world that serves you as normal. It's also the power to remain silent in the face of racial inequity. It's the power to weigh the need for protest or confrontation against the discomfort or inconvenience of speaking up. It's getting to choose when and where you want to take a stand. It's knowing that you and your humanity are safe.

And what a privilege that is.

Understanding the Reading

1. Why is it important to understand racism not just as conscious acts but also as the consequences of historic inequities?
2. How does the author define systemic racism?
3. How should we understand the term *white privilege* when we know many white people have struggled, worked hard, and may or may not have access to health services, jobs, or adequate housing?
4. Give examples of "the power of normal." What do these examples symbolize?
5. How does the author explain the wealth gap between white, black, and Hispanic households, given the same amount of education and hours worked?
6. What are some of the laws and policies that structured the wealth gap in the United States?

Suggestion for Responding

1. Initiate a conversation or panel discussion on white privilege in your classroom or with a group of friends. Deal with the protests, confusion, and frustrations as a sort of mediator. *Note*: It is important that this be a civil conversation, albeit a difficult one. Insist on everyone remaining respectful.

28

Native Americans vs. the U.S. Government

MICHAEL DORRIS

The turn of the twentieth century was an unhappy time for the Native people of America. Their total population was at its lowest ebb, the vast majority of their land had been taken away, their religions were outlawed, their children removed from home and incarcerated in hostile institutions where it was deemed a crime to so much as speak in one's own language. In 1900 few Native Americans were citizens and as a group they constituted the poorest, unhealthiest, and least likely to survive—much less succeed—population in all of the United States. And yet they not only survived but also survived as a culturally intact group of peoples; against all odds, tribes maintained their languages and wisdom, guarded their art and music and literature, and for the most part, chose to continue to be Indians rather than assimilate and disappear.

The U.S. government, however, continued to advocate a melting-pot policy, and in 1924 Congress passed the Curtis Act, which conferred American citizenship on all native-born Indians. In many areas, such a change in status did not mean automatic access to the ballot box, however, and Native "citizens" remained disenfranchised "persons under guardianship" in Arizona and New Mexico until 1948.

Nevertheless, citizenship did, in the minds of some congressmen and others, abrogate the rights to special status which were guaranteed through treaty. Questions like "How can we have treaties with our own citizens?" (with its correlative answer: "We can't, therefore throw out the treaties and open up the land!!") should have been asked and answered before any such act was passed. *If* it had been made clear that United States citizenship meant abandonment of Native American identity, and *if* the opinion of Native American people had been solicited, it is improbable that even a significant minority of Indian people would have opted for it in 1924.

In effect, the Curtis Act was tantamount to the American government deciding to celebrate the Bicentennial in 1976 by unilaterally declaring all inhabitants of the Western Hemisphere "American citizens" and then immediately forcing any (former) Brazilian, Canadian, or Venezuelan engaging in international trade to comply with U.S. tariff restrictions and oil prices. Such an expanded Monroe Doctrine precludes all argument. The American experiment with instant naturalization is not unique: The Portuguese tried it in Angola, the Belgians in Zaire, and the French in Algeria—but somehow most Africans apparently never *felt* like Europeans. Most Native Americans didn't, either, but by the twentieth century they lacked the population or resources to successfully dispute the denial of their sovereignty.

Four years later, a blue-ribbon congressional committee chaired by Lewis Meriam issued a report on conditions in Indian country. Its aim was to assess the effects of the Dawes[1] and Curtis acts and to inform the government of the progress these pieces of legislation had made possible for Native American people. The situation on reservations in 1928, however, yielded little in the way of optimistic forecast. Since 1887 conditions had universally worsened: The educational level was in most cases lower, the poverty greater, the death rate higher (and for younger people) than at any time previous to the enactment of the "benevolent" policies. Federal enforcement of the misguided and totally unjust severalty laws[2] was, in effect, cultural genocide.

In 1934, President Roosevelt appointed the anthropologist John Collier as Commissioner of Indian Affairs. Unlike too many of his predecessors in office, Collier actually knew something of at least one Native society (Pueblo) and had long opposed the Allotment policy[3] for both its inhumanity and its naiveté. His major achievement was to assist in the development and passage of the Indian Reorganization Act (the Wheeler-Howard Act), a policy which sought to undo most of the provisions of the Dawes Act and begin to remedy the disasters recounted in the Meriam Report of 1928.

Almost half a century, however, was a long time, and it was beyond realistic possibility that either the land base or the cultural, educational, and economic health of Native American societies could be restored as they were in 1880.

The Wheeler-Howard Act aimed to revive the traditional "bilateral, contractual relationship between the government and the tribes." Commissioner Collier emphasized the Native American right to a kind of self-determination and banned any further allotment of tribal land. The Indian Reorganization Act further authorized severely limited appropriations to purchase new holdings and reclaim certain lost property; it also established a federal loan policy for Native groups and reaffirmed the concept of self-government on reservations.

Many tribes opposed this legislation, however, on the basis of the restrictions and regulations it placed on the participating tribes. The act, for instance, prohibited any individual transfer of tribal land without governmental approval, and it required that all tribal governments conform to a single political system based on majority rule. No tribe was eligible for a single benefit of the act unless it agreed to it *in toto*, and therefore its acceptance necessarily became widespread.

The period following the Collier administration and extending into the early 1950s was one in which many Americans seemed to forget about Indians and assumed that *at last* "they" had finally vanished as predicted. The national interest was focused on World War II and the Korean War, and domestic treaties seemed a thing of the far-distant past.

After one of these "dormant cycles," the public and its government usually seem particularly piqued and frustrated to discover that Native Americans are still very much alive and intact. Once again in the 1950s, as in the 1880s, the presumptuous and thoroughly invalid assumption was made that if Indians had not chosen to disappear into the melting pot, something sinister was to blame. It seems never to have occurred to those in power that Crows or Yakimas, for instance, simply preferred being Crows or Yakimas!

As usual, the federal government, liberal "friends of the Indian," and rural land developers concluded that special status, and the reservation system in particular, were somehow retarding Native assimilation, and therefore it was decided, once again, to breach all legal precepts of international and U.S. law and unilaterally break treaty agreements. It was further concluded that if some Native Americans insisted that they didn't want to change their relationship with the government, they simply didn't know what was good for them. The rivers were still running, the grass was still growing, but the promises made by the American government and written to apply in perpetuity could not exist for even a century without twice being violated.

A committee was therefore appointed to divide, like Gaul,[4] all reservations into three parts: the "prosperous," the "marginal," and the "poor." Even with this license, only a handful of tribes could be found to fit, by any stretch of the imagination, into the first category, and these were marked for quick termination. The implications of this policy are clear: Apparently Congress regarded reservations as transitory steps between "primitive" and "modern" society. As soon as a group achieved a margin of success (according to the ethnocentric standards of American culture), a reservation ceased to have a rationale for existence. This self-serving attitude totally ignores both the political circumstances which brought about the reservation system in the first place (e.g., aboriginal right of title) and the legal treaties and sanctions which supposedly protected it.

Two of the most economically self-sustaining tribes, the Klamath in Oregon and the Menominee in Wisconsin, were located in timberland areas and operated logging industries. The government exerted tremendous pressure, employing levers of doubtful legal and ethical practice, and the manipulation of misunderstanding, to force these tribes to submit to termination. Whether this consent was ever actually granted in either case is a debatable point, but it is clear that neither group, had it sufficiently understood the policy, would have agreed.

Termination meant the absolute cessation, in exchange for a monetary settlement, of any special treaty arrangements or status which existed between the tribe and its members and the U.S. government. Upon termination, the Menominees would be expected, in legal effect, to cease being Indians and to somehow turn themselves into Wisconsonians overnight. On a date set by the government, the dependent, sovereign Menominee Nation, hundreds of years old, would become simply another county within the state.

Historical retrospect clearly shows that in all cases the termination policy was even more ill conceived and socially disruptive than the Allotment policy had been before it—and just as illegal. The net effects of termination were the loss of large amounts of valuable land by the tribes involved, plus an enormous psychological blow to thousands of Indian people. The fallacy of the policy was patently obvious so quickly that it was suspended shortly after implementation, sparing other tribes similar losses. To date, one of the victimized tribes, the Menominee, has, through persistent and valiant efforts of a group of its members, managed to be reestablished as a reservation in 1973. But as a direct result of termination, the new Menominee lands were much smaller and poorer than the reservation had been before 1953.

Subsequent government policies aimed at assimilating the Native American were more subtle. Among these were the urban relocation programs, often hastily conceived and poorly managed attempts to induce Native Americans to migrate to cities. A substantial percentage of the participants in these programs eventually returned, frustrated and cynical, to their reservations.

[1975]

Terms

1. Dawes Act: The federal law that abolished tribal organizations and allotted 160 acres to the head of each family.

2. Severalty Laws: Laws mandating that land must be held by individuals rather than in common by the whole group.
3. Allotment Policy: The distribution of reservation land under the Dawes Act and the opening of undistributed land to whites.
4. Gaul: An ancient name for what are now France and Belgium. Julius Caesar opened his history with the statement "All Gaul is divided into three parts."

Understanding the Reading

1. What effect did the Curtis Act have on Native Americans?
2. What were conditions like on reservations in 1928?
3. What were the benefits and restrictions of the Indian Reorganization Act?
4. What was "termination," and what were its effects?

Suggestions for Responding

1. Dorris presents the analogy of the U.S. government unilaterally declaring all inhabitants of the Western Hemisphere to be American citizens. Suppose this actually happened, and write about how you would respond personally if you were a citizen of one of the annexed countries.
2. Research one of the governmental policies Dorris mentions; explain what it was supposed to do and what it actually did.

29

Urban Native Americans

ROBERTA FISKE-RUSCIANO

The term "urban Native Indians" is problematic for most non–Native Americans. Whether thinking of Native Americans brings forth positive, negative, or neutral images, most non-natives do not imagine natives as members of an urban, technological society, and this lack of urban image has led to a blindness regarding the presence and needs of Native Americans in the cities. Identification of the urban Native American has therefore been one of the central problems surrounding government policymaking regarding American Indians since the early 1960s. The U.S. census data counts 67 percent of Native Americans and Alaska natives living outside designated native areas. A large proportion is living in metropolitan areas.

Relocation and Migration

All members of a federally recognized tribe in the United States, according to the U.S. Constitution, are due certain benefits and services, by right of their heritage. This unique legal relationship with the U.S. government was never meant to end once an individual moved to a metropolitan area, but in effect that is what has happened. In the mid-1950s, the Bureau of Indian Affairs (BIA), in accord with Congress, began the Voluntary Relocation Program. BIA officers on each reservation were instructed to "sell" the idea of city living to likely candidates. Individuals, and sometimes families, were given a one-way ticket to the chosen city, where housing and employment awaited, all arranged by the BIA. Subsistence money was guaranteed for six weeks, after which these newest immigrants were on their own. It was informally known as a "sink-or-swim policy." As anthropologist Sol Tax noted twenty years after relocation, however, "Indians don't sink or swim, they float."

Most Native Americans who arrived in the city under the relocation program left as soon as they got a good look at their new way of life. Many of the jobs were unskilled, and Native Americans found they were able to afford only the worst housing available in the city. Under these conditions, transition to city dwelling was, for many, impossible. Yet the BIA did not recognize the shortcomings of its multimillion-dollar program and continued to relocate as many Native Americans as possible. Noticing that many of their clients were returning to their reservations, the BIA began relocating people as far away from their reservations as could be managed, to make it as difficult as possible to return. Part of the plan was to terminate the reservations eventually. Watt Spade and Willard Walker illustrate one Native American view of this phase of the relocation program. They wrote of overhearing two Native American men humorously discussing the government's wanting to land a man on the moon. It could be done, one man said, but nobody knew how to get the man home again after he landed on the moon. All the government had to do, he said, was put a Native American in the rocket ship and tell him he was being relocated: "Then, after he

got to the moon, that Indian would find his own way home again and the government wouldn't have to figure that part out at all." The Voluntary Relocation Program was a failure according to its own goals. This program was based on the prejudiced notion that Native American culture and life-ways will, and should, disappear. The BIA and the U.S. Congress of the 1950s counted on America's cities to speed that process.

Most Native Americans presently living in urban areas did not arrive through the relocation program but migrated independently, usually looking for employment, and settled near relatives or friends from their reservation or hometown. Many are permanent residents, but many are transient—relocating within the city, going from city to city, or spending part of the year in the city and part on the reservation. There is no known "typical" pattern of migration; tribal nations, families, and individuals differ according to their needs. A family may live in the city during the winter so the children can stay in school, then leave for the reservation in the summer. Construction workers are often busy in the cities during the warm months and leave in the winter. The powwow season and harvests also draw many urban Native Americans back to the reservations. Jeanne Guillemin points out in *Urban Renegades* that the young Micmac women of Boston often prefer to return to their kin in the Canadian Maritime Provinces when it is time to give birth. There they receive the physical, emotional, and spiritual support they need and avoid the frightening aspects of the city, such as its clinics and hospitals. The frequent moving to and from the reservation or hometown and within the city is one factor in the urban Native American's past invisibility or elusiveness.

Urban Native American Identity

Another factor until recently has been their reluctance to identify themselves as Native Americans to non–Native Americans in the city. In 1976 the director of the American Indian Health Service in Chicago illustrated this problem with an anecdote. A young man had been playing baseball and had been hit hard by the bat. When he was taken to the emergency room, he removed all his turquoise beads, giving them to a friend to keep for him, and stuffed his long braids inside his baseball cap; he said, "Now the receptionist will think I'm a Mexican." His friend said they frequently try to pass as Mexicans in order to be treated better. The urban Native Americans' attempts to remain unidentified, coupled with the tremendous mobility of individuals and families, has made it impossible in past years for the U.S. Census to come close to an accurate count in the cities. In the 1990 U.S. Census, however, there was a huge increase in people identifying themselves as Native Americans, Eskimos, and Aleuts. As the increase cannot be completely explained by actual population growth, there is much speculation regarding what has made so many more Native Americans willing to be identified. Some cynical observers insist that the motive must be monetary: to obtain funds and services that are due Native Americans under the law. One thing that scholars studying Native American culture have learned over the decades, however, is that Native Americans usually cannot be coaxed to take a particular course of action because of the promise of money. Most Native Americans living in cities do not receive federal funds or services of any kind, because of distrust of Native American or non–Native American agencies and a preference for finding survival strategies among one another.

In the past, most sociological studies have focused on the atypical urban Native American—the one most visible, "lying in the gutter," cut off from kin. It is important to learn how most urban Native Americans (neither the upper middle-class professionals nor the indigent) have found their way in this foreign environment, maintaining strong kin relationships and networks and not necessarily assimilating. Native Americans have arrived in cities all over the United States for many reasons; work opportunities and education are the most commonly cited. Guillemin states another very important reason in her chapter "The City as Adventure." For the Micmac of Canada, she points out, going to Boston is seen as extending one's tribal boundaries. While trying to survive in this environment, the young Micmac learn much about coping with conditions as they meet them in the South End, a settling ground for immigrants from all over the world. Their risk-taking and networking are important parts of a young urban Native American's education. Flexibility is seen as one key to their tribal nation's survival. While it is often assumed that cities temper and neutralize (if not actually melt) the unique cultures of their residents, in this case a native people is claiming the city as their own and using it for their own purposes—to strengthen themselves as members of a Native American nation as well as to survive and enjoy themselves. Some cities,

such as Chicago, have operated high-quality schools for Native American children as further insurance against their losing precious traditions and ways of thinking. To combat cycles of poverty and ill health, many cities with large Native populations have indigenous-inspired and indigenous run programs, such as San Francisco's Native Mentorship in Public Health Program, which focuses on physical, mental, and spiritual wellness for young Native Americans. Minneapolis has a 212-apartment complex, Little Earth of United Tribes, that gives preference to Native Americans.

Gambling as Urban Legacy

One clear consequence of Native Americans learning to deal with the bureaucratic state has been the success stories of Native American nations using the existing laws to repair damages done to their nations, such as bringing an economic base to their reservation. One example comes from the small Pequot Nation in Ledyard, Connecticut. In response to a 1988 ruling holding that federal law allows recognized Native American tribes to have gambling on reservations if the state in which they live allows some sort of gambling off the reservation, the Pequots set up what is now the largest gambling casino in the world, the Foxwoods Resort and Casino. The gambling question affects reservations all over the country; from California to New Jersey, Native Americans are debating the serious question of what effects the presence of casinos would have on their reservations. Many are now in operation. Although most reservation casinos are not located in large metropolitan areas, the situation clearly involves the bringing of some aspects of the city (in concentrated doses) to the reservation. Although various forms of gambling have existed traditionally among many Native American nations, the dangers and problems that seem to surround non-Native American casino centers worry many people, alongside the hopefulness that sudden wealth will solve many personal and cultural problems. After thirty years of watching, it is not surprising that both great advantages and challenges have arrived.

Many young adults have returned to the reservations, as there is increased employment. Numbers of the working poor have declined, there are better educational and health resources, and consequently mortality has decreased. In general, the tribal nations with successful casinos have more choices available to them. Although details of the sharing of the profits are not known, according to Linda Gorman (*National Bureau of Economic Research*, May 30, 2018), Foxwoods Pequot tribe gave Connecticut $350 million in 2002 so that no other gambling non-Indian casino license would be granted in the Bridgeport area.

"Indian gaming" creates jobs for Native and non-Native people in the area, thus allowing tribes to be self-sufficient. Challenges that arrive with gaming, such as corruption, gambling addictions, and divisiveness within tribes, are being watched and handled according to each tribe's policies. The ability to deal with rapid social change and the need to protect their traditions are definitely a balancing act—one that requires resilience. Many of the same questions that have concerned Native peoples for generations—about the quality of life left for their people—continue to worry them, whether they are on an impoverished reservation, in a large city, or on a reservation that has made casino gambling the economic base of its people's lives.

[1995, 2012, 2018]

References

Fiske, Roberta. "Native American Artists in Chicago." In *A Report on the Chicago Ethnic Arts Project*. Washington, D.C.: Library of Congress, American Folklife Center, 1978.

Gorman, Linda. *National Bureau of Economic Research*, May 30, 2018.

Guillemin, Jeanne. *Urban Renegades*. New York: Columbia University Press, 1975.

Johnson, Kirk. "Seeking Lost Culture at a Powwow: Pequots Draw Ritual Dancers across U.S. with Rich Prizes." *The New York Times*, September 19, 1993, 52.

Kaufman, Michael T. "A James Bond with $100 Tries Out a Tribal Casino." *The New York Times*, March 18, 1994, C1.

Lurie, Nancy. "The Contemporary American Indian Scene." In *North American Indians in Historical Perspective*, edited by Eleanor Burke Leacock and Nancy Lurie. New York: Random House, 1971.

Spade, Watt, and Willard Walker. "Relocation." In *The Way: An Anthology of American Indian Life*, edited by Shirley Hill Witt and Stan Steiner. New York: Alfred A. Knopf, 1972.

Understanding the Reading

1. What was the purpose of the Voluntary Relocation Program?
2. Why was it a failure?
3. Why do Native Americans go to cities to live?
4. Why have they been reluctant, until recently, to be identified as Indians in urban areas?
5. What is one survival strategy they have learned, as a result of dealing with the bureaucratic state?

Suggestions for Responding

1. Research which American Indians live nearest to you. How do they make a living?
2. Look for data on the general health and other socioeconomic markers of Indians in any U.S. urban area.

30

Sex, Class, and Race Intersections: Visions of Women of Color

CAROL LEE SANCHEZ

*"As I understand it," said the American Indian [to one of the Puritan fathers], "you propose to civilize me."
"Exactly."
"You want to get me out of the habit of idleness and teach me to work."
"That is the idea."
"And then lead me to simplify my methods and invent things to make my work lighter."
"Yes."
"And after that I'll become ambitious to get rich so that I won't have to work at all." "Naturally."
"Well, what's the use of taking such a roundabout way of getting just where I started from? I don't have to work now."*

—American jokelore

To identify Indian is to identify with an invisible or vanished people; it is to identify with a set of basic assumptions and beliefs held by *all* who are not Indian about the indigenous peoples of the Americas. Even among the Spanish-speaking Mestizos or mezclados,[1] there is a strong preference to "disappear" their Indian blood, to disassociate from their Indian beginnings. To be Indian is to be considered "colorful," spiritual, connected to the earth, simplistic, and disappointing if not dressed in buckskin and feathers;

shocking if a city-dweller and even more shocking if an educator or other type of professional. That's the positive side.

On the negative side, to be Indian is to be thought of as primitive, alcoholic, ignorant (as in "Dumb Indian"), better off dead (as in "the only good Indian is a dead Indian" or "I didn't know there was any of you folks still left"), unskilled, non-competitive, immoral, pagan or heathen, untrustworthy (as in "Indian giver") and frightening. To be Indian is to be the primary model that is used to promote racism in this country.

How can that happen, you ask? Bad press. One hundred and fifty years of the most consistently vicious press imaginable. Newspapers, dime novels, textbooks and fifty years of visual media have portrayed and continue to portray Indians as savage, blood-thirsty, immoral, inhuman people. When there's a touch of social consciousness attached, you will find the once "blood-thirsty," "white-killer savage" portrayed as a pitiful drunk, a loser, an outcast or a mix-blood not welcomed by, or trusted by, either race. For fifty years, children in this country have been raised to kill Indians mentally, subconsciously through the visual media, until it is an automatic reflex. That shocks you? Then I have made my point.

Let me quote from Helen Hunt Jackson's book, *A Century of Dishonor*, from the introduction written by Bishop H. B. Whipple of Minnesota, who charged that

the American people have accepted as truth the teachings that the Indians were a degraded, brutal race of savages, who it was the will of God should perish at the approach of civilization. If they do not say with our Puritan fathers that these are the Hittites[2] who are to be driven out before the saints of the Lord, they do accept the teaching that manifest destiny[3] will drive the Indians from the earth. The inexorable has no tears or pity at the cries of anguish of the doomed race.

This race still struggles to stay alive. Tribe by tribe, pockets of Indian people here and there. One million two hundred thousand people identify as Indians—raised and socialized as Indian—as of the 1980 census; yet Cowboys and Indians is still played every day by children all over America of every creed, color, and nationality. Well—it's harmless, isn't it? Just kids playing kill Indians. It's all history. But it's still happening every day, and costumes are sold and the cheap western is still rolling out of Hollywood, the old shoot-'em-up westerns playing on afternoon kid shows, late night T.V. Would you allow your children to play Nazis and Jews? Blacks and KKKs? Complete with costume? Yes! It is a horrifying thought, but in thinking about it you can see how easy it is to dismiss an entire race of people as barbaric and savage, and how almost impossible it is, after this has been inculcated in you, to relate to an Indian or a group of Indians today. For example, how many famous Indians do you know offhand? Certainly the great warrior chiefs come to mind first, and of course the three most famous Indian "Princesses"—Pocahontas, Sacajawea and La Malinche. Did you get past ten? Can you name at least five Indian women you know personally or have heard about? That's just counting on one hand, folks.

As Indians, we have endured. We are still here. We have survived everything that European "civilization" has imposed on us. There are approximately 130 different Indian languages still spoken in North America of the some 300 spoken at contact; 180 different Tribes incorporated and recognized by the Federal Government of the approximately 280 that once existed, with an additional 15–25 unrecognized Tribes that are lumped together on a reservation with other Tribes. We still have Women's Societies and there are at least 30 active women-centered Mother-Rite Cultures[4] existing and practicing their everyday life in that manner, on this continent.

We have been displaced, relocated, removed, terminated, educated, acculturated and in our hearts and minds we will always "go back to the blanket"[5] as long as we are still connected to our families, our Tribes and our land.

The Indian Way is a different way. It is a respectful way. The basic teachings in every Tribe that exists today as a Tribe in the Western Hemisphere are based on respect for all the things our Mother gave us. If we neglect her or anger her, she will make our lives very difficult and we always know that we have a hardship on ourselves and on our children. We are raised to be cautious and concerned for the *future* of our people, and that is how we raise our children—because *they* are *our* future. Your "civilization" has made all of us very sick and has made our mother earth sick and out of balance. Your kind of thinking and education has brought the whole world to the brink of total disaster, whereas the thinking and education among my people forbids the practice of almost everything Euro-Americans, in particular, value.

Those of you who are socialists and marxists have an ideology, but where in this country do you live communally on a common land base from generation to generation? Indians, who have a way of life instead of an ideology, do live on communal lands and don't accumulate anything—for the sake of accumulation.

Radicals look at reservation Indians and get very upset about their poverty conditions. But poverty to us is not the same thing as poverty is to you. Our poverty is that we can't be who we are. We can't hunt or fish or grow our food because our basic resources and the right to use them in traditional ways are denied us. In order to live well, we must be able to provide for ourselves in such a way that we can continue living as we always have. We still don't believe in being slaves to the "domineering" culture systems. Consequently, we are accused of many things based on those standards and values that make no sense to us.

You want us to act like you, to be like you so that we will be more acceptable, more likeable. You should try to be more like us regarding communal co-existence; respect and care for all living things and for the earth, the waters, and the atmosphere; respect for human dignity and the right to be who they are.

During the 1930s, 1940s and 1950s, relocation programs caused many Indians to become lost in the big cities of the United States and there were many casualties from alcoholism, vagrancy and petty crime. Most Indians were/are jailed for assault and battery in barroom brawls because the spiritual and psychological violation of Indian people trying to live in the dominant (domineering) culture generally forces us to numb ourselves as frequently as possible. That is difficult, if not impossible, for you to understand. White science studies dead things and creates poisonous substances to kill and maim the creatures as well as the humans. You call that progress. Indians call it insanity. Our science studies living things; how they interact and how they maintain a balanced existence. Your science disregards—even denies—the spirit world: ours believes in it and remains connected to it. We fast, pray to our ancestors, call on them when we dance and it rains—at Laguna, at Acoma, at Hopi—still, today. We fight among ourselves, we have border disputes, we struggle to exist in a modern context with our lands full of timber, uranium, coal, oil, gasoline, precious metals and semi-precious stones; full—because we are taught to

take only what we need and not because we are too ignorant to know what to do with all those resources. We are caught in the bind between private corporations and the government—"our guardian"—because they/you want all those resources. "Indians certainly don't need them"—and your people will do *anything* to get their hands on our mineral-rich lands. They will legislate, stir up internal conflicts, cause inter-Tribal conflicts, dangle huge amounts of monies as compensation for perpetual contracts and promise lifetime economic security. If we object, or sue to protect our lands, these suits will be held in litigation for fifteen to twenty years with "white" interests benefiting in the interim. Some of us give up and sell out, but there are many of us learning to hold out and many many more of us going back to the old ways of thinking, because we see that our ancestors were right and that the old ways were better ways. So, more Indians are going "back to the blanket," back to "Indian time," with less stress, fewer dominant (domineering) culture activities and occupations. Modern Indians are recreating Indian ways once again. All this leads to my vision as an Indian woman. It is my hope:

1. that you—all you non-Indians—study and learn about our systems of thought and internal social and scientific practices, leaving your patriarchal anthropology and history textbooks, academic training and methodologies at home or in the closet on a dusty shelf.

2. that your faculties, conference organizers, community organizers stop giving lip service to including a "Native American" for this or that with the appended phrase: "if we only knew one!" Go find one. There are hundreds of resource lists or Indian-run agencies, hundreds of Indian women in organizations all over the country—active and available with valuable contributions to make.

3. that you will strongly discourage or STOP the publication of any and all articles *about* Indians *written by non-Indians*, and publish work written by Indians about ourselves—whether you agree with us, approve of us or not.

4. that you will *stop colonizing us* and reinterpreting *our* experience.

5. that you will *listen* to us and *learn* from us. We carry ancient traditions that are thousands of years old. We are modern and wear clothes like yours and handle all the trappings of your "civi-

lization" as well as ours; maintain your Christianity as well as our ancient religions, and we are still connected to our ancestors, and our land base. You are the foreigners as long as you continue to believe in the progress that destroys our Mother.

You are not taught to respect our perfected cultures or our scientific achievements which have just recently been re-evaluated by your social scientists and "deemed worthy" of respect. Again, let me restate that 150 years of bad press will certainly make it extremely difficult for most white people to accept these "primitive" achievements without immediately attempting to connect them to aliens from outer space, Egyptians, Vikings, Asians and whatever sophisticated "others" you have been educated to acknowledge as those who showed the "New World" peoples "The Way." Interestingly, the only continents that were ever "discovered" (historically) where people already lived are North and South America. Who discovered Europe? Who discovered Africa? Who discovered Asia? Trade routes, yes—continents, no. Manifest Destiny will continue to reign as long as we teach our children that Columbus "discovered" America. Even this "fact" is untrue. He actually discovered an island in the Caribbean and *failed* to discover Cathay!

When we consistently make ourselves aware of these "historical facts" that are presented by the Conqueror—the white man—only then can all of us benefit from cultural traditions that are ten to thirty thousand years old. It is time for us to *share* the best of all our traditions and cultures, all over the world; and it is our duty and responsibility as the women of the world to make this positive contribution in any and every way we can, or we will ultimately become losers, as the Native Race of this hemisphere lost some four hundred years ago.

[1988]

Terms

1. Mestizos or Mezclados: The Latin American name for the offspring of a Native American and a Spaniard.
2. Hittites: Ancient non-black peoples of Asia Minor and Syria.
3. Manifest Destiny: A nineteenth-century belief that white people had the duty and right to control and develop the entire North American continent.

4. Mother-Rite Cultures: Societies in which motherhood is the central kinship bond and women are highly valued and have considerable influence.
5. "Go back to the blanket": A phrase used by missionaries and white educators referring to "educated" Indian children who rejected white "civilized" values and returned to their native culture.

Understanding the Reading

1. What are the positive and negative stereotypes of American Indians?
2. What does Sanchez mean when she says, "Children of this country have been raised to kill Indians"?
3. How does Sanchez characterize the Indian way?
4. Why do you think Sanchez objects to "articles about Indians written by non-Indians"?
5. What point is Sanchez making by her list of hopes?

Suggestions for Responding

1. Name and identify all the Native Americans you can think of. What does your list show you?
2. Write a summary of what you learned and thought about Indians when you were a child. Analyze how this correlates with Sanchez's assertions about cultural stereotypes of Indians.

31

Crimes against Humanity

WARD CHURCHILL

During the past couple of seasons, there has been an increasing wave of controversy regarding the names of professional sports teams like the Atlanta "Braves," Cleveland "Indians," Washington "Redskins," and Kansas City "Chiefs." The issue extends to the names of college teams like Florida State University "Seminoles," University of Illinois "Fighting Illini," and so on, right on down to high school outfits like the Lamar (Colorado) "Savages." Also involved have been team adoption of "mascots," replete with feathers, buckskins, beads, spears and "warpaint" (some fans have opted to adorn themselves in the same fashion), and nifty little "pep" gestures like the "Indian Chant" and "Tomahawk Chop."

A substantial number of American Indians have protested that use of native names, images and symbols as sports team mascots and the like is, by definition, a virulently racist practice. Given the historical relationship between Indians and non-Indians during what has been called the "Conquest of America," American Indian Movement leader (and American Indian Anti-Defamation Council founder) Russell Means has compared the practice to contemporary Germans naming their soccer teams the "Jews," "Hebrews," and "Yids," while adorning their uniforms with grotesque caricatures of Jewish faces taken from the Nazis' anti-Semitic propaganda of the 1930s. Numerous demonstrations have occurred in conjunction with games—most notably during the November 15, 1992 match-up between the Chiefs and Redskins in Kansas City—by angry Indians and their supporters.

In response, a number of players—especially African Americans and other minority athletes—have been trotted out by professional team owners like Ted Turner, as well as university and public school officials, to announce that they mean not to insult but to honor native people. They have been joined by the television networks and most major newspapers, all of which have editorialized that Indian discomfort with the situation is "no big deal," insisting that the whole thing is just "good, clean fun." The country needs more such fun, they've argued, and "a few disgruntled Native Americans" have no right to undermine the nation's enjoyment of its leisure time by complaining. This is especially the case, some have argued, "in hard times like these." It has even been contended that Indian outrage at being systematically degraded—rather than the degradation itself—creates "a serious barrier to the sort of intergroup communication so necessary in a multicultural society such as ours."

Okay, let's communicate. We are frankly dubious that those advancing such positions really believe their own rhetoric, but, just for the sake of argument, let's accept the premise that they are sincere. If what they say is true, then isn't it time we spread such "inoffensiveness" and "good cheer" around among *all* groups so that *everybody* can participate *equally* in fostering the round of national laughs they call for? Sure it is—the country can't have too much fun or "intergroup involvement"—so the more, the merrier. Simple consistency demands that anyone who thinks

the Tomahawk Chop is a swell pastime must be just as hearty in their endorsement of the following ideas—by the logic used to defend the defamation of American Indians—to help us all really start yukking it up.

First, as a counterpart to the Redskins, we need an NFL team called "Niggers" to honor Afro-Americans. Half-time festivities for fans might include a simulated stewing of the opposing coach in a large pot while players and cheerleaders dance around it, garbed in leopard skins and wearing fake bones in their noses. This concept obviously goes along with the kind of gaiety attending the Chop, but also with the actions of the Kansas City Chiefs, whose team members—prominently including black team members—lately appeared on a poster looking "fierce" and "savage" by way of wearing Indian regalia. Just a bit of harmless "morale boosting," says the Chiefs' front office. You bet.

So that the newly formed Niggers sports club won't end up too out of sync while expressing the "spirit" and "identity" of Afro-Americans in the above fashion, a baseball franchise—let's call this one the "Sambos"—should be formed. How about a basketball team called the "Spearchuckers"? A hockey team called the "Jungle Bunnies"? Maybe the "essence" of these teams could be depicted by images of tiny black faces adorned with huge pairs of lips. The players could appear on TV every week or so gnawing on chicken legs and spitting watermelon seeds at one another. Catchy, eh? Well, there's "nothing to be upset about," according to those who love wearing "war bonnets" to the Super Bowl or having "Chief Illiniwik" dance around the sports arenas of Urbana, Illinois.

And why stop there? There are plenty of other groups to include. "Hispanics"? They can be "represented" by the Galveston "Greasers" and San Diego "Spics," at least until the Wisconsin "Wetbacks" and Baltimore "Beaners" get off the ground. Asian Americans? How about the "Slopes," "Dinks," "Gooks," and "Zipperheads"? Owners of the latter teams might get their logo ideas from editorial page cartoons printed in the nation's newspapers during World War II: slant-eyes, buck teeth, big glasses, but nothing racially insulting or derogatory, according to the editors and artists involved at the time. Indeed, this Second World War–vintage stuff can be seen as just another barrel of laughs, at least by what current editors say are their "local standards" concerning American Indians.

Let's see. Who's been left out? Teams like the Kansas City "Kikes," Hanover "Honkies," San Leandro "Shylocks," Daytona "Dagos," and Pittsburgh "Polacks" will fill a certain social void among white folk. Have a religious belief? Let's all go for the gusto and gear up the Milwaukee "Mackerel Snappers" and Hollywood "Holy Rollers." The Fighting Irish of Notre Dame can be rechristened the "Drunken Irish" or "Papist Pigs." Issues of gender and sexual preference can be addressed through creation of teams like the St. Louis "Sluts," Boston "Bimbos," Detroit "Dykes," and the Fresno "Fags." How about the Gainesville "Gimps" and Richmond "Retards," so the physically and mentally impaired won't be excluded from our fun and games?

Now, don't go getting "overly sensitive" out there. None of this is demeaning or insulting, at least not when it's being done to Indians. Just ask the folks who are doing it, or their apologists like Andy Rooney in the national media. They'll tell you—as in fact they *have* been telling you—that there's been no harm done, regardless of what their victims think, feel, or say. The situation is exactly the same as when those with precisely the same mentality used to insist that Step 'n' Fetchit was okay, or Rochester on the Jack Benny Show, or Amos and Andy, Charlie Chan, the Frito Bandito, or any of the other cutesy symbols making up the lexicon of American racism. Have we communicated yet?

Let's get just a little bit real here. The notion of "fun" embodied in rituals like the Tomahawk Chop must be understood for what it is. There's not a single non-Indian example used above which can be considered socially acceptable in even the most marginal sense. The reasons are obvious enough. So why is it different where American Indians are concerned? One can only conclude that, in contrast to the other groups at issue, Indians are (falsely) perceived as being too few, and therefore too weak, to defend themselves effectively against racist and otherwise offensive behavior.

Fortunately, there are some glimmers of hope. A few teams and their fans have gotten the message and have responded appropriately. Stanford University, which opted to drop the name "Indians" from Stanford, has experienced no resulting dropoff in attendance. Meanwhile, the local newspaper in Portland, Oregon, recently decided its long-standing editorial policy prohibiting use of racial epithets should include derogatory team names. The Redskins, for instance, are now referred to as "the Washington team," and will continue to be described in this way until the franchise adopts an inoffensive moniker (newspaper sales in Portland have suffered no decline as a result).

Such examples are to be applauded and encouraged. They stand as figurative beacons in the night, proving beyond all doubt that it is quite possible to indulge in the pleasure of athletics without accepting blatant racism into the bargain.

On October 16, 1946, a man named Julius Streicher mounted the steps of a gallows. Moments later he was dead, the sentence of an international tribunal composed of representatives of the United States, France, Great Britain, and the Soviet Union having been imposed. Streicher's body was then cremated, and—so horrendous were his crimes thought to have been—his ashes dumped into an unspecified German river so that "no one should ever know a particular place to go for reasons of mourning his memory."

Julius Streicher had been convicted at Nuremberg, Germany, of what were termed "Crimes against Humanity." The lead prosecutor in his case—Justice Robert Jackson of the U.S. Supreme Court—had not argued that the defendant had killed anyone, nor that he had personally committed any especially violent act. Nor was it contended that Streicher had held any particularly important position in the German government during the period in which the so-called Third Reich had exterminated some 6,000,000 Jews, as well as several million Gypsies, Poles, Slavs, homosexuals, and other *untermenschen* (subhumans).

The sole offense for which the accused was ordered put to death was in having served as publisher/editor of a Bavarian tabloid titled *Der Sturmer* during the early to mid-1930s, years before the Nazi genocide actually began. In this capacity, he had penned a long series of virulently anti-Semitic editorials and "news" stories, usually accompanied by cartoons and other images graphically depicting Jews in extraordinarily derogatory fashion. This, the prosecution asserted, had done much to "dehumanize" the targets of his distortion in the mind of the German public. In turn, such dehumanization had made it possible—or at least easier—for average Germans to later indulge in the outright liquidation of Jewish "vermin." The tribunal agreed, holding that Streicher was therefore complicit in genocide and deserving of death by hanging.

During his remarks to the Nuremberg tribunal, Justice Jackson observed that, in implementing its sentences, the participating powers were morally and legally binding themselves to adhere forever after to the same standards of conduct that were being applied to Streicher and the other Nazi leaders. In the alternative, he said, the victorious allies would have committed "pure murder" at Nuremberg—no different in substance from that carried out by those they presumed to judge—rather than establishing the "permanent benchmark for justice" which was intended.

Yet, in the United States of Robert Jackson, the indigenous American Indian population had already been reduced, in a process which is ongoing to this day, from perhaps 12.5 million in the year 1500 to fewer than 250,000 by the beginning of the twentieth century. This was accomplished, according to official sources, "largely through the cruelty of [Euro-American] settlers," and an informal but clear governmental policy which had made it an articulated goal to "exterminate these red vermin," or at least whole segments of them.

Bounties had been placed on the scalps of Indians—any Indians—in places as diverse as Georgia, Kentucky, Texas, the Dakotas, Oregon, and California, and had been maintained until resident Indian populations were decimated or disappeared altogether. Entire peoples such as the Cherokee had been reduced to half their size through a policy of forced removal from their homelands east of the Mississippi River to what were then considered less preferable areas in the West.

Others, such as the Navajo, suffered the same fate while under military guard for years on end. The United States Army had also perpetrated a long series of wholesale massacres of Indians at places like Horseshoe Bend, Bear River, Sand Creek, the Washita River, the Marias River, Camp Robinson, and Wounded Knee.

Through it all, hundreds of popular novels—each competing with the next to make Indians appear more grotesque, menacing, and inhuman—were sold in the tens of millions of copies in the United States. Plainly, the Euro-American public was being conditioned to see Indians in such a way as to allow their eradication to continue. And continue it did until the Manifest Destiny[1] of the United States—a direct precursor to what Hitler would subsequently call *Lebensraumpolitik* (the politics of living space)—was consummated.

By 1900, the national project of "clearing" Native Americans from their land and replacing them with "superior" Anglo-American settlers was complete; the indigenous population had been reduced by as much as 98 percent while approximately 97.5 percent of their original territory had "passed" to the invaders. The survivors had been concentrated, out of sight and mind of the public, on scattered "reservations," all of them under the self-assigned "plenary" (full) power of the federal government. There was, of course, no Nuremberg-style tribunal passing judgment on those who had fostered such circumstances in North America. No U.S. official or private citizen was ever imprisoned—never mind hanged—for implementing or propagandizing what had been done. Nor had the process of genocide afflicting Indians been completed. Instead, it merely changed form.

Between the 1880s and the 1980s, nearly half of all Native American children were coercively transferred from their own families, communities, and cultures to those of the conquering society. This was done through compulsory attendance at remote boarding schools, often hundreds of miles from their homes, where native children were kept for years on end while being systematically "deculturated" (indoctrinated to think and act in the manner of Euro Americans rather than as Indians). It was also accomplished through a pervasive foster home and adoption program—including "blind" adoptions, where children would be permanently denied information as to who they were/are and where they'd come from—placing native youths in non-Indian homes.

The express purpose of all this was to facilitate a U.S. governmental policy to bring about the "assimilation" (dissolution) of indigenous societies. In other words, Indian cultures as such were to be caused to disappear. Such policy objectives are directly contrary to the United Nations 1948 Convention on Punishment and Prevention of the Crime of Genocide, an element of international law arising from the Nuremberg proceedings. The forced "transfer of the children" of a targeted "racial, ethnical, or religious group" is explicitly prohibited as a genocidal activity under the Convention's second article.

Article II of the Genocide Convention also expressly prohibits involuntary sterilization as a means of "preventing births among" a targeted population. Yet, in 1975, it was conceded by the U.S. government that its Indian Health Service (IHS), then a subpart of the Bureau of Indian Affairs (BIA), was even then conducting a secret program of involuntary sterilization that had affected approximately 40 percent of all Indian women. The program was allegedly discontinued, and the IHS was transferred to the Public Health Service, but no one was punished. In 1990, it came out that the IHS was inoculating Inuit children in Alaska with hepatitis-B vaccine. The vaccine had already been banned by the World Health Organization as having a demonstrated correlation with the HIV syndrome which is itself correlated to AIDS. As this is written, a "field test" of hepatitis-A vaccine, also HIV-correlated, is being conducted on Indian reservations in the northern plains region.

The Genocide Convention makes it a "crime against humanity" to create conditions leading to the destruction of an identifiable human group, as such. Yet the BIA has utilized the government's plenary prerogatives to negotiate mineral leases "on behalf of" Indian peoples, paying a fraction of standard royalty rates. The result has been "super profits" for a number of preferred U.S. corporations. Meanwhile, Indians, whose reservations ironically turned out to be in some of the most mineral-rich areas of North America, which makes us the nominally wealthiest segment of the continent's population, live in dire poverty.

By the government's own data in the mid-1980s, Indians received the lowest annual and lifetime per capita incomes of any aggregate population group in the United States. Concomitantly, we suffer the highest rate of infant mortality, death by exposure and malnutrition, disease, and the like. Under such circumstances, alcoholism and other escapist forms of substance abuse are endemic in the Indian community, a situation which leads both to a general physical debilitation of the population and to a catastrophic accident rate. Teen suicide among Indians is several times the national average.

The average life expectancy of a reservation-based Native American man is barely forty-five years; women can expect to live less than three years longer.

Such itemizations could be continued at great length, including matters like the radioactive contamination of large portions of contemporary Indian Country, the forced relocation of traditional Navajos, and so on. But the point should be made: Genocide, as defined in international law, is a continuing fact of day-to-day life (and death) for North America's native peoples. Yet there has been—and is—only the barest flicker of public concern about, or even consciousness of, this reality. Absent any serious expression of public outrage, no one is punished and the process continues.

A salient reason for public acquiescence before the ongoing holocaust in Native North America has been a continuation of the popular legacy, often through more effective media. Since 1925, Hollywood has released more than 2,000 films, many of them rerun frequently on television, portraying Indians as strange, perverted, ridiculous, and often dangerous things of the past. Moreover, we are habitually presented to mass audiences one-dimensionally, devoid of recognizable human motivations and emotions; Indians thus serve as props, little more. We have thus been thoroughly and systematically dehumanized.

Nor is this the extent of it. Everywhere, we are used as logos, as mascots, as jokes: "Big Chief" writing tablets, "Red Man" chewing tobacco, "Winnebago" campers, "Navajo" and "Cherokee" and "Pontiac" and "Cadillac" pickups and automobiles. There are the Cleveland "Indians," the Kansas City "Chiefs," the Atlanta "Braves," and the Washington "Redskins" professional sports teams—not to mention those in thousands of colleges, high schools, and elementary schools across the country—each with their own degrading caricatures and parodies of Indians and/or things Indian. Pop fiction continues in the same vein, including an unending stream of New Age manuals purporting to expose the inner works of indigenous spirituality in everything from pseudo-philosophical to do-it-yourself styles. Blond yuppies from Beverly Hills amble about the country claiming to be reincarnated seventeenth-century Cheyenne Ushamans ready to perform previously secret ceremonies.

In effect, a concerted, sustained, and in some ways accelerating effort has gone into making Indians unreal. It is thus of obvious importance that the American public begin to think about the implications of such things the next time they witness a gaggle of face-painted and war-bonneted buffoons doing the "Tomahawk Chop" at a baseball or football game. It is necessary that they think about the implications of the grade-school teacher adorning their child in turkey feathers to commemorate Thanksgiving. Think about the significance of John Wayne or Charlton Heston killing a dozen "savages" with a single bullet the next time a western comes on TV. Think about why Land-o-Lakes finds it appropriate to market its butter with the stereotyped image of an "Indian princess" on the wrapper. Think about what it means when non-Indian academics profess—as they often do—to "know more about Indians than Indians do themselves." Think about the significance of charlatans like Carlos Castaneda and Jamake Highwater and Mary Summer Rain and Lynn Andrews churning out "Indian" best-sellers, one after the other, while Indians typically can't get into print.

Think about the real situation of American Indians. Think about Julius Streicher. Remember Justice Jackson's admonition. Understand that the treatment of Indians in American popular culture is not "cute" or "amusing" or just "good, clean fun."

Know that it causes real pain and real suffering to real people. Know that it threatens our very survival. And know that this is just as much a crime against humanity as anything the Nazis ever did. It is likely that the indigenous people of the United States will never demand that those guilty of such criminal activity be punished for their deeds. But the least we have the right to expect—indeed, to demand—is that such practices finally be brought to a halt.

[1993]

Term

1. Manifest Destiny: A nineteenth-century belief that white people had the duty and right to control and develop the entire North American continent.

Understanding the Reading

1. Why do American Indians object to the use of Indian names, images, and symbols?
2. How has such usage been justified by non-Indians?
3. How does Churchill expose the racism and degradation of this practice?
4. How is this practice beginning to change?
5. Why was Julius Streicher executed after World War II?
6. What caused the dramatic decline in the Native American population?
7. What happened to Native American children between the 1880s and the 1980s?
8. What is the U.N. Genocide Convention, and how has it been violated in the United States?
9. What are the conditions of life in the Indian community?
10. How have Indians been portrayed in the mass media?

Suggestions for Responding

1. Write a short essay explaining why you think American Indians have been singled out by the sports industry.

2. Write a letter to the editor of your local newspaper stating your position on the exploitation of Native American images.

32

Anti-Semitism in the United States

Robert Cherry

From most accounts, it appears that anti-Semitism was most intense during the period 1877–1927, from the time Joseph Seligman was refused admittance to the Grand Hotel in Saratoga, New York, until Henry Ford publicly apologized for anti-Semitic articles in his Dearborn Press.[1] Prior to this period, there were examples of anti-Semitism, beginning with the reluctance of Peter Stuyvesant to allow the first group of Jews to enter New York in 1654. Anti-Semitism also was part of the Know-Nothing party's[2] anti-immigration campaign in the 1850s and General Grant's policies during the Civil War. However, anti-Semitism became widespread only during the latter part of the nineteenth century.

Oscar Handlin and Richard Hofstadter identify anti-Semitism with the short-lived agrarian Populist movement[3] of the 1890s. They contend that the Populists associated traditional Jewish stereotypes with the evils faced by the yeomanry. Increasingly forced into debt peonage, the yeomanry demanded elimination of the gold standard. However, President Cleveland pursued a scheme with the Rothschild banking empire[4] to protect the gold standard. This led many Populists to attack Jews for what they perceived as Jewish control of world finance. Also, the yeomanry often divided society into those who engaged in productive labor and those who did not. Typically, Jews in rural areas were identified with nonproductive labor—that is, they were commercial and financial middlemen who gained income from the work of others.

Other historians claim that early twentieth century anti-Semitism was associated with xenophobic fears fueled by mass immigration. Later Jewish immigrants tended to be poorer, less skilled, and less urbanized than the Jews who had emigrated from Germany during the 1850s. They were considered a dangerous criminal element. In 1908 New York City's police commissioner Theodore Bingham suggested that half of all criminals were Jews. The 1910 report of the

Dillingham commission claimed that large numbers of Jews scattered throughout the United States seduced and kept girls in prostitution and that many were petty thieves, pickpockets, and gamblers. The report stated, "Jews comprise the largest proportion of alien prisoners under sentence for offenses against chastity."

During this era, Jews were not pictured simply as petty criminals. The stereotypic Jewish businessman was one who manipulated laws and engaged in white-collar crimes, especially insurance fraud. Michael N. Dobkowski gives numerous examples of how these stereotypes became part of the popular culture. In describing a Jewish businessman, *Puck*, a popular New York City humor magazine, noted that "despite hard times, he has had two failures and three fires." It claimed, "There is only one thing [their] race hates more than pork—asbestos." So pervasive were these images that the Anti-Defamation League (ADL)[5] in 1913 noted, "Whenever a theatre producer wishes to depict a betrayer of the public trust, a white slaver or other criminal, the actor is directed to present himself as a Jew." Indeed, for more than fifty years, *Roget's Thesaurus* included the word *Jew* as a synonym for usurer, cheat, extortioner, and schemer.

Some historians, including John Higham, believe that anti-Semitism was more significant among the elite than among either the rural yeomanry or the middle-class xenophobic nativists. Higham notes that the patrician class, typified by Henry and Brooks Adams, realized that the industrialization process was transforming the United States into a materialistic, pragmatic society that had less concern for tradition and culture than previously. This transformation, which meant the end of patrician hegemony over political and economic affairs, was thought to be the result of Jewish influence.

According to Higham, the patrician class believed that Jewish commercial values undermined basic American traditions. While most became defeatist, some, including Henry Cabot Lodge and John J. Chapman, attempted to reduce Jewish influence. In 1896 Lodge proposed legislation requiring immigrants to be literate in the language of their country of origin rather than in another language. Since most Polish and Russian Jews were literate in Yiddish but not in Polish or Russian, this would have made them ineligible for immigration. Lodge's legislative proposal was defeated, and Jewish immigration continued. Chapman was an active urban reformer who did not have anti-Semitic values until the time of World War I. Dobkowski contends that his inability to reform urban society led him to agree with Henry Adams that the reason for urban decay was growing Jewish influence.

Dobkowski documents how progressive muckrakers,[6] including George Kibbe Turner, Jacob Riis, and Emily Balch, echoed many of the charges against Jews made by the patrician class. Lamenting the decay of cities, Turner considered Jewish immigrants to be at the "core of this festering human cancer." Riis believed that the lack of social values among Jewish immigrants was overwhelming urban society. He thought that recent Jewish immigrants believed that "money is God. Life itself is of little value compared with even the leanest bank account." Even Balch, a leading defender of social welfare reforms, accepted negative Jewish stereotypes.

Liberal sociologist E. A. Ross believed that Jewish immigrants were cunning in their ability to use their wit to undermine business ethics and to commercialize professions and journalism. He claimed that attempts to exclude Jews from professional associations and social clubs had nothing to do with discrimination; instead, they reflected a strong desire not to associate with individuals from an immoral culture. Tom Watson, a former Populist and later KKK leader, used Ross's writings to justify his organization's anti-Semitism.

These examples of anti-Semitic views sometimes provide the basis for contentions that Jews faced discrimination similar to that of other groups. Thomas Sowell implies this when he states, "Anti-Semitism in the United States assumed growing and unprecedented proportions in the last quarter of the nineteenth century with the mass arrival of eastern European Jews. . . . [H]elp wanted ads began to specify 'Christian,' as they had once specified 'Protestant' to exclude the Irish."

This is an incorrect assessment. During the last quarter of the nineteenth century, the United States adopted a reservation program for American Indians, an exclusionary policy for Orientals, Jim Crow laws for blacks, and an anti-immigration movement to harass Italian and Polish newcomers. In contrast, before World War I, Jewish immigrants faced few anti-Semitic barriers to their advancement. For example, in 1910 it was estimated that only 0.3 percent of employment advertisements specified Christians and no colleges had adopted restrictive entrance policies.

Only after World War I and the Bolshevik Revolution when xenophobic fears peaked did anti-Semitic restrictions become significant. Zosa Szakowski documents the vigorous attack on Jews during the anti-immigrant Palmer raids[7] in 1919. In 1920, 10 percent of employment ads specified Christians, rising to 13.3 percent by 1926. Stephen Steinberg summarizes the restrictive entrance policies many prestigious universities, including Columbia and Harvard, adopted at that time to reduce Jewish enrollment.

At about this time, Henry Ford began publishing anti-Semitic tracts in his Dearborn Press. Like Ross, Ford was a Progressive. He supported Wilson,[8] social legislation, antilynching laws, and urban reforms. Unlike Ross, Ford had nothing but praise for the ordinary Jewish businessman, and he could count Jews among his personal friends. However, Ford thought that industrialists were at the mercy of financial institutions controlled by international Jewry.

Adopting a similar perspective, Robert La Follette introduced a petition to Congress in 1923 assigning responsibility for World War I to Jewish international bankers. This petition also asserted that Wilson, Lloyd George, Clemenceau, and Orlando[9]—the officials in charge of negotiating the peace treaty at Versailles—were surrounded by Jewish advisors.

World's Work and other liberal publications also complained that Jews were not 100 percent American. They identified Jews with draft dodgers and war profiteers, but also complained that Jews, though taking advantage of the opportunities given by democracy, had not taken "the one essential act of a democratic society. . . . They are not willing to lose their identity." By the end of the decade, however, after immigration restrictions laws had been passed and the anticommunist hysteria had subsided, anti-Semitism again subsided to a minimum level.

[1989]

Terms

1. Dearborn Press: The publisher of the very conservative, anti-Semitic magazine the *Dearborn Independent*.
2. Know-Nothing Party: A political movement in the mid-nineteenth century that was antagonistic to Catholics and immigrants.
3. Populist movement: A political movement advocating the rights of the common people.
4. Rothschild banking empire: An international financial empire created by a Jewish banking

dynasty during the first half of the nineteenth century.
5. Anti-Defamation League (ADL): A Jewish civil rights organization.
6. Muckrakers: Investigative reporters who focused on corruption.
7. Palmer raids: Raids authorized by Attorney General A. Mitchell Palmer, who zealously enforced the Espionage Act of 1917 to suppress antiwar and socialist publications.
8. Wilson: Woodrow Wilson, Democratic president of the United States, 1913–1921.
9. Lloyd George, Clemenceau, and Orlando: David Lloyd George, British prime minister, 1916–1922; Georges Clemenceau, French premier, 1906–1909, 1917; Vittorio Emanuele Orlando, Italian prime minister, 1917–1919.

Understanding the Reading

1. Explain why the Populists attacked Jews.
2. What stereotypes were assigned to Jews in the early part of the twentieth century?
3. Why were the elites anti-Semitic?
4. What other justifications have been given to rationalize anti-Semitism?

Suggestions for Responding

1. Describe the Jewish stereotype that underlies the various beliefs Cherry discusses, and explain its inconsistencies.
2. Do you agree with the claim by *World's Work* that losing one's identity is "the one essential act of a democratic society"? Why or why not?

33

Behind Barbed Wire

JOHN HERSEY

On March 31, 1942, there appeared on notice boards in certain communities on the Western Seaboard of the United States a number of broadsides bearing the ominous title "Civilian Exclusion Orders." These bulletins warned all residents of Japanese descent that they were going to have to move out of their homes. No mention was made of where they would have to go. One member of each family was directed to report for instructions at neighboring control stations.

The Japanese attack on Pearl Harbor had taken place a little less than four months earlier. These Exclusion Orders cast a wide net. There were about 125,000 persons of Japanese ancestry scattered along the coastal tier of states then, and seven out of ten of them, having been born there, were full-fledged citizens of the United States; yet no distinction between alien and native was made among those summoned to control stations. The United States had declared war on Germany and Italy, as well as Japan, but no German or Italian enemy aliens, to say nothing of German Americans or Italian Americans, were subjected to these blanket Exclusion Orders. Only "Japanese aliens and non-aliens," as the official euphemism put it.

Each person who responded to the summons had to register the names of all family members and was told to show up at a certain time and place, a few days later, with all of them, bringing along only such baggage as they could carry by hand—for a trip to a destination unknown. Names had become numbers. "Henry went to the control station to register the family," wrote a Japanese American woman years later. "He came home with twenty tags, all numbered 10710, tags to be attached to each piece of baggage, and one to hang from our coat lapels. From then on, we were known as Family No. 10710." "I lost my identity," another woman would assert, describing the replacement of her name by a number. "I lost my privacy and dignity."

There followed a period of devastating uncertainty and anxiety. "We were given eight days to liquidate our possessions," one of the evacuees testified at an investigation by the Department of Justice many years later. The time allowed varied from place to place. "We had about two weeks," another recalled, "to do something. Either lease the property or sell everything." Another: "While in Modesto, the final notice for evacuation came with a four-day notice." Under the circumstances, the evacuees had to dispose of their businesses, their homes and their personal possessions at panic prices to hostile buyers.

"It is difficult," one man would later testify, "to describe the feeling of despair and humiliation experienced by all of us as we watched the Caucasians coming to look over our possessions and offering such nominal amounts, knowing we had no recourse but to accept whatever they were offering because we did not know what the future held for us." One

woman sold a thirty-seven-room hotel for $300. A man who owned a pickup truck, and had just bought a set of new tires and a new battery for $125, asked only that amount of a prospective buyer. "The man 'bought' our pickup for $25." One homeowner, in despair, wanted to burn his house down. "I went to the storage shed to get the gasoline tank and pour the gasoline on my house, but my wife . . . said don't do it, maybe somebody can use this house; we are civilized people, not savages."

By far, the greatest number of Nisei—the term for first-generation Japanese Americans that came to be used as the generic word for all ethnic Japanese living in America—were in agriculture, growing fruit, vegetables, nursery plants and specialty crops. They had worked wonders in the soil. They owned about one-fiftieth of the arable land in the three Pacific Coast states, and what they had made of their farms is suggested by the fact that the average value per acre of all farms in the three states in 1940 was roughly $38, while an acre on a Nisei farm was worth, on average, $280.

But now the farmers had to clear out in a matter of days. The Mother's Day crop of flowers, the richest harvest of the year, was about to be gathered; it had to be abandoned. An owner of one of the largest nurseries in southern California, unable to dispose of his stock, gave it all to the Veterans Hospital adjoining his land. A strawberry grower asked for a deferral of his evacuation summons for a few days, so he could harvest his crop. Denied the permission, he bitterly plowed the berries under. The next day, the Federal Bureau of Investigation charged him with an act of sabotage and put him in jail.

Assured by authorities that they could store property and reclaim it after the war, many put their chattels in impromptu warehouses—homes and garages and outbuildings—only to have the stored goods, before long, vandalized or stolen. Some leased their property but never received rents. Some were cheated by their tenants, who sold the property as if it were their own.

On the day of departure, evacuees found themselves herded into groups of about 500, mostly at railroad and bus stations. They wore their numbered tags and carried hand-baggage containing possessions that they had packed in fear and perplexity, not knowing where they were going. They embarked on buses and trains. Some trains had blacked-out windows. Uniformed guards carrying weapons patrolled the cars.

"To this day," one woman recalled long afterward, "I can remember vividly the plight of the elderly, some on stretchers, orphans herded onto the train by caretakers, and especially a young couple with four preschool children.

"The mother had two frightened toddlers hanging on to her coat. In her arms, she carried two crying babies. The father had diapers and other baby paraphernalia strapped to his back. In his hands he struggled with duffel bag and suitcase."

Each group was unloaded, after its trip, at one of sixteen assembly centers, most of which were located at fairgrounds and racetracks. There seeing barbed wire and searchlights, and under the guard of guns, these "aliens and non-aliens" were forced to realize that all among them—even those who had sons or brothers in the U.S. Army—were considered to be dangerous people. At the entrance to the Tanforan Assembly Center, one man later remembered, "stood two lines of troops with rifles and fixed bayonets pointed at the evacuees as they walked between the soldiers to the prison compound. Overwhelmed with bitterness and blind with rage, I screamed every obscenity I knew at the armed guards, daring them to shoot me." Most evacuees were silent, dazed. Many wept.

A typical assembly center was at the Santa Anita race track. Each family was allotted a space in the horse stalls of about 200 square feet, furnished with cots, blankets and pillows; the evacuees had to make their own pallets, filling mattress shells with straw. There were three large mess halls, in which 2,000 people at a time stood in line with tin plates and cups, to be served mass-cooked food that cost an average of 39 cents per person per day—rough fare, usually overcooked, such as brined liver, which, one testified, "would bounce if dropped."

"We lined up," another later wrote, "for mail, for checks, for meals, for showers, for washrooms, for laundry tubs, for toilets. . . ." Medical care, under jurisdiction of the Public Health Service, was provided by evacuee doctors and nurses who were recruited to serve their fellow inmates in an improvised clinic, supplied at first with nothing more than mineral oil, iodine, aspirin, sulfa ointment, Kaopectate and alcohol. Toilets were communal, without compartments. The evacuees bathed in what had been horse showers, with a partition between the men's and the women's section. When the women complained that men were climbing the partition and looking at them, a camp official responded, "Are you sure you women are not climbing the walls to look at the men?"

Toward the end of May 1942, evacuees began to be transferred from these temporary assembly centers to thirteen permanent concentration camps—generally called by the more decorous name of "relocation centers"—where they would be held prisoner until several months before the end of the war. By Nov. 1, some 106,770 internees had been put behind barbed wire in six western states and Arkansas.

Thus began the bitterest national shame of the Second World War for the sweet land of liberty: the mass incarceration, on racial grounds alone, on false evidence of military necessity, and in contempt of their supposedly inalienable rights, of an entire class of American citizens—along with others who were not citizens in the country of their choice only because that country had long denied people of their race the right to naturalize. (A 1924 federal law had cut off all Japanese immigration and naturalization; it was not rescinded until 1952.)

"My mother, two sisters, niece, nephew, and I left" by train, one recalled in later years. "Father joined us later. Brother left earlier by bus. We took whatever we could carry. So much we left behind, but the most valuable thing I lost was my freedom."

The Manzanar camp was quickly built in the desert country of east-central California. Its second director, a humane and farsighted man named Ralph Merritt, realized that history ought to have some testimony of what its victims had managed to salvage from an unprecedented American social crime. He had seen the consummate artistry of photographs taken in nearby Yosemite National Park by a friend of his, Ansel Adams, and he invited the great photographer to come to the camp to capture its woes and its marvels on film.

"Moved," Adams would later write, "by the human story unfolding in the encirclement of desert and mountains, and by the wish to identify my photography . . . with the tragic momentum of the times, I came to Manzanar with my cameras in the fall of 1943."

Adams' photographs restore energy to the sorry record—and remind us that this very word "record" in its ancient origins meant "to bring back the heart."

But first it seems appropriate to re-engage the mind, for the stories of Manzanar and the other camps raise grave questions for the American polity: Could such a thing occur again? How did this slippage in the most precious traditions of a free country come about?

The Japanese attack on Pearl Harbor on Dec. 7, 1941, threw the American psyche into a state of shock. Despite four years' demonstration of the skill and dispatch—and cruelty—of the Japanese invasion of China, American military commanders in the Philippines and elsewhere had issued boastful statements, over and over again, about how quickly the "Japs," as they were scornfully called, would be wiped out if they dared attack American installations.

Then suddenly, within hours, the U.S. Pacific Fleet was crippled at anchor. Most of the U.S. air arm in the Philippines was wrecked on the ground. American pride dissolved overnight into American rage and hysteria—and nowhere so disastrously as on the country's western shores.

President Franklin D. Roosevelt promptly proclaimed, and Congress voted, a state of war against Japan, and within days the other Axis powers, Germany and Italy, also became belligerents. The president issued orders that classified nationals of those countries as enemy aliens. These orders gave responsibility for carrying out certain restrictions against enemy aliens of all three countries to Attorney General Francis Biddle and the Department of Justice. Biddle was given authority to establish prohibited zones, from which enemy aliens could be moved at will; to seize as contraband any weapons and other articles as required for national security; to freeze enemy aliens' funds, and to intern any of them who might be deemed dangerous. These were perfectly normal wartime precautions against enemy aliens only, for which there had been statutory precedent under President Woodrow Wilson in the First World War.

With great speed and efficiency, beginning on the very night of the attack, the Justice Department arrested certain marked enemy aliens of all three belligerent nations. Within three days, 857 Germans, 147 Italians and 1,291 Japanese (367 of them on the Hawaiian Islands, 924 on the continent) had been rounded up.

On the night of Dec. 8, when Pearl Harbor jitters were at their highest pitch, San Francisco suffered a false alarm of an air incursion. Military and/or naval radio trackers reported that enemy aircraft were soaring in over the Bay Area and later that they had turned back to sea without attacking. Planes of the Second Interceptor Command took off from Portland, Ore., and searched as far as 600 miles offshore

for a nonexistent Japanese aircraft carrier, from which the enemy planes were assumed to have been launched. At the first alarm, sirens sounded a warning, and San Francisco was supposed to be blacked out at once. But skyscrapers blazed, neon lights winked at hundreds of night spots, and Alcatraz was like a heap of sparkling diamonds in the bay.

Enter, the next morning, to center stage, a military figure in a high state of excitation. As commanding officer of the Fourth Army and Western Defense Command, Lieut. Gen. John L. DeWitt was charged with making sure that there would be no Pearl Harbors on the West Coast. That morning, a meeting at City Hall was called with Mayor Angelo Rossi and 200 of the city's civic leaders, and as *Life* magazine would put it, DeWitt "almost split with rage."

"You people," he said to them, "do not seem to realize we are at war. So get this: Last night there were planes over this community. They were enemy planes. I mean Japanese planes. And they were tracked out to sea. You think it was a hoax? It is damned nonsense for sensible people to think that the Army and Navy would practice such a hoax on San Francisco."

He shouted that it might have been "a good thing" if some bombs *had* been dropped. "It might have awakened some of the fools in this community who refuse to realize that this is a war."

On the night of this "air attack," one of DeWitt's subordinates, Maj. Gen. Joseph W. Stilwell, later to be the famous "Vinegar Joe" of the doomed campaigns in Burma and China, wrote in pencil in a dime-store notebook that he used as a diary, "Fourth Army"—obviously meaning its headquarters—"kind of jittery." Two nights later, DeWitt and his staff, hearing that there was to be an armed uprising of 20,000 Nisei in the San Francisco area, whipped up a plan to put all of them in military custody. The plan fortunately was aborted by the local F.B.I.[1] chief of station, Nat Pieper, who told the Army that the "reliable source" for their news of the uprising was a flake whom Pieper had once employed and had had to dismiss because of his "wild imaginings."

Next, on Dec. 13, came "reliable information" that an enemy attack on Los Angeles was imminent, and DeWitt's staff drafted a general alarm that would have advised all civilians to leave the city. Fortunately, it was never broadcast. That night, General Stilwell wrote in his notebook that General DeWitt was a "jackass."

The first week of the war brought news of one setback after another. The Japanese struck at Midway, Wake, the Philippines, Hong Kong, the Malay Peninsula and Thailand. On Dec. 13, they captured Guam. The American dream of invulnerability had suddenly been replaced by a feeling that the Japanese could do just about anything they wanted to do—including landing at any point along DeWitt's vast coastal command.

Two days after Pearl Harbor, Navy Secretary Frank Knox went to Hawaii to try to find out what had gone wrong there. On Dec. 15, he returned to the mainland from his scouting trip and called a press conference at which he said, "I think the most effective fifth-column work[2] of the entire war was done in Hawaii, with the possible exception of Norway." He carried back to Washington this report of treachery by resident Japanese, "both from the shores and from the sampans," and his absurdly impracticable recommendation that all those with Japanese blood be evacuated from Oahu.

His charges were quickly denied, in confidential reports, by J. Edgar Hoover of the F.B.I.; by John Franklin Carter, a journalist whom Roosevelt had enlisted to give him intelligence reports; and, after a few days, by Lieut. Gen. Delos C. Emmons, the newly appointed commanding officer in the Hawaiian Islands. But Frank Knox's statement was never denied by the Government—which, from Pearl Harbor to V-J Day, would record not a single case of sabotage by a Japanese alien or a Japanese American worse than the plowing under of strawberries.

In 1943, when General DeWitt would submit to the secretary of war his "Final Report" on the removal of the Japanese from the West Coast, one of its first assertions would be "The evacuation was impelled by military necessity." DeWitt wrote, "There were hundreds of reports nightly of signal lights visible from the coast, and of intercepts of unidentified radio transmissions."

Hoover scornfully ridiculed the "hysteria and lack of judgment" of DeWitt's Military Intelligence Division. An official of the Federal Communications Commission reported on the question of radio intercepts, "I have never seen an organization that was so hopeless to cope with radio intelligence requirements. . . . The personnel is unskilled and untrained. . . . As a matter of fact, the Army air stations have been reported by the Signal Corps station as Jap enemy stations."

DeWitt urged random spot raids on homes of ethnic Japanese to seize "subversive" weapons and cam-

eras. Attorney General Biddle stipulated that raiders should follow the constitutional requirement of finding probable cause for arrest, but DeWitt argued that being of Japanese descent was in itself probable cause. He insisted on searches without warrants, even of the homes of citizens. Yet the Justice Department concluded from F.B.I. reports, "We have not found a single machine gun, nor have we found any gun in any circumstances indicating that it was to be used in a manner helpful to our enemies. We have not found a camera which we have reason to believe was for use in espionage."

When it came right down to it, the mere fact of having Japanese blood and skin was, to DeWitt, enough basis for suspicion. When he wrote in his "Final Report" of the way the ethnic Japanese population was scattered through his Defense Command, he used the military term "deployed"—"in excess of 115,000 persons deployed along the Pacific Coast"—as if these people, these farmers and merchants and house servants, had been posted by plan, poised for attack.

Testifying before a Congressional subcommittee, DeWitt would say, as if this alone proved the military necessity he was trying to assert, "A Jap is a Jap."

The news from the Pacific after the first shock of Pearl Harbor grew worse and worse, and nerves in the Presidio[3] tightened. On Dec. 24 and 25, 1941, the Japanese took Wake Island and Hong Kong. On Dec. 27, Manila fell, and U.S. forces retreated to the Bataan Peninsula.

On Dec. 19, DeWitt urged on the War Department "that action be initiated at the earliest practicable date to collect all alien subjects fourteen years of age and over, of enemy nations and remove them" to inland places, where they should be kept "under restraint after removal." This recommendation covered only aliens—Germans and Italians as well as Japanese.

Toward the end of the month, according to Roger Daniels, who has written two authoritative books on the evacuation, DeWitt began talking by phone—outside the normal chain of command, without telling his superiors—with an officer he knew in Washington, Maj. Gen. Allen W. Gullion. Gullion was Provost Marshal General, the Army's top law enforcement officer. Since the fall of France in June 1940, he had been concerning himself with the question of how the military could acquire legal control over civilians in wartime—in case there should be a domestic fifth column—and DeWitt, evidently stung by the ridicule of his alarms by civilian agencies like the F.B.I. and the F.C.C.,[4] was much attracted by Gullion's views.

Gullion had the chief of his Aliens Division, Major Karl R. Bendetsen, draft a memorandum proposing that the president "place in the hands of the Secretary of War the right to take over aliens when he thought it was necessary."

In one of their turn-of-the-year conferences, Bendetsen outlined to DeWitt plans for surveillance and control of West Coast Nisei; if the Justice Department wouldn't do the job, Bendetsen told DeWitt, then it would be up to the Army—really, to the two of them—to do it. According to notes taken at the session, DeWitt went along with Bendetsen, saying that he had "little confidence that the enemy aliens are law-abiding or loyal in any sense of the word. Some of them, yes; many, no. Particularly the Japanese. I have no confidence in their loyalty whatsoever."

In organizations like the Native Sons of the Golden West and the American Legion, clamor for the incarceration of all Nisei was growing. Congressman Leland Ford of Los Angeles argued for their removal with a most peculiar logic. On Jan. 16, he wrote to Secretary of War Henry L. Stimson a formal recommendation "that all Japanese, whether citizens or not, be placed in inland concentration camps. As justification for this, I submit that if an American-born Japanese, who is a citizen, is really patriotic and wishes to make his contribution to the safety and welfare of this country, right here is his opportunity to do so. . . . Millions of other native-born citizens are willing to lay down their lives, which is a far greater sacrifice, of course, than being placed in a concentration camp."

There were, in fact, lots of patriotic Nisei. Many of them were fiercely and showily patriotic precisely because so many "real Americans" doubted their fidelity. Some had joined together in the Japanese-American Citizens League, which did all it could to flaunt its members' loyalty. Their idealistic creed, adopted before Pearl Harbor, said, "Although some individuals may discriminate against me, I shall never become bitter or lose faith, for I know that such persons are not representative of the majority of American people."

Nisei in many cities and towns helped with civil defense. Furthermore, many young Nisei volunteered for the Army. (In Italy and France, the Japanese American 442d Combat Regimental Team would turn out to be one of the most decorated units in the entire United States Army—with seven Presidential Distinguished Unit Citations, one Congressional Medal of Honor, 47 Distinguished Service Crosses, 350 Silver Stars, 810 Bronze Stars and more than 3,600 Purple Hearts. President Truman, attaching a Presidential Distinguished Unit Citation to the regimental colors, would say, "You fought not only the enemy, but you fought prejudice. . . .")

DeWitt's anxieties, however, flowered more and more, and they soon bore fruit. On Jan. 21, 1942, he recommended to Secretary Stimson the establishment of 86 "prohibited zones" in California, from which all "enemy" aliens would be removed, as well as a handful of larger "restricted zones," where they would be kept under close surveillance.

On Jan. 25, persuaded by DeWitt's reports of danger, Stimson recommended to Biddle that these zones be established. Since this request touched only enemy aliens, and meant moving them in most cases for very short distances, Biddle acceded.

At the beginning of February, voices raised on the West Coast against Japanese Americans became more and more shrill. The *Los Angeles Times* took up the cry that Japanese citizens were just as much enemies as Japanese aliens: "A viper is nonetheless a viper wherever the egg is hatched—so a Japanese-American, born of Japanese parents, grows up to be a Japanese, not an American." California's liberal Governor, Culbert L. Olson, who had earlier taken the position that Japanese Americans should continue in wartime to enjoy their constitutional rights, reversed himself in a radio address. Evidently on information from DeWitt, he said, "It is known that there are Japanese residents of California who have sought to aid the Japanese enemy by way of communicating information, or have shown indications of preparation for fifth column activities." He hinted that there might have to be large-scale removals.

Biddle wanted to issue a press release jointly with the Army, designed to calm public fears on the West Coast about sabotage and espionage, and on Feb. 4, he, Assistant Attorney General James Rowe Jr., J. Edgar Hoover, Stimson, McCloy, Gullion and Bendetsen met to discuss it. Gullion later described this encounter:

[The Justice officials] said there is too much hysteria about this thing; said these Western Congressmen are just nuts about it and the people getting hysterical and there is no evidence whatsoever of any reason for disturbing citizens, and the Department of Justice—Rowe started it and Biddle finished it—the Department of Justice will [have] nothing whatsoever to do with any interference with citizens, whether they are Japanese or not. They made me a little sore, and I said, well listen, Mr. Biddle, do you mean to tell me that if the Army, the men on the ground, determine it is a military necessity to move citizens, Jap citizens, that you won't help me? He didn't give a direct answer, he said the Department of Justice would be through if we interfered with citizens and writ of habeas corpus,[5] etc.

When DeWitt, on Feb. 9, asked for the establishment of much larger prohibited zones in Washington, Oregon and Arizona, Biddle refused to go along. "Your [recommendations] of prohibited areas . . . include the cities of Portland, Seattle, and Tacoma," he wrote, "and therefore contemplate a mass evacuation of many thousands. . . . No reasons were given for this mass evacuation. . . . The Department of Justice is not physically equipped to carry out any mass evacuation."

If there were to be any question of evacuating citizens, the Attorney General wanted no part of it—yet, in washing his hands of this eventuality, he now conceded that the Army might justify doing this as a "military necessity. . . . Such action, therefore, should in my opinion, be taken by the War Department and not by the Department of Justice."

Two days later, Stimson went over Biddle's head to Roosevelt. Unable to fit an appointment into a busy day, the president talked with Stimson on the phone. The secretary told Roosevelt that the Justice Department was dragging its feet and asked whether he would authorize the Army to move American citizens of Japanese ancestry as well as aliens away from sensitive areas. Further, he asked whether the president would favor evacuating more than 100,000 from the entire West Coast, 70,000 living in major urban areas, or small numbers living around critical zones, such as aircraft factories, "even though that would be more complicated and tension-producing than total evacuation."

Right after Stimson hung up, Assistant Secretary John J. McCloy jubilantly called Bendetsen in San Francisco to say that the president had declined to make a specific decision about numbers himself but had decided to cut out the Justice Department and

had given the Army "*carte blanche*[6] to do what we want to." Roosevelt's only urging was to "be reasonable as you can."

The very next day—so promptly as to suggest that there had been some orchestration—the most influential newspaper pundit in the country, Walter Lippmann, in a column titled "The Fifth Column on the Coast," [laid] out the basis for advocating the removal of citizens as well as aliens. "The Pacific Coast," he wrote, "is in imminent danger of a combined attack from within and without. . . . It is a fact that the Japanese Navy has been reconnoitering the coast more or less continuously. . . . There is an assumption [in Washington] that a citizen may not be interfered with unless he has committed an overt act. . . . The Pacific Coast is officially a combat zone. Some part of it may at any moment be a battlefield. And nobody ought to be on a battlefield who has no good reason for being there. There is plenty of room elsewhere for him to exercise his rights."

The day after the Lippmann article, the entire Pacific Coast Congressional delegation signed and delivered to Roosevelt a resolution urging "the immediate evacuation of all persons of Japanese lineage and all others, aliens and citizens alike, whose presence shall be deemed dangerous or inimical to the defense of the United States from . . . the entire strategic areas of the states of California, Oregon, and Washington, and the Territory of Alaska."

On Feb. 14, freed by Roosevelt's green light to the Army, doubtless encouraged by Lippmann and by the vociferousness of the West Coast press and West Coast congressmen, DeWitt finally submitted to Stimson his recommendation for "Evacuation of Japanese and Other Subversive Persons from the Pacific Coast," to be carried out by his command. In justifying the "military necessity" of such an action, DeWitt wrote that ". . . along the vital Pacific Coast over 112,000 potential enemies, of Japanese extraction, are at large today. There are indications that these are organized and ready for concerted action at a favorable opportunity. The very fact that no sabotage has taken place to date is a disturbing and confirming indication that such action will be taken."

Here was logic worthy of *Animal Farm*[7]: Proof that all ethnic Japanese were "ready for concerted action" lay in their not having taken it yet.

On Feb. 17, Biddle, in a letter to the president, made a last-ditch protest. "My last advice from the War Department," he wrote, "is that there is no evidence of imminent attack and from the F.B.I. that there is no evidence of planned sabotage."

The protest came too late. By this time, the attorney general—whose voice had been absolutely solo in reminding those in power of central values in the Bill of Rights—was not only ignored but also brutally vilified. Congressman Leland Ford told later of a call to Biddle: "I gave them 24 hours' notice that unless they would issue a mass evacuation notice I would drag the whole matter out on the floor of the House and of the Senate and give the bastards everything we could with both barrels. I told them they had given us the runaround long enough . . . and that if they would not take immediate action, we would clear the goddamned office out in one sweep."

On the day Biddle transmitted his final protest to Roosevelt, Stimson convened a meeting with War Department aides to plan a presidential order enabling a mass evacuation under Army supervision. Gullion was sent off to draft it.

That evening, McCloy, Gullion and Bendetsen went to Biddle's house, and Gullion read his draft aloud to the Attorney General. The order was to be sweeping and open-ended. Basing the president's right as commander in chief to issue it on a war powers act that dated back to the First World War, it authorized "the Secretary of War, and the military commanders whom he may from time to time designate . . . to prescribe military areas . . . from which any or all persons may be excluded, and with respect to which, the right of any person to enter, remain in, or leave shall be subject to whatever restriction the Secretary of War or the appropriate military commander may impose in his discretion."

On Feb. 19, 1942, Roosevelt set his signature to Executive Order No. 9066, "Authorizing the Secretary of War to Prescribe Military Areas."

The next day, Secretary Stimson formally appointed DeWitt "the military commander to carry out the duties and responsibilities" under Executive Order 9066. He specified that DeWitt should not bother to remove persons of Italian descent. There was widespread affection for Italian Americans. The mayor of San Francisco was one, and the baseball stars Joe and Dom DiMaggio, whose parents were aliens, were among the most popular idols in the country. "I don't care so much about the Italians," Biddle later quoted Roosevelt as having said in his cavalier way. "They are a lot of opera singers."

Stimson took a slightly harder line on German aliens, though he never authorized evacuating German Americans. Instructions to DeWitt were that German aliens who were "bona fide refugees" should be given "special consideration." In any case, the F.B.I. had long since taken into custody German aliens who had been marked as potentially subversive.

As to ethnic Japanese, the message was clear. Classes 1 and 2 of those who were to be moved out were "Japanese Aliens" and "American Citizens of Japanese Lineage." A sharp racist line had been drawn.

Congress had set up a Select Committee to investigate the need for what it euphemistically called "National Defense Migration." Testifying in San Francisco on Feb. 21, Earl Warren, then Attorney General of California, echoed DeWitt's amazing "proof" of trouble to come. "Unfortunately [many] are of the opinion that because we have had no sabotage and no fifth column activities in this State . . . that none have been planned for us," Warren said. "But I take the view that this is the most ominous sign in our whole situation. It convinces me more than perhaps any other factor that the sabotage we are to get, the fifth column activities we are to get, are timed just like Pearl Harbor was timed and just like the invasion of France, and of Denmark, and of Norway, and all of those other countries."

Two evenings later, almost as if designed to make irrational fears like these seem plausible, a Japanese submarine, the I-17, having recently returned to the coastal waters, fired about 25 five-and-a-half-inch shells at some oil storage tanks on an otherwise empty hillside west of Santa Barbara. There were no casualties. But was this a prelude to an invasion?

The next night, the Army detected nonexistent enemy airplanes over Los Angeles, and at 2:25 A.M., an antiaircraft battery opened fire. Other gun crews, hearing the explosions, began firing, and within a couple of hours, 1,430 three-inch shells had gone off above the city. Their fragments rained down, causing a fair amount of damage to automobiles. It took quite a while before this happening could be given the joking title it came finally to bear: "The Battle of Los Angeles." At the time, it reinforced the public's panic.

On Feb. 27, the Cabinet in Washington met to discuss how the evacuations should be carried out. Bendetsen had been arguing that the Army should not bear the burden of administering the removals because, as he said in a phone call to the State Department, the Army's job was "to kill Japanese, not to save Japanese." And indeed, the Cabinet did decide that day that the "resettlement" should be handled by a new civilian agency, which would eventually be called the War Relocation Authority. Milton S. Eisenhower, an official of the Department of Agriculture, brother of the popular general who would one day be elected president, was put in charge of it. The Army would round up the evacuees and move them to temporary collection centers, and then the civilian W.R.A. would settle and hold them for the duration of the war in permanent camps.

On March 2, DeWitt established as Military Area No. 1—the field of hottest imaginary danger—the entire western halves of Washington, Oregon and California, and the southern half of Arizona. Presumably somewhat cooler was Military Area No. 2, comprising the remainder of the four states.

DeWitt did not yet, however, issue any orders for actual removals, because in Washington, Gullion had realized that there was no law on the books that made a civilian's disobedience of a military command a crime, so there was no way for DeWitt to force anyone to move. Gullion's office therefore went to work drawing up a statute—something absolutely new in American legal history—that would invent such a crime. DeWitt urged that imprisonment be mandatory, and that the crime be classified as a felony because, he argued, "you have a greater liberty to enforce a felony than you have to enforce a misdemeanor, *viz*, You can shoot a man to prevent the commission of a felony."

On March 9, Stimson submitted to Congress the proposed legislation, which would subject any civilian who flouted a military order in a military area to a year in jail and a fine of $5,000. Only one person in either chamber rose in debate to challenge the measure: the archconservative Senator Robert A. Taft of Ohio, who would be known in later years as "Mr. Republican." This bill, he said, was "the 'sloppiest' criminal law I have ever read or seen anywhere."

When it came to a vote, not a single member of either chamber voted against the bill, which was signed into law by Roosevelt on March 21. The way was cleared. On March 31, 1942, with the posting of Civilian Exclusion Orders, the cruel capture of the ethnic Japanese was set in motion.

By early 1943, McCloy and others in the War Department and Army had clearly seen that "military necessity" could no longer, by the wildest imagining, justify keeping loyal American citizens of Japanese ancestry—or loyal aliens—away from the West Coast in

"pens." DeWitt was horrified, but the War Department had had enough of his obsessive fears and complaints. He was relieved of his Western Defense Command that fall.

In the spring of 1944, the War Department finally urged the president to dissolve the camps. Others, however, urged caution. "The question appears to be largely a political one," wrote Under Secretary of State Edward Stettinius Jr., in a memo to the president. Roosevelt would be running for a fourth term in November. The evacuees would have to wait.

At the first Cabinet meeting after Roosevelt's re-election, it was decided that all evacuees who passed loyalty reviews could, at last, go home.

They went home to a bitter freedom. It took more than a year to empty all the camps. Given train fare and $25, the evacuees returned to the coast, many to learn that their goods had been stolen or sold; their land had been seized for unpaid taxes; strangers had taken possession of their homes. Jobs were plentiful, but not for the returning detainees, who met with notices: "No Japs Wanted." Housing was hard to find; whole families moved into single rooms.

One man, who had a brother still overseas with the 442d Regimental Combat Team, would testify that his mother "finally had enough money for a down payment on a house. We purchased the house in 1946 and tried to move in, only to find two Caucasian men sitting on the front steps with a court injunction prohibiting us from moving in because of a restrictive covenant.[8] If we moved in, we would be subject to a $1,000 fine and/or one year in the County Jail."

One ordeal had ended; another had begun.

[1988]

Terms

1. F.B.I.: Federal Bureau of Investigation.
2. Fifth-column work: Secret subversive activities aiding an invading enemy.
3. The Presidio: The U.S. Army post in San Francisco that served as DeWitt's headquarters.
4. F.C.C.: Federal Communications Commission.
5. Writ of habeas corpus: An order to release or bring a prisoner before a court.
6. *Carte blanche*: Full discretionary power.
7. *Animal Farm*: A satirical novel by George Orwell with the climactic slogan "All animals are equal, but some animals are more equal than others."
8. Restrictive covenant: A law prohibiting certain ethnic groups from residing in a given area.

Understanding the Reading

1. What were the Civilian Exclusion Orders?
2. What was the economic impact of the orders?
3. In what ways were the Japanese Americans treated like criminals?
4. What were conditions like at the Assembly Centers?
5. What was Lieutenant General DeWitt's response to the supposed San Francisco fly-over by Japanese planes?
6. What was the single case of sabotage by a Japanese American?
7. What were some of the problems with the Military Intelligence Division?
8. What were some of the most bizarre justifications offered in support of the evacuation?
9. What was the 442d Combat Regimental Team, and what was its service record like?
10. What triggered the "Battle of Los Angeles"?
11. Why did evacuation have to wait for Congress to act?
12. What problems did Japanese Americans face after they left the camps?

Suggestions for Responding

1. Hersey raises the question of whether such an incident as the relocation program could occur again. How would you answer him?
2. Imagine you were a Japanese American attending a West Coast university at the time of the evacuation order. How would you have reacted?
3. Explain DeWitt's role in the evacuation.

34

Asian Americans Battle "Model Minority" Stereotype

ROBERT DASELER

For decades, Asian Americans have borne the peculiar burden of being the "model minority." Their signal success, especially in technical and scientific fields, has resulted in their being viewed more favorably than other American minorities, who supposedly lack their initiative.

The idea that Asians can serve as a model for other minorities seems to have originated in the 1960s,

during the heyday of the civil rights movement. In a 1966 *New York Times Magazine* article, Berkeley sociologist William Petersen wrote, "By any criterion of good citizenship that we choose, the Japanese Americans are better than any other group in our society, including native-born whites. They have established this remarkable record, moreover, by their own almost totally unaided effort." Later in the article, Petersen, having further elaborated the accomplishments of Japanese Americans, made the invidious comparison to other minorities: "This is not true (or, at best, less true) of such 'non-whites' as Negroes, Indians, Mexicans, Chinese, and Filipinos."

Despite the fact that Petersen included Chinese and Filipinos on his list of less successful minorities, the idea spread that Asians generally work hard, send their children to college, rise rapidly in American society, and are "by any criterion of good citizenship that we choose" better than, for example, African Americans, Latinos, and Native Americans.

Although Petersen did not explicitly state that other minorities ought to emulate Japanese Americans or other Asian Americans, the notion of Asians as a model minority acquired a certain popular acceptance in the 1970s and 1980s.

According to Ruth Gim, a Pomona College psychologist whose family emigrated to this country from Korea in 1970, the "model minority" tag stereotypes Asians, denying their many social, psychological, and financial difficulties and falsifying the actual record of their assimilation into American culture.

In Gim's view, the model minority image is dangerous to Asian Americans because it results in the denial of their actual needs, it imposes a set of expectations for Asian Americans that they do not create for themselves ("Someone else is prescribing to us what we should be"), and it biases their relations with other minorities.

Gim also believes that there was an implicit message behind the development of the myth of the model minority: "It was sending a message to the other minorities, saying, 'Why can't you be like them?' It was trying to use one minority group to send a message to another minority group." Many Asian Americans came quite naturally to resent the dubious distinction of being hailed as models for other minorities.

A study, released by UCLA in May, pointed out that Asian Americans are just as likely to be impoverished and disadvantaged as they are to be economically successful. According to Paul Ong, editor of the report, "It's been an uphill battle to get decision-makers and the population overall to realize that the Asian Pacific American population is a diverse one." The UCLA study paints a picture of a rapidly growing population (the 1990 Census said the nation's Asian and Pacific Islander population totaled 7,273,662, more than double the 1980 total) whose veneer of success camouflages some disturbing struggles.

At a series of luncheons sponsored by Pomona's Asian American Resource Center during the spring semester, Gim, who directs the center, and other speakers examined the myth, trying to understand its origins, the reasons for its widespread acceptance (even among many Asian Americans), and its dangers.

Promoting Super-Achievers

Gim, who teaches courses in Asian American studies and psychology at Pomona, was the lead-off speaker in the series. Promoting Asians as super-achievers was, in effect, a tactic that conservatives could use to undercut criticism of mainstream culture by dissidents within the minority communities, Gim said.

In fact, Petersen, in his 1966 piece, emphasized the point that discrimination against Japanese Americans had been, if anything, more virulent than discrimination against other minorities. The implication of the Petersen article was clear: if other minorities did not prosper, it was because they were not as industrious or as determined as the Japanese.

By holding up Asian Americans as a model for other minorities, mainstream culture could, in effect, deny that racial prejudice was to blame for unemployment and poverty among African Americans, Latinos, and others. Drawing attention to the success of thousands of Asian Americans was, in other words, an indirect way of placing the blame for racial inequality upon the minorities themselves, rather than the dominant culture. Gim believes that embedded in the model minority myth was an assumption of cultural determinism: that Asian cultures are superior to other cultures, and for that reason, Asians tend to rise to the top of whatever culture they enter. She asserts that this presumption of Asian superiority is actually harmful for Asian Americans, especially those who are not academic superstars.

Gim also notes, ironically, that the model minority portrayal of Asian Americans is in stark contrast to the "Yellow Peril" image of them promulgated earlier in the century.

In the years prior to World War II, the prevailing view of Asians was represented by the figure of Charlie Chan, the movie detective who outwitted (usually Irish) policemen to solve crimes. Chan was an icon of the "inscrutable" Oriental: astute, mysterious, and ultimately risible. (Although he possessed a good vocabulary, his grammar was defective.)

Gim points out that many Asian Americans have internalized the "model minority" image, resulting in a narrowing of their social horizons. They know they are expected to enter technical and scientific fields—mathematics, engineering, medicine, economics—but not the humanities. Asian American students who do *not* do well in math or technical subjects often feel that they have not lived up to the expectations they have inherited. Asian American students do not have the freedom to be mediocre.

Furthermore, those who want to study history, sociology, or art often feel they are stepping over an invisible line between what is and is not an appropriate career path.

Contrary to the myth of invulnerability, Asian American students have a significantly higher rate of major depression and diagnosed schizophrenia than European Americans. "The superficial view seems to support the model minority image," Gim says, "but when you dig deeper, you find that cultural factors influence the underutilization of psychological services by Asian American students."

Moreover, the severity of psychiatric problems reported by Asian American students belies the image of them as programmed automatons.

The pressure on these students is coming not only from the culture, of course, but primarily from their families, who often steer the students into traditional and lucrative professions.

The concluding speaker in the series, Linus Yamane, as assistant professor of economics at Pitzer College, further debunked the myth by noting that, while the average family income of Asian Americans, $42,250, is higher than that for European Americans, $36,920, the proportion of Asian Americans living below the poverty line is much higher than for European Americans.

Yamane also pointed out that Asian American families tend to be larger than families of European Americans, somewhat vitiating their higher average income.

Yamane drew a complex picture of Asians in the United States, saying that poverty rates for Chinese, Japanese, and Korean families are lower than for

European Americans, while poverty rates for Filipino and Native American families are higher.

Yamane also argued that discrimination against Asians in the work force varies with their ethnic background. Japanese and Korean males are found to do as well as European American males with comparable education, but Chinese and Filipino males do less well, and Native American men earn about 30 percent less, on the average, than European American males with comparable education.

MANAGEMENT GLASS CEILING

Yamane believes that there is a "glass ceiling" for Asian Americans in management. Studies appear to show that, while Asian Americans rise rapidly in the lower ranks of organizations, they are excluded from higher managerial positions.

Between Gim and Yamane came three other speakers. One of these was David Yoo, a historian at Claremont McKenna College, whose specialty is ethnicity, immigration, and race. Yoo characterized the model minority view of Asian Americans as just the latest wrinkle in the evolution of the stereotype of Asians in America.

Proclaiming Asian Americans to be a model minority "works against the true notion of a multicultural America," Yoo says. "It reinforces a racial hierarchy, which is kept intact if you can pit one minority against another."

Yoo believes that embracing Asians as exemplary gives people an excuse not to ask more fundamental questions about race and inequality.

While debunking the model-minority image as a myth, Gim, Yamane, and Yoo agree that there is some truth to the characterization of Asian Americans as high achievers. The proportion of Asian American students at highly selective colleges and universities is itself an indicator that at least a few ethnic groups within the Asian American community place high status on education, discipline, and intellectual distinction.

In March, homosexuality in the Asian Pacific Islander communities was discussed by Eric Reyes, a member of the Asian Pacific AIDS Intervention Team in Los Angeles, and Alice Y. Hom, a doctoral candidate in history at The Claremont Graduate School; and Jack Ling, a psychologist and environmental consultant, spoke on the subject of Asian American gangs. Reyes, Hom, and Ling highlighted aspects of the Asian American experience that conflict with the model-minority stereotype.

The number of Asian American students at The Claremont Colleges and in the University of California system does not signify that the story of Asian Americans is one of unalloyed success and social advance. Stereotyping, a pervasive sense of being suspended between two strong cultures, high stress levels, and a concern about loss of identity also are elements in the story.

Asian American students tend, for the most part, to associate with one another, and sometimes this leads to resentment by European American students, who view the Asians as cliquish and unfriendly.

A Pomona sophomore, who asked that his name not be mentioned, is a good example of the Asian American student who has taken the traditional path toward a career. With a double major in chemistry and Chinese, he is conforming, at least for the moment, to his father's expectation that he should become a doctor.

"He has one thing in mind," this young man says of his father, who was raised in Taiwan. "He thinks medicine is the best way to go."

A graduate of a prep school at which there was "a substantial" number of Asian students, the young man associated primarily with other Asian students in high school. At Pomona College, too, he associates with other Asians more than with Caucasian students. "Just for some reason, a lot of the people I know happen to be Asian," he says. He thinks that Koreans tend to be more cliquish than other Asians, though.

This sophomore learned about the model minority myth when he took Ruth Gim's "Asian American Perspectives" class as a freshman.

"You can apply it to some people," he says, "but I don't think you can apply it to Asians as a whole. Asians do work hard and try to do well in school. I think the model-minority myth could be applied to a lot of my friends, but a lot of my Caucasian friends would fit the myth, too, if they were Asians."

A recent graduate, who also asked for anonymity, chose a nontraditional major for a student whose parents were born, as the sophomore's were, in Taiwan. She majored in sociology and women's studies, and in her senior thesis, she compared the cultural sensitivity of two centers for battered women: one mainstream, the other for Pacific Islanders and Asians.

Except for her social sciences major, she believes that "I do fall into what people would call a model-minority category." That is, she works hard, attends a prestigious college, and will pursue graduate studies. She also acknowledges the generational linguistic and class privileges that have allowed her to achieve these goals.

She is troubled by the stereotype, however. "I think it's very dangerous," she says. "It creates suspicion between groups, and it prevents us from forming coalitions in our similar struggle." She says that majoring in sociology and women's studies wasn't something she planned. "I could barely do the natural sciences," she admits. So she switched into a field in which she had an interest . . . and could excel.

She graduated from a high school in Cerritos, California, in which the Asian Pacific Islander enrollment was 75 percent.

"It was the most comfortable social environment I was ever in or that I expect I ever will be in," she says. "It was difficult adjusting to Pomona, where suddenly I was the minority. I was not a part of the dominant culture."

Although being in the majority was pleasant, she now believes that "she would have benefited more from high school if there had been a greater diversity of students, particularly more African American and Latino students."

She took a course from Gim, who helped her put the Asian American experience in perspective. "It really allowed me to see the Asian American contributions to American history," she says.

Growing up in Riverside and Orange counties, Gim found that there were two ways for her to compensate for being a minority: "I made sure I did better academically [than other students]. I don't think I really was smarter than other kids, but I made sure I worked harder. The other defense mechanism was that I dressed well."

Gim hopes that the increasing number of Asian American courses will help Asian American students find their own identity in a dominantly European American culture, without having to rely upon stereotypes imposed either by that culture or by their own minority culture.

"I am more American than most Americans walking around," Gim asserts. "I really believe that. I don't think most people realize what it is to be an American. I believe I have a better understanding and appreciation of what it means to be an American because of my bicultural background."

[1994]

Understanding the Reading

1. What led to the development of the myth that Asian Americans are a "model minority"?
2. Why is this image dangerous for Asian Americans?
3. What is the reality of life in the United States for Asian/Pacific Americans?
4. What impact has the model-minority image of Asian Americans had on other minorities?
5. How has it affected Asian Americans themselves?
6. How are Asian Americans affected by the "glass ceiling"?
7. How do Asian American students tend to behave in college?
8. How do college classes in Asian American studies affect Asian American students?

Suggestions for Responding

1. Think about Hersey's description of Japanese Americans during World War II and write an explanation of why you think their image has changed so much in the past sixty years.
2. Write a short essay explaining how your life has been affected by a stereotype that others have applied to you.

35

Jim Crow Revived in Cyberspace

GREG PALAST AND MARTIN LUTHER KING III

Birmingham, Ala.—Astonishingly, and sadly, four decades after the Rev. Martin Luther King Jr. marched in Birmingham, we must ask again, "Do African Americans have the unimpeded right to vote in the United States?"

In 1963, Dr. King's determined and courageous band faced water hoses and police attack dogs to call attention to the thicket of Jim Crow laws—including poll taxes and so-called "literacy" tests—that stood in the way of black Americans' right to have their ballots cast and counted. Today, there is a new and real threat to minority voters, this time from cyberspace: computerized purges of voter rolls.

The menace first appeared in Florida in the November 2000 presidential election. While the media chased butterfly ballots and hanging chads, a much more sinister and devastating attack on voting rights went almost undetected.

In the two years before the elections, the Florida secretary of state's office quietly ordered the removal of 94,000 voters from the registries. Supposedly, these were convicted felons who may not vote in Florida. Instead, the overwhelming majority were innocent of any crime—and just over half were black or Hispanic.

We are not guessing about the race of the disenfranchised: A voter's color is listed next to his or her name in most Southern states. (Ironically, this racial ID is required by the Voting Rights Act of 1965, a King legacy.)

How did mass expulsion of legal voters occur? At the heart of the ethnic purge of voting rights was the creation of a central voter file for Florida placed in the hands of an elected, and therefore partisan, official. Computerization and a 1998 "reform" law meant to prevent voter fraud allowed for a politically and racially biased purge of thousands of registered voters on the flimsiest of grounds.

Voters whose name, birth date and gender loosely matched that of a felon anywhere in America were targeted for removal. And so one Thomas Butler (of several in Florida) was tagged because a "Thomas Butler Cooper Jr." of Ohio was convicted of a crime. The legacy of slavery—commonality of black names—aided the racial bias of the "scrub list."

Florida was the first state to create, computerize and purge lists of allegedly "ineligible" voters. Meant as a reform, in the hands of partisan officials it became a weapon of mass voting rights destruction. (The fact that Mr. Cooper's conviction date is shown on state files as "1/30/2007" underscores other dangers of computerizing our democracy.)

You'd think that Congress and President Bush would run from imitating Florida's disastrous system. Astonishingly, Congress adopted the absurdly named "Help America Vote Act," which requires every state to replicate Florida's system of centralized, computerized voter files before the 2004 election.

The controls on the 50 secretaries of state are few—and the temptation to purge voters of the opposition party enormous. African Americans, whose vote concentrates in one party, are an easy and obvious target.

The act also lays a minefield of other impediments to black voters: an effective rollback of the easy voter registration methods of the Motor Voter Act; new identification requirements at polling stations; and

perilous incentives for fault-prone and fraud-susceptible touch-screen voting machines.

No, we are not rehashing the who-really-won fight from the 2000 presidential election. But we have no intention of "getting over it." We are moving on, but on to a new nationwide call and petition drive to restore and protect the rights of all Americans and monitor the implementation of frighteningly ill-conceived new state and federal voting "reform" laws.

Four decades ago, the opposition to the civil right to vote was easy to identify: night riders wearing white sheets and burning crosses. Today, the threat comes from partisan politicians wearing pinstripe suits and clutching laptops.

Jim Crow has moved into cyberspace—harder to detect, craftier in operation, shifting shape into the electronic guardian of a new electoral segregation.

[2003]

Understanding the Reading

1. What does the title "Jim Crow Revived in Cyberspace" mean?
2. How exactly were minority voters targeted in this example?
3. How has Congress reacted to this allegation, since the 2000 election?

Suggestions for Responding

1. Make a list of ways minorities have been nonviolently disenfranchised in the United States throughout history.
2. Have a class discussion on how the possibility of computer fraud and improprieties could be eliminated from future U.S. elections.

36

It's Not Just Starbucks: White Fear Is an American Problem

RENÉE GRAHAM

April 16, 2018

Driving while black. Walking while black.

Shopping while black. Selling CDs while black. Listening to music in a car while black.

Asking for directions while black. Sitting in Starbucks while black.

To be black is to always be in the wrong place at the wrong time because, in America, there is never a right place for black people.

Several recent events again drove home that point like a stake through the heart. Two black men in Philadelphia were arrested at a Starbucks for being two black men in Starbucks. They hadn't ordered anything and were waiting for a friend. This was enough to make a Starbucks employee call the police.

Starbucks will close its U.S. stores May 29 for racial-bias education.

Not long after several officers arrived, the men were perp-walked off the premises in handcuffs. Hours later, they were released without charges.

Three years ago, the coffeehouse chain launched its quickly aborted "Race Together" campaign to spark conversations about race. Now it's in the piping-hot center of another debate about racial profiling. A video of the incident has been viewed more than nine million times, and the story is now a national headline.

For black people, this video has been viral forever. This is what we live with every damn day.

This isn't a Starbucks problem. It could have been a fast food restaurant, a mall—or a street in Cambridge. Last Friday police responded to a report of a naked man on Massachusetts Avenue. A video shows Selorm Ohene, a black twenty-one-year-old Harvard student, being struck several times after he was already pinned to the ground by three Cambridge police officers and an MBTA transit cop. Cambridge mayor Marc C. McGovern called the incident "disturbing."

Everything black people do is weighted by irrational white fear. It's mentally exhausting to always be on guard, even during mundane moments like waiting in a coffee shop—or asking for directions.

Last week, Brennan Walker, a fourteen-year-old African American, had to walk to his Rochester Hills, Michigan, school after missing the bus. When he got lost on his four-mile trek, Walker went to a house and knocked on the door, hoping to get directions. The woman who answered accused him of trying to break in—then it got worse. A white man, wielding a shotgun, ran at the teen. His shot missed Walker, who took off as soon as he saw the gun.

Jeffrey Craig Zeigler, fifty-three, has been charged with assault with intent to murder and possession of a firearm in the commission of a felony. Walker said

he chose that house because he saw a neighborhood-watch sticker and thought it would be safe.

Years ago, when I was dating a white woman, I used to half-joke that being with her meant that if we got lost in a predominately white area, she could be the one to ask for directions. Before GPS, I would often opt for squinting at maps and driving miles out of my way rather than asking for help. Even with my lousy sense of direction, I wouldn't run the risk of ending up in jail or dead because someone criminalized my blackness.

After Trayvon Martin was shot to death in 2012, the media became obsessed with "the talk" that many black parents have with their sons about how to behave around white people, especially cops. I never got a version of that conversation. Still, I always knew not to reach into my bag in a store unless I'm in full view of the cashier or to leave the house without ID.

When you're black, you just know. Just as the two men in Starbucks knew not to do anything that would further escalate an already ridiculous predicament.

On *Good Morning America*, Starbucks CEO Kevin Johnson called what happened to those two black men "reprehensible" and plans to meet with them to apologize personally. *GMA* host Robin Roberts called this "a teachable moment," but I don't believe that. This nation has had several centuries' worth of teachable moments, and little is ever learned. Yes, there has been progress, but that's slight consolation when you can still be arrested simply for sitting in a coffee shop.

Nothing will ever change until a majority of white people in this nation stop perceiving black existence as sinister and suspicious. Talking about racism may hurt white people's feelings, but their unchecked racism continues to endanger our black lives.

Understanding the Reading

1. What does the author see as frustrating and urgent?
2. Do you agree that there is a pattern of white response to blacks that must be changed in the United States? Why or why not?
3. Decide on two specific strategies that could combat undeserved violence and always being suspected.

Suggestions for Responding

1. Discuss the consequences of Americans constantly seeing each other as enemies.

2. What would U.S. society be like if we assumed that we are all living in a civil society and act accordingly?

37

Emmett Louis Till, 1941–1955

SOUTHERN POVERTY LAW CENTER

Mamie Till was a devoted, well-educated mother who taught her son that a person's worth did not depend on the color of his or her skin. Nevertheless, when she put 14-year-old Emmett on a train bound for Mississippi in the summer of 1955, she warned him, "If you have to get down on your knees and bow when a white person goes past, do it willingly."

It was not in Emmett Till to bow down. Raised in a working-class section of Chicago, he was bold and self-assured. He didn't understand the timid attitude of his Southern cousins toward whites. He even tried to impress them by showing them a photo of some white Chicago youths, claiming the girl in the picture was his girlfriend.

One day he took the photo out of his wallet and showed it to a group of boys standing outside a country store in Money, Mississippi. The boys dared him to speak to a white woman in the store. Emmett walked in confidently, bought some candy from Carolyn Bryant, the wife of the store owner, and said "Bye baby" on his way out.

Within hours, nearly everyone in town had heard at least one version of the incident. Some said Emmett had asked Mrs. Bryant for a date; others said he whistled at her. Whatever the details were, Roy Bryant was outraged that a black youth had been disrespectful to his wife. That weekend, Bryant and his half-brother J. W. Milam went looking for Till. They came to the cotton field shack that belonged to Mose Wright, a 64-year-old farmer and grandfather of Emmett Till's cousin. Bryant demanded to see "the boy that did the talking." Wright reluctantly got Till out of bed. As the white men took Emmett Till away, they told Wright not to cause any trouble or he'd "never live to be 65."

A magazine writer later paid Milam to describe what happened that night. Milam said he and Bryant beat Emmett Till, shot him in the head, wired a 75-pound cotton gin fan to his neck and dumped his body in the Tallahatchie River.

When asked why he did it, Milam responded, "Well, what else could I do? He thought he was as good as any white man."

So the World Could See

Till's body was found three days later—a bullet in the skull, one eye gouged out and the head crushed in on one side. The face was unrecognizable. Mose Wright knew it was Till only because of a signet ring that remained on one finger. The ring had belonged to Emmett's father Louis, who had died ten years earlier, and bore his initials L.T.

Mamie Till demanded the body of her son be sent back to Chicago. Then she ordered an open-casket funeral so the world could see what had been done to Emmett. *Jet* magazine published a picture of the horribly disfigured corpse. Thousands viewed the body and attended the funeral.

All over the country, blacks and sympathetic whites were horrified by the killing. Thousands of people sent money to the NAACP[1] to support its legal efforts on behalf of black victims.

In the meantime, J. W. Milam and Roy Bryant faced murder charges. They admitted they kidnapped and beat Emmett Till, but claimed they left him alive. Ignoring nationwide criticism, white Mississippians raised $10,000 to pay the legal expenses for Milam and Bryant. Five white local lawyers volunteered to represent them at the murder trial.

Mose Wright risked his life to testify against the men. In a courtroom filled with reporters and white spectators, the frail black farmer stood and identified Bryant and Milam as the men who took Emmett away.

Wright's act of courage didn't convince the all-white jury. After deliberating just over an hour, the jury returned a verdict of not guilty.

The murder of Emmett Till was the spark that set the civil rights movement on fire. For those who would become leaders of that movement, the martyred 14-year-old was a symbol of the struggle for equality.

"The Emmett Till case shook the foundations of Mississippi," said Myrlie Evers, widow of civil rights leader Medgar Evers, ". . . because it said even a child was not safe from racism and bigotry and death."

NAACP Executive Director Roy Wilkins said white Mississippians "had to prove they were superior . . . by taking away a 14-year-old boy."

Fred Shuttlesworth, who eight years later would

lead the fight for integration in Birmingham, said, "The fact that Emmett Till, a young black man, could be found floating down the river in Mississippi just set in concrete the determination of the people to move forward . . . only God can know how many Negroes have come up missing, dead and killed under this system with which we live."

[1989]

Term

1. NAACP: National Association for the Advancement of Colored People.

Understanding the Reading

1. What did Emmett Till do to provoke the white Southerners?
2. What did Bryant and Milam do to Till?
3. What were the charges and the verdict against Bryant and Milam?
4. Nationally, what effect did Till's death produce, and why?

Suggestion for Responding

1. Write a short essay explaining why an incident like this could or could not happen today; support your position with some specific examples.

38

Blacks Feel Indignities

ROBERT ANTHONY WATTS

Joe Reed grew up in the birthplace of the civil rights movement, hearing haunting stories from his relatives about the horrors of segregation.

But when Reed considers the impact of racism on his life, his mind moves north from Montgomery, Ala., to the corridors of power of Congress, where he began working as a legislative aide this year.

Reed repeatedly was stopped by lobbyists sponsoring receptions and asked to produce identification, while white aides walked in without question. Sometimes he was turned away, told the gatherings were restricted to members of Congress, only to learn later that was a lie.

"It makes you angry," says Reed, who is 23. "It makes you feel second class. No matter how far you go, no matter how well-dressed you are, you're still black."

For many black Americans, these kinds of snubs and slights are common experiences in restaurants, stores and social settings.

Usually subtle and almost never involving slurs, the incidents are far less obvious than Jim Crow laws that prevailed in the South three decades ago.

But still, many blacks say, such behavior is jarring, leads to simmering anger and widens the racial divide in America. They say they rarely share the slights with white friends and co-workers, fearing they'll be considered overly sensitive.

In one of the most notable examples, some blacks contend they were given poor or no service at restaurants run by the Denny's chain and asked to pre-pay for their meals.

Six black Secret Service agents filed suit against the chain in May, alleging that they were waited on, then ignored and not served, while white agents sitting nearby in the Annapolis, Md., outlet received prompt service.

The agents' lawsuit came on the heels of a similar suit filed by 32 blacks in California against Denny's, which has signed a nondiscrimination settlement in which it admitted no wrongdoing. The chain did, however, say it would stop certain practices, such as asking customers in some restaurants to pre-pay.

Dr. Carl Bell, a Chicago psychiatrist known for his work on racism, says such behavior is called "micro-insults" or "micro-aggressions." The experiences can be particularly frustrating for blacks, he says, because they are so personal and subjective.

"How do you prove that someone jumped in line in front of you?" Bell said. "You go into a store and look at a suit, the guy takes you to the cheapest suits in the store. How can you prove racial bias in that? It's not hard evidence. . . . White people can blow you off and say, 'No, you're just touchy.' And you walk away feeling, maybe I was."

But in Reed's case, one of his white colleagues, Ken Mullinax, also noticed the difference in treatment on Capitol Hill. Both men worked for U.S. Rep. Earl Hilliard, an Alabama Democrat, before Reed left to start law school at the University of Pittsburgh.

"It's weird," said Mullinax, who often was the lone white among Hilliard aides attending the receptions.

"We all go together, and every time, they let me walk right in."

But black aides "are always stopped and questioned," he said. "It has happened so many times now, I can't think it's anything else but a black-white issue."

Reed said snubs continued in the receptions, where lobbyists seemed reluctant to shake his hand, uninterested in what he has to say and more attentive to white aides.

"Sometimes you almost want to cry, but you start to believe it sometimes," he said. "You start to feel like, 'Is there really something wrong with me?'"

Many blacks—especially those who grew up under segregation—say such modern-day insults, even subtle ones, are jolting because they occur at moments when they feel they have escaped the burden of race.

"As bad as segregation is, the rules are clear," said Melvin Sikes, a retired black psychologist in Austin, Texas, who still is angry over an experience three years ago with a cab driver. "If you are prepared to be hit—even if you are hit—you know how to absorb it. This, you don't know how to deal with."

Sikes and his wife, Zeta, say their 1990 anniversary weekend was ruined when a cab driver bypassed them and picked up a white couple.

After returning from a wonderful celebration aboard a dinner train in nearby San Antonio, the couple had walked to the street to hail a cab. A white couple came up behind them, Sikes said, and agreed to wait for a second cab.

But when the first cab arrived and Sikes reached to open the door for his wife, the cab rolled past, he said, pulling up to the white couple, who, after a short exchange with the driver, climbed inside.

"Had it been 20 years ago, it wouldn't have bothered me, because that was the story of my life," said Mrs. Sikes, 75, who grew up at a time when blacks couldn't vote in Texas. "But in 1990, I certainly didn't expect that."

Unable to forget the experience, the couple cut short a planned stay out of town and returned home.

Michael Thurmond, a lawyer and former chairman of the Black Caucus in the Georgia Legislature, remembers the sting of leaving an elegant reception for lawmakers at the Ritz-Carlton hotel in Atlanta last year and being asked by an elderly white woman, and then her husband, to retrieve their car.

Thurmond, dressed in a $250 tailor-made blazer, white shirt and silk tie, was standing by the hotel door waiting for his car when the wife approached him. Thurmond says he politely told her he was not an employee.

But when her husband asked moments later, Thurmond angrily snapped at the man, who stammered an apology and nervously walked away.

"I was really ticked," Thurmond said. "Here I am being entertained upstairs as chairman of the black caucus with all these business people trying to shake your hand, and you come downstairs and get mistaken for a parking attendant."

[1993]

Understanding the Reading

1. How was legislative aide John Reed treated in Congress?
2. How did Denny's treat six black Secret Service agents?
3. What is a "micro-insult" or "micro-aggression"?
4. How did Ken Mullinax react to the treatment of his black colleague?
5. What indignity did Melvin Sikes experience?
6. Describe Michael Thurmond's experience at an Atlanta hotel.

Suggestion for Responding

1. How do you think blacks should respond to "micro-insults"?

Suggestions for Responding to Part IV

1. Research and report on a specific example of racism in American history, such as the Cherokee removal and the Trail of Tears, anti-Semitic quotas in admission to colleges such as Harvard in the 1920s, restrictive covenants, the "scientific" studies that "proved" racial inferiority on the basis of such characteristics as brain size and physique, or the treatment of Mexican citizens under the treaty of Guadalupe Hidalgo.

2. Investigate a minority "first," such as baseball player Jackie Robinson; athlete James Thorpe; Harriet Tubman, the "Moses" of the Underground Railroad; Virginia governor Eugene Wilder; Arctic explorer Matthew Henson; Rosa Parks, the woman whose arrest prompted the Montgomery bus boycott; Olympic athlete Jesse Owens; Olympic gold medalist Kristi Yamaguchi; Supreme Court justice Thurgood Marshall; tennis champion Arthur Ashe; heavyweight boxing champion Joe Lewis; poet Phillis Wheatley; Jean Baptiste Point du Sable, founder of Chicago; Nobel peace prize winner Ralph Bunche; congressional representatives Hiram Fong and Daniel Inouye; Academy Award winner Sidney Poitier; Springfield, Ohio, mayor Robert C. Henry; Senator Edward Brooke; Dr. Daniel Hale Williams, the physician who performed the first open-heart surgery; President Barack Obama; or any of the many others. Report on their achievements, and focus on the racial barriers they faced and overcame.

3. Imagine you are a member of a different race, and write an autobiography in which you analyze the impact that your new race has on your opportunities and accomplishments.

4. Research how the stereotype of one racial or ethnic group in America evolved—for example, the image of Native Americans as noble savages evolving into the drunken Indian or the inscrutable Chinese into the model minority. Analyze how historical contexts influenced the various characterizations and how each variation benefited the dominant culture.

5. In American society, it is almost impossible not to be affected in some way by racism. Write a critical analysis of a manifestation of your own racism.

Part V
Power and Sexism

Two generations ago, traditional gender roles were accepted as natural, normal, even inevitable. Men were expected to be strong, unemotional, aggressive, competitive, and devoted to concerns of the outside world; women were to be gentle, emotional, passive, nurturing, and devoted to home and family. Those who violated these norms were labeled deviant. A man whose eyes appeared to moisten in public was immediately perceived as less than fully qualified to be U.S. president. An ambitious middle-class woman who wanted more than a domestic role was declared by psychiatrists to be suffering from a psychological personality disorder. This fit the supposed ideal for white, middle-class families. The millions of non-white individuals and families, and recent immigrants streaming into metropolitan areas, did not have the possibility of choosing to be a homemaker without pay.

The word *sexism* did not exist until approximately fifty years ago. In the early 1960s, everyone assumed that women had the same rights and opportunities that men had and that they were content with their domestic role, caring for their homes and families. Magazines, movies, television, school textbooks, church leaders, politicians—everyone, everywhere, including most women—extolled the virtues of the traditional division of labor: man the breadwinner and woman the homemaker.

However, economic reality was already making this ideal more and more difficult for white, middle-class women to maintain. Increasingly, they had to work outside the home, but working women were also expected to continue to serve as wife and mother. In the workplace, however, they were restricted in the kinds of jobs they could get. Newspapers printed ads under separate "Help Wanted—Male" and "Help Wanted—Female" listings, shunting even women with college degrees, for example, into secretarial rather than professional positions. Paying less for women's work was considered natural because men were regarded as the family breadwinners.

In 1963, Betty Friedan published *The Feminine Mystique*, in which she investigated the unhappiness and malaise that haunted the well-educated suburban homemaker. Suddenly, everybody began talking about the "woman problem." Women organized **consciousness-raising groups**, where they shared their experiences as women. Simple as this sounds, this sharing almost immediately altered the way people saw the gendered social system. Problems previously regarded as personal were revealed to be part of a larger web of social limitations that society imposed on women simply because of their sex.

The value of women and a women-centered perspective and the advocacy of social, political, and economic equality for both women and men became the widely accepted and widely debated platform of modern feminism. Scrutinizing every facet of society through a feminist lens revealed that fundamental gender inequality was (and still is) embedded in the entire social system. The system was exposed as **patriarchal**, meaning that it is hierarchical and that its structures of power, value, and culture are **androcentric**—that is, they are male-centered and male-dominated. Every aspect of society—employment, education, religion, media, law, economic arrangements, and even the family—reinforced and maintained men's social superiority and women's social inferiority and subordination.

As soon as feminist analysis exposed the inherent

inequities of this system, women organized to change it. Equating the position of all women with that of blacks, they coined the term *sexism* to emphasize the correspondence between racism and the discriminatory treatment to which women were subjected. **Sexism** is the subordination of an individual man or woman or a group of men or women and the assumption of the superiority of an individual woman or man or a group of women or men, based solely on sex. Like racism, sexism is reflected in both individual and institutional acts, decisions, habits, procedures, and policies that neglect, overlook, exploit, subjugate, or maintain the subordination of an individual man or woman or all men or women.

Feminist activism throughout the past forty years has changed society dramatically. Textbooks from basal readers to medical volumes are scrupulously edited to eliminate blatant sexism and gender stereotyping. Women today have access to higher education and professional training, and they are represented in nearly every occupation from carpentry and mining to the clergy and the securities market. Men are more likely to share housework and childcare responsibilities. Advertisements present women taking business trips (other than to the supermarket) and climbing telephone poles.

These changes have led many of us to believe that women in the United States have come closer to achieving equality with men than most other women in the world. In fact, however, when it comes to women's nonagricultural wage as a percentage of men's, the United States ranks behind thirty other countries—including Hungary, Tanzania, Vietnam, Jordan, Zambia, and most of Western Europe. In 2018, American women earned 79 percent of what men earned, even when the comparisons were adjusted for education and experience. (This is four cents higher than in 1995. If we stay at this rate of change, we will see women on par with men in 138 years.)

We begin with *The American Prospect*'s "Citizenship and Violence" (reading 39), focusing upon the tension of some states with the power of the federal government as it is deliberated whether violence against women within a relationship falls under civil rights or the privacy due to "domestic relations."

Abigail Geiger and Kim Parker show us women's gender gains and gaps in the United States in reading 40. In reading 41, Nikki Graf of the Pew Research Center writes of "Sexual Harassment at Work in the Era of #MeToo."

One of the most serious problems women and men face in the workplace is **sexual harassment**, which is unwanted, unsolicited, and nonreciprocated sexual behavior or attention. The testimony by Anita Hill before the Senate Judiciary Committee finally brought this issue fully into the public awareness. She contested the qualifications of Clarence Thomas to serve on the U.S. Supreme Court, charging that he had sexually harassed her when she worked for him at the Equal Employment Opportunity Commission.

Sexist attitudes and beliefs and homophobia continue to be challenged on many fronts. Author Kate Stephenson (reading 42) describes how women trying to break into the building trades still have to endure extreme sexual harassment and humiliation simply to keep their jobs.

Violence is the use of physical force to control the behavior of another person, to compel him or her to follow a certain course of action or enforced inaction, to coerce him or her into acting or thinking in whatever way the person with power dictates, and to leave the victim with no alternative except compliance. In other words, violence—physical, verbal, emotional, and sexual—is used to enforce the dominance of the perpetrator and the subordination of the victim.

Spouse beating is the most common and least reported crime in this country, afflicting men and women of all races, classes, and ages. According to FBI statistics, a woman is beaten by her husband or partner every eighteen seconds. Furthermore, battery is not confined to marital relationships.

In "Why Doesn't She Just Leave?" (reading 43), Clarethia Ellerbe brings us face to face with specific methods of controlling a woman in an intimate relationship, with and without the threat of physical violence. The author first interviews an aunt, who had been in a physically violent marriage for almost forty years. Next, she interviews a man who straightforwardly explains his methods of being a "controller": "I start by building her ego . . . send her flowers. . . . She now opens up. . . . I listen to every word she has to say. . . . This is my opportunity to find out which of her girlfriends or family members has the strongest influence on her. . . . I start planning how to eliminate that person from her circle." It is an unforgettable window into the insidiousness of emotional and psychological abuse.

The threat of **rape**, of being forced to have sex without consent, is a real threat for men and women, but especially for women. A woman is raped every six minutes, and one out of every three women will be raped in her lifetime. Notwithstanding the frequency with which this crime occurs, rape victims are still treated with skepticism, even by friends and family. If a rape survivor decides to press charges against his or her attacker and the case goes to trial, the defense may try to introduce the plaintiff's behavior into the proceedings and may well claim that he or she enticed the assailant or that he or she wanted or enjoyed it.

Readings 44 and 45 address this issue. One of the most important points James A. Doyle makes is that rape is an act of dominance, not sex; he explains why, despite general recognition of this fact, society tends to **blame the victim**, accusing him or her of being somehow responsible for what was done. Doyle also examines how **pornography**, some of which links violence against women with sexuality, contributes to the degradation of women. On a lighter note, the anonymous sketch "'The Rape' of Mr. Smith" (reading 45) tellingly exposes the injustice of our societal attitudes toward and treatment of rape victims.

Concluding part V, reading 46 by Ilyse Hogue reviews the precarious status of *Roe v. Wade* as it turns forty-five years old, and reading 47, by Liz Shu-

ler of the AFL-CIO, describes how U.S. unions are fighting for families.

In the last twenty years, until the Trump administration, it was generally not considered civil behavior to openly express racist, classist, and, to a lesser extent, sexist attitudes. Although racism and sexism may have been less visible, both remain well entrenched in our culture and within ourselves. They continue to distort our perceptions of one another and to impair our interpersonal behavior. They constrict the educational, economic, social, and cultural opportunities of people of color, women, and in the LGBTQ community. As always, it poisons the one who hates. Bad as this situation is, even worse has been the use of law and violence to oppress some groups and to serve the interests of others. We shall watch carefully to see what effects the Trump administration will have as we enter a phase of our history that sharply contrasts with the previous administration. After Trump's first year in office, our country experienced tremendous pushback from many sectors of society in the forms of demonstrations, courtrooms reversing judgments made by President Trump, and movements signaling social unrest around seriously dangerous human rights violations.

39

Citizenship and Violence

THE AMERICAN PROSPECT

Why, when the issue is violence against women, do some people talk about sex? While some violence directed at women is sexualized, calling it "sex" softens the brutality, implicates the victim as possibly an inciter or a participant, and offers the perpetrator the justification of lust.

Think also about the phrase "domestic violence." True, a good deal of violence against women does occur inside houses, but the coziness assumed to reside within the "domestic" stands in contrast to the cruelty of violence imposed by someone so close.

Linking violence against women to sex and domestic life illustrates more than a problem of rhetoric; it demonstrates the ongoing effects of laws that have treated women unequally. For centuries, state laws wove notions of sex and domesticity into a fabric of toleration of violence against women. And now that federal law is trying to protect women from the residue of that discrimination, objectors are arguing that federal remedies are unconstitutional—because violence against women is about sex and the home, which they say are state, not federal, concerns.

Two centuries ago, husbands had the prerogative of beating their wives. One century ago, state courts constructed rules about the sanctity of the home, thereby justifying under a rubric of privacy a reluctance to interfere when men beat or raped their wives. Indeed, up until about 10 years ago, under the U.S. military code, a man could not be convicted of the rape of his wife because the code defined rape as "the act of sexual intercourse with a female not his wife, by force and without her permission."

In short, the law decided which harms against women were tolerable. And even when those exemptions no longer exist, police, prosecutors, juries, and judges continue to be influenced by the long-standing assumption that women do not have rights of bodily integrity equal to those of men.

But law is not static. Particularly when civil rights are at issue, Congress has often enabled groups that have suffered discrimination under state laws to turn to federal courts for protection.

Recall that after the Civil War, some states did not allow African Americans to marry. When Congress considered federal remedies, some opponents responded that marriage was a matter of "domestic relations"—outside the purview of Congress. Congress concluded otherwise; federal civil rights law guaranteed newly freed slaves the right to marry.

In the early part of the twentieth century, labor's opponents argued that employment relations were personal relations, a matter for state, not federal, governance, but Congress began to pass labor laws, including legislation protecting the right of workers to unionize.

These federal laws now seem unremarkable. Yet, in a case currently before the U.S. Supreme Court, opponents of the Violence Against Women Act (VAWA), passed by Congress in 1994, are once again raising the familiar themes of personal relations and states' rights.

Congress enacted VAWA after four years of hearings and many revisions; it crafted a multifaceted statute that provides substantial funding to state, tribal, and local programs to combat violence against women. VAWA also authorizes federal criminal prosecutions in limited circumstances—for example, if a person crosses state lines to harm an intimate partner already protected by a permanent state court order. And VAWA includes a new civil rights remedy for victims of gender-based violence akin to the remedy already on the books for race discrimination: VAWA lets plaintiffs sue assailants for damages, in either state or federal court, upon proof that a crime of violence was motivated by "animus based on gender."

Now at issue before the Supreme Court is the constitutionality of this one aspect of VAWA, the civil remedy. Thus far, most of the federal judges who have considered it have upheld it. However, one federal appellate court, the Fourth Circuit, thought otherwise, holding that neither the Constitution's Commerce Clause nor the Fourteenth Amendment enabled Congress to create federal court remedies for victims of gender-based violence. . . .

The Fourth Circuit's view that VAWA harms states' rights is not shared by many representatives of state government. When the legislation was pending, the attorneys general of 38 states told Congress that VAWA's civil rights provisions would be a useful supplement to—not a displacement of—state remedies. At the time, few laws in the United States still expressly exculpated men who had attacked their wives. But many prosecutors worried that the residue of both legal and social attitudes about violence against women results in systematically less protection for women victims of violence than for men.

States did more than worry. In the 1980s and 1990s, the chief justices of more than half the states commissioned task forces to explore the treatment of women in their courts. What they learned was powerful and disheartening. Connecticut's task force concluded, for example, that "women are treated differently from men in the justice system, and because of it, many suffer from unfairness." From states as different as California, Georgia, Maryland, Minnesota, and Kentucky, reports came that women victims of violence faced special hurdles—their claims of injury were often discounted, their testimony often disbelieved.

The record of systemic discrimination was before Congress when it enacted VAWA. And that record explains why, in 1999, the National Association of Attorneys General supported the reauthorization of VAWA and 36 states signed onto a brief filed in the current Supreme Court case, urging that the civil rights remedy be upheld. (Only one state—Alabama—argued for invalidation.)

Power is surely at stake here, but not only how to allocate it between state and federal governments. Also at issue is the Supreme Court's ability to override congressional enactments. Will the Court now ignore congressional fact-finding and substitute its own? Will it change its current interpretation of the Commerce Clause and cut back on Congress's power to legislate in this sphere?

To understand why the Court should not, first focus on the Fourth Circuit's argument that violence against women is about sex, crimes, family life, and the home, and that states have exclusive dominion here. That claim is untrue, and as policy it would be unwise.

Federal law oversees state criminal law and family law in a variety of contexts. States cannot, for example, enforce criminal laws discriminatorily, nor can they forbid interracial marriage. Outside the domain of civil rights, many other federal laws define and structure relations that could be termed "domestic"—like welfare law (requiring beneficiaries to work, so that children need to be in child care programs), the Equal Retirement Income Security Act (creating marital property rights in pensions), or tax law (defining economic obligations by reference to marital status).

The point is not that Congress has taken over state law, but rather that state and federal governance—overlapping, often cooperative—is the norm in virtually all fields of human endeavor in the United States, family life and criminal law included.

Second, focus on Congress's powers over interstate commerce. Since the 1930s, the Constitution has been understood as permitting Congress to regulate not only commercial transactions themselves but also activities substantially related to commerce. Since the 1960s, the Constitution has been understood as permitting Congress to remove obstacles to engaging in commerce—especially discriminatory obstacles. Before enacting VAWA, Congress heard testimony from both business executives and individuals detailing not only that violence has an economic effect on the GDP but also that violence against women limits women's full participation as economic actors. Congress learned both that women were beaten to prevent them from going to work and that the threat of violence restricted women's employment options.

At the time, VAWA's opponents predicted its civil rights remedy would open the floodgates to lawsuits having little or nothing to do with commerce. Yet to date, only about 50 decisions have been reported under the civil rights remedy, and of those, more than 40 percent involved allegations of attacks in commercial or educational settings. Indeed, the case before the Supreme Court involves a young woman allegedly raped by two students at her college, one of whom explained publicly that he liked to "get girls drunk and fuck the shit out of them."

Third, consider Congress's power to enforce the Fourteenth Amendment, forbidding states to deny equal protection of the laws. Opponents of VAWA argue that violence inflicted by individuals is a private act, not state action. But state laws have failed to protect women's physical security equally with men's. State prosecutors have told Congress that inequality continues. Congress can therefore fashion proportionate remedies, as it has done before to protect blacks from racially motivated violence.

VAWA, in other words, is an ordinary exercise of congressional powers, executed in a "federalism-friendly" fashion to provide complementary means of rights enforcement. Its opponents want to identify women with the home, focus on violence in bedrooms, and confine a woman's remedies to whatever is available in the locality in which she finds herself. What they fail to understand is that the federal government has an obligation to secure women's physical safety and to protect women's rights to participate in the national economy free from the threat of targeted violence. VAWA is not about sex, and it is not about a family any of us would want to be in; citizenship in the nation is what is at stake.

[2001]

[Editor's note: According to the Woodhull Freedom Foundation (Levy), the reauthorization for the Violence Against Women Act is up in September 2018, and it is at great risk. The Department of Justice is responsible for carrying this out, and head of the DOJ Jeff Sessions voted against it in 2013. Even if it is reauthorized, the source of funding and its maintenance over the next decade are central concerns—2018]

Understanding the Reading

1. Give two examples in U.S. history where states have fought with the federal government over jurisdiction concerning "domestic relations."
2. How does violence against women affect our country's economy?
3. Give at least two arguments of supporters of the Violence Against Women Act that explain why this act is constitutional.

Suggestions for Responding

1. Research your state's laws that pertain to violence against women.
2. Was VAWA reauthorized in 2018? If so, under what conditions?

40

For Women's History Month, a Look at Gender Gains—and Gaps—in the United States

ABIGAIL GEIGER AND KIM PARKER

March 15, 2018

Over the past half-century, women have strengthened their position in the labor force and boosted their economic standing by making gains in labor force participation, wages, and access to more lucrative occupations. But their progress on some fronts has stagnated in recent years, and large gender gaps persist at the top levels of leadership in government and business.

Here are some key findings about gender gains and gaps in America.

1. Women make up 47 percent of the U.S. labor force, up from 30 percent in 1950—but growth has stagnated. The share of women in the labor force generally grew throughout the second half of the twentieth century, but it has since leveled off. Projections from the Bureau of Labor Statistics indicate that in the coming decades women will continue to make up slightly less than half of the labor force.
2. Women have seen steady growth in labor force participation over the past several decades, but that, too, has leveled off. In 2017, 57 percent of working-age women (ages sixteen and older) were either employed or looking for work. That's higher than it was in 1980 (51 percent) but down somewhat from its peak of 60 percent in 1999.

   One of the main drivers of increased labor force participation among women over the decades has been the sharp increase in the share of mothers in the workforce. Nearly three-quarters (73 percent) of mothers with children younger than eighteen were in the labor force in 2000, up from 47 percent in 1975 (the first year for which data on mothers' labor force participation are available). That share has remained relatively stable since about 2000.

   Men's presence in the labor force has been on the decline in recent decades. In 1980, 77 percent of working-age men (ages sixteen and older) were employed or looking for work; in 2017, 69 percent were in the labor force.
3. Growing wages for women have helped narrow the gender pay gap, though women still lag behind men in pay. Women's median hourly earnings were $16 in 2016, up from $12.48 in 1980 (after adjusting for inflation). Men earned a median hourly wage of $19.23 in 2016, down slightly from $19.42 in 1980.

   In other words, in 2016, the median working woman earned eighty-three cents for every dollar earned by men, compared with sixty-four cents for every man's dollar in 1980. For workers ages twenty-five to thirty-four, the wage gap is smaller: in 2016, women in this group earned ninety cents for every dollar a man in the same age group made. White and Asian women have narrowed the wage gap with white men to a much greater degree than black and Hispanic women.

Women's increasing wages have been driven in part by their increased presence in more lucrative occupations. For example, women today are just as likely as men to be working in managerial positions. In 1980, men were twice as likely as women to have these types of jobs.

4. Women have made gains in educational attainment, which has contributed to their progress in the workforce at large. Among adults ages twenty-five to sixty-four, women are now more likely than men to have a four-year college degree. In 2017, 38 percent of these women and 33 percent of men had a bachelor's degree.

Women are also outpacing men in postgraduate education. In 2017, 14 percent of women ages twenty-five to sixty-four had an advanced degree, compared with 12 percent of men. In 1992, a higher share of men (9 percent) than women (6 percent) in this age group had an advanced degree.

5. Women still lag in top leadership positions in business and government. Women have made inroads in a wide range of leadership positions in recent decades, but they only account for about 20 percent of members of Congress and about a quarter of state legislature members. Women made up roughly 5 percent of Fortune 500 company CEOs in the first quarter of 2017 and about 20 percent of Fortune 500 board members in 2016. As of March 2018, there are six female governors and five females in executive branch cabinet-level positions.

Most Americans say women are equally as capable of leading as men are. But many say there aren't more women in top business or political positions because women are held to higher standards than men and have to do more to prove themselves (43 percent say this for business positions, 38 percent for political offices). Similar numbers say that electorate and corporate America are just not ready to put more women in top leadership positions.

[Article published in part.]

Understanding the Reading

1. Why are U.S. women significantly more likely to be college educated than men?
2. What do you think the consequences of this will be for our society?
3. How would you explain why women lag behind men in government and business leadership roles in the United States, in spite of their educational attainments?

Suggestions for Responding

1. Interview one or two women in leadership roles, asking about their experiences.
2. Do you think there should be a quota for women in business leadership, such as CEOs, in order to counter age-old sexist attitudes? (This exists in several countries.)

41

Sexual Harassment at Work in the Era of #MeToo

Nikki Graf

Recent allegations against prominent men in entertainment, politics, the media, and other industries have sparked increased attention to the issue of sexual harassment and assault, in turn raising questions about the treatment of the accused and the accusers and what lies ahead for men and women in the workplace.

A new Pew Research Center survey finds that, when it comes to sexual harassment in the workplace, more Americans think men getting away with it and female accusers not being believed are major problems than say the same about employers firing men before finding out all the facts or women making false accusations. And while these attitudes differ somewhat by gender, they vary most dramatically between Democrats and Republicans.

The nationally representative survey of 6,251 adults was conducted online from February 26 to March 11, 2018, using Pew Research Center's American Trends Panel.

Many Americans also believe the increased focus on sexual harassment and assault poses new challenges for men as they navigate their interactions with women at work. About half (51 percent) say the recent developments have made it harder for men to know how to interact with women in the workplace. Only 12 percent say this increased focus has made it easier for men, and 36 percent say it hasn't made much difference.

At the same time, Americans see little upside for women's workplace opportunities as a result of the increased focus on sexual harassment and assault. Just 28 percent say it will lead to more opportunities for women in the workplace in the long run, while a somewhat smaller share (20 percent) say it will lead to fewer opportunities and 51 percent say it won't make much of a difference.

The survey also finds that 59 percent of women and 27 percent of men say they have personally received unwanted sexual advances or verbal or physical harassment of a sexual nature, whether in or outside of a work context. Among women who say they have been sexually harassed, more than half (55 percent) say it has happened both in and outside of work settings.

[Article published in part.]

Understanding the Reading

1. What potential challenges for workers exist with more focus on harassment in the workplace?
2. Have a class discussion on the short-term and long-term effects this focus will have in the workplace.

Suggestions for Responding

1. Have discussions with an older generation, both male and female, on this topic. Report on what you find.
2. Have similar discussions with people not brought up in the United States. Are there differences?

42

Breaking Down Gender Bias in the Construction Industry

KATE STEPHENSON

March 8, 2017

The construction industry is dominated by male workers, but a critical labor shortage is an opportu-

nity to usher in change. The construction trades have long been among the industries with the lowest percentage of gender diversity in the workforce. As of 2015, less than 3 percent of workers in the construction and extraction trades were women—data on the percentage of lesbian, gay, bisexual, transgender, and queer (LGBTQ) workers in the trades is not available—and the design field is not much better off. According to a 2012 survey of AIA member firms, only 16 percent of the AIA's membership is female. Forty-nine percent of architecture students and 39 percent of interns are women, but just 17 percent are firm principals and partners. And these numbers have not changed significantly in the last thirty years.

Why does it matter? We have a huge shortage of skilled labor in the trades right now. According to the Associated Builders and Contractors, 1.6 million new skilled workers will be needed between now and 2022. We can double the number of people available to fill this need by actively recruiting, supporting, and creating training programs for women, transgender, and gender-nonconforming people.

Often, the construction trades are looked down upon by our society and our education system. The industry is not necessarily seen as a place where one can learn professional skills, experience career advancement, or be compensated with a living wage and benefits. We need to change this perception of our industry: jobs in the building trades, engineering, and design can be lifelong careers that support families, providing employment with relatively high wages, especially for women. According to a *New York Times* article from 2011, the gender wage gap in construction is lower than in any other sector, and women earn 92.2 cents on the dollar of what men earn.

With our community's focus on high-performance construction, integrated process, and building science and technology, the construction profession is becoming more sophisticated and requires a more diverse set of skills. Increasing the profile of our industry will also help attract a diverse workforce that includes more women and gender-nonconforming workers.

What are the barriers to increasing gender diversity? Clearly, there is a lack of role models. Traditional gender stereotyping begins when children are very young, and it is reinforced when girls are encouraged to play with dolls and boys are encouraged to play with trucks and toy tools. Often those raised as boys gain building experience by helping their dads with projects around the house, while those raised as girls, even those who express an interest in carpentry, don't have the same experience working with tools and building materials.

This connects to ideas of leadership, "toughness," and prowess with physical or spatial problem solving. By the time kids are in high school, there may be a sharp gender divide in confidence with these skills—one that has nothing to do with natural talent. Instead, it is the result of socialization and unequal access based on stereotypes about talents correlating with gender. The end result is that when it comes to hiring a laborer or carpenter on the crew, it's more likely that a male will be hired over a female because they are perceived to be stronger and have more previous experience.

Gender stereotypes also frequently play into how students are "tracked" or exposed to career counseling in high school. Those raised as boys are more often encouraged to pursue vocational trades such as carpentry, welding, plumbing, and electrical while those raised as girls are typically pushed toward health care, cosmetology, and education. And that's assuming they have access to vocational education at all—regardless of gender, the availability of vocational education has been decreasing steadily over the past fifty years.

What will it take to change our field? We all know that equality and equity are not synonymous. Equality is treating everyone the same. Equity is giving everyone what they need to be successful. What we need is gender equity. On a practical level, that means putting in extra effort to attract, recruit, train, and retain employees in order to increase gender diversity.

Here are a few basic ways to make your business more equitable:

- Use gender-neutral language in job postings and job descriptions.
- Respect everyone's self-identification—call everyone by their preferred name and pronoun.
- Ensure that adequate gender-neutral restroom facilities are available on every job site.
- Ensure that all crew members have properly fitting personal protective equipment. (It can often be unsafe for smaller people to use "standard" PPE.)
- Develop and enforce a zero-tolerance sexual harassment policy—not only for your employees but also for all subs on a job site.
- Connect with tradeswomen organizations and post your jobs on their websites.
- Be willing to challenge your assumptions about

an applicant's ability to perform the work—give people a chance to prove themselves.
- Make it a priority to hire and work with other subcontractors or vendors that are women or trans owned and/or make it a priority to hire women, trans, and gender-nonconforming people.

Surveys of women and LGBTQ workers in the construction industry (including engineers, architects, and specialty trades) consistently show that these employees are frequently the target of harassment and discrimination by their co-workers.

Some of this treatment is explicitly sexual harassment, while some is subtler and, at times, even well intentioned. For example, some men see it as just being polite to offer to carry something for a woman, but the offer implies that women or smaller-bodied people can't lift heavy things or perform the same tasks as their co-workers.

Every female or gender-nonconforming contractor I know can tell a dozen horror stories of inappropriate things said to them on a job site. Some are directed at making them feel uncomfortable, unwanted, and disrespected as an authority or leader despite their skills and qualifications. Others—which are often chalked up to "locker room talk"—use vulgar or explicit language.

Changing the company culture is important. Changing these workplace dynamics takes a real intention on the part of business owners and managers. It's one thing to go out of your way to hire women, transgender, and gender-nonconforming people in your company, but you also need to do the work to change your company culture so those people feel welcome and thrive in that work environment.

Here are some tips for retention:

- Sponsor and offer an apprenticeship program to young women, trans, and gender-nonconforming people and promote the career opportunities available in the trades.
- Offer a buddy system that starts from the job offer stage and assists women, trans, and gender-nonconforming people to form relationships, build networks, and transition successfully to the company.
- End isolation on worksites by assigning women, trans, and gender-nonconforming people, especially those new to the trades, in pairs or more.
- Guarantee pay equity within your company.

- Offer flexibility—family-friendly work schedules will make your business more attractive to all genders.
- Change the company's culture to embrace diversity and flexibility as an ongoing commitment to the entire workforce—not just "special treatment" for women, trans, and gender-nonconforming people.

What are the rewards? According to cumulative Gallup Workplace Studies, companies with inclusive cultures do better on several indicators than those that are not inclusive: customer satisfaction +39 percent, productivity +22 percent, profitability +27 percent, and turnover down by 22 percent.

As leaders in the fields of renewable energy, green building, building science, and sustainable design, our success and the success of our industry is contingent on creating inclusive and equitable companies. To support this work, a number of members of the Northeast Sustainable Energy Association have collaborated to produce "Breaking Down Gender Bias: A Toolkit for Construction Business Owners." It's full of practical tips you can use to introduce these issues into your workplace, either as a business owner or as an employee.

Understanding the Reading

1. Why are there so few women in the construction industry, in spite of the urgent need for more workers?
2. How does the industry's culture need to change to be able to recruit women, trans, and gender-nonconforming people?
3. What should society do to encourage recruitment in this industry if, in fact, we see value in worker diversity?
4. What is the difference between worker equality and worker equity?

Suggestion for Responding

1. Interview a woman you know who works in a traditionally male field about her experience, asking questions about whether she has experienced harassment on the job.

43
Why Doesn't She Just Leave?

Clarethia Ellerbe

On the first night of a university course I was taking, "Gender, War and Peace," the class viewed a film called *Speak Truth to Power*. Rita Moreno was one of the actors reading the testimony of a Russian woman who had created a hotline for abused women. After the film, the class discussed the film's contents, but spoke very little on the subject of domestic violence. This made me wonder whether the topic was taboo, or just something that people do not feel comfortable discussing. Or is it something that society is not aware of, or feels that it only happens in a certain part of society?

Before viewing this film I had never really given domestic violence much consideration. As I sat there listening to Rita Moreno, a celebrity reading the words of a woman fighting domestic violence, it made me want to do some research on how deeply it cuts. From my research, I learned that when people hear the words "domestic violence," they often think of the physical aspect of it, such as pushing, shoving, hitting, twisting arms, punching, choking and slapping. While the abuser and the victim are in the relationship, they are not willing to admit to themselves or anyone else that they are in an abusive relationship. A co-worker once told me that her husband could beat her the night before and she could wear a one-piece bathing suit the next day, and you, as the observer, could not detect her bruises. I asked her how he was able to accomplish this. She had no answer, but her statement did make me wonder about the abuser's view of domestic violence. Observing relationships of some of my family and friends, I decided to ask the ones that appeared to be in abusive relationships, or have been in the past.

Interview I

The following story is told to me by my aunt, who was in an abusive marriage for almost forty years: "At the age of sixteen, I met my husband, and I enjoyed a wonderful, romantic courtship with him. Then people began to make comments, like: 'Why would a pretty girl like you get married to an ugly duckling'; that is when my problems started. The comments led him to thoughts of jealousy, verbal and mental abuse, and eventually physical abuse.

"It got to the point where he painted our windows black and did not allow me and the children to visit with relatives or friends. I had choke marks on my neck and wore these bruises as if they were some kind of trophy. Along with my bruises, I received cuts, wounds and black eyes. My head was banged against the walls, doors, the floor, and the refrigerator, and during all this time I thought he loved me. When people used to ask me about the beatings I was taking from my husband, I would say, 'If a man doesn't beat you every now and then, he doesn't love you.' I strongly believed that all his hitting was about him loving me, and teaching me the right way to go in life. It makes me laugh when I tell someone that my husband was going to teach me the right things to do. I have asked myself a thousand times, 'What could my husband have taught me, as dumb as he was?' I'm glad that my husband didn't love me to death! But it would be nice if one day he came to me and asked me to forgive him."

Interview II

Joe is a friend of the family, and we grew up in the same town. He likes to call himself a controller. This is his story about his method for control: "When I first meet someone who I want to be in my life, I start by building her ego, you know, like telling her things I know women like to hear. I tell her how beautiful she is, and I might add something like how lucky I am to have found her. Women love it when a man talks like that to them, especially when the guy tells them that they are a cut above all the common Janes.

"After the first few dates I send her flowers or some other token gift. You know, not an expensive gift, but just something to make her feel good about herself. By now, she is thanking her lucky stars that she finally met the man of her dreams. I know how women like to brag to their girlfriends about meeting the man of their dreams. Soon I have her all happy and excited about the start of her ideal relationship with her ideal man. She now opens up and begins to talk freely about what she wants. I listen to every word she has to say. She talks about her girlfriends, as well as her family, at this stage of the game. This is my opportunity to find out which of her girlfriends or family members has the strongest influence in her life.

"After I learn the name of the strongest person in her life, I start planning how to eliminate that person from her circle of friends. Because I know that this person is strong, I know that this person will not let me treat her friend in an unkind way. I know that she will come between me and my woman, once she sees me trying to mistreat her friend. Women have something called 'sisterhood,' and once they get this sisterhood working there is nothing in the world that a man can do to break this bond. I am not strong enough to break that bond; it is a bond that will take me out of life so fast I wouldn't know what hit me. We men are afraid of the sisterhood bond; women don't really know how powerful that sisterhood is. We men keep you women fighting amongst yourselves, so you guys cannot form that strong bond.

"But once I eliminate her strongest friend, it is easy to keep her away from her other friends, coworkers, as well as interfering family members. I am now in control. My strategy is to control her completely and make her totally dependent on me, to the point where she cannot make her own decisions without first asking me, which also includes when and where to go to the bathroom. Feeling powerful and feeling the need for more control, I begin to downplay all her achievements she made before she met me. It doesn't matter if she had a better job than me, or if she owns her own home, or has a car and I don't. I am constantly telling her that if it weren't for me, she would have nothing. I am the one who makes her look good in the eyes of her friends, her coworkers, and family. I make her look respectable in the neighborhood, as well as to her female friends and family. I make her feel like all of her friends are jealous of her good man."

While doing this research I learned that an abused person's perceptions are altered by the abuse, and that domestic violence has nothing to do with conflict resolution. It has a purpose of its own. That purpose is to establish a relationship of power over and control of the partner.

[2003]

References

Aunt "Jane," personal communication, 2003 Domestic Abuse & Sexual Assault Intervention Services (www.dasi.org)

Domestic Violence Statistical Summary (www.fultonpd.com/stats.htm)

Dr. Susan Forward and Joan Torres (1987). *Men Who Hate Women & the Women Who Love Them*

"Joe," personal communication, 2003

MSN Learning and Research—Domestic Violence (http://encarta.msn.com/encnet/refpages/ RefArticle.aspx?refid = 762529482)

Understanding the Reading

1. What kinds of abuse are featured in this essay?
2. Why did the author's aunt stay with her husband for so long?
3. How does Joe control women?
4. Why does Joe control women?
5. What is his greatest obstacle?

Suggestions for Responding

1. Interview someone who was in an abusive relationship (without asking why he or she stood for it).
2. Share stories in the class of people you have known who were in abusive relationships.
3. Invite a representative from a women's shelter to speak to the class.

44

Rape and Sexual Assault

JAMES A. DOYLE

Few words strike as much terror in a person's heart as rape. Few human acts are so fraught with misinformation and misconception as rape. Few other acts so degrade a human being as rape. And few other acts show the imbalance of power between men and women and men's quest for domination over women as rape does.

Rape is first and foremost an act of *violence*, an attempted or completed sexual assault instigated by one or more persons against another human being. The historical roots of rape run deep in the patriarchal tradition of male violence toward women. Rape, to be understood, must not be seen as simply a violent sexual act of a few lunatics or pathologically disordered persons, but rather a violent sexual act performed by many and reinforced by the dominant patriarchal values coming to the fore in their most twisted and disturbing forms in our culture. A few cultures may be less prone to violent sexual acts between males and females, but ours and most others are definitely "rape-prone" cultures. No discussion of power and its imbalance between women and men would be complete without a discussion of rape.

We will first take up the issue of rape as an act of dominance (not sex) and of power (not pathology) that is ingrained in the very fiber of the male's gender role. Next we will attempt to put the statistics of rape in perspective by trying to give some scope to the enormity of the act of rape in the everyday lives of many women and some men. And then we will note the rising concern and some of the actions taken among feminists and nonfeminists alike over the issue of rape as a social phenomenon of epidemic proportions and not merely an isolated criminal act affecting a few.

Rape and Power

Throughout most of this century those who influenced what others thought about rape saw it as a "victim-precipitated phenomenon." Sigmund Freud, in his study of the female personality, theorized that the female was more "masochistic" than the male and that rape—either in fantasy or in fact—was the one sexual act wherein the female acted out her masochism to the utmost. However, such nonsense was soon dismissed by the psychiatric and psychological communities who began to speculate that rape was the result of a disordered or aberrant sexual impulse within a certain small group of men. Today, however, rape—whether the victim is female or male—is seen as an act of power or dominance of one person over another. Recently, some social scientists have noted that rape is one of the most terrifying means used by men to dominate other men inside and outside of prison. To focus on rape as a power or dominance act we need only analyze how rape is used in prison:

> Rape in prison is rarely a sexual act, but one of violence, politics and an acting out of power roles. "Most of your homosexual rapes [are] a macho thing," says Col. Walter Pence, the Chief of Security here at the Louisiana State Penitentiary at Angola. "It's basically one guy saying to another: 'I'm a better man than you and I'm gonna turn you out ["turn you out" is prison slang for rape] to prove it.' I've investigated about a hundred cases personally, and I've not seen one that's just an act of passion. It's definitely a macho/power thing among the inmates."

A prime ingredient in rape is the element of aggression that is so deeply embedded in the male's gender role. For many men, aggression is one of the major ways of proving their masculinity and manhood, especially among those men who feel some sense of powerlessness in their lives. The male-as-dominant or male-as-aggressor is a theme so central to many men's self-concept that it literally carries over into their sexual lives. Sex, in fact, may be the one area where the average man can still prove his masculinity when few other areas can be found for him to prove himself manly or in control, or the dominant one in a relationship. Diana Russell addresses this issue when she declares that rape is not the act of a disturbed male, but rather an act of an overconforming male. She writes:

> Rape is not so much a deviant act as an over-conforming act. Rape may be understood as an extreme acting-out of qualities that are regarded as super masculine in this and many other societies: aggression, force, power, strength, toughness, dominance, competitiveness. To win, to be superior, to be successful, to conquer—all demonstrate masculinity to those who subscribe to common cultural notions of masculinity, i.e., the *masculine mystique*. And it would be surprising if these notions of masculinity did not find expression in men's sexual behavior. Indeed, sex may be the arena where these notions of masculinity are most intensely played out, particularly by men who feel powerless in the rest of their lives, and hence, whose masculinity is threatened by this sense of powerlessness.

The fusion of aggression and sexuality for many men can be seen when we examine the area of sexual arousal as stimulated by graphic scenes of rape. Initially, researchers found that convicted rapists were more sexually aroused by depictions of violent sexuality than were men who had not raped. Thus it was thought that rapists must have a very low threshold for sexual arousal, and that the least little provocation would set off a male rapist (e.g., a woman who would assertively say "no" to sexual advances or even put up a fight was enough to trigger off a rapist, or so it was thought). In more recent studies, however, when men who had never raped were exposed to depictions of sexual assault, they reported a heightened sexual arousal from such scenes and an increase in their rape fantasies. Another disquieting note is that when

nonrapist males were shown depictions of sexual assault, they reported the possibility that they would even consider using force themselves in their sexual relations. The research appears to suggest that most men (i.e., rapists and nonrapists) find violence a stimulant to heighten or arouse their sexual feelings. There is evidence that seems to indicate that males in general find sexuality related at some level to an expression of aggression, and in turn aggression heightens their sexual fantasies or actual sexual behaviors.

In summary, we can say that sexual assault or rape is first and foremost an act of sexual violence that to some degree draws upon the sexual fantasies of the rapist; it is linked to the rapist's need to show superiority and dominance over another.

The Problem of Numbers

Rape is one of the most underreported of all serious crimes in the United States and in other countries as well. When we try to get a true picture of the enormity of its incidence, we find the issue complicated by the lack of reliable rape statistics. The crime of rape presents some uniquely confounding problems.

One problem we encounter is the simple fact that many, if not most, rape victims simply refuse to come forward and report to the authorities incidents of sexual violence. For many rape victims, a sense of shame or guilt or self-blame about their role in the rape assaults may be enough to prevent them from coming forward and pressing charges. Those who do press charges, however, are apt to meet with questions, accusations, and other degrading and humiliating experiences by the very authorities that are sworn to uphold the laws of society that make the rape of a person a serious felony.

Another problem is that when rape victims do press charges against their assailants, their life histories, especially sexual activities, are dragged before the public. In many instances, the public seems willing to blame the victim for the assault rather than the rapist. The reason for such an attribution of guilt to the victim rather than to the assailant seems to lie in the fact that many people have a tendency to blame others for their misfortunes, as if the world we live in was and is a "just world" where bad things happen only to those who somehow bring on or somehow deserve the consequences of their acts. Consequently, a likely result of such a "just world" orientation is that, more often than not, the defenders of rapists will try to show that the rape victims acted in such a manner as to infer their complicity in the sexual assaults or that they "had it coming" because of their actions. We find such a courtroom tactic used by many defense attorneys, and it was one that apparently did not work in the much publicized 1984 New Bedford, Massachusetts, gang-rape case. There the rape victim's motives for stopping at a bar were questioned and inferences were made impugning her behavior while in the bar. For example, during the trial, it was pointed out that the rape victim had talked with several of the accused rapists before the gang rape occurred. (If the mere act of talking is sufficient cause in some people's minds for a group of men to rape a woman, then we indeed have a twisted view of the causes of rape.)

Thus, with all the barriers preventing the victims of sexual assault from coming forward, it is no wonder that rape continues to be one of the most underreported crimes. Even so, the Federal Bureau of Investigation reported that in the decade between 1967 and 1977 the number of reported rapes doubled in the United States. I have noted that

during 1977 alone, over 63,000 cases of rape were reported by the FBI. The most shocking feature of these statistics is that rape is considered by many experts in crime statistics to be one of the *least* reported violent crimes. The best available estimates suggest that for every one reported rape case there are anywhere from three to ten unreported cases. The conservative estimate of three means that over a quarter of a million women were forcibly raped in the United States in 1977!

While we have no absolute statistics for the total number of completed or attempted rapes committed annually in North America, we can estimate the probability of a woman being the victim of sexual assault during her lifetime. Allan Johnson estimated that "Nationally, a *conservative* estimate is that, under current conditions, 20–30 percent of girls now twelve years old will suffer a violent sexual attack during the remainder of their lives." Even with this estimate, however, we should keep in mind that this percentage excludes females under twelve, married women, and male rape victims. The enormity of the incidence of rape becomes even more staggering when we note that untold numbers of children under twelve are often the victims of sexual assault, as well as the many cases of male rape both inside and outside of prison.

Rape as a Social Concern

Due to the mounting concern over women's rights heralded by the reemergent women's movement, sexual assaults and their debilitating consequences for the victims have become one of the more pressing central issues of the 1970s and 1980s. Consequently, many social scientists have turned their attention toward understanding the dynamics of rapists and their motives, the institutional and cultural factors promoting rape, and of course, the various factors affecting the assault on rape victims and their reactions.

To combat the growing number of rapes, more and more people are beginning to think in terms of prevention and not only of ways to deal with the debilitating aftermath of sexual assault. Many different ways have been suggested to stop the growing wave of sexual assaults in our society.

Two such preventive approaches commonly thought of are, first, a "restrictive approach" that focuses on women changing their life-styles (e.g., not going out alone or not talking to strangers), and second, an "assertive approach" that suggests that women learn martial arts in order to fight back if assaulted. Both of these approaches, however, have some drawbacks. The restrictive approach, asking women to change their pattern of living, is an affront to women. Do we ask merchants to stop keeping money in their cash registers to prevent robberies? Why then should women change, for example, their dress or their social habits? The assertive approach has one possible value: the demise of the myth of the "defenseless woman." However, one problem with this approach is that many times in order to coerce a victim a rapist uses a deadly weapon, which totally nullifies any preventive action or force a victim may take to ward off an assailant.

Along with teaching young children and women to skillfully defend themselves, it seems that a broader based attack against sexual assaults should be taken against the social and institutional factors that promote sexual violence in our society. Two additional areas should be addressed if we are to see a reduction and, hopefully, an elimination in sexual assaults in our society. First, we need to examine the male's gender role with its prescriptive aggressive element, especially aggression against women. Aggression and violence are still seen by many as an integral part of the male's gender role. One way to reduce sexual assault in our society would be to redefine the male gender role, incorporating nonaggressive or nonviolent elements rather than aggressiveness. Of course, many people would object to such a major change in the male role, fearing that our country would fall prey to its national enemies who may wish to attack a nation of nonaggressive men.

Another controversial change that would reduce the number of sexual assaults is an open attack on hard-core and violence-oriented pornography and the multi-million dollar business that supports it. First of all, we should dismiss the notion that only males find sexually explicit materials arousing. Research has found that men *as well as* women find various kinds of erotic material sexually stimulating. However, the pornography industry has mainly directed its sales to a male audience. Although some erotic material does not focus on violent sexual aggression, a large proportion of the male-oriented pornography that is sold in stores across our country portrays the female as the victim of physical and sexual assault.

Researchers Neil Malamuth and Edward Donnerstein have found that exposure to violent pornography generally increases sexual arousal as well as negative attitudes toward women and favorable attitudes toward sexual assault. Thus one possible way to reduce the sexual violence in our society against women would be to eliminate such material. However, those who oppose such a plan immediately bring up the issue of a person's First Amendment rights, which guarantee freedom of speech; such opposition, however, misinterprets the Constitution and its intent.

Would society be as accepting if various media presented graphic anti-Semitic portrayals of Jews being shoved into gas chambers or American Indians being shot for sport for their land? And yet many people support the multi-million dollar industry that shows women assaulted and maimed for the sake of sexual stimulation.

If our society is to rectify the age-old problem of unequal power between females and males, we need to challenge many of our behaviors, our attitudes, and our social institutions that continue to cast women in an inferior role. Until that day, the problem of inequality between the genders is everyone's concern.

[1985]

Understanding the Reading

1. How does rape reflect patriarchal values?
2. How have theories about rape changed during the past one hundred years, and how is it viewed today?
3. How is rape an act of an overconforming male?
4. How are aggression and sexuality related for most men?
5. Why is it difficult to know accurately the incidence of rape?
6. Why do people tend to "blame the victim" of sexual assault?
7. Explain the difference between the "restrictive approach" and the "assertive approach" to rape prevention and what is wrong with each.
8. What social and institutional factors promote sexual violence?

Suggestions for Responding

1. Doyle proposes that the male role be changed to eliminate its emphasis on aggression. Do you think this is desirable or not? Why? How might we go about making such a change?
2. Doyle also proposes that eliminating violent pornography is one way to reduce violence against women, and he dismisses the claim that this would be an infringement of First Amendment rights. Do you agree or disagree with his position? Why?

45

"The Rape" of Mr. Smith

UNKNOWN

The law discriminates against rape victims in a manner which would not be tolerated by victims of any other crime. In the following example, a holdup victim is asked questions similar in form to those usually asked a victim of rape.

"Mr. Smith, you were held up at gunpoint on the corner of 16th & Locust?"

"Yes."

"Did you struggle with the robber?"

"No."

"Why not?"

"He was armed."

"Then you made a conscious decision to comply with his demands rather than to resist?"

"Yes."

"Did you scream? Cry out?"

"No. I was afraid."

"I see. Have you ever been held up before?"

"No."

"Have you ever given money away?"

"Yes, of course—"

"And did you do so willingly?"

"What are you getting at?"

"Well, let's put it like this, Mr. Smith. You've given away money in the past—in fact, you have quite a reputation for philanthropy. How can we be sure that you weren't *contriving* to have your money taken from you by force?"

"Listen, if I wanted—"

"Never mind. What time did this holdup take place, Mr. Smith?"

"About 11 P.M."

"You were out on the streets at 11 P.M.? Doing what?"

"Just walking."

"Just walking? You know that it's dangerous being out on the street that late at night. Weren't you aware that you could have been held up?"

"I hadn't thought about it."

"What were you wearing at the time, Mr. Smith?"

"Let's see. A suit. Yes, a suit."

"An *expensive* suit?"

"Well—yes."

"In other words, Mr. Smith, you were walking around the streets late at night in a suit that practically *advertised* the fact that you might be a good target for some easy money, isn't that so? I mean, if we didn't know better, Mr. Smith, we might even think you were *asking* for this to happen, mightn't we?"

"Look, can't we talk about the past history of the guy who *did* this to me?"

"I'm afraid not, Mr. Smith. I don't think you would want to violate his rights, now, would you?"

Naturally, the line of questioning, the innuendo, is ludicrous—as well as inadmissible as any sort of cross-examination—unless we are talking about parallel questions in a rape case. The time of night, the victim's previous history of "giving away" that which was taken by force, the clothing—all of these are held against the victim. Society's posture on rape, and the manifestation of that posture in the courts, helps account for the fact that so few rapes are reported.

[n.d.]

Understanding the Reading

1. In what way are rape victims often discriminated against, when they are being questioned initially?
2. Why would an officer of the law imply that the victim was "asking for it"?
3. With present-day DNA technology, do you think that society's attitude toward investigating rape has changed? Why or why not?

Suggestion for Responding

1. Why do you think rape victims are treated so differently from victims of other crimes?

46

Roe v. Wade *Turns Forty-Five, but There's No Time to Celebrate*

ILYSE HOGUE

I woke up anxious the morning after Donald Trump's inauguration a year ago—the same weekend as the forty-fourth anniversary of *Roe v. Wade*. For six weeks following Trump's election, I observed the growing excitement about a march on Washington. A march where women would come together to protest not only Trump's election but also systemic misogyny and sexism.

Anticipation of the march was a bright spot in an otherwise dismal environment as we contemplated our lives—and our country—under a Trump administration with Mike Pence as vice president. On the freezing cold morning of the Women's March, the stakes felt inexplicably high, and it was hard to know how the day would play out.

The number of women and allies who showed up that day was inspiring. It was the largest single-day public demonstration in our country's history, and it did not stop at our borders. People marched in multiple countries in addition to all fifty states. I expected large turnouts in big cities like New York, Chicago, and Los Angeles, but when images started pouring in from the marches in small towns, I knew something profound had been unleashed. Singer-songwriter Carole King helped lead a march in Stanley, Idaho: population sixty-three. From Carbondale, Colorado, to Longville, Minnesota, to Greenville, South Carolina, the energy was palpable, and the message was clear. The resistance was alive, thanks to women—and allies—all over the world.

As she watched this new movement rise, Rabbi Sharon Brous observed, "Once it happens in a generation that a spirit of resistance is awakened. This is one of those moments—our children will ask us 'Where were you when our country was thrust into a lion's den of demagoguery and division?'"

And thrust into a lion's den, we were.

From my vantage point as president of NARAL Pro-Choice America, it's clear that 2017 was the year in which the horrors we'd watched creep across the country through red states and small towns found a welcome home in our federal politics. Newly empowered antiabortion organizations and their representatives in Congress advanced multiple abortion bans. President Trump put an antiabortion justice on the Supreme Court and stacked our nation's lower courts with right-wing ideologues who will continue to reshape the country in Trump's image for generations to come. And leaders of a dangerous and out-of-step antiabortion movement took up residency in multiple federal agencies, working quietly to undo some of our most reliable protections. For years, women have had to battle for their rights; each day of 2017 felt like war.

But on this historic forty-fifth anniversary of *Roe v. Wade*, we see widespread proof that our resistance last year, anchored in the Women's March, created a new feminist movement, one that NARAL—and our more than 1.2 million members—were made for. Through grit, determination, and optimism in the face of overwhelming threats, prochoice women actually made 2017 a year of progress on abortion rights. We didn't just resist—we persisted, and we actually advanced and expanded reproductive freedom across the country.

Nevada passed several prochoice measures, including laws requiring health insurance plans to cover a twelve-month supply of contraception at once—all in a state with a Republican governor.

Oregon enacted truly revolutionary legislation that enshrines women's constitutionally protected right to abortion through *Roe v. Wade* into state law. The state also passed legislation requiring insurance companies to cover FDA-approved contraceptives and abortion services without cost sharing, greatly expanding access to affordable care.

The 2018 midterm elections will be the most important day of political reckoning in my lifetime. Like Nevada, Washington State also enacted a law requiring health insurance plans to cover a twelve-month supply of contraception at once, giving women more control over their bodies and lives without worrying about how to access birth control on a regular basis.

Delaware passed landmark legislation codifying a woman's right to access abortion and repealed the state's unconstitutional ban.

NARAL's Missouri chapter helped pass a groundbreaking nondiscrimination law in St. Louis that would prevent employers and landlords from punishing women because of their reproductive choices. This was one of our most significant victories of the year—and proof that we can organize effectively in a red state.

Looking back on 2017, I am heartbroken for those most impacted by Trump's hateful agenda and enraged at the way he drags our country's reputation through the mud.

I am also hopeful.

It brings me hope when prochoice-elected officials, at all levels of government, fight diligently, not just to resist the bad policies coming from the antiabortion movement but also to pass and strengthen good policies that protect and expand reproductive freedom. It brings me hope when advocates unite in their activism across generations, religion, and race. And it brings me hope when this countrywide movement, from Oregon to Maine, results in multiple pieces of landmark legislation that protect the right to an abortion and birth control access in anticipation of attacks from Trump and his antiabortion colleagues.

The fight for women's rights isn't just about access to reproductive health care. It's also about a fundamental fight for our freedom. Journalist Jill Filipovic nailed it when she wrote, "Opposition to abortion appears to be not so much about fetal life, as about controlling women. It's about discomfort with the female power and progress facilitated by abortion rights."

The 2018 midterm elections will be the most important day of political reckoning in my lifetime. After a series of candidates won in 2017 by running on their values and not shying away from abortion rights, women must remain steadfast in our support for candidates who trust us and hold out-of-touch, antiabortion politicians accountable when they fall short. And as antiabortion legislators and organizations continue to feel emboldened in their efforts to eliminate access to abortion and contraception, women—and the legislators who stand with us—must continue to push proactive, prochoice policy in state houses across the country.

We face the most righteous struggle of our time. Women's freedoms are under unprecedented attack, but they are also the igniting spark of unity, momentum, and change. Last year, our challenge was to turn the energy of the Women's March into tangible action. Our job in 2018 is to turn our success into accountability for all those who challenge our rights and freedoms.

Understanding the Reading

1. What is it about the Trump administration that makes the author so anxious?
2. Describe the Women's March as it happened across the country. Besides reproductive rights, what was it about?
3. List some of the policies states have passed in opposition to the present administration.

Suggestion for Responding

1. Discuss the following issue in class—a woman's right to choose versus not being allowed to choose whether to terminate a pregnancy. Consider these contexts: the woman's life is in danger, or she is pregnant because she was raped. Do these contexts change your decision? (Keep in mind that you are making social policy, not a personal choice.)

47

Unions Are Fighting for Families

LIZ SHULER

February 9, 2018

Women in the workplace have made major strides. Women currently make up 48 percent of the workforce and are the sole or primary breadwinner for 40 percent of families in the United States. Yet most family responsibilities still rest on women's shoulders, and, too often, women put in a full day's work only to come home and clock in for a second shift.

As secretary-treasurer of the AFL-CIO, I am constantly in awe of the powerful work the 6.8 million women of the labor movement do to advance issues that matter. Consider this: In the past decade, there has been tremendous momentum at the state and local level, with millions of working people winning the freedom to take time off to care for family, and labor unions have been at the center of these wins. Which might explain why states with higher union density are more likely to have paid sick leave and paid family and medical leave laws. And when unions are strong, women are strong. Unions make a difference for women in dollars and cents—$222, to be exact. That's how much more the typical woman in a union job makes in a week compared with a woman in a nonunion job.

Beyond supporting working women, the labor movement has always advocated for policies that promote a full-employment economy at wages high enough to allow working people to support their families. We work to combat policies that erode the rights of working people and make sure they're rewarded for the wealth they help create. To achieve this goal, we support a broad range of policies, including restoring the minimum wage to a living wage, restoring overtime protections, prevailing wage standards, and putting an end to wage theft and the rampant misclassification of employees as independent contractors. The AFL-CIO adopted this working people's Bill of Rights at our recent convention to demand that all working people have the right to:

- A Good Job with Fair Wages: Everyone who wants to work has the right to a good job where we earn wages that allow us to support ourselves and our families.
- Quality Health Care: Regardless of income, job, or a preexisting condition.
- A Safe Job: Free from harassment and violence.
- Paid Time Off and Flexible, Predictable Scheduling: To spend time with family or care for ourselves or a loved one.
- Freedom from Discrimination: In hiring, firing, and promotions.
- Retire with Dignity: And financial security.
- Education: Public K–12, higher education, and career training that advances our knowledge and skills without leaving us in debt.
- Freedom to Join Together: With our co-workers for better wages and working conditions, whether we are in a union or not.
- A Voice in Democracy: To freely exercise our

democratic voice through voting and civic participation.

Building on recent victories, state legislators have demonstrated that they are #FightingForFamilies in 2018 by introducing legislation to advance some of these policies in states across the country, and union members have been advocating alongside them. Sixteen states have bills pending for paid family and medical leave in 2018. Thirteen states are considering bills for equal pay, and thirteen states are considering paid sick days. Sixteen states are considering measures to prevent employment discrimination against LGBT workers. Ten states have bills to ensure pregnant workers' rights. And that's just the beginning.

Young workers, immigrants, women, LGBT people, and communities of color are coming together to advance changes that will improve our lives. When we join in union, we are a formidable force—a political force. Together, we can make equal pay, paid leave, and fair scheduling the law of the land. Together, we can lead a movement to change the world and build an economy that works for us all. Together, we can reject quiet acceptance and build an America where all working women can sustain their families and realize their dreams.

Women fight and win battles every day. By stand-ing and negotiating together, we will continue to make the world a better place for all of us. Unions are rejecting the status quo and are working to build an America where all working people can sustain their families and realize their dreams.

Understanding the Reading

1. Do you agree that unions are good for workers? Why or why not?
2. What are the differences in working conditions in states where unions exist?
3. As you read the AFL-CIO's Working People's Bill of Rights, give your own ideas about this document.

Suggestions for Responding

1. Discuss the basic idea of unions. Why would a government be against unions when they strengthen economies?
2. Some people have spent their adult lives struggling to organize different kinds of unions: migrant farm workers, steel workers, and factory workers. Research some of these union organizers. What role do unions play in American life today?

Suggestions for Responding to Part V

1. Write a research report on the male–female pay differentials in the field you have chosen as a career. If at all possible, try to control for differences in the education and experience of the two groups.
2. Investigate the federal Women's Education Equity Program to find out what kinds of research it conducts and the kinds of services it provides to public schools. If there is a similar agency in your state or area school district, learn about its activities and services.
3. Research the initial entry of women into higher education—in women's colleges such as Mount Holyoke in 1837 and Vassar in 1865 and at the coeducational Oberlin College in 1832. How did the educational and extracurricular experiences differ in the two kinds of institutions? How were women treated differently from men at Oberlin?

4. If you are heterosexual, attend a meeting of the gay and/or lesbian group or center on your campus. Find out what its priorities are, and explore ways that you could help reduce the prejudice and discrimination it faces.
5. Title IX of the Education Amendments of 1972 prohibits sex discrimination in all federally funded educational programs. Its intent is to encourage equity in athletic programs, requiring colleges and universities to provide and equally support comparable sports offerings for women and men. See whether your school is in compliance. How many sports are offered for women and for men? How many women and men participate? Are budgets for the two overall programs equitable? Are scheduling and access to facilities fair to both women and men? Do the number and rank of the coaches reflect appropriate gender balance?

176 Power / Power and Sexism

6. Investigate and report on a governmental or volunteer organization formed to protect rape victims or victims of domestic violence to learn what support is available to women in your area.

7. The Cleary Act demands that colleges disclose and *give full access to* rape statistics on campus. Is your college in compliance with the Cleary Act? If you have never seen these statistics, take action by inviting the appropriate administrators to your classroom. Make demands and write letters to your school newspaper.

Part VI
Power and Classism

MOST AMERICANS LIKE TO THINK OF OURS AS A CLASS-less society, and thus we tend to ignore class as an aspect of our lives. If we do think of class, most of us tend to identify ourselves as middle class. Historically, the sense of a classless nation arose because most early European immigrants were neither nobility nor serfs, but rather generally "commoners"—farmers, artisans, trades workers, and such. Due to the abundance of land on this continent, these early immigrants could also become property owners and enjoy a substantial degree of autonomy. From the beginning, of course, this view of a middle-class nation was inaccurate because, among other things, it ignored slaves, indentured servants, Native Americans, and others whose reality did not meet this idyll. Additionally, in the colonial era, white land-owning males constituted only about 7 percent of the population.

Socioeconomic inequities became more generalized and pronounced with the nineteenth-century onset of the **Industrial Revolution**, the transformation of methods of production, transportation, and communication through the substitution of machines for hand labor. This mechanization of production systems brought about massive social and economic changes, and America began developing an identifiable class structure. More and more people moved from being relatively self-sufficient and independent to being wage earners working for and dependent on factory and business owners.

This shift signaled the growth of **capitalism**, an economic system characterized by private (or corporate) ownership of capital assets and by free-market determination of prices, production, and distribution of goods. The capitalist system was reinforced by a belief in **free enterprise**, the freedom of private businesses to operate competitively for profit with minimal government regulation, except to protect public interest and keep a balance in the national economy.

Satisfaction of unfettered capitalist interests, with little government regulation, inevitably resulted in an inequitable distribution of power, resources, and property. To realize maximum profits, as it was understood and practiced at that time, it was in the employers' interest to pay the lowest possible wages to the workers and to require the highest possible production from them, an arrangement that seriously disadvantaged the workers. This inequality led wage earners, during the latter decades of the nineteenth century and the first half of the twentieth, to respond by organizing and forming **unions** to advance their interests, to collectively improve wages and working conditions, and to enhance job security. Union successes, however, were uneven as the owners often had the law (and private police forces) enforcing their interests.

Capitalism also created a number of "panics" and **depressions**, periods of drastic decline in the national economy characterized by decreasing business, falling prices, and rising unemployment. Although both owners and workers suffered from these economic declines, hard times fell most heavily on the latter, especially during the Great Depression of the 1930s, which led to the social reforms of President Franklin D. Roosevelt's New Deal.

New Deal social policies included farm supports; federal reforms of the financial system; national control of the stock market, banking, and public utilities; the development of public works projects and housing programs; relief for the unemployed; minimum wage standards; and the Social Security system. Some people bitterly complained that these policies conflicted with the values of capitalism and free enterprise and that they moved this country toward socialism. However, in socialism the means of production are owned collectively or governmentally. Also, in socialism everyone equally owns the aspects of production and their distribution. In the United States the nature of the system was and remains free market, even with some government regulations, as long as the means of production are privately owned. Redistributive regulations, such as fair pay, provisions for health care and old age, do not make it socialist. Many nations consider such mechanisms as good investments in their workers (i.e., happy, healthy workers produce more).

Nonetheless, New Deal social programs and post–World War II economic prosperity led to the growth of a broad middle class during the 1950s and 1960s, but ended in the 1970s, when wage growth for full-time wage and salary workers became stagnant. Since 1980, there has been a definite redistribution of wealth upward (i.e., to the wealthiest percentage of the population), with no evidence of the wealth "trickling down" to the middle and lower classes. The share of income going to the middle one-fifth of Americans in 2010 shrank to its lowest level ever (Center on Budget and Policy Priorities, June 25, 2010). President Trump's tax bill of 2017 has resulted in the largest redistribution of wealth in thirty years— nearly two-thirds of the tax bill benefits go to the top 1 percent, producing an extreme gap in wealth. This particular redistribution of wealth away from the poor and middle class represents fewer people having health insurance, less funding for public schools, and many other traditional federal responsibilities. According to Christopher Ingraham (*Washington Post*, December 6, 2017), "This kind of extreme inequality is bad for the economy . . . [It represents less access to important resources such as quality education and healthcare, which in turn leads to] large amounts of wasted potential and lower social mobility, which directly harms economic growth."

Most Americans are more conscious of the problems and impediments caused by race and gender than we are of those based on socioeconomic class. Class in America is difficult to define because we are reluctant to talk about it and because the boundaries between classes are blurred. **Class** is related to relative wealth, but socioeconomic culture is also a com-

ponent, as is relative access to power. Roughly, we tend to speak of the upper class, upper middle class, middle class, working class, poor, and underclass, but in the United States these categories are fluid and dependent on context. (In some other cultures, "class" is a much more permanent idea, regardless of one's personal wealth.)

Despite definitional difficulties, class is a reality in the United States, as are the related stereotypes, prejudices, and discrimination that provide the basis for our classism. Because of **classism**, wealthy and financially better off people are privileged and assigned high status, whereas poor and working-class people and their cultures are stigmatized and disadvantaged simply because of their relative wealth. It should come as no surprise to anyone that those at the top of the economic hierarchy benefit most from classist values, and those at the bottom suffer the most from classism.

Race has a substantial impact on economic prosperity. More specifically, the median **net worth** of white households in 2017 was approximately ten times that of black households. (In 2000 the median net worth of white households was roughly eight times that of black households.) According to Brian Thompson (*Forbes*, February 18, 2018), "By 2020 black and Latino households are projected to lose even more wealth: 18 percent for the former, 12 percent for the latter."

The official federal **poverty line** is based on the cost of a "Thrifty Food Plan," which is not considered nutritionally adequate for long-term use, multiplied by three to account for nonfood expenses and adjusted for family size and for changes in the consumer price index. It is not adequate to cover such essential expenses as child care.

Our social stereotype of the "lazy, freeloading poor" notwithstanding, two million people who worked full time year-round in 2016 were below the official poverty line. In addition, the **Federal Reserve Board**, which controls the money supply, interest rates, and inflation, sets policies that keep millions of people unemployed in order to control inflation.

Gender is as critical a factor in determining socioeconomic class as race is. According to Legal Momentum, in 2018 70 percent of the nation's poor are women and children. "Women in America are still 35 percent more likely than men to be poor in America, with single mothers facing the highest risks." The reasons given: segregation into low-paying work, gender wage gap, inadequate social safety net, and lack of affordable childcare. There are also the costs of pregnancy, violence, and abuse. The wage gap alone is 79 percent of what men make with similar education and work experience, and although not legal, it persists because of traditional norms, especially of streamlining women into less lucrative positions, but also because of lack of transparency and accountability. With political will this could be changed.

A number of misconceptions about welfare are accepted as truths by American society. First, when Americans refer to "welfare," they are referring to Temporary Assistance for Needy Families, but also food stamps, public housing, and occasionally Medicaid (although the latter is increasingly thought of as having a separate status). In spite of the stereotypes and political climate of 2018, "welfare" recipients (TANF) are not long-time users who are mostly non-white. According to the Huffington Post (February 5, 2018, Delaney and Edwards-Levy), "Medicaid had more than 70 million beneficiaries in 2016, of whom 43 percent were white, 18 percent black, and 30 percent Hispanic. Of 45 million food recipients that year, 36.2 percent were white, 25.6 percent black, 17.2 percent Hispanic and 15.5 percent unknown." Furthermore, most families using these government safety nets are off them within three years.

The economic realities have substantial adverse effects on our nation's children. According to the American Community Survey (NCCP 2018), the U.S. population is made up of one-quarter children, who represent a third of the poorest in the population. "41 percent (29.8 million) of America's children were living on the brink of poverty in 2016—including more than 5 million infants and toddlers under age three" (Basic Facts About Low-Income Children). According to the Children's Defense Fund, poor children are twice as likely as other children to die from birth defects; three times as likely to die from all causes; four times as likely to die from fires; and five times as likely to suffer from infectious diseases and parasites. It seems clear that children are the greatest victims of poverty.

According to economist Edward Wolff, we should be concerned with this huge disparity for two reasons: first, it is unethical to have such inequality. Also, "the divisiveness that comes out of large disparities in incomes and wealth, is actually reflected in poor economic performances of a country" ("The Wealth Divide: The Growing Gap in the United States Between the Rich and the Rest," *Multinational Monitor* 24, no. 5 [May 2003]: 6.)

As we listen to many politicians speak of reducing and eventually erasing the nation's antipoverty programs that have given much relief to children and their families, we know precisely the consequences of such policies. They represent deep disrespect for the poor and a deprivation of human rights. "A nation's greatness is measured by how it treats its weakest members" (Mahatma Gandhi). The Preamble to the U.S. Constitution includes our promise "to promote the general welfare." It is how we struggle to form a more perfect union and establish justice.

To most of us, classism tends to be less visible than racism or sexism. Moreover, we also believe that we live in a **meritocracy**, in which advancement is based on ability or achievement. Thus, we hold to the myth that, although people cannot determine their race or sex, individuals can control their economic well-being and are responsible for their economic success or failure. As a result, we tend to blame poor people for their poverty. The readings in part VI show that such beliefs and stereotypes misrepresent reality.

Part VI opens with several analyses of the current economic conditions in our society. First, in reading 48, billionaire Warren Buffett urges the United States to "stop coddling the superrich" by giving them a lower tax rate than most of the middle class. In reading 49, Albert Hunt analyzes the reasons behind our growing prison population.

Many of our social assumptions and practices contribute to class distinctions and classism and reinforce discrimination, which can be unconscious and unintentional. Robert Cherry (reading 50), for example, examines how discrimination is **institutionalized**—that is, how the various parts of our social system work together to create a self-perpetuating cycle of discrimination and economic disadvantage. For instance, people with lower educational levels have limited access to good jobs with good pay, whereas affordable housing is available only in neighborhoods with poor schools, which means the next generation is doomed to lower educational levels and on and on.

Other economic practices intentionally discriminate against poor people. For example, "redlining," decisions by banks and insurance companies not to invest in certain areas—most often, older, inner-city, and minority neighborhoods—contributes to their increasing impoverishment and deterioration.

Ashley Jardina (reading 51) writes on the peculiar

understanding and attitude the U.S. public has to charity versus "welfare." Finally, reading 52 by Alexander C. Kaufman examines a water crisis in New York state that becomes an enormous political problem for local politicians as they face environmental racism.

These readings give us an unflattering image of ourselves as a society, making these class issues difficult for us to digest and making it even harder for us to do something about them. It is tempting to deny the structural and individual elements of classism and to hold onto the myths about poverty and the rewards of hard work and discipline. However, as citizens of the world in the twenty-first century, we must not comfort ourselves with a dismissive rationalization, such as "for ye have the poor always with you." Instead, we as a society must provide for the least privileged and most oppressed among us if the American community that we all value is to remain strong and a true world leader.

48

Warren Buffett Calls for Higher Taxes for U.S. Super-Rich

Graeme Wearden

Warren Buffett, at the 2010 meeting of his Berkshire Hathaway investment group, says that billionaires like himself have been "coddled" by Congress.

In the process of accumulating one of the greatest fortunes the world has ever seen, Warren Buffett stands apart from the average squillionaire. Not for him the clichés of lavish mansions and superyachts, preferring instead his modest home in Omaha, Nebraska, and nights in with burger and cherry cola.

Now Buffett has added to his list of atypical pronouncements by saying that America's super-rich should pay more tax if the country's debt problems are ever to be solved.

Writing in the *New York Times* on Monday, Buffett argued that the richest members of U.S. society are indulged with an unfairly generous tax regime and are not making a fair contribution to repairing the country's finances.

"While the poor and middle class fight for us in Afghanistan, and while most Americans struggle to make ends meet, we mega-rich continue to get our extraordinary tax breaks," wrote Buffett, whose personal fortune was estimated at $50bn (£30bn) by *Forbes* this year [Ed.: $786b by *Forbes* in 2017] , making him the third richest person in the world behind Carlos Slim and Bill Gates.

"These and other blessings are showered upon us by legislators in Washington who feel compelled to protect us, much as if we were spotted owls or some other endangered species. It's nice to have friends in high places," the 80-year old investor added.

Buffett, known as the Sage of Omaha, built his fortune on a no-frills investment strategy and was a fierce critic of the exotic financial investments that brought the banking system to its knees in 2008, dubbing them instruments of financial mass destruction.

A long-time critic of the U.S. tax system, he has calculated that he handed over 17.4 percent of his income as tax last year—a lower proportion than any of the 20 other people who work in his office.

Under the debt ceiling deal agreed in Washington, a "super committee" of 12 congressmen and senators must find $1.5tn worth of savings and cuts to help cut America's national debt. Tax rises are hugely unpopular with elements within the Republican party, with the Tea Party movement adamant that America should balance its books by cutting public spending.

Buffett argues that this super-committee should raise the tax rate paid by those earning more than $1m a year, including earnings from capital gains which are currently taxed at a lower rate than ordinary income. Those raking in upward of $10m a year could then pay even more.

The package of tax cuts brought in by President George W. Bush are set to expire at the end of 2012, although they could be extended. Many of the leading Republicans who hope to challenge Barack Obama at the next presidential election have argued for lower taxation to stimulate the U.S. economy.

On Saturday Rick Perry, the governor of Texas, argued that it was an "injustice" that almost a half of all Americans currently pay no federal income tax.

"Spreading the wealth punishes success while setting America on a course for greater dependency on government," Perry argued as he announced his bid for the 2012 Republican nomination.

Buffett argues that the U.S. policymakers should be looking at the other end of the spectrum. As he put it, "My friends and I have been coddled long enough by a billionaire-friendly Congress. It's time for our government to get serious about shared sacrifice."

[2011]

Understanding the Reading

1. In the context of this article, how does Warren Buffett disagree with Congress about how to solve our nation's debt crisis?

2. Why does the middle class pay a higher percentage of their income than the mega-wealthy in the United States?

3. With which statement do you agree: "Spreading the wealth punishes success" (i.e., the very wealthy should not pay more taxes), or "It is time for shared sacrifice" (i.e., the very wealthy have an obligation to pay higher taxes)?

Suggestions for Responding

1. Choose four European nations (perhaps Germany, France, Denmark, and Spain) and compare what they get for their taxes, as opposed to what U.S. citizens get for their taxes.

2. Have a classroom discussion about where tax money should be spent to ensure a flourishing economy.

49

Bulging Jails Are Other American Exception

ALBERT R. HUNT

One area where the United States indisputably leads the world is incarceration.

There are 2.3 million people behind bars, almost one in every 100 Americans. The federal prison population has more than doubled over the past 15 years, and one in nine black children has a parent in jail. Proportionally, the United States has four times as many prisoners as Israel, six times more than Canada or China, eight times more than Germany and 13 times more than Japan.

With just a little more than 4 percent of the world's population, the United States accounts for a quarter of the planet's prisoners, and has more inmates than the leading 35 European countries combined. Almost all the other nations with high per capita prison rates are in the developing world.

There's also a national election in America soon. This issue isn't on the agenda. It's almost never come up with Republican presidential candidates; one of the few exceptions was a debate in September when the audience cheered the governor of Texas, Rick Perry, because his state has carried out a record number of executions.

Barack Obama, the first black president, rarely mentions this question or how it disproportionately affects minorities. More than 60 percent of America's prisoners are black or Hispanic, though these groups comprise less than 30 percent of the population.

"We've had a race to incarcerate that has been driven by politics, racially coded, get-tough appeals," says Michelle Alexander, a law professor at Ohio State University who wrote "The New Jim Crow: Mass Incarceration in the Age of Colorblindness."

Escalating Costs

The escalating cost of the criminal-justice system is an important factor in the fiscal challenges around the country. Nowhere is that more evident than in California, which is struggling to obey a court order requiring it to reduce its overcrowded prisons by 40,000 inmates.

Today there are 140,000 convicts in California's state prisons, who cost about $50,000 each per year. The state spends more on prisons than it does on higher education.

Yet the prisons are so crowded—as many as 54 inmates have to share one toilet—that Conrad Murray, the doctor convicted in the death of the pop star Michael Jackson, may be able to avoid most prison time.

California isn't unique. In Raleigh County, West Virginia, the county commission has worried that the cost of housing inmates at its Southern Regional Jail may imperil basic services, including education. That problem is exacerbated as the state keeps more prisoners longer at such regional facilities to alleviate its overcrowding problems.

The prison explosion hasn't been driven by an increase in crime. In fact, the crime rate, notably for violent offenses, is dropping across the United States, a phenomenon that began about 20 years ago.

The latest FBI figures show that murder, rape and robberies have fallen to an almost half-century low; to be sure, they remain higher than in other major industrialized countries.

There are many theories for this decline. The most accepted is that community police work in major metropolitan areas has improved markedly, focusing on potential high-crime areas. There are countless other hypotheses, even ranging to controversial claims that more accessible abortion has reduced a number of unwanted children who would be more likely to commit crimes.

However, one other likely explanation is that more than a few would-be criminals are locked up. Scholars such as James Q. Wilson have noted that the longer prison terms that are being handed down may matter more than the conviction rates.

This comes at a clear cost. For those who do ultimately get out, being an ex-con means about a 40 percent decrease in annual earnings. Moreover, research suggests that kids from homes where a father is in jail do considerably less well in life and are more prone to becoming criminals themselves.

"Without Fathers"

"People ask why so many black kids are growing up without fathers," says Alexander. "A big part of the answer is mass incarceration."

It seems clear that the U.S. penal system discriminates against minorities. Some of this is socioeconomic, as poorer people, disproportionately blacks and Hispanics, may commit more crimes.

Much of the inmate explosion and racial disparities however, grow out of the way America treats illegal drugs. It began several decades ago with harsher penalties for crimes involving crack cocaine, which was more widely used by blacks, than powder cocaine, which was more likely to involve whites. A larger issue is how the American criminal justice system differentiates in its treatment of drug sellers—who get the book thrown at them—versus drug users, who, at most, get a slap on the wrist.

A hypothetical example: A black kid is arrested for selling cocaine to the members of a fraternity at an elite university. The seller gets sent away for 25 years. The fraternity is put on probation for a semester by the university and nothing else.

In all likelihood, the convicted seller is quickly replaced and few of the fraternity kids change their drug-use habits. The lesson: neither the supply nor the demand has changed, and the prison population grows.

Given their budgetary difficulties, about half the states are actually reducing their prison populations. Smart selective policies are cost-effective. Many criminologists and sociologists believe the proclivity to commit crimes diminishes with age; the recidivism rate for convicts over 30 is relatively low, and most analysis suggests that parole and probation are far cheaper for taxpayers than incarceration.

Nevertheless, the politics of the crime issue cuts against any rational approach. Even if recidivism rates are low, it's the failures that attract attention. In 1988, the Democratic presidential nominee, Michael Dukakis, was savaged when it was revealed that one convict furloughed under his watch, the now infamous Willie Horton, committed a rape while at large. Four years ago, the former governor of Arkansas, Mike Huckabee, a Republican, was hurt in his bid for his party's nomination by reports of crimes committed by felons he had paroled.

"One case where a parolee does something very wrong is sensationalized," Alexander says, "and many, many others are kept behind bars for a long time."

[2011]

Understanding the Reading

1. Why does America have the highest prison population in the world proportionally?

2. If the violent crime rate is dropping in the United States, then why are the prisons bulging?
3. How will California solve its budgetary problems related to its prison system?

Suggestion for Responding

1. Have a classroom discussion on the fact that the United States spends more money on prisons than on education.

50
Institutionalized Discrimination

ROBERT CHERRY

Individuals and institutions may use decision-making procedures that inadvertently discriminate and reinforce inequalities. For example, income differentials can cause unequal access to education even though the school system does not intend to discriminate; locational decisions of firms may have the unintended impact of reducing access to jobs. Similarly, when housing is segregated by income (race), all individuals do not have equal access to job information, as higher-income (white) households will tend to have greater access to job information through personal contacts than lower-income (black) households. Thus, employers will have more higher-income white applicants than if housing was distributed without regard to race or income. Also, employers attempting to reduce their screening costs might rely on group stereotypes rather than more individualized information when deciding which applicants to interview.

In none of these instances is discrimination consciously undertaken, but disadvantaged groups, having unequal access to education, job information, and the interviewing process, are nonetheless harmed. Though unintentional, these problems reinforce the "vicious cycle" of poverty.

Income Differentials and Educational Attainment

Income constraints place heavy burdens on the allocation decisions of low-income households. Often they must "choose" to do without many necessities, such as education. In addition, children from low-income households often have explicit household responsibilities that take time away from school activities. This may involve responsibility for household activities (baby-sitting, shopping, and so on) or earning income. In either case, economists would argue that on average low-income students have a greater opportunity cost[1] on their time than high-income students.

Since their opportunity costs are greater, lower-income students rationally allocate less time to studying and school-related activities than equally motivated higher-income students.

At the college level, even the availability of low-cost public institutions does not necessarily equalize the economic cost of education to all students. Just as at the elementary and secondary school level, lower-income students have a greater opportunity cost on their time than comparable higher-income students. Even if family responsibilities are negligible, students still require income for their own support. This invariably requires lower-income students to work at least part-time while attending school and has often led to the sending of male but not female offspring to college.

The level of income required is influenced by whether the student can live at home while attending college. Historically, public colleges were located in rural areas. For example, none of the original campuses of the Big Ten or Big Eight colleges are located in the states' largest metropolitan areas. The original campus of the University of Illinois is not located in Chicago and the University of Missouri is not located in St. Louis or Kansas City. Thus, not only did lower-income students have to pay for room and board away from home, but it was usually difficult to find part-time employment in these rural communities. This implies that even the availability of low-cost public colleges did not necessarily place the lower-income student on an equal footing with more prosperous students.

Theoretically, low-income youths with appropriate abilities and motivation should be able to borrow money to finance their education. As long as the economic returns from schooling are greater than the interest rate, students will gain from borrowing rather than forgoing additional education. The equalizing of economic costs can occur only if all students of equal promise can borrow at the same rates. Financial institutions, however, cannot accept expectations or probabilities of future income as sufficient collateral for loans. They require bank accounts or other tradable

assets, which are normally held by upper-income but not lower-income households. Thus, students from lower-income households cannot borrow readily for education without government intervention.

It also appears that schools in poorer neighborhoods tend to have larger classes and weaker teachers. John Owen found that within the same city, as the mean neighborhood income rose by 1 percent, class size decreased by 0.24 percent and the verbal ability of teachers rose by 0.11 percent. This inequality is even more glaring when comparisons are made between cities. Owen found that for each 1 percent increase in the mean income of a city, there was a rise of 0.73 percent in real expenditures per student and a 1.20 percent increase in the verbal ability of teachers. Thus, students living in poorer neighborhoods in poorer cities have a double disadvantage.

If higher opportunity costs and lower-quality education were not sufficient to discourage educational attainment, Bennett Harrison found that for black inner-city youths, incomes are hardly affected by increases in educational attainment. He notes, "[A]s their education increases, blacks move into new occupations, but their earnings are hardly affected at all by anything short of a college degree, and there is no effect whatever on their chances of finding themselves without a job over the course of the year." Thus, independent of conscious discrimination by the educational system, we should expect low-income minority youths to have lower educational attainment than white youths, even when ability and motivation are held constant.

During the 1970s, a number of policies were implemented in an attempt to compensate for the influence of family income on educational attainment. First, legislatures began funding state universities in larger urban areas. Second, court rulings forced states to change funding formulas so that per capita funding from wealthy and poor communities within each state would become more equal. Third, guaranteed student loans reduced the disadvantage low-income students faced when attempting to finance their education.

Differential Impact of Incomplete Information

In the most simplified labor models, it is assumed that workers and firms act with complete information: Workers know the jobs that are available, and firms know the productivity of job seekers. In this situation, competitive firms would hire the best applicants for the jobs available, and workers would gain the maximum wage obtainable.

Economists have recently developed models in which information has a price; it is only "purchased" up to the point at which its benefits are at least as great as its costs. Neither firms nor workers rationally attempt to gain complete information concerning the labor market opportunities available. Workers find that some additional job information is not worth its cost, while firms find that some information on the productivity of applicants is not worth the additional personnel expenses. Liberals have argued that when workers and firms rationally decide to act on the basis of optimal rather than complete information, biases are generated.

Let us begin by analyzing how firms decide the optimal productivity information they should obtain. A firm benefits from additional productivity information if it translates into hiring a more profitable work force. A firm must weigh this increased profitability against the cost involved in seeking the additional information. After some point, it is likely that the benefits from additional information are insufficient to outweigh its cost. Even though the firm realizes additional information would probably result in hiring a somewhat more productive worker than otherwise, it knows that the added screening expenses would be even greater.

When a strong profit motive and wide productivity differentials among applicants are present, extensive screening will occur. This is the case with professional sports teams, especially since television revenues have transformed ownership from a hobby to a profit-making activity. Liberals believe, however, that in the vast majority of situations, productivity differentials among applicants are quite small and benefits from extensive screening are minimal.

Liberals suggest that the initial screening of applicants is often done with very little individual productivity information available. For firms with a large number of relatively equally qualified applicants, there is no reason to spend much time determining which applicants should be interviewed. These firms simply take a few minutes (seconds) to look over applications and select a promising group to interview. The employer realizes that such a superficial procedure will undoubtedly eliminate some job applicants who are slightly more productive than those selected for interviews. Since productivity differentials are perceived to be minor, however, this loss is not sufficient to warrant a more extensive (expensive) screening procedure.

There would be no discrimination if the job applicants victimized were random, but let us see why the screening method might cause the consistent victimization of individuals from disadvantaged groups. Suppose a firm considering college graduates for trainee positions decides that it has many equally qualified candidates. Looking at résumés, the firm can quickly identify each applicant's race, sex, and college attended. If the firm has enough applicants from better colleges, it is likely to say, "All things being equal, students from these colleges are likely to be more qualified than applicants who attended weaker colleges." Thus, the firm dismisses applicants from the weaker colleges, even though it realizes that weaker schools produce some qualified applicants. The firm has nothing against qualified graduates of weaker colleges. It simply reasons that the extra effort required to identify them is not worth the expense.

However unintentional, highly qualified graduates from weaker schools are discriminated against. Discrimination occurs because this screening method determines the selection for interviews on the basis of group characteristics rather than individual information. More generally, highly qualified applicants from any group that is perceived to have below-average productivity would be discriminated against by this superficial screening method.

Suppose employers believe that black and female applicants are typically less productive than their white male counterparts. If the firm has sufficient white male applicants, it will not interview black or female applicants. The firm will decide that although there are some black and female applicants who are slightly more productive than some white male applicants, it is not worth the added expense to identify them. The process by which individuals are discriminated against when firms use group characteristics to screen individuals is usually called statistical discrimination.

Statistical discrimination can occur indirectly. A firm hiring workers for on-the-job training may be primarily interested in selecting applicants who will stay an extended period of time. The firm does not want to invest training in individuals who will leave the firm quickly. Presumably, if the firm had a sufficient number of applicants who worked more than four years with their previous employer, it would not choose to interview applicants with more unstable work experience. Again, the firm reasons that although there are likely to be some qualified applicants among those with an unstable work record, it is too costly to identify them. This method of screening is likely to discriminate because of the nature of seniority systems, which operate on a "last hired, first fired" basis. Many minorities and women have unstable work records because they are hired last and fired first. Thus, even when firms do not use racial or gender stereotypes, they discriminate, since women and minorities are more likely to come from weaker schools and have more unstable work records than equally qualified white male applicants.

Financial and Occupational Effects

Many economists believe the job market is divided between good (primary) and bad (secondary) jobs. Good jobs have characteristics such as on-the-job training and promotions through well-organized internal labor markets. Bad jobs have little on-the-job training and minimum chance for promotions; they are dead-end jobs. Since on-the-job training is a significant aspect of primary-sector jobs, employment stability and behavioral traits are often more important than formal education and general skills. Both conservative and liberal economists agree that workers who do not possess the proper behavioral traits, such as low absenteeism and punctuality, will not be employed in the primary sector. Most liberals believe that many women and minority workers who possess the proper behavioral traits also will not find jobs in the primary sector as a result of statistical discrimination.

Facing discrimination in the primary sector, many qualified female and minority workers shift to secondary labor markets. As a result, secondary employers have a greater supply of workers and can reduce wages and standards for working conditions. Primary employers and majority workers also benefit from statistical discrimination. Since majority workers face less competition, more of them will gain primary employment than they would in the absence of statistical discrimination.

Primary employers may have to pay somewhat higher wages and employ somewhat less productive workers as a result of statistical discrimination, but the reduced screening costs more than compensate for the higher wages and productivity losses. Moreover, many primary employers also hire secondary workers. For them, the higher cost of primary employees will be offset by the resulting reduction in wages paid to secondary workers and their somewhat higher productivity.

Since primary workers, primary employers, and secondary employers benefit from statistical discrimination, there are identifiable forces opposed to change. Thus, rather than the market disciplining decision makers, statistical discrimination creates groups having a financial stake in its perpetuation.

Applicants and Their Search for Job Information

For job seekers, the cheapest source of job information is personal contacts, including neighbors and relatives and their acquaintances. Additional information can be obtained from newspaper advertisements and government employment offices. The most costly information is obtained from private employment agencies. A significant difference in the cost of job information would occur if one individual had few personal contacts and was forced to use private employment services, while another individual had extensive personal contacts. All things being equal, the individual with the lower cost of obtaining information would be better informed and hence more likely to obtain higher earnings.

The job information minorities receive from their search effort is likely to be less valuable than the job information received by their white counterparts. The fact that an individual is recommended by a personal contact might be sufficient reason to grant the person an interview. Those who obtain information from newspaper ads or government employment services do not have this advantage. This distinction is summed up in the adage "It's not what you know but who you know that counts."

Low-income (minority) individuals tend to have fewer contacts than high-income (white) individuals of equal abilities and motivation. High-income (white) individuals tend to have many neighbors or relatives who have good jobs, own businesses, or are involved in their firm's hiring decisions. Low-income (minority) individuals, having few personal contacts, are forced to spend additional time and money to obtain job information. Even if the job information is as valuable as that obtained by their white counterparts, minorities might give up searching for employment sooner because it is more costly. They do not do so because they are less able or less motivated; they simply face greater expenses.

Affirmative Action

Affirmative action legislation is the major government attempt at counteracting the discriminatory features of the hiring process. Affirmative action assumes that discrimination results from employment decisions based on incomplete information. The role of the government is simply to encourage firms to hire all qualified applicants by forcing them to gather individualized productivity information.

Guidelines stipulate that all government agencies and private firms doing business with the government must publicly announce job openings at least forty-five days prior to the termination of acceptance of applications. This provision attempts to offset the information inequality disadvantaged workers face. More importantly, these employers must interview a minimum number of applicants from groups that tend to be victims of statistical discrimination.

It is important to remember the difference between affirmative action and quotas. Under affirmative action, there is no requirement to hire; employers are required only to interview female and minority applicants and make sure they have access to job information. Quotas are more drastic actions reserved for situations in which firms are not making good faith efforts to seek out and hire qualified female and minority applicants. For example, if a firm attempts to circumvent affirmative action guidelines by announcing job openings in papers that reach only the white community or, after interviewing applicants, uses discriminatory procedures to eliminate women from employment, the government can impose quotas. Thus, quotas are imposed only when it is demonstrated that the lack of female or minority employment reflects something more conscious than the unintentional effects of incomplete information.

Besides the government, some private groups have attempted to compensate for unequal access to information. Women's groups have attempted to set up networks to aid female job applicants for management positions. Female executives are encouraged to share as much information as possible with other women to offset the traditional networking done by men. In many areas, male networking is referred to as the old boy network, and entry into it has historically been critical to obtaining the most desirable jobs. Thus, the lack of personal contacts is at least partially offset by networks that direct job information to disadvantaged workers and provide low-cost productivity information to firms.

Skill and Locational Mismatches

Many individuals reject the view that groups are held back due to external pressures by noting that "when we came to America, we faced discrimination but were able to overcome it." In particular, these individuals often believe that internal inadequacies are responsible for the seemingly permanent economic problems minorities face. One response is to argue that the discrimination minorities face is more severe and their economic resources fewer than those of European immigrants at the turn of the century. Another response dominated the U.S. Riot Commission's assessment of black poverty. This presidential commission, which was created to study the causes of the urban rebellions of the late 1960s, noted,

> When the European immigrants were arriving in large numbers, America was becoming an urban-industrial society. To build its major cities and industries, America needed great pools of unskilled labor. Since World War II . . . America's urban-industrial society has matured: unskilled labor is far less essential than before, and blue-collar jobs of all kinds are decreasing in numbers and importance as sources of new employment. . . . The Negro, unlike the immigrant, found little opportunity in the city; he had arrived too late, and the unskilled labor he had to offer was no longer needed.

This commission, commonly known as the Kerner commission, avoided blaming either the victims (culture of poverty) or society (discrimination) for black economic problems; they were simply the result of technological change. To compensate for the higher skill levels required for entry-level positions, the Kerner commission recommended extensive job-training programs. Supposedly, once these skills were obtained, blacks would enter the employment mainstream and racial income disparities would diminish.

Job-training programs became the centerpiece of the liberal War on Poverty initiated during the Johnson administration. To an extent, these job-training programs complemented compensatory educational programs. Whereas the compensatory programs attempted to develop general skills, job-training programs attempted to develop specific job-related skills. Whereas the compensatory programs were attempts to increase white-collar skills, job-training programs were attempts to increase blue-collar skills.

The government's involvement in job-training programs was pragmatic; it sought upward mobility in ways that would not conflict with the interests of other groups. Thus, it did not aggressively institute training programs that would conflict with the objectives of many craft unions. This meant that in many of the construction trades, which had historically restricted membership, the government accepted union prerogatives. Job-training success also was impeded by the seeming irrelevance of many of the skills taught, and there were complaints that training programs did not use the latest equipment and the newest methods.

Many liberals discounted these complaints. They agreed with conservatives that the problems disadvantaged groups faced stemmed from their internal inadequacies. These liberals thought the actual technical skills developed were irrelevant; what was critical was the development of the proper behavioral traits of punctuality and low absenteeism. These liberals also recommended more restrictive programs that would train only the least deficient of the disadvantaged group. In contrast, those liberals who believed that external pressures, particularly discrimination, were dominant proposed costly training programs and a more aggressive approach to craft unions.

Job-training success also was impeded by the shifting of blue-collar jobs out of Northeastern and Midwestern urban areas. After World War II, technological changes decreased the viability of central city locations. First, trucking replaced the railroads as the major transportation mode. When firms delivered their output (and received their input) on railcars, central city locations were ideal. When trucking became dominant, traffic tie-ups made those locations too costly. Indeed, recognizing these costs, the federal government built a new interstate highway system so that travelers could bypass congested central city areas.

Second, new technologies emphasized assembly-line techniques that required one-level production. No longer could manufacturing firms use factory buildings in which they operated on a number of floors. High land costs made it too expensive to build one-level plants in urban centers, so manufacturing firms began to locate in industrial parks near the new interstate highways on the outskirts of urban areas. This intensified minority employment problems, as most minorities continued to live in the inner city.

Minorities with the proper behavioral requirements, education, and skills have difficulty obtaining employment due to these locational mismatches. Inner-city residents are likely to lack the financial ability to commute to suburban jobs. They are unlikely to own a car or to earn a sufficient income to justify the extensive commuting required, even if public transportation is available. Minorities also are less likely to have access to these jobs because they have fewer personal contacts working in suburban locations.

Liberals have offered a number of recommendations to offset locational mismatches. Some economists have favored government subsidies to transportation networks that would bring inner-city workers to suburban employment locations. These subsidies would be cost-effective if the added employment generated greater income tax revenues and government spending reductions. Other economists have favored subsidizing firms to relocate in targeted inner-city zones. This approach was even endorsed by President Reagan under the catchy name "Free Enterprise Zones."

[1989]

Term

1. Opportunity Cost: The relative proportion of time or resources that can be invested in a given activity.

Understanding the Reading

1. In what ways does having a lower income level limit one's educational attainment?
2. Explain what Cherry means by "purchasing information" and how it affects discriminatory employment practices or statistical discrimination.
3. What causes higher wages in the primary sector and lower wages in the secondary sector?
4. How are low-income people disadvantaged in their job searches?
5. Explain how affirmative action is supposed to work and how it differs from quotas.
6. What were the objectives and problems of job training as a solution to minority unemployment or underemployment?

Suggestions for Responding

1. Apply Cherry's analysis to the circumstances described in one of the selections in part VI.

2. Write a brief essay in which you speculate on how the "cycle of poverty" that Cherry describes might be broken.

51

Why People Love "Assistance to the Poor" But Hate "Welfare"

Ashley Jardina

January 29, 2018

Last spring, in a highly publicized meeting with members of the Congressional Black Caucus, President Donald Trump received some startling news. One of the members mentioned to Trump that pushing forward with "welfare reform" would be hurtful to her constituents, "not all of whom are black."

"Really?" Trump replied. "Then what are they?"

Statistically, they were probably white. But given the United States' history with the word *welfare*, it's not all that surprising that Trump was confused.

Despite the fact that white Americans benefit more from government assistance than people of color, means-tested aid is primarily associated with black people and other people of color—particularly when the term *welfare* is used. For many Americans, the word *welfare* conjures up a host of disparaging stereotypes so strongly linked to stigmatized beliefs about racial groups that—along with crime—it is arguably one of the most racialized terms in the country.

White People's Racial Attitudes Are the Single Most Important Influence on Their Views on Welfare

Martin Gilens, a professor of political science at Princeton University, has studied the relationship between whites' racial attitudes and their opinion on welfare extensively. In one study, he finds that white people's racial attitudes are the single most important influence on their views on welfare. In other words, white people who are more prejudiced toward black people are also significantly more opposed to welfare. Numerous studies in the social sciences have substantiated this claim.

That has tremendous consequences for the types of policies that are proposed and passed. Public support for programs associated with the term *welfare* is generally weaker than support for other programs, like unemployment insurance, primarily because welfare is so strongly linked to the negative attitudes that white people possess about black people. However, the public is willing to support redistributive benefits generally when they are not called welfare. For example, in 2014, 58 percent of white people thought that we are spending too much on welfare, whereas only 16 percent reported that we are spending too much on the poor.

These same racial attitudes also structure the way policies are designed. They inform which groups we think are deserving of assistance, and which are not. Nicholas Winter, for instance, notes that part of why Social Security is so relatively popular compared to welfare is because of how both policies are racialized. Social Security, he argues, has been framed as a policy that is universal—that is, it benefits all groups—and as one that has been contrasted with welfare as an earned reward for hard work (stereotypes associated with white people), rather than a handout for the lazy and dependent (stereotypes associated with black people).

In contrast, negative beliefs about the beneficiaries of programs we think of as welfare have arguably led to a system of surveillance and sanctions. After Reagan popularized the disparaging stereotype of the "welfare queen" in the 1980s, Bill Clinton passed welfare reform policies that restricted access to benefits to satisfy racist attitudes. In addition to placing significant and often unfair burdens on the individuals seeking assistance, these restrictions—like required drug testing of program applicants, restrictions on where benefits can be spent, and specifications on what types of work count toward required hours—relied on stereotypes and reinforced the belief that beneficiaries of these programs are undeserving. According to work by Joe Soss and Sanford F. Schram, more people believed that welfare benefits lead to dependency in 2003 than in 1989.

The media have played a significant role in establishing the link between poverty, welfare, and race in the public mind. According to Gilens, these trends were forged in the 1960s, when race riots drew the nation's attention to the black urban poor. In just three years—from 1964 to 1967—the percentage of poverty news stories that featured images of black people grew from 27 percent to 72 percent. These trends have persisted in the present day.

But both Gilens's and Winter's work suggests that the media can also help promote antipoverty legislation by avoiding racialized terms, like *welfare*, to talk about public assistance. But if they keep leaning specifically on the term *welfare*—as they have during Speaker Ryan's recent push to cut antipoverty programs by referring to them as *welfare reform*—then otherwise popular policies may be dragged down with the word's racialized history.

Understanding the Reading

1. How are welfare recipients portrayed in the media?
2. In what ways does the welfare stereotype not fit reality?
3. Why do you think the present administration uses the term *welfare* rather than *assistance to the poor*?

Suggestions for Responding

1. Interview someone who is or has benefited from federal antipoverty programs and describe how he or she differs from the stereotypes mentioned in this article.
2. Interview someone from an older generation about what they think of short-term assistance to the poor.

52

The Tainted Water Crisis in Upstate New York That Andrew Cuomo Can't Shake

Alexander C. Kaufman

March 9, 2018

NEWBURGH, N.Y.—Lately, Wayne Vradenburgh daydreams about a demotion.

Vradenburgh has spent his entire career working for the water department of Newburgh, an Upstate New York city of twenty-eight thousand people, most of whom are Hispanic or black. He started as an assistant water maintenance mechanic at eighteen, repairing fire hydrants. Two decades later, in 2016, he took the top job of superintendent. He made plans to fix leaky pipes and mostly just aspired to keep things running smoothly for the poverty-stricken city of dilapidated brownstones nestled on the Hudson River.

Then, a mere two weeks after he took over, state health officials pulled up in his driveway. They had grim news: Lake Washington, the 1.3-billion-gallon reservoir that had served the city since the 1880s, had tested positive for a dangerous chemical. Vradenburgh soon found himself frantically studying the names of tongue-twister chemicals he'd never heard of, going head to head with state and federal agencies, and working seventy-hour weeks overseeing $50 million in emergency projects.

"It's been a whirlwind ever since," said Vradenburgh, forty, as he brushed his hand through his hoary hair, which contrasted starkly with his sandy brown, neatly trimmed beard. "I've got a lot more grays now."

The contamination started back in 1990, when the nearby Stewart Air National Guard Base, home to the 105th Airlift Wing of the New York Air National Guard, spilled four thousand gallons of fire-fighting foam into a stream that flows directly into Lake Washington. That foam contained perfluorooctane sulfonate, or PFOS, an invisible, flavorless industrial chemical that clings to water molecules. PFOS has been linked to cancer, thyroid problems, and chronic kidney disease, and it can accelerate puberty, delay mammary gland development, lower sperm count, and raise cholesterol.

The Pentagon has continued to use the foam, discharging it into pools near the airbase. Even now, the Department of Defense has only put some restrictions on its use as it researches an alternative. Even if they had stopped, the Environmental Protection Agency classifies the chemical as "extremely persistent," meaning that it takes many years to naturally degrade.

Despite this, PFOS is not federally regulated. In January 2009, the EPA issued an advisory in response to a contamination in Alabama, stating that the chemical only posed a health risk in concentrations of at least two hundred parts per trillion. For its sister compound, perfluorooctanoic acid, or PFOA, the EPA warned against concentrations any higher than four hundred parts per trillion.

New York already had a PFOA contamination crisis under way when Newburgh's situation came to light. In late 2015, Hoosick Falls, a sleepy former mill town about two and a half hours north of Newburgh, discovered dangerously high levels of PFOA in its water. As parallels emerged between Hoosick Falls and the lead contamination in Flint, Michigan, New York governor Andrew Cuomo (D)—keen to avoid the national criticism that Michigan's leaders received—decided in January 2016 to make New York the first state to regulate PFOA as a hazardous substance. The state added PFOS to the list of hazardous chemicals in April 2016, a first step toward setting limits on maximum allowable levels.

Those moves awoke Newburgh to its own chemical crisis. Samples taken from Lake Washington in 2014 contained PFOS levels of up to 243 parts per trillion. In Silver Stream, they were as high as 286 parts per trillion. In drainage pools at the air base, that figure climbed to 5,900 parts per trillion. Near the airstrip, contamination levels skyrocketed as high as 1.9 million parts per trillion. Recognizing the urgency of the problem, the EPA in May 2016 issued a new health advisory lowering the health risk threshold to 70 parts per trillion.

That prompted Newburgh to declare a state of emergency, which temporarily banned filling swimming pools and watering lawns. The city stopped drawing water from Lake Washington and switched over to the Catskills Reservoir, the highly regulated source of New York City's water. In August 2016, the Cuomo administration designated the air base a state Superfund site, giving the state authority to petition the Department of Defense to clean up the contamination.

The state has nearly completed construction on a new water treatment plant that will filter out PFOS. But officials in Newburgh say they don't just want the PFOS cleaned from their water—they want the toxic chemicals removed at the source. State health officials say the Department of Defense hasn't moved to do so, despite getting $25 million in the defense spending bill last year for PFOS and PFOA remediation.

But Newburgh's elected officials say the state should be doing more, too. And late last month, it announced plans to sue the state, the Department of Defense, several other federal agencies, and two private companies for contaminating the water in the first place.

The lawsuits aim to force the Cuomo administration to take radical steps to change the way the state manages its watersheds, taking authority away from cities, towns, and villages and putting it in the hands of the state Department of Health. That would require the governor to push for new regulatory powers from a Republican-controlled legislature to take

on the military and big corporate polluters, officials say.

Cuomo has chastised the city for filing the suit, arguing that his administration is already doing everything it can. But city officials say it's their best hope for forcing someone to take responsibility for tainting their water. "The states must declare their inherent police powers on this matter, and the feds must quit their game of selective federalism," said Newburgh city manager Michael Ciaravino. "Everything is landing on local governments' heads."

"A Band-Aid Approach"

For decades, the Newburgh Water Department was housed in three plain two-story, red-brick buildings less than half a mile northeast from Lake Washington, on the quiet, tree-lined Little Britain Road. But construction at the department has been almost nonstop recently.

First, backhoes exhumed a 1.3-million-gallon tank from beneath a grassy field and replaced it with a 1.5-million-gallon above-ground concrete dome and, beside that, a two-story red barn. Inside the barn, eighteen sea-green cylinders, twenty-seven feet tall and twelve feet in circumference, now whir like a giant engine. This is the new granular activated carbon filter that will remove the PFOS from Newburgh's water.

Calgon Carbon Corporation, the Pittsburgh-based filter manufacturer, said this site is the biggest of the forty-five PFOS filtration systems it's installed across the country in the past two years. The company has sold activated carbon filters for decades to strain out bacterial and chemical contaminants, and it only began selling systems to treat PFOS contamination two years ago. The company says those systems now make up 2 percent of its global sales, or roughly $15 million.

For now, the tanks hold untainted water from the Catskills Reservoir, pumping 3.1 million gallons into the town's pipes and taps each day. But that's just to work out the kinks. At some point in the coming weeks, the city plans to run its inaugural tests on water from Lake Washington, allowing it to flow through the screens of the shed-sized brick intake building that juts out on a dirt peninsula into the middle of the reservoir and, with the pull of gravity, gush through pipes into the new filtration system tanks. The filtered water will be tested for PFOS, the results of which will take two weeks.

But the city says just cleaning the chemical out of the water isn't enough.

"The state has gone ahead with this Band-Aid approach, putting granular activated carbon filters at the end of the pipe to try to treat whatever chemicals would come into the system," Alan Knauf, the attorney leading Newburgh's lawsuits, told HuffPost. "The problem is they're just treating contaminated water, there's the possibility of a breakthrough of some of the chemicals, and eventually there will be a breakthrough."

It's Vradenburgh's job to keep that from happening. Standing next to one of the tanks last week, he demonstrated how he will collect samples by turning one of four nozzles and pouring a splash of clear water into a cup. He swirled it around, then dumped it into a bucket. The weekly tests are expected to cost the water department $1,200 a month, nearly doubling what it used to pay for standard bacterial testing. The state has agreed to cover the costs.

"This is the rest of my career," Vradenburgh said. He sighed and stared up the tank. For him, the effort is worth it; he lives just two miles from the plant and has a three-year-old daughter and one-month-old son. "But I'll make sure that we're good."

Strokes, Seizures, and Severe Migraines

For some residents, the plant is too little, too late. At a city council meeting last week, the packed recreation center erupted in applause when Beatrice Harris, twenty-nine, stepped up to the microphone and thanked the city for its decision to sue the state. "Personally, I think that is one of the best decisions this city has ever made," she said.

Harris moved to Newburgh in 2006. Three years later, she met Julius Harris and fell in love. In a twenty-two-slide PowerPoint she put together for a presentation on water contamination at the local library, she shows two pictures of them together in 2009, with the captions "used to smile all the time" and "feeling safe." They married in 2013.

The next slide shows her in a hospital bed, unconscious and hooked up to IV drips.

"Had my first stroke in 2013," she said. "And it got worse over the years. Now I have permanent neurological issues as a result. Not to mention I'm premenopausal, and I'm only twenty-nine."

"Strokes, seizures, right-sided weakness, severe migraines," she added. "I have had a pretty rough adult life."

She's convinced that the PFOS-laced water from Lake Washington is to blame. Harris and her husband started the Environmental Alliance of Newburgh last year to make people aware of PFOS and advocate for a complete cleanup. She is skeptical of the new filtration system. "There really is no right way to filter this out of water, no matter what they say," she said outside the council meeting. "That's bullshit to me."

State health officials insist it's too early to tell whether Newburgh is experiencing increased rates of cancer or other PFOS-related diseases. The state Department of Health started a review of New York's reported cancer cases last year, including the geographic location of each diagnosis. Once that review is complete, the agency plans to produce a report by the end of the year examining the rate and types of cancer diagnoses in Newburgh.

Yet data on PFOA- and PFOS-related diseases remain scarce. The Department of Defense's budget this year includes funding for the Centers for Disease Control and Prevention to perform a first-of-its-kind longitudinal study of the noncancer health effects of the chemicals. That could provide crucial big-picture context to the body of research linking the chemicals to thyroid disease and developmental problems.

"There's emerging evidence to suggest there's certain concerns for health effects," said Brad Hutton, deputy commissioner at the New York State Department of Health's Office of Public Health. "[But] there's quite a bit of gaps in information, including what are the levels of exposure that bring those health effects."

A Familiar Story

The health impacts of exposure to perfluorinated chemicals are clearer in places such as Hoosick Falls. The village, about an hour northeast of Albany, was built around two chemical plants that produced Teflon products. In 2011, scientists studying a massive PFOA contamination near a DuPont plant in Parkersburg, West Virginia, began releasing findings linking the chemical to a host of diseases, including kidney and thyroid cancer. In 2014, residents in Hoosick Falls became concerned about unusually high rates of kidney cancer and thyroid disease and began urging the village and state officials to test the water. In late 2015, after a resident's privately run tests yielded alarming results, the state finally stepped in and found dangerously high levels of PFOA in the groundwater.

That finding is what prompted New York to list PFOA as a hazardous substance in January 2016. Yet the state issued notices advising the public that their water was safe to drink even as federal regulators said otherwise, actively disputing the EPA's concerns. At that point, the Cuomo administration had already waited more than a year do anything about the contamination, despite knowing that the PFOA levels in Hoosick Falls exceeded federal guidelines, according to a Politico investigation published in March 2016.

In July 2016, Cuomo signed legislation to make it easier for municipalities like Hoosick Falls to sue polluters—in the village's case, two giant chemical manufacturers—over water contamination. But cleanup efforts stalled. Hoosick Falls residents soon grew so frustrated by the state's failure to do anything to eliminate the contamination that they staged a protest outside the governor's office in November 2016. The state finished installing a filtration system in Hoosick Falls in February 2017, and it also established a Drinking Water Quality Council in September to address drinking water problems across the state.

But Judith Enck, New York's former regional EPA administrator for eight years under President Barack Obama, described the council as mired in "bureaucratic malaise." It's met just three times and is still working on making a final recommendation on safe levels of PFOA and PFOS. Hutton, the Health Department official, said that the council is "at the real close endgame of getting a recommended level."

In Hoosick Falls' case, the village sued Saint-Gobain Performance Plastics and Honeywell International, the chemical companies that at different points operated the plant that polluted the groundwater. The governor supported that suit, and officials announced a $330,251 settlement with the companies last week.

But now Newburgh is targeting Cuomo, and the governor has come out swinging. At a press conference at Marist College in Poughkeepsie late last month, Cuomo criticized the city for its impending lawsuit. "Why they would threaten litigation—you know—they have to feed lawyers," Cuomo said.

Michael G. Ciaravino, Newburgh's city manager, scoffed at the governor's remark. "We're a city that's facing 12 firefighter layoffs," he told HuffPost. "We have a lot of financial challenges. The last thing we want to do is enrich lawyers."

What Ciaravino does want is for the state to take control over the watershed. It wouldn't be an unprecedented move. In 1997, New York adopted rules that gave regulators in New York City and the towns located on its watershed new powers under the state Department of Health to protect the Catskills Reservoir and any tributaries that feed it. The rules, called the Watershed Rules and Regulations, established a unified code mandating the same standards for zoning, permitting, and wastewater treatment across the entire watershed.

The rest of the state relies on drinking water regulations passed in the early 1900s. As a result, water rules generally address pollution sources such as cesspools, garbage, animal manure, and industrial discharges, but make no mention of modern contaminants such as sediment, fertilizer, pesticides, and road salt, according to a memo from Hudson Valley Regional Council, a county agency in Newburgh.

"What we see in the case of New York City is the world-class example of protecting drinking water at its source," said Dan Shapley, the water quality program director at the New York–based watchdog group Riverkeeper. "But those same rules and regulations have not been updated for other communities in New York State for 100 years or close to it."

Newburgh is a paradigm of the problems that the current web of water jurisdictions creates. The state owns the air base that polluted the stream that feeds Lake Washington, but it leases the property to the federal government. One quarter of the reservoir is located in the town of Newburgh, a separate, confusingly larger neighboring municipality of roughly thirty thousand people, located to the city's north and west. The other 75 percent is technically part of the town of New Windsor. The City of Newburgh pays property taxes to both of them.

Then there's the development issue. In recent years, the town of Newburgh has been building up a strip of big-box retailers on Route 300, a thoroughfare that runs along the western bank of Lake Washington. Shapley warned that runoff from stores poses yet another risk to the water.

Changing watershed regulations across the state would require transferring many zoning and permitting powers from towns and villages to larger municipal bodies, such as counties or even the state itself. The constitutional grounds to do so are solid, according to John Nolon, a law professor at Pace University and counsel at the school's Land Use Law Center.

There aren't legal obstacles to solving the problem, Nolon said, but introducing a bill to strip towns of key powers could be career suicide for a state law-maker. "That is a politically very fraught task, because state legislators within the Assembly or Senate, they're all local politicians and they all run for office," he said. "When they go home, it's difficult for them to say, 'We just took away the town's power to deter-mine its future.'"

No Political Clout

If the state committed an original sin in Newburgh's contamination case, Ciaravino sees it not as the 1990 PFOS spill but as the state's classification of Silver Stream as a Class D stream, which allowed the Department of Defense to obtain permits to dis-charge into it in the first place. The stream should have been designated under Class A, meaning that it provides drinking water and therefore should not be used for waste.

"It was a simple error in labeling on the map," said Martin Brand, deputy commissioner for remediation at the New York State Department of Environmental Conservation. He declined to comment on "whether it was appropriate to discharge [into the stream] or not," noting that PFOS was not regulated until 2016. Yet he insisted the body of water was "all appropri-ately mapped."

The Department of Defense did not respond to repeated calls and emails requesting comment.

For the last two years, Silver Stream has been sev-ered from Lake Washington by a thick steel diversion gate, locked with three chained-together, rust-cov-ered wheel cranks. Cut off from the lake, the stream gushes over a cement dam and through the woods and into the Hudson River. The lake remains stag-nant, full of water with a contaminant that won't dis-integrate anytime soon.

A dam overflows with water diverted from Silver Stream, the body of water that would normally feed into the Lake Washington reservoir but was discov-ered to be contaminated with the chemical PFOS.

Ciaravino worries Newburgh may have one thing stacked against it that a village like Hoosick Falls doesn't: Hoosick Falls is nearly 98 percent white, according to census data. Newburgh is 52 percent Hispanic and 26 percent black. Historically, studies show those demographics suffer worse from pollution than white Americans and receive far fewer resources to mitigate it.

Even without the PFOS contamination, New-burgh's water is dirty. The Environmental Working Group's tap water database shows levels of trihalo-methanes—cancer-causing contaminants that form during the water treatment process—roughly three times higher than the state and national average, though still within legal limits. Chromium, a carcino-genic pollutant linked to industrial waste, appears at levels three times EWG's guidelines, which are based on combined state and EPA advisories. And that's just based on the data available in 2015.

"Maybe we just don't have the political juice over the last 20 years to advocate for our own safety needs," Ciaravino said.

Even if Newburgh fails to force the state to take more drastic action to clean up the contamination and change the way watershed jurisdictions work, its lawsuit could open the doors to a flood of litigation against the Defense Department, one of the nation's top polluters.

The military is responsible for 140 federal Super-fund sites, according to the EPA—more than any other civil entity. And the problem could be much bigger. The Pentagon identified 391 "active and closed instal-lations with known or suspected releases of PFOS and PFOA" as of December 2016, according to a Govern-ment Accountability Office report released last Octo-ber. The report warned that there are still holes in the Defense Department's internal data.

"Almost every military base, almost every fire-fighter-training session, used massive amounts of PFOS," Enck told HuffPost. "We are really in the middle of an emerging national crisis."

Understanding the Readings

1. How did the PFOS get into the aquifer of New-burgh, New York?
2. Why is this story about racism?
3. Why is it important to note that Newburgh's stream was labeled Class D instead of Class A? What is being done to remedy the situation?

Suggestions for Responding

1. Research toxic sites in your county.
2. Research the history and work of the Riverkeep-ers, an environmentalist group.

Suggestions for Responding to Part VI

1. Write an autobiographical analysis of your economic life from as far back as you can remember. Besides describing changing circumstances over time, analyze the impact economic class has had on your sense of self-worth, feelings, opportunities, and experiences—as well as the effects change has had on others' responses to you.

2. Alternatively, imagine a twenty-one-year-old woman, divorced and with a three-year-old child. She has graduated from high school but has not gone to college. She has not worked since her child was born. While she was in high school, she worked during the summers and sometimes after school for minimum wage in retail stores and fast food restaurants. Her ex-husband has not paid any child support, though legally he is required to do so. Her parents are no longer living, and she has no sisters or brothers. How is she going to support herself and her three-year-old child?

   Looking at the classifieds of a local newspaper, find this woman a job. Find out what her yearly salary would be, and calculate her monthly income from that projected salary. Do not forget how much she will have to pay for income taxes and FICA deductions. (Information about the percentages for these deductions should be available in your library.)

   After you write your report on your findings, draw some conclusions from comparing her finances with the poverty line, which is approximately $15,130 a year for a two-person family in 2012, and with your local welfare payment for a two-person family. What do these comparisons show?

3. In 1995, federal politicians from both parties committed themselves to "ending welfare as we know it." From what you *know* (not believe) about welfare and from the readings in part VI, try (either alone or with a small group) to create a policy that would improve our welfare system or social safety net.

4. After reading part VI, identify what you feel is the central economic problem facing our nation today. Research this problem either in the library or in your community and write a paper concretely describing the problem and what you think should be done to address it.

Part VII
Race, Class, and Gender during the Obama and Trump Administrations: A Comparative Look

"There are years that ask questions and years that answer."

—Zora Neale Hurston, *Their Eyes Were Watching God*

MOST OF US HAVE HEARD IT SAID ABOUT THE YEAR 2001: "After 9/11, everything changed." Certainly for the broken families who lost loved ones in the World Trade Center, the Pentagon, and the hijacked planes that crashed, life is immeasurably changed. But the sentence implies more—it refers to how we feel about ourselves and others in the world, and from this has issued a large debate nationwide and worldwide. Whether or not "everything changed" depends on the reactions of individual citizens and of governments. As for individual behavior, after 9/11, there were basically three ways of carrying on day to day. One was to "cocoon"—basically, to go about one's business with very little social interaction and to stay close to home. The second way was to want revenge and, so, to direct anger toward those nearby and afar. The third way was to become very involved with some sort of community service or cause that the person highly valued. Many people wanted to do something to heal themselves and the world. As for national reactions, the global outpouring of sympathy and grief for the United States quickly changed when the George W. Bush administration announced that there were ties between Saddam Hussein and the terrorist group Al Qaeda, and that Iraq had weapons of mass destruction. Ignoring the warnings from the United Nations Security Council, the United States invaded and occupied Iraq from 2003 to 2011, at great loss of American and Iraqi life, based on false claims of Iraq having weapons of mass destruction and ties to Al Qaeda.

What happened within the United States was equally upsetting and designed to quell any critics. With the passage of the Patriot Act, the federal government was given more power than any other administration to do surveillance on our own people, circumvent due process and First Amendment rights, prevent citizens from traveling, incarcerate whomever it sees fit, and demand access to student records from universities. Combine these policies of no checks and balances with deep troubles in the U.S. economy and anxiety over the safety of family members serving in Iraq and Afghanistan, and we see a movement of citizenry ready for change. The dialogues and "town meetings" going on all over America have been about revisiting our core values. Do we have a greater sense of unity as Americans now, or not? Does this sense cross racial, ethnic, and gender boundaries, or do we use these boundaries to structure how people see themselves and others in the world? Has being afraid made us **xenophobic**—highly fearful of anyone of foreign origin? Or perhaps mistrusting the dramatic, military approach to global and domestic problem solving, do we look forward to the time when we can again call on each other for resources, healing many of the rifts, especially with those living within America and with our traditional allies? As for law-abiding immigrants, who have been recently marginalized by an atmosphere of fear, we definitely look forward to the time when we will not feel *compelled* to fly or wear an American flag, as an attempt to not be targeted because of our accent, color of skin, or country of origin. This part of the text is dedicated to Americans, new and old, who are willing to help heal a wounded nation and world by active citizenship and faith that we can learn from our history.

We begin part VII with reading 53, in which Michael Dimock writes of "How America Changed During Barack Obama's Presidency." Analyzing this Pew study, the author focuses on legislative and policy changes made partly to minimize the economic crisis from the recession's fallout, and to respond to urgent social demands, all in the context of rapidly changing public opinion and demographic changes.

In reading 54, Nilagia McCoy brings us the highlights of a conversation with *The Atlantic*'s Adam Serwer on the politics of racism in Trump's America. In reading 55, Annalisa Merelli analyzes specific changes in federal policies under the Trump administration that limit women's rights and creates a culture of distrust in women's decisions.

Michael J. Brogan's essay "Environmental Justice in the Age of Trump" (reading 56) focuses upon the Trump administration's approach to protecting the air, water, ground, and, therefore, our people and all living things, from deadly pollutants. Here we especially examine the crises of the most vulnerable, underserved communities, recognizing that this is a public health emergency. The final essay in part VII is Victor Thompson's "The Power to Count: Citizenship and the Census." The author focuses upon a recent request from the secretary of commerce to quickly insert a question about U.S. citizenship for the 2020 census. There are many concerns about this request, most importantly, the politicization of the census, possibly leading to a less transparent process of collecting and reporting important data.

These articles challenge us all to share ideas, analyze, and make proposals for serious problem solving. If every classroom becomes a temporary think tank, it encourages us to make strides here and in the world.

53

How America Changed during Barack Obama's Presidency

Michael Dimock

Barack Obama campaigned for the U.S. presidency on a platform of change. As he prepares to leave office, the country he led for eight years is undeniably different. Profound social, demographic and technological changes have swept across the United States during Obama's tenure, as have important shifts in government policy and public opinion.

Apple released its first iPhone during Obama's 2007 campaign, and he announced his vice presidential pick—Joe Biden—on a two-year-old platform called Twitter. Today, use of smartphones and social media has become the norm in U.S. society, not the exception.

The election of the nation's first black president raised hopes that race relations in the United States would improve, especially among black voters. But by 2016, following a spate of high-profile deaths of black Americans during encounters with police and protests by the Black Lives Matter movement and other groups, many Americans—especially blacks—described race relations as generally bad.

The U.S. economy is in much better shape now than it was in the aftermath of the Great Recession, which cost millions of Americans their homes and jobs and led Obama to push through a roughly $800 billion stimulus package as one of his first orders of business. Unemployment has plummeted from 10 percent in late 2009 to below 5 percent today; the Dow Jones Industrial Average has more than doubled.

But by some measures, the country faces serious economic challenges: A steady hollowing of the middle class, for example, continued during Obama's presidency, and income inequality reached its highest point since 1928.

Obama's election quickly elevated America's image abroad, especially in Europe, where George W. Bush was deeply unpopular following the U.S. invasion of Iraq. In 2009, shortly after Obama took office, residents in many countries expressed a sharp increase in confidence in the ability of the U.S. president to do the right thing in international affairs. While Obama remained largely popular internationally throughout his tenure, there were exceptions, including in Russia and key Muslim nations. And Americans themselves became more wary of international engagement.

Views on some high-profile social issues shifted rapidly. Eight states and the District of Columbia legalized marijuana for recreational purposes, a legal shift accompanied by a striking reversal in public opinion: For the first time on record, a majority of Americans now support legalization of the drug.

As it often does, the Supreme Court settled momentous legal battles during Obama's tenure, and in 2015, it overturned long-standing bans on same-sex marriage, effectively legalizing such unions nationwide. Even before the court issued its landmark ruling in *Obergefell v. Hodges*, a majority of Americans said for the first time that they favored same-sex marriage.

[Article published in part.]

Understanding the Reading

1. Identify some of the major changes that occurred during Obama's presidency, especially legislative ones.
2. What did Europe think of Obama's election?

Suggestions for Responding

1. Collect testimonials from people of different backgrounds of what they liked or disliked about the Obama presidency.
2. Research the requirements that Obama's Affordable Care Act required of insurance companies (especially "no denial of care because of prior conditions"), and compare that with the present-day health care debate.

54

The Atlantic's *Adam Serwer: The Politics of Racism in Trump's America*

Nilagia McCoy

March 27, 2018—Adam Serwer, senior editor at *The Atlantic*, discussed the role of race and class in U.S. politics, and its media coverage, during a visit to the

Shorenstein Center. Below are some highlights of his conversation with Shorenstein Center Director Nicco Mele, as well as the full audio. The Shorenstein Center's podcast is also available on iTunes, Google Play, iHeartRadio, and Stitcher.

Narratives about Race and Politics

"The nature of American politics is always to want to hold white people blameless when they act out of racism. In the case of [David] Duke, the reality is that in the 1990s, if it had been up to the white people of Louisiana, the state would have sent a Klansman to the U.S. Senate . . . faced with that, I think the impulse is to say we can't really be that terrible, and so you have to find some rationalization, some explanation for why what is happening in front of your eyes is not actually happening. I think that same impulse was at work with Donald Trump's candidacy."

The nature of American politics is always to want to hold white people blameless when they act out of racism.

"The press is largely white . . . they don't want to think of their friends and relatives and people they have close personal relationships with as having what is perceived as this incredible character flaw. So I think it's easier for people to tell themselves that that's not what's going on, as opposed to saying straight out what it is. I think that's partially why you see a big distinction . . . in the way Trump is written about from journalists of color than you often do with white journalists . . . there's an awareness of explicit subtext with journalists of color. We're cognizant of the fact that Trump is talking about us and people like us in a way that I think is easier for white journalists to dismiss."

Race and Class

"I want to distinguish between two things, between the idea that the white working class is suffering, and the idea that white working class suffering is the explanation for Trump. There's no question that in a country like ours where almost all of the wage gains of the past 30–40 years have accrued almost entirely to people at the top of the income scale, that people below that, particularly people in the working class or poor, are struggling. The question is, to what extent are you willing to buy into a solution to that problem that blames other people on the basis of race?"

"People of color of similar class backgrounds did

not like those solutions, and they didn't like them because they were targeted by them . . . The economic factors that affected the white working class affected the black and Latino working classes even more deeply, and there was no corresponding drive toward extremism. After the [2008] recession you didn't see Nation of Islam membership suddenly swelling as a result of black wealth being systematically destroyed by unscrupulous banks . . . the framing of this election was that it was a rebellion of the working class, and the story is much more complicated than that."

Preparing for 2020 Election Media Coverage

The federal government is an amazing repository of official knowledge, and when you have control over those types of things, you are able to manipulate the press in ways that we've seen a million times before.

"The real issue is going to be [that] the Trump administration has shown a lack of restraint when it comes to using the levers of the federal government for political purposes, and I think it will be very difficult for the press to deal with that . . . for example, there was a Department of Homeland Security report a while ago that said that most terrorism was caused by immigrants, but . . . essentially it defined homegrown terrorism by white supremacists as not [being] terrorism."

"The federal government is an amazing repository of official knowledge, and when you have control over those types of things, you are able to manipulate the press in ways that we've seen a million times before. When you look at the war in Iraq, selective leaks to the press were part of the way that the case for the war was built. This time around in 2020, the Trump administration, which arguably has an even less intimate relationship with the truth than the Bush administration, is going to be able to manipulate that official knowledge in ways that I think the press is not necessarily prepared for."

The Democratic Party's Response to "Trumpism"

"I think the Democrats are in a difficult place, because they have to figure out a way to appeal to the broadest section of white voters . . . no one wants to say that Trump is racist in part because if you do that, you taint his voters, and Democrats who want to reach out to those voters don't want to make those people feel bad, because otherwise, they might not vote Democratic. So Democrats have to figure out a critique of Trump that brings more white voters into their camp while also not making their black and Latino constituents feel as though their concerns are being sidelined or dismissed. We have yet to see how good the post-Obama Democrats actually are at politics."

The Future U.S. Politics and Race Relations

"I do think that people can change. I think that people are capable of being better. And I think that while the [*Atlantic*] essay is a strong case for the inevitability of history affecting the present, people can make different choices, and people can decide to reject the politics of white identity. We'll see whether the nation is capable of it, but I certainly don't think it's inevitable that this is how our politics are going to be forever just because the politics of white identity have dominated America in the past."

Understanding the Reading

1. How does Adam Serwer explain our denial of white racism in our population?
2. What is an important difference between the idea of acknowledging the suffering of the working class according to Adam Serwer and that of Donald Trump?
3. Why did the Homeland Security report say that terrorism acts in the United States are caused by immigrants, without calling the white supremacists terrorists?
4. Why does Serwer say the Democratic Party is in a difficult position concerning the topic of racism?

Suggestion for Responding

1. Have a classroom discussion on who can be a terrorist. Does a person's race or ethnicity make a difference? If the person is a soldier with a uniform, can he or she be a terrorist?

55

The Trump Administration Isn't Just Curtailing Women's Rights; It's Systematically Eroding Trust in Women

ANNALISA MERELLI

October 14, 2017

Since its earliest days, it has been clear that the Trump administration was going to chip away at women's rights and gender equality. Nine months in, here are some of the things it has done:

- January: Reinstated the Mexico City Policy, which cuts aid funding to any international organization that so much as mentions to a pregnant woman that abortion is one of her options
- April: Cut funding to the UN Population Fund, which provides reproductive health in more than 150 countries
- July: Promoted the idea (paywall) that most reports of college sexual assault are false
- August: Scrapped a rule that would have made pay disparities more visible by requiring many U.S. companies to report on pay rates by race and gender
- August: Removed a key report on college sexual assault—which found, among other things, that very few assault reports are false—from the White House website
- September: Issued new guidance on how colleges should investigate sexual assault, requiring a higher burden of proof
- October: Curtailed the right to birth control enshrined in Obamacare

But these moves don't only block the progress of gender equality. They have a sinister side-effect: undermining the word of women, making them seem undeserving of trust, thus weakening their voices and their complaints.

It is hard not to see this as a deliberate intention. The president is a noted misogynist who has nominated men to government jobs at a higher rate than any of the last three presidents. His administration doesn't trust women, and it doesn't want its citizens to trust them, either.

Perhaps the clearest example is its recent change to the guidelines on how colleges should investigate sexual assault, which is considered a violation of Title IX, the piece of law that prohibits discrimination on campuses.

The Barack Obama administration issued new Title IX guidelines to help colleges deal with accusations of assault more quickly (giving a deadline for investigating assault reports) and made the victim's word alone enough to begin an investigation (since in most cases, assault or rape accusations are down to the victim's word against the perpetrator's).

Education secretary Betsy DeVos recently amended these guidelines. After saying in a speech that people accused of sexual assault needed more protecting from the assumption of guilt, she introduced changes such as letting schools allow both victim and perpetrator to appeal a decision (previously, only victims could appeal), getting rid of the deadline for investigations, and saying that under Title IX "schools must address sexual misconduct that is severe, persistent or pervasive"—implying that not all sexual misconduct should be addressed.

But the administration isn't just changing the policies on investigating sexual assault—it's also attacking the facts that justified those policies.

The Obama guidelines were based on the understanding that the vast majority of accusations of rape on campus are legitimate. This was the finding of a 2014 White House report on sexual assault, which said that only 2–10 percent of rape reports are false (pdf, p. 16). It also found that 20 percent of female students suffer sexual assault (p. 1), but only 12 percent of assaults are reported, and that young men who admit to rape or attempted rape have done it an average of six times (p. 14).

The report was published on the White House website during the Obama administration. It remained there until the Trump administration quietly removed it at the end of August, though it's still on the archived Obama White House site.

Meanwhile, the administration has been promoting another set of data through Candice Jackson, the head of civil rights at the Education Department. Without providing evidence, she claimed (paywall) that 90 percent of assault accusations "fall into the category of 'we were both drunk,' 'we broke up, and six months later I found myself under a Title IX investigation because she just decided that our last sleeping together was not quite right.'" Jackson also said that in most cases the men aren't accused of forcing

themselves on women against their will—implying that an assault isn't really an assault unless the woman fights back. (In reality, a woman may be too afraid, or indeed drunk, to resist or say no, but that doesn't mean she consents.)

"I think this sends a very strong message," says Mellissa Withers, a global health professor at the University of Southern California whose work focuses on sexual assault and gender-based violence. "Of course, we don't want anyone who is innocent to be accused," she says, but false accusations are so rare that the new guidelines seem like a deliberate attempt to promote suspicions that women who report an assault may be lying. This runs contrary to decades of scientific literature on rape reporting.

This is an approach that perpetuates a fundamental lack of trust in women—something that in turn is fertile ground for limiting their rights. The same mindset runs through the proposed ban on abortion after the twentieth week of pregnancy, introduced by a conservative Republican member of the House of Representatives, which passed a House vote on Oct. 3.

The proposal, which focuses on saving the lives of future healthy babies from their murderous mothers, seems to believe women capriciously and frequently resort to late-term abortions. In reality, only 1.3 percent of abortions happen after the twentieth week, according to the Centers for Disease Control. Typically they're because of certain health problems with the fetus that don't become apparent until later in pregnancy, such as some genetic conditions. The justification for the measure—that fetuses as young as 20 weeks can supposedly feel pain—is also scientifically flimsy.

Trusting women's judgment would mean believing that they make sensible decisions, even when that decision is to end a pregnancy late or report an abuse with no evidence other than what they themselves experienced. But if their credibility is systematically undermined, it's easier to diminish their worth. That ultimately makes it easier to justify paying them less, not choosing them for political office, ignoring their voices, and taking away their rights over their bodies.

Understanding the Reading

1. What is the Trump administration's attitude toward domestic and international agencies that provide reproductive health care?
2. What actions have been taken by the Trump

administration to undo the Obama guidelines concerning campus rape?

3. What is the basis for these changes of policies that were meant to protect women?

Suggestions for Responding

1. Research your campus's policies and their enactment concerning rape.
2. Find what agencies and care facilities exist in your community for reproductive health aside from private physicians.

56

Environmental Justice in the Age of Trump

MICHAEL J. BROGAN

Introduction

This essay examines the impact of the Trump administration's approach to protecting clean air and water for communities most vulnerable to environmental injustice. The examination of the Trump administration's environmental record, as of this writing, is done so through the lens of Environmental Justice. This concept is defined as a linkage between social justice and environmental rights. The Trump administration has sought to reduce the role of the federal government on this issue, by reducing and streamlining resources for environmental protection. As part of this approach, the administration has sought to eliminate the U.S. EPA Office of Environmental Justice (OEJ) through the budget process. The administration's actions signal an unwillingness to help communities most vulnerable to environmental injustice.

This essay is organized in three parts. The first is a brief overview of Environmental Justice in the United States. The second is a review of the attempt by the Trump administration to no longer fund the U.S. EPA's Office of Environmental Justice. Finally, we will analyze the implications of actions undertaken by the Trump Administration on communities that are fighting to secure clean air and water.

Overall, the Environmental Justice movement seeks to increase the voice of communities that have been underserved under the existing environmental regulatory regime through a deliberative approach to environmental policymaking. Environmental Justice differs from more traditional environmental rights movements over the past fifty years, as it equally places the interconnections between environmental problems, social justice and public health.

Another distinction between environmental justice and traditional environmental movements is membership. In traditional environmental movements, membership has often had a middle to upper class bias. Environmental justice movements broaden their coalition to include people of color and groups that have worked on social justice issues. Membership in environmental justice movements stems from the framing of environmental problems as both a poor people's and a civil rights movement. By doing so, the movement has broadened the appeal to individuals and groups that normally would not gravitate towards environmental problems and opened up new avenues for grassroots participation.

A third distinction of environmental justice movements compared to traditional environmentalism is over the focus of problems and solutions to environmental problems. Traditional environmentalism has focused on technology and scientific evidence as the means for defining environmental problems and solutions. In this context, humans and social problems associated with environmental degradation tend to be discounted in the policy process. Environmental Justice movements have taken a more democratic approach to environmental policy, by making social problems equal to environmental ones and seeking lasting solutions that improve both the environment and the communities that have been historically underserved.

Overview of Environmental Justice in the United States

To understand the context of Environmental Justice in the United States, it must first be situated within the broader context of environmental politics—the context is over concerns as to how humanity organizes itself relative to the environment and how the environment sustains human impact (Layzer 2010: 2). Disputes in environmental politics, therefore, tend to be "contests over values" that focus on the effect of humans on the environment. Conflict in the environmental policy process stems from the adversarial nature of our value system—a system that values economic growth and protecting the environment. What is contested, therefore, is the severity of how much humans contribute to issues of public health and pollution, and whether government intervention seeking a remedy for these issues would not hurt economic growth.

Clowney and Mosto (2009) contend that Environmental Justice movements arose from debates over the trade-off of societal values and environmental degradation in shaping environmental policy. Overuse of natural resources for raw materials and energy production in the name of economic growth, often did not impact society equally in terms of costs. Not only did economic growth come at the expense of environmental conditions, but it also became more acute in areas most vulnerable.

Historically, the focus on economic growth resulted in environmental policy being ill suited to help vulnerable communities. The adaption of environmental movements to include human social circumstances and value systems gave new opportunities to expand membership. Now it was not only issues of pollution that drove environmental politics but also connecting how pollution created new forms of injustice—new extremes of wealth and poverty directly connected to differential environmental conditions in communities based upon social stratification.

Estimating the Magnitude of Environmental Justice

To identify the magnitude of risk to vulnerable communities, this section conducts a brief multivariate analysis of the U.S. EPA's EJSCREEN data. The data is used to identify factors related to environmental justice, public health and environmental conditions. To define demographic factors used to analyze risk, the EJSCREEN provides the following variables at the U.S. census tract level: percent of low income in a U.S. census block less than or equal to twice the federal poverty level; percent of minority in a population in a U.S. census tract who identify racial status as other than "white"; percent of population that is linguistically isolated, percent of population under age of five and percent of population over sixty-five, and finally the percent of buildings built before 1960.

Based on the data, environmental justice issues are significantly most acute in the poorest communities. For instance, in estimating the impact of communities who have populations at the 95th percentile in terms of living at or below the poverty level, and having high minority populations, we can expect that

these communities to be at 95th level for air toxic quality cancer risk (other things being equal). In communities that have populations of 98 percent minority and 89 percent or higher living at the federal poverty level, we can also expect that community to be in the 95th percentile of living in an area with high levels of air toxic respiratory hazards. Communities with high minority populations and high poverty levels are in the 75th percentile in areas that are below the federal standard of being at or above Particle Matter 2.5m (measured in micrometers).

In addition to air quality indicators, the poorest communities in the nation are more likely to be at or above the 90th percentile of being in proximity to the following environmental hazards: superfund sites, facilities that have higher potential for chemical accidents, and hazardous waste management facilities. Proximity of poor communities to siting problems associated with poor public health and environmental conditions are also significant in regards to wastewater discharge and to high traffic areas. Being in proximity to waste-water discharge facilities results in increased rates of flooding, runoff and pollution. Communities that are at the 95th percentile for minority population and in the 95th percentile of people living at or below the poverty line, are in the 85th percentile of being in close proximity to waste-water discharge facilities. Further, minority and poorer communities are in the 87th percentile of living near high traffic areas. For these areas, air quality issues related to car emissions and increases in ozone levels during the summer months put residents at risk for respiratory issues.

Environmental Justice as a Form of U.S. Public Policy

In 1994, President Clinton implemented executive order 12898. The order defined the role of the U.S. federal government in relation to environmental justice. The order stipulated that "each Federal agency shall make achieving environmental justice part of its mission by identifying and addressing, as appropriate, disproportionately high and adverse human health or environmental effects of its programs, policies, and activities on minority populations and low-income populations" (Office of the U.S. President 1994: 1). The order effectively addressed environmental justice issues, by including marginalized segments of society in the decision-making process. The executive directive and definition of environmental justice at the federal level added two dimensions to U.S. federal environmental policy (Holifield 2001). First, it includes measures that examine the distribution of environmental quality among different communities (distributive justice). Second, programs expand the procedural process by which citizens have access to participate in the decision-making process that impact environments (procedural justice).

Two years prior to President Clinton's executive order, the U.S. EPA created the Office of Environmental Equity (the predecessor to the Office of Environmental Justice) based upon recommendations from the EPA Environmental Equity Work Group. The primary goal of the office is "to ensure that all people, regardless of race, national origin or income, are protected from disproportionate impacts of environmental hazards" (U.S. Environmental Protection Agency, Office of Environmental Justice 2000).

The office classified marginalized communities as minority and/or low-income groups who have been excluded from the environmental policy-setting and/ or decision-making process in the past. The office targets communities that have been subject to a disproportionate impact from environmental hazards and experienced a disparate implementation and lack of enforcement of environmental regulations, requirements, practices and activities in their communities (U.S. Environmental Protection Agency, Office of Environmental Justice 2000). The expansion of defining marginalized communities, and by including input from stakeholders who live in them, ensured they would no longer be left out of the policy process.

The primary mission of the office is to ensure that agencies that receive funding from the U.S. EPA do not act in a discriminatory manner. Its mission stems from the U.S. Civil Rights Act of 1964 (Title VI) which prohibited federal assistance to organizations and agencies that racially discriminate.

The Office of Environmental Justice has been pivotal in successfully fulfilling the dimensions of distributive and procedural in U.S. environmental policy. It has done so by providing technical assistance, enforcement and grants to over 1,400 communities (Ali 2017). The office has distributed more than $24M on these efforts. In 2017, the Office awarded 36 grants for lead exposure, Other Toxic Substances Clean Water, Clean Air, Land Remediation, Green Infrastructure, Solid Waste Disposal, and Environmental Education.

Types of projects funded by the office include a $30K grant to the Friends of Van Cortlandt Park

"Wetland Stewardship for a Healthier Bronx Watershed" project. The project reduces runoff issues from Van Cortlandt Lake and Tibbetts Brook into the sewer. The project also funds educational training, outreach and projects designed to empower students to become more aware of runoff issues on communities, with well-developed knowledge and tools to combat this problem through ecological and technological efforts.

Another example of the impact the office has had on vulnerable communities is awarding a $30K grant to deal with high rates for children being exposed to lead in the Near Northwest Neighborhood of South Bend, IN. The grant was prompted from a study that found 31 percent of children in the tract tested over the blood level of 5 micrograms per deciliter (EPA 2017). The grant was used to partner with the city health department to do outreach to families with children under the age of seven to inform of the risks and prevention strategies of dealing with lead exposure.

Criticizing and Attempting to Eliminate the Office of Environmental Justice

Though the office of Environmental Justice has had many successes, this has not come without criticism for its ability to enforce Title VI complaints on behalf of communities of color (ProPublica 2015). The primary complaint about the office is that it has denied investigation of complaints, failed to investigate or resolve complaints with informal agreements. Environmental groups and impacted communities have sued the office over unreasonable delays and inaction.

Though these complaints do point to a pattern of an inability to enforce the office's primary mission, its very existence came into threat with the election of President Donald Trump and his appointment of Secretary of U.S. EPA Scott Pruitt. Perhaps the most brazen of the Trump administration's efforts to eliminate the office was to zero out its budget. This was done via the Office of Management and Budget (OMB) budget request to Congress for fiscal year 2019. For FY19, the office's budget was set to zero. The final budget was a cut of -$4.7M, leaving funding at approximately $2M for the year. As part of this total, all funds for "Hazardous Substance Superfund" related to this program were zeroed out. The rationale for the cuts by Administrator Pruitt were a commitment to create "a leaner, more accountable, less intrusive, and more effective Government" (U.S. EPA 2018).

The objective of zeroing out the office's budget is to consolidate all programs related to environmental justice into the EPA's Office of Policy (OP). Remaining funding includes $2 million to support the Environmental Justice Small Grants program, Environmental Justice Technical Assistance for Communities and to continue providing EJSCREEN data. According to the administration, consolidating and streamlining resources to the Office of Policy is to accomplish better integration overall. The Trump administration argues the move strengthens and complements work already being done by other offices. For the administration, reorganization would provide better support to vulnerable communities both to improve public health and to protect the environment, as well as to spur economic growth.

So what does this cut in funding mean for Environmental Justice efforts? The most likely outcomes from the Trump administration's attempt to defund the office include: reducing employee morale, hindering capacity efforts of the office that previously had only modest funding compared to other initiatives at the agency, and further marginalization of the communities that require the most help and attention from the federal government.

The first outcome has already occurred at the agency. Staff reductions of more than 3,200 employees since the Trump administration took power, means fewer people to do an ever-increasing workload (*New York Times* 2017). Reductions in the agency are most acute in the science division of the agency resulting in decreases in accumulated expertise and knowledge of protecting air and water.

Second, declining policy capacity issues to carry out the office's mission are a problem. Loss of expertise among EPA employees, a diminished ability of the Office of Environmental Justice to coordinate, mobilize and distribute resources, constrain the ability of employees to carry out the office's mission (Lindquist 2006). Capacity tools needed for successful policy implementation include being able to provide information, train, educate, and resources needed to enable individuals and groups with the ability to make decisions and carry out activities (Schneider and Ingram 1990). Cutting the office's budget by -57 percent reduces overall capacity to provide these tools. The reductions increase likelihood of failure for the office.

A final, and related, outcome: The Trump adminis-

tration's refusal to acknowledge evidence of a significant relationship between structural socio-economic stratification and public health and environmental conditions. Findings from an analysis of the EJSCREEN point to systemic problems for the nation's poorest communities. The actions by the Trump administration point to a failure in the near and long term. Funding cuts mean a reduction in grants to communities who need support. The primary function of the office—to provide grants, oversight and enforcement—has been reduced and can only support vulnerable communities on a limited basis at best. Issues related to air and water quality and public health, therefore, cannot be fully addressed. Communities that have been effectively left behind by society will fall further back.

Discussion

The EPA's Office of Environmental Justice was set up to target communities that have been subject to a disproportionate impact from environmental hazards and have been underserved in the enforcement of environmental regulations enacted to protect all residents. Since its inception, the office has had a positive impact on minority, low-income, tribal and indigenous communities (EPA 2017). It has positively contributed to the lowering of fine particle air pollution matter (by 2016 there was 92 percent standard compliance), small community drinking water compliance (by 2016 an improvement of 57 percent), and meeting tribal drinking water standards (by 2016, 92 percent of tribal communities met this standard).

The Trump administration's approach to environmental justice has been adversarial to the office's mission and accomplishments. The zeroing out of the office's budget by the administration is based on the rationale of streamlining resources. But by consolidating resources, the administration has not provided a clear rationale as to how environmental justice issues will remain a priority. These actions also remove the significance of hope to vulnerable communities that social and environmental issues have a specific and defined purpose within the environmental policy domain. Consolidation and streamlining ignore the significance of the office and the role of the federal government in fighting environmental racism.

It is also unclear how the competing goals of protecting public health and dealing with pollution while at the same time facilitating economic growth in vulnerable communities will be accomplished by zeroing out the Office of Environmental Justice and by reassigning duties to the Office of Policy. In fact, the opposite goal is likely to occur. The Trump administration's approach would make issues of public health and environmental pollution worse as a result of the diminished regulatory role of the U.S. EPA. In order to have economic growth, there needs to be viable communities that are safe, healthy and not situated by environmental hazards. The Trump administration ignores these factors and provides little in terms of substance or style in giving hope to vulnerable communities.

A further complication related to the reorganization of OEJ is over the priorities pushed forward by staff of the Office of Policy. The OP at the U.S. EPA is staffed by administration appointees, as well as by career professionals at the agency. Karl Brooks, former acting chief of EPA's Office of Administration and Resources Management, stated that the tension between these two groups of employees can be problematic in meeting the overall mission of the agency. He argues that "objective, unvarnished" advice from career professionals can be "diluted" or "overridden" by political appointees whose primary mission is to carry out the direction of the administration's own political priorities.

So, what is at stake? The ideologically driven approach of the Trump administration to environmental justice could result in major setbacks for vulnerable communities. For most of his career, EPA Administrator Pruitt has been an adversary to environmental regulation. (As attorney general of Oklahoma he sued the federal government over the Clean Air Act.) In his short tenure, Pruitt has been accused of stalling on implementing and enforcing existing regulations tied to clean air and public health. It should come as no surprise as impacted communities related to environmental justice issues are now put at increased risk under this administration. The reality of the Trump administration is that now the impact of risk for these communities will be larger and more far reaching than what has occurred under prior administrations.

[2018]

Bibliography

Ali, Santago Mustafa. 2017, March 8. *Letter of Resignation to Administrator Pruitt*.

Bogardus, Kevin. 2017, September 7. "Top Brass Tout Reorganization in Email to Staff." *E&E News*. Accessed April 14, 2018, https://www.eenews.net/stories/1060060007/print.

Clowney, David, and Pat Mosto. 2009. *Earthcare: An Anthology in Environmental Ethics*. Lanham, MD: Rowman & Littlefield.

Friedman, Lisa, Marina Affo, and Derek Kravitz. 2017, December 22. "E.P.A. Officials, Disheartened by Agency's Direction, Are Leaving in Droves." *New York Times*. Accessed April 8, 2018, https://www.nytimes.com/2017/12/22/climate/epa-buyouts-pruitt.html.

Garcia, Lisa. 2018, January 23. "Pruitt's Attacks on Environmental Protections Hit People of Color Hardest." *Huffington Post*. Accessed April 22, 2018, https://www.huffingtonpost.com/entry/opinion-garcia-pruitt-environmental-justice_us_5a565eede4b03bc4d03d77b2.

Gogal, Danny. 2017, November 6. "25 Years of Environmental Justice at the EPA." *The EPA Blog*. https://blog.epa.gov/blog/2017/11/25-years-of-environmental-justice-at-the-epa/.

Holifield, Ryan. 2001. "Defining Environmental Justice and Environmental Racism." *Urban Geography* 22: 78–90.

Layzer, Judith. 2010. *Environmental Case: Translating Values into Policy*. Washington, D.C.: CQ Press.

Lindquist, E. A. 2006. "Organizing for Policy Implementation: The Emergence and Role of Implementation Units in Policy Design and Oversight." *Journal of Comparative Policy Analysis* 8, no. 4.

Lombardi, Kristin, Talia Buford, and Ronnie Greene. 2015, August 3. "Environmental Racism Persists, and the EPA Is One Reason Why." Center for Public Integrity. Accessed April 23, 2018, https://www.publicintegrity.org/2015/08/03/17668/environmental-racism-persists-and-epa-one-reason-why.

Office of the U.S. President. 1994, February 11. "Federal Actions to Address Environmental Justice in Minority Populations and Low-Income Populations: Executive Order: 12898." http://www.eahcp.org/documents/1994_Clinton_ExecutiveOrder12898.pdf.

Schneider, Anne, and Helen Ingram. 1990. "The Behavioral Assumptions of Policy Tools." *Journal of Politics* 52: 510–29.

U.S. EPA. 2018. "FY2018 Budget in Brief." Accessed April 23, 2018, https://www.epa.gov/sites/produc

tion/files/2017-05/documents/fy-2018-budget-in
-brief.pdf.

U.S. EPA Office of Environmental Justice. 2017.
"2017 Environmental Justice Small Grants Program." Accessed April 24, 2018, https://www.epa
.gov/sites/production/files/2017-10/documents/
ejsg _2017_project_summaries.pdf.

Understanding the Reading

1. Why and how is the Trump administration eliminating the U.S. Environmental Protection Agency
office of Environmental Justice?
2. What effects will this have for people of the
United States?
3. Describe the Environmental Justice movement,
and why is it also considered to be a public health
movement?
4. Why is the Civil Rights Act of 1964 (Title VI)
important to this movement's strategies?

Suggestions for Responding

1. As a class, research and identify examples of
underserved populations in the United States that
are plagued by various pollutants in the air, water,
and soil. Also identify the health consequences
evident in each specific area.
2. What business interests are served by ignoring
accountability and culpability?

57

The Power to Count: Citizenship and the Census

Victor Thompson

Globally, almost half of all countries conducted a
census or population register in the 2010 census
round with a question on citizenship. This number
increased from approximately 28 percent of all countries in 1990 to 42 percent in 2010. It varies considerably by region of the world with only two-thirds of
Oceania and Europe asking a question on citizenship,
while less than one-third of North and South American countries ask a question on citizenship (Kukutai
and Thompson 2018). In short, citizenship questions
are somewhat commonplace around the globe and

likely to become even more common. The question
itself is neither unique nor controversial. Indeed, in
an effort to standardize some parts of the census taking apparatus, the United Nations recommends that
all member nations include a question on citizenship
as a core topic on the census (United Nations 2017).
The recommendations remain open in terms of
whether the question is asked as part of a 100 percent
census count or is gathered through a sample.

In the United States, citizenship data is already
collected using the American Community Survey
(ACS) by asking "Is this person a citizen of the United
States?" There are several possible responses based
on whether one was born in the United States, a
dependency, abroad to U.S. citizens, by naturalization, or not a citizen. The ACS is a monthly survey
administered by the U.S. Census Bureau that goes
out to approximately 3.5 million persons per year. It
replaces the "long-form" version of the U.S. decennial census, which until 2000 was a key source of
data for detailed social, demographic and economic
questions not included on the "short-form" questionnaire, which is mailed out to every household on a
decennial basis. Much like the "short form," all questions on the ACS are federally mandated and necessary for the implementation of some policies (U.S.
Census Bureau 2016). Before inclusion, most questions undergo years of testing, typically 3–5 years,
before they are finalized. This includes listening to
proposals for new questions or changes, assessing the
merit of changes/proposals, exploring wording option
and language, followed by field testing and public
comment before final implementation. It is a long
and tedious task but circumventing this process has
the potential to corrupt data, lower response rates,
and produce unexpected results.

A key distinction between the ACS and the "short
form" decennial census is that it is generally agreed
upon that only results from the short form can be
used for determining actual counts of the population
to be used for Congressional redistricting. Congressional redistricting is a process through which states
redraw their Congressional district boundaries every
ten years so that districts have roughly equal numbers
of people residing in them. Demographic forces associated with migration patterns, fertility rates and mortality rates mean that districts are always changing.
Unfortunately, the Reapportionment Act of 1929
capped the total number of congressional districts to
435, meaning ultimately that it is a zero-sum game.
Losses in one part of the country mean gains in

another part of the country or vice versa. Similarly, loss of representation means loss of political power and resources. Thus, the political goal of political parties is to minimize the losses in districts where your party dominates and maximize gains in districts where you hold less power. This zero-sum game will become relevant to the citizenship question shortly. But first, we must examine the origins of the proposal to include citizenship on the decennial census.

On March 26, 2018, President Trump's newly appointed secretary of commerce Wilbur Ross sent a request to Under Secretary Kelley titled "Reinstatement of a Citizenship Question on the 2020 Decennial Census Questionnaire." It appeared to come out of nowhere only a few days before the federal deadline for introducing new questions to the Census, catching Census Bureau employees and others off-guard with what appeared to be a general disregard for the standard timeline for introducing new questions to the U.S. Census. The claim, according to the request, was that the Department of Justice (DOJ) and the courts needed citizenship for determining census block level citizenship voting age population ("CVAP") for determining violations of Section 2 of the Voting Rights Act, which protects minority population voting rights. While it is not unusual to have requests for questions that seem politically motivated, it was highly unusual to demand an immediate change like this with such short notice (Ross 2018). This immediately raised flags around Washington and among technocrats who regularly work with Census data. Why the urgency? Why was the DOJ, under newly elected President Trump, rarely an advocate of Civil Rights, so concerned about Section 2 violations? Was it all a ruse? Were there other motives? And what's the deal with CVAP?

To answer these questions and to return to the question of redistricting, one must first locate the origins of the request. Ostensibly, the request is framed around Civil Rights legislation and violations of Section 2 of the Voting Rights Act. Few however take these claims seriously. The genesis of Wilbur Ross's request is more likely a byproduct of fallout from a relatively simple but important court case: *Evenwel v. Abbott on Redistricting* 578 (2016). Historically, it is left to individual states to redistrict every ten years based on the total population of people living in their districts. Generally, as the population of states change, so too does the number of representatives they have in Congress. Population increases translate into increased representation and population de-

creases lead to decreased representation. To date, all states use the total population of people living in a district to determine these numbers. This reflects the language of the Constitution which says that "Representatives shall be apportioned among the several States according to their respective numbers, counting the whole number of persons in each State, excluding Indians not taxed."

Sue Evenwel, a Texan, and her co-plaintiff argued this was not fair. Her logic was based on the idea that if districts are roughly the same size of persons but have different number of eligible voters across districts, then someone's vote in a district with lots of eligible voters counts "less" in theory than the person from a district with fewer eligible voters, simply because they are one out of a greater total number of voters (e.g., 1/350,000 vs. 1/200,000). This is common in districts in Texas and thus, Evenwel argued, it was unfair and violated the "one person, one vote" principle of the Equal Protection Clause of the Fourteenth Amendment of the United States Constitution. Despite the fact that Evenwel was suing the State of Texas, she found some support among the administration. The Governor of Texas was supportive of the claim that eligible voters should be used to determine district population size, not total population. "One voter, one vote" was more appealing to a Governor concerned about maintaining a strong Republican power base than the status quo of "one person, one vote," primarily because the "one voter, one vote" scenario almost always produced a significant advantage for Republicans.

The U.S. Supreme Court ruled against Evenwel and upheld the status quo. Interestingly, had they not ruled against Evenwel, and were states to adopt the eligible voters model, nearly every district in the United States would need to be redrawn as they would in their current state be unconstitutional. Instead, states, the Supreme Court argued, would be allowed to use total population as the number for determining the size of congressional districts, preserving the principle of "one person, one vote." The Court however failed to settle the question of what are the best means for determining Congressional district sizes and left it open for future cases. While it seems evident after Evenwel that "eligible voters" cannot be used as a means for counting district sizes, there are other possibilities being proposed. Texas, not coincidentally, has already proposed using citizenship voting age population (CVAP) to count districts. Yes, the very same CVAP that Secretary Ross proposes is so important for the enforcement of Section 2 of the Civil Rights Act. This would have similar consequences on the power distribution in most states, lending a sizeable advantage to Republicans across states (Beveridge 2016). The problem of course though is only "short form" data can be used for determining population counts so new categories would need to be added to the "short form" to identify CVAP since we may not use the ACS for counting the total population. Namely, citizenship status would need to be added to the decennial census. Once included, states could attempt to redistrict based on these counts rather than the total population, though it is almost certain that court cases challenging the Constitutionality of such a move will soon follow.

This brings us to our current predicament. On one side, we have a political right confronting countervailing demographic shifts that is hell-bent on preserving power at all costs, even if it means changing the rules of the game. On the other side, we have Census bureaucrats and the political left expressing concerns about the motivations and timing of the addition of a citizenship question on the U.S. Census. Initially, Census bureaucrats articulated a response, formulated most forcefully in a letter penned by former U.S. Census Bureau directors to Secretary Wilbur Ross, by pointing out the risks of such a change at this stage in the process. With only two years left to prepare, and limited testing, their concern was that the citizenship question would lower response rates, corrupt data, and increase errors on the decennial Census. The ACLU, NAACP, Urban League, LULAC, and other organizations quickly denounced the new citizenship question as politically motivated and dangerous. Ironically, the nation's institutions most often at the forefront of Civil Rights legislation were the ones most vehemently opposed to the inclusion of a citizenship question, despite Secretary Ross's claim that it was for the enforcement of Civil Rights legislation. This was soon followed by a coalition of 19 attorney generals led by Attorney General Schneiderman from New York, suing the federal government on behalf of their constituents. The collective sentiment from the left and those involved most directly with administering the U.S. Census was that including citizenship on the census is wrong-headed and irresponsible.

The first, and perhaps most immediate concern, raised by most of these groups was timing. Typically, questions undergo several years of testing and retesting before final approval. This is important as it gives

the Census Bureau time to test the effects of new questions, question order, and question format on the census. Not doing so, runs the risk of increasing non-response rates, misunderstandings, and other forms of data contamination associated with poorly designed questions. Even something as minor as switching the order of questions, as was done with the Hispanic/non-Hispanic question on the 1990 and 2000 census can have a significant effect on population characteristics and takes years of testing. "Any effort to ascertain citizenship," says the Census Bureau, "will inevitably jeopardize the overall accuracy of the population count" (486 F. Supp. 564, 568 D.D.C. 1980).

Another concern is one of cost. The U.S. Census Bureau has been underfunded for years. Attempts to request additional funds were eventually met with a small infusion of money, though costs will continue to rise as we approach 2020. Furthermore, the inclusion of citizenship will likely indirectly increase costs by increasing non-response rates to the census, something everyone agrees is likely with the addition of citizenship. Because every non-response must be followed up, sometimes multiple times, the cost can add up very quickly. The reasons for this non-response are complex, but focus groups suggest that there are already concerns about the confidentiality of questions and trust with the data, in particular among Spanish-speaking respondents. Fears about immigration raids, deportation, and the use of census data for spying on respondents were all cited as major concerns for individuals involved in these focus groups. The lack of trust identified in these focus groups translated to either increases in non-response rates or deceptive responses (CSM 2017). This is an ongoing concern by Census administrators that seems to coincide with the current political climate.

The response by Secretary Wilbur Ross to these concerns was largely dismissive. In regards to response rates, and issues around trust, Secretary Ross felt that the "need for accurate citizenship data and the limited burden that the reinstatement of the citizenship question would impose outweigh fears about a potentially lower response rate." He suggested that lack of trust in the government's ability to collect data on the public had little to do with the inclusion or exclusion of the citizenship question and that to date no one has "provided evidence that reinstating a citizenship question on the decennial census would materially decrease response rates among those who generally distrusted government and government information collection efforts, disliked the current administration, or feared law."

Admittedly, Secretary Ross recognized there would be some increase in expense associated with a change but it would be minimal. He argued that the current use of citizenship on the ACS obviated the claim that extensive testing and re-testing needed to be done, thereby decreasing implementation costs significantly. Indeed, Secretary Ross claimed, opposition to the inclusion of a citizenship question were unfounded or based on little or no evidence. To his credit, Secretary Ross is correct. There is very little evidence about the effects of what adding a citizenship question would do to the Census, but there is good reason for this. Namely, there has been little research on the effects of such a change. It is one thing to claim that there is no evidence to support an argument after conducting tests only to find little or no support for one's claims. It is another to deny the research entirely and claim no evidence exists to support a claim. The latter scenario is closer to what we have with the current adoption of the citizenship question on the decennial Census under the Trump administration. At the directive of Secretary Ross, we will be adding an untested, last minute question to the decennial census with little knowledge about what impact it will have on the overall accuracy of the census. And this is where most tension around the new citizenship question derives.

In an era of changing demographics, politicians are worried about the effects of these changing demographics on the distribution of votes across the country. The Census is but one site of the coming political battles we will see going in to the twenty-first century as political parties jockey for power in a world in flux. The old principle of "one person, one vote" puts Republicans at a disadvantage and dilutes their political power as more non-whites and immigrants enter the country who traditionally vote Democrat. Interestingly, with only a few tweaks to the system, the Republicans stand to gain significant leverage in the ability to control the redistricting of Congressional districts by changing the ways in which we count the population for redistricting. This seems on its surface somewhat superficial, but the power to count and the ability to dictate how counting will take place cannot be understated. By changing the process by which we allocate congressional seats, Republicans can gain significant advantages across the country, giving the Republican Party lasting power well in to the twenty-first century. While much opposition exists, this is

but one battle in a larger political war that may or may not pay off. It is a gamble, but a gamble worth taking. It is a dangerous gamble though and should come with a warning. The very same tools that are used to gain power in the present may be turned on them at some point in an attempt to take power back.

Opponents stand by their claims that the last-minute inclusion of a citizenship question is an irresponsible way to enact policy. While some oppose it entirely or see it as unnecessary given its current presence on the ACS, others see it as rushed and sloppy. There is no monolithic opposition to it, but there are concerns about how it will be implemented. Claims that it is needed for enforcement of Section 2 of the Voting Rights Act are met with an air of suspicion as no court has ever requested a need for CVAP data on the decennial Census to enforce Section 2 of the Voting Rights Act. Likewise, we have sufficient ACS data on citizenship down to the block group readily available, so it seems hard to believe that suddenly there is a need for block level information on citizenship. Opponents are most worried however, not about a depression in response rates, which would be an added bonus for conservatives, but about the politicization of the Census in ways that dilute the power of individuals and consolidate political power by changing the rules of the game.

In the end, the inclusion of citizenship may or may not be as bad as opponents to its inclusion suggest. It seems likely to increase non-response rates, but that was already happening so it is difficult to identify causal order. Other countries certainly count using citizenship, and the UN recommends it as a variable to include on all censuses. The bigger concern we should have as citizens of a democracy is the politicization of the census in a haphazard way that pays little attention to the rational, scientific logic of the U.S. Census Bureau and prioritizes the immediate needs of a political party over the interests of its citizens. The most irresponsible thing we can do is begin implementation of a question that has never been tested in a field environment and is already a politically charged question in a polarized political climate.

Perhaps even more worrisome is the second mandate to the Wilbur Ross request, which has so far received less publicity, but may be just as dangerous. Namely, the mandate to link administrative data across sources and explore its feasibility as a means for determining total populations. One of the unique things about the decennial census is that it is a relatively transparent process, open to public input and simple to understand. Big data linkages of administrative data will likely be done behind the scenes and "off the radar" with little or no input from the public. The fact that we can discuss in an open venue the costs and benefits of adding citizenship to the census suggest we have some input in to the final product and is a testament to the democratic process. My fear with linked administrative data sets is that this process will be less transparent and as a result less democratic. But that is a battle for another day.

References

Beveridge, Andrew A. 2016. The Threat to Representation for Children and Non-Citizens: An Analysis of the Potential Impact of *Evenwel v. Abbott on Redistricting*. https://static.socialexplorer.com/evenwel/Evenwell_Impact_Report.pdf.

Center for Survey Measurement (CSM). 2017. Respondent Confidentiality Concerns. U.S. Census Bureau.

Hartnett, C. (2000). Principles and Recommendations for Population and Housing Censuses, Revision 1–United Nations, New York, 1998. *Journal of Government Information*, 27(2), 250–254.

Kukutai, Thau, and Victor Thompson. (2018). Ethnicity Counts? dataset, National Institute of Demographic and Economic and Analysis.

Ross, Wilbur. 2018. Reinstatement of a Citizenship Question on the 2020 Decennial Census Questionnaire. March 26, 2018. U.S. Department of Commerce.

United Nations. 2017. *Principles and Recommendations for Population and Housing Censuses, Revision 3*. United Nations.

U.S. Census Bureau. 2016. *American Community Survey: Why We Ask*.

U.S. Census Bureau. 2017. https://www2.census.gov/programs-surveys/acs/about/qbyqfact/2016/AmericanCommunitySurveyPopulationQuestions.pdf.

Understanding the Reading

1. What probable effect would suddenly adding a citizenship question on the ten-year U.S. Census (population register) have on the response rate?

2. Republicans want to change their district counts so only eligible voters are counted. How would this help them stay in power?

3. Why is the author concerned about the "politicization of the census"?

Suggestion for Responding

1. Become familiar with the term "gerrymandering" and be able to explain how and why strangely shaped Congressional districts are created.

Suggestions for Responding to Part VII

1. Read an American newspaper of note (e.g., *New York Times, Washington Post, L.A. Times*, or *Chicago Tribune*) at least three times a week, looking for news of world interest and opinion pieces on the op-ed page. Also read a foreign newspaper (onlinenewspapers.com) and compare news coverage of the same story. Divide the class so that some are especially responsible for each continent or region of the world. Take note of which newspapers are state controlled (*Arab News* or *China Daily*, for example). Also note that the rest of the world seems to know much more about the United States than we do about the rest of the world.

2. Research whether your surrounding community has received refugees from abroad. Find creative ways to discover how they are faring. Are the children happy in school? Are the parents working? Are they underemployed? Are these families considered an integral part of the community? Research how other parts of the country react toward their refugees.

3. Research two activist groups: the Feminist Majority and Women's International League for Peace and Freedom (WILPF). The Feminist Majority, founded in 1987, has a very useful human rights watch newswire (feminist.org), which includes world news as well as national news. WILPF is nearly one hundred years old (Jane Addams was its first president) and is an official nongovernmental organization, recognized by the United Nations. It, too, works locally, nationally, and

worldwide. Invite speakers to your class representing each of these two agencies. Ask the WILPF representative about "The Raging Grannies."

4. Have a class discussion on ways of balancing national security with respect for civil rights. Compare America's ideals with what you see implemented by our different levels of government.

5. Compare the United States with other countries' reactions and solutions to "difference" as they struggle with their rapidly changing population. For example, France has a policy of not publicly wearing religious symbols and religious articles of clothing, such as the hijab, niqab, and yarmulke.

Suggestions for Responding to Power

Research one manifestation of racism and sexism or classism that you read about in this book. As an individual, you will want to focus on what may seem to be a very small part of the problem, but a group could investigate a broader problem, breaking it into its component parts, with each group member assuming responsibility for one aspect.

As a group, you could investigate sexual harassment; as an individual, you could focus on something like sexual harassment on your campus. A group could look at housing segregation; individually, you could consider redlining (refusing credit to residents and businesses in certain locations) in your community. A group could research the issue of domestic battery, but individually you could research the cycle of violence. Or a group could examine current incidents of racial or homophobic harassment, but one person could concentrate on his or her campus or community.

Other broad areas for research include government policies affecting Native Americans; "scientific proof" of the inferiority of a racial, religious, or gender group; racist, sexist, or homophobic social policies; the race and/or gender wage gap; one facet of the history of racism or sexism in American law; organized racism, historically or at present; a manifestation of discrimination in education or employment; or the federal government's response or nonresponse to a community in crisis—one affluent and another with a large poor population.

Report on both the causes and the effects of the problem. Also include information about efforts that have already been made to alleviate or at least ameliorate the problem, and discuss how effective or unsuccessful they have been and why.

If your instructor plans to have you develop a "plan for action" in response to *Power*, you probably want to select a topic for this assignment that particularly concerns you and that you would like to see changed.

As with earlier assignments, your instructor may ask you or your group to present your findings orally to your classmates.

Change

CHANGE IS NOT ONLY POSSIBLE but also an inevitable part of life. Seasons pass. We grow older. This kind of natural change is beyond our control. We adjust to many changes without taking much notice. Conversely, there is **social change**, caused and controlled by people acting individually and collectively. Most of us think of social change as resulting from mass **social movements**, coalitions of groups and individuals seeking to revise social policies and transform social institutions. We recognize the strategies and achievements of the major American social movements that have affected the groups we have been reading about: abolition and civil rights, labor unions and consumer rights, woman suffrage and women's liberation, and gay and lesbian rights. This kind of direct collective action is probably the most effective way to promote social change, but it requires the strong commitment of many people who agree and will act on common objectives. However, social change does not necessarily depend on large-scale political activism. In fact, each of us in our daily life participates in the processes of social change.

You may think this does not apply to you. For example, you may never have been interested in social issues, much less consider yourself a social activist, but this does not mean you have no impact on the shape of society. You may not consider yourself prejudiced, but when a friend tells you a racial joke, you might laugh so you will not offend her. Your laughter, however, indicates your approval of the joke's racist assumptions and, without your being aware of it, you have added one more stitch to the racist fabric of our society. In contrast, had you made a quiet comment that you do not care for that kind of joke, you could have begun to unravel at least one little thread. Both what you do and what you do not do influence social values.

Many of the issues raised in the first two divisions of this book are very disturbing. Because stereotypes are arbitrary oversimplifications, they blind us to the individuality of members of stereotyped groups and the rich potential of our diverse society. Prejudice, in turn, rests on such stereotyped thinking and encourages discrimination, sexism, heterosexism, racism, and classism. These "isms" support the beliefs and behaviors that lead to the pervasive neglect, exploitation, subordination, and oppression of women, minorities, the LGBTQ community, and the poor. This is a problem not just for members of these groups but for all Americans because systemic exclusion of so many people from full participation diminishes society by depriving us of their full skills, talents, wisdom, and creativity. Moreover, prejudiced convictions, and the behaviors that grow out of them, violate the most basic tenets of American society, the principles of freedom, equality, and justice. In other words, the practice of marginalizing groups is *a way of thinking*—it is not because of the presence of that group that discrimination occurs. Without a "traditional" group to oppress, another must be found, unless this behavior is no longer tolerated.

As troubling and discouraging as an awareness of these social problems may be, we do not need to accept them as inevitable or unalterable. They can be changed, and we can be instrumental in the process of effecting such change. We already have begun that process by learning about these issues, for we cannot begin to address a problem until we see and understand it. But such knowledge is only the first step.

This division, *Change*, is intended to show how to make the changes we want. Part VIII, *Taking Action*, gives us an understanding of the nature and dynamics of social change. By learning the step-by-step process of creating social change, we can see how to be more effective contributors to society. Of course, not everyone desires or supports certain social changes. In fact, some people will try to obstruct our efforts; others will resort to direct action to inhibit certain changes. However, people continue to exert their energies to make things better, at least according to their values. Part IX, *Change Makers*, explores how people have worked to change their own lives and the world around them. This final section of the text challenges us to apply the knowledge we have gained and to articulate problems and possible solutions to the specific circumstances of this millennium. Together these readings will increase our sense of our ability to control our own lives and to influence the society in which we live.

Part VIII
Taking Action

AT ONE TIME OR ANOTHER, WE ALL WANT TO CHANGE something—our looks, our behavior, what happens to us or to others. This is one reason you are in school: you want your life to be different than it otherwise would be. Part VIII provides information about how to make change occur—how to think about problems, how to plan what we want to do, and how to do it. When we understand the way to approach change logically, we are better able to initiate and effect change ourselves.

This part describes a six-step process to effect change. By the end of part VIII, you will understand both how social change is created and how to make such change yourself.

The first basic step in the process is **identifying the problem**. We tend initially to see a problem in its broadest form, such as the general issue of homelessness. But that problem is so extensive that it feels overwhelming, so we are likely just to shrug our shoulders and dismiss it. After all, "What can one person do?" We *can* do something, though. First, we must learn as much as we can about the specific issues that underlie the larger problem. This information will help us identify and define a specific, concrete issue to work on. Homelessness, for example, has numerous causes for us to consider: an apartment fire, high rents and low incomes in the community, job loss, family breakups, and neglected addictions or mental illness. Another way of thinking about this issue is to think about its consequences, such as lack of economic resources, sanitary facilities, or safety.

The first selection (reading 58) focuses on the attorney general of the United States, Eric Holder Jr., who has promised to use the full weight of his office's authority to protect the basic right of U.S. citizens to vote in the next election. Meanwhile, some states are instituting laws that target minorities, the poor, and students. Preventing these groups from voting has become an important strategy for certain power holders.

This brings us to the second step in the change process: **identifying the desired outcome**—that is, defining what specific change we would like to see. In reading 59, Arturo Madrid considers his personal experiences of being seen as the "other" and concludes that America and Americans must come to terms with the diversity of our society, his desired outcome. In reading 60, Derek Schork, as a teenager, tries (in a very dramatic way) to elicit an apology from a middle-aged man, who mistakenly concludes that he is parking in a handicapped space illegally. In the following essay (reading 61), Ricard Tolman gives us five ways to help prevent domestic violence, the lynchpin being the involvement and commitment of men.

The third step is **developing strategies** for realizing the goal. Our first idea is probably not our best idea. We are better off considering many alternatives. Brainstorming—letting our minds wander freely—is a good approach. Take plenty of time, alone or with a group, to generate as many different ideas as possible. At this stage, do not censor yourself in any way; in fact, try to be as imaginative and creative as possible because what might at first seem an unrealistic strategy can sometimes trigger an original, workable solution. This is what Charlotte Bunch is doing in reading 62 as she explores ways of bringing her feminist vision to bear on the public arena. Her "anything is possible" approach results in her suggesting many inventive tactics that most of us never would have dreamed of. Similarly, Andrew Kimbrell (reading 63) explores ways that men can work for change in their relationships with their families, with the environment, and in the community. Try brainstorming tactics that could be used to help homeless persons get jobs; see how many you can list. You might realize, for instance, that, without a home, even qualified people have nowhere to receive responses to job applications. You could help solve this problem by figuring out a way to provide them with a mailing address.

Step four is **developing a plan for action**. Select the most appropriate strategies from your brainstorming and figure how to implement them. Be realistic. Consider what resources you have access to: time, energy, people, money, materials, and so on. Think about how you can augment them. After brainstorming about everything that needs to be done, develop a time line—a schedule of what needs to be done and in what order.

What could you do to help homeless people receive mail service? Probably very little by yourself, but if you interest others in working with you, you might create an effective solution. For example, you could solicit funds to pay rent on a post office box and distribute its contents at a prearranged location once a day. You could approach a church that already has a soup kitchen to feed homeless persons and offer to help church members establish a mail service for homeless jobseekers at the church's address. There are many other ways to tackle this problem. Once you settle on your approach, develop your plan: the resources you need, your time frame, whom you need to work with you, and so on.

Once you have carefully mapped out your action project, your next step, the fifth, is **implementing the plan**. One major difficulty you will face at this stage is motivating people, getting them to act, to agree with you or your analysis of the problem, to support or perhaps even just to accept the desirability of the change you wish to implement. This is often the most crucial part of effecting social change. People resist change because we all tend to be more comfortable with the familiar, even when we realize that it is not perfect; we all value the security of living with what we already know.

Taking action and creating social change is easiest, of course, if you have the power and authority to require people to change their attitude and behavior. However, seemingly powerless people can also create tremendous changes by organizing and working together. For example, the March for Our Lives took place in Washington, D.C., and many other cities and towns all over the world in 2018, as a response to the gun massacre in Parkland, Florida. Throughout the country, small groups of youth have worked together to articulate what their goals are and to devise strategies to achieve gun control. They have successfully used social media, and the movement is strengthening.

The final step in any good plan for social change is **evaluating your actions**—assessing the effectiveness of your endeavor and identifying the reasons for its successes and its disappointments. This is a very important step. Appraising the degree of your achievement can enhance your sense of a job well done, contributing to the satisfaction of everyone working with you. Identifying weaknesses in your project can help you plan better strategies to use in future actions. Evaluation is not simply a matter of determining whether the plan worked; it is much more a function of one's beliefs and expectations. People determine the relative success of a project based on a wide variety of standards, values, attitudes, and expectations. What one person considers a success another may perceive to be a failure.

Evaluative judgments differ when they rest on different priorities or value systems. In reading 64, "Freedom for the Thought We Hate," Gerald Gunther, a law professor, evaluates college and university policies that prohibit racist, sexist, and other types of harassing language or acts on their campuses. He opposes them because he believes they violate our constitutional freedom of speech.

The final reading, "The Oklahoma Teachers' Strike Is Twenty-Six Years in the Making," is written by Jon Hazell. Twenty-six years of fighting for respect and funding for public schools can be seen as failure or success, but it clearly represents an unstoppable force of committed educators, responding to their children's diminishing access to an excellent education.

An awareness of these six steps makes it easier for us to work for social changes that we desire. However, change is never easy. Each step requires a substantial investment of time and thought, and the more basic or extensive the desired change is, the more difficult it will be to achieve. Successful action demands thorough research, careful thought, strong motivation, extensive planning, and lots of time. If you commit yourself, however, you can do more than you probably think you can.

58

Attorney General Eric Holder Speaks at the Lyndon Baines Johnson Library and Museum

Eric Holder

Thank you, Mark [Updegrove]. It is a pleasure to be with you—and to join so many friends, colleagues, and critical partners in welcoming some of our nation's most dedicated and effective civil rights champions—as well as the many University of Texas law students who are here, and who will lead this work into the future.

I'd also like to thank Mark and his staff, as well as the Lyndon Baines Johnson Library and Museum's board members and community of supporters, for providing a forum for today's conversation—and for all that you do, not only to honor the life and legacy of our thirty-sixth commander-in-chief but also to build upon his historic efforts to ensure the strength, integrity, and future of our democracy.

Nearly half a century has passed since a national tragedy catapulted Lyndon Johnson to the presidency, and at the same time launched a new chapter in America's story. Those of us who lived through those painful days will never forget LBJ's first presidential speech—to a nation in mourning, and in desperate need of strong and steady leadership. After quoting the 1961 inaugural address in which President Kennedy famously declared, "Let us begin," President Johnson outlined the unfinished business of the civil rights agenda. Then—with three simple words—he gave voice to the goals of his presidency, and issued a challenge that has echoed through the ages: "Let us continue."

In fulfilling this directive, President Johnson—and the many leaders, activists, and ordinary citizens who shared his vision and determination—set our country on a course toward remarkable, once-unimaginable, progress. Together, they opened new doors of opportunity, helping to ensure equal access to schools and public spaces, to restaurants and workplaces, and—perhaps most important of all—to the ballot box. Our great nation was transformed.

In 1965, when President Johnson signed the landmark Voting Rights Act into law, he proclaimed that, "the right to vote is the basic right, without which all others are meaningless."

Today, as attorney general, I have the privilege—and the solemn duty—of enforcing this law, and the other civil rights reforms that President Johnson championed. This work is among the Justice Department's most important priorities. And our efforts honor the generations of Americans who have taken extraordinary risks, and willingly confronted hatred, bias, and ignorance—as well as billy clubs and fire hoses, bullets and bombs—to ensure that their children, and all American citizens, would have the chance to participate in the work of their government. The right to vote is not only the cornerstone of our system of government—it is the lifeblood of our democracy. And no force has proved more powerful—or more integral to the success of the great American experiment—than efforts to expand the franchise.

Despite this history, and despite our nation's long tradition of extending voting rights—to non-property owners and women, to people of color and Native Americans, and to younger Americans—today, a growing number of our fellow citizens are worried about the same disparities, divisions, and problems that—nearly five decades ago—LBJ devoted his presidency to addressing. In my travels across this country, I've heard a consistent drumbeat of concern from many Americans, who—often for the first time in their lives—now have reason to believe that we are failing to live up to one of our nation's most noble, and essential, ideals.

As Congressman John Lewis described it, in a speech on the House floor this summer, the voting rights that he worked throughout his life—and nearly gave his life—to ensure are, "under attack . . . [by] a deliberate and systematic attempt to prevent millions of elderly voters, young voters, students, [and] minority and low-income voters from exercising their constitutional right to engage in the democratic process." Not only was he referring to the all-too-common deceptive practices we've been fighting for years. He was echoing more recent concerns about some of the state-level voting law changes we've seen this legislative season.

Since January, more than a dozen states have advanced new voting measures. Some of these new laws are currently under review by the Justice Department, based on our obligations under the Voting Rights Act. Texas and South Carolina, for example, have enacted laws establishing new photo identification requirements that we're reviewing. We're also examining a number of changes that Florida has made to its electoral process, including changes to the procedures governing third-party voter registration organizations, as well as changes to early voting procedures, including the number of days in the early voting period.

Although I cannot go into detail about the ongoing review of these and other state-law changes, I can assure you that it will be thorough—and fair. We will examine the facts, and we will apply the law. If a state passes a new voting law and meets its burden of showing that the law is not discriminatory, we will follow the law and approve the change. And where a state can't meet this burden, we will object as part of our obligation under Section 5 of the Voting Rights Act.

As many of you know—and as I hope the law students here are learning—Section 5 was put in place decades ago because of a well-documented history of voter discrimination in all or parts of the sixteen states to which it applies. Within these "covered jurisdictions," any proposed change in voting procedures or practices—from moving a polling location to enacting a statewide redistricting plan—must be "precleared"—that is, approved—either by the Justice Department or by a panel of federal judges.

Without question, Sections 5's preclearance process has been a powerful tool in combating discrimination for decades. In 2006, it was reauthorized with overwhelming bipartisan support—passing the House by a vote of 390 to 33, and the Senate by a vote of 98 to zero—before being signed into law by President Bush.

Despite the long history of support for Section 5, this keystone of our voting rights laws is now being challenged five years after its reauthorization as unconstitutional in no fewer than five lawsuits. Each of these lawsuits claims that we've attained a new era of electoral equality, that America in 2011 has moved beyond the challenges of 1965, and that Section 5 is no longer necessary.

I wish this were the case. The reality is that—in jurisdictions across the country—both overt and subtle forms of discrimination remain all too common. And we don't have to look far to see recent proof.

For example, in October, the Justice Department objected to a redistricting plan in East Feliciana Parish, Louisiana, where the map-drawer began the process by meeting exclusively with white officeholders—and never consulted black officeholders. The result was a map that diminished the electoral opportunity of African Americans. After the Justice Department objected, the parish enacted a new, nondiscriminatory map.

And, here in Texas, just two months ago, the department argued in court filings that proposed redistricting plans for both the state House and the Texas congressional delegation are impermissible, because the state has failed to show the absence of discrimination. The most recent Census data indicated that Texas has gained more than 4 million new residents—the vast majority of whom are Hispanic—and that this growth allows for four new congressional seats. However, this state has proposed adding zero additional seats in which Hispanics would have the electoral opportunity envisioned by the Voting Rights Act. Federal courts are still considering this matter, and we intend to argue vigorously at trial that this is precisely the kind of discrimination that Section 5 was intended to block.

To those who argue that Section 5 is no longer necessary—these and other examples are proof that we still need this critical tool to combat discrimination and safeguard the right to vote.

As concerns about the protection of this right and the integrity of our election systems become an increasingly prominent part of our national dialogue—we must consider some important questions. It is time to ask: what kind of nation—and what kind of people—do we want to be? Are we willing to allow this era—our era—to be remembered as the age when our nation's proud tradition of expanding the franchise ended? Are we willing to allow this time—our time—to be recorded in history as the age when the long-held belief that, in this country, every citizen has the chance—and the right—to help shape their government, became a relic of our past, instead of a guidepost for our future?

For me—and for our nation's Department of Justice—the answers are clear. We need election systems that are free from fraud, discrimination, and partisan influence—and that are more, not less, accessible to the citizens of this country.

Under this administration, our Civil Rights Division—and its Voting Section—have taken meaningful steps to ensure integrity, independence, and transparency in our enforcement of the Voting Rights Act. We have worked successfully and comprehensively to protect the voting rights of U.S. service members and veterans, and to enforce other laws that protect Americans living abroad, citizens with disabilities, and language minorities. As part of our aggressive enforcement of the "Motor Voter" law, this year alone, we filed two statewide lawsuits to enforce the requirement that voter registration opportunities be made available at a wider variety of government offices—beyond just the local Department of Motor Vehicles. And we're seeing promising results from this work. For example, after filing a lawsuit in Rhode Island, we reached an agreement with state agencies that resulted in more voters being registered in the first full month after our lawsuit than in the entire previous two-year reporting period.

We're also working to ensure that the protections for language minorities included in the Voting Rights Act are aggressively enforced. These protections now apply to more than 19 million voting-age citizens. These are our Spanish-speaking friends and neighbors, our Chinese-speaking friends and neighbors, and a large and growing part of all our communities. In just the past year, we've filed three lawsuits to protect their rights. And, today, we're actively reviewing nationwide compliance.

But the Justice Department can't do it all. Ensuring that every veteran, every senior, every college student, and every eligible citizen has the right to vote must become our common cause. And, for all Americans, protecting this right, ensuring meaningful access, and combating discrimination must be viewed, not only as a legal issue—but as a moral imperative.

Just as we recently saw in Maine—where voters last month overturned a legislative proposal to end same-day voter registration—the ability to shape our laws remains in the hands of the American people.

Tonight, I'd like to highlight three areas where public support will be crucial in driving progress—and advancing much-needed reforms. The first involves deceptive election practices—and dishonest efforts to prevent certain voters from casting their ballots.

Over the years, we've seen all sorts of attempts to gain partisan advantage by keeping people away from the polls—from literacy tests and poll taxes, to misinformation campaigns telling people that Election Day has been moved, or that only one adult per household can cast a ballot. Before the 2004 elections, fliers were distributed in minority neighborhoods in Milwaukee, falsely claiming that "[I]f anybody in your family has ever been found guilty [of a crime], you can't vote in the presidential election"—and you risk a 10-year prison sentence if you do. Two years later, 14,000 Latino voters in Orange County, California, received mailings, warning in Spanish, "[If] you are

an immigrant, voting in a federal election is a crime that can result in jail time." Both of these blatant falsehoods likely deterred some eligible citizens from going to the polls.

And, just last week, the campaign manager of a Maryland gubernatorial candidate was convicted on election fraud charges for approving anonymous "robocalls" that went out on Election Day last year to more than 100,000 voters in the state's two largest majority-black jurisdictions. These calls encouraged voters to stay home—telling them to "relax" because their preferred candidate had already wrapped up a victory.

In an effort to deter and punish such harmful practices, during his first year in the U.S. Senate, President Obama introduced legislation that would establish tough criminal penalties for those who engage in fraudulent voting practices—and would help to ensure that citizens have complete and accurate information about where and when to vote. Unfortunately, this proposal did not move forward. But I'm pleased to announce that—tomorrow—Senators Charles Schumer and Ben Cardin will reintroduce this legislation, in an even stronger form. I applaud their leadership—and I look forward to working with them as Congress considers this important legislation.

The second area for reform is the need for neutrality in redistricting efforts. Districts should be drawn to promote fair and effective representation for all—not merely to undercut electoral competition and protect incumbents. If we allow only those who hold elected office to select their constituents—instead of enabling voters to choose their representatives—the strength and legitimacy of our democracy will suffer.

One final area for reform that merits our strongest support is the growing effort—which is already underway in several states—to modernize voter registration. Today, the single biggest barrier to voting in this country is our antiquated registration system. According to the Census Bureau, of the 75 million adult citizens who failed to vote in the last presidential election, 60 million of them were not registered and, therefore, not eligible to cast a ballot.

All eligible citizens can and should be automatically registered to vote. The ability to vote is a right—it is not a privilege. Under our current system, many voters must follow cumbersome and needlessly complex voter registration rules. And every election season, state and local officials have to manually process a crush of new applications—most of them handwritten—leaving the system riddled with errors, and, too often, creating chaos at the polls.

Fortunately, modern technology provides a straightforward fix for these problems—if we have the political will to bring our election systems into the twenty-first century. It should be the government's responsibility to automatically register citizens to vote, by compiling—from databases that already exist—a list of all eligible residents in each jurisdiction. Of course, these lists would be used solely to administer elections—and would protect essential privacy rights.

We must also address the fact that although one in nine Americans move every year, their voter registration often does not move with them. Many would-be voters don't realize this until they've missed the deadline for registering, which can fall a full month before Election Day. Election officials should work together to establish a program of permanent, portable registration—so that voters who move can vote at their new polling place on Election Day. Until that happens, we should implement fail-safe procedures to correct voter-roll errors and omissions, by allowing every voter to cast a regular, nonprovisional ballot on Election Day. Several states have already taken this step, and it's been shown to increase turnout by at least three to five percentage points.

These modernization efforts would not only improve the integrity of our elections, they would also save precious taxpayer dollars.

Despite these benefits, there will always be those who say that easing registration hurdles will only lead to voter fraud. Let me be clear: voter fraud is not acceptable—and will not be tolerated by this Justice Department. But as I learned early in my career—as a prosecutor in the Justice Department's Public Integrity Section, where I actually investigated and prosecuted voting-fraud cases—making voter registration easier is simply not likely, by itself, to make our elections more susceptible to fraud. Indeed, those on all sides of this debate have acknowledged that in-person voting fraud is uncommon. We must be honest about this. And we must recognize that our ability to ensure the strength and integrity of our election systems—and to advance the reforms necessary to achieve this—depends on whether the American people are informed, engaged, and willing to demand commonsense solutions that make voting more accessible. Politicians may not readily alter the very systems under which they were elected. Only we, the people, can bring about meaningful change.

So speak out. Raise awareness about what's at stake. Call on our political parties to resist the temptation to suppress certain votes in the hope of attaining electoral success and, instead, encourage and work with the parties to achieve this success by appealing to more voters. And urge policymakers at every level to reevaluate our election systems—and to reform them in ways that encourage, not limit, participation.

Today, we cannot—and must not—take the right to vote for granted. Nor can we shirk the sacred responsibility that falls upon our shoulders.

Throughout his presidency, Lyndon Johnson frequently pointed out that, "America was the first nation in the history of the world to be founded with a purpose—to right wrong, [and] to do justice." Over the last two centuries, the fulfillment of this purpose has taken many forms—acts of protest and compassion, declarations of war and peace, and a range of efforts to make certain that, as another great president said, "government of . . . by . . . [and] for the people shall not perish from the Earth."

Today, there are competing visions about how our government should move forward. That's what the democratic process is all about—creating space for thoughtful debate, creating opportunity for citizens to voice their opinions, and ultimately letting the people chart their course. Our nation has worked, and even fought, to help people around the world establish such a process—most recently during the wave of civil rights uprisings known as the Arab Spring. Here at home, honoring our democracy demands that we remove any and all barriers to voting—a goal that all American citizens of all political backgrounds must share.

Despite so many decades of struggle, sacrifice, and achievement—we must remain ever vigilant in safeguarding our most basic and important right. Too many recent actions have the potential to reverse the progress that defines us—and has made this nation exceptional, as well as an example for all the world. We must be true to the arc of America's history, which compels us to be more inclusive with regard to the franchise. And we must never forget the purpose that—more than two centuries ago—inspired our nation's founding, and now must guide us forward.

So, let us act—with optimism and without delay. Let us rise to the challenges—and overcome the divisions—of our time. Let us signal to the world that—in America today—the pursuit of a more perfect union lives on.

And, in the spirit of Lyndon Baines Johnson, let us continue.

[2011]

Understanding the Reading

1. Why is there so much attention on voters' rights in this speech?
2. What are a few ways to intentionally discriminate against certain U.S. voters?
3. Why does Eric Holder say that our voting system is antiquated, and how could it be modernized?

Suggestions for Responding

1. Have a class discussion on patterns of discrimination against voters and voter identification fraud.
2. What are your state's laws about students voting?

59

Diversity and Its Discontents

ARTURO MADRID

My name is Arturo Madrid. I am a citizen of the United States, as are my parents and as were my grandparents and my great-grandparents. My ancestors' presence in what is now the United States antedates Plymouth Rock, even without taking into account any American Indian heritage I might have.

I do not, however, fit those mental sets that define America and Americans. My physical appearance, my speech patterns, my name, and my profession (a professor of Spanish) create a text that confuses the reader. My normal experience is to be asked, "And where are *you* from?" My response depends on my mood. Passive-aggressive, I answer, "From here." Aggressive-passive, I ask, "Do you mean where I am originally from?" But ultimately my answer to those follow-up questions that will ask about origins will be that we have always been from here.

Overcoming my resentment I try to educate, knowing that nine times out of ten my words fall on inattentive ears. I have spent most of my adult life explaining who I am not. I am exotic, but—as Richard Rodriguez of *Hunger of Memory* fame so painfully found out—not exotic enough . . . not Peruvian, or Pakistani, or whatever. I am, however, very clearly the *other*, if only your everyday, garden-variety, domestic

other. I will share with you another phenomenon that I have been a part of, that of being a missing person, and how I came late to that awareness. But I've always known that I was the *other*, even before I knew the vocabulary or understood the significance of otherness.

I grew up in an isolated and historically marginal part of the United States, a small mountain village in the state of New Mexico, the eldest child of parents native to that region, whose ancestors had always lived there. In those vast and empty spaces people who look like me, speak as I do, and have names like mine predominate. But the *americanos* lived among us: the descendants of those nineteenth-century immigrants who dispossessed us of our lands; missionaries who came to convert us and stayed to live among us; artists who became enchanted with our land and humanscape and went native; refugees from unhealthy climes, crowded spaces, unpleasant circumstances; and, of course, the inhabitants of Los Alamos,[1] whose sociocultural distance from us was accentuated by the fact that they occupied a space removed from and proscribed to us. More importantly, however, they—*los americanos*—were omnipresent (and almost exclusively so) in newspapers, newsmagazines, books, on radio, in movies, and, ultimately, on television.

Despite the operating myth of the day, school did not erase my otherness. It did try to deny it, and in doing so only accentuated it. To this day what takes place in schools is more socialization than education, but when I was in elementary school—and given where I was—socialization was everything. School was where one became an American, because there was a pervasive and systematic denial by the society that surrounded us that we were Americans. That denial was both explicit and implicit.

Quite beyond saluting the flag and pledging allegiance to it (a very intense and meaningful action, given that the United States was involved in a war and our brothers, cousins, uncles, and fathers were on the front lines), becoming American was learning English, and its corollary: not speaking Spanish. Until very recently ours was a proscribed language, either *de jure*—by rule, by policy, by law—or *de facto*—by practice, implicitly (if not explicitly), through social and political and economic pressure. I do not argue that learning English was not appropriate. On the contrary. Like it or not, and we had no basis to make any judgments on that matter, we were Americans by virtue of having been born Americans, and English was the common language of Americans. And there was a myth, a pervasive myth, to the effect that if only we learned to speak English well—and particularly without an accent—we would be welcomed into the American fellowship.

Sam Hayakawa[2] and the official English movement folks notwithstanding, the true text was not our speech, but rather our names and our appearance, for we would always have an accent, however perfect our pronunciation, however excellent our enunciation, however divine our diction. That accent would be heard in our pigmentation, our physiognomy, our names. We were, in short, the *other*.

Being the *other* involves contradictory phenomena. On the one hand, being the *other* frequently means being invisible. Ralph Ellison wrote eloquently about that experience in his magisterial novel, *Invisible Man*. On the other hand, being the *other* sometimes involves sticking out like a sore thumb. What is she/he doing here?

For some of us being the *other* is only annoying; for others it is debilitating; for still others it is damning. Many try to flee otherness by taking on protective colorations that provide invisibility, whether of dress or speech or manner or name. Only a fortunate few succeed. For the majority of us otherness is permanently sealed by physical appearance. For the rest, otherness is betrayed by ways of being, speaking, or doing.

The first half of my life I spent downplaying the significance and consequences of otherness. The second half has seen me wrestling to understand its complex and deeply ingrained realities; striving to fathom why otherness denies us a voice or visibility or validity in American society and its institutions; struggling to make otherness familiar, reasonable, even normal to my fellow Americans.

I spoke earlier of another phenomenon that I am a part of: that of being a missing person. Growing up in northern New Mexico I had only a slight sense of us being missing persons. *Hispanos*, as we called (and call) ourselves in New Mexico, were very much a part of the fabric of the society, and there were *hispano* professionals everywhere about me: doctors, lawyers, schoolteachers, and administrators. My people owned businesses, ran organizations, and were both appointed and elected public officials.

My awareness of our absence from the larger institutional life of the society became sharper when I went off to college, but even then it was attenuated

by the circumstances of history and geography. The demography of Albuquerque still strongly reflected its historical and cultural origins, despite the influx of Midwesterners and Easterners. Moreover, many of my classmates at the University of New Mexico were *hispanos*, and even some of my professors. I thought that would pertain at UCLA, where I began graduate studies in 1960. Los Angeles had a very large Mexican population and that population was visible even in and around Westwood and on the campus. Many of the groundskeepers and food-service personnel at UCLA were Mexican. But Mexican American students were few and mostly invisible, and I do not recall seeing or knowing a single Mexican American (or, for that matter, African American, Asian, or American Indian) professional on the staff or faculty of that institution during the five years I was there. Needless to say, people like me were not present in any capacity at Dartmouth College, the site of my first teaching appointment, and of course were not even part of the institutional or individual mind-set. I knew then that we—a we that had come to encompass American Indians, Asian Americans, African Americans, Puerto Ricans, and women—were truly missing persons in American institutional life.

Over the past three decades the *de jure* and *de facto* types of segregation that have historically characterized American institutions have been under assault. As a consequence, minorities and women have become part of American institutional life. Although there are still many areas where we are not to be found, the missing persons phenomenon is not as pervasive as it once was. However, the presence of the *other*, particularly minorities, in institutions and in institutional life resembles what we call in Spanish a *flor de tierra* (a surface phenomenon): we are spare plants whose roots do not go deep, vulnerable to inclemencies of an economic, or political, or social nature.

Our entrance into and our status in institutional life are not unlike a scenario set forth by my grandmother's pastor when she informed him that she and her family were leaving their mountain village to relocate to the Rio Grande Valley. When he asked her to promise that she would remain true to the faith and continue to involve herself in it, she asked why he thought she would do otherwise. "Doña Trinidad," he told her, "in the Valley there is no Spanish church. There is only an American church." "But," she protested, "I read and speak English and would be able to worship there." The pastor responded, "It is possible that they will not admit you, and even if they do, they might not accept you. And that is why I want you to promise me that you are going to go to church. Because if they don't let you in through the front door, I want you to go in through the back door. And if you can't get in through the back door, go in the side door. And if you are unable to enter through the side door I want you to go in through the window. What is important is that you enter and stay."

Some of us entered institutional life through the front door; others through the back door; and still others through side doors. Many, if not most, of us came in through windows, and continue to come in through windows. Of those who entered through the front door, some never made it past the lobby; others were ushered into corners and niches. Those who entered through back and side doors inevitably have remained in back and side rooms. And those who entered through windows found enclosures built around them. For, despite the lip service given to the goal of the integration of minorities into institutional life, what has frequently occurred instead is ghetto-ization, marginalization, isolation.

Not only have the entry points been limited, but the dynamics have also been singularly conflictive. Gaining entry and its corollary, gaining space, have frequently come as a consequence of demands made on institutions and institutional officers. Rather than entering institutions more or less passively, minori-ties have of necessity entered them actively, even aggressively. Rather than waiting to receive, they have demanded. Institutional relations have thus been adversarial, infused with specific and general-ized tensions.

The nature of the entrance and the nature of the space occupied have greatly influenced the view and attitude of the majority population within those insti-tutions. All of us are put into the same box—that is, no matter what the individual reality, the assessment of the individual is inevitably conditioned by a per-ception that is held of the class. Whatever our his-tory, whatever our record, whatever our validations, whatever our accomplishments, by and large we are perceived unidimensionally and dealt with accord-ingly. I remember an experience I had in this regard, atypical only in its explicitness. A few years ago I allowed myself to be persuaded to seek the presidency of a well-known state university. I was invited for an interview and presented myself before the selection committee, which included members of the board of trustees. The opening question of that brief but mem-

orable interview was directed at me by a member of that august body. "Dr. Madrid," he asked, "why does a one-dimensional person like you think he can be the president of a multidimensional institution like ours?" Over the past four decades America's demog-raphy has undergone significant changes. Since 1965 the principal demographic growth we have experi-enced in the United States has been of peoples whose national origins are non-European. This population growth has occurred both through birth and through immigration. A few years ago discussion of the national birthrate had a scare dimension: the high—"inordinately high"—birthrate of the Hispanic popu-lation. The popular discourse was informed by words such as "breeding." Several years later, as a conse-quence of careful tracking by government agencies, we now know that what has happened is that the birthrate of the majority population has decreased. When viewed historically and comparatively, the minority populations (for the most part) have also had a decline in birthrate, but not one as great as that of the majority.

There are additional demographic changes that should give us something to think about. African Americans are now to be found in significant num-bers in every major urban center in the nation. His-panic Americans now number over 15 million people, and although they are a regionally concentrated (and highly urbanized) population, there is a Hispanic community in almost every major urban center of the United States. American Indians, heretofore a small and rural population, are increasingly more numer-ous and urban. The Asian American population, which has historically consisted of small and concen-trated communities of Chinese, Filipino, and Japa-nese Americans, has doubled over the past decade, its complexion changed by the addition of Cambodians, Koreans, Hmongs, Vietnamese, et al.

Prior to the Immigration Act of 1965,[3] 69 percent of immigration was from Europe. By far the largest number of immigrants to the United States since 1965 have been from the Americas and from Asia: 34 percent are from Asia; another 34 percent are from Central and South America; 16 percent are from Europe; 10 percent are from the Caribbean; the remaining 6 percent are from other continents and Canada. As was the case with previous immigration waves, the current one consists principally of young people: 60 percent are between the ages of 16 and 44. Thus, for the next few decades, we will continue to see a growth in the percentage of non-European-origin Americans as compared to European Americans.

To sum up, we now live in one of the most demographically diverse nations in the world, and one that is increasingly more so.

During the same period social and economic change seems to have accelerated. Who would have imagined at mid-century that the prototypical middle-class family (working husband, wife as homemaker, two children) would for all intents and purposes disappear? Who could have anticipated the rise in teenage pregnancies, children in poverty, drug use? Who among us understood the implications of an aging population?

We live in an age of continuous and intense change, a world in which what held true yesterday does not today, and certainly will not tomorrow. What change does, moreover, is bring about even more change. The only constant we have at this point in our national development is change. And change is threatening. The older we get the more likely we are to be anxious about change, and the greater our desire to maintain the status quo.

Evident in our public life is a fear of change, whether economic or moral. Some who fear change are responsive to the call of economic protectionism, others to the message of moral protectionism. Parenthetically, I have referred to the movement to require more of students without in turn giving them more as academic protectionism. And the pronouncements of E. D. Hirsch and Allan Bloom[4] are, I believe, informed by intellectual protectionism. Much more serious, however, is the dark side of the populism[5] which underlies this evergoing protectionism—the resentment of the *other.* An excellent and fascinating example of that aspect of populism is the cry for linguistic protectionism—for making English the official language of the United States. And who among us is unaware of the tensions that underlie immigration reform, of the underside of demographic protectionism?

A matter of increasing concern is whether this new protectionism, and the mistrust of the *other* which accompanies it, is not making more significant inroads than we have supposed in higher education. Specifically, I wish to discuss the question of whether a goal (quality) and a reality (demographic diversity) have been erroneously placed in conflict, and, if so, what problems this perception of conflict might present.

As part of my scholarship, I turn to dictionaries for both origins and meanings of words. Quality, according to the *Oxford English Dictionary*, has multiple meanings. One set defines quality as being an essential character, a distinctive and inherent feature. A second describes it as a degree of excellence, of conformity to standards, as superiority in kind. A third makes reference to social status, particularly to persons of high social status. A fourth talks about quality as being a special or distinguishing attribute, as being a desirable trait. Quality is highly desirable in both principle and practice. We all aspire to it in our own person, in our experiences, in our acquisitions and products, and of course we all want to be associated with people and operations of quality.

But let us move away from the various dictionary meanings of the word and to our own sense of what it represents and of how we feel about it. First of all, we consider quality finite—that is, it is limited with respect to quantity; it has very few manifestations; it is not widely distributed. I have it and you have it, but they don't. We associate quality with homogeneity, with uniformity, with standardization, with order, regularity, neatness. All too often we equate it with smoothness, glibness, slickness, elegance. Certainly it is always expensive. We tend to identify it with those who lead, with the rich and famous. And, when you come right down to it, it's inherent. Either you've got or you ain't.

Diversity, from the Latin *divertere*, meaning to turn aside, to go different ways, to differ, is the condition of being different or having differences, is an instance of being different. Its companion word, diverse, means differing, unlike, distinct; having or capable of having various forms; composed of unlike or distinct elements. Diversity is lack of standardization, of regularity, of orderliness, homogeneity, conformity, uniformity. Diversity introduces complications, is difficult to organize, is troublesome to manage, is problematical. Diversity is irregular, disorderly, uneven, rough. The way we use the word diversity gives us away. Something is too diverse, is extremely diverse. We want a little diversity.

When we talk about diversity, we are talking about the *other,* whatever that other might be: someone of different gender, race, class, national origin; somebody at a greater or lesser distance from the norm; someone outside the set; someone who possesses a different set of characteristics, features, or attributes; someone who does not fall within the taxonomies we use daily and with which we are comfortable; someone who does not fit into the mental configurations that give our lives order and meaning.

In short, diversity is desirable only in principle, not in practice. Long live diversity . . . as long as it conforms to my standards, my mind set, my view of life, my sense of order. We desire, we like, we admire diversity, not unlike the way the French (and others) appreciate women—that is, *Vive la différence!*—as long as it stays in its place.

What I find paradoxical about and lacking in this debate is that diversity is the natural order of things. Evolution produces diversity. Margaret Visser, writing about food in her latest book, *Much Depends on Dinner*, makes an eloquent statement in this regard:

Machines like, demand, and produce uniformity. But nature loathes it: her strength lies in multiplicity and in differences. Sameness in biology means fewer possibilities and therefore weakness.

The United States, by its very nature, by its very development, is the essence of diversity. It is diverse in its geography, population, institutions, technology; its social, cultural, and intellectual modes. It is a society that at its best does not consider quality to be monolithic in form or finite in quantity, or to be inherent in class. Quality in our society proceeds in large measure out of the stimulus of diverse modes of thinking and acting; out of the creativity made possible by the different ways in which we approach things; out of diversion from paths or modes hallowed by tradition.

One of the principal strengths of our society is its ability to address, on a continuing and substantive basis, the real economic, political, and social problems that have faced and continue to face us. What makes the United States so attractive to immigrants is the protections and opportunities it offers; what keeps our society together is tolerance for cultural, religious, social, political, and even linguistic difference; what makes us a unique, dynamic, and extraordinary nation is the power and creativity of our diversity.

The true history of the United States is one of struggle against intolerance, against oppression, against xenophobia, against those forces that have prohibited persons from participating in the larger life of the society on the basis of their race, their gender, their religion, their national origin, their linguistic and cultural background. These phenomena are not consigned to the past. They remain with us and frequently take on virulent dimensions.

If you believe, as I do, that the well-being of a society is directly related to the degree and extent to which all of its citizens participate in its institutions, then you will have to agree that we have a challenge before us. In view of the extraordinary changes that are taking place in our society we need to take up the struggle again, irritating, grating, troublesome, unfashionable, unpleasant as it is. As educated and educator members of this society we have a special responsibility for ensuring that all American institutions, not just our elementary and secondary schools, our juvenile halls, or our jails, reflect the diversity of our society. Not to do so is to risk greater alienation on the part of a growing segment of our society; is to risk increased social tension in an already conflictive world; and, ultimately, is to risk the survival of a range of institutions that, for all their defects and deficiencies, provide us the opportunity and the freedom to improve our individual and collective lot.

Let me urge you to reflect on these two words— quality and diversity—and on the mental sets and behaviors that flow out of them. And let me urge you further to struggle against the notion that quality is finite in quantity, limited in its manifestations, or restricted by considerations of class, gender, race, or national origin; or that quality manifests itself only in leaders and not in followers, in managers and not in workers, in breeders and not in drones; or that it has to be associated with verbal agility or elegance of personal style; or that it cannot be seeded, nurtured, or developed.

Because diversity—the *other*—is among us, it will define and determine our lives in ways that we still do not fully appreciate, whether that other is women (no longer bound by tradition, house, and family); or Asians, African Americans, Indians, and Hispanics (no longer invisible, regional, or marginal); or our newest immigrants (no longer distant, exotic, alien). Given the changing profile of America, will we come to terms with diversity in our personal and professional lives? Will we begin to recognize the diverse forms that quality can take? If so, we will thus initiate the process of making quality limitless in its manifestations, infinite in quantity, unrestricted with respect to its origins, and more importantly, virulently contagious.

I hope we will. And that we will further join together to expand—not to close—the circle.

[1990]

Terms

1. Los Alamos: The military installation where scientists developed the atomic bomb.
2. Sam Hayakawa: The former president of San Francisco State University and an outspoken opponent of bilingual education.
3. Immigration Act of 1965: The federal law that abolished the national-origins quota system of immigration.
4. E. D. Hirsch and Allan Bloom: The authors, respectively, of *Cultural Illiteracy* and *The Closing of the American Mind*, both of which advocate a traditional curriculum.
5. Populism: A political philosophy that gives primacy to the needs of common people.

Understanding the Reading

1. Why does Madrid resent being asked where he is from?
2. What does he mean by being "other"?
3. What does he mean by referring to himself as "invisible" or a "missing person"?
4. What is the distinction between a school's erasing otherness and denying it?
5. Why did his grandmother's pastor feel that it was important for her to enter the church and stay?
6. What does Madrid mean by saying he is perceived unidimensionally?
7. Why does he find *breeding* an offensive term?
8. What point is Madrid making by giving the various dictionary meanings of *quality* and *diversity*?

Suggestion for Responding

1. Do you agree or disagree with Madrid that diversity is the basis for the "quality" of the United States? Why?

60

Breakfast at Perkins

DEREK SCHORK

Yes, stereotypes and prejudices have been a part of my thinking. I don't think anyone can honestly say that they have not had a prejudiced thought at one time or another, especially in the wake of 9/11. I'd rather not go into detail about these thoughts, as I am not particularly proud of them. However, there was one time that comes to mind when I was victimized by a stereotype. It made me very angry at the time, but now almost three years later, it's very easy for me and my friends, especially those who were there, to laugh about.

This story takes place on an early spring morning of my senior year in high school. You must know that I have a below-the-knee amputation of my left leg. This particular morning I was wearing jeans. Keep that in mind as you read on. A group of friends and I decided to go out for breakfast instead of going to school on time. When I pulled into the parking lot at Perkins Restaurant, I saw that there weren't any available parking spots on this side of the lot. Legally I am allowed to park in a handicapped spot and I have the designation that hangs from my mirror. I was running late and all of my friends were already inside, so I parked in one of the handicapped spots. As I got out of my car with my friend Jamie, an older man (mid-50s) was walking into the restaurant, when he stopped and looked at us and said, "Which one of you is handicapped? You should be ashamed of yourselves." This made me irate. Who was he to question us about where we parked? He made the stereotype of seeing two kids wearing long pants (so he couldn't see my prosthesis) and he assumed that there was no way a kid could be handicapped. Well, I started yelling at him to turn around, as I rolled up my pant leg. He wouldn't turn around, which made me even madder. At this point I think he realized that he had made a mistake but wouldn't admit it. So I continued to try to get his attention, this time by taking off my leg and hopping after him into the restaurant. Perkins Restaurant was not prepared for this scene—evident by the stunned looks on the faces of everyone as a cursing kid hopped in with leg in hand. The hostess tried to calm me down as the man walked to his seat and I reattached myself. My friends were having a good laugh as I went and sat down and explained to them what happened. If the old man had asked me nicely instead of making a stupid assumption, I would have had no problem explaining to him why I parked there. This story is now legendary among my friends. At least now it's a good story to tell.

[2002]

Understanding the Reading

1. Why weren't Schork and his friends in school on this particular morning?

2. Why did the man outside Perkins Restaurant assume he was parking illegally?
3. What made Schork so angry? What did he do?
4. What could have solved this problem?

Suggestion for Responding

1. Share memories with your classmates of someone making erroneous assumptions, about you or someone else, because of a physical aspect of that person. Share your own mistaken judgments as well.

61

Five Ways to Help Prevent Domestic Violence

RICHARD TOLMAN

Associated Press, March 1, 2018

Can President Donald Trump's recent repudiation of domestic violence actually help prevent it?

Rob Porter, a high-level aide to Trump, was accused of serial domestic violence by his two ex-wives. The controversy dominated news coverage earlier this month. Trump publicly denounced domestic violence one week after Porter resigned, saying "I'm totally opposed to domestic violence of any kind."

Those who called for such a statement by the president may be motivated by the belief that when powerful men convincingly call out abusers, society's acceptance of domestic violence can be diminished.

There is not a lot of research to support this commonsense idea. But there is a growing body of work with men and boys that research shows can be effective in diminishing domestic violence.

This is a significant evolution in the field. Since the establishment of the first domestic violence shelters in the 1970s, domestic violence policies and services have rightly focused most attention on survivors and meeting their needs for safety and healing.

Increasingly, though, domestic violence organizations are adopting approaches that involve men and boys in domestic violence prevention. The idea is that by addressing the root causes, these programs can stop domestic violence from occurring in the first place.

I am a professor who studies how to intervene and prevent men's violence against women. Our research team has researched the effectiveness of programs that involve boys and men in domestic violence prevention efforts.

Much of the work being done with men and boys is not well known, despite the fact that this is a thriving movement. Here is a snapshot of some of those efforts, both global and local, and what we know about their effectiveness.

1. Sports and Prevention

Some efforts to involve men are directed in the arena of sports because, well, men like sports. They venerate sports figures and identify with teams. Reports of domestic violence perpetrated by athletes have grown more common. This has led to visible efforts by sports organizations to respond with sanctions for perpetrators and to become part of prevention efforts, like the NFL's No More. The seriousness and effectiveness of these efforts are yet to be determined.

But sports have also been the site of innovative and effective interventions for youth. Coaching Boys into Men provides high school athletic coaches with the resources they need to help prevent relationship abuse, harassment, and sexual assault by their players.

The program's curriculum includes coach-to-athlete trainings that model respect and promote healthy relationships. It also includes a card series to help coaches incorporate themes of teamwork, integrity, fair play, and respect into their daily practice and routine.

Coaching Boys into Men has been rigorously evaluated and found to be effective in reducing dating violence, and it is being widely implemented in the United States and replicated in other countries.

2. Transition to Fatherhood

A prime risk factor for future abuse is the exposure of children to violence. Preventing abuse in new families would reduce children's exposure to violence and thus the potential for future violence.

One promising strategy is to involve men in prevention efforts as they move into fatherhood. Research shows that a caring and supportive relationship with their fathers reduces the risk of harsh physical discipline by the next generation of parents, for both fathers and mothers. Positive fathering predicts warmer and more positive parenting by adult sons when they become fathers.

Strategies that could be used in this area include engaging men at prenatal visits such as ultrasound appointments, which the vast majority of men in the United States attend, and at in-home visits during pregnancy and after the birth of a child.

Global campaigns such as MenCare seek to improve caregiving by fathers and address partner violence. MenCare's programs ask men to become more equitable partners and provide them with opportunities to learn and practice parenting skills. They promote policy change, like paid parental leave. And they conduct media campaigns to inspire men and their communities to support men's caregiving.

3. Preventing Dating Abuse

Studies document high levels of dating violence beginning in middle school. When it comes to prevention, one could argue that programs must intervene early or the effort will be wasted, because stopping abuse before it becomes an entrenched pattern is more likely to be effective in preventing relationship violence.

School-based abuse prevention programs like Safe Dates and Fourth R have shown some success in changing attitudes and behavior. The Safe Dates program, for example, uses nine fifty-minute sessions, a student-performed forty-five-minute play, and a poster contest to explore topics on how to cultivate caring relationships, overcome gender stereotypes, and help friends.

4. Bystander Programs

"Bystander" prevention programs, increasingly commonplace on college campuses, build skills to recognize, respond to, and disrupt behavior that might lead to sexual assault or intimate partner violence.

Some examples of bystander behavior include telling a man who is saying disrespectful things about women to stop or helping a woman who is being harassed to get away from a situation in which she could be harmed. Teens involved in bystander interventions are more likely to intervene to prevent victimization of their peers.

5. Motivating Men to Be Allies

Our research group surveyed men around the world who have been involved in efforts to prevent violence against women. The survey revealed that many men who get involved have a personal experience with violence—as child witnesses or survivors of their own child abuse. Still others find their way to prevention efforts through a commitment to social justice.

Importantly, we found that many men are receptive to violence prevention efforts when they tune in to survivors' experiences.

Given that men are moved by learning about survivors' experiences, the visibility of and emotional power of the #MeToo movement and the remarkable and vivid accounts of White House aide Rob Portman's ex-wives can lead men to get involved in ending violence against women.

Whatever the pathway, men's involvement in preventing domestic violence in their families, workplaces, and communities can be part of the global effort to promote safety and equality for women and to end victimization in all its forms.

Understanding the Reading

1. How are efforts today more effective in preventing domestic violence than in the 1970s?
2. Why has Coaching Boys into Men been so effective globally?
3. How do people motivate men to be allies in this initiative, and why are men receptive?

Suggestion for Responding

1. Have a class discussion of your own ideas about preventing domestic violence. Which of the article's strategies would you most like to see in your school or community?

62

Going Public with Our Vision

CHARLOTTE BUNCH

Transformational Politics and Practical Visions

To bring the feminist vision to bear on all issues and to counter the right-wing agenda for the future, require that we engage in multiple strategies for action. We must work on many fronts at once. If a movement becomes a single issue or single strategy, it runs the danger of losing its overall vision and diminishing its support, since different classes of people feel most intensely the pressure of different issues. So while we may say at any given moment that one issue is particularly crucial, it is important that work be done on other aspects of the changes we need at the same time. The task is not finding "the right issue," but bringing clear political analysis to each issue showing how it connects to other problems and to a broad-based feminist view of change in society.

Feminist concerns are not isolated, and oppression does not happen one-by-one-by-one in separate categories. I don't experience homophobia as a separate and distinct category from economic discrimination as a woman. I don't view racism as unconnected to militarism and patriarchal domination of the world.

In order to discuss the specific strategies necessary to get through this transition and bring feminism into the public arena more forcefully, we must first be clear that feminism is a transformational politics. As such, feminism brings a perspective to *any* issue and cannot and must not be limited to a separate ghetto called "women's issues." When dealing with any issue, whether it is budgets or biogenetics or wife battering, feminism as a political perspective is about change in structures—about ending domination and resisting oppression. Feminism is not just incorporating women into existing institutions.

As a politics of transformation, feminism is also relevant to more than a constituency of women. Feminism is a vision born of women that we must offer to and demand of men. I'm tired of letting men off the hook by saying that we don't know whether they can be feminists, just as I can and must struggle to be antiracist. If feminism is to be a transforming perspective in the world, then men must also be challenged by it.

This does not mean that we do not also need spaces and organizations for women only. Women need and want and have the right to places where we gather strength and celebrate our culture and make plans only with women. But as a political vision, feminism addresses the future for men as well as for women, for boys as well as for girls, and we must be clear that it is a politics for the future of the world, not just for an isolated handful of the converted.

If we are clear about feminism as a transformational politics, we can develop viable public alternatives to Reaganism and all patriarchal policies. These would be policy statements of how we think the world could be organized in various areas if a feminist approach is taken.

We need feminist budgets for every town, state, and nation. For example, you could take the state budget in Montana, whatever it is, take the same amount of money and prepare a budget of how you would reorganize the use of that money if feminists had control of the state government. When you finish that one, you can do a federal budget. And when you finish that, take on the UN budget! Budgets are good indicators of priorities. If we publicized our approaches, people could see that there are alternatives, that we are talking about something different, and they would get a clearer idea of what a feminist perspective means in practical terms.

I would also like to see feminist plans for housing, transportation, criminal justice, child care, education, agriculture, and so on. We need serious discussion as feminists about how we deal with the issues of defense, not only by doing critiques of militarism but also by deciding how to cope with the competing powers and threats in this world, as they exist right now. We're not going to solve many of the problems immediately, but we have to put forward other policies and practices, so people can see the difference. If we start with how things are now, then we can talk about how to move, step-by-step, toward policies that are based on very different assumptions and values.

To use such feminist policy statements, when we engage in electoral politics for example, would give people a clear and public statement of what it means to elect a feminist. We would also have something concrete to hold a candidate accountable to after election. To work to elect feminists with clear policy content makes a campaign focus on feminism as a transforming politics rather than just on personality or on adding women without clear political statements of what they represent. It can make electoral politics part of a strategy for change rather than isolated from the movement or a substitute for other action.

Developing such policies is particularly important now because the Reagan crowd is also about a "revolution" in social policies. We could call it reactionary, but if revolution means massive change in government policies, that is what Reagan is pulling off right now. We need a creative counter to these policy changes that is not just a return to where we were in the past. We have to put forward approaches that both deal with the problems that we had before

Reagan and reveal the antiwoman, patriarchal, racist, and sexist assumptions of the right wing.

Organizing for Action

Perhaps the most important thing that we need to do, which underlies everything I've said, is organize. Organize. Organize. Organize. All the great ideas in the world, even feminist budgets, will mean little if we don't also organize people to act on them. We have to organize in a variety of ways.

We need to take what has been the decentralized strength of the women's movement—a multitude of separate women's projects and individuals whose lives have been radically affected by feminism—and find lasting forms for bringing that to more political power. The feminist movement has a wonderful array of creative small groups and projects. Nevertheless, when these don't have any voice in something larger, a lot of their potential power is lost simply because what is learned and done is limited to a small circle and has no larger outlet to affect the public. I don't want to abandon the small-group approach to working, but those groups need to band together into larger units that can have a political impact beyond their numbers. This can take the form of citywide or issue-based alliances, which still preserve each group's autonomy. Such feminist alliances then become the basis for coalitions—as a feminist force—with other progressive groups. If we organize ourselves to join coalitions as a community, rather than having women going into other groups one by one, we have a better chance of keeping our feminist values and perspectives in the forefront of that coalition work.

We can utilize the grass-roots decentralized nature of feminism well in organizing around policy changes today, because it is at the state and local level where most of the battles with the right wing are presently focused. But to do that effectively we have to learn how to get our supporters out—to be visible about their politics. If we are trying to influence policy, the policymakers must know that our people are reliable; if we say that a hundred thousand women will be in Washington, D.C., or a thousand in Billings, Montana, they have to know that they will be there.

The agenda for change is often set by the kind of organizing that goes on around specific issues—particularly ones that are very visible and of considerable interest to people, such as reproductive rights or the Family Protection Act.[1] Whatever the issue, as long as it is one that affects people's lives, the task of the organizer is to show how it connects to other issues of oppression, such as racism, and also to illustrate what that issue means in terms of a vision for the future. The Family Protection Act has demonstrated well these connections as its supporters have sought to bring back the patriarchal order through policies against gays, against assistance to battered women and children, against freedom in the schools, and against the organizing of workers into unions, and so on. It provides a clear case for discussing feminist versus antifeminist perspectives on life.

Another task of organizers is to devise strategies to activate people who care, but who aren't politically active. I saw a chain letter circulating among women artists, which, instead of having people send a dollar, said, "Write a letter to Senator So and So (participating in the hearings on abortion), and then send this letter to eight of your friends who want reproductive rights but who aren't doing anything about it."

One mistake we often make is to act as if there is nothing that supporters can do politically if they can't be activists twenty-four hours a day, seven days a week. We must provide channels of action for people who have ten minutes a day or an hour a week, because that very action ties them closer to caring and being willing to risk or move toward a feminist vision. We must mobilize the constituency we have of concerned individuals, recognizing that many of them are very busy just trying to survive and care for their children or parents.

One of Jerry Falwell's[2] organizations sends a little cardboard church to its local supporters, who deposit a quarter a day, and at the end of the week, they dump the money out and send it to Falwell. We can learn something from this approach, which provides a daily connection to one's supporters. When I see community resources—health clinics, women's centers, whatever—closing because they're no longer getting outside support, I worry about our connections to our supporters. This movement did not start with government money. This movement started in the streets and it started with the support of women, and it can only survive if it is supported by us.

I have no objections to feminists getting government money or applying for grants as long as we remember that when they don't give us the money, we have to figure out other ways to do what has to be done by ourselves. We have to go back to our own resources if we believe in what we're doing. If the peasants of Latin America have supported the Catholic Church over the centuries, I don't see any reason why the feminists and gay men and lesbians of North America cannot support our movements.

Coalitions: The Bottom Line

Coalitions with other progressive groups are important, but we must be clear about what makes them viable. The basis of coalitions is integrity and respect for what each group describes as its bottom line. Now that's not always easy. But with honest struggle over what each group feels is its necessary, critical minimum demand, coalitions can work. If we are to make compromises on where we put our time and energy, it has to be within that framework. Coalitions don't succeed simply for ideological or charitable reasons. They succeed out of a sense that we need each other, and that none of our constituencies can be mobilized effectively if we abandon their bottom-line concerns. Therefore, we have to know where the critical points are for each group in a coalition.

This is a difficult process, but I saw it work in Houston at the National Women's Conference[3] in 1977. As one of the people organizing the lesbian caucus, I can tell you there were moments in that process when I was ready to scream over the homophobia we encountered. But we knew our bottom line and were clear about what compromises we could and could not accept. If it had been an event comprised only of feminists, we would have said more about lesbianism. But as a large, diverse conference, we saw our task as coalescing a critical mass recognition and support of the issue of sexual preference through working as part of the broad-based feminist coalition there.

In order to get this recognition, we had to organize our constituency so that other groups would want our support. We were clear that we would not support a compromise that left us out—that we had to have that mutual respect to make the coalition work. But the success of lesbians was based on the fact that we had organized at the state and local level as well as nationally. Our people were there and others knew we had the numbers. Many women realized that they had a lot more to gain by mobilizing our support for the overall plan by including us, than by alienating us, and creating a very public nuisance. Coalitions are possible, but they are only effective when you have mutual respect; when you have a clearly articulated bottom line; and when you have your own group mobilized for action. If you haven't got your own

group organized, your own power base, then, when the crunch comes, no matter how politically correct or charitable people feel, they are going to align with the groups they feel will make them stronger.

We need more feminist alliances or coalitions that do not coalesce around only one event, but that establish themselves over time as representing a variety of groups and types of action, from electoral and media work to demonstrations or public education. Such ongoing political action groups are usually multi-issue and their strength lies in bringing groups together for concerted action on a city- or statewide basis. These groups then become a reliable basis for coalitions with other progressive organizations.

Going Public

I think that it is crucial for the feminist movement to become more public. By going public, I mean we need to move beyond the boundaries of our subculture. This does not mean giving up the women's community, which remains our strength, our base, the roots of our analysis and of our sustenance. But to go more public in actions that are visible beyond our circles, demonstrating to the world that feminists have not rolled over and played dead as the media sometimes implies.

Going public involves statements about our visions for change. This can be through vehicles such as feminist policy statements on housing or the budget, as well as by demonstrating the passion of our visions with militancy, such as the civil disobedience and fasting women did in the struggle for ratification of the ERA.[4] Such actions make our issues dramatically visible, seen as matters of life and death. These also capture the public imagination and re-create some of that spirit of discovery that accompanied the early years of women's liberation. We need more creative community or media-oriented events that bring that instant recognition of what is at stake and inspire people to talk about those issues.

One of the important things that I remember about the early days of the women's movement is that we talked about feminism—incessantly. We talked in the laundromat, we talked on our jobs, we talked to everybody because we were so excited about what we were discovering. And that talk spread—it excited other women, whether they agreed with us or not. The primary method by which women have become feminists is through talk, through consciousness-raising, and through talk with other feminists. It was not through the government or even the media, but through ourselves. And they cannot take that away. They can deny us money, but they cannot take away ourselves, and the way that this movement has grown is through our "beings"—through being active in the world and being visible.

We have to go public by moving out of what may be comfortable places and engage with women who don't necessarily call themselves feminists. You can go public a hundred different ways—whether that is through media-oriented action or by talking to women on the job or at established women's places. In going public, we risk the vulnerability that goes with such interaction, but the rewards are worth it. The challenge to our ideas that comes with it enables us and our ideas to expand and be more inclusive and more powerful. The interaction that comes with seeing feminism in relation to situations that are not familiar to us, or seeing women of different class or race or geographic backgrounds taking feminism in new directions, is a very good tonic for "tired feminists."

The growth of feminism depends precisely on this interaction—of different generations of feminists and of challenges that make our ideas change and go farther than when they started. If we believe that our visions are visions for the world and not just for a cult, then we have to risk them. For if our ideas cannot survive the test of being engaged in the world more broadly, more publicly, then feminism isn't developed enough yet, and that engagement will help us to know how to remold feminism and make it more viable. For if feminism is to be a force for change in the world, it too must grow and change; if we hoard it or try to hang onto it, we will only take it to the grave with us.

Going public with our visions is ultimately the only way that feminism can become a powerful force for change. There is no way that we can get more people wanting to be feminists and supporting and expanding our visions if they can't even see them, if they never even hear about feminism from feminists rather than the media, and if they don't sense what we care about and believe in. To be seen as an alternative vision for the world, we first have to be seen. It's that simple and it's that important.

Another part of going public is coming out as feminists—in places where we might feel more comfortable not using the word or even discussing the ideas. An academic study has shown what movement activists have said for years—that the most effective counter to homophobia is "knowing one"—that is, people's antigay ideas change most when they realize that they know and care about someone who is gay. But this change would never occur if no one came out, and therefore most people could go on not realizing that they know one of "us" and accepting society's homophobia unchallenged.

"Coming out" as feminists has a similar power. It forces people to get beyond their media stereotypes and deal concretely with a feminist person and with ideas and visions as embodied by that person. Just as coming out for lesbians and gay men has to be decided on a personal basis, so too does coming out as a feminist. Still, it is important to recognize the political power of the personal action and to see that it is useful in advancing feminism and combating the power of the right wing, which includes the effort to intimidate us into going back into closets of fear and adopting apolitical life-styles.

Coming out and going public make it possible for us to communicate our feminist visions to people—the majority of whom I believe would welcome alternatives to the state of the world and have not necessarily accepted the right-wing's visions. They want alternatives to living behind closed doors in fear of violence on the streets and contamination in the air; they want decent work that does not destroy or demean them; they want to be able to affirm freedom and justice, but they may not believe that it is possible. We have to show them that we care about those same things and that our movement is about feminist struggles to create visions of new possibilities in the world, beginning with the struggle for possibilities for women and moving outward from there.

We need to invite people to join us in this struggle, approaching them with something to offer, rather than rejecting them as if they were enemies, or ignoring them as if they were not what we think they should be. If we invite them to join us in trying to become and create something different, we engage in politics as a process of seduction as well as of confrontation. Feminism must be a process of seeing and invoking the best in people as well as in confronting the worst. In this we may discover new ways of moving politically that will enable feminist visions to emerge and to provide the leadership so desperately needed to prevent the patriarchal militaristic destruction of the planet.

This is our challenge in the 1980s. It is the particular moment that we have been given in human evolution and in the struggle between the forces of justice and domination. We are the inheritors of a proud and living tradition of creators, dreamers, resisters, and organizers who have engaged in the struggle before us, and we shall pass it on to the next generation. However long each of us lives, that's how much time we have, for this is a lifetime process and a lifetime commitment.

[1987]

Terms

1. Family Protection Act: A 1981 congressional bill to repeal federal laws that promote equal rights for women, including coeducational school-related activities and protection for battered wives, and to provide tax incentives for married mothers to stay at home.
2. Jerry Falwell: The founder of the Moral Majority, a conservative political organization.
3. National Women's Conference: As part of the United Nations Decade for Women, each member country held a meeting to establish its national priorities for improving the status of women.
4. ERA: Equal Rights Amendment.

Understanding the Reading

1. Why does Bunch believe that feminism should not be limited to women's issues?
2. What does *transformational politics* mean?
3. List Bunch's strategies for achieving a feminist transformation.
4. What actions does she suggest?
5. What advantages does she see in "going public"?

Suggestion for Responding

1. Choose one strategy Bunch suggests, such as a feminist budget or coalition formation, and explore the social effects it could have.

63

A Manifesto for Men

ANDREW KIMBRELL

As many of us come to mourn the lost fathers and sons of the last decades and seek to reestablish our ties to each other and to the earth, we need to find ways to change the political, social, and economic structures that have created this crisis. A "wild man" weekend in the woods, or intense man-to-man discussions, can be key experiences in self-discovery and personal empowerment. But these personal experiences are not enough to reverse the victimization of men. As the men's movement gathers strength, it is critical that this increasing sense of personal liberation be channeled into political action. Without significant changes in our society there will only be continued hopelessness and frustration for men. Moreover, a coordinated movement pressing for the liberation of men could be a key factor in ensuring that the struggle for a sustainable future for humanity and the earth succeeds.

What follows is a brief political platform for men, a short manifesto with which we can begin the process of organizing men as a positive political force working for a better future. This is the next step for the men's movement.

Fathers and Children

Political efforts focusing on the family must reassert men's bonds with the family and reverse the "lost father" syndrome. While any long-term plan for men's liberation requires significant changes in the very structure of our work and economic institutions, a number of intermediate steps are possible: We need to take a leadership role in supporting parental leave legislation, which gives working parents the right to take time from work to care for children or other family members. And we need to target the Bush administration for vetoing this vital legislation. Also needed is pro-child tax relief such as greatly expanding the young child tax credit, which would provide income relief and tax breaks to families at a point when children need the most parental care and when income may be the lowest.

We should also be in the forefront of the movement pushing for changes in the workplace including more flexible hours, part-time work, job sharing, and home-based employment. As economic analyst William R. Mattox Jr. notes, a simple step toward making home-based employment more viable would be to loosen restrictions on claiming home office expenses as a tax deduction for parents. Men must also work strenuously in the legal arena to promote more liberal visitation rights for non-custodial parents and to assert appropriateness of the father as a custodial parent. Non-traditional family structures should also be given more recognition in our society, with acknowledgment of men's important roles as stepfathers, foster fathers, uncles, brothers, and mentors. We must seek legislative ways to recognize many men's commitments that do not fit traditional definitions of family.

Ecology as Male Politics

A sustainable environment is not merely one issue among others. It is the crux of all issues in our age, including men's politics. The ecological struggles of our time offer a unique forum in which men can express their renewed sense of the wild and their traditional roles as creators, defenders of the family, and careful stewards of the earth.

The alienation of men from their rootedness to the land has deprived us all of what John Muir[1] called the "heart of wilderness." As part of our efforts to re-experience the wild in ourselves, we should actively become involved in experiencing the wilderness firsthand and organize support for the protection of nature and endangered species. Men should also become what Robert Bly[2] has called "inner warriors" for the earth, involving themselves in non-violent civil disobedience to protect wilderness areas from further destruction.

An important aspect of the masculine ethic is defense of family. Pesticides and other toxic pollutants that poison our food, homes, water, and air represent a real danger, especially to children. Men need to be adamant in their call for limitations on the use of chemicals.

Wendell Berry[3] has pointed out that the ecological crisis is also a crisis of agriculture. If men are to recapture a true sense of stewardship and husbandry and affirm the "seedbearing," creative capacity of the male, they must, to the extent possible, become involved in sustainable agriculture and organic farming and gardening. We should also initiate and support legislation that sustains our farming communities.

Men in the Classrooms and Community

In many communities, especially inner cities, men are absent not only from homes but also from the schools. Men must support the current efforts by black men's groups around the country to implement male-only early-grade classes taught by men. These programs provide role models and a surrogate paternal presence for young black males. We should also commit ourselves to having a far greater male presence in all elementary school education. Recent studies have shown that male grade school students have a higher level of achievement when they are taught by male teachers. Part-time or full-time home schooling options can also be helpful in providing men a great opportunity to be teachers—not just temperaments—to their children.

We need to revive our concern for community. Community-based boys' clubs, scout troops, sports leagues, and big brother programs have achieved significant success in helping fatherless male children find self-esteem. Men's groups must work to strengthen these organizations.

Men's Minds, Men's Bodies, and Work

Men need to join together to fight threats to male health including suicide, drug and alcohol abuse, AIDS, and stress diseases. We should support active prevention and education efforts aimed at these deadly threats. Most importantly, men need to be leaders in initiating and supporting holistic and psychotherapeutic approaches that directly link many of these health threats to the coercive nature of the male mystique and the current economic system. Changes in diet, reduction of drug and alcohol use, less stressful work environments, greater nurturing of and caring for men by other men, and fighting racism, hopelessness, and homelessness are all important, interconnected aspects of any male health initiative.

Men without Hope or Homes

Men need to support measures that promote small business and entrepreneurship, which will allow more people to engage in crafts and human-scale, community-oriented enterprises. Also important is a commitment to appropriate, human-scale technologies such as renewable energy sources. Industrial and other inappropriate technologies have led to men's dispossession, degradation—and increasingly to unemployment.

A related struggle is eliminating racism. No group of men is more dispossessed than minority men. White men should support and network with African American and other minority men's groups. Violence and discrimination against men because of their sexual preference should also be challenged.

Men, who represent more than four-fifths of the

homeless, can no longer ignore this increasing social tragedy. Men's councils should develop support groups for the homeless in their communities.

The Holocaust of Men

As the primary victims of mechanized war, men must oppose this continued slaughter. Men need to realize that the traditional male concepts of the noble warrior are undermined and caricatured in the technological nightmare of modern warfare. Men must together become prime movers in dismantling the military-industrial establishment and redistributing defense spending toward a sustainable environment and protection of family, school, and community.

Men's Action Network

No area of the men's political agenda will be realized until men can establish a network of activists to create collective action. A first step might be to create a high-profile national coalition of the men's councils that are growing around the country. This coalition, which could be called the Men's Action Network (MAN), could call for a national conference to define a comprehensive platform of men's concerns and to provide the political muscle to implement those ideas.

A Man Could Stand Up

The current generation of men face a unique moment in history. Though often still trapped by economic coercion and psychological co-option, we are beginning to see that there is a profound choice ahead. Will we choose to remain subservient tools of social and environmental destruction or to fight for rediscovery of the male as a full partner and participant in family, community, and the earth? Will we remain mesmerized by the male mystique, or will we reclaim the true meaning of our masculinity?

There is a world to gain. The male mystique, in which many of today's men—especially the most politically powerful—are trapped, is threatening the family and the planet with irreversible destruction. A men's movement based on the recovery of masculinity could renew much of the world we have lost. By changing types of work and work hours, we could break our subordination to corporate managers and return much of our work and lives to the household. We could once again be teaching, nurturing pres-

ences to our children. By devoting ourselves to meaningful work with appropriate technology, we could recover independence in our work and our spirit. By caring for each other, we could recover the dignity of our gender and heal the wounds of addiction and self-destruction. By becoming husbands to the earth, we could protect the wild and recover our creative connections with the forces and rhythms of nature.

Ultimately we must help fashion a world without the daily frustration and sorrow of having to view each other as a collection of competitors instead of a community of friends. We must celebrate the essence and rituals of our masculinity. We can no longer passively submit to the destruction of the household, the demise of self employment, the disintegration of family and community, and the desecration of our earth.

Shortly after the First World War, Ford Madox Ford, one of this century's greatest writers, depicted twentieth-century men as continually pinned down in their trenches, unable to stand up for fear of annihilation. As the century closes, men remain pinned down by an economic and political system that daily forces millions of us into meaningless work, powerless lives, and self-destruction. The time has come for men to stand up.

[1991]

Terms

1. John Muir: An American naturalist and conservationist.
2. Robert Bly: The author of *Iron John* and advocate of the men's movement, which emphasizes men's exploring their inner maleness and bonding with other men.
3. Wendell Berry: A contemporary American writer and university professor who has a special interest in the environment.

Understanding the Reading

1. Why does Kimbrell think men need to focus on family?
2. Why would environmental activism be especially beneficial to men?
3. What can men do to improve their communities?
4. How can men improve their health?
5. Why should men be concerned about war?
6. What does Kimbrell see as the benefits men would gain by implementing his program?

Suggestion for Responding

1. Do you agree or disagree with Kimbrell that men have been victimized by society? Why?

64

Freedom for the Thought We Hate

GERALD GUNTHER

I am deeply troubled by current efforts—however well intentioned—to place new limits on freedom of expression at this and other campuses. Such limits not only are incompatible with the mission and meaning of university but also send exactly the wrong message from academia to society as a whole. University campuses should exhibit greater, not less, freedom of expression than prevails in society at large.

Proponents of new limits argue that historic First Amendment rights must be balanced against the university's commitment to the diversity of ideas and persons. Clearly, there is ample room and need for vigorous university action to combat racial and other discrimination. But curbing freedom of speech is the wrong way to do so. The proper answer to bad speech is usually more and better speech—not new laws, litigation, and repression.

Lest it be thought that I am insensitive to the pain imposed by expressions of racial or religious hatred, let me say that I have suffered that pain and empathize with others under similar verbal assault. My deep belief in the principles of the First Amendment arises in part from my own experiences. I received my elementary education in a public school in a very small town in Nazi Germany. There I was subjected to vehement anti-Semitic remarks from my teacher, classmates, and others—"Judensau" (Jew pig) was far from the harshest. I can assure you that they hurt.

More generally, I lived in a country where ideological orthodoxy reigned and where the opportunity for dissent was severely limited.

The lesson I have drawn from my childhood in Nazi Germany and my happier adult life in this country is the need to walk the sometimes difficult path of denouncing the bigots' hateful ideas with all my power, yet at the same time challenging any community's attempt to suppress hateful ideas by force of law.

Obviously, given my own experience, I do *not* quarrel with the claim that *words* can do harm. But I firmly deny that a showing of harm suffices to deny First Amendment protection, and I insist on the elementary First Amendment principle that our Constitution usually protects even offensive, harmful expression.

That is why—at the risk of being thought callous or doctrinaire—I recently opposed attempts by some members of my university community to enlarge the area of forbidden speech to prohibit not only "personal abuse" but also "defamation of groups"—expression "that by accepted community standards . . . pejoratively characterizes persons or groups on the basis of personal or cultural differences." Such proposals, in my view, seriously undervalue the First Amendment and far too readily endanger its precious content. Limitations on free expression beyond those established by law should be eschewed in an institution committed to diversity and the First Amendment.

In explaining my position, I will avoid extensive legal arguments. Instead, I want to speak from the heart, on the basis of my own background and of my understanding of First Amendment principles—principles supported by an ever larger number of scholars and Supreme Court justices, especially since the days of the Warren Court.[1]

Among the core principles is that any official effort to suppress expression must be viewed with the greatest skepticism and suspicion. Only in very narrow, urgent circumstances should government or similar institutions be permitted to inhibit speech. True, there are certain categories of speech that may be prohibited, but the number and scope of these categories has steadily shrunk over the last fifty years. Face-to-face insults are one such category; incitement to immediate illegal action is another. But opinions expressed in debates and arguments about a wide range of political and social issues should not be suppressed simply because of disagreement with those views, with the content of the expression.

Similarly, speech should not and cannot be banned simply because it is "offensive" to substantial parts of a majority of the community. The refusal to suppress offensive speech is one of the most difficult obligations the free speech principle imposes upon all of us; yet it is also one of the First Amendment's greatest glories—indeed, it is a central test of a community's commitment to free speech.

The Supreme Court's 1989 decision to allow flag-burning as a form of political protest, in *Texas v. John-*

son, warrants careful pondering by all those who continue to advocate campus restraints on "racist speech." As Justice Brennan's majority opinion in *Johnson* reminded, "If there is a bedrock principle underlying the First Amendment, it is that the Government may not prohibit the expression of an idea itself offensive or disagreeable." In refusing to place flag-burning outside the First Amendment, moreover, the *Johnson* majority insisted (in words especially apt for the "racist speech" debate), "The First Amendment does not guarantee that other concepts virtually sacred to our Nation as a whole—*such as the principle that discrimination on the basis of race is odious and destructive*—will go unquestioned in the marketplace of ideas. We decline, therefore, to create for the flag an exception to the joust of principles protected by the First Amendment." (Italics added.)

Campus proponents of restricting offensive speech are currently relying for justification on the Supreme Court's allegedly repeated reiteration that "fighting words" constitute an exception to the First Amendment. Such an exception has indeed been recognized in a number of lower court cases. However, there has only been *one* case in the history of the Supreme Court in which a majority of the justices has ever found a statement to be a punishable resort to "fighting words." That was *Chaplinsky v. New Hampshire*, a nearly fifty-year-old case involving words which would very likely not be found punishable today.

More significant is what has happened in the nearly half-century since: Despite repeated appeals to the Supreme Court to recognize the applicability of the "fighting words" exception by affirming challenged convictions, the court has in every instance refused. One must wonder about the strength of an exception that, while theoretically recognized, has for so long not been found apt in practice.

The phenomenon of racist and other offensive speech is not a new one in the history of the First Amendment. In recent decades, for example, well-meaning (but in my view misguided) majorities have sought to suppress not only racist speech but also anti-war and anti-draft speech, civil rights demonstrators, the Nazis and Ku Klux Klan, and left-wing groups.

Typically, it is people on the extremes of the political spectrum (including those who advocate overthrow of our constitutional system and those who would not protect their opponents' right to dissent were they the majority) who feel the brunt of repression and have found protection in the First Amendment; typically, it is well-meaning people in the majority who believe their sensibilities, their sense of outrage, justify restraints.

Those in power in a community recurrently seek to repress speech they find abhorrent, and their efforts are understandable human impulses. Yet freedom of expression—and especially the protection of dissident speech, the most important function of the First Amendment—is an anti-majoritarian principle. Is it too much to hope that, especially on a university campus, a majority can be persuaded of the value of freedom of expression and of the resultant need to curb our impulses to repress dissident views?

The principles to which I appeal are not new. They have been expressed, for example, by the most distinguished Supreme Court justices ever since the beginning of the court's confrontations with First Amendment issues nearly seventy years ago. These principles are reflected in the words of so imperfect a First Amendment defender as Justice Oliver Wendell Holmes: "If there is any principle of the Constitution that more imperatively calls for attachment than any other it is the principle of free thought—not free thought for those who agree with us but freedom for the thought that we hate." This is the principle most elaborately and eloquently addressed by Justice Louis D. Brandeis, who reminded us that the First Amendment rests on a belief "in the power of reason as applied through public discussion" and therefore bars "silence coerced by law—the argument of force in its worst form."

This theme, first articulated in dissents, has repeatedly been voiced in majority opinions in more recent decades. It underlies Justice Douglas's remark in striking down a conviction under a law banning speech that "stirs the public to anger": "A function of free speech [is] to invite dispute. . . . Speech is often provocative and challenging. That is why freedom of speech [is ordinarily] protected against censorship or punishment."

It also underlies Justice William J. Brennan's comment about our "profound national commitment to the principle that debate on public issues should be uninhibited, robust and wide-open, and that it may well include vehement, caustic and sometimes unpleasantly sharp attacks"—a comment he followed with a reminder that constitutional protection "does not turn upon the truth, popularity or social utility of the ideas and beliefs which are offered."

These principles underlie as well the repeated insistence by Justice John Marshall Harlan, again in majority opinions, that the mere "inutility or immorality" of a message cannot justify its repression, and that the state may not punish because of "the underlying content of the message." Moreover, Justice Harlan, in one of the finest First Amendment opinions on the books, noted, in words that we would ignore at our peril at this time,

> The constitutional right of free expression is powerful medicine in a society as diverse and populous as ours. . . . To many, the immediate consequence of this freedom may often appear to be only verbal tumult, discord and even offensive utterance. These are, however, within established limits, in truth necessary side effects of the broader enduring values which the process of open debate permits us to achieve. That the air may at times seem filled with verbal cacophony is, in this sense, not a sign of weakness but of strength.

In this same passage, Justice Harlan warned that a power to ban speech merely because it is offensive is an "inherently boundless" notion, and added that "we think it is largely because governmental officials cannot make principled distinctions in this area that the Constitution leaves matters of taste and style so largely to the individual." (The Justice made these comments while overturning the conviction of an antiwar protestor for "offensive conduct." The defendant had worn, in a courthouse corridor, a jacket bearing the words "Fuck the draft.")

I restate these principles and repeat these words for reasons going far beyond the fact that they are familiar to me as a First Amendment scholar. I believe—in my heart as well as my mind—that these principles and ideals are not only established but also right. I hope that the entire academic community will seriously reflect upon the risks to free expression, lest we weaken hard-won liberties at our universities and, by example, in this nation.

[1990]

Term

1. Warren Court: The Supreme Court under Chief Justice Earl Warren, which passed down such decisions as the prohibition of school segregation.

Understanding the Reading

1. Why does Gunther describe his childhood in Germany?

2. Why does he argue that speech "should not . . . be banned simply because it is 'offensive'"?
3. What connection does Gunther make between flag-burning and racist speech?
4. Why does he object to the use of the concept of "fighting words" to prohibit racist speech?
5. Explain each of the quotations of the five Supreme Court justices.

Suggestion for Responding

1. Gunther presents a persuasive advocacy of freedom of speech. Develop an argument in favor of some restrictions.

65

The Oklahoma Teachers' Strike Is Twenty-Six Years in the Making

JON HAZELL

The teachers' strike in Oklahoma is twenty-six years in the making. For two and a half decades, our state's public education system has been groaning under the growing weight of defunding and disrespect—and now the teachers of Oklahoma are at a breaking point.

In 1992, Oklahoma voters passed State Question 640, which requires that any bill to raise revenue must receive a 75 percent supermajority vote in both legislative chambers and be signed by the governor. As a result, any small legislative group that has an issue with a bill or just wants to play political games can shut down meaningful progress. This effectively eliminates the option of raising taxes to fund public education. Since the passage of State Question 640, only one small revenue-raising bill has passed—a 2004 tax on tobacco.

Next, the Oklahoma legislature cut various taxes in hopes of luring companies to the state with the promise of lower taxes (or sometimes no taxes, in the form of long-term tax credits). Their philosophy was that the jobs these businesses would bring into the state would result in more people putting money into the economy through economic activities and taxes. But at the same time, Oklahoma began implementing cuts to personal income taxes, leading to a half-billion-dollar cut to the tax base on which public schools depend.

Another major mistake Oklahoma made was tying a large amount of education funding to the oil and gas industry: a large part of the education budget comes from the Gross Production Tax (GPT) of oil and gas wells. Given the volatility of that industry, this decision was extremely unwise.

A few years back, when gas was $4 a gallon, the oil companies asked that the GPT be lowered from 7 percent to 1 percent so they could invest in drilling research and development. The government obliged. When the oil industry basically tanked and its tax contributions dried up, the 75 percent supermajority rule and the industry's political influence ensured that the state could not raise the GPT to its previous rate.

All of a sudden, Oklahoma found itself with a $1 billion annual revenue hole. It's had that hole for five years now. Oklahoma also has one of the lowest property tax rates anywhere, and over the years, much of that money—which is supposed to go to education—has been siphoned off to help make up for all of the budget holes. Another growing problem is that the federal government dictates the allocation of the federal dollars we receive, and very little of it goes to education.

There are more causes for the cracks we're seeing in the state today—these are just some of the factors that have led us to this dire, and extremely complex, breaking point.

The state's budget crisis necessitated cuts to many agencies in the state. In the past five years alone, common education in Oklahoma has been cut 28 percent, and the state leads the nation in education cuts. These cuts have been devastating. Teacher salaries in Oklahoma are among the lowest in the nation, and my colleagues and I have not had a raise in ten years.

Our teachers are able to drive across the border to Texas or Arkansas and make tens of thousands of dollars more. A teacher who is fresh out of college can go to Texas and begin teaching at a higher salary than Oklahoma educators who have been teaching for two decades. Last year's Oklahoma Teacher of the Year was forced to move to Texas because he couldn't support his family on his Oklahoma salary. He and his wife—also a teacher—immediately made $40,000 more between them. The salary disparity has caused a mass exodus of teachers, and in response, Oklahoma emergency certified around five thousand teachers in the last three years alone.

The teacher shortage hits students hard, too. Fewer teachers means larger class sizes; it is not uncommon to see classes of thirty-five or forty students or more. To make matters worse, many schools can no longer afford to employ a full support staff, and the result is that teachers have been placed in an impossible situation. They are not teaching under the conditions necessary to provide every child with the quality education they deserve.

And as the money allocated to the general funding formula has dissipated, schools can no longer provide the resources—like textbooks and technology—that teachers need to prepare our children for the twenty-first-century world. When you consider that our teachers and schools are evaluated on how their students perform compared to students nationwide who do not face these same obstacles, perhaps you can begin to grasp the frustration and pressure so many of our teachers feel. Now, that frustration has finally boiled over.

I supplement my teaching income with two other jobs. My wife, who has been a second-grade teacher for the past thirty-four years, works two jobs.

Our legislators must finally realize that an education system is the most critical component of a successful society. The teachers who have stayed and fought a courageous battle under extremely difficult circumstances deserve their immediate attention, respect, and help in the form of real and tangible resources.

That means paying teachers a living wage. It means providing schools with enough funding to hire qualified teachers to fill every classroom, so that every child has a qualified teacher and every classroom has a manageable number of students. It means funding for textbooks that have all of the pages in them and aren't held together by duct tape. It means providing the funding necessary to provide updated technology that students need to be able to compete on a level playing field with other students across the country. And it means providing enough funding so that teachers don't have to spend money out of their own pockets to buy basic classroom supplies.

I have taken issue with the way some educators have responded during this time, but I take no issue with their justified frustration and feelings of hopelessness. As an Oklahoma teacher for thirty-five years, I get it: I have endured and suffered as much as all of them. I supplement my teaching income with two other jobs—jobs I enjoy, but jobs nonetheless. When my wife is not in the classroom, she sells real estate. It's unacceptable that it takes five jobs between two people to ensure a middle-class existence.

The state of Oklahoma has neglected education for far too long. We can point fingers and blame whomever we wish; as I have already shown, there is plenty of blame to go around. But the time to enact real solutions is right now. Oklahoma has taken a good first step this week in passing a $480 million revenue package to help education, and the legislators who worked tirelessly to make that happen deserve our thanks. But there is much more catching up that needs to be done. It is past time to stop blaming and start fixing.

Jon Hazell has taught anatomy and physiology, biology, and an adaptive environmental science class for special needs students at Durant High School for thirty-five years. He is the current Oklahoma State Teacher of the Year.

Understanding the Reading

1. In response to drastic funding cuts from the federal government, what errors has Oklahoma made that have resulted in disastrous cuts to the public schools' budgets?
2. What have been the effects on teachers for students?
3. What have state lawmakers done recently to reverse some of the crises the defunding has caused?

Suggestion for Responding

1. Research other states that have had teachers' strikes recently. Why is this happening, and what have been the results of the strikes?

Suggestions for Responding to Part VIII

Action Project for Social Change

The readings in part VIII have tried to show that you can actually do something to effect social change. Now it is time to put what you have learned into practice. Simply follow the steps described in the introduction to part VIII, commit yourself, and take action.

First, identify something as a problem, such as becoming aware of sexism in the media. You then need to have a desire to do something about the problem, and you need to figure out specifically what it is that you find offensive and what you want to achieve.

Then, alone or together with whoever else is going to join you in your action, brainstorm about possible actions you could realistically take. You could write to the producers of videos or to a specific network; you could try to organize a boycott; or you could undertake other, different actions. Then plan your action project, considering what you will do, when you will do it, and how you will evaluate the success of your project. Finally, do it and become a change maker yourself.

Part IX
Change Makers

WE USUALLY THINK OF CHANGE MAKERS AS THE MOVERS and shakers of the world, those larger-than-life people who "really make a difference": perhaps, George Washington, Abraham Lincoln, Martin Luther King, Rosa Parks, and just maybe social worker Jane Addams. Part IX is not about people of such heroic proportions, however. Instead, it is about people like ourselves, people we can see as "real."

The people we will read about here are young and old. "Mother" Jones (reading 66) was a fifty-year-old widow when she first became a union organizer of coal miners of all ages.

Readings 67, 68, and 69 give some insight into the civil rights movement, possibly the most enveloping and dynamic social movement of the past century, one that has transformed American society. Over a century ago, Ida B. Wells-Barnett, who was orphaned at age fourteen and who took responsibility for her younger siblings, challenged the practice of white lynching of blacks; she earned an international reputation and eventually became a cofounder of the National Association for the Advancement of Colored People. The ultimate successes of the civil rights movement depended on similar dedication and commitment of many people whose names are not widely known today. For example, the report by the Southern Poverty Law Center summarizes the decades-long struggle of hundreds of individuals, taking stands by themselves, but more often cooperating in groups, to demonstrate the unfair policies and practices that kept blacks subordinate in most areas of society.

Anne Moody, a college student from an impoverished southern black family, was willing to face violence from white high school students—taking beatings, being sprayed with paint and condiments—to stand up for the right of blacks to eat at a public lunch counter. Similarly, college student Muriel Tillinghast risked rape and other violence to assert blacks' rights during the Freedom Summer activism.

Readings 70 and 71 introduce change makers from the most impoverished group in the United States, Native American women. Despite their lack of resources, they are improving life on their reservations. Michael Ryan tells how, despite obstructive government regulations and lack of funds, three women created on their Yakima, Washington, reservation a college that in eight years graduated over four hundred students. Next, Ann Davis introduces us to the indefatigable Cecilia Fire Thunder, who has organized her tribal sisters to transform life and politics on their Lakota reservation. Reading 72, "Claiming Respect for Ancestral Remains," describes the dedicated work of the Repatriation Committee of the Caddo Nation of Oklahoma.

The final article, new to this edition, highlights the promise of the American Dream, its successes and its remaining challenges. Reading 73, "The Weinstein Effect," is by Linda Burstyn. She writes, "It's the story of a country that likes to think of itself as a leader in gender equality, but in fact, has a long way to go.

"All of us can learn important lessons from the change makers who speak in these pages. As we think of abridged human rights on the job, in school, in public areas, dealing with the quality of our air, water, and soil, we can, perhaps, compare our plight to that of the well-known frog in a pot of water that is slowly heating up. The frog might be happy with his pot of water, unaware that it will soon be boiling water. However, as everyday people committed to social change, we are aware of so many of our fellow Americans who have recently planned, organized, and carried out ongoing movements. The youth of America from many states (and now many countries in solidarity), are continuing their movement that holds our lawmakers directly responsible and call on those old enough to vote to use their vote to challenge and change the country's gun laws. Extraordinary social change is nearly always multipronged—generated from varied sources and different layers of society. In recent years we have seen women and men demanding more respect and rights as workers, women, Natives, students, immigrants, African Americans, Muslims—in the name of all our children and the American Dream.

66

Victory at Arnot

MARY HARRIS "MOTHER" JONES[1]

Before 1899 the coal fields of Pennsylvania were not organized. Immigrants poured into the country and they worked cheap. There was always a surplus of immigrant labor, solicited in Europe by the coal companies, so as to keep wages down to barest living. Hours of work down underground were cruelly long. Fourteen hours a day was not uncommon, thirteen, twelve. The life or limb of the miner was unprotected by any laws. Families lived in company owned shacks that were not fit for their pigs. Children died by the hundreds due to the ignorance and poverty of their parents.

Often I have helped lay out for burial the babies of the miners, and the mothers could scarce conceal their relief at the little ones' deaths. Another was already on its way, destined, if a boy, for the breakers; if a girl, for the silk mills where the other brothers and sisters already worked.

The United Mine Workers decided to organize these fields and work for human conditions for human beings. Organizers were put to work. Whenever the spirit of the men in the mines grew strong enough a strike was called.

In Arnot, Pennsylvania, a strike had been going on four or five months. The men were becoming discouraged. The coal company sent the doctors, the school teachers, the preachers and their wives to the homes of the miners to get them to sign a document that they would go back to work.

The president of the district, Mr. Wilson, and an organizer, Tom Haggerty, got despondent. The signatures were overwhelmingly in favor of returning on Monday.

Haggerty suggested that they send for me. Saturday morning they telephoned to Barnesboro, where I was organizing, for me to come at once or they would lose the strike.

"Oh Mother," Haggerty said. "Come over quick and help us! The boys are that despondent! They are going back Monday."

I told him that I was holding a meeting that night but that I would leave early Sunday morning.

I started at daybreak. At Roaring Branch, the nearest train connection with Arnot, the secretary of the Arnot Union, a young boy, William Bouncer, met me with a horse and buggy. We drove sixteen miles over rough mountain roads. It was biting cold. We got into Arnot Sunday noon, and I was placed in the coal company's hotel, the only hotel in town. I made some objections, but Bouncer said, "Mother, we have engaged this room for you, and if it is not occupied, they will never rent us another."

Sunday afternoon I held a meeting. It was not as large a gathering as those we had later, but I stirred up the poor wretches that did come.

"You've got to take the pledge," I said. "Rise and pledge to stick to your brothers and the union till the strike's won!"

The men shuffled their feet but the women rose, their babies in their arms, and pledged themselves to see that no one went to work in the morning.

"The meeting stands adjourned till ten o'clock tomorrow morning," I said. "Everyone come and see that the slaves that think to go back to their masters come along with you."

I returned to my room at the hotel. I wasn't called down to supper but after the general manager of the mines and all of the other guests had gone to church, the housekeeper stole up to my room and asked me to come down and get a cup of tea.

At eleven o'clock that night the housekeeper again knocked at my door and told me that I had to give up my room; that she was told it belonged to a teacher. "It's a shame, mother," she whispered, as she helped me into my coat.

I found little Bouncer sitting on guard down in the lobby. He took me up the mountain to a miner's house. A cold wind almost blew the bonnet from my head. At the miner's shack I knocked.

A man's voice shouted, "Who is there?" "Mother Jones," said I.

A light came in the tiny window. The door opened. "And did they put you out, Mother?" "They did that."

"I told Mary they might do that," said the miner. He held the oil lamp with the thumb and his little finger and I could see that the others were off. His face was young but his body was bent over.

He insisted on my sleeping in the only bed, with his wife. He slept with his head on his arms on the kitchen table. Early in the morning his wife rose to keep the children quiet, so that I might sleep a little later as I was very tired.

At eight o'clock she came into my room, crying. "Mother, are you awake?"

245

"Yes, I am awake."

"Well, you must get up. The sheriff is here to put us out for keeping you. This house belongs to the Company."

The family gathered up all their earthly belongings, which weren't much, took down all the holy pictures, and put them in a wagon, and they with all their neighbors went to the meeting. The sight of that wagon with the sticks of furniture and the holy pictures and the children, with the father and mother and myself walking along through the streets, turned the tide. It made the men so angry that they decided not to go back that morning to the mines. Instead, they came to the meeting where they determined not to give up the strike until they had won the victory.

Then the company tried to bring in scabs.[2] I told the men to stay home with the children for a change and let the women attend to the scabs. I organized an army of women housekeepers. On a given day they were to bring their mops and brooms and "the army" would charge the scabs up at the mines. The general manager, the sheriff and the corporation hirelings heard of our plans and were on hand. The day came, and the women came with the mops and brooms and pails of water.

I decided not to go up to the Drip Mouth myself, for I knew they would arrest me and that might rout the army. I selected as leader an Irish woman who had a most picturesque appearance. She had slept late and her husband had told her to hurry up and get into the army. She had grabbed a red petticoat and slipped it over a thick cotton night gown. She wore a black stocking and a white one. She had tied a little red fringed shawl over her wild red hair. Her face was red and her eyes were mad. I looked at her and felt that she could raise a rumpus.

I said, "You lead the army up to the Drip Mouth. Take that tin dishpan you have with you and your hammer, and when the scabs and the mules come up, begin to hammer and howl. Then all of you hammer and howl and be ready to chase the scabs with your mops and brooms. Don't be afraid of anyone."

Up the mountain side, yelling and hollering, she led the women, and when the mules came up with the scabs and the coal, she began beating on the dishpan and hollering, and all the army joined in with her. The sheriff tapped her on the shoulder.

"My dear lady," said he, "remember the mules. Don't frighten them."

She took the old tin pan and she hit him with it, and she hollered, "To hell with you and the mules!"

He fell over and dropped into the creek. Then the mules began to rebel against scabbing. They bucked and kicked the scab drivers and started off for the barn. The scabs started running downhill, followed by the army of women with their mops and pails and brooms.

A poll parrot in a nearby shack screamed at the superintendent, "Got hell, did you? Got hell?"

There was a great big doctor in the crowd, a company lap dog. He had a little satchel in his hand and he said to me, impudent like, "Mrs. Jones, I have a warrant for you."

"All right," said I. "Keep it in your pill bag until I come for it. I am going to hold a meeting now."

From that day on the women kept continual watch on the mines to see that the company did not bring in scabs. Every day women with brooms or mops in one hand and babies in the other arm, wrapped in little blankets, went to the mines and watched that no one went in. And all night long they kept watch. They were heroic women. In the long years to come the nation will pay them high tribute for they were fighting for the advancement of a great country.

I held meetings throughout the surrounding country. The company was spending money among the farmers, urging them not to do anything for the miners. I went out with an old wagon and a union mule that had gone on strike, and a miner's little boy for a driver. I held meetings among the farmers and won them to the side of the strikers.

Sometimes it was twelve or one o'clock in the morning when I would get home, the little boy asleep on my arm and I driving the mule. Sometimes it was several degrees below zero. The winds whistled down the mountains and drove the snow and sleet in our faces. My hands and feet were often numb. We were all living on dry bread and black coffee. I slept in a room that never had a fire in it, and I often woke up in the morning to find snow covering the outside covers of the bed.

There was a place near Arnot called Sweedy Town, and the company's agents went there to get the Swedes to break the strike. I was holding a meeting among the farmers when I heard of the company's efforts. I got the young farmers to get on their horses and go over to Sweedy Town and see that no Swede left town. They took clotheslines for lassos and any Swede seen moving in the direction of Arnot was brought back quick enough.

After months of terrible hardships the strike was about won. The mines were not working. The spirit of the men was splendid. President Wilson had come home from the western part of the state. I was staying at his home. The family had gone to bed. We sat up late talking over matters when there came a knock at the door. A very cautious knock.

"Come in," said Mr. Wilson.

Three men entered. They looked at me uneasily and Mr. Wilson asked me to step in an adjoining room. They talked the strike over and called President Wilson's attention to the fact that there were mortgages on his little home, held by the bank which was owned by the coal company, and they said, "We will take the mortgage off your home and give you $25,000 in cash if you will just leave and let the strike die out."

I shall never forget his reply: "Gentlemen, if you come to visit my family, the hospitality of the whole house is yours. But if you come to bribe me with dollars to betray my manhood and my brothers who trust me, I want you to leave this door and never come here again."

The strike lasted a few weeks longer. Meantime, President Wilson, when strikers were evicted, cleaned out his barn and took care of the evicted miners until homes could be provided. One by one he killed his chickens and his hogs. Everything that he had he shared. He ate dry bread and drank chicory. He knew every hardship that the rank and file of the organization knew. We do not have such leaders now.

The last of February the company put up a notice that all demands were conceded.

"Did you get the use of the hall for us to hold meetings?" said the women.

"No, we didn't ask for that."

"Then the strike is on again," said they. They got the hall, and when the president, Mr. Wilson, returned from the convention in Cincinnati, he shed tears of joy and gratitude.

I was going to leave for the central fields, and before I left, the union held a victory meeting in Bloosburg. The women came for miles in a raging snow storm for that meeting, little children trailing on their skirts, and babies under their shawls. Many of the miners had walked miles. It was one night of real joy and a great celebration. I bade them all good bye. A little boy called out, "Don't leave us, Mother. Don't leave us!" The dear little children kissed my hands. We spent the whole night in Bloosburg rejoicing. The men opened a few of the freight cars out on a siding and helped themselves to boxes of beer. Old

and young talked and sang all night long and to the credit of the company no one was interfered with.

Those were the days before the extensive use of gun men, of military, of jails, of police clubs. There had been no bloodshed. There had been no riots. And the victory was due to the army of women with their mops and brooms.

A year afterward they celebrated the anniversary of the victory. They presented me with a gold watch but I declined to accept it, for I felt it was the price of the bread of the little children. I have not been in Arnot since but in my travels over the country I often meet the men and boys who carried through the strike so heroically.

[1925]

Terms

1. Mary Harris "Mother" Jones: After the loss of her four children and her husband in a yellow fever epidemic and the destruction of her dressmaking shop in the Chicago fire of 1871, "Mother" Jones became a legendary labor union organizer.
2. Scabs: Strike breakers.

Understanding the Reading

1. What were the miners' lives like?
2. Why was Mother Jones not called down to supper, and what was the real reason that she had to give up her room at the hotel?
3. What was the effect of the sheriff's putting the family who sheltered her out of their house?
4. Why did Mother Jones organize an "army of women" rather than men to face the scabs?
5. Why did the miners finally win the strike?

Suggestion for Responding

1. Describe a time when you joined with others to organize for change.

67

Free at Last

SOUTHERN POVERTY LAW CENTER

By 1910, blacks were caught in a degrading system of total segregation throughout the South. Through "Jim Crow" laws (named after a black minstrel in a popular song), blacks were ordered to use separate restrooms, water fountains, restaurants, waiting rooms, swimming pools, libraries, and bus seats.

The United States Supreme Court gave its approval to Jim Crow segregation in the 1896 case of *Plessy v. Ferguson.* The Court said separate facilities were legal as long as they were equal. In practice, Southern states never provided equal facilities to black people—only separate ones.

Frederick Douglass[1] tried to expose the inherent contradictions in the law of the land: "So far as the colored people of the country are concerned," he said, "the Constitution is but a stupendous sham . . . fair without and foul within, keeping the promise to the eye and breaking it to the heart."

Despite Douglass's eloquent arguments, it would be generations before the nation lived up to its promises.

Fighting Jim Crow

Just as slaves had revolted against being someone else's property, the newly freed blacks revolted peacefully against the forces of racism. Ida B. Wells (later Wells-Barnett) began a crusade against lynching at age 19 that inspired a national gathering of black leaders in 1893 to call for an anti-lynch law.

George Henry White, the only black U.S. congressman at the turn of the century, was a bold spokesman for equal rights. The former slave from North Carolina sponsored the first anti-lynching bill and insisted that the federal government enforce the constitutional amendments. In a speech to his fellow congressmen, White asked, "How long will you sit in your seats and hear and see the principles that underlie the foundations of this government sapped away little by little?"

One of the strongest critiques of American racism was offered by W. E. B. DuBois, a Harvard-educated sociologist. In *The Souls of Black Folk*, DuBois said American society had to be transformed if blacks were to achieve full equality.

DuBois, along with other black and white leaders, established the National Association for the Advancement of Colored People (NAACP) in 1910. The NAACP launched a legal campaign against racial injustice, began documenting racist violence, and published a magazine called *Crisis*. By 1940, NAACP membership reached 50,000.

As blacks were organizing for reform, white supremacists were organizing to stop them. By the time the NAACP was 10 years old, two million whites belonged to the Ku Klux Klan. During the 1920s, Klansmen held high positions in government throughout the country.

In the South, Klan violence surged. Blacks moved North in record numbers, hoping to escape racial terrorism and to find better jobs. Although they faced poverty, unequal education, and discrimination in the North as well, racial restrictions there were less harsh. Blacks could even vote in Northern states. Indeed, by 1944, the black vote was a significant factor in 16 states outside the South.

Bringing Democracy Home

With the election of President Franklin Delano Roosevelt, black Americans finally had an ally in the White House. Black leaders were included among the president's advisers. Roosevelt's New Deal made welfare and jobs available to blacks as well as whites. A more liberal Supreme Court issued rulings against bus segregation and all-white political primaries. Black labor leader A. Philip Randolph scored a major victory when he convinced President Roosevelt to issue an Executive Order banning racial discrimination in all defense industries.

The demand for equal rights surged after World War II, when black soldiers returned from battling the racist horrors of Nazi Germany only to find they remained victims of racism at home.

Determined to bring democracy to America, blacks sought new strategies. Seeing Mohandas Gandhi[2] lead the Indian masses in peaceful demonstrations for independence, the Congress of Racial Equality (CORE) decided to put the philosophy of nonviolence to work in America.

After much training and discussion, black and white members of CORE entered segregated restaurants, quietly sat down, and refused to leave until they were served. They did not raise their voices in anger or strike back if attacked. In a few Northern cities, their persistent demonstrations succeeded in integrating some restaurants.

After the Supreme Court outlawed segregation on interstate buses in 1946, CORE members set out on a "Journey of Reconciliation" to test whether the laws were being obeyed. Blacks and whites rode together on buses through the South and endured harassment without retaliating.

While the sit-ins and freedom rides of the 1940s served as models for the next generation of civil rights activists, they did not capture the broad support that was necessary to overturn segregation. The CORE victories were quiet ones, representing the determination of relatively few people.

The major battles against segregation were being fought in courtrooms and legislatures. Growing pressure from black leaders after World War II forced President Harry Truman to integrate the armed forces and to establish a civil rights commission. In 1947, that commission issued a report called *To Secure These Rights* that exposed racial injustices and called for the elimination of segregation in America.

By that time, half a million blacks belonged to the NAACP. Lawsuits brought by the NAACP had forced many school districts to improve black schools. Then, in 1950, NAACP lawyers began building the case that would force the Supreme Court to outlaw segregated schools and mark the beginning of the modern civil rights movement.

A Movement of the People

Linda Brown's parents could not understand why their 7-year-old daughter should have to ride long distances each day to a rundown black school when there was a much better white school in their own neighborhood of Topeka, Kansas. Harry Briggs of Clarendon, South Carolina, was outraged that his five children had to attend schools which operated on one-fourth the amount of money given to white schools. Ethel Belton took her complaints to the Delaware Board of Education when her children were forced to ride a bus for nearly two hours each day instead of walking to their neighborhood high school in Claymont. In Farmville, Virginia, 16-year-old Barbara Johns led her fellow high school students on a strike for a better school.

All over the country, black students and parents were angered over the conditions of their schools. NAACP lawyers studied their grievances and decided that it was not enough to keep fighting for equal facilities. They wanted all schools integrated.

A team of NAACP lawyers used the Topeka, Clarendon, Claymont and Farmville examples to argue that segregation itself was unconstitutional. They lost in the lower courts, but when they took their cause to the Supreme Court, the justices ruled they were right.

On May 17, 1954, the Supreme Court unanimously ruled that segregated schools "are inherently unequal." The Court explained that even if separate

schools for blacks and whites had the same physical facilities, there could be no true equality as long as segregation itself existed. To separate black children "solely because of their race," the Court wrote, "generates a feeling of inferiority as to their status in the community that may affect their hearts and minds in a way very unlikely ever to be undone."

The *Brown v. Board of Education* ruling enraged many Southern whites who did not believe blacks deserved the same education as whites and didn't want their children attending schools with black children. Southern governors announced they would not abide by the Court's ruling, and White Citizens' Councils were organized to oppose school integration. Mississippi legislators passed a law abolishing compulsory school attendance. A declaration called the Southern Manifesto was issued by 96 Southern congressmen, demanding that the Court reverse the *Brown* decision.

Despite the opposition by many whites, the *Brown* decision gave great hope to blacks. Even when the Supreme Court refused to order immediate integration (calling instead for schools to act "with all deliberate speed"), black Americans knew that times were changing. And they were eager for expanded rights in other areas as well.

Walking for Justice

Four days after the Supreme Court handed down the *Brown* ruling, Jo Ann Robinson wrote a letter as president of the Women's Political Council to the mayor of Montgomery, Alabama. She represented a large group of black women, she said, and was asking for fair treatment on city buses.

Blacks, who made up 75 percent of Montgomery's bus riders, were forced to enter the buses in front, pay the driver, and re-enter the bus from the rear, where they could only sit in designated "colored" seats. If all the "white" seats were full, blacks had to give up their seats.

Women and children had been arrested for refusing to give up their seats. Others who challenged the bus drivers were slapped or beaten. Hilliard Brooks, 22, was shot dead by police in 1952 after an argument with a bus driver.

Every day, black housekeepers rode all the way home after work, jammed together in the aisles, while 10 rows of "white" seats remained empty.

Blacks could shut down the city's bus system if they wanted to, Jo Ann Robinson told the mayor.

"More and more of our people are already arranging with neighbors and friends to ride to keep from being insulted and humiliated by bus drivers."

The mayor said segregation was the law and he could not change it.

On December 1, 1955, Rosa Parks was riding home from her job as a department store seamstress. The bus was full when a white man boarded. The driver stopped the bus and ordered Mrs. Parks along with three other blacks to vacate a row so the white man could sit down. Three of the blacks stood up. Rosa Parks kept her seat and was arrested.

Jo Ann Robinson and the Women's Political Council immediately began to organize a bus boycott with the support of NAACP leader E. D. Nixon. Prominent blacks hurriedly formed the Montgomery Improvement Association and selected a newcomer in town, Dr. Martin Luther King Jr., to be their leader.

On the night of December 5, a crowd of 15,000 gathered at Holt Street Church to hear the young preacher speak. "There comes a time that people get tired," King told the crowd. "We are here this evening to say to those who have mistreated us so long that we are tired—tired of being segregated and humiliated; tired of being kicked about by the brutal feet of oppression. . . . We have no alternative but to protest."

"And we are not wrong in what we are doing," he said. "If we are wrong, the Supreme Court of this nation is wrong. If we are wrong, God Almighty is wrong!"

If the bus boycott was peaceful and guided by love, King said, justice would be won. Historians in future generations, King predicted, "will have to pause and say, 'There lived a great people—a black people—who injected new meaning and dignity into the veins of civilization.'"

For 381 days, black people did not ride the buses in Montgomery. They organized carpools and walked long distances, remaining nonviolent even when harassed and beaten by angry whites. When Dr. King's home was bombed, they only became more determined. City officials tried to outlaw the boycott, but still the buses traveled empty.

On December 21, 1956, blacks returned to the buses in triumph. The U.S. Supreme Court had outlawed bus segregation in Montgomery in response to a lawsuit brought by the boycotters with the help of the NAACP. The boycotters' victory showed the entire white South that all blacks, not just civil rights leaders, were opposed to segregation. It demonstrated that poor and middle-class blacks could unite

to launch a successful protest movement, overcoming both official counterattacks and racist terror. And it showed the world that nonviolent resistance could work—even in Montgomery, the capital of the Confederate States during the Civil War.

King went on to establish an organization of black clergy, called the Southern Christian Leadership Conference, that raised funds for integration campaigns throughout the South. Black Southern ministers, following the example of King in Montgomery, became the spiritual force behind the nonviolent movement. Using the lessons of Montgomery, blacks challenged bus segregation in Tallahassee and Atlanta.

But when they tried to integrate schools and other public facilities, blacks discovered the lengths to which whites would go to preserve white supremacy. A black student admitted to the University of Alabama by federal court order was promptly expelled. The State of Virginia closed all public schools in Prince Edward County to avoid integration. Some communities filled in their public swimming pools and closed their tennis courts, and others removed library seats, rather than let blacks and whites share the facilities.

Blacks who challenged segregation received little help from the federal government. President Eisenhower had no enthusiasm for the *Brown* decision, and he desperately wanted to avoid segregation disputes.

Finally, in 1957, a crisis in Little Rock, Arkansas, forced Eisenhower to act.

Nine Pioneers in Little Rock

On September 4, 1957, Governor Orval Faubus ordered troops to surround Central High School in Little Rock, to keep nine black teenagers from entering. Despite the *Brown* ruling, which said black students had a right to attend integrated schools, Governor Faubus was determined to keep the schools segregated.

That afternoon, a federal judge ordered Faubus to let the black students attend the white school. The next day, when 15-year-old Elizabeth Eckford set out for class, she was mobbed, spit upon and cursed by angry whites. When she finally made her way to the front steps of Central High, National Guard soldiers turned her away.

An outraged federal judge again ordered the governor to let the children go to school. Faubus removed the troops but gave the black children no protection. The nine black children made it to their first class but had to be sent home when a violent white mob gathered outside the school. Faubus said the disturbance proved the school should not be integrated.

President Eisenhower had a choice: he could either send in federal troops to protect the children or allow a governor to defy the Constitution. Saying "our personal opinions have no bearing on the matter of enforcement," the president ordered in troops. For the rest of the school year, U.S. soldiers walked alongside the Little Rock nine as they went from class to class.

The next year, Governor Faubus shut down all the public schools rather than integrate them. A year later, the U.S. Supreme Court ruled that "evasive schemes" could not be used to avoid integration, and the Little Rock schools were finally opened to black and white students.

Although the Little Rock case did not end the long battle for school integration, it proved the federal government would not tolerate brazen defiance of federal law by state officials. It also served as an example for President John F. Kennedy, who in 1962 ordered federal troops to protect James Meredith as he became the first black student to attend the University of Mississippi.

[1989]

Terms

1. Frederick Douglass: An escaped slave, who became a leading abolitionist.
2. Mohandas Gandhi: A Hindu nationalist and spiritual leader, who led the "passive resistance" movement to get the British out of India.

Understanding the Reading

1. What were Jim Crow laws?
2. How did the newly freed blacks respond to them?
3. How did Franklin Roosevelt's presidency benefit black Americans?
4. What gains did CORE achieve?
5. Explain the Supreme Court ruling in *Brown v. Board of Education*.
6. What made the Montgomery bus boycott effective?
7. What tactics did whites use to avoid school desegregation?

Suggestions for Responding

1. Imagine that you were an African American in the South in the first half of the twentieth century. Choose one example of Jim Crow segregation (separate schools, restrooms, waiting rooms, drinking fountains; prohibitions on voting; rules about having to ride in the back of the bus) and describe your experience. What would you realistically do in such circumstances?
2. Learn more details about one specific example of southern white resistance to school integration, and write a brief report on it.

68

The Movement

ANNE MOODY

I had counted on graduating in the spring of 1963, but, as it turned out, I couldn't because some of my credits still had to be cleared with Natchez College. A year before, this would have seemed like a terrible disaster, but now I hardly even felt disappointed. I had a good excuse to stay on campus for the summer and work with the Movement, and this was what I really wanted to do. I couldn't go home again anyway, and I couldn't go to New Orleans—I didn't have money enough for bus fare.

During my senior year at Tougaloo, my family hadn't sent me one penny. I had only the small amount of money I had earned at Maple Hill. I couldn't afford to eat at school or live in the dorms, so I had gotten permission to move off campus. I had to prove that I could finish school, even if I had to go hungry every day. I knew Raymond and Miss Pearl were just waiting to see me drop out. But something happened to me as I got more and more involved in the Movement. It no longer seemed important to prove anything. I had found something outside myself that gave meaning to my life.

I had become very friendly with my social science professor, John Salter, who was in charge of NAACP[1] activities on campus. All during the year, while the NAACP conducted a boycott of the downtown stores in Jackson, I had been one of Salter's most faithful canvassers and church speakers. During the last week of school, he told me that sit-in demonstrations were about to start in Jackson and that he wanted me to be the spokesman for a team that would sit-in at Woolworth's lunch counter. The two other demonstrators would be classmates of mine, Memphis and Pearlena. Pearlena was a dedicated NAACP worker, but Memphis had not been very involved in the Movement on campus. It seemed that the organization had had a rough time finding students who were in a position to go to jail. I had nothing to lose one way or the other. Around ten o'clock the morning of the demonstrations, NAACP headquarters alerted the news services. As a result, the police department was also informed, but neither the policemen nor the newsmen knew exactly where or when the demonstrations would start. They stationed themselves along Capitol Street and waited.

To divert attention from the sit-in at Woolworth's, the picketing started at J. C. Penney's a good fifteen minutes before. The pickets were allowed to walk up and down in front of the store three or four times before they were arrested. At exactly 11 A.M., Pearlena, Memphis, and I entered Woolworth's from the rear entrance. We separated as soon as we stepped into the store, and made small purchases from various counters. Pearlena had given Memphis her watch. He was to let us know when it was 11:14. At 11:14 we were to join him near the lunch counter and at exactly 11:15 we were to take seats at it.

Seconds before 11:15 we were occupying three seats at the previously segregated Woolworth's lunch counter. In the beginning the waitresses seemed to ignore us, as if they really didn't know what was going on. Our waitress walked past us a couple of times before she noticed we had started to write our own orders down and realized we wanted service. She asked us what we wanted. We began to read to her from our order slips. She told us that we would be served at the back counter, which was for Negroes.

"We would like to be served here," I said.

The waitress started to repeat what she had said, then stopped in the middle of the sentence. She turned the lights out behind the counter, and she and the other waitresses almost ran to the back of the store, deserting all their white customers. I guess they thought that violence would start immediately after the whites at the counter realized what was going on. There were five or six other people at the counter. A couple of them just got up and walked away. A girl sitting next to me finished her banana split before leaving. A middle-aged white woman who had not yet been served rose from her seat and came over to us.

"I'd like to stay here with you," she said, "but my husband is waiting."

The newsmen came in just as she was leaving. They must have discovered what was going on shortly after some of the people began to leave the store. One of the newsmen ran behind the woman who spoke to us and asked her to identify herself. She refused to give her name, but said she was a native of Vicksburg and a former resident of California. When asked why she had said what she had said to us, she replied, "I am in sympathy with the Negro movement." By this time a crowd of cameramen and reporters had gathered around us taking pictures and asking questions, such as Where were we from? Why did we sit-in? What organization sponsored it? Were we students? From what school? How were we classified?

I told them that we were all students at Tougaloo College, that we were represented by no particular organization, and that we planned to stay there even after the store closed. "All we want is service," was my reply to one of them. After they had finished probing for about twenty minutes, they were almost ready to leave.

At noon, students from a nearby white high school started pouring in to Woolworth's. When they first saw us they were sort of surprised. They didn't know how to react. A few started to heckle and the newsmen became interested again. Then the white students started chanting all kinds of anti-Negro slogans. We were called a little bit of everything. The rest of the seats except the three we were occupying had been roped off to prevent others from sitting down. A couple of the boys took one end of the rope and made it into a hangman's noose. Several attempts were made to put it around our necks. The crowds grew as more students and adults came in for lunch.

We kept our eyes straight forward and did not look at the crowd except for occasional glances to see what was going on. All of a sudden I saw a face I remembered—the drunkard from the bus station sit-in. My eyes lingered on him just long enough for us to recognize each other. Today he was drunk too, so I don't think he remembered where he had seen me before. He took out a knife, opened it, put it in his pocket, and then began to pace the floor. At this point, I told Memphis and Pearlena what was going on. Memphis suggested that we pray. We bowed our heads, and all hell broke loose. A man rushed forward, threw Memphis from his seat, and slapped my face. Then another man who worked in the store threw me against an adjoining counter.

Down on my knees on the floor, I saw Memphis lying near the lunch counter with blood running out of the corners of his mouth. As he tried to protect his face, the man who'd thrown him down kept kicking him against the head. If he had worn hard-soled shoes instead of sneakers, the first kick probably would have killed Memphis. Finally a man dressed in plain clothes identified himself as a police officer and arrested Memphis and his attacker.

Pearlena had been thrown to the floor. She and I got back on our stools after Memphis was arrested. There were some white Tougaloo teachers in the crowd. They asked Pearlena and me whether we wanted to leave. They said that things were getting too rough. We didn't know what to do. While we were trying to make up our minds, we were joined by Joan Trumpauer. Now there were three of us and we were integrated. The crowd began to chant, "Communists, Communists, Communists." Some old man in the crowd ordered the students to take us off the stools.

"Which one should I get first?" a big husky boy said.

"That white nigger," the old man said.

The boy lifted Joan from the counter by her waist and carried her out of the store. Simultaneously, I was snatched from my stool by two high school students. I was dragged about thirty feet toward the door by my hair when someone made them turn me loose. As I was getting up off the floor, I saw Joan coming back inside. We started back to the center of the counter to join Pearlena. Lois Chaffee, a white Tougaloo faculty member, was now sitting next to her. So Joan and I just climbed across the rope at the front end of the counter and sat down. There were now four of us, two whites and two Negroes, all women. The mob started smearing us with ketchup, mustard, sugar, pies, and everything on the counter. Soon Joan and I were joined by John Salter, but the moment he sat down he was hit on the jaw with what appeared to be brass knuckles. Blood gushed from his face and someone threw salt into the open wound. Ed King, Tougaloo's chaplain, rushed to him.

At the other end of the counter, Lois and Pearlena were joined by George Raymond, a CORE[2] field worker and a student from Jackson State College. Then a Negro high school boy sat down next to me. The mob took spray paint from the counter and sprayed it on the new demonstrators. The high school student had on a white shirt; the word "nigger" was written on his back with red spray paint.

We sat there for three hours taking a beating when the manager decided to close the store because the mob had begun to go wild with stuff from other counters. He begged and begged everyone to leave. But even after fifteen minutes of begging, no one budged. They would not leave until we did. Then Dr. Beittel, the president of Tougaloo College, came running in. He said he had just heard what was happening.

About ninety policemen were standing outside the store; they had been watching the whole thing through the windows but had not come in to stop the mob or do anything. President Beittel went outside and asked Captain Ray to come and escort us out. The captain refused, stating the manager had to invite him in before he could enter the premises, so Dr. Beittel himself brought us out. He had told the police that they had better protect us after we were outside the store. When we got outside, the policemen formed a single line that blocked the mob from us. However, they were allowed to throw at us everything they had collected. Within ten minutes, we were picked up by Reverend King in his station wagon and taken to the NAACP headquarters on Lynch Street.

After the sit-in, all I could think of was how sick Mississippi whites were. They believed so much in the segregated Southern way of life, they would kill to preserve it. I sat there in the NAACP office and thought of how many times they had killed when this way of life was threatened. I knew that the killing had just begun. "Many more will die before it is over with," I thought. Before the sit-in, I had always hated the whites in Mississippi. Now I knew it was impossible for me to hate sickness. The whites had a disease, an incurable disease in its final stage. What were our chances against such a disease? I thought of the students, the young Negroes who had just begun to protest, as young interns. When these young interns got older, I thought, they would be the best doctors in the world for social problems.

Before we were taken back to campus, I wanted to get my hair washed. It was stiff with dried mustard, ketchup and sugar. I stopped in at a beauty shop across the street from the NAACP office. I didn't have on any shoes because I had lost them when I was dragged across the floor at Woolworth's. My stockings were sticking to my legs from the mustard that had dried on them. The hairdresser took one look at me and said, "My land, you were in the sit-in, huh?"

"Yes," I answered. "Do you have time to wash my hair and style it?"

254 Change / Change Makers

"Right away," she said, and she meant right away. There were three other ladies already waiting, but they seemed glad to let me go ahead of them. The hairdresser was real nice. She even took my stockings off and washed my legs while my hair was drying.

There was a mass rally that night at the Pearl Street Church in Jackson, and the place was packed. People were standing two abreast in the aisles. Before the speakers began, all the sit-inners walked out on the stage and were introduced by Medgar Evers.[3] People stood and applauded for what seemed like thirty minutes or more. Medgar told the audience that this was just the beginning of such demonstrations. He asked them to pledge themselves to unite in a massive offensive against segregation in Jackson, and throughout the state. The rally ended with "We Shall Overcome" and sent home hundreds of determined people. It seemed as though Mississippi Negroes were about to get together at last.

[1968]

Terms

1. NAACP: National Association for the Advancement of Colored People.
2. CORE: Congress of Racial Equality.
3. Medgar Evers: The NAACP field secretary in Mississippi, who was assassinated a few weeks after this event.

Understanding the Reading

1. How do you account for the various reactions of the whites at the lunch counter when the demonstrators sat down?
2. Why did the high school students respond differently than these people did?
3. Explain the reaction of the women in the beauty shop.

Suggestion for Responding

1. Explain how Moody's experience illustrates the various features of nonviolent resistance.

69

Freedom Is a Constant Struggle

Muriel Tillinghast

Three days after I graduated, I decided I was going to Mississippi. I didn't know what was going to happen after that, but I was definitely going to go. Now, it was already bad enough that I had let my hair grow natural—that eliminated about 90 percent of the discussion in my house—but when I decided to go to Mississippi, everyone got on my case. My parents, my family—people weren't *talking* to me.

We knew that something momentous was occurring down South. People were operating in very small groups, but they were operating in many different places. At that point the press had not yet decided what political perspective they were going to take on events in the South, so they were actually showing all this activity on television. This was a source of encouragement for us and helped to tie the lines of communication together. Of course, that didn't last. Later on, I'm sure the press boys sat down in a large room and said, "Enough of this, let's move on."

Now, I was basically a Northerner—folks from Washington, D.C., like to think that they're from the North. I had already had some experiences on the eastern shore of Maryland, which will let you know immediately that you're not North, but I hadn't really gotten ready for Mississippi. We all spent a week at the orientation center in Oxford, Ohio. SNCC[1] sent up its people, who told us all these tales about what folks had to go through just in terms of a normal life struggle. We knew that Mississippi was going to be a special place. And for all of us who went, we know we didn't come back the same.

Heading South

So we went to Mississippi after spending a week getting ready for something you really couldn't get ready for. We headed in on Greyhound buses. People were singing and talking and joking around on the bus, but when we hit that Mississippi line there was silence. People got dropped off at various projects one by one in the dead of night. I was dropped off in Greenville. We made a point of distinguishing Greenville from Greenwood. Green*ville* was relatively liberal. If you were in Green*wood*, you were in deep. I still had hope.

In all honesty I spent my first two weeks in the office upstairs because I didn't know quite how I was going to be able to survive Mississippi. After a while it dawned on me that I would never get anybody to register that way, so I started coming downstairs and cautiously going out into the town. I functioned like a shadow on the wall, just getting used to walking in the streets.

Charles Cobb was my project director. About a month after I got to Mississippi, Charles looked at me and said, "You know, I want to do something else. So I'm going to leave you in charge of this project. You look like you can handle it." Right, sure thing . . .

I was in charge of three counties: Washington, Sharkey, and Issaquena. In Mississippi, you learn the county structure like the back of your hand, because the basis of power politics is the county structure. Greenville, which was the base of our operations, was the Washington County seat. It was the town in a county of hamlets. Sharkey County was the home of the Klan in that part of Mississippi. Issaquena was a black county, and it was sort of discounted at the time.

By and large we took our mandate from Stokely Carmichael (Kwame Toure), who was the project chief in our area. We were young, and we were just beginning to learn what politics and power were all about. We began to find out that power is monolithic, particularly in places where there is not a lot of competition.

People in Mississippi knew about us long before we had even gotten there. We didn't realize it at first, but we were under constant surveillance. For instance, a young white volunteer was doing some research at the library, which was in the same building as the police station, on the second floor. As she was coming out of the library, the police chief said to her, "Come here, I want to show you something." He took her to a room, and in that room was a file drawer, and in that file drawer were pictures of everybody in our project. We had no idea that they were watching us this closely. And they had pictures of every kind of activity, taken day and night, because they were using infrared.

Well, these pictures may not mean anything right now, but there were times when the political pressure really got to us. For example, we had some young gay men who were in our project, and I remember very tearfully putting one of them on the bus. He said, "Muriel, I can't have those pictures shown." I didn't even know that anything was going on, but the bot-tom line is that everybody's privacy was invaded. And that's *before* we had even registered anybody to vote.

In these little country towns, as soon as a foreign-sounding motor comes across the road in the middle of the night, people know that a stranger is there. You need never make an announcement. You can stay in the house all day—someone knows. "I heard a different motor last night. It stopped about two doors down the street." And they start making inquiries. There were instances when the police just opened the door and came through the house looking for us and never said a word to any of the people who lived there. Not that they were going to rough us up at that point, but someone knew that someone was keeping company with people who weren't local.

In order to encourage people to vote, we had to explain what was going on in the country and why they were in the situation that they were in. We tried to convince them of the importance of their participation in the voting process by showing them who was actually on the voting rolls—for instance, half the local cemetery! Sometimes we were able to register only a few people—why risk your life simply to sign a piece of paper or register at the county courthouse—but as people gradually came to trust us, they would talk to their neighbors, and the numbers swelled.

The Heart of the Black Belt

Later I moved out of Greenville and into Issaquena County. Until I got to Mississippi, I didn't know anything about black counties. I began to find out that there were these towns like Mound Bayou, outside of Holly Springs, where blacks had settled after the Emancipation Proclamation and established their own base.

Most people in the North don't understand why blacks are so poor. They don't realize that when black people left slavery, they left with nothing—I mean *nothing*. Whatever they were wearing, those were the clothes that they took with them into their new life. Whatever beans or seeds they could gather, that was going to be food. They didn't own the land they were standing on—they were immediately trespassing. And in Mississippi trespassing was a serious crime—as serious as selling a kilo of cocaine in New York City today. You were going to go to jail and your minimum time was going to be five years—just for standing on the land.

So the people had to move, and when they moved, they moved under pain of death, because the same people who had always kept black people enslaved were again at work hunting down those bands of blacks who were leaving by foot. Black people had no way of defending themselves. They had to travel by night, gathering up at certain places—word gets around on the grapevine. And they began to establish themselves in various places, even in the state of Mississippi. Issaquena was one of those places. It was sort of a long county, and very sparsely settled. Counting everybody standing up, the county seat at Mayersville had 50 people.

Some of you may be familiar with the name of Unita Blackwell. She made a name for herself over time as the mayor of Mayersville and as an activist, but when I met Unita, she was just an ordinary housewife. She and her husband, Jeremiah Blackwell, were the first ones to offer us a safe haven in Issaquena. That's really how we operated. We would be invited in by one household, and based on that household's sense of us as individuals and where we were going as an organization—because they knew that we were not alone—they would introduce us to someone else. This would be our next contact. And if this sounds like we were operating under war conditions, we were. You did not talk to *anybody* unless someone said it was okay. And it wasn't that obvious who was safe to talk to, because you never knew whether you were talking to the State Sovereignty Commission.

The State Sovereignty Commission was an intelligence-gathering force. It was set up by the government of the state of Mississippi. Hundreds of thousands of dollars of state taxpayers' money—including black taxpayers' money—was used to finance all this surveillance. It was responsible for gathering and spreading disinformation early in the game. Early on we thought it was *mis*information—that they just didn't get it straight—but it was really *dis*information that was deliberately designed to undermine public support for the activities that we were engaged in.

You had to be careful about who you spoke to because you could be trailed back to your base. Wherever you were staying, those people were as vulnerable to midnight raids as you were on the streets. So when they allowed you to sleep on their floor or in their best bed in the corner of their house, whatever the accommodations were, they were putting themselves in jeopardy. As Bob Moses used to say, "Mississippi needs no exaggeration." It was its own exaggeration.

I remember one family of cotton pickers that I stayed with—two adults and five kids. They were in Hollandale, a nasty little town on the highway between Greenville and Mayersville. This family was at the very bottom of the economic ladder. They worked by permission on someone else's land. They worked from sun up to sun down with no breaks. It was as close to slavery as I hope I ever see in life. I usually made a point of eating somewhere else, but one night they said, "No, you eat with us." I'll never forget that dinner. It was cornbread and a huge pot of water into which they cut three or four frankfurters. For them that was a *good* dinner.

Founding a Freedom School

We also started a Freedom School. Why? Well, out of natural curiosity schoolchildren wanted to know, "Why can't we vote?" So there was a need to put this particular situation into some sort of historical context. And as you talked about the history of black people in this country, you began to see another kind of development taking place in the young people. Before they would let certain things in school go by unchallenged. They might not like something, but they wouldn't question it. Our presence gave them a support base, and they began to have the courage to say certain things, or not to read certain things, or to bring other materials to the classroom. This was unheard of. And it wouldn't take long before those kids would be sent home—first one kid, then another, and by the time a week had passed, there would be 20 kids who had been told by the principal, "Don't come back!"

Now the school system was segregated—these were black kids in black schools—so how could this be happening? To understand that, you have to understand the power relations in the South. You don't get to be a black principal in a black school in Mississippi unless you are an acceptable political commodity—pure and simple. And you quickly become *un*acceptable when you start having alien thoughts, like why can't we register to vote and what is this Grandfather Clause anyway—just normal conversation. But that wasn't considered normal conversation—that was considered subversive, and these young people had to be plucked out before they spread the cancer to the rest of the student population. So even though most of us tried to maintain a low profile, it didn't take long for brush fires to occur.

Sheriff Davis Builds a Jail

Even though Issaquena was a black county, all the people who had any power were white, including Sheriff Davis. When our paths crossed, which they did all too frequently, we would greet each other—"How ya doin'?"—because Mississippi is country-like in that way. The first time I saw Sheriff Davis coming down the road he had a pickup truck. By the next week the pickup truck had a kind of metal grating on the top. One day he stopped me and said, "You like that, you like what I got? Well, that's for y'all."

And then Sheriff Davis told us that he was building a one-room jail out of cinder blocks—just for us! And did we like that? It was big enough to stand up in, you could sit down, and of course it was out there in the middle of the hot sun. When we told him he was really wasting his time, Sheriff Davis said, "Well, I know you're gonna do something. I know you are, and I'll keep up with you." Sometimes when we would go walking down the street, there was Sheriff Davis's car, coming right behind us. He'd sit in the front and wait, and sometimes we'd go past the person's house and go to somebody else's house in the back, because we didn't want to lead him directly to our next possible registrant.

I don't think we understand what people risked when they took those steps. As soon as we had made contact with people, as soon as they went to the courthouse to register, their boss would be right there. If they worked in the cotton fields, oftentimes they were dismissed immediately. Or they'd be cut off of their welfare rations. The power system was consolidated on the notion that no, you will not move up, you will not challenge us in any way.

Welcoming the Klan

Then we began to look at other things that were going on. Why could some people plant cotton when others couldn't? There were these gentlemen farmers who planted nothing but made an awful lot of money, and then there were people who were planting cotton but were barely able to get it ginned. So, early on, we began to deal with the cotton allotment system. Well, when we began to run people for the cotton allotment board, we hit the economic bell. And that brought out the Klan.

Sometimes the Klan seemed benign compared to some of the other rabid, racist organizations, like the Association for the Preservation of the White Race,

who made no bones about the fact that if they saw you, they were going to kill you.

One time I called a meeting of tractor workers, thinking that I was going to organize *black* tractor workers, and I walked right dead into a nest of Klansmen who had gotten the same word. I don't know who had told them, but they were there. As I approached them in my car—carefully—I was wondering who were all these white men standing at the church steps. They knew something was wrong because the place of the meeting was a black church, and they didn't look happy. I kind of looked at them. They kind of looked at me. I said, "You here for the meetin'?" and they said, "Yeah. You called the meetin'?" I said, "No. I'm just looking for the person who called the meetin'." And I kind of backed on out and left.

All of us learned how to be patient, how to play for the occasion, because your life could turn on a dime. Later you might laugh, but at the time it wouldn't seem so funny. Like the time I ran into the police car. Now, you should have seen me jump out of my car all incensed, carrying on about this and that, with this poor white volunteer sitting next to me. He just knew we were dead. But this policeman was so disgusted with me that he just told me to get a move on.

Life Lessons

One of the things I have learned about doing political work is that you may not be serious, or you may not know how serious a step you're taking, but when the opposition see anybody treading on their territory, they're *always* serious.

We had so many near misses, so many close calls, and we had nobody to depend on but ourselves. If you had a problem, you sure couldn't call a cop! Which is almost the same situation in which the black community finds itself in the inner cities today. If you have a problem and you call the cop, the cop is going to give you a *bigger* problem. So we learned to handle things ourselves as best we could.

Most of all we learned that people in Mississippi were a very special group of people. They were our country's peasant base. They were incredible in their wisdom, and many had extreme courage. I can remember this guy, Applewhite. Now Applewhite was a placid, nondescript kind of guy. You were never quite sure whether what you had to say registered. I didn't like riding with Applewhite because I felt that if I was going to get pushed into something, I was going to be on my own. One day we were riding down the road, and I said to Applewhite, "Do you have anything in this car in case we get stopped?" Well, you would never know what was going on in Applewhite's head—he had a perfect poker face. "Open up the glove compartment," he said. "Check down underneath the seat on my side. And on your side. Listen, we may not survive, but we sure could blaze a few holes." I said, "That's the way I want to go."

I learned that people aren't always what they appear. At the same time you're trying to organize them, they're trying to figure out where you are in this constellation of players. Are you going to be around when the action goes down? Am I talking to the State Sovereignty Commission? And essentially, is what you're telling me true? That's why we always encouraged people to read. We always encouraged people to discuss. Nothing that we did was cloaked in any kind of secrecy, which is the way I've continued to operate.

So that was my life for two years. It was about day-to-day survival but it was also about how you transform a community that really had not been touched in over 100 years by any outside force—how you get it to join the twentieth century and get enough players inside that loop to be able to carry it on after you leave. On the whole, I think we were very successful. We paid some very, very high prices for it, but I think most of us would have done it again.

[1994]

Term

1. SNCC: Student Nonviolent Coordinating Committee.

Understanding the Reading

1. How were the volunteers prepared for going to Mississippi?
2. What were Tillinghast's responsibilities in Mississippi?
3. In what ways were the volunteers threatened by law enforcement?
4. How did the volunteers persuade people to register to vote?
5. Why were southern blacks so poor?
6. What was the State Sovereignty Commission?
7. What was the Freedom School, and why was it established?
8. What tactics did Sheriff Davis use to intimidate the volunteers?

9. Why did Tillinghast feel the volunteers had to handle problems on their own?
10. How did she feel about the Mississippi blacks?

Suggestions for Responding

1. List the various resistance tactics white Mississippians used, and rank-order them based on your sense of their effectiveness, justifying your choices.
2. Consider one of the experiences Tillinghast describes, and write a short narrative or essay describing how you think you might have reacted to it. Comment on how you wish you might have reacted instead.

70

"Don't Tell Us It Can't Be Done"

Michael Ryan

Martha Yallup, Sister Kathleen Ross, and their colleagues made something wonderful happen on the Yakima Indian Reservation in Washington State a decade ago. In a poor area where higher education was almost inaccessible, they began to train Head Start[1] teachers from the Indian communities. It was hard work, but it was doubly rewarding. Not only did the program give adults new skills, but it also helped provide a leg up for the children born into the grueling poverty of the reservation. For Martha, the tribe's Head Start director, and Sister Kathleen, the academic vice president of Fort Wright College in Spokane, the program was a splendid example of how a private college and a community group could work together to change lives.

Then disaster struck.

"In 1980, the board of Fort Wright decided to close the college," Sister Kathleen recalls. "I had the job of coming down here and telling Martha that we were going to have to end the program because the home campus was closing. I gave her the bad news, and I remember she just looked at me and said: 'No, it's not closing.'"

Instead of sitting by and watching their dream die, Martha Yallup got together with a colleague, Violet Rau, and Sister Kathleen and decided on a plan of incredible daring: They would start a college on their own.

The idea seemed as doomed as it was courageous. The reservation was no place to raise the funds needed to start a college from scratch. And Fort Wright was in no position to help much. A small liberal-arts school run by the Catholic Sisters of the Holy Names of Jesus and Mary, it had been driven out of business by competition from larger, better-financed schools. And, although Martha and Violet were confident, virtually nobody believed in them—except Sister Kathleen. "People on the reservation said, 'You're crazy. It's going to fail,'" Martha recalls.

But Martha and Violet went to work on the reservation, lining up community leaders, public officials and business people to form a board of directors for the new college—and to start raising money for it. Back in Spokane, Sister Kathleen persuaded college officials to keep Fort Wright open through the spring of 1982. Then the hard work began.

First, the new college needed recognition from the IRS[2] so that it could accept donations. Sister Kathleen fought her way through the agency's bureaucracy and emerged with official recognition. Then the women tried to persuade the authorities to transfer Fort Wright's accreditation to their new school. "Our philosophy had always been 'If you don't ask, you don't get,'" Martha says with a laugh. They failed, but they made a strong enough case that they were granted candidate status—the last step before full accreditation. That meant that their new school's courses could be recognized for full credit by other institutions.

But they had one more obstacle to clear: A college designed for some of the poorest people in the country would have to be able to offer financial aid. And the federal government's rule held that a school must be in business two years before its students qualify for federal loans. "We went to the top person in the Seattle office," Sister Kathleen says, "and he said, 'There's got to be a way,' so I asked him if I could see the book of regulations." She found a section that allowed the government to authorize financial aid when a school is sold to a new owner. It was clearly intended to cover vocational schools, but the rule didn't say that explicitly. "The guy looked at me like I was crazy," Sister Kathleen recalls. "Then he said, 'Why not?'" Sister Kathleen and her board of directors purchased their education program from Fort Wright for $1, and a new college was born.

The day I went to visit, Heritage College had been in business for eight years. It is a nondenominational institution—although a small group of nuns still holds key administrative positions at the school. Sister Kathleen Ross has been the president since before the college opened its doors. Martha Yallup, now the deputy director of the Yakima tribe's Department of Human Services, was the board's first chair and still serves as its secretary.

But the story that began with the determination of a handful of courageous women has become a story of courage and determination on the part of hundreds. This year, Heritage College will confer 199 degrees and certificates. The average Heritage student is 35 and, as the faculty likes to say, "place-bound"—inhibited by family and work commitments from traveling the 90 minutes it takes to get to the nearest college off the reservation. For most of the students, college is a dream which could never have come true without Heritage.

If you want to know how great the accomplishment of Sister Kathleen, Martha Yallup and the others is, meet Hipolito Mendez. He may be the typical Heritage student—an industrious, outgoing man who works part-time to pay his tuition and speaks eagerly of his planned career as a high school teacher. He is also a 47-year-old father of five. "My wife and I had a business, and it went down the tubes," he says. "We decided, 'Now's the time to go back to school and do something with our lives.' But we discovered we just couldn't afford to go to the state university. There wasn't much hope for us. Then we heard about Heritage."

Admittedly, he says, it felt strange for a man in middle age to become a college student, but Mendez found that Heritage's emphasis on personalized education eased his transition. "The first week, I was apprehensive," he says. "After that, I fit right in." Next fall, he will begin a new life as an educator—and his wife, Paula, will start teaching elementary school as well.

Or look at how Heritage has changed the life of Edith Walsey, 32. "If this college wasn't here, I wouldn't have gone to college, because of my family and my tradition and my husband," she confides. "I'm from the Warm Springs reservation in Oregon. The teachers here understand my customs. At first, it was kind of hard for me. My husband wasn't for me going to school. We have three children. Now he takes care of them while I'm in class and working part-time. I'm a junior studying computers. When I graduate, I hope to go home and work with my tribe."

In its eight years of existence, Heritage has grown from a three-room cottage to a set of buildings on the campus of a former elementary school in the reservation town of Toppenish. It now has 25 full-time faculty, an additional 70 or so part-time, and more than 400 degree-holding alumni. These are impressive statistics, but not as impressive as the testimonial one recent graduate gave Sister Kathleen last year. A native of the reservation, she had gone away to college but dropped out, feeling uncomfortable in an alien culture. Then she heard about Heritage. She enrolled and finished her degree. In one sentence, she summed up the magic of the school. As she told Sister Kathleen, "You allowed me not to be a failure."

[1991]

[Editor's note: Heritage College became Heritage University in 2004. As of fall 2017, it has 1,010 degree-seeking students for undergraduate and graduate degrees.]

Terms

1. Head Start: A federal program for disadvantaged preschoolers.
2. IRS: Internal Revenue Service.

Understanding the Reading

1. What problems did Yallup, Rau, and Sister Kathleen face in starting Heritage College?
2. How did they overcome each of them?
3. Evaluate the effectiveness of the project.

Suggestion for Responding

1. Describe a time when you faced what seemed to be impossible obstacles, and explain how you tackled them, alone or with the help of others.

71

Cecilia Fire Thunder: She Inspires Her People

ANN DAVIS

Cecilia Fire Thunder hunches over a doll she's making, clamping one more silver buckle on the belt before she fastens it to a dark blue, shell-decorated dress. The kitchen table where she works is a cluttered stage of tall, elegant Plains Indian women, hands outstretched with an eagle wing fan or holding a fringed shawl close in to their waists.

Her small trailer home on the Pine Ridge reservation in South Dakota is a Frankenstein's[1] laboratory—plastic bags full of arms, legs, and torsos bulge beneath the planter, overflow behind the TV. Corpses waiting for heads line the sofa.

Fire Thunder sits back and studies the doll, reading glasses perched at the end of her nose. "Some of that old stuff is ugly," she mutters, attaching a small buckskin bag to the belt. "I like my bodies to resemble bodies—they don't have to look like stuffed tamales."

When Fire Thunder started making dolls a few years ago, her original impetus was simple: to reflect contemporary Plains Indian women, the friends she dances with at pow-wows around the Midwest. When her foot-high dolls won her awards and trips to Washington, D.C., to demonstrate dollmaking techniques at the Smithsonian, she took it in stride. Making art is part of her life, and speaking in public goes with the territory.

You might think dollmaking an utterly apolitical activity. Not for Fire Thunder. Even her dolls are lessons in history and cultural values. The cowrie shells on her traditional dolls reveal the extensive trade routes existing between tribes on the West Coast and the Great Plains. The tanned hides are a vehicle to talk about the Lakota's relation to other life forms and their philosophy of natural harmony.

When she talks to non-Indian audiences, Fire Thunder uses the dolls to clear away misconceptions about Native Americans. When she speaks in local schools, she uses her dolls to talk about traditional values and the problems of drugs and alcohol.

"I talk to high school kids, not about how it should be, but about how it is," Fire Thunder said. Instead of lecturing about the evils of substance abuse, Fire Thunder asks them pointblank how many still do drugs, even after years of being preached at in the schools. Most raise their hands. Then they tell her about growing up in alcoholic homes, about nights of no sleep, worrying whether they'll get beat up by a drunk adult.

Even though students understand that drugs and alcohol are bad for them, Fire Thunder believes they will not change their behavior until adult problem drinkers admit it and share their experiences with younger people.

Fire Thunder says that part of the reason she can reach Indian people at a gut level is because she is one of them. She can tell jokes that non-Indians could never get away with, jokes that in a humorous way reveal people's dysfunctional behavior to themselves. For instance, what is Indian love? Answer: a black eye and a hickie.

"The gift I have is my humor, my gift to communicate," Fire Thunder said. "No white person can say what I say." She believes it is up to Indian people to solve their own problems.

When asked whether she ever gets overwhelmed by all the work, Fire Thunder says no. "My passion is what I do. The most important thing I have is that I know who I am," she says. "I still have a lot of quirks, but my identity is pretty strong. And I know when to play."

Out on the dance floor in the Rapid City Civic Center, Fire Thunder wears her traditional women's dress, decorated with cowrie shells and a handsome silver belt. Like the Pied Piper,[2] she breaks away from the movement of the group and leads a long snakeline of women in and out around a kaleidoscope of feathers and swirling fringe. She bends her head to hear a joke, laughs and continues her swinging walk, head tilted back elegantly, like one of her dolls. She's easy to pick out among hundreds of dancers. "If you feel good about yourself, you're just going to shine," says Cecilia Fire Thunder, and she does.

Fire Thunder goes non-stop. A dazzling public speaker, organizer in her home community of the Pine Ridge reservation, a founder of the Oglala Lakota Women's Society, registered nurse, mother, political lobbyist, pow-wow enthusiast, traditional dollmaker, KILI radio personality: you might think this enough for a lifetime or two. But this summer, Fire Thunder, who ran for tribal president—and lost—was also appointed tribal health planner for the Pine Ridge reservation and charged with building the first comprehensive plan to fight alcoholism.

Many community groups approved when Fire Thunder was appointed to the sensitive political post. "If anyone can do it, she can," was the comment heard frequently around the tribal office, according to Taylor Little White Man, executive director of the Oglala Sioux Tribe.

Like her dolls, she is tall and captivating with deep brown eyes, a brilliant smile and abundant energy. And some internal switch seems to have locked in the "on" position when Fire Thunder was born. It's an intensity that delights some and frustrates others. Her rebelliousness infuriated the nuns at Red Cloud Indian School, a Catholic boarding school she

attended until tenth grade. The nuns tried to convince the head priest not to let her come back; she was too influential with the other girls.

She rebelled most against the violence: How the religious brothers beat boys with thick belt-straps outside the girls' classroom windows. How the nuns humiliated "bad" girls by forcing them to bend over a big piano in front of the class, pulling down their panties and smacking them with rulers. How they did things so bad that Fire Thunder won't tell me about them.

"They hurt us to make us cry because once you cried, they'd defeated you," she said.

It took Fire Thunder years to undo the emotional damage caused by the boarding school, an internalized violence she feels she carried into her relationship with her children. "In order to do what I do, you have to confront your own devils, because something or someone will remind you of your past," Fire Thunder said. Fire Thunder's attempts at easing children's suffering is a constant in her work as community organizer, health planner, speaker, even dollmaker.

Inspired by her meeting with organizer Eileen Iron Cloud at a pow-wow in Colorado, and their discussions about empowering women and influencing state legislation at Pine Ridge, Fire Thunder, along with Iron Cloud, formed the Oglala Lakota Women's Society in 1987.

Fire Thunder recounts Lakota spiritual tradition, saying that thousands of years ago a woman gave her people a pipe and told them how to pray with it in ceremonies. This woman who came among the people was the inspiration for the women's society, says Fire Thunder. Through the society, women are able to air their concerns about community and tribal affairs.

Repeatedly, the number one issue on the nine reservations was alcohol. Not a surprising statistic, since some nine out of ten people on Pine Ridge are alcoholic.

"Part of community organizing is getting people to tell you what you already know," Fire Thunder said.

Now that women had identified their major focus, the group decided to take on the candidates for tribal election. Fire Thunder talked about sober leadership on her radio show; the women's society sent out 1,000 mailings urging voters to support sober leaders. At stump speeches, women badgered the candidates to state whether they still drank. "We didn't care who you were, what you did, what kind of past you had,"

Fire Thunder said. "If you were sober, we were gonna vote for you."

Though their criteria were crude, their results were impressive: after the smoke cleared on election night, eleven of the sixteen new tribal council members were declared non-drinkers.

The domestic violence was next. Tribal law had required that women sign a complaint against abusive partners before the police would act. In 1988, the women's society lobbied for and won a mandatory arrest law for domestic violence. Since fall of last year, whenever there is probable cause of domestic abuse, the perpetrator automatically spends the night in jail. The complaint is signed by the arresting officer. At first, a lot of "men in shock" were sitting in jail cells, Fire Thunder said. The women's society was criticized as "manhaters" and the trial court briefly tried to overturn the law. But most have now come to accept mandatory arrest as reality.

Part of the women's focus was on helping abusive men to change. Through their efforts, they won a grant to provide counseling to men who batter. "We did this because we also love our men," Fire Thunder said. "We want them to understand their rage and anger."

The society's other main concern was child sexual abuse. In 1988, the group staged a candlelight march in support of National Child Abuse Prevention Month. Last year, they went one step further by letting abused children speak out about their experience. In a two-hour show broadcast live on radio station KILI, six children talked about how it felt to be beaten, raped, ridiculed and neglected. "In those two hours, we reached more people in the listening audience than with anything else we ever did," Fire Thunder said.

Such confrontational tactics have not always made her a popular figure. She and others in the women's society have been accused of butting into other people's business. Some reservation people have complained that women's groups are not "traditional."

But Fire Thunder brushes off the criticism, saying she is motivated more by the pain of children than the fear of criticism. "When oppression is so great, there's no nice way to get to the heart of the people," she said. "The only way was 'shock treatment'—hit 'em hard and shake 'em up. Now that they've accomplished an awareness of issues on Pine Ridge, their tactics can change," she said.

The fierce pace of the women's society has slowed in the past year. Iron Cloud says the group lost its focus. She has been studying organizing models and believes that the women's society needs to reorient itself to keep all women involved, rather than having a few do all the work.

Fire Thunder believes everyone just got worn out. "We pulled back because we had to. For three years, we gave 150 percent of everything in our lives" to the women's society, she says. Fire Thunder agrees the group needs to restructure itself for the next phase of work.

Some say Fire Thunder sold out when she accepted a position with the tribal government this summer. "They say, 'Oh, they're gonna shut her up,'" Fire Thunder says. "But I took the position with the understanding that I could do more."

Though Iron Cloud counseled her not to take the new job, she believes Fire Thunder has the strength to hang in there and not sell out to political interests.

Perhaps she will. Fire Thunder has already written grants for half a million dollars and taken charge of the committee overseeing a new plan to house all alcohol programs under one roof. She says the tribe has a lot of catching up to do to enable people to face the pain of their addictions.

[1991]

Terms

1. Frankenstein: A fictional scientist who created a monster that destroyed its maker.
2. Pied Piper: A legendary piper whose music charmed first the rats and then the village children into following him out of town forever.

Understanding the Reading

1. What tactics does Fire Thunder use in her work with high school students?
2. What is the purpose of the Oglala Lakota Women's Society?
3. What tactics did Fire Thunder employ to combat alcoholism on the Lakota reservation?
4. How did she address the problem of domestic violence?
5. What did she do about the problem of child abuse?

Suggestion for Responding

1. The article reports that the Women's Society has lost its earlier momentum. Using your knowledge

about the change process, what advice would you give them (or a similar group working on some community problem) about the one specific outcome that you feel is most necessary? Explain its priority and the strategies you would recommend to realize that outcome.

72

Claiming Respect for Ancestral Remains: Repatriation and the Caddo Nation of Oklahoma

ROBERT L. CAST, BOBBY GONZALEZ, AND TIMOTHY K. PERTTULA

Since the passage of the Native American Graves Protection and Repatriation Act (NAGPRA) in 1990, the Caddo Nation of Oklahoma has repatriated hundreds of sets of prehistoric and historic Caddo human remains and thousands of associated and unassociated funerary objects. At least 130 museum facilities have human remains and funerary objects culturally affiliated to the Caddo. In this article, we discuss the importance of repatriation to the Caddo Nation and the role of the Caddo Repatriation Committee within the tribal government, and we provide concrete examples of several repatriation efforts and accomplishments.

The Caddo have one primary burial tradition with particularly important implications for the repatriation and reburial of human remains and funerary objects.

Caddo spiritual belief dictates that funerary objects (such as ceramic vessels) are to be placed in the grave of the deceased person as containers to hold and provide sustenance for them on their journey in the afterlife. If these objects are separated from the person, the Caddo believe that this journey has been interrupted. A large part of our NAGPRA work is spent obtaining information and documentation to reunite funerary objects with human remains so they can then be reburied to fulfill this traditional Caddo need. Sometimes, unfortunately, this cannot be accomplished because of the great dispersion of human remains and funerary offerings from sites and burials among several different museum facilities.

Organization

The Caddo peoples lived in contiguous portions of Arkansas, Louisiana, Oklahoma and Texas (an area of about 180,000 square km) from time immemorial until they were removed—first by treaty with the United States of America in 1835, and then through force of arms from the Brazos Reserve by Texans in 1859—from their traditional homelands and forced to resettle in western Oklahoma. This painful history of forced migration gives contemporary repatriation efforts particular significance.

The Caddo Nation Repatriation Committee was formed through a tribal resolution in 1996. The committee consists of traditional elders that still speak the language and actively participate in hosting and attending annual dances; teaching Caddo songs and dances to young people; and performing the reburial ceremonies of human remains and associated funerary objects culturally affiliated to the Caddo Nation under NAGPRA. The committee has been instrumental in providing insight and guidance by attending regular meetings with Caddo Nation Cultural Preservation Department (CPD) staff and addressing the sensitive issues of repatriation, burial practices and traditions, reburial of human remains and associated funerary objects, and the education of the general public about the Caddo through exhibits in the Caddo Nation Heritage Museum in Binger, OK.

Through input from the Repatriation Committee, the Caddo's CPD has developed agreements with museums and repositories that have collections in their possession and control that fall under NAGPRA regulation. These agreements focus on the treatment, care and handling of Caddo funerary objects, objects of cultural patrimony, and sacred objects, with an emphasis on insuring the traditional treatment of items in the collections. For example, the Caddo believe that a light of some sort should be left on where any human remains are being housed. To date, the Caddo have agreements with Northwestern State University (in Natchitoches, LA), the Sam Noble Oklahoma Museum of Natural History at the University of Oklahoma, the Texas Archeological Research Laboratory at the University of Texas, and the Arkansas Archeological Survey.

Consultation

Through these agreements, the Repatriation Committee has had an important role in consultations addressing the analysis of human remains and funerary objects in archeological research being done on Caddo sites and with collections from the Caddo Nation's original homelands. One of the stipulations of the agreements addresses the need for students and researchers interested in doing work with any collections defined as being culturally affiliated with the Caddo to consult with the Caddo before beginning a research project where these collections may be needed as part of ongoing research or comparative analysis. There are a handful of archaeologists and anthropologists with an interest in the Caddo who have requested input on a variety of research proposals, ranging from documenting the temporal and spatial distributions of Caddo pottery found in burials; to determining the importance of maize in the prehistoric Caddo diet; and to bioarchaeological analysis of human crania, especially the distinctive Caddo practice of cranial modeling.

The Repatriation Committee makes its recommendations of support or opposition to these proposals and analyses on a case-by-case basis. Oftentimes, a researcher may presuppose that the Repatriation Committee will deny any request involving the analysis of human remains; however, this historically has not been the case. Any types of destructive analysis of human remains (for purposes of radiocarbon dating or isotope analysis) certainly tend to be taboo, but there have been several instances where the Repatriation Committee has approved destructive analysis.

Through this collaborative process, researchers who plan to work with collections that are culturally affiliated to the Caddo quickly learn they must communicate effectively, be ready to ask and answer many questions, and be prepared to consult appropriately about their specific research interests. They must also be prepared to share their results with the committee, and to have their findings scrutinized by the CPD and our archeological consultants. This collegial process of consultation and information-sharing helps to not only better prepare graduate students for their future in the discipline but also better prepare our staff and committee members for understanding the variety of complex research approaches being proposed by universities and repositories continuing to work with collections affiliated with Native American tribes.

Repatriation

The actual repatriation of human remains, funerary objects, sacred objects, and objects of cultural patri-

mony has been variable. In some cases putting all the pieces of a NAGPRA puzzle back together, such as finding which institution has human remains and which institution (that just happens to be a thousand miles away) has associated funerary objects, is a daunting task. We have completed NAGPRA repatriations that took years of careful negotiation to accomplish, and we have also repatriated skulls and funerary objects while standing in a parking lot. In that particular non-NAGPRA case, the human remains and objects had been given to an individual from a known looter, who then returned them to us.

We have also repatriated human remains and funerary objects under the National Museum of the American Indian Act from the Natchitoches National Fish Hatchery in Louisiana, and have collaborated with a wide variety of other government entities on repatriation efforts in recent years. Working in conjunction with representatives of the Federal Highway Administration and the Texas Department of Transportation, after five years of consultation the Caddo were able to see that 27 individuals and their associated funerary objects, recovered in excavations at a sixteenth-and seventeenth-century Caddo cemetery, were reburied in a local cemetery in Mount Pleasant, TX. These repatriations are milestones for the Caddo people. Having ancestral Caddo remains and funerary objects finally treated with some modicum of respect is a large part of what the CPD, the Repatriation Committee and the Caddo Nation strive to achieve.

[2010]

Understanding the Reading

1. What is NAGPRA, and why is it important to Native Americans and non–Native Americans?
2. Name some burial traditions that are especially important to the Caddo Nation of Oklahoma.
3. Besides working in cooperative relationships with many governmental and educational entities and with other native tribes, has the Repatriation Committee had success in returning remains and funerary objects to their burial sites?

Suggestion for Responding

1. Discuss why this is such an important topic, especially for Native Americans.

73

The Weinstein Effect

LINDA BURSTYN

January 4, 2018

Like any good movie, the story of the downfall of Harvey Weinstein resonates because it's more than a story about one man and the women who accused him of harassment, rape, and assault.

It's the story of many men in power and many women victimized. And it's the story of not just Hollywood but also Silicon Valley and Capitol Hill. Newsrooms and sports teams. Big business and small. Hotels and restaurants, and farms and assembly lines.

It's the story of the many industries and companies where supervisors and bosses have, at least until now, turned a blind eye—or even given a wink and a nod—toward allegations of harassment and assault.

It's the story of a country that likes to think of itself as a leader in gender equality but in fact has a long way to go.

For the moment, there's been some reckoning. Powerful men have been brought down by women who've accused them of sexual harassment or assault, and the torrent of accusations shows no indication of abating.

In the weeks since the Harvey Weinstein article appeared in *The New York Times*, more than one hundred women have come forward with allegations of sexual harassment or assault or rape by the movie mogul. Comedian Louis C.K. saw the release of his latest movie canceled and ties to media companies FX Networks and FX Productions severed after five women accused him of sexual harassment. Gal Gadot—a.k.a. Wonder Woman—refused to sign on for a superhero movie sequel unless director and producer Brett Ratner, accused of sexual harassment by six women, is cut from the franchise.

MSNBC commentator Mark Halperin was fired after a dozen women accused him of sexual harassment. Roy Price, Amazon Studios chief; Leon Wieseltier of *The New Republic* and *The Atlantic* magazines; Michael Oreskes, NPR chief editor—all gone after women came forward to expose them.

Women senators and congresswomen have recounted their own stories of sexual harassment. Allegations have surfaced in legislatures in Minnesota, Kentucky, Illinois, Oregon, and Rhode Island, while in Sacramento, California, nearly two hundred women added their names to a letter detailing an environment of pervasive sexual wrongdoing in the statehouse. Women farmworkers joined the "Take Back the Workplace March" in Los Angeles to demand an end to decades of abuse by foremen, and women hotel workers are insisting on protections that shield them from hotel guests who harass and assault them.

At press time, nearly two million women and men had come forward using the hashtag #MeToo to recount their own experiences with sexual harassment and assault. The hashtag has gone viral globally, trending in eighty-five countries, according to news accounts. A local variant in France, #BalanceTonPorc (roughly translated as "squeal on your pig"), urged users to name their alleged abusers.

There is no doubt that as the numbers of women speaking out increase, others will feel comfortable coming forward as well. Still, it will pass, as all moments do, and what will be left behind? Will the shrugging culture of "boys will be boys" give way to a new culture that allows women to be women—as equals—in the workplace?

What can be done to ensure that when the waters recede from this watershed moment, the land that's revealed underneath is forever changed?

Feminists had been working since the 1970s to have sexual harassment in the workplace defined as illegal discrimination, but it wasn't until 1986 that the Supreme Court, in the case *Meritor Savings Bank v. Vinson*, ruled that sexual harassment was a violation of Title VII of the Civil Rights Act of 1964.

Five years later, when Anita Hill came forward to speak out against Supreme Court nominee Clarence Thomas, the country—especially women—got a three-day lesson about what sexual harassment looked like and how the law prohibits it. At the time of her testimony, 60 percent of Americans didn't believe Hill. Perhaps more people would have believed her if the other women who had worked with Thomas and were prepared to testify about his inappropriate behavior had been allowed to testify before the Senate Judiciary Committee. Thomas, who denied all allegations, was confirmed as a Supreme Court justice by a vote of 52 to 48.

Many predicted that the treatment of Hill by the Judiciary Committee would discourage women from coming forward, but in the aftermath of her testimony, the EEOC saw a more than twofold rise in sexual harassment claims by women. Moreover, Hill's testimony contributed to the passage of the Civil Rights Act of 1991, which expanded the remedies available to victims of workplace discrimination. The law provided, for the first time, that women could sue for punitive damages in cases of sex discrimination, though the damages were capped at $300,000 per individual plaintiff.

And then there was the presidential election of 2016 featuring Donald Trump's "grab them by the pussy" remarks. Trump's victory in the election—despite losing the popular vote by nearly three million votes—radicalized women throughout the country. Some 5.9 million marched the day after his inauguration; a tsunami of women wore pink "pussy hats" in repudiation of Trump and his misogynistic agenda.

Millions more have marched and protested since the massive Women's Marches. Thousands of women have stepped forward to run for political office, winning big in November. And millions of women have joined the #MeToo movement, speaking out against sexual harassment when they see it.

The anger is real, and the backlash to Trump is helping fuel a shift in the way women are believed and the way they're treated in the workplace. "This moment feels like a new opportunity to finally get at the cultural pieces that have allowed harassment and workplace violence to persist," NWLC's Andrea Graves observes.

Perhaps it's true. Perhaps this is "the moment" so many women have been waiting for. Perhaps, as unlikely as it may seem, the election of Trump, putting a harasser in the White House, will usher in an era of positive change in America. Two things are for sure: This is only the tip of the iceberg. And Pandora's box has been opened.

Understanding the Reading

1. Describe what the "Weinstein Effect" is according to this article.
2. List some of the ways this movement is affecting the United States.
3. How has the Civil Rights Act of 1991 given strength to women in 2018?

Suggestions for Responding

1. Will this movement get stronger and broader or not?
2. Have a class discussion about whether this movement serves justice.

Suggestions for Responding to Part IX

1. Write a personal essay describing yourself as a change maker. Make clear what problem you decided to work on, how you chose to attack it, what happened, and how successful (or unsuccessful) your effort was.
2. Make an oral presentation to the class about your action project, briefly covering thepoints raised in question 1.

3. Research a civil rights activist or organization, focusing on one particular action he, she, or they undertook. Write an essay describing and evaluating the project.
4. Investigate a group on your campus or in your community that is working to implement change.

Suggestions for Responding to Change

Throughout history, important social and economic change has been the result of organized movements. The following assignments are intended to give you a better understanding of organized nongovernmental forces that have changed life in America.

1. Research the origins of a specific labor union, such as the American Federation of Labor and

Congress of Industrial Organizations (AFL-CIO); Actors' Equity Association; Knights of Labor; National Women's Trade Union League; National Consumers League; International Workers of the World; National Education Association; Longshoremen's and Warehousemen's Union; United Farm Workers of America; 9–5; Teamsters; Association of

Federal, State, County and Municipal Employees; International Ladies' Garment Workers Union; and so on. Write a report on the forces that led to the initial organizing and the obstacles the organizers faced.

2. Research and report on the strategies used by the abolition movement, and analyze their effectiveness.

3. Research and report on the strategies used by the National Woman Suffrage Association, the American Woman Suffrage Association, or the National American Woman Suffrage Association, and analyze the effectiveness of the organization.

4. In the post–Civil War years, women organized for a number of purposes. Research one of these organizations, such as the women's club movement, the temperance movement, settlement houses, or the National Consumer League, and report on their short-term and long-term achievements.

5. Write a biography of a major historical change maker, focusing on his or her contributions to the larger movement of which he or she was a part. Consider such activists as Lucretia Mott, Sarah and Angelina Grimké, William Lloyd Garrison, Frederick Douglass, Elizabeth Cady Stanton, Susan B. Anthony, Carrie Chapman Catt, Mary McLeod Bethune, Frances Willard, Mary Church Terrell, Jane Addams, Florence Kelley, Lillian Wald, Louis Brandeis, Sophie Loeb, Emma Goldman, Elizabeth Gurley Flynn, Rose Schneiderman, Mary Anderson, Abigail Scott Duniway, Thurgood Marshall, or Morris Dees.

6. Research and report on the goals and strategies used by one of the civil rights organizations of the 1950s and 1960s—for example, the Student Non-Violent Coordinating Committee, Southern Christian Leadership Conference, National Association for the Advancement of Colored People, Congress of Racial Equality, Black Panthers, American Indian Movement, La Raza Unida, National Organization for Women, National Abortion Rights Action League, or National Association for the Legalization of Marijuana.

7. Identify someone in your community who has effected a change that has had a direct impact on you, your family, or your friends or neighbors. Go to your local library or newspaper morgue and review the clipping file on this person; arrange for an interview if you can. Report on what motivated the person, what resources he or she had to make this effort effective, and what obstacles he or she had to overcome; assess the value of this person's efforts.

8. Invite one or more members of an Arab American association or a Muslim American community to speak to your class or university. If possible, combine this with a member of a Japanese American community who was imprisoned in a relocation camp during World War II or who had a family member imprisoned in the camps. Discuss the consequences to all Americans when civil liberties are suspended for any group.

9. As a class, watch at least the first twenty minutes of the film *Skokie* and discuss the following questions: (a) As a citizen (Jew or non-Jew) of the town of Skokie, Illinois, home to many Holocaust survivors and their descendants, how would you react if neo-Nazis marched down your street? (b) As the judge responsible for issuing or denying permits for public demonstrations, would you give a permit to these neo-Nazis to demonstrate in Skokie? (c) As the mayor of Skokie, how would you react? (d) As the head of the American Civil Liberties Union, would you accept the neo-Nazis' demand for protection of their First Amendment rights, even though many of your members would consequently leave, and also knowing that if the neo-Nazis ever came to power, the first thing they would do would be to suspend freedom of speech? Remember, as head of the ACLU you are dedicated to the protection of the liberties outlined in the Bill of Rights.

10. Be in touch with a church organization, mosque, temple, or nongovernmental organization that can guide your class to help residents in distress, be it homelessness, illiteracy, or other needs. Find out what is needed and encourage your community to help.

Credits

project, Free at Last, Southern Poverty Law Center, www.tolerance.org. Used by permission of the Southern Poverty Law Center.

Chapter 38: "Blacks Feel Indignities" by Robert Anthony Watts. Reprinted by permission of Associated Press via the YGS Group.

Chapter 39: "Citizenship and Violence" by *The American Prospect*. Copyright © 2001 by *The American Prospect*, Prospect.org. Used with permission of *The American Prospect*. All rights reserved.

Chapter 40: "For Women's History Month, a Look at Gender Gains—and Gender Gaps—in the United States" by Abigail Geiger and Kim Parker. Pew Research Center, March 15, 2018. Copyright © 2018. Reprinted with permission.

Chapter 41: "Sexual Harassment at Work in the Era of #MeToo" by Nikki Graf. Pew Research Center, April 4, 2018. Copyright © 2018. Reprinted with permission.

Chapter 42: "Breaking Down Gender Bias in the Construction Industry" by Kate Stephenson. *Building Energy* (Spring 2017). Copyright © 2017. Reprinted by permission of the author. *Building Energy* is a publication of the Northeast Sustainable Energy Association (NESEA).

Chapter 43: "Why Doesn't She Just Leave?" by Clarethia Ellerbe. Copyright © 2003. Published with permission of the author.

Chapter 44: "Rape and Sexual Assault" by James A. Doyle. From *Sex and Gender*, 5th edition. Copyright © 1985 by Times Mirror Higher Education Group, Inc. Reprinted by permission of the McGraw-Hill Companies. All rights reserved.

Chapter 45: "'The Rape' of Mr. Smith." Author unknown.

Chapter 46: "*Roe v. Wade* Turns Forty-Five, but There's No Time to Celebrate" by Ilyse Hogue. *Huffington Post*, January 22, 2018. Copyright © 2018. Reprinted with permission.

Chapter 47: "Unions Are Fighting for Families" by Liz Shuler. Copyright © Liz Shuler and AFL-CIO. Reprinted with permission.

Chapter 48: "Warren Buffett Calls for Higher Taxes for U.S. Super-Rich" by Graeme Wearden. *Guardian*, August 15, 2011. Copyright © 2011. Used by permission.

Chapter 49: "Bulging Jails Are Other American Exception" by Albert R. Hunt. Bloomberg News, November 20, 2011. Used by permission.

Chapter 50: "Institutionalized Discrimination" by Robert Cherry. From *Discrimination: Its Economic Impact on Blacks, Women, and Jews* by Robert D. Cherry. Copyright © 1989 by Lexington Books, an imprint of Rowman & Littlefield. Reprinted with permission.

Chapter 51: "Why People Love 'Assistance to the Poor' But Hate 'Welfare'" by Ashley Jardina. talkpoverty.org, January 29, 2018. Copyright © 2018. Reprinted by permission of the author.

Chapter 52: "The Tainted Water Crisis in Upstate New York That Andrew Cuomo Can't Shake" by Alexander C. Kaufman. *Huffington Post*, March 9, 2018. Reprinted from Huffington Post. Copyright © 2018. Oath, Inc. Used under license. All rights reserved.

Chapter 53: "How America Changed during Barack Obama's Presidency" by Michael Dimock. Pew Research Center, January 10, 2017. Copyright © 2017. Reprinted by permission.

Chapter 54: "*The Atlantic*'s Adam Serwer: The Politics of Racism in Trump's America" by Nilagia McCoy. "The Politics of Racism in Trump's America" is based on a talk given by Adam Serwer, senior editor at *The Atlantic*, at Harvard Kennedy School, March 24, 2018. Adapted and summarized by Nilagia McCoy, Shorenstein Center on Media, Politics, and Public Policy. Copyright © 2018. Reprinted with permission.

Chapter 55: "The Trump Administration Isn't Just Curtailing Women's Rights; It's Systematically Eroding Trust in Women" by Annalisa Merelli. *qz.com*, October 14, 2014. Reproduced with permission of Atlantic Monthly Group, Inc., in the format book via Copyright Clearance Center.

Chapter 56: "Environmental Justice in the Age of Trump" by Michael J. Brogan. Copyright © 2018 by Michael J. Brogan. Reprinted by permission of the author.

Chapter 57: "The Power to Count: Citizenship and the Census" by Victor Thompson. Copyright © Victor Thompson. Reprinted by permission of the author.

Chapter 58: "Attorney General Eric Holder Speaks at the Lyndon Baines Johnson Library and Museum." Austin, Texas, December 13, 2011.

Index

abortion. *See* reproductive rights and health care

ACS. *See* American Community Survey

Adams, Ansel, 140

ADL. *See* Anti-Defamation League

affirmative action, 15, 17, 122, 187

AFL-CIO, 174–75

Afro DZ ak (Peter Shungu), 4, 6

Alexander, Michelle, 182, 183

Alien Act (1798), 104

America First, ix

American Anthropological Association, 4, 6–8

American Community Survey (ACS), 208

American Dream: change makers and, 244; myth of, 73; upward mobility and, 74

American individualism, 1

Americanization, 8–9

ancestry testing, 3, 32–33

Anti-Defamation League (ADL), 137, 138

antigovernment groups, 118

anti-Semitism, 94; *The Eternal Jew* and, 102; Know-Nothing Party and, 136; Lodge and, 137; of Nazis, 7; Palmer raids and, 138; Populist movement and, 136, 138

assimilation, 4; Franklin, J., on, 12; of Native Americans, 123, 124, 125, 134

Association for the Preservation of the White Race, 257

athletes, 51

Baia, Ashley, 19

Baldwin, James, 98–99; on *Birth of a Nation*, 102

Batista, Fulgencio, 39, 40

battered women, 158

Bay of Pigs operation, 41

Bell, Carl, 154

Bendetsen, Karl R., 143, 144

Benjamin, Harry: hormone therapy and, 56; sexual orientation scale of, 58

Bennett, Jacob, 119

Berry, Wendell, 236, 237

BIA. *See* Bureau of Indian Affairs

Biddle, Francis, 141, 142, 143–45

Bingham, Sallie, 74, 83–86

birther movement, 97

Birth of a Nation (1915): Baldwin on, 102; birther movement and, 97; Black Lives Matter and, 103; "brother against brother" tragedy in, 97–98; costs of Civil War in, 99–100; KKK in, 94, 96; Lincoln portrayed in, 100; mistrust of black women and, 99; mulatto in, 98, 99, 100; rape in, 101; slavery in, 96, 97–98; "snake in Eden" reference in, 97; structural racism in, 96

Black Lives Matter, 102–3; *Birth of a Nation* and, 103

Blackwell, Unita, 256

Bloom, Allan, 226, 228

Bly, Robert, 236, 237

Border Patrol. *See* Immigration and Customs Enforcement

Bouncer, William, 245

Brand, Martin, 194

Brennan, William J., 239

Brogan, Michael J., 198, 203–7

Brown, Jerry, 104

Brown v. Board of Education, 250

Bryant, Roy, 153

Buffett, Warren, 179, 181

Bunch, Charlotte, 217, 230–35

Bureau of Indian Affairs (BIA): involuntary sterilization and, 134; mineral-rich lands and, 135; urban Native Americans and, 126

Burstyn, Linda, 243, 265–66

Bush, George W., 181, 197, 199

Butler, Matthew C., 105

bystander programs, 230

CAA. *See* Cuban Adjustment Act

Caddo Nation Cultural Preservation Department (CPD), 263–64

Caddo Repatriation Committee: consultation with, 263–64; forming of, 263

CANF. *See* Cuban American National Foundation

capitalism, 177, 178

Carson, Ben, 89

Cast, Robert L., 263–64

Castro, Fidel, 39, 40; Trump and, 34–35

Census Bureau, U.S., 36, 38, 221; ACS and, 208; citizenship question on decennial census and, 208, 209, 210–11; funding for, 210; Ross, W., and, 209, 210, 211

change, x, 215; Madrid on, 226. *See also* taking action

change makers, x, 216; American Dream and, 244; Caddo Repatriation Committee and, 263–64; in civil rights movement, 243, 248–58; Fire Thunder as, 260–62; Hill as, 158, 265–66; Jones as, 243, 245–47; Moody as, 243, 251–54; Native American, 243, 260–64; Tillinghast as, 243, 254–58; "Weinstein Effect" and, 265–66; Yallup and Ross, K., as, 258–59, 260

Chaplinsky v. New Hampshire, 239

Cherry, Robert, 136–38, 179, 183–89

child sexual abuse, 262

Chinese Exclusion Act (1882), 105, 107

Churchill, Ward, 94, 131–36

Ciaravino, Michael G., 193, 194

citizenship: ACS and, 208; African Americans and, 12; CVAP and, 209–10; decennial census and, 208, 209, 210–11; VAWA and, 162; Voting Rights Act and, 209

citizenship voting age population (CVAP), 209–10

Civilian Exclusion Orders and Japanese internment camps (1942–1944): Adams on, 140; assembly centers and, 140; Battle of Los Angeles and, 145; Bendetsen and, 143, 145; Biddle and, 141, 142, 143–45; criminal law bill for, 146; DeWitt and, 141, 143, 145, 146; dissolving, 146; evacuation day for, 138–40; Gullion and, 143–44, 145, 146; Lippmann supporting, 144; McCloy and, 144, 145, 146; Nisei and, 139, 141, 143; Pearl Harbor attack and, 141; possessions and, 139; racism after, 146; relocation centers for, 140; restrictive covenant and, 146; Roosevelt and, 141, 142, 144, 146; Stimson and, 143, 144, 145, 146; War Relocation Authority for, 146

Civil Rights Act (1964), 120; Title VI of, 205; Title VII of, 57, 265

civil rights movement: *Brown v. Board of Education* and, 250; bus boycott and, 250; change makers in, 243,

248–58; civil rights commission and, 249; CORE and, 248–49; Moody and, 251–54; NAACP and, 248, 249, 250, 251–52; school segregation and, 249, 250–51, 256; Till and, 153–54; Tillinghast and, 243, 254–58. *See also* King, Martin Luther, Jr.

Civil War, 10, 100–101

Clair, Matthew, 119

class and economics, 2, 73; appearance and, 75; corporate tax and, 78; G.I. Bill and, 80; homelessness and, 88–89, 217; housing and, 87–88; identity, 75–80; measuring, 75–76; multiculturalism and, 76–77; race and, 199; railroad building and, 78; relationships and, 76; rich women and, 74, 83–86; shame and, 88; upward mobility and, 74; visibility and, 77–79; Williams on, 74, 86–88; worker strikes and, 78–79, 82; work structure and, 77. *See also* power and classism; Zandy, Janet

class consciousness, 77, 81

classism. *See* power and classism

Clinton, Bill, 189, 205

Cloud, Eileen Iron, 261

Cobb, Charles, 255

Collier, John, 124

Collins, Cory, 94, 118–23

Collins, Francis, 32

colonialism, 7

coming out, 51–52

Congress of Racial Equality (CORE), 248–49

Constitution, U.S.: First Amendment of, 171, 197, 238–40; Fourteenth Amendment to, 56, 161; Franklin, J., on, 9; Obama, B., on, 4, 14; Three-Fifths Compromise in, 98

construction industry, and gender bias: career counseling and, 165; children and, 165; company culture and, 165–66

CORE. *See* Congress of Racial Equality

Counter, S. Allen, 33

CPD. *See* Caddo Nation Cultural Preservation Department

Crevecoeur, Hector St. Jean de, 8–9, 10

criminal justice system: cost of, 182, 183; minorities in, 182–83; in

politics, 182; prison population and, 183; rape in prison, 168; recidivism and, 183; violent crimes and, 182

Cuba: Batista in, 39, 40; Bay of Pigs operation and, 41; Castro in, 34, 39, 40; economic embargo against, 35; Eisenhower and, 35, 41; exile from, 41–42; Lansky and, 40; leaders of, 44; racism in, 26

Cuban Adjustment Act (CAA), 38, 43

Cuban American National Foundation (CANF), 39, 39n7

Cuban exiles, 41nn11–12; adaption of, 44; CAA and, 38, 43; characteristics of, 36–37, 43; Cold War policies and, 35; collectivism and, 39, 41; Cuban residency and, 36; Cuban Revolution and, 39–40; Democrats and, 35, 37, 39; Fernandez and, 35, 44; Haitian refugees compared to, 111; Hispanic/Latinos and, 42; income and, 43; Martí as, 37; Mas Canosa and, 43–44; Obama, B., and, 35, 39; political affiliation of, 37–38; repatriation of, 44; terror cells and, 42n13; Trump vote and, 38–39, 42, 43–44; U.S. immigration policy and, 35, 38, 40–41, 43; vintages of, 36, 36n3, 37, 38, 39, 43; "Wet-foot/Dry-foot" policy and, 35, 43

Cumpián, Carlos, 4, 31–32

Cuomo, Andrew, 191, 193

CVAP. *See* citizenship voting age population

DACA. *See* Deferred Action for Childhood Arrivals

Daseler, Robert, 94, 147–50

Davis, Ann, 243, 260–63

Dawes Act, 124, 125

Dearborn Press, 136, 138

Deferred Action for Childhood Arrivals (DACA), 114, 115

Denis, Jeffrey S., 119

Department of Homeland Security (DHS): creation of, 113; immigration and, 108–9, 113

Detention and Removal Operations (DRO), 114

DeVos, Betsy, 202

DeWitt, John L., 141, 143, 145, 146

DHS. *See* Department of Homeland Security

Diaz, Mercedes, 5, 34–44

Dimock, Michael, 198, 199

disabilities, 217, 228

domestic violence, 166; controller interview on, 167; Native Americans and, 262; prevention of, 229–30; sisterhood bond and, 167

Dorris, Michael, 94, 123–25

Douglass, Frederick, 248, 251

Doyle, James A., 159, 168–71

Dreams from My Father (Obama, B.), 15–16

Dred Scott case, 98

DRO. *See* Detention and Removal Operations

DuBois, W. E. B., 248

Duke, David, 117, 200

Duster, Troy, 32

education, 111, 149; Cuban exiles and, 36; institutionalized discrimination and, 183–84; labor force and gender and, 163; men's movement and, 236; Native Americans and, 127, 134; Oklahoma teacher strike and, 240–42; power and classism and, 179, 183, 184; women and, 158, 163, 164, 165

Eisenhower, Dwight D.: *Brown v. Board of Education* and, 250; Faubus and, 250–51; Cuba and, 35, 41

Ellerbe, Clarethia, 158, 166–68

Employment Non-Discrimination Act (ENDA), 57

Enck, Judith, 193, 194

Enhanced Border Security and Visa Entry Reform Act (2002), 113

environmental justice, 203–7; Clinton and, 205; environmental politics and, 203; men's movement and, 236, 237; public health and, 203, 204, 206, 207; risk to vulnerable communities and, 205; traditional environmentalism compared to, 203

Environmental Protection Agency (EPA): EJSCREEN of, 204, 206; OEJ and, 203, 207; Office of Environmental Equity of, 205; Pruitt

at, 205–6, 207; Trump administration and, 205–7

Equal Rights Amendment, 233, 235

The Eternal Jew, 102

Evenwel v. Abbott on Redistricting 578, 209

Evers, Medgar, 254

FAIR. *See* Federation for American Immigration Reform

Falwell, Jerry, 232, 235

Family Protection Act, 232, 235

Faubus, Orval, 250–51

Fears, Darryl, 4, 25–27

Federation for American Immigration Reform (FAIR), 109, 112

The Feminine Mystique (Friedan), 157

feminism, 230–35; budgets for, 231; coalitions and, 233; National Women's Conference and, 233, 235; organizing and, 232; policies for, 231–32; power and sexism and, 158; transformational politics and, 231

Fernandez, Miguel: IMPAC started by, 35; Republican support by, 35; Trump and, 35, 44

Fire Thunder, Cecilia, 260–62; background of, 261; cultural values and, 260; Oglala Lakota Women's Society and, 261–62

First Amendment, U.S. Constitution, 171; *Chaplinsky v. New Hampshire* and, 239; Patriot Act and, 197; Supreme Court justices on, 238–40; *Texas v. Johnson* and, 238–39; university campuses and, 238, 239

Fiske-Rusciano, Roberta, 94, 125–28

five-sex system, 50

Fong Yue Ting v. United States, 105

Ford, Ford Madox, 237

Ford, Henry, 136, 138

Fourteenth Amendment, U.S. Constitution: transgender rights and, 56; VAWA and, 161

Franklin, Benjamin, 73

Franklin, John Hope, 4, 8–14; on African Americans, 10–12; on Anglo-Saxon complex, 10; on assimilation, 12; on Crevecoeur, 8–9, 10; on defining ethnicity, 10, 13; on Jefferson, 11; on nativism, 9–10; on public policy and

ethnicity, 12; slavery and, 11; on Statue of Liberty, 12–13; U.S. Constitution for, 9

Franz, Barbara, 109–17

Freedom School, 256

free enterprise, 177

Frej, Willa, 94, 103–4

Freud, Sigmund, 168

Friedan, Betty, 157

Froese, Paul, 53

Fullwiley, Duana, 32, 33, 34

gambling, 127–28

Gandhi, Mohandas, 248, 251

Gaul, 124, 125

Geiger, Abigail, 158, 162–63

gender and sexual identity, ix, 2; anatomical sex and, 58; coming out and, 51–52; femininity and, 49; five-sex system and, 50; homophobia and, 158, 234; intersexuals and, 50; masculinity and, 49, 54–56, 169, 237; military and, 50, 57; Olympic athletes and, 51; Rippon, and, 51–52; same-sex marriage and, 57, 199; sexual orientation and, 50, 57; transgender rights and, 50, 56–58; women's rights and, 201–3. *See also* transgender individuals

gender pay gap, 162–63

gender roles, 50, 157; male, 54–56; socialization and, 49

genetic science: ancestry testing and, 3, 32–33; Counter and, 33; disease probability and, 33, 34; Fullwiley on, 32, 33, 34; Genographic Project and, 33–34; racism and, 34; Wells and, 33–34

Genocide Convention, U.N., 134

Genographic Project, 33–34

Gentleman's Agreement, 105, 106, 108

G.I. Bill (Public Law 346), 80

Gilens, Martin, 189–90

Gim, Ruth, 147, 148, 149, 150

Gingrich, Newt, 99

Gone with the Wind, 96

Gonzalez, Bobby, 263–64

Graf, Nikki, 158, 163–64

Graham, Renée, 151–53

Great Chain of Being, 7

Griffith, D. W., 98, 99

Guillemin, Jeanne, 126, 127

Gullion, Allen W., 143–44, 145, 146

guns and gun control: faith and, 52, 53; masculinity and, 53; Obama, B., on, 52; racism and, 52–53; violence statistics and, 53–54

Gunther, Gerald, 218, 238–40; anti-Semitism and, 238

Gwaltney, John Langston, 27–29

H-2 visa program, 109

Haggerty, Tom, 245

Haitians, 111

Hamilton, Alexander, 78

Harlan, John Marshall, 239–40

Harris, Beatrice, 192

Harrison, Bennett, 184

hate groups, 117–18; male supremacy groups as, 118. *See also* white supremacists

Hayakawa, Sam, 224, 228

Hazell, Jon, 218, 240–42

Head, Tom, 50, 56–58

health care. *See* public health; reproductive rights and health care

Hersey, John, 94, 138–47

Hill, Anita: as change maker, 265–66; testimony before Senate of, 158, 265, 266; Thomas and, 265

Hirsch, E. D., 226, 228

Hittites, 129, 131

Hogue, Ilyse, 159, 172–74

Holder, Eric, Jr., 217, 219–23

Holmes, Oliver Wendell, 239

homelessness: causes of, 217; by city, 88–89; federal government and, 89; income gap and, 88, 89; men's movement and, 236, 237; taking action on, 217, 218

homophobia, 158, 234

Hunt, Albert R., 182–83

Hurston, Zora Neale, 197

Hussein, Saddam, 197

ICE. *See* Immigration and Customs Enforcement

identity. *See* gender and sexual identity; racial and ethnic identity

IHS. Indian Health Service

Illegal Immigration Reform and Immigration Responsibility Act (IIRIRA) (1996), 111–13, 116

immigration, ix, 94; Alien Act and, 104; anti-Catholicism and, 104; Asiatic barred zone and, 105–6; border wall for, 115, 116; Chinese Exclusion Act and, 105, 107; Cuban exiles and, 35, 38, 40–41,

43; DHS and, 108–9, 113; Displaced Persons Act and War Bridges Act and, 107; Enhanced Border Security and Visa Entry Reform Act and, 113; FAIR and, 109, 112; *Fong Yue Ting v. United States* and, 105; Gentleman's Agreement and, 105, 106, 108; H-2 visa program and, 109; Haitians and, 111; IIRIRA and, 111–13, 116; Immigration Act (1965), 225, 228; Immigration Act (1990), 110–11; Immigration and Nationality Act, 108, 110; INS enforcing, 112, 112n10, 113, 114, 116; IRCA on, 109–10, 111, 115–16; literacy tests and, 105; McCarran-Walter Act for, 107; Mexican repatriation and, 107; National Origins Act and, 106, 107; nativism and, 104–5, 115; Obama, B., and, 114–15; "Operation Wetback" and, 107; Patriot Act and, 109, 113, 197; post-9/11, 113–14, 116; Proposition 187 and, 111, 111n7; refoulement and, 111, 116; Refugee Act and, 108; second preference for, 108; seventh preference and, 108; Sutter's Mill and, 104, 108; terrorism and, 113–14; Trump and, 103–4, 115; unaccompanied children and, 114; Welfare and Illegal Immigration Reform and Immigration Control Acts, 109, 112, 116

Immigration and Customs Enforcement (ICE): DRO division of, 114; Oakland raid by, 94, 103–4; Obama, B., and, 114; Schwab quitting, 103–4

Immigration and Naturalization Service (INS), 112, 112n10, 113, 114, 116

Immigration Partnership & Coalition Fund (IMPAC), 35

Immigration Reform and Control Act (IRCA) (1986), 109–10, 111, 115–16

income inequality, 199

Indian Health Service (IHS), 134–35

Indian Reorganization Act. *See* Wheeler-Howard Act

Industrial Revolution, 177

Ingraham, Christopher, 178

INS. *See* Immigration and Naturalization Service

institutionalized discrimination, 183–89; affirmative action and, 15, 17, 122, 187; classism and, 179; education and, 183–84; financial and occupation effects of, 186; firm hiring information as, 184–86; income and, 183, 184; job seeker information as, 186; job-training programs and, 187–88; Kerner commission and, 187; opportunity costs and, 184, 188; quotas and, 187; racism and, 92; seniority systems and, 186; skill and locational mismatches as, 187–88

institutionalized racism, 93, 95

involuntary sterilization, 134–35

IRCA. *See* Immigration Reform and Control Act

Jackson, Candice, 202

Jackson, Robert, 133–34

Japanese internment camps. *See* Civilian Exclusion Orders and Japanese internment camps

Jardina, Ashley, 179–80, 189–90

Jefferson, Thomas, 11

Jim Crow, 13, 16, 37, 119; DuBois and, 248; overt racism and, 93; *Plessy v. Ferguson* and, 26, 248; Roosevelt and, 248; Wells-Barnett fighting, 248; White and, 248

Johnson, Allan, 170

Johnson, Kevin, 152

Johnson, Lyndon B., 222; Voting Rights Act and, 219

Jones, Mary Harris "Mother," 243, 245–47; Bouncer and, 245; family of, 247; female protesters and, 245–46; Haggerty and, 245; scabs and, 246; on United Mine Workers, 245; on winning strike, 247

Jorgensen, Christine, 56; Stearns and, 58, 60, 63

Kaufman, Alexander C., 180, 190–94

Kendall, Francis E., 119

Kennedy, John F., 39, 41, 219, 251

Kerner commission, 187

Kimberlin, Sara, 89

Kimbrell, Andrew, 217–18, 235–38

King, Martin Luther, Jr., 150, 250

King, Martin Luther, III, 94, 150–51

Know-Nothing Party, 138; anti-

Semitism and, 136; nativism and, 104–5, 108
Knox, Frank, 142
Ku Klux Klan (KKK), 12; in *Birth of a Nation*, 94, 96; decline of, 117; in government, 248; Tillinghast and, 257

labor force, and gender, 157; construction industry and, 164–66; education and, 163; equity and, 165; gender discrimination and, 163; leadership positions in, 163; unions and, 174–75; wage gap and, 158, 162–63, 179. *See also* sexual harassment in the workplace
labor history. *See* worker strikes
Lansky, Meyer, 40
Latin America, whiteness and blackness in: class and, 26–27; Martins and, 25, 27; Neinstein on, 27; slavery and, 26
Lewis, John, 219
Lewontin, Richard, 32
Liberating Memory: Our Work and Our Working-Class Consciousness (Zandy), 81
Lincoln, Abraham, 73; in *Birth of a Nation*, 100
Lippmann, Walter, 144
Lodge, Henry Cabot, 137
The Long Walk Home, 102
Lopez-Gottardi, Cristina, 38
Ludlow Massacre, 78–79, 82

Madrid, Arturo, 217, 223–28; on birth rate, 225; change and, 226; on demographic changes, 225–26; diversity for, 226–27; education of, 223; family of, 223; missing persons and, 223, 224; on otherness, 223, 224, 226, 227; on quality, 226, 227
male role stereotype: characteristics of, 54–55; cost of, 55–56
MAN. *See* Men's Action Network
Manifest Destiny, 129, 131, 134, 136
marriage equality. *See* same-sex marriage
Martí, Jose, 37
Martin, Trayvon, 152
Martins, Maria, 25, 27
Mas Canosa, Jorge, 44
masculinity, 49; guns and, 53; male

role stereotype and, 54–56; men's movement and, 237; rape and, 169
McCloy, John J., 143, 145, 146
McCoy, Nilagia, 198, 199–201
McIntosh, Peggy, 118, 120, 121
Means, Russell, 132
media: 2020 election and, 200; Native Americans in, 135; social, 199; Trump and, 200
Mele, Nicco, 200
Mencken, F. Carson, 53
Mendez, Hipolito, 259
Men's Action Network (MAN), 237
men's movement, 235–38; education and, 236; environmental justice and, 236, 237; health and, 236, 237; homelessness and, 236, 237; masculinity and, 237; policy for fathers and children in, 235–36; warfare and, 237
Merelli, Annalisa, 198, 201–3
meritocracy, 179
Meritor Savings Bank v. Vinson, 265
mestizos, 26, 128, 131
#MeToo movement, 158, 230; "Weinstein Effect" and, 265, 266
mezclados, 128, 131
micro-aggressions, 154, 155
Milam, J. W., 153
miscegenation, 6
model minority stereotype, 147–50; Gim on, 147, 148, 149, 150; homosexuality and, 149; management glass ceiling and, 149–50; Ong on, 147–48; Petersen on, 147, 148; psychological services and, 149; superachievers and, 148–49; Yamane and, 149; Yellow Peril compared to, 148; Yoo and, 149
Modestin, Yvette, 25
Montilla, Jillian, 4, 30–31
Moody, Anne, 243; Evers and, 254; NAACP and, 251–52, 253; at sit-in, 251–54
Moreno, Rita, 166
Moyers, Bill, 102
muckrakers, 137, 138
Muir, John, 237
mulatto: in *Birth of a Nation*, 98, 99, 100; rape and, 98–99
Mullinax, Ken, 154–55
multiculturalism, ix, 75; class and economics and, 76–77
Murillo, Luis, 26

NAACP. *See* National Association for the Advancement of Colored People
NAGPRA. *See* Native American Graves Protection and Repatriation Act
NARAL Pro-Choice America, 173
National Association for the Advancement of Colored People (NAACP), 106; *Brown v. Board of Education* and, 250; bus boycott and, 250; civil rights movement and, 248, 249, 250, 251–52; DuBois and, 249; Moody and, 251–52, 253
National Origins Act (1924), 106, 107
National Women's Conference, 233, 235
Native American Graves Protection and Repatriation Act (NAGPRA), 263, 264
Native Americans, 3; alcohol and, 129, 130, 135, 261–62; Allotment policy for, 124, 125; assimilation of, 123, 124, 125, 134; BIA and, 126, 134; Caddo Repatriation Committee and, 263–64; change makers, 243, 260–64; child sexual abuse and, 262; Collier and, 124; Cowboys and Indians and, 129; Cumpián and, 4, 31–32; Curtis Act and, 123, 124, 125; Dawes Act and, 124, 125; deculturation of, 134; domestic violence and, 262; education of, 127, 134; Fire Thunder and, 260–62; genocide of, 134–36; "go back to the blanket" for, 129, 131; IHS and, 134–35; involuntary sterilization of, 134–35; Klamath Nation, 124–25; and Manifest Destiny, 129, 131, 134, 136; mass media portrayal of, 135; Menominee Nation, 124–25; mineral-rich lands of, 130, 135; poverty for, 130; power and racism and, 94, 123–25, 128–36; Qoyawayma and, 23–25; severalty laws on, 124, 125; Thanksgiving for, 4, 31, 135; urban, 125–28; Wheeler-Howard Act and, 124. *See also* sport teams and Native Americans
nativism: Franklin, J., on, 9–10; immigration and, 104–5, 115;

Know-Nothing Party and, 104–5, 108; Proposition 187 and, 111, 111n7

Nazis, 7, 102, 117, 132, 134, 238; black soldiers and, 248

Neinstein, Jose, 26–27

Nisei (first-generation Japanese Americans), 139, 141, 143. *See also* Civilian Exclusion Orders and Japanese internment camps

Nolon, John, 193–94

Nuremberg tribunal, 133–34

Obama, Barack, x, 73, 182; Baia and, 19; birther movement and, 97; campaign of, 15, 18–19; Constitution and, 4, 14; Cuban exiles and, 35, 39; DACA and, 114, 115; on economic opportunity, 16–17; family of, 14, 16; guns and, 52; ICE and, 114; immigration and, 114–15; income inequality and, 199; international popularity of, 199; on legalized discrimination, 16; as mixed race, 98; rape and sexual assault guidelines of, 202; social media and, 199; stimulus package of, 199; Title IX and, 202; transgender rights and, 57; "Toward a More Perfect Union," 14–20; at Trinity United Church of Christ, 15–16; voting rights and, 221; on white and black anger, 17; Wright and, 15–16, 17, 18

Obama, Michelle, 99

Obergefell v. Hodges, 199

Office of Environmental Justice (OEJ), 203, 207

Oglala Lakota Women's Society, 261–62

Ohene, Selorm, 152

Oklahoma teachers' strike, 240–42

Ong, Paul, 147–48

opportunity cost, 184, 188

Order of the Star Spangled Banner, 9–10

overt racism, 93; Till and, 94

Owen, John, 184

Palast, Greg, 94, 150–51

Paley, Grace: Christmas play and, 20–23; neighbors of, 21; parents of, 20, 21, 22

Palmer raids, 138

Parker, Kim, 158, 162–63

Parks, Rosa, 250

passing, 29

patriarchal systems and traditions, 157, 168, 231, 232

Patriot Act (2001), 109, 113, 197

perfluorooctane sulfonate (PFOS), 190, 191, 192, 194

perfluorooctanoic acid (PFOA), 190–91, 192–93

Perry, Rick, 181

Perttula, Timothy K., 263–64

Petersen, William, 147, 148

PFOA. *See* perfluorooctanoic acid

PFOS. *See* perfluorooctane sulfonate

Plessy v. Ferguson, 26, 248

pogrom, 21, 22

Populist movement, 136, 138, 228; other and, 226; Watson and, 137

pornography, 159, 171

Porter, Rob, 229

post-9/11 era: immigration in, 113–14, 116; prejudice in, 228; xenophobia in, 197

power, ix; discrimination and, 92; hierarchy, 91; marginalization and, 91; prejudice and, 92; stereotypes and, 91–92, 94

power and classism: Buffett and, 179, 181; capitalism and, 177, 178; children and, 179; education and, 179, 183, 184; free enterprise and, 177; income inequality and, 199; Industrial Revolution and, 177; meritocracy and, 179; New Deal and, 177–78; poverty line and, 178; race and, 178; TANF and, 179; Trump tax bill and, 178; War on Poverty and, 187; water crisis and, 180, 190–94; welfare and, 189–90. *See also* criminal justice system; institutionalized discrimination

power and racism, x; anti-Semitism and, 94, 102, 136–38, 238; Collins on, 94, 118–23; in Cuba, 26; Frej and, 94, 103–4; guns and gun control and, 52–54; model minority stereotype and, 147–50; Native Americans and, 94, 123–25, 128–36; personhood and, 102; racial discrimination and prejudice and, 93, 94; restrictive covenants and, 13, 93, 146; Sanchez and, 94, 128–31; Till and, 94, 153–54; urban Native

Americans and, 125–28; welfare and, 189–90; white fear and, 151–52; white privilege and, 77, 94, 118–23; World War II Japanese internment camps and, 94, 138–47. *See also Birth of a Nation*; Civilian Exclusion Orders and Japanese internment camps; immigration; Jim Crow

power and sexism: consciousness-raising groups for, 157; construction industry and, 164–66; education and, 158, 163, 165; feminist activism and, 158; origins of sexism, 157–58; patriarchal systems and, 157; reproductive health care and, 173–74; sexual harassment in the workplace and, 158, 163–64, 265–66; traditional gender roles and, 157. *See also* labor force, and gender; violence against women; Violence Against Women Act

prejudice, 215; in post-9/11 era, 228; power and, 92; racial, 93–94

Price, Karen, 51–52

privilege. *See* white privilege

propaganda, 102

Protestant work ethic, 73

Pruitt, Scott, 205–6, 207

public health, 204, 205, 206, 207. *See also* reproductive rights and health care

Public Law 346 (G.I. Bill), 80

Qoyawayma, Polingaysi, 23–25; on hidden meanings, 24; stick meaning for, 23–24

racial and ethnic identity, ix, 1–2; African American exclusion and, 11–12; African cultures and, 4; Afro DZ ak on, 4, 6; Americanization and, 8–9; ancestry testing and, 3, 32–33; colonialism and, 7; cultural heritage and, 4; Cumpián and, 4, 31–32; difference between, 3; Fears and, 4, 25–27; Franklin, J., on, 4, 8–14; genetic science and, 3, 32–34; Great Chain of Being and, 7; groups with, 93; Gwaltney and, 27–29; miscegenation and, 6; Montilla and, 4, 30–31; Nazis and, 7; Obama, B., on, 4, 14–20; Paley and, 4, 20–23; people of color who do not feel

black and, 4, 25–27; Qoyawayma
and, 23–25; racial myths and, 7;
social constructs and, 3–4, 7–8,
32; "Statement on Race" and, 4,
6–8. *See also* Cuban exiles
racial bias, 119
racialization, 119
racism: overt, 93, 95; structural, 96;
systemic, 119, 121. *See also* power
and racism; subtle racism
railroad strike (1877), 78
rape and sexual assault, 158;
aggression and, 168–69, 170–71;
in *Birth of a Nation*, 101; colleges
and, 201, 202; DeVos and, 202;
dominance and power and,
168–69; masculinity and, 169;
mulatto and, 98–99; Obama, B.,
and, 202; patriarchal values and,
168; prevention, 170–71; in
prison, 168; questions in case of,
171–72; reporting, 169–70;
slavery and, 98–99; victim blaming
and, 159, 171–72; violent pornography and, 159, 171
Rau, Violet, 258–59
Reagan, Ronald, 188, 189, 231–32
Reapportionment Act (1929), 208
redistricting: decennial census and,
209, 211; *Evenwel v. Abbott on
Redistricting 578*, 209
Reed, Joe, 154, 155
refoulement, 111, 116
repatriation of ancestral remains,
263–64
reproductive rights and health care:
involuntary sterilization and,
134–35; Mexico City Policy and,
201; *Roe v. Wade* and, 159, 172,
173
restrictive covenants, 13, 93; Civilian
Exclusion Orders and, 146
rich women, 83–86; expectations of,
84–85; invisibility of, 84; slave
mentality and, 85; recommendations for, 86
Rippon, Adam, 51–52
Roberts, Robin, 152
Robinson, Jo Ann, 250
Roe v. Wade, 159, 172, 173
Roosevelt, Franklin D.: Civilian
Exclusion Orders and Japanese
internment camps and, 141, 142,
144, 146; New Deal of, 177–78,
248

Ros-Lehtinen, Ileana, 44
Ross, E. A., 137
Ross, Kathleen, 258–59, 260
Ross, Wilbur, 209, 210, 211
Rothschild banking empire, 136, 138
Rubio, Marco, 44
Rusciano, Frank Louis, 94, 96–103
Russell, Diana, 169
Ryan, Michael, 243, 258–60

Salter, John, 251–52, 253
same-sex marriage, 57; *Obergefell v.
Hodges* and, 199
Sanchez, Carol Lee, 94, 128–31; on
Cowboys and Indians, 129; "go
back to the blanket" and, 129,
131; mineral-rich lands and, 130;
poverty for, 130
sanctuary cities, 104
Schaaf, Libby, 103, 104
school segregation, 249, 250–51, 256
Schork, Derek, 217, 228–29
Schwab, James, 103–4
Senate, U.S., 106, 109, 220; Hill
testimony before, 158, 265, 266
Serwer, Adam, 198, 199–201
Sessions, Jeff, 103, 104, 162
sexism. *See* power and sexism
sexual harassment in the workplace,
163–64; Civil Rights Act and, 265,
266; Hill and, 158, 265–66;
Meritor Savings Bank v. Vinson
and, 265
sexual identity. *See* gender and sexual
identity
sexual orientation: Benjamin scale of,
58; laws on, 50
Shapley, Dan, 193
Sherman, William Tecumseh, 100
Shuler, Liz, 159, 174–75
Shungu, Peter. *See* Afro DZ ak
Siddiqui, Sabena, 74, 88–89
Sikes, Melvin, 155
slavery, 119, 256; after abolishment
of, 26; in *Birth of a Nation*, 96,
97–98; *Dred Scott* decision and,
98; Franklin, J., on, 11; in Latin
America, 26; rape and, 98–99;
Three-Fifths Compromise and, 98
Smith, Jeremy Adam, 52–54
SNCC. *See* Student Nonviolent
Coordinating Committee
social media, 199
Soelle, Dorothee, 80
Sopo, Giancarlo, 38

Southern Poverty Law Center
(SPLC), 117–18, 243, 247–51; on
Till, 94, 153–54
Sowell, Thomas, 137
sport teams and Native Americans:
controversy and, 131–32;
genocide and, 135–36; mass
media and, 135; Means on, 132;
offensive names for, 132–33;
protesting, 132, 133
Starbucks, 152
"Statement on Race" (American
Anthropological Association), 4,
6–8; colonialism and, 7; Great
Chain of Being and, 7; physical
variation and, 6–7; status and, 8
State Sovereignty Commission, 256,
258
Statue of Liberty, 12–13
Stearns, Jessica R., 58–70; as aviation
cadet navigator, 63; in Brooklyn,
60; charter flying of, 65; as
commercial pilot, 65, 66, 69;
counseling for, 65; daughter of,
64, 66, 67; doctors for, 64, 64–66;
early farm life of, 59–60; female
clothes for, 59, 62, 63; firing of,
68, 69; flight lessons for, 62; foster
family of, 62, 63; grandparents of,
59, 60; hormone treatment for,
64–65, 66; Jorgensen and, 58, 60,
63; lawsuit of, 50, 68, 69; media
and, 69; name of, 67; pilots
treatment of, 68, 69; relationships
of, 63–64, 66, 70; at school, 60,
61; sex reassignment surgery for,
67–69; sexual orientation of, 70;
support for, 68, 69; in Vietnam
War, 64; Wollman and, 66
Stephenson, Kate, 158, 164–66
stereotypes, 215; male role, 54–56;
power and, 91–92, 94. *See also*
model minority stereotype
Stimson, Henry L., 143, 144, 145,
146
Streicher, Julius, 133
Stroud, Angela, 52, 53, 54
Student Nonviolent Coordinating
Committee (SNCC), 254, 258
subtle racism: on Capitol Hill,
154–55; at Denny's, 154; micro-
aggressions and, 154; Mullinax on,
154–55; Reed and, 154, 155;
Sikes and, 155; Thurmond and,
155

Sutter's Mill, 104, 108
systemic racism, 119, 121

taking action, 217–18; developing
    plan for, 218; developing strategies
    for, 217, 218; domestic violence
    prevention as, 229–30; evaluation
    and, 218; feminism and, 230–35;
    First Amendment and, 238–40;
    Holder and., 217, 219–23; on
    homelessness, 217, 218; identi-
    fying problem for, 217; identifying
    specific change and, 217; imple-
    menting plan for, 218; Madrid
    and, 217, 223–28; men's
    movement and, 235–38;
    Oklahoma teachers' strike as,
    240–42; Schork and, 217,
    228–29; Tolman on, 217, 229–30
tax: breaks to wealthy, 178, 181;
    Buffett and, 181; corporate share
    of, 78; Trump tax bill and, 178
Temporary Assistance for Needy
    Families (TANF), 179
terrorism, 94, 102, 112, 113–14, 116,
    197. *See also* white supremacists
Texas v. Johnson, 238–39
Thanksgiving, 4, 31, 135
Thomas, Clarence, 158, 265
Thompson, Doug Cooper, 50, 54–56
Thompson, Victor, 198, 208–12
Thurmond, Michael, 155
Till, Emmett Louis, 94, 153–54
Tillinghast, Muriel, 243, 254–58;
    Blackwell and, 256; Cobb and,
    255; Freedom School and, 256;
    KKK and, 257; life lessons of,
    257–58; Sheriff Davis and, 257;
    SNCC and, 254; State Sovereignty
    Commission and, 256, 258
Title VI, of Civil Rights Act, 205
Title VII, of Civil Rights Act, 57, 265
Title IX, of Education Amendments
    (1972), 202
Tolman, Ricard, 217, 229–30
transformational politics, 231
transgender individuals: Benjamin
    and, 56, 58; hormone therapy for,
    56, 58; Jorgensen and, 56, 58, 60,
    63; sexual assignment surgery for,
    50. *See also* Stearns, Jessica R.
transgender rights, 50, 56–58; ENDA
    and, 57; Fourteenth Amendment
    and, 56; Obama, B., and, 57
transsexual, 57, 58–70

Truman, Harry, 249
Trump, Donald, x, 73; America First
    and, ix; CAA and, 38, 43; Castro
    and, 34–35; Cuban exiles vote for,
    38–39, 42, 43–44; EPA and,
    205–7; Fernandez and, 35, 44;
    "grab them by the pussy" remarks
    of, 266; human rights violations
    and, 159; on ICE Oakland raid,
    103–4; immigration and, 103–4,
    115; media and, 200; midterm
    elections and, 173; political divi-
    sions and, 35; "snake in Eden"
    reference of, 97; tax bill of, 178;
    on welfare, 189; white suprema-
    cists and, 94, 117; Women's
    March and, 172, 266; women's
    rights and, 172, 173, 201–3

United Nations, 134
urban Native Americans, 125–28;
    BIA and, 126; gambling and,
    127–28; identity of, 126–27; relo-
    cation and migration of, 125–26;
    unemployment, 127; Voluntary
    Relocation Program for, 126

VAWA. *See* Violence Against Women
    Act
Venter, Craig, 32
violence against women: dating abuse
    and, 230; domestic violence as,
    166–67, 229–30, 262; justice
    system and, 160–61; men as allies
    and, 230; sex and, 160; "Weinstein
    Effect" and, 265–66. *See also* rape
    and sexual assault
Violence Against Women Act
    (VAWA): civil remedy of, 160;
    Fourteenth Amendment and, 161;
    reauthorization of, 161, 162
Visser, Margaret, 227
voter disenfranchisement, 150–51
voting: CVAP and, 209–10; *Evenwel
    v. Abbott on Redistricting* 578 and,
    209; Holder and, 217; portable
    registration for, 222; redistricting
    and, 209, 211; voter fraud, 222
voting rights: election fraud and, 221;
    Holder on, 217, 219–23; Obama,
    B., and, 221; Three-Fifths
    Compromise and, 98
Voting Rights Act: citizenship and,
    209; Johnson, L. B., and, 219;
    language minorities and, 221;

Motor Voter law and, 220–21;
    Section 5 of, 220
Vradenburgh, Wayne, 190, 192

wage gap, 158, 162, 179
Wakefield, Rosa, 27–29
Walker, Brennan, 152
Walsey, Edith, 259
War on Poverty, 187
Warren, Earl, 145, 238, 240
Washington, George, 78, 82
water crisis, New York, 180; band-aid
    approach to, 191–92; Ciaravino
    and, 193, 194; Cuomo and, 191,
    193; development and, 193–94;
    Harris on, 192; health impacts of,
    192–93; lawsuits over, 191, 193;
    PFOA and, 190–91, 192–93;
    PFOS and, 190, 191, 192, 194;
    Vradenburgh and, 190, 192
Watson, Tom, 137
Watts, Robert Anthony, 94, 154–55
Wearden, Graeme, 181–82
Weinstein, Harvey, 265
"Weinstein Effect": #MeToo
    movement and, 265, 266;
    Women's March and, 266
welfare: race and, 189–90; Trump on,
    189
Welfare and Illegal Immigration
    Reform and Immigration Control
    Acts (1996), 109, 112, 116
Wells, Spencer, 33–34
Wells-Barnett, Ida B., 243; Jim Crow
    fought by, 248
Wheeler-Howard Act (Indian Reorga-
    nization Act), 124
Whipple, Bishop H. B., 129
white fear, 151–52
white privilege, 77; arrests and, 121;
    in Australia, 121; Bennett on, 119;
    Collins on, 94, 118–23; hiring
    and, 120;
    #IfTheyGunnedMeDown
    campaign and, 121; inheritance
    and, 122; Kendall on, 119;
    McIntosh and, 118, 120, 121; as
    power of accumulated power,
    121–23; power of benefit of the
    doubt and, 120–21; as power of
    normal, 120; racism and, 118–19,
    121; wealth and, 121–22; zoning
    and, 122
white supremacists: alt-right as, 117;

KKK as, 12, 94, 96, 117, 248, 257; Trump and, 94, 117
Williams, Randall, 74, 86–88
Winter, Nicholas, 189, 190
Withers, Mellissa, 202
Wolff, Edward, 179
Wollman, Leo, 66
women, rich. *See* rich women
Women's March, 172, 173, 174; "Weinstein Effect" and, 266
women's rights, 172, 173, 174, 201–3. *See also specific topics*
Workers Memorial Day, 81–82
worker strikes: Ludlow Massacre and, 78–79, 82; railroad, 78

World War II, 94, 122; aftermath of Pearl Harbor attack during, 142–46; Bendetsen and, 143, 145; enemy alien orders in, 141, 143; Knox and, 142; Pearl Harbor attack during, 141, 142. *See also* Civilian Exclusion Orders and Japanese internment camps
Wright, Jeremiah, 15–16, 17, 18

xenophobia, 116, 197

Yallup, Martha, 258–59
Yamane, Linus, 149
Yoo, David, 149

Zandy, Janet, 74, 75–83; on class identity, 75–77; on history of class disparity, 78–79, 80; *Liberating Memory: Our Work and Our Working-Class Consciousness* by, 81; Ludlow Massacre and, 78–79, 82; Pam Am Flight 103 bombing and, 79; on power, 75, 76, 77, 79, 80; student experiences and, 82–83; on visibility, 77–79; Workers Memorial Day and, 81–82; working-class women and literary culture, 80–81
Zeigler, Jeffrey Craig, 152

Ingram Content Group UK Ltd.
Milton Keynes UK
UKHW031536190523
422023UK00019B/417

9 781538 114933